SUMMER JOBS IN THE USA

2004–2005

THOMSON

PETERSON'S™

Australia • Canada • Mexico • Singapore • Spain • United Kingdom • United States

About The Thomson Corporation and Peterson's

The Thomson Corporation, with 2002 revenues of US$7.8 billion, is a global leader in providing integrated information solutions to business and professional customers. The Corporation's common shares are listed on the Toronto and New York stock exchanges (TSX: TOC; NYSE: TOC). Its learning businesses and brands serve the needs of individuals, learning institutions, corporations, and government agencies with products and services for both traditional and distributed learning. Peterson's (www.petersons.com) is a leading provider of education information and advice, with books and online resources focusing on education search, test preparation, and financial aid. Its Web site offers searchable databases and interactive tools for contacting educational institutions, online practice tests and instruction, and planning tools for securing financial aid. Peterson's serves 110 million education consumers annually.

For more information, contact Peterson's, 2000 Lenox Drive, Lawrenceville, NJ 08648; 800-338-3282; or find us on the World Wide Web at www.petersons.com/about.

ISSN 1064-6701
ISBN 0-7689-1270-9

Printed in Canada

10 9 8 7 6 5 4 3 2 1   05 04 03

Sixth Edition

CONTENTS

HOW TO USE THIS BOOK

What are you going to do to make this summer special? You already have a good start. *Summer Jobs in the USA 2004–2005* is an indispensable catalog of interesting and enriching summer work experiences for students or anyone looking for summer employment. You'll find detailed, up-to-date information on more than 55,000 positions offered across the country and abroad—from counselors, instructors, and lifeguards to theater stagehands, wilderness guides, and office clerical workers. The list is long, and many of these jobs require little or no previous experience.

SEARCH BY YOUR INTERESTS

There are many different ways you can use *Summer Jobs in the USA 2004–2005* to find the right work opportunity. If your primary consideration is the geographic location of a job (if, for instance, you'd like to spend the summer working near your hometown or in a particular area of the country), you can turn directly to the **State-by-State Listings**, where employers are listed alphabetically by state. The **Canadian Listings** and **Locations Outside North America Listings** sections feature summer employment opportunities in Canada and elsewhere.

Another way you can put *Summer Jobs in the USA 2004–2005* to work for you is by looking for jobs according to the services they provide. The opportunities featured in this book are divided into fifteen main areas, which are listed in the **Category Index** at the back of the book. If you know, for instance, that you want to work at an amusement or theme park, the **Category Index** lists all such employers that are featured in the book. Use the following list of categories as your guide:

Accommodations and Food Services
Ambulatory Health Care Services
Amusement and Theme Parks
Business and Professional Organizations
Educational Services
Manufacturing
Nature Parks and Environmental Institutions
Performing Arts Companies
Professional, Scientific, and Technical Services
Public Administration
Recreation Industries
Recreational and Vacation Camps
Religious Organizations
Retail Trade
Social Assistance

Of course, if you already know the name of the employer you want to contact, you can simply turn to the **Employer Index** for a page reference to the description of that employer's job opportunities.

If you're interested in knowing what kinds of jobs are most readily available, turn to the **Job Types Index**. It lists the most frequently cited job types in the book and the facilities that offer them.

READ THE EMPLOYER PROFILES

Once you have found an employer that interests you, you can read about the opportunities provided. The **General Information** section of each profile provides details about the location, size, focus, and special features of the facility. You can check the **Profile of Summer Employees** to get an idea of who your coworkers might be. **Employment Information** includes descriptions of available jobs as well as important details about when positions are available, salaries, and special requirements. Any **Benefits,** such as meals, laundry facilities, health insurance, or the possibility of college credit, and **Preemployment Training,** such as leadership skills or accident prevention and safety, are also noted. The **Contact** paragraph provides you with information on how the employer wants you to apply for a position and the application deadline.

International applicants for any of the positions found in this guide should pay special attention to valuable information found in the **Employment Information** section. If international students are encouraged to apply for available positions, a sentence stating such will appear at the end of this section, along with any special application procedures required of international applicants, such as referral through an agency designed to handle these applications.

The data in this book were collected in the spring and summer of 2003 from employers eager to fill staff vacancies with high-quality, motivated workers. A representative of each employer completed a questionnaire to describe the job opportunities to be offered specifically for the summer of 2004, but more than likely in subsequent summers as well. In some cases, additional information was obtained through secondary research. Since the data were collected in 2003, you should check with the employer before applying for or accepting a position to verify that all information in the profiles is still accurate and up-to-date. A phone call to the contact person listed in the profile or a visit to the employer's Web site (address is in the **Contact** section) will provide you with even more information about the employer and the type of employment that is available. Peterson's does not assume responsibility for the hiring policies or actions of these employers.

LEARN HOW TO APPLY

Summer Jobs in the USA 2004–2005 features four articles that provide additional help in your search for a summer job. If you are just learning how to apply for a summer job, be sure to read "Looking for a Summer Job?" "Look Into Summer Jobs Carefully" provides valuable information for those pursuing summer work as a salesperson. International job hunters are strongly urged to read "International Applicants for Summer Employment in the U.S." "Do You Want to Work Temporarily in Canada?" tells you the steps you need to take before you begin a summer job in Canada; the article outlines procedures you and your Canadian employer must follow for you to receive employment authorization.

Remember, all of the employers listed in this book are actively looking for your help—they are waiting for your application! We hope that this book will help make your summer a fun, interesting, and profitable experience.

ABBREVIATION CHART

The following are abbreviations commonly used in this book:

ACA	American Camping Association
AHSE	Association for Horsemanship Safety and Education
ALS	Advanced Life Saving
ARC	American Red Cross
BUNAC	British University North American Club
CAA	Camp Archery Association
CIT	Counselor-in-Training
CPR	Cardiopulmonary Resuscitation
EMR	Educationally Mentally Retarded
EMT	Emergency Medical Technician
EOE	Equal Opportunity Employer
HSA	Horsemanship Safety Association
ICCP	International Camp Counselors Program
IDC	Instructor Development Center
LD	Learning Disabled
LPN	Licensed Practical Nurse
NAUI	National Association of Underwater Instructors
NRA	National Rifle Association
PADI	Professional Association of Diving Instructors
RN	Registered Nurse
SASE	Self-addressed, stamped envelope
SCI	Small-Craft Instructor
SLS	Senior Life Saving
WSI	Water Safety Instructor

LOOKING FOR A SUMMER JOB?

by Shirley J. Longshore

As an older teenager or young adult concerned about your future, working at a job—for pay or not—is an important, if not mandatory, summer undertaking. If you've never done it, looking for a job may seem intimidating, but it's not. Hundreds of thousands of young people *do* find interesting and rewarding jobs every summer.

Many young adults turn to summer employment not only to pay for college expenses but also to earn spending money or even to help out their families. Competition for these jobs can be stiff, but keep in mind that summer employment can provide the background you'll need to compete aggressively both with other college-bound students when applying to schools *and* with other job seekers when looking for a full-time job. Guidance counselors, admissions officers, and corporate human-resource managers look for college and job applications that display outside activities, work experiences, and additional credentials. A good summer job record is a plus that colleges and employers now routinely expect to see.

"Strong academics are not enough any more," says a college admissions officer at a small university in Georgia. "We're looking very hard at what else students are doing, how they use their time, and what other skills they are acquiring. Even the less competitive colleges are becoming much more demanding in evaluating prospective students." If you don't need to earn money, working as a volunteer will also give you a competitive edge.

GET STARTED NOW

Landing the summer job that will add to the bottom line in your bank book and bolster your resume is harder than it used to be. The competition can be tough, but you can overcome the obstacles. To increase your chances for success, you must be willing to work at mounting an organized, targeted job search; the sooner you get started, the better!

"The key is to start early," emphasizes the personnel director of a large state park that employs many young people each summer. "You can't wait until May and then see what's around, because there truly won't be anything left. I see this over and over. We have all of our hiring done, and then we get call after call and letter after letter from panicked, although qualified, students who are just applying much

---

Shirley J. Longshore is a writer, editor, and communications consultant. Her articles about business, work, and education have appeared in national publications.

too late." A job seeker fortunate enough to get his or her application in early and who is hired also has the opportunity to ensure a somewhat more secure summer job situation throughout the rest of high school or college; those who prove themselves valuable will likely have first crack at getting the job back the following summer.

PREPARE YOUR RESUME AND COVER LETTER

Your resume should be limited to one page and must communicate your strong points by detailing relevant experience and describing your background. It should present you in a way that will interest an employer enough to arrange an interview.

"I had a student this year who said he didn't have to be convinced that a summer job was important, but he didn't have a clue how to begin looking for one," says a guidance counselor at a large public high school in Florida. "High school students look at me like I'm from outer space when I tell them that, first, they should write a resume. They say things like: 'What would I put on it? I have no real skills; I've never done much of anything. A resume is for older people looking for real jobs.' But when we look at the clubs they have participated in, after-school activities, volunteer work, and baby-sitting jobs, we can often work up quite a list together. It gives young people an idea of what they have to offer an employer."

Everyone has the makings of a resume in their background—even those just starting out. You simply have to look at your past thoroughly. Don't overlook any activities that could enhance your credentials. Don't forget the computer knowledge you gained in school. Do you teach Sunday school? Have you worked in your town's recreation program? Do you assist in a shelter for the homeless or collect newspapers for recycling? All of these activities require skills that can be translated into proven experience for an employer. At the very least, participating in these kinds of activities will show that you are focused, well-rounded, community-minded, responsible, and trustworthy.

A resume should also list people who will give you good recommendations. (Before listing anyone as a reference, check to make sure he or she is willing to be listed.) To prepare a reference list, create a separate page with your name, address, and phone number followed by the names, addresses, and phone numbers of 2 to 4 people who will verify your skills and testify to the qualities that will convince the employer to hire you.

You may want to tailor your resume to appeal to a particular employer—using a computer makes this easy. Perhaps you are intrigued by a counselor's job at an academic-oriented camp. The resume for that position should contain an item that mentions that you put the skill you show in math to good use tutoring a third-grader after school. Phrase the item: "Demonstrated maturity and responsibility tutoring third-grade student in math in after-school sessions." With this entry on your resume, you are showcasing both a skill at an academic subject and experience working with a younger person. If you're using a computer, this item can easily be deleted from the resume you'll send in application to a job that doesn't involve academics or supervising children.

Your resume should also include items mentioning any athletics training you have had, such as swimming lessons, ballet classes, and team memberships. These activities demand those qualities employers look for—self-discipline, high energy, dedication, and a desire for self-improvement.

A college student from Massachusetts didn't think his experience as head cook for the school's international club's dinners was very important. "I just did it for fun," the student admitted. "But then I saw an opening for an assistant chef at a lodge for the summer between my junior and senior years, and I realized I could parlay that experience into a job. It worked."

The best resume is one that is straightforward and clearly presented. If you're composing one for the first time, you should take advantage of the knowledge of older siblings or friends—talk with them and ask to see their resumes. Remember, it must state relevant information about you and your skills.

This is where a strong cover letter comes into play. A cover letter serves as your introduction to a potential employer and, hopefully, will interest him or her enough to want to read your resume. A cover letter should draw the reader's attention to those experiences that best relate to the qualifications required for a particular job. For example, if a camp is looking for counselors to lead activities, your letter should mention your involvement in school plays (an item on your resume) and suggest that this experience would enable you to confidently instruct campers in drama or in a stage production. Although a cover letter should be brief and to the point, it doesn't hurt to help the resume reader along by flagging pertinent information. Sell yourself!

My Resume Is Ready—Now What?

After you've identified your skills and written your resume, you need to consider what you want to get out of your summer job. Ask yourself: What do I enjoy doing? What am I really good at? What would I like to learn more about? What work experience would enhance my chances at future opportunities? Do I love to be outdoors in the summer, or do I really prefer the air-conditioned comfort of an office? Is this the time to go far away from home, or would I rather stay close by? Do I need to make money? Keep in mind that some jobs may be too costly for you. If you need to earn money to cover college expenses, for instance, you may not want your pay to be eaten away by transportation and room-and-board costs.

After answering the questions above, turn to this guide's **Category Index** to zero in on the kinds of opportunities that make sense for you. The listings go beyond what you'll find in your local community through the usual pavement-pounding, want-ad-answering, asking-around methods. The jobs in this guide are located all over. Some may be in your geographic area, and others may be hundreds or thousands of miles away. Included are camps, resorts, summer theaters, conservation and environmental programs, lodges, ranches, conference and training centers, national parks, and amusement and theme parks that normally hire many young people for each busy summer season. The possibilities are endless, so you don't have to worry about ending up in a job in which you have little interest.

Keep in mind that many summer employers provide on-site training in the particular skills needed for their jobs, so don't be discouraged if your skills don't match exactly. These people are generally looking for qualities other than direct experience—motivation, interest, and the desire to learn. When you read about a position, *read between the lines* to see what kind of employee is really being sought.

WINNING INTERVIEWS

Once you have contacted the employers you'd like to work for, think about how you'll present yourself at interviews. An interview may take place over the phone or in a face-to-face meeting. In either case, it's a chance for you and the employer to get a better sense of each other.

Remember, an interview goes both ways. It is also an opportunity for you to ask any questions and to decide whether you really want the job. You may want to ask about specific duties, hours, pay, what benefits are provided (such as room and board), and when hiring decisions will be made. Always write a brief, sincere thank-you note to follow up an interview, even if it was very short or conducted by telephone.

It's important to dress appropriately for an in-person interview. Bring with you any credentials that are required (e.g., working papers, birth certificate, school records, or Social Security card). If you don't have a Social Security card, you can, and should, get one right away. You can start the process by calling 800-772-1213, the nationwide toll-free number for Social Security information.

Finding a good summer job opportunity is not an impossible task. There are jobs out there. You have a good shot at landing one if you prepare your resume, start going after the jobs you know about early, and present yourself both on paper and in person in the best possible light.

SAMPLE COVER LETTER

ANNE MEREDITH

421 South Street
Apartment 2C
City Line, NJ 07685
821-663-4121

218 Tower Hall
State University
Brighton, PA 62451
580-341-6840

January 4, 2004

Name of person in charge, title
Name of camp or resort
Street address
Town, state, zip code

Dear Mr. or Ms. (last name):

I saw the listing describing your summer program in <u>Summer Jobs in the USA 2004–2005</u>. It states that you are hiring a Waterfront Director, a summer position for which I would like to apply.

As you will see from the attached resume, I am qualified for such a position. I taught swimming, was a lifeguard, coached a swim team, and swam on my high school team for four years. I was named to the Junior Varsity Swim Team at State University in both my freshman and sophomore years.

I am experienced at supervising and teaching both adults and children in swimming and waterfront safety. I enjoy working with people and sharing my expertise with them. Your summer program sounds like one in which my skills would be fully utilized.

I would appreciate the opportunity to explore this position with you further. I would be happy to talk with you by telephone or to arrange a personal interview during my winter break, which is until the end of this month.

Thank you for your consideration. I look forward to hearing from you soon. You can reach me at my home number in City Line until January 27th.

Sincerely,

Anne Meredith

SAMPLE RESUME

ANNE MEREDITH

421 South Street
Apartment 2C
City Line, NJ 07685
821-663-4121

218 Tower Hall
State University
Brighton, PA 62451
580-341-6840

EDUCATION: State University, Brighton, PA
Expected date of graduation, 2005
Major: Biology GPA: 3.4 Degree track: B.S.

HONORS: Dean's List, first semester, State University
Science Scholar Award, City Line High School
State Merit Scholarship Winner

EXPERIENCE: Head Lifeguard/Swimming Coach
River Edge Athletic Club, Edgeton, NJ
Summer 2002–2003
    Responsibilities included scheduling and overseeing the
    summer staff of ten lifeguards and serving as one of two
    coaches for the club's competitive children's swim team (35
    members). I also gave private swimming lessons to club
    members.

Lifeguard
YWCA, City Line, NJ; Winter 2001–2002

Swimming Instructor/Lifeguard
River Edge Athletic Club, Edgeton, NJ; Summer 2001 and 2000

Assistant Swimming Instructor (3- to 5-year-olds)
YWCA, City Line, NJ; Summer 1999

Day Camp Helper (9- and 10-year-olds)
YWCA, City Line, NJ; Summer 1998

ACTIVITIES: Swim Team, Junior Varsity, State University, 2002–2003
Glee Club, State University, 2002–2003
Swim Team, YWCA, City Line, NJ, 2000–2001
    Captain, 2000–2001
Junior-Senior Chorus, City Line High School, 1999–2001
Youth Group, St. John's Church, 1999–2002
    President, 2002
Springvale Nursing Home, volunteer visitor, 2001–2002

SKILLS: Red Cross Certification, Lifesaving
Fluent in Spanish
Teaching experience with children and adults
Computer skills: Microsoft Word

LOOK INTO SUMMER JOBS CAREFULLY

Some newspaper ads promise great summer jobs for students—offering travel and good pay. Many of these summer jobs require long hours of selling and traveling in car pools in a van and sharing cheap motels with others on the sales team.

To entice you to sign up, some of these companies offer examples of students who made big money selling for them. But such promises of huge earnings often are misleading because the companies use examples of students who also were paid commissions to recruit others to join the company. People who just sell the company's products earn a great deal less and often do it under less than ideal working conditions.

Moreover, because students often are hired as independent contractors, the company assumes no responsibility for its actions. It likewise may provide no unemployment insurance or Workers' Compensation benefits.

It is your responsibility to know the laws about selling in the state in which you are working. For example, if you get arrested for not having a state transient merchant's license, it would probably be your responsibility to get yourself out of jail—not the company's.

Your ability to sell and your personal motivation will determine how much money you make. Some students have complained that they could have earned more money working at a minimum-wage restaurant job based on the number of hours they spent selling.

Be sure to check out any company before you sign up for a job. Some unscrupulous companies make students work long hours for little pay in dangerous communities. Some of these same companies put their recruits through emotional and physical abuse.

Before you sign up:

- Ask the company detailed questions about the working conditions and income potential.

- Ask what will happen if you get injured on the job or need to quit in the middle of the summer.

- Ask the company how you will get home in case of an emergency.

- Ask how and when you will be paid and what room and board accommodations the company will provide.

Reprinted with the permission of the North Dakota Attorney General's Office, Consumer Protection Division.

INTERNATIONAL APPLICANTS FOR SUMMER EMPLOYMENT IN THE U.S.

by Elizabeth Chazottes

Nothing is more exciting and rewarding than an international summer job in the United States. For years, international students have been spending their summers in the U.S. to learn American methods of business, to perfect their English skills, to make international connections that last a lifetime, and to just have fun! However, since the events of September 11, 2001, things have become a bit more complex for international students in general. There are still plenty of opportunities, but you must be well-informed. Take the time to learn about your options and which opportunities will best meet your needs. The better prepared you are, the more successful your experience will be. Begin your search well in advance—a year is not too soon to begin narrowing your options, and certainly six to nine months before you want to come to the U.S. is none too soon to firm up your plans. With the recent changes in visa laws and enhanced security and oversight by the new Department of Homeland Security, advance planning is a necessity.

In an effort to provide guidance that is as accurate as possible for students from outside the United States, each employer listed in *Summer Jobs in the USA 2004–2005* has been asked if applications will be accepted from international students. Peterson's has also asked if the employer is willing to undertake the necessary steps—either directly with the U.S. Bureau of Citizenship and Immigration Services (BCIS) in the Department of Homeland Security (DHS) or through an educational exchange organization—to make it possible for the student to secure a proper U.S. visa that will allow him or her to complete the program and legally receive a salary or stipend, if applicable, while in the United States. There are significant penalties for employers who hire foreign nationals illegally. It should be noted that the former Immigration and Naturalization Service (INS) functions have been divided and now fall under the new Department of Homeland Security, with the service and benefit functions under the BCIS and the enforcement function under the Bureau of Immigration and Customs Enforcement (BICE).

All international students interested in coming to the U.S. for a summer job should make sure they are clear on what they can and cannot do in the workplace

---

Elizabeth Chazottes is the Executive Director and CEO of the Association for International Practical Training and has written numerous articles on international training, overseas employment, and international human resources issues.

with the type of visa they have been issued. Foreign nationals can be deported and barred from returning to the United States for violating their visa status. If an employer in the United States offers you a summer job, make certain that both you *and* the employer know and follow the requirements of U.S. law *before* you leave home.

Passports

In order to get a U.S. visa that permits summer employment, you must have a valid passport from your own country. Your passport must be valid for six months beyond the date on which you expect to leave the United States. A number of countries have special passport validity agreements with the United States under which a passport is considered to be valid for six months beyond the expiration date stated in the passport. In order to avoid last-minute problems, you should contact U.S. consular officials as early as possible to determine the exact requirement for your country.

Visas

Unlike many countries, the United States does not issue work permits or residence permits or require police registration. Instead, what an individual may or may not do while in the United States depends entirely on the specific type of visa granted. As a result, the United States has the world's most complex visa system—there are currently more than eighty different kinds of nonimmigrant visas! Of particular interest to the international applicant is the fact that although an individual may be a full-time student in his or her own country, a student visa for admission to the United States applies only to people attending an American school for full-time study. Therefore, the three kinds of student visas (F-1, J-1, and M) cannot be used by a student coming to the United States uniquely for a summer job experience.

As a general rule, there are only four U.S. visas that are likely to be suitable for students coming to the United States for summer employment:

H-2B Temporary Worker: U.S. companies may use this visa to temporarily employ skilled or unskilled foreign nationals when there is a temporary need and there are no qualified U.S. workers available. There is a two-step process involved that must be initiated by the U.S. employer. First, the employer must request a *temporary labor certification* from the state employment service office serving the area in which the proposed employment is to be offered. Once the state office processes the temporary labor certification, the request must then be forwarded to the U.S. Department of Labor's regional office for a final determination. The employer has to demonstrate (a) that a real job exists (i.e., not a job made up to suit the particular background of the foreign national); (b) that substantial efforts have been made to fill the job with a U.S. citizen; (c) that no qualified U.S. citizens can be found for the job; and (d) that the job to be filled is of a one-time, seasonal, peak-load, or intermittent nature. Once the labor certification is approved, a visa petition must then be filed by the employer with the BCIS. There are also annual limits on the number of H-2B admissions permitted. Once the limit is attained, no new petitions are accepted by BCIS until the next fiscal year (October 1). This process can be rather lengthy, so the U.S. employer should initiate it well in advance.

H-3 Trainee: This visa is used by U.S. companies to bring foreign employees to the U.S. to participate in established company training programs. The U.S. employer must submit the H-3 application to the BCIS Service District Office that covers the area in which the person will work. The application must include a detailed training plan to show what the trainee will do in the U.S., including how much time will be spent in *classroom and other instruction* and how much time will be devoted to *on-the-job training.* Information on the position the individual will fill when he or she returns to his or her home country is also required. The company must demonstrate that the training is provided with the intent to employ the individual abroad upon completion of training or to provide skills that will increase the value of the individual to a foreign business. Any productive work must be incidental to the training program. The employer must also show that the training program provides knowledge or experience that is unavailable in the individual's own country.

J-1 Exchange Visitor: J-1 visa programs are managed by approved organizations or sponsors, such as U.S. government agencies, schools and universities, hospitals, companies, and private nonprofit educational exchange organizations. The Bureau of Educational and Cultural Affairs of the U.S. Department of State, formerly the U.S. Information Agency, has authority over these programs. There are thirteen different J-1 categories, each with its own specific rules and regulations. Among these categories are those that permit international high school students, university students, trainees, au pairs, camp counselors, and researchers to participate in programs in the U.S. Each sponsor is granted a program description that specifies the activities that are permitted for participants in the sponsor's program.

Of the thirteen J-1 categories, the *summer work travel* category is suitable for many international students desiring to come to the U.S. for short-term summer jobs. This category permits university and postsecondary school students to work in any job they may find during the summer months (November to February for students from the Southern Hemisphere). No extensions of visas are permitted, and changes to other J-1 visa categories are not allowed. Preplacement is required for 50 percent of the participants, and students should check with the U.S. sponsoring organization about specific requirements. The Council on International Educational Exchange (CIEE) is the largest and one of the oldest of these programs, but many other programs also now operate summer work travel programs. A full list is available on the Department of State's Web site at http://exchanges.state.gov/education/jexchanges/private/SWT_Sponsors_112602.pdf.

A second type of additional J-1 visa is for placements in summer camps for *camp counselor* experience. Participants must be at least 18 years old. Placements are limited to a maximum of four months and must be for genuine camp counseling assignments in accredited U.S. camps. The YMCA, Camp America, Summer Camp USA, and InterExchange operate several of the better-known camp counselor programs. The full list of all approved programs is available at http://exchanges.state.gov/education/jexchanges/private/CampCounselor_Sponsors.pdf.

International Applicants for Summer Employment in the U.S.

The *trainee* category can also be the right one for international students. This category permits individuals to come to the U.S. to receive on-the-job practical training or participate in a structured internship in their field for periods of three weeks to a maximum of eighteen months. A detailed training program must be prepared by the U.S. host employer, specifying the objectives and skills to be learned as well as the length of time required to complete the program. A trainee cannot replace a U.S. worker but comes to the U.S. to acquire skills and knowledge in U.S. methodology. The number of trainee programs has grown over the years. Two of the long-standing trainee exchange organizations for students are the International Association of Students in Economics and Business Management (AIESEC)—for business and economics students—and the International Association for the Exchange of Students for Technical Experience (IAESTE)—for students in technical fields. The Council on International Educational Exchange (CIEE) is the largest of the student trainee programs, followed by the Association for International Practical Training (AIPT), which brings in students and professionals from some eighty countries annually. Other programs are also available that deal primarily with trainees from specific countries or regions of the world or specific industries. There are a number of private businesses and corporations that have their own J-1 trainee programs. Some U.S. universities also run trainee programs. A complete list of sponsors is available at http://exchanges.state.gov/education/jexchanges/private/Training_Sponsors.pdf.

It should be noted that in some cases, an individual coming to the United States on the J-1 visa may be subject to something called the *two-year foreign residence requirement*. Some countries have asked the U.S. government to establish a *skills list* for its citizens. If the person's field is included on the skills list for his or her country, that means that this particular skill is greatly needed in the home country, and it will generally be necessary for the individual to return to his or her country after completing a program in the U.S. Someone subject to this residence requirement must return to his or her home country for a minimum of two years before coming back to the United States with most of the nonimmigrant visas or as a *permanent resident*. Most European countries do not have skills lists, but many other countries do. If the ability to return to the United States within a two-year period after training is of concern, you should get specific information regarding this from U.S. consular officials. Also, participants who receive funding from the sending foreign government or the U.S. government may also be subject to the two-year residency requirement.

A fourth J-1 category available to students is the *au pair* program. Au pair programs allow participants to live with and participate in the home life of an American host family while providing child-care services and attending a U.S. postsecondary educational institution. The au pair participant cannot provide child-care services for more than 45 hours per week. All participants must register and attend classes offered by an accredited U.S. postsecondary institution. Au pairs must be between the ages of 18 and 26, secondary school graduates or the equivalent, and proficient in spoken English.

There is a separate component of the au pair program called *EduCare,* which is for families who have only school-aged children and require child care before and after school. The au pair participating in the EduCare program cannot provide child-care services for more than a total of 30 hours per week. Au pairs must also complete academic course work during their program. A complete list of au pair and EduCare sponsors is available at http://exchanges.state.gov/education/jexchanges/private/AuPair_Sponsors.pdf.

There are strong indications that a new category specifically for interns will be created in the near future with similar requirements as for the trainee category but permitting stays of up to twelve months.

And lastly, there is the Q visa:

Q International Cultural Exchange Visitor: The Q visa allows the U.S. employer to apply to BCIS for permission to hire a person over 18 years of age from another country for a period of not more than fifteen months. The purpose of the program is for the international participant to work or train and to share or demonstrate his or her own culture with Americans. A frequently cited example of a major Q employer is the EPCOT Center at Walt Disney World in Florida. Another example would be a museum or a department of a museum devoted to the art and culture of the student's home country.

The *cultural component* must be an integral part of the employment or training offered. The employer must demonstrate that the individual to be hired is fully able to communicate with Americans about his or her culture, as well as being fully qualified for the work aspects of the position. Substantial documentation is required as part of the employer's application.

VISA PROCEDURES

Recently, the U.S. has updated its visa policies and procedures to increase security. It will likely take you longer to get a visa than it used to, and you will find that new security measures have been put into place. For details that may apply specifically to your country, see information posted by your nearest U.S. consulate or embassy. Specific country information can be found online at http://travel.state.gov/links.html.

If an employer's applications for an H-2B, H-3, or Q visa are successful, the District Office of the Bureau of Citizenship and Immigration Services will advise the U.S. embassy in the student's country. The student can then obtain the visa and travel to the U.S.

In the case of the J-1 visa, the sponsoring organization arranging the program issues a U.S. government document called a DS-2019 (a Certificate of Eligibility). The DS-2019, which is sent to the student, is used to apply for the J-1 visa in his or her own country.

You will also be required to complete at least two forms, the DS-156 Nonimmigrant Visa Application and, for all males between the ages of 16 and 45, the DS-157 Supplemental Nonimmigrant Visa Application. All J-1 Exchange Visitor visa applicants must also complete the DS-158 Contact Information and Work History. Copies of these forms are available to download online at http://travel.state.gov/visaforms.html. There is currently a visa application fee of $100, and in some instances additional reciprocity fees may apply. The application fee is mandatory and is not refundable under any circumstances, even if you are denied your visa or later decide not to come to the U.S.

In-person interviews have become mandatory for most individuals as of August 1, 2003. Because of the delays in obtaining interview appointments at U.S. embassies and consulates, many sponsors try to provide the DS-2019 up to ninety days in advance. You may not, however, enter the U.S. more than thirty days before the start date of your program. As soon as you receive your visa document, you should immediately contact the nearest U.S. embassy or consulate to obtain an appointment for a visa interview. It may take three to four weeks to obtain an appointment; in some parts of the world, waits of three to six months are not unusual. Some U.S. embassies and consulates use a toll telephone number, where you pay a per-minute charge to obtain an interview appointment. Once you have your interview, make sure you arrive on time and have all the necessary paperwork with you. Interviews typically last less than 3 minutes, so you need to be well prepared. Visa issuance may be the same day or it may require a return visit. Again, check the Web for the U.S. embassy or consulate where you will be applying for specific requirements and information, as it may vary from country to country.

As of 2004, as part of the increased security measures, it becomes mandatory for all visa applicants to provide "biometrics" to obtain a visa. Information can be found on the Web at http://travel.state.gov/links.html.

Upon entering the United States, the admitting BCIS inspector issues a Form I-94 (Arrival/Departure Record) to H-2B, H-3, and Q visa holders, which notes the specific visa granted and the date when the Permit to Stay expires. J-1 visa holders are issued a Permit to Stay with the notation "D/S" (for duration of status). This means that J-1 participants may remain in the U.S. as long as they are engaged in their programs or until the end date of their IAP-66, plus thirty days. The I-94 form (and DS-2019 for the J-1 categories) is the only documentation needed for the student to proceed to the workplace and begin the assignment.

SEVIS

The Student and Exchange Visitor Information System, or SEVIS, was put into place beginning in early 2003. SEVIS is an Internet-based system that maintains accurate and current information on nonimmigrant students (F and M visa), exchange visitors (J visa), and their dependents (F-2, M-2, and J-2). SEVIS enables schools and program sponsors to transmit electronic information and event notifications, via the Internet, to the Bureau of Immigration and Customs Enforcement and Department of State throughout a student or exchange visitor's stay in the United States. SEVIS requires that all sponsors submit information on all J-1 exchange visitors (as well as F and M visa students) and any accompanying dependents. Once the information has been submitted by the sponsoring organization or school, SEVIS will actually generate the DS-2019 form for signature by the sponsor. This form is then sent to the participant to be used to obtain the J-1 visa. Once the J-1 visa participant enters the U.S., the sponsor will be notified through the SEVIS system and then has thirty days to "validate" that the participant has arrived at his or her site of activity and to provide a U.S. street address (not a P.O. box). It becomes extremely important for the participants to notify the sponsor upon their arrival at the host employer or work site of their U.S. home address. If they do not inform the sponsor of their arrival within thirty days, they will "time-out" of the SEVIS system and become deportable. It is also important for participants to notify their U.S. sponsors of any change of address or change of program, as this information is all tracked through the SEVIS system. Enforcement of SEVIS is through the Department of Homeland Security's Bureau of Immigration and Customs Enforcement.

EMPLOYMENT ELIGIBILITY VERIFICATION

U.S. law requires employers to examine documentation proving that persons hired are either citizens of the United States or noncitizens legally authorized for employment during their stay in the United States. Essentially, the law requires that within three business days after a person is hired, the employer must *physically examine* documentation that (a) establishes proof of the new employee's identity and (b) establishes that the person is either a U.S. citizen or is a noncitizen who has the legal right to be employed in the United States. The law requires that a record of the verification process be maintained in the employer's files for a period of three years after the date of hiring. For this purpose, the BCIS has developed the I-9 form. Virtually all kinds of employment are covered, from a full-time job with a large employer such as IBM to selling hamburgers part-time at the local McDonald's.

Certainly, all of the jobs listed in *Summer Jobs in the USA 2004–2005* will require you and your employer to complete the I-9 form. The I-9 form has two parts. The top half must be filled out by the employee—you. You then present the form, together with your documentation, to your employer, who completes the bottom half of the form.

SOCIAL SECURITY NUMBER

In most cases, you will need to obtain a Social Security number for U.S. employment. It is widely used in the United States as a basic identification number—in most automated payroll systems, in university enrollment systems, and for transactions such as opening a bank account. Individuals entering the U.S. on the F, J, M, and Q visas are usually exempt from the U.S. Social Security tax, but those entering on other visas (such as H-2B or H-3) can expect to have the tax withheld from their pay. Even if you are exempt from paying Social Security tax, you will still need to obtain a Social Security number.

Because of enhanced security requirements, the Social Security Administration now requires independent verification that the individual has entered the U.S. in legal status from the BCIS. Upon entry into the U.S., this information should be available to the Social Security Administration within ten days in most cases; however, much longer delays have been reported. Without this independent verification, a Social Security number will not be issued. Social Security regulations require that you apply in person, and it is advised that you do this approximately ten to fourteen days after arrival (no sooner), as this will give the BCIS time to get your visa and arrival information into the system, allowing the Social Security Administration to verify your information and issue you a number.

It will be important for you to provide full documentation that clearly shows you have a visa that permits employment. The Social Security official to whom you submit your application will want to see your passport, your I-94 form, visa documents (DS-2019), and any documents related to your work placement. If you do not present the proper documentation, a Social Security card marked "Not Valid for Employment" will be issued. If this happens, you will not be able to receive a salary or stipend during the program. If you have any problems getting your Social Security card, you should contact your sponsoring organization for assistance.

INCOME TAX

As a general rule, individuals coming to the United States on any of the visas discussed in this article will be subject to U.S. income tax (and possibly state and local income tax) on the money they earn while in the country. H-2B workers are required to obtain a Certificate of Compliance, or Sailing Permit, before departure from the U.S. The Sailing Permit is evidence that they have paid whatever taxes may be due the U.S. government. H-3, J-1, and Q visa holders are exempt from this requirement. However, they are not exempt from filing an income tax return. Between January 1 and April 15 of the year following your employment, you will have to submit an income tax return (Form 1040EZ or Form 1040) to the IRS. The 1040EZ is used if you have no dependents, earned less than $50,000 of income, and have no travel expense deductions. If you have remained in the country from one year to the next, you also must submit a Form 8843 to verify your nonresident status. Tax regulations and procedures are not simple, and you should seek help from your employer and/or your sponsoring organization if you are participating in a J-1 program. You may also wish to secure a copy of IRS Publication 519, *U.S. Tax Guide for Aliens,* which is available free of charge from the Internal Revenue Service. Forms are available online at http://www.irs.gov/formspubs/index.html.

FULL-TIME STUDENTS AT U.S. SCHOOLS

Individuals enrolled at U.S. colleges and universities for full-time academic study are usually admitted on the basis of the F-1 (student), M-1 (student), or student category of the J-1 visa. In each case, summer employment may be possible before graduation, after graduation, or both. When such employment may take place, the length of time allowed and what the employment is called (practical training, curricular practical training, academic training) depends on the specific visa and circumstances of the individual student. A number of schools in the United States offer academic courses—usually known as cooperative education programs—that combine periods of study with periods of practical training employment. Under certain conditions, students from other countries who are enrolled as regular, full-time students in a cooperative education program are allowed to undertake the practical training assignments (which are usually paid) in the same manner as U.S. students. For information on enrollment in cooperative education programs and the American colleges and universities that offer these opportunities, contact:

Cooperative Education and Internship Association
4190 S. Highland Drive, Suite 211
Salt Lake City, Utah 84124
Telephone: 801-984-2026
Fax: 801-984-2027
World Wide Web: http://www.ceiainc.org

Whether enrolled in a cooperative education program (either before or after graduation) and regardless of the type of visa (M-1, F-1, or J-1), the student remains under the legal sponsorship of his or her college, university, or, in the case of some J-1 students, Exchange Visitor Program sponsor. Therefore, students should seek assistance from the international student adviser at their school.

Visa Violations or Overstays

U.S. immigration laws have become more restrictive, and the monitoring of foreign nationals in the U.S. has intensified. With increased homeland security issues, all international visitors, trainees, and temporary work visa holders should make sure that they fully understand their responsibilities under the particular visa they use to enter the U.S. It is extremely important that you know exactly what you are permitted to do on the type of visa you have been granted and how long you are permitted to remain in the United States. If you have any questions about this, please check with your program sponsor, employer, or the BCIS. If your program ends early, you are not permitted to remain in the United States. You must either return home upon completion of your work program or take the steps necessary to legally remain in the United States. There are severe penalties for foreign nationals who overstay their visas or violate their status. You could be barred from returning to the U.S. for ten years or longer if you violate your visa status, even unintentionally.

In Conclusion

Most countries have very strict regulations regarding employment for noncitizens in order to protect job opportunities for their own citizens. The United States is no different. What is different, however, is the U.S. system of visas and the rules and regulations that apply to each type (and subtype) of visa. The process of acquiring the proper visa takes a good deal of time (sometimes as long as one year) and can often be frustrating and confusing. Therefore, it is important to plan ahead and contact prospective employers as early as possible to ensure that the employer has sufficient time to undertake the paperwork involved. If you have applied to or have been accepted by a trainee program, make sure that the employer knows the name of the organization, because each sponsoring organization has its own internal procedures that must be followed. Security concerns in the U.S. have added additional requirements for individuals wanting to come to the U.S., so be prepared to answer questions and deal with new and changing procedures. Prepare well in advance, ask lots of questions, and make sure you understand what needs to be done. If you do your research and begin early, you will soon be on your way to a fulfilling work experience in the United States.

DO YOU WANT TO WORK TEMPORARILY IN CANADA?

What You Need to Know

If you wish to work temporarily in Canada, you will likely be required to have an **employment authorization.** An employment authorization is issued by an immigration officer after a Human Resources Centre approves your job offer.

This article outlines what you and your employer must do *before* you arrive in Canada. For additional advice, contact the Canadian Embassy, High Commission, or Consulate General near you.

Additional procedures may be required if you wish to work in Quebec. For further information, contact the Canadian Embassy abroad.

What Your Employer Must Do

Your employer must give details of your job offer to a Human Resources Centre. An employment counselor will check to determine if your offer of employment meets the prevailing wages and working conditions for the occupation concerned. A check will also be made to see if the job cannot be filled by a suitably qualified and available Canadian or permanent resident. If these conditions are met, the Human Resources Centre will approve your job offer. They will then issue a confirmation of offer of employment and send this to the Canadian Embassy, High Commission, or Consulate General in your country.

The employer will be provided with a copy of the confirmation of offer of employment, to be forwarded to you. Your employer is responsible for arranging your workers' compensation and medical coverage when you arrive in Canada.

Some jobs may be exempt from Human Resources Centre approval, and either the centre or a visa office at a Canadian embassy or consulate can advise you on this.

What You Must Do

The Canadian visa office near you will contact you upon receipt of your confirmation of offer of employment. You may be asked to go to an interview or to send some information by mail. You may also be asked to have a medical checkup,

Produced by Communications Branch, Citizenship and Immigration Canada. Reproduced with the permission of Citizenship and Immigration Canada and Public Works and Government Services Canada, 2000. For more information, please visit http://www.cic.gc.ca.

which you will have to pay for yourself. If you qualify and have all the necessary documents, you will receive an employment authorization and will possibly have a separate visitor visa placed in your passport.

The employment authorization will state that you can work at a specific job for a specific period of time for a specific employer. You will need to produce the authorization when you arrive in Canada, as well as your passport, visa (if issued), and airline tickets.

There is a processing fee when you submit an application for an employment authorization. There are no refunds if your application is refused. Request the brochure on immigration fees by calling Public Enquiries or ask an immigration officer for fee information.

Different procedures exist for citizens or permanent residents of the United States. You should seek clarification from the nearest Canadian embassy or consulate; general procedures are stated later in this article.

An employment authorization will not be issued to you to come to Canada to look for work. *It is valid only for the specific job, the specific amount of time, and the employer stated on the form.*

WHEN YOU ARRIVE IN CANADA

When you arrive at the port of entry to Canada, show your confirmation of offer of employment, your employment authorization, and other papers to an immigration officer. You will be given forms to fill out so that you can get a Social Insurance Number (SIN). These forms and proper identification, such as a birth certificate, should be taken to a counselor at a Human Resources Centre, who can help you if you have trouble filling them out. When you receive your SIN card, you will have to give your number to your employer.

Your employment authorization is not a contract. Your job can be ended by you or your employer at any time. However, if your duties change or the job is to be extended, you must contact immigration right away, before the expiry date of your current authorization. You can do this by calling the Canadian Citizenship and Immigration Call Centre at 888-242-2100 (toll-free).

SOME WORKERS CAN APPLY AT A PORT OF ENTRY

Most foreign workers must apply for employment authorization outside of Canada, but if you are a resident of the United States, Greenland, or St. Pierre and Miquelon, you can apply for an employment authorization when you arrive at a port of entry to Canada. To apply this way, you must produce your confirmation of offer of employment and other papers when you arrive at the port of entry. Remember that you must find out what papers you will need *before* arriving in Canada. Check with the Canadian Embassy, High Commission, or Consulate General.

REMEMBER

- There is a nonrefundable fee to process a request for an employment authorization.

- Most foreign workers must get their employment authorizations before arriving in Canada. Visitors *cannot* obtain employment authorization while in Canada.

- You must follow the terms of your employment authorization while in Canada. If you do not, you may be asked to leave the country.

- Human Resources Centre staff in Canada and Canadian government representatives in your home country cannot help you find a job.

- If you want to work temporarily or if you have further questions about working in Canada, contact the nearest Canadian Embassy, High Commission, or Consulate General.

- This is not a legal document. For precise, legal information consult the Immigration Act and Regulations.

STATE-BY-STATE LISTINGS

ALABAMA

CAMP LANEY FOR BOYS
916 WEST RIVER ROAD
MENTONE, ALABAMA 35984

General Information Traditional summer camp for boys ages 8-14 with a ropes course, archery, riflery, horseback, tennis, team sports, swimming, canoeing, and mountain biking. Optional activities include rock climbing and white-water rafting. Established in 1959. 120-acre facility located 58 miles from Chattanooga, Tennessee. Features: beautiful river; mountain bike trails; climbing wall; extensive ropes course; surrounding woods; 3 tennis courts.

Profile of Summer Employees Total number: 55; typical ages: 19–22. 100% men; 5% high school students; 95% college students. Nonsmokers preferred.

Employment Information Openings are from June 1 to August 9. Jobs available: ▶ 3–4 *horseback staff* (minimum age 18) experienced with horses (or training provided) at $2100–$3000 per season ▶ 7–9 *ropes course staff* (minimum age 18) with provided training at $2100–$2700 per season ▶ *waterfront staff* (minimum age 18) with provided Red Cross lifeguarding training at $2100–$2800 per season. Applicants must submit formal organization application, three personal references. An in-person interview is required. International applicants accepted; must apply through a recognized agency.

Benefits and Preemployment Training Free housing, free meals, health insurance, willing to provide letters of recommendation, willing to complete paperwork for educational credit, willing to act as a professional reference, and opportunity to attend seminars/workshops. Preemployment training is required and includes accident prevention and safety, first aid, CPR, interpersonal skills, leadership skills.

Contact Associate Director, Camp Laney for Boys. Telephone: 800-648-2919. Fax: 256-634-4098. E-mail: info@camplaney.com. World Wide Web: http://www.camplaney.com. Contact by e-mail, phone, or through World Wide Web site. Application deadline: continuous.

CAMP SKYLINE
4888 ALABAMA HIGHWAY 117
MENTONE, ALABAMA 35984

General Information Residential camp located on top of Lookout Mountain serving 275–315 girls. Campers select a "six-a-day" schedule from more than 20 activities. Established in 1947. 80-acre facility located 50 miles from Chattanooga, Tennessee. Features: river access; three oval riding rings; western trails; hut row cabins; triplex; lodge, Riverside Hotel; large gymnasium; arts and crafts building; tennis, volleyball, basketball courts; circus; spacious dining hall.

Profile of Summer Employees Total number: 125–140; typical ages: 18–24. 5% men; 95% women; 6% minorities; 23% high school students; 43% college students; 5% retirees; 2% non-U.S. citizens; 31% local applicants. Nonsmokers preferred.

Employment Information Openings are from June 8 to August 1. Jobs available: ▶ 10–20 *Christian leadership instructors* (minimum age 18) ▶ 4–6 *canoeing instructors* (minimum age 18) ▶ 5 *cheerleading/flag twirling/baton twirling instructors* (minimum age 17) ▶ 5–8 *circus staff* (minimum age 18) ▶ 10 *fine and performing arts instructors (music, dance, arts and crafts, and drama)* (minimum age 17) ▶ 10–12 *lifeguards and swimming instructors* (minimum age 17) with WSI certification ▶ 2–3 *nature specialists* (minimum age 18) ▶ 3–4 *riflery instructors* (minimum age 18) ▶ 15–20 *ropes course and climbing tower instructors* (minimum age 18) ▶ 8–10 *sports instructors* (minimum age 17) with skills including archery, tennis, swimming, diving, horseback riding, and gymnastics. Applicants must submit formal organization application, four personal references. An in-person interview is recommended, but a telephone interview is acceptable. International applicants accepted; must obtain own visa, obtain own working papers, apply through a recognized agency.

Benefits and Preemployment Training Free housing, free meals, willing to provide letters of recommendation, and on-the-job training. Preemployment training is required and includes accident prevention and safety, first aid, CPR, leadership skills.

Contact Sally C. Johnson, Director, Camp Skyline, PO Box 287, Mentone, Alabama 35984. Telephone: 800-448-9279. Fax: 256-634-3018. E-mail: info@campskyline.com. World Wide Web: http://www.campskyline.com. Contact by e-mail, fax, mail, phone, or through World Wide Web site. Application deadline: continuous.

THE SOUTHWESTERN COMPANY, ALABAMA
See The Southwestern Company on page 297 for complete description.

STUDENT CONSERVATION ASSOCIATION (SCA), ALABAMA
See Student Conservation Association (SCA), New Hampshire on page 200 for complete description.

ALASKA

A CHRISTIAN MINISTRY IN THE NATIONAL PARKS–ALASKA
See A Christian Ministry in the National Parks–Maine on page 107 for complete description.

ALASKA STATE PARKS VOLUNTEER PROGRAM
550 WEST 7TH AVENUE, SUITE 1380
ANCHORAGE, ALASKA 99501-3561

General Information Program offering volunteer positions in state parks throughout the state of Alaska. Established in 1970. 3,300,000-acre facility. Features: wilderness; wildlife.

Profile of Summer Employees Total number: 184; typical ages: 18–70. 45% college students; 50% retirees; 5% local applicants.

Employment Information Openings are from May 15 to October 15. Winter break positions also offered. Jobs available: ▶ 6 *backcountry ranger assistants* (minimum age 18) with outdoor experience, good physical condition, familiarity with hand and power tools, and some education in natural resources at $200–$300 per month ▶ 15 *natural history interpreters* (minimum age 18) with outdoor experience, good people skills, and some education in natural resources at $200–$300 per month ▶ 5 *park caretakers* (minimum age 18) with outdoor experience, good people skills, and good physical condition at $200–$300 per month ▶ 20 *ranger assistants* (minimum age 18) with outdoor experience, good people skills, good physical condition, and some education in natural resources at $100–$300 per month ▶ 15 *trail crew* (minimum age 18) with outdoor experience, good physical condition, familiar with hand and power tools, and some education in natural resources at $200–$300 per month. Applicants must submit a formal organization application, letter of interest, resume, personal reference, letter of recommendation. A telephone interview is required.

Benefits and Preemployment Training Free housing, on-the-job training, willing to complete paperwork for educational credit, and expense allowance for food. Preemployment training is required.

Contact Lynn Wibbenmeyer, Volunteer Coordinator, Alaska State Parks Volunteer Program. Telephone: 907-269-8708. Fax: 907-269-8907. E-mail: volunteer@dnr.state.ak.us. World Wide Web: http://www.dnr.state.ak.us/parks/vip. Contact by e-mail, fax, mail, phone, or through World Wide Web site. Application deadline: April 1.

AMERICA & PACIFIC TOURS, INC. (A&P)
430 K STREET
ANCHORAGE, ALASKA 99501

General Information Japanese land operator for Japanese tourists providing planned, individualized, and special guided trips of Alaska. Established in 1970. Features: main office; boys' condominium (1); girls' condominium (1); Fairbanks office; Tokyo, Japan office; Palmer Land only Alaska.

Profile of Summer Employees Total number: 15. 50% men; 50% women; 90% college students; 50% non-U.S. citizens; 50% local applicants. Nonsmokers preferred.

Employment Information Openings are from June 1 to September 30. Winter break and year-round positions also offered. Jobs available: ▶ 1 *accounting* (minimum age 22) with accounting skills at $1800–$2000 per month ▶ 1–2 *bookkeepers* (minimum age 23) with ability to speak Japanese and English at $1800–$1900 per month ▶ 10–15 *tour guides and office workers* (minimum age 20) with current driver's license and fluency in Japanese (salary depends upon experience as guide) at $1400–$3000 per month. Applicants must submit a letter of interest, resume. A telephone interview is required. International applicants accepted.

Benefits and Preemployment Training Housing at a cost, on-the-job training, and willing to complete paperwork for educational credit. Preemployment training is optional.

Contact Keizo Sugimoto, President, America & Pacific Tours, Inc. (A&P), PO Box 10-1068, Anchorage, Alaska 99510. Telephone: 907-272-9401. Fax: 907-272-0251. E-mail: aptours@alaska. com. World Wide Web: http://www.aptoursalaska.com. Contact by e-mail, fax, or phone. Application deadline: continuous.

CAMP TOGOWOODS
WASILLA, ALASKA 99654

General Information Residential program of traditional camping activities for girls ages 7–17. Established in 1958. 260-acre facility located 50 miles from Anchorage. Features: freshwater lake; wooded setting; hiking trails.

Profile of Summer Employees Total number: 26–28; typical ages: 18–50. 5% men; 95% women; 24% minorities; 95% college students; 10% non-U.S. citizens; 38% local applicants. Nonsmokers required.

Employment Information Openings are from June to August. Jobs available: ▶ 1 *art director* (minimum age 21) at $2200 per season ▶ 1 *assistant director* (minimum age 21) at $2200 per season ▶ 2 *cooks* (minimum age 18) at $2000 per season ▶ 12 *counselors* (minimum age 21) first aid and CPR certifications required at $2000 per season ▶ 1 *environmental education director* (minimum age 21) at $2200 per season ▶ 1 *food service director* (minimum age 21) at $2200 per season ▶ 1 *health care director* (minimum age 21) with RN license or EMT and current CPR certification at $2200 per season ▶ 2 *lifeguards* (minimum age 18) with lifeguard certification (waterfront lifeguarding preferred) at $2000 per season ▶ 1 *waterfront director* (minimum age 21) with SCS certification, lifeguard training, and waterfront lifeguarding at $2200 per season ▶ 4 *wilderness counselors* (minimum age 21) with wilderness trip-leading experience preferred; wilderness first aid and CPR required at $2000 per season ▶ 1 *wilderness program director* (minimum age 21) with experience leading wilderness trips at $2200 per season. Applicants must submit formal organization application, three personal references. An in-person interview is recommended, but a telephone interview is acceptable. International applicants accepted; must apply through a recognized agency.

Benefits and Preemployment Training Free housing, free meals, health insurance, willing to provide letters of recommendation, on-the-job training, willing to complete paperwork for educational credit, willing to act as a professional reference, and travel stipend. Preemployment training is required and includes accident prevention and safety, interpersonal skills, leadership skills, supervision training.

Contact Laura Pettersen, Camp Director, Girl Scouts Susitna Council, Camp Togowoods, HC 30, Box 5400, Wasilla, Alaska 99687. Telephone: 907-376-1310. Fax: 907-376-1358. E-mail: camptogo@alaska.net. World Wide Web: http://www.girlscouts.ak.org. Contact by e-mail, fax, mail, or phone. Application deadline: continuous.

KATMAILAND INC.
4125 AIRCRAFT DRIVE
ANCHORAGE, ALASKA 99502

General Information Katmailand Inc. operates three lodges and a restaurant in Katmail National Park. Established in 1949. 4-acre facility. Features: wooded setting; photography; hiking; kayaking; fishing; scenic mountains.

Profile of Summer Employees Total number: 58; typical ages: 22–38. 70% men; 30% women; 85% college students; 15% local applicants.

Employment Information Openings are from May 20 to September 20. Jobs available: ▶ *administrators/auditors/front desk staff* with extensive bookkeeping experience; responsibilities include: front desk operation, customer service, cash handling, credit cards, and ten key and typing 40 wpm ▶ *assistant chef/head chef* with responsibilities including assisting in prep work, baking, stocking, cleaning, and other assigned tasks ▶ *auditors* ▶ *bartenders* ▶ *bus drivers* (minimum age 25) with good communication skills and good physical condition; must have Commercial Driver's License allowing operation of school bus with multiple passengers ▶ *dishwashers* ▶ *driver/laborers* (minimum age 25) with customer service skills and commercial driver's license; responsibilities include cleaning of facility, float planes, dumping garbage daily, greeting guests at airport or pier, and loading luggage ▶ *head maintenance workers* with well rounded background; must have knowledge of carpentry, plumbing, and welding skills ▶ *house supervisors* with responsibilities that include overseeing housekeeping, bartender, and storekeeper ▶ 5–10 *housekeepers/food service workers* (minimum age 18) with responsibilities that include cleaning guest's cabins, doing laundry, waiting tables during meal hours, busing tables, helping in kitchen, and having ability to lift 40 pounds, and customer service at $5.65 per hour ▶ *inn keepers* with responsibilities including overseeing all kitchen operations, including ordering, inventory, quality control, special diet requests, cleaning guest cabins, and waiting/busing tables ▶ *sport fishing guides* with extensive fishing experience, knowledge of fly-fishing, casting, trolling, fly-tying, and spin fishing, boat handling skills and maintenance experience. Must have OUPC six pack license and three years Alaska guiding experience ▶ *storekeepers* with knowledge of fishing and responsibilities that include: inventory control, pricing, stocking, display, daily reports, balancing cash, and being in charge of rental equipment. Applicants must submit a formal organization application, three personal references, three letters of recommendation. A telephone interview is required. International applicants accepted; must obtain own visa, obtain own working papers.

Benefits and Preemployment Training Free housing, free meals, on-the-job training, and airfare from Anchorage to Lodge. Preemployment training is required and includes accident prevention and safety, first aid, CPR.

Contact Jim Albert, Brooks Lodge Manager, Katmailand Inc., 4125 Aircraft Drive, Anchorage, Alaska 99502. E-mail: job@katmailand.com. World Wide Web: http://www.katmailand.com. Contact by e-mail, mail, or through World Wide Web site. No phone calls. Application deadline: continuous.

THE SOUTHWESTERN COMPANY, ALASKA
See The Southwestern Company on page 297 for complete description.

STUDENT CONSERVATION ASSOCIATION (SCA), ALASKA
See Student Conservation Association (SCA), New Hampshire on page 200 for complete description.

ARIZONA

A CHRISTIAN MINISTRY IN THE NATIONAL PARKS– ARIZONA
See A Christian Ministry in the National Parks–Maine on page 107 for complete description.

CENTER FOR TALENTED YOUTH/JOHNS HOPKINS UNIVERSITY–ARIZONA STATE UNIVERSITY
TEMPE, ARIZONA
See Center for Talented Youth/Johns Hopkins University on page 131 for complete description.

GRAND CANYON NATIONAL PARK LODGES
PO BOX 699
GRAND CANYON, ARIZONA 86023

General Information National park concessioner providing all hotel, restaurant, retail, and transportation services on the south rim of the Grand Canyon. Established in 1903. 640-acre facility located 90 miles from Flagstaff. Features: Grand Canyon; San Francisco Peaks; Sedona/Red Rock Wilderness Area; Kendrick Mountain Wilderness Area; Lake Powell/NRA; Lake Havasu.

Profile of Summer Employees Total number: 1,220; typical ages: 18–42. 50% men; 50% women; 30% minorities; 20% college students; 20% retirees; 10% non-U.S. citizens; 30% local applicants.

Employment Information Openings are from February 15 to October 20. Spring break, winter break, and year-round positions also offered. Jobs available: ▶ 30–40 *cafeteria workers* (minimum age 18) at $6.25 per hour ▶ 15–25 *cashiers* (minimum age 18) with experience cashiering in food service at $6.25 per hour ▶ 10–15 *cooks' helpers* (minimum age 18) with some food service experience at $6.60 per hour ▶ 20–30 *cooks-I,II,III* (minimum age 18) with a minimum of 6 months restaurant cooking experience at $6.75–$9.36 per hour ▶ 80–100 *guest room attendants* (minimum age 18) at $6.25 per hour ▶ 15–25 *guest service agents* (minimum age 18) with hotel front desk or previous customer service experience at $6.76 per hour ▶ 10–12 *hosts/hostesses* (minimum age 15) with a minimum of 6 months restaurant experience at $6.25 per hour ▶ 50–70 *kitchen/utility personnel* (minimum age 18) at $6.25 per hour ▶ 40–50 *retail clerks* (minimum age 18) with cashier and/or retail sales experience at $6.25 per hour. Applicants must submit formal organization application. An in-person interview is recommended, but a telephone interview is acceptable. International applicants accepted; must apply through a recognized agency.

Benefits and Preemployment Training Meals at a cost, free housing, formal training, possible full-time employment, health insurance, names of contacts, on-the-job training, willing to complete paperwork for educational credit, opportunity to attend seminars/workshops, and living in a National Park. Preemployment training is required and includes accident prevention and safety, general information about company and park.

Contact Rob Gossard, Staffing Manager, Grand Canyon National Park Lodges. Telephone: 928-638-2343. Fax: 928-638-2361. E-mail: jobs@grandcanyonlodges.com. Contact by e-mail, fax, mail, or phone. Application deadline: continuous.

ORME SUMMER CAMP
1000 ORME ROAD
MAYER, ARIZONA 86333

General Information Residential coed camp serving up to 200 campers with a wide variety of indoor and outdoor activities, including mountain biking, horseback riding, and desert survival/ rock climbing. Established in 1929. 40,000-acre facility located 70 miles from Phoenix. Features: swimming pool; complete gymnasium with weight room; riflery range; high desert climate; 40,000 acres for horseback riding; fully equipped boarding school campus.

Profile of Summer Employees Total number: 45; typical ages: 19–24. 50% men; 50% women; 2% minorities; 10% high school students; 80% college students; 1% retirees; 18% non-U.S. citizens; 10% local applicants. Nonsmokers preferred.

Employment Information Openings are from June 1 to August 14. Jobs available: ▶ 5–10 *general counselors* (minimum age 19) with driver's license and some experience at $1300–$1400 per season ▶ 1–2 *horsemanship staff* (minimum age 21) with driver's license and extensive experience with horses and children at $1400–$1600 per season ▶ 1–2 *outdoor adventure/ survival instructors* (minimum age 21) with Outward Bound or NOLS completion or equivalent and driver's license at $1500–$1600 per season ▶ 1 *photo journalist* (minimum age 19) with experience with digital camera and basic computer competency at $1300–$1400 per season ▶ 1–2 *pool assistants* (minimum age 19) with WSI and lifeguard certification at $1300–$1400 per season ▶ 1 *riflery instructor* (minimum age 19) with driver's license and riflery safety courses at $1500–$1600 per season ▶ 1–3 *senior counselors* (minimum age 20) with one year of college completed, driver's license, and experience working with children in camp setting at $1500–$1600 per season. Applicants must submit formal organization application, writing sample, three personal references, three letters of recommendation. A telephone interview is required. International applicants accepted; must obtain own visa, obtain own working papers, apply through a recognized agency.

Benefits and Preemployment Training Free housing, free meals, willing to provide letters of recommendation, on-the-job training, willing to act as a professional reference, and travel reimbursement. Preemployment training is required and includes accident prevention and safety, first aid, CPR, interpersonal skills, leadership skills.

Contact Mr. Tim Magill, Director, Orme Summer Camp, HC 63, Box 3040, Mayer, Arizona 86333. Telephone: 928-632-7601. Fax: 928-632-7605. E-mail: tmagill@ormeschool.org. World Wide Web: http://www.ormecamp.org. Contact by e-mail, fax, mail, or phone. Application deadline: March 15.

THE SOUTHWESTERN COMPANY, ARIZONA
See The Southwestern Company on page 297 for complete description.

STIVERS STAFFING SERVICES–ARIZONA
See Stivers Staffing Services–Illinois on page 96 for complete description.

STUDENT CONSERVATION ASSOCIATION (SCA), ARIZONA
See Student Conservation Association (SCA), New Hampshire on page 200 for complete description.

ARKANSAS

THE SOUTHWESTERN COMPANY, ARKANSAS
See The Southwestern Company on page 297 for complete description.

STUDENT CONSERVATION ASSOCIATION (SCA), ARKANSAS
See Student Conservation Association (SCA), New Hampshire on page 200 for complete description.

CALIFORNIA

ACADEMY BY THE SEA/CAMP PACIFIC
2605 CARLSBAD BOULEVARD
CARLSBAD, CALIFORNIA 92008
General Information Nonprofit, private camp that hires camp counselors, teachers, and administrative staff. Established in 1943. 16-acre facility located 35 miles from San Diego. Features: ocean front campus; 4 tennis courts; ocean front recreation center; swimming pool; dormitories; athletic fields.

Profile of Summer Employees Total number: 100; typical ages: 20–40. 60% men; 40% women; 2% high school students; 30% college students; 20% non-U.S. citizens; 10% local applicants. Nonsmokers preferred.

Employment Information Openings are from June 15 to August 5. Jobs available: ▶ 1–12 *camp counselors* (minimum age 21) at $2100–$2500 per season ▶ 1–5 *camp nurses* (minimum age 25) at $3600–$4500 per season ▶ 10–20 *teachers* (minimum age 21) with degree required at $3000–$3500 per season. Applicants must submit formal organization application, letter of interest, resume, academic transcripts, two personal references, letter of recommendation. An in-person interview is required. International applicants accepted; must apply through a recognized agency.

Benefits and Preemployment Training Free housing, free meals, possible full-time employment, willing to provide letters of recommendation, names of contacts, on-the-job training, willing to act as a professional reference, and opportunity to attend seminars/workshops. Preemployment training is required and includes accident prevention and safety, first aid, CPR, interpersonal skills, leadership skills.

Contact Lori Adlfinger, Associate Director, Academy by the Sea/Camp Pacific, PO Box 3000, Carlsbad, California 92018. Fax: 760-729-1574. E-mail: info@abts.com. World Wide Web: http://www.abts.com. Contact by e-mail, fax, or mail. No phone calls. Application deadline: continuous.

A CHRISTIAN MINISTRY IN THE NATIONAL PARKS–CALIFORNIA

See A Christian Ministry in the National Parks–Maine on page 107 for complete description.

ADVATECH PACIFIC, INC.
2015 PARK AVENUE, SUITE 8
REDLANDS, CALIFORNIA 92373

General Information Engineering and development firm specializing in support of aerospace and defense industries. Conducts engineering analysis and develops engineering applications software. Established in 1995. Located 60 miles from Los Angeles.

Profile of Summer Employees Total number: 20; typical ages: 21–24. 50% minorities; 100% college students. Nonsmokers required.

Employment Information Year-round positions also offered. Jobs available: ▶ 1–2 *engineering assistants* with engineering background with structures, design, or fluids at $10–$20 per hour ▶ 1–2 *marketing/finance assistants* with excellent verbal and writing skills, multi-lingual desirable at $6–$10 per hour ▶ 1–2 *programming assistants* with background in C++, GUI, UNIX, and Motif desirable at $10–$20 per hour. Applicants must submit resume. An in-person interview is required.

Benefits and Preemployment Training Possible full-time employment, on-the-job training, and willing to act as a professional reference.

Contact Sheila Snider, Business Manager, Advatech Pacific, Inc., 2015 Park Avenue, Suite 8, Redlands, California 92373. Fax: 909-798-9368. E-mail: info@advatechpacific.com. World Wide Web: http://www.advatechpacific.com. Contact by e-mail, fax, or through World Wide Web site. No phone calls. Application deadline: continuous.

ADVENTURE CITY
10120 BEACH BOULEVARD
STANTON, CALIFORNIA 90680

General Information Small child amusement park with rides. Established in 1994. 3-acre facility located 1 mile from Anaheim. Features: 10 adult and child capacity rides; food service; rock climbing wall; children's theater; petting farm; game room.

Profile of Summer Employees Total number: 90–100; typical ages: 15–75. 40% men; 60% women; 50% minorities; 40% high school students; 40% college students; 5% retirees; 5% non-U.S. citizens; 20% local applicants. Nonsmokers required.

Employment Information Openings are from January to December. Year-round positions also offered. Jobs available: ▶ 5–10 *food service staff* (minimum age 16) with friendly, outgoing personality at $6.75 per hour ▶ 5–10 *merchandise salespersons* (minimum age 15) with friendly, outgoing personality at $6.75 per hour ▶ 1–5 *redemption/game room workers* (minimum age 15) with friendly, outgoing personality at $6.75 per hour ▶ 5–10 *ride operators* (minimum age 18) with friendly, outgoing personality at $6.75 per hour. Applicants must submit formal organization application, resume, three personal references. An in-person interview is required. International applicants accepted; must obtain own visa, obtain own working papers, apply through a recognized agency.

Benefits and Preemployment Training Possible full-time employment, on-the-job training, willing to complete paperwork for educational credit, and reduced cost meals. Preemployment training is required and includes accident prevention and safety, interpersonal skills, leadership skills.

Contact Bob Brazelton, Human Resources Representative, Adventure City, 1238 South Beach Boulevard, Anaheim, California 92804. Telephone: 714-236-9300 Ext. 503. Fax: 714-827-2992. E-mail: adventurecity@prodigy.net. World Wide Web: http://www.adventurecity.com. Contact by fax, mail, or phone. Application deadline: continuous.

ADVENTURE CONNECTION, INC.
986 LOTUS ROAD
LOTUS, CALIFORNIA 95651

General Information River trips for children and adults ages 7 and up. Established in 1983. 25-acre facility located 45 miles from Sacramento. Features: river-side camp; volleyball court.

Profile of Summer Employees Total number: 30; typical ages: 20–50. 50% men; 50% women; 20% minorities; 35% college students; 15% retirees; 10% non-U.S. citizens; 50% local applicants.

Employment Information Openings are from April 1 to October 15. Spring break positions also offered. Jobs available: ▶ *food packer/ordering staff* (minimum age 18) with driver's license (noncommercial license acceptable), training provided at $7–$10 per hour ▶ 25 *river guides* (minimum age 18) with experience guiding or completion of guide school and first aid/CPR certification at $60–$110 per day. Applicants must submit a formal organization application, resume, personal reference, letter of recommendation. An in-person interview is recommended, but a telephone interview is acceptable. International applicants accepted.

Benefits and Preemployment Training Free housing, formal training, willing to provide letters of recommendation, on-the-job training, willing to complete paperwork for educational credit, willing to act as a professional reference, and opportunity to attend seminars/workshops. Preemployment training is required and includes accident prevention and safety, first aid, CPR, interpersonal skills, leadership skills, swiftwater rescue, natural and human history, interpretive training.

Contact Nate Rangel, President, Adventure Connection, Inc., PO Box 475, Coloma, California 95613. Telephone: 800-556-6060. Fax: 530-626-9268. E-mail: getwet@raftcalifornia.com. World Wide Web: http://www.raftcalifornia.com. Contact by e-mail, fax, mail, or phone. Application deadline: continuous.

BAR 717 RANCH/CAMP TRINITY
STAR ROUTE BOX 150
HAYFORK, CALIFORNIA 96041

General Information Coed ranch offering horsemanship, swimming, hiking, crafts, animal care, ranch work projects, pottery, and the teaching of responsibility. Established in 1930.

450-acre facility located 80 miles from Redding. Features: located on pristine river; surrounded by acres of pristine forest; barn with 30 horses; miles of trails for horseback riding, hiking, and backpacking; high and low ropes course; large organic gardens.

Profile of Summer Employees Total number: 50; typical ages: 18–60. 50% men; 50% women; 10% minorities; 1% high school students; 90% college students; 5% retirees; 10% non-U.S. citizens; 10% local applicants. Nonsmokers required.

Employment Information Openings are from June 20 to September 1. Jobs available: ▶ 30 *counselors* (minimum age 19) with 2 years of college completed (or equivalent work experience), lifesaving, first aid/CPR, and wilderness first aid training at $195–$245 per week ▶ 6–10 *junior counselors* (minimum age 18) with lifesaving, first aid/CPR training at $185–$195 per week ▶ 4–6 *kitchen staff members* (minimum age 18) at $185 per week. Applicants must submit formal organization application, two personal references. An in-person interview is recommended, but a telephone interview is acceptable. International applicants accepted; must obtain own visa, obtain own working papers, apply through a recognized agency.

Benefits and Preemployment Training Housing at a cost, meals at a cost, willing to provide letters of recommendation, on-the-job training, willing to complete paperwork for educational credit, and willing to act as a professional reference. Preemployment training is required and includes accident prevention and safety, first aid, CPR, interpersonal skills, leadership skills.

Contact Gretchen Collard, Staff Director, Bar 717 Ranch/Camp Trinity, Star Route Box 150, Hayfork, California 96041. Telephone: 530-628-5992. Fax: 530-628-9392. E-mail: gretchen@bar717.com. World Wide Web: http://www.bar717.com. Contact by e-mail, fax, mail, phone, or through World Wide Web site. Application deadline: May 15.

CAMP JCA SHALOM
34342 MULHOLLAND HIGHWAY
MALIBU, CALIFORNIA 90265

General Information Residential Jewish camp offering a warm, supportive atmosphere for campers ages 7–17. Established in 1961. 135-acre facility located 40 miles from Los Angeles. Features: wooded setting in mountains; ropes course; swimming pool; archery range.

Profile of Summer Employees Total number: 90; typical age: 18. 50% men; 50% women; 10% minorities; 20% high school students; 78% college students; 10% non-U.S. citizens; 70% local applicants. Nonsmokers preferred.

Employment Information Openings are from June to August. Spring break and winter break positions also offered. Jobs available: ▶ 1 *Jewish education director* (minimum age 21) with knowledge of Jewish traditions, culture, history, and entertainment, as well as the ability to develop and lead camp-wide programs, including all-day Shabbat programs at $1000–$3000 per season ▶ 1–5 *bus drivers* (minimum age 18) with current Class B California driver's license and a clean driving record (knowledge of mountain driving extremely helpful) at $1000–$3000 per season ▶ 40–60 *counselors* (minimum age 18) at $1000–$3000 per season ▶ 1–4 *registered nurses* with RN and ability to run the infirmary, supervise nurse's aide, and interact well with parents at $1000–$3000 per season ▶ 1 *ropes course leader* (minimum age 21) with ability to lead groups through high and low elements at $1000–$3000 per season ▶ 1 *song leader* with ability to lead camp-wide singing of American and Hebrew folk songs, highly spirited nature, and guitar-playing skills at $1000–$3000 per season ▶ 5 *swimming and water safety instructors* with CPR, ALS, and WSI certifications at $1000–$3000 per season ▶ 2 *teen travel leaders* (minimum age 21) with college degree, knowledge of outdoors (experience with children essential), and current first aid and CPR certification at $1000–$3000 per season ▶ 3–4 *unit heads* (minimum age 21) with college degree, three years of camping experience, and good Jewish program skills (graduate training or social work experience helpful) at $1000–$3000 per season. Applicants must submit formal organization application, three personal references, three letters of recommendation. An in-person interview is recommended, but a telephone interview is acceptable. International applicants accepted; must apply through a recognized agency.

Benefits and Preemployment Training Free housing and on-the-job training. Preemployment training is optional and includes accident prevention and safety, interpersonal skills, leadership skills.

Contact Mr. Joel Charnick, Camp Director, Camp JCA Shalom, 34342 Mulholland Highway, Malibu, California 90265. Telephone: 818-889-5500. Fax: 818-889-5132. World Wide Web: http://www.campjcashalom.com. Contact by mail, phone, or through World Wide Web site. Application deadline: continuous.

CAMP LA JOLLA
176 C AVENUE
CORONADO, CALIFORNIA 92118

General Information Weight-loss/fitness camp for ages 8 and older serving separate age and gender groups in fitness, sports, nutrition, behavior modification, field trips, beach visits, theater arts, and arts and crafts; emphasis on healthy lifestyle. Established in 1979. 50-acre facility located 10 miles from San Diego. Features: beachside location; numerous athletic fields; outdoor swimming pool; 35 million dollar workout facility; university dormitories–suite style.

Profile of Summer Employees Total number: 86. 20% men; 80% women; 25% minorities; 5% high school students; 95% college students; 30% local applicants. Nonsmokers required.

Employment Information Openings are from June 14 to August 25. Year-round positions also offered. Jobs available: ▶ *aerobics instructors* at $900–$1600 per season ▶ 3 *behavior modification specialists* at $900–$1600 per season ▶ 15 *counselors* at $900–$1600 per season ▶ 10 *exercise specialists* with WSI and lifeguard certification at $900–$1600 per season ▶ 2 *nurses* with RN, EMT, or LPN license at $2000–$2600 per season ▶ 3 *nutritionists* at $900–$1600 per season ▶ 10 *personal trainers* at $900–$1600 per season ▶ *tennis instructors* at $900–$1600 per season. Applicants must submit a formal organization application, personal reference, letter of recommendation. An in-person interview is recommended, but a telephone interview is acceptable.

Benefits and Preemployment Training Free housing, free meals, willing to provide letters of recommendation, on-the-job training, willing to complete paperwork for educational credit, willing to act as a professional reference, and internship opportunities available. Preemployment training is required and includes accident prevention and safety, first aid, interpersonal skills, leadership skills.

Contact Nancy Lenhart, Director, Camp La Jolla, 176 C Avenue, Coronado, California 92118. Telephone: 800-825-8746. Fax: 619-435-8188. E-mail: camplj@aol.com. World Wide Web: http://www.camplajolla.com. Contact by e-mail, fax, mail, phone, or through World Wide Web site. Application deadline: June 1.

CAMP LAKOTA
11220 DOROTHY LANE
FRAZIER PARK, CALIFORNIA 93225

General Information Residential camp serving 140 girls ages 7–17 weekly and emphasizing traditional activities, horsemanship, and Girl Scout programs. Established in 1949. 58-acre facility located 75 miles from Los Angeles. Features: pine forest setting; strong equestrian program; heated swimming pool; adjacent to National Forest.

Profile of Summer Employees Total number: 40; typical ages: 18–35. 5% men; 95% women; 30% minorities; 5% high school students; 95% college students; 20% non-U.S. citizens; 2% local applicants. Nonsmokers required.

Employment Information Openings are from June 1 to August 25. Year-round positions also offered. Jobs available: ▶ 1 *assistant cook* (minimum age 18) at $165–$190 per week ▶ 1 *head cook* (minimum age 21) with food preparation experience at $235–$265 per week ▶ 1 *health supervisor* (minimum age 21) with RN license (preferred), EMT, or LVN at $295–$315 per week

▶ 3 *kitchen staff members* (minimum age 16) at $120–$191 per week ▶ 1 *leadership director* (minimum age 21) with experience as a camp counselor or equivalent at $165–$195 per week ▶ 1 *maintenance person* (minimum age 21) with driver's license at $162–$186 per week ▶ 1 *pool director* (minimum age 18) with lifeguard, CPR, and standard first aid certification (WSI preferred) at $164–$186 per week ▶ 1 *program director* (minimum age 21) with camp experience required at $200–$230 per week ▶ 1 *riding director* (minimum age 21) with CHA certification or equivalent (preferred) at $210–$235 per week ▶ 15 *unit counselors* (minimum age 18) at $150–$185 per week ▶ 7 *unit leaders* (minimum age 21) at $165–$195 per week ▶ 2–3 *wranglers* (minimum age 16)' with horse experience at $160–$187 per week. Applicants must submit formal organization application, three personal references. An in-person interview is recommended, but a telephone interview is acceptable. International applicants accepted; must apply through a recognized agency.

Benefits and Preemployment Training Free housing, free meals, willing to provide letters of recommendation, on-the-job training, and willing to complete paperwork for educational credit. Preemployment training is required and includes accident prevention and safety, first aid, CPR, interpersonal skills, leadership skills, program skills, group building activities.

Contact Connie Scharff, Outdoor Program/Property Director, Camp Lakota, 9421 Winnetka Avenue, Chatsworth, California 91311. Telephone: 818-886-1801 EXT. 31. Fax: 818-407-4840. E-mail: cscharff@sfvgsc.org. World Wide Web: http://www.sfvgsc.org. Contact by e-mail, fax, mail, phone, or through World Wide Web site. Application deadline: continuous.

CASTILLEJA SCHOOL
1310 BRYANT STREET
PALO ALTO, CALIFORNIA 94301

General Information All-girls, day school grades 6-12 and summer day camp with full enrichment program. Established in 1907. Affiliated with National Association of Independent Schools, Secondary School Admission Test Board. 5-acre facility located 30 miles from San Francisco. Features: competitive pool; beautiful campus; theater; full gymnasium; excellent dining services.

Profile of Summer Employees Total number: 25; typical ages: 19–30. 20% men; 80% women; 33% minorities; 75% college students; 98% local applicants.

Employment Information Openings are from June 12 to August 9. Jobs available: ▶ 23–26 *camp counselors* with one year out of high school at $3200 per season ▶ *lifeguards/counselors* with current lifeguard certification at $3200 per season. Applicants must submit a formal organization application, three personal references. An in-person interview is recommended, but a telephone interview is acceptable. International applicants accepted; must obtain own visa, obtain own working papers.

Benefits and Preemployment Training Free meals, willing to provide letters of recommendation, willing to complete paperwork for educational credit, and willing to act as a professional reference. Preemployment training is required and includes accident prevention and safety, first aid, CPR, interpersonal skills, leadership skills, the culture of the program.

Contact Katy Roybal, Camp Director, Castilleja School. Telephone: 650-328-3160 Ext. 440. Fax: 650-326-8036. E-mail: katy_roybal@castilleja.org. World Wide Web: http://www.castilleja. org. Contact by e-mail, phone, or through World Wide Web site. Application deadline: continuous.

CATALINA ISLAND CAMPS
HOWLANDS LANDING
AVALON, CALIFORNIA 90704

General Information Private summer camp for children ages 7-15. Established in 1926. 27-acre facility located 26 miles from Los Angeles. Features: private ocean cove; Catalina Island; oceanfront property; skin diving; sailing; sea kayaking.

Profile of Summer Employees Total number: 75; typical ages: 20–25. 50% men; 50% women; 10% minorities; 90% college students; 10% non-U.S. citizens; 10% local applicants.

Employment Information Openings are from June 2 to August 23. Year-round positions also offered. Jobs available: ▶ 35–40 *activity specialists* (minimum age 19) with first aid, CPR, and lifeguard (waterfront) certifications at $165–$180 per week ▶ 20 *cabin counselors* (minimum age 19) with first aid and CPR certification at $165–$180 per week. Applicants must submit formal organization application, two personal references. An in-person interview is recommended, but a telephone interview is acceptable. International applicants accepted; must obtain own visa, apply through a recognized agency.

Benefits and Preemployment Training Free housing, free meals, formal training, willing to provide letters of recommendation, on-the-job training, willing to complete paperwork for educational credit, willing to act as a professional reference, and opportunity to attend seminars/workshops. Preemployment training is required and includes accident prevention and safety, first aid, CPR, interpersonal skills, leadership skills, lifeguarding.

Contact Sam Cover, Assistant Director, Catalina Island Camps, PO Box 94146, Pasadena, California 91109. Telephone: 800-696-CAMP. Fax: 626-794-1401. E-mail: jobs@catalinaislandcamps.com. World Wide Web: http://www.catalinaislandcamps.com. Contact by e-mail, fax, mail, phone, or through World Wide Web site. Application deadline: continuous.

CENTER FOR STUDENT MISSIONS
PO BOX 900
DANA POINT, CALIFORNIA 92629-0900

General Information Organization which links Christian suburban/rural groups to service and mission opportunities in urban areas. Established in 1988.

Profile of Summer Employees Total number: 83; typical ages: 19–25. 40% men; 60% women; 15% minorities; 99% college students; 1% retirees. Nonsmokers preferred.

Employment Information Openings are from May 20 to August 31. Jobs available: ▶ 1–10 *city hosts* (minimum age 18) with CPR/first aid certification and membership in Christian church at $450 per month. Applicants must submit a formal organization application, 3 to 4 personal references, site visit (required). An in-person interview is required.

Benefits and Preemployment Training Free housing, possible full-time employment, willing to provide letters of recommendation, on-the-job training, willing to complete paperwork for educational credit, and most meals free. Preemployment training is required and includes accident prevention and safety, first aid, CPR, interpersonal skills, leadership skills.

Contact Kyle Becchetti, Vice President of Operations, Center for Student Missions. Telephone: 949-248-8200. Fax: 949-248-7753. E-mail: info@csm.org. World Wide Web: http://www.csm.org. Contact through World Wide Web site. Application deadline: continuous.

CENTER FOR STUDENT MISSIONS–LOS ANGELES
LOS ANGELES, CALIFORNIA
See Center for Student Missions above for complete description.

CENTER FOR STUDENT MISSIONS–SAN FRANCISCO
SAN FRANCISCO, CALIFORNIA
See Center for Student Missions above for complete description.

CENTER FOR TALENTED YOUTH/JOHNS HOPKINS UNIVERSITY–LOYOLA MARYMOUNT UNIVERSITY
LOS ANGELES, CALIFORNIA
See Center for Talented Youth/Johns Hopkins University on page 131 for complete description.

CENTER FOR TALENTED YOUTH/JOHNS HOPKINS UNIVERSITY–MIRMAN SCHOOL

WEST LOS ANGELES, CALIFORNIA
See Center for Talented Youth/Johns Hopkins University on page 131 for complete description.

CENTER FOR TALENTED YOUTH/JOHNS HOPKINS UNIVERSITY–STANFORD UNIVERSITY

PALO ALTO, CALIFORNIA
See Center for Talented Youth/Johns Hopkins University on page 131 for complete description.

CENTER FOR TALENTED YOUTH/JOHNS HOPKINS UNIVERSITY–UNIVERSITY OF CALIFORNIA, SANTA CRUZ

SANTA CRUZ, CALIFORNIA
See Center for Talented Youth/Johns Hopkins University on page 131 for complete description.

CYBERCAMPS–CONCORDIA UNIVERSITY

IRVINE, CALIFORNIA
See Cybercamps–University of Washington on page 326 for complete description.

CYBERCAMPS–DEANZA COLLEGE

CUPERTINO, CALIFORNIA
See Cybercamps–University of Washington on page 326 for complete description.

CYBERCAMPS–STANFORD UNIVERSITY

STANFORD, CALIFORNIA
See Cybercamps–University of Washington on page 326 for complete description.

CYBERCAMPS–UC IRVINE

IRVINE, CALIFORNIA
See Cybercamps–University of Washington on page 326 for complete description.

CYBERCAMPS–UCLA

LOS ANGELES, CALIFORNIA
See Cybercamps–University of Washington on page 326 for complete description.

CYBERCAMPS–UC SAN DIEGO (UCSD)

LA JOLLA, CALIFORNIA
See Cybercamps–University of Washington on page 326 for complete description.

CYBERCAMPS–UNIVERSITY OF CALIFORNIA AT BERKELEY

BERKELEY, CALIFORNIA
See Cybercamps–University of Washington on page 326 for complete description.

DOUGLAS RANCH CAMPS
33200 EAST CARMEL VALLEY ROAD
CARMEL VALLEY, CALIFORNIA 93924

General Information Private, traditional, residential summer camp for 120 children ages 7–14. Structured program in horseback riding, swimming, archery, tennis, riflery, and crafts. Focus is on improving social skills, leadership, and confidence in a positive and fun environment. Established in 1925. 120-acre facility located 15 miles from Carmel. Features: large oval pool; central lodge and dining hall; 4 tennis courts; private hiking and riding trails; shady oak trees on hillside; 15 miles to ocean.

Profile of Summer Employees Total number: 40; typical ages: 19–24. 45% men; 55% women; 15% minorities; 85% college students; 5% retirees; 10% non-U.S. citizens; 20% local applicants. Nonsmokers required.

Employment Information Openings are from June 13 to August 25. Jobs available: ▶ 2–5 *archery instructors* (minimum age 18) with camp, school, or archery team experience and at least one year of college completed at $2200–$2750 per season ▶ 2–5 *crafts instructors* (minimum age 18) with experience working with children, teaching and/or experience with arts and crafts, and at least one year of college completed at $2200–$2750 per season ▶ 30–32 *general counselors* (minimum age 18) with experience working with children, at least one year of college completed, and general experience in at least one activity (riding, swimming, tennis, archery, riflery, crafts, ballsports) at $2200–$2750 per season ▶ 2–3 *kitchen assistants* (minimum age 18) with experience in general food preparation and dishwashing, and at least one year of college completed at $2200–$2750 per season ▶ 4–10 *riding instructors* (minimum age 18) with experience giving riding lessons, at least one year of college complete, and teaching children riding, saddling, and/or general horse care at $2200–$2750 per season ▶ 2–5 *riflery instructors* (minimum age 18) with camp, school, or riflery team experience and at least one year of college completed at $2200–$2750 per season ▶ 4–10 *swimming instructors* (minimum age 18) with WSI and/or lifeguard certification, experience on club or team, and at least one year of college completed at $2200–$2750 per season ▶ 2–5 *tennis instructors* (minimum age 18) with experience on tennis team, club, or in teaching and at least one year of college completed at $2200–$2750 per season. Applicants must submit formal organization application, two personal references, two letters of recommendation. An in-person interview is recommended, but a telephone interview is acceptable. International applicants accepted; must apply through a recognized agency.

Benefits and Preemployment Training Free housing, free meals, formal training, health insurance, willing to provide letters of recommendation, on-the-job training, willing to complete paperwork for educational credit, willing to act as a professional reference, and CPR and first aid certification. Preemployment training is required and includes accident prevention and safety, first aid, CPR, interpersonal skills, leadership skills, child psychology and development, team building.

Contact J. P. O'Conner, Director, Douglas Ranch Camps, 33200 East Carmel Valley Road, Carmel Valley, California 93924. Telephone: 831-659-2761. Fax: 831-659-5690. E-mail: director@ douglascamp.com. World Wide Web: http://www.douglascamp.com. Contact by e-mail, fax, mail, phone, or through World Wide Web site. Application deadline: June 1.

DRAKESBAD GUEST RANCH
END OF WARNER VALLEY ROAD
CHESTER, CALIFORNIA 96020

General Information Rustic guest ranch in the heart of Lassen Volcanic National Park. Established in 1974. 100-acre facility located 120 miles from Reno, Nevada. Features: National Park setting; hot spring pool; horse stable; no electricity or television; hiking trails; fishing stream.

Profile of Summer Employees Total number: 22; typical ages: 20–26. 15% men; 85% women; 10% minorities; 80% college students; 5% retirees; 75% non-U.S. citizens; 10% local applicants. Nonsmokers preferred.

Employment Information Openings are from June 1 to October 15. Jobs available: ▶ 2–3 *grill cooks* (minimum age 18) with cooking, food safety, and sanitation experience at $8–$9 per hour ▶ 5–6 *housekeepers/groundskeepers/waitstaff/children's program staff/kitchen maintenance* (minimum age 18) with knowledge of children's games and crafts at $7–$8 per hour ▶ 1–2 *kitchen help/food staff* (minimum age 18) at $7–$8 per hour ▶ 1 *kitchen maintenance staff* (minimum age 18) at $7–$8 per hour ▶ 1 *maintenance/groundskeeper* (minimum age 18) with technical skills at $7–$8 per hour ▶ 1 *masseuse* (minimum age 21) with health therapist certification at $25 per hour (part-time) ▶ 3–4 *store clerks/cashiers* (minimum age 18) with driver's license at $7–$8 per hour ▶ 3–4 *waitstaff* (minimum age 18) at $7–$8 per hour ▶ 1–2 *wranglers* (minimum age 21) with first aid and CPR certification, 5 years horsemanship, and 2 years stable hand experience at $7–$8 per hour. Applicants must submit letter of interest, resume, photograph, e-mail address, Web site application (preferred). An in-person interview is recommended, but a telephone interview is acceptable. International applicants accepted; must apply through a recognized agency.

Benefits and Preemployment Training Housing at a cost, meals at a cost, willing to provide letters of recommendation, and on-the-job training. Preemployment training is required and includes accident prevention and safety, CPR, interpersonal skills.

Contact Ed Fiebiger, Ranch Host, Drakesbad Guest Ranch, 2150 North Main Street, Red Bluff, California 96080. Fax: 530-529-4511. E-mail: billie@goldrush.com. World Wide Web: http://www.drakesbad.com. Contact by e-mail or through World Wide Web site. No phone calls. Application deadline: March 15.

ELITE EDUCATIONAL INSTITUTE
4009 WILSHIRE BOULEVARD, #200
LOS ANGELES, CALIFORNIA 90010

General Information Academic enrichment and college preparation. Established in 1985.

Profile of Summer Employees Total number: 200; typical ages: 25–35. 70% men; 30% women. Nonsmokers preferred.

Employment Information Openings are from June 20 to August 25. Jobs available: ▶ 10–20 *SAT-verbal, math/junior high verbal, math instructors* (minimum age 25) with teaching experience required at $20–$35 per hour. Applicants must submit a formal organization application, letter of interest, resume, screening exam. An in-person interview is required.

Benefits and Preemployment Training Formal training, possible full-time employment, health insurance, willing to provide letters of recommendation, and opportunity to attend seminars/workshops. Preemployment training is optional and includes teacher training.

Contact Wonna Kim, Program Director, Elite Educational Institute, 4009 Wilshire Boulevard #200, Los Angeles, California 90010. Fax: 213-365-1253. E-mail: wonna.kim@eliteprep.com. World Wide Web: http://eliteprep.com. Contact by e-mail or fax. No phone calls. Application deadline: continuous.

GIRL SCOUTS OF THE SAN FERNANDO VALLEY
9421 WINNETKA AVENUE
CHATSWORTH, CALIFORNIA 91311

General Information Nonprofit organization serving the girls of the San Fernando Valley. 58-acre facility located 80 miles from Los Angeles. Features: forest setting; mountainous terrain; horseback riding; heated swimming pool; rustic living; tripping and leadership programs.

Profile of Summer Employees Total number: 40; typical ages: 18–25. 2% men; 98% women; 45% minorities; 2% high school students; 96% college students; 20% non-U.S. citizens; 80% local applicants. Nonsmokers required.

Employment Information Openings are from June 9 to August 25. Jobs available: ▶ 3–5 *cooks/ kitchen aides* (minimum age 16) with kitchen experience at $1600–$4200 per season ▶ 1–5 *lifeguard* (minimum age 18) with lifeguard certification and previous experience at $2000– $2200 per season ▶ 2–4 *program specialists-art/nature/archery/leadership* (minimum age 18) with experience at $2000–$2200 per season ▶ 10–22 *unit counselors* (minimum age 18) with previous child care experience preferred at $1900–$2150 per season ▶ 3–5 *wrangler/riding instructors* (minimum age 18) with horseback instructional experience needed at $2000–$3900 per season. Applicants must submit formal organization application, resume, three personal references. An in-person interview is recommended, but a telephone interview is acceptable. International applicants accepted; must apply through a recognized agency.

Benefits and Preemployment Training Free housing, free meals, formal training, health insurance, willing to provide letters of recommendation, on-the-job training, willing to complete paperwork for educational credit, willing to act as a professional reference, and opportunity to attend seminars/workshops. Preemployment training is required and includes accident prevention and safety, first aid, CPR, leadership skills, program and risk management training.

Contact Connie Scharff, Program/Property Director, Girl Scouts of the San Fernando Valley. Fax: 818-407-4840. E-mail: camplakota@sfvgsc.org. World Wide Web: http://www.sfvgsc.org. Contact by e-mail, fax, mail, or through World Wide Web site. No phone calls. Application deadline: continuous.

GIRL SCOUTS OF TIERRA DEL ORO
3005 GOLD CANAL DRIVE
RANCHO CORDOVA, CALIFORNIA 95670

General Information Nonprofit organization for girls. Established in 1921. 176-acre facility located 90 miles from Stockton. Features: wooded setting; canoe lake; rustic; swimming lake; archery; 5000 foot elevation.

Profile of Summer Employees Total number: 48; typical ages: 18–27. 1% men; 99% women; 30% minorities; 1% high school students; 98% college students; 1% retirees; 10% non-U.S. citizens; 70% local applicants. Nonsmokers required.

Employment Information Openings are from May 30 to August 18. Jobs available: ▶ 1 *assistant camp director* (minimum age 21) with administrative, supervisory and camp experience, knowledge of Girl Scout program; Class B driver's license required at $72–$75 per day ▶ 1 *assistant cook* (minimum age 19) with experience preparing food for large groups at $61–$63 per day ▶ 20 *assistant unit leaders* (minimum age 18) with experience in camping and/or group leadership at $46–$48 per day ▶ 1 *business manager* (minimum age 21) with business and purchasing experience and Class B driver's license required at $50–$53 per day ▶ 1 *health supervisor* (minimum age 21) with state license or registered as an MD, PA, RN, LVN, or EMT; current first aid training and CPR at $84–$89 per day ▶ 3 *kitchen assistants* (minimum age 16) with some kitchen experience and dishwashing helpful at $43–$45 per day ▶ 1 *kitchen manager* (minimum age 21) with menu planning ability and experience cooking for large groups (100 plus) at $75–$78 per day ▶ 1 *leadership assistant* (minimum age 19) with previous camp experience, skills in activity programming, teen communication, camp craft, and supervision; valid driver's license at $48–$51 per day ▶ 1 *leadership director* (minimum age 21) with previous camp experience, skills in activity programming, teen communication, camp craft, and supervision; valid driver's license at $50–$53 per day ▶ 1 *maintenance support* (minimum age 18) with a valid driver's license, carpentry, plumbing, and electrical aptitude; willingness to take direction at $53–$55 per day ▶ 1 *program manager* (minimum age 21) with supervisory and camp experience required and knowledge of Girl Scout program at $56–$59 per day ▶ 3 *program specialists (arts and crafts, science and nature, archery)* (minimum age 19) with extensive knowledge and experience related to the specific program area at $48–$51 per day ▶ 2 *trip adventure leaders* (minimum age 21) with extensive outdoor skills and backpacking experience and certification as EMT in wilderness first aid, or willingness to obtain at $50–$53 per day

California

▶ 1 *trip coordinator* (minimum age 21) with previous camp experience and California/equivalent Class B driver's license, or willingness to obtain at $48–$51 per day ▶ 4 *unit leaders* (minimum age 21) with experience with children in groups, supervisory experience (preferred), and valid driver's license at $48–$51 per day ▶ 3 *waterfront assistants* (minimum age 18) with current lifeguard, first aid, and CPR certifications; canoeing experience helpful at $48–$51 per day ▶ 1 *waterfront director* (minimum age 21) with current WSI, lifeguard, first aid, and CPR certifications; canoeing skills, supervisory and waterfront experience at $51–$54 per day. Applicants must submit formal organization application, three personal references. An in-person interview is recommended, but a telephone interview is acceptable. International applicants accepted; must apply through a recognized agency.

Benefits and Preemployment Training Free housing, free meals, formal training, health insurance, on-the-job training, willing to complete paperwork for educational credit, and opportunity to attend seminars/workshops. Preemployment training is required and includes accident prevention and safety, first aid, CPR, interpersonal skills, leadership skills, songs, games, lifeguarding (occasionally).

Contact Joy Galloway, Camp Director, Girl Scouts of Tierra del Oro. Telephone: 916-638-4475. Fax: 916-638-8452. E-mail: joy_galloway@tdogs.org. World Wide Web: http://www.tdogs.org. Contact by e-mail, fax, mail, phone, or through World Wide Web site. Application deadline: continuous.

GOLD ARROW CAMP
HUNTINGTON LAKE, CALIFORNIA 93634

General Information Private residential camp for boys and girls ages 6–14. Established in 1933. 27-acre facility located 65 miles from Fresno. Features: freshwater lake; creek; Sierra National Forest; island outpost camp; natural rock climbing area.

Profile of Summer Employees Total number: 100; typical ages: 19–28. 55% men; 45% women; 10% minorities; 80% college students; 5% retirees; 10% non-U.S. citizens; 15% local applicants. Nonsmokers required.

Employment Information Openings are from June 20 to August 28. Jobs available: ▶ 30–33 *activity counselors* (minimum age 19) with CPR (lifeguard certification for waterfront positions) at $1658 per season, plus room and board ▶ 30–32 *group counselors* (minimum age 19) with CPR certification at $1658 per season, plus room and board ▶ 2–10 *kitchen staff* (minimum age 19) at $200–$225 per week ▶ 2–5 *maintenance staff/drivers* (minimum age 21) with class B commercial driver's license at $200–$225 per week. Applicants must submit formal organization application, two personal references, two letters of recommendation. An in-person interview is recommended, but a telephone interview is acceptable. International applicants accepted; must apply through a recognized agency.

Benefits and Preemployment Training Free housing, free meals, formal training, willing to provide letters of recommendation, willing to complete paperwork for educational credit, willing to act as a professional reference, opportunity to attend seminars/workshops, and travel reimbursement. Preemployment training is required and includes accident prevention and safety, first aid, interpersonal skills, leadership skills.

Contact Steven Monke, Director, Gold Arrow Camp, 2900 Bristol Street, Suite A-107, Costa Mesa, California 92626. Telephone: 800-554-2267. Fax: 714-424-0844. E-mail: mail@goldarrowcamp.com. World Wide Web: http://www.goldarrowcamp.com. Contact by e-mail, phone, or through World Wide Web site. Application deadline: continuous.

GRIFFITH PARK BOYS CAMP
4730 CRYSTAL SPRINGS DRIVE
LOS ANGELES, CALIFORNIA 90027

General Information Camp for boys, ages 6-14, including arts and crafts, climbing wall, high ropes course, athletic field, pool, 16 heated-air conditioned cabins, dining hall, and kitchen.

Established in 1926. Features: 32 foot climbing wall; high ropes course; archery range; swimming pool; athletic field; arts and crafts area.

Profile of Summer Employees Total number: 35–50; typical ages: 18–30. 99% men; 1% women; 85% minorities; 1% high school students; 99% college students; 100% local applicants. Nonsmokers preferred.

Employment Information Openings are from June 13 to August 31. Jobs available: ▶ 25–35 *camp counselors* (minimum age 18) at $260–$350 per week. Applicants must submit a formal organization application. An in-person interview is required.

Benefits and Preemployment Training Free housing, free meals, willing to provide letters of recommendation, on-the-job training, and willing to complete paperwork for educational credit. Preemployment training is required and includes accident prevention and safety, first aid, CPR, interpersonal skills, leadership skills.

Contact Roger Williams, Camp Director, Griffith Park Boys Camp. Telephone: 323-664-0571. Fax: 323-913-4170. E-mail: griffithparkboyscamp@rap.lacity.org. Contact by e-mail, fax, mail, or phone. Application deadline: June 15.

HIDDEN VILLA SUMMER CAMP
26870 MOODY ROAD
LOS ALTOS HILLS, CALIFORNIA 94022

General Information Multi-cultural environmental summer camp. Established in 1945. 1,600-acre facility located near Palo Alto.

Profile of Summer Employees Total number: 80; typical ages: 17–40. 30% men; 70% women; 30% minorities; 2% high school students; 60% college students; 2% non-U.S. citizens; 20% local applicants. Nonsmokers preferred.

Employment Information Openings are from June 8 to August 23. Jobs available: ▶ 40–50 *camp counselors* (minimum age 18) with experience with children, group settings, and rustic living at $235–$310 per week ▶ 2–4 *cooks* (minimum age 21) with experience in a food service environment, managing meals, and planning menus at $650–$700 per week. Applicants must submit formal organization application, resume. An in-person interview is recommended, but a telephone interview is acceptable. International applicants accepted; must obtain own visa, obtain own working papers, apply through a recognized agency.

Benefits and Preemployment Training Free housing, free meals, formal training, willing to provide letters of recommendation, names of contacts, on-the-job training, willing to complete paperwork for educational credit, and willing to act as a professional reference. Preemployment training is required and includes accident prevention and safety, first aid, CPR, interpersonal skills, leadership skills, policies and procedures.

Contact José G. Arzate, Assistant Director, Hidden Villa Summer Camp. Telephone: 650-949-8641. Fax: 650-948-1916. E-mail: camp@hiddenvilla.org. World Wide Web: http://www.hiddenvilla.org. Contact by e-mail, phone, or through World Wide Web site. Application deadline: May 1.

HUNEWILL GUEST RANCH
TWIN LAKES ROAD
BRIDGEPORT, CALIFORNIA 93517

General Information Guest ranch accommodating 45–55 guests weekly. Established in 1931. 4,800-acre facility located 120 miles from Reno, Nevada. Features: lush mountain meadows; surrounding mountains; mountain lakes nearby; 180 horses; 26 rooms; Victorian-style ranch house and dining room.

Profile of Summer Employees Total number: 20; typical ages: 18–25. 25% men; 75% women; 5% high school students; 80% college students; 15% local applicants. Nonsmokers required.

Employment Information Openings are from May 15 to October 1. Jobs available: ▶ 1 *breakfast/ pastry chef* (minimum age 18) with experience baking for groups at $457 per week ▶ 3 *cabin* *staff members* (minimum age 18) with ability to work quickly and eye for neatness at $381.46–$423.77 per week ▶ 1 *cook* with cooking experience or cooking school certification at $2080–$2100 per month ▶ 1 *gardener* (minimum age 18) with experience with lawn mowers, some landscaping, and an aptitude for gardening at $381–$423 per week ▶ 1 *kitchen janitorial* (minimum age 18) physically able to do manual labor and have an eye for neatness at $381–$423 per week ▶ 1 *maintenance person* (minimum age 18) with general plumbing, electrical, and carpentry ability, including fence building and some work with livestock at $381.46–$423.77 per week ▶ 2 *waiters/waitresses* (minimum age 18) with experience at $411–$457 per week ▶ 3–6 *wranglers* (minimum age 18) with extensive horse experience and good people skills at $381–$423 per week. Applicants must submit resume, three personal references, three letters of recommendation. A telephone interview is required. International applicants accepted; must obtain own visa, obtain own working papers, apply through a recognized agency.

Benefits and Preemployment Training Meals at a cost, free housing, willing to provide letters of recommendation, and on-the-job training.

Contact Betsy Hunewill Elliott, Assistant Manager, Hunewill Guest Ranch, 205 Hunewill Lane, Wellington, Nevada 89444. Telephone: 702-465-2238. E-mail: raftere@qnet.com. World Wide Web: http://www.hunewillranch.com. Contact by e-mail, mail, phone, or through World Wide Web site. Application deadline: continuous.

IDYLLWILD ARTS SUMMER PROGRAM
PO BOX 38
IDYLLWILD, CALIFORNIA 92549

General Information Nonprofit educational organization that offers intensive summer instruction to students of all ages and abilities. Established in 1946. 205-acre facility located 110 miles from Los Angeles. Features: mountain campus; state of the art film studio; new art gallery; large dance studios; air conditioned practice rooms; modern dormitories.

Profile of Summer Employees Total number: 350; typical ages: 19–25. 40% men; 60% women; 20% minorities; 95% college students; 10% local applicants. Nonsmokers preferred.

Employment Information Openings are from June 20 to August 25. Jobs available: ▶ 30–35 *resident advisors* (minimum age 19) with 1 year of college at $200 per week ▶ 5–6 *teaching assistants* (minimum age 21) with visual arts background and teaching experience at $200 per week ▶ 4–6 *tech assistants* (minimum age 19) with theater tech experience at $200 per week. Applicants must submit a formal organization application, resume, three personal references. A telephone interview is required. International applicants accepted; must obtain own visa, obtain own working papers.

Benefits and Preemployment Training Free housing, free meals, willing to provide letters of recommendation, on-the-job training, willing to complete paperwork for educational credit, willing to act as a professional reference, opportunity to attend seminars/workshops, and workers compensation, Cal SDI. Preemployment training is required and includes accident prevention and safety, first aid, CPR, interpersonal skills, leadership skills.

Contact Emma Showalter, Assistant Director, Idyllwild Arts Summer Program. Telephone: 909-659-2171 Ext. 369. Fax: 909-659-5463. E-mail: iasumpro@aol.com. World Wide Web: http://www.idyllwildarts.org. Contact by e-mail, fax, mail, or phone. Application deadline: March 15.

JAMESON RANCH CAMP
GLENNVILLE, CALIFORNIA 93226

General Information Jameson Ranch Camp connects children to a self-sufficient ranch lifestyle where campers grow some of the food and help with the farm animals. Established in 1934. 520-acre facility located 40 miles from Bakersfield. Features: 5000-ft. elevation in Sierras; mountain setting; closest neighbors 4 miles away; property borders National Forest; freshwater lake with great fishing; cattle ranch.

Profile of Summer Employees Total number: 30; typical ages: 19–55. 50% men; 50% women; 20% minorities; 90% college students; 5% retirees; 10% non-U.S. citizens; 5% local applicants. Nonsmokers required.

Employment Information Openings are from June 10 to August 26. Jobs available: ▶ 1 *archery instructor* (minimum age 19) with archery experience at $2700 per season ▶ 2 *crafts instructors* (minimum age 19) with crafts or art experience at $2700 per season ▶ 1 *drama instructor* (minimum age 19) with some theater background at $2700 per season ▶ 1 *head cook* (minimum age 21) with experience in the field at $2700 per season ▶ 2 *horse instructors* (minimum age 19) with Western riding and bareback riding experience at $2700 per season ▶ 1 *horse vaulting instructor* (minimum age 19) with some horse vaulting experience at $2700 per season ▶ 2 *kitchen persons* (minimum age 19) with some food service experience at $2700 per season ▶ 4 *lifeguards* (minimum age 19) with ALS certification or equivalent at $2700 per season ▶ 1 *mountain biking instructor* (minimum age 19) with good technique in mountain biking and bike maintenance skills required at $2700 per season ▶ 1 *photography instructor* (minimum age 19) with darkroom and photo composition experience required at $2700 per season ▶ 1 *riflery instructor* (minimum age 19) with riflery and hunter's safety experience at $2700 per season ▶ 1 *rock climbing instructor* (minimum age 19) with technical expertise and extensive climbing experience at $2700 per season ▶ 2 *swimming instructors* (minimum age 19) with WSI certification and lifeguard certification at $2700 per season. Applicants must submit formal organization application, letter of interest, resume, four personal references. An in-person interview is recommended, but a telephone interview is acceptable. International applicants accepted; must apply through a recognized agency.

Benefits and Preemployment Training Free housing, free meals, formal training, willing to provide letters of recommendation, on-the-job training, willing to complete paperwork for educational credit, and willing to act as a professional reference. Preemployment training is required and includes accident prevention and safety, interpersonal skills, leadership skills.

Contact Ross Jameson, Owner/Director, Jameson Ranch Camp, PO Box 459, Glennville, California 93226. Telephone: 661-536-8888. Fax: 661-536-8896. E-mail: thejamesons@ jamesonranchcamp.com. World Wide Web: http://www.jamesonranchcamp.com. Contact by e-mail, fax, mail, phone, or through World Wide Web site. Application deadline: continuous.

LOS ANGELES DESIGNERS' THEATRE
BOX 1883
STUDIO CITY, CALIFORNIA 91614-0883

General Information Summer theater that produces stage productions and teaches theatrical producing, including the legal aspects of production. Established in 1970.

Profile of Summer Employees Total number: 100; typical ages: 20–60. 50% men; 50% women; 40% minorities; 5% high school students; 30% college students; 65% local applicants. Nonsmokers required.

Employment Information Openings are from January 1 to December 31. Jobs available: ▶ *actors and actresses* salary per show negotiable with experience ▶ 1 *box office/house manager* at a negotiable salary per show ▶ 3–5 *carpenters* salary per show negotiable with experience ▶ 1 *choreographer* salary per show negotiable with experience ▶ 1–6 *costume designers* salary per show/production negotiable with experience ▶ 4–6 *crew members* salary per show negotiable ▶ 2–3 *cutters/drapers (first hands)/sewing machine operators* salary per show/per costume negotiable with experience ▶ 6 *directors* with experience at a negotiable salary per show/ production ▶ 2–4 *electricians* salary per show negotiable with experience ▶ 1–6 *lighting designers* salary per show/production negotiable with experience ▶ 1 *musical director* salary per show negotiable with experience ▶ 1 *program/graphics designer* license fee per image negotiable ▶ 1–6 *property designers* at a negotiable salary per show/production ▶ 1–6 *set designers* salary per show/production negotiable with experience ▶ *singers and dancers* salary per show negotiable with experience ▶ 1–6 *sound designers* salary per show/production negotiable with experience. Applicants must submit a letter of interest, resume, portfolio (for designers only), I-9 form.

Benefits and Preemployment Training Willing to provide letters of recommendation, names of contacts, on-the-job training, willing to complete paperwork for educational credit, and willing to act as a professional reference.

Contact Richard Niederberg, Artistic Director, Los Angeles Designers' Theatre, PO Box 1883, Attn: PS04, Studio City, California 91614-0883. E-mail: ladesigners@juno.com. Contact by e-mail. No phone calls. Application deadline: continuous.

RAWHIDE RANCH
PO BOX 216
BONSALL, CALIFORNIA 92003

General Information Camp that teaches children how to ride horses and take care of farm animals. Established in 1964. 36-acre facility located 13 miles from Escondido. Features: old western town setting; vaulting arena; horseback riding arena; covered arena and rodeo arena; over 40 horses and ponies; teepees, covered wagons, and a fort dormitory.

Profile of Summer Employees Total number: 48; typical ages: 20–25. 20% men; 80% women; 80% college students; 15% non-U.S. citizens; 5% local applicants. Nonsmokers preferred.

Employment Information Openings are from June 8 to August 23. Jobs available: ▶ 10–12 *program staff* (minimum age 18) at $6.75 per hour ▶ 36 *summer camp counselors* (minimum age 20) at $1900 per season. Applicants must submit formal organization application, three personal references, 3 job references. An in-person interview is recommended, but a telephone interview is acceptable. International applicants accepted; must apply through a recognized agency.

Benefits and Preemployment Training Free housing, free meals, possible full-time employment, on-the-job training, and willing to complete paperwork for educational credit. Preemployment training is required and includes leadership skills, animal care skills.

Contact Paul Tate, Co-Director, Rawhide Ranch, United States. Telephone: 760-758-0083. Fax: 760-758-0440. E-mail: paul@rawhideranch.com. World Wide Web: http://www.rawhideranch. com. Contact through World Wide Web site. Application deadline: continuous.

SANTA CATALINA SCHOOL SUMMER CAMP
1500 MARK THOMAS DRIVE
MONTEREY, CALIFORNIA 93940

General Information Residential and day camp for girls ages 8–14 with an emphasis on performing and fine arts and athletics. Established in 1953. 35-acre facility located 90 miles from San Jose. Features: 6 tennis courts; heated swimming pool; modern dormitories; library; weight room; computer labs.

Profile of Summer Employees Total number: 50; typical ages: 18–24. 100% women; 20% minorities; 100% college students. Nonsmokers required.

Employment Information Openings are from June 15 to July 30. Jobs available: ▶ 18 *counselors* (minimum age 18) with one year of college completed at $1350–$1550 per season. Applicants must submit a formal organization application, two letters of recommendation. A telephone interview is required.

Benefits and Preemployment Training Free housing, free meals, willing to provide letters of recommendation, and on-the-job training. Preemployment training is required and includes accident prevention and safety, first aid, CPR, interpersonal skills, leadership skills.

Contact Mrs. Deirdre Gonzales, Director of Summer Programs, Santa Catalina School Summer Camp, 1500 Mark Thomas Drive, Monterey, California 93940. Telephone: 831-655-9386. Fax: 831-649-3056. E-mail: summercamp@santacatalina.org. World Wide Web: http://www.santacatalina. org. Contact by e-mail, mail, or phone. Application deadline: continuous.

SARATOGA SPRINGS PICNIC, CAMPGROUNDS, AND DAY CAMP
22801 BIG BASIN HIGHWAY
SARATOGA, CALIFORNIA 95070

General Information Full-service corporate picnic facility serving 50-2000 guests daily. Services include catering, beverages, an entertainment package, and a summer camp serving children ages 7-12. Established in 1972. 14-acre facility located 10 miles from San Jose. Features: wooded setting; 2 year-round streams; fabulous barbecued food; RV and tent campsites; 6 private picnic groves; general store/arcade.

Profile of Summer Employees Total number: 40–50; typical age: 14. 25% minorities; 60% high school students; 15% college students; 5% retirees; 95% local applicants.

Employment Information Openings are from May 1 to October 31. Jobs available: ▶ 10–15 *barbecue cooks* (minimum age 18) at $10–$15 per hour ▶ 1 *lifeguard supervisor* (minimum age 18) with supervisory experience, two years lifeguarding experience, and certifications at $10–$13 per hour ▶ 4–8 *lifeguards* (minimum age 16) with lifeguard certification at $10–$13 per hour ▶ 5–10 *maintenance/parking attendants* (minimum age 14) at $7.25–$12 per hour ▶ 1 *recreation director* (minimum age 18) with ability to supervise, schedule, and manage employees at $12–$16 per hour ▶ 15–20 *recreation leaders* (minimum age 14) at $6.75–$12 per hour ▶ 2–4 *recreation supervisors* (minimum age 18) at $8–$12 per hour. Applicants must submit a formal organization application. An in-person interview is required. International applicants accepted; must obtain own visa.

Benefits and Preemployment Training Formal training, willing to provide letters of recommendation, and on-the-job training. Preemployment training is required and includes certain positions only.

Contact Mimi Giannini, Director of Human Resources, Saratoga Springs Picnic, Campgrounds, and Day Camp. Telephone: 408-867-3016. Fax: 408-867-0766. E-mail: mimi@saratoga-springs. com. World Wide Web: http://www.saratoga-springs.com. Contact by e-mail, fax, mail, or phone. Application deadline: continuous.

SHAFFER'S HIGH SIERRA CAMP
248 SAN MARIN DRIVE
NOVATO, CALIFORNIA 94945

General Information Non-competitive, largely team-based wilderness adventure program for boys and girls ages 9-16; activities include sailing, kayaking, rock climbing, backpacking, mountain biking, archery, volleyball, ropes course, drama, and arts and crafts. Established in 2000. 22-acre facility located 35 miles from Truckee. Features: tipis and cabins; setting in Tahoe National Forest; over 70 mountain lakes; on peaceful headwaters of North Yuba River; miles of hiking/biking trails.

Profile of Summer Employees Total number: 25; typical ages: 19–28. 50% men; 50% women; 5% minorities; 75% college students; 20% non-U.S. citizens; 80% local applicants. Nonsmokers required.

Employment Information Openings are from January 1 to May 31. Jobs available: ▶ 1–2 *archery specialists/counselors* (minimum age 19) with current first aid/CPR certification and relevant experience; 18 year-olds with 1 year of college are also eligible at $250–$300 per week ▶ 1–2 *arts/crafts specialists/counselors* (minimum age 19) with current first aid/CPR certification and arts/crafts experience; 18 year-olds with 1 year of college are also eligible at $250–$300 per week ▶ 1–2 *drama/theatre arts specialists/counselors* (minimum age 19) with current first aid and CPR certification and relevant experience; 18 year-olds with 1 year of college are also eligible at $250–$300 per week ▶ 1–2 *games specialists (volleyball, frisbee, golf, group games)/ counselors* (minimum age 19) with current first aid/CPR certification and relevant experience; 18 year-olds with 1 year of college are also eligible at $250–$300 per week ▶ 1–2 *lakefront specialists/counselors* (minimum age 19) with current CPR/first aid certification, open water lifeguard certification, and sailing, kayaking, and windsurfing experience; 18 year-olds with 1 year of college are also eligible at $275–$300 per week ▶ 2–3 *mountain biking specialists/ counselors* (minimum age 19) with current first aid and CPR certification and basic bike repair/ maintenance skills; 18 year-olds with 1 year of college are also eligible at $250–$300 per week ▶ 1 *program director* (minimum age 23) with experience in the position or as an assistant director; current CPR and first aid certification required at $500–$700 per week ▶ 2–4 *rock climbing/ropes course specialists/counselors* (minimum age 19) with current first aid/CPR certification; relevant experience; 18 year-olds with 1 year of college are also eligible at $250– $300 per week ▶ 1–2 *waterfront specialists/counselors* (minimum age 19) with current first aid/CPR certification and lifeguard certification; 18 year-olds with 1 year of college are also eligible at $275–$300 per week. Applicants must submit formal organization application, three personal references. A telephone interview is required. International applicants accepted; must apply through a recognized agency.

Benefits and Preemployment Training Free housing, free meals, willing to provide letters of recommendation, on-the-job training, willing to complete paperwork for educational credit, willing to act as a professional reference, and opportunity to attend seminars/workshops. Preemployment training is required and includes accident prevention and safety, interpersonal skills, leadership skills.

Contact Lisa Shaffer, Director, Shaffer's High Sierra Camp. Telephone: 800-516-3513. Fax: 415-897-0316. E-mail: jobs@highsierracamp.com. World Wide Web: http://www.highsierracamp. com. Contact by e-mail. Application deadline: continuous.

SIERRA SERVICE PROJECT
PO BOX 992
CARMICHAEL, CALIFORNIA 94618

General Information United Methodist-related service organization offering a Christian service learning program to church youth groups and home repair work to Native American communities. Established in 1975. Features: school or church locations; rural; some desert locations; some lake-side locations; small towns; Indian reservations.

Profile of Summer Employees Total number: 35; typical ages: 19–35. 50% men; 50% women; 10% minorities; 90% college students; 5% non-U.S. citizens. Nonsmokers preferred.

Employment Information Openings are from June 15 to August 18. Jobs available: ▶ *cooks* (minimum age 19) at $1900–$2100 per season ▶ 2–4 *home repair coordinators* (minimum age 19) with youth ministry experience and ability to teach at $3000–$3200 per season ▶ 5 *program directors/spiritual life directors* (minimum age 19) with youth ministry experience and program creation experience at $3000–$3200 per season ▶ 10 *supply coordinators* (minimum age 19) at $1900–$2100 per season. Applicants must submit a formal organization application, three personal references, two letters of recommendation. An in-person interview is recommended, but a telephone interview is acceptable.

Benefits and Preemployment Training Free housing, free meals, formal training, willing to provide letters of recommendation, on-the-job training, willing to complete paperwork for educational credit, and willing to act as a professional reference. Preemployment training is required and includes accident prevention and safety, interpersonal skills, leadership skills.

Contact Rick Eaton, Executive Director, Sierra Service Project, PO Box 992, Carmichael, California 95609. Telephone: 916-488-6441. Fax: 916-483-0917. E-mail: director@ sierraserviceproject.org. World Wide Web: http://www.sierraserviceproject.org. Contact by e-mail, fax, mail, or phone. Application deadline: March 1.

THE SOUTHWESTERN COMPANY, CALIFORNIA
See The Southwestern Company on page 297 for complete description.

STEVENSON SCHOOL SUMMER CAMP
3152 FOREST LAKE ROAD
PEBBLE BEACH, CALIFORNIA 93953

General Information Residential and day summer camp for children aged 10-15. Established in 1972. Located 5 miles from Monterey. Features: golf courses; ocean; pool; tennis courts; high school dormitories; close to Big Sur.

Profile of Summer Employees Total number: 40; typical ages: 18–35. 55% men; 45% women; 80% college students; 1% non-U.S. citizens; 3% local applicants. Nonsmokers preferred.

Employment Information Openings are from June 15 to July 25. Jobs available: ▶ 5–15 *camp counselors* with high school diploma required at $1800–$3000 per season. Applicants must submit a formal organization application, letter of interest, personal reference. A telephone interview is required. International applicants accepted; must obtain own visa, obtain own working papers.

Benefits and Preemployment Training Free housing and free meals. Preemployment training is required and includes accident prevention and safety, interpersonal skills, leadership skills.

Contact Ellen Meranze, Director of Summer Camp, Stevenson School Summer Camp, 3152 Forest Lake Road, Pebble Beach, California 93953. Fax: 831-625-5208. E-mail: summercamp@ rlstevenson.org. World Wide Web: http://www.rlstevenson.org. Contact by e-mail. No phone calls. Application deadline: March 1.

STIVERS STAFFING SERVICES–CALIFORNIA
See Stivers Staffing Services–Illinois on page 96 for complete description.

STUDENT CONSERVATION ASSOCIATION (SCA), CALIFORNIA
See Student Conservation Association (SCA), New Hampshire on page 200 for complete description.

SUMMER DISCOVERY AT UCLA
UNIVERSITY OF CALIFORNIA, LOS ANGELES
LOS ANGELES, CALIFORNIA 90024

General Information Precollege enrichment program for high school students at University of California, Los Angeles. Established in 1986. Features: sport facilities; beaches; mountains; lakes; major cities nearby; college towns.

Profile of Summer Employees Total number: 50; typical ages: 21–35. 45% men; 55% women; 10% minorities; 60% college students. Nonsmokers required.

Employment Information Openings are from June to August. Jobs available: ▶ 50 *resident counselors* (minimum age 21) with experience working with high school students/children at $200 per week. Applicants must submit a formal organization application, resume, three personal references. An in-person interview is required. International applicants accepted; must obtain own visa, obtain own working papers.

Benefits and Preemployment Training Free housing, free meals, possible full-time employment, on-the-job training, willing to complete paperwork for educational credit, and willing to act as a professional reference. Preemployment training is required and includes accident prevention and safety, CPR, leadership skills.

Contact Rouel Belleza, Operations, Summer Discovery at UCLA, 1326 Old Northern Boulevard, Roslyn, New York 11576, United States. Telephone: 516-621-3939. Fax: 516-625-3438. E-mail: staff@summerfun.com. World Wide Web: http://www.summerfun.com. Contact by e-mail, fax, phone, or through World Wide Web site. Application deadline: continuous.

SUMMER DISCOVERY AT UC SAN DIEGO
UNIVERSITY OF CALIFORNIA, SAN DIEGO
SAN DIEGO, CALIFORNIA

General Information Precollege enrichment program for high school students at University of California, San Diego. Features: sports facilities; beaches; mountains; lakes; major cities nearby; college towns.

Employment Information Openings are from June to August. Jobs available: ▶ *resident counselors* (minimum age 21) with experience working with high school students/children at $200 per week. Applicants must submit a formal organization application, resume, three personal references. An in-person interview is required.

Benefits and Preemployment Training Free housing, free meals, possible full-time employment, on-the-job training, willing to complete paperwork for educational credit, and willing to act as a professional reference. Preemployment training is required and includes accident prevention and safety, CPR, leadership skills.

Contact Rouel Belleza, Operations, Summer Discovery at UC San Diego, 1326 Old Northern Boulevard, Roslyn, New York 11576. Telephone: 516-621-3939. Fax: 516-625-3438. E-mail: staff@summerfun.com. World Wide Web: http://www.summerfun.com. Contact by e-mail, fax, phone, or through World Wide Web site. Application deadline: continuous.

SUMMER DISCOVERY AT UC SANTA BARBARA
UNIVERSITY OF CALIFORNIA, SANTA BARBARA
SANTA BARBARA, CALIFORNIA

General Information Precollege enrichment program for high school students at University of California, Santa Barbara. Features: sports facilities; beaches; mountains; lakes; major cities nearby; college towns.

Employment Information Openings are from June to August. Jobs available: ▶ *resident counselors* (minimum age 21) with experience working with high school students/children at $200 per week. Applicants must submit a formal organization application, resume, three personal references. An in-person interview is required.

Benefits and Preemployment Training Free housing, free meals, possible full-time employment, on-the-job training, willing to complete paperwork for educational credit, and willing to act as a professional reference. Preemployment training is required and includes accident prevention and safety, CPR, leadership skills.

Contact Rouel Belleza, Operations, Summer Discovery at UC Santa Barbara, 1326 Old Northern Boulevard, Roslyn, New York 11576. Telephone: 516-621-3939. Fax: 516-625-3438. E-mail: staff@summerfun.com. World Wide Web: http://www.summerfun.com. Contact by e-mail, fax, phone, or through World Wide Web site. Application deadline: continuous.

SUPERCAMP-CLAREMONT COLLEGES
CLAREMONT COLLEGES
CLAREMONT, CALIFORNIA 91711

General Information Residential program for teens that includes life skills and academic courses designed to build self-confidence and lifelong learning skills. Established in 1981. Located 60 miles from Los Angeles. Features: university dormitories; outdoor ropes course.

Profile of Summer Employees Total number: 27–30; typical ages: 18–25. 40% men; 60% women; 80% college students; 10% non-U.S. citizens. Nonsmokers preferred.

Employment Information Openings are from June to August. Jobs available: ▶ 10 *counselors* with college degree plus PPS credential or master's degree in counseling or MFCC license at $900 to $1500 per 10 day session ▶ 4–10 *facilitators* with presentation skills, college degree, and teaching credentials preferred at $1300 to $2350 per 10 day session ▶ 1 *logistics manager* with excellent organizational skills and high school diploma at $600 to $1100 per 10 day session ▶ 2 *nurses* with RN license at $600 to $1300 per 10 day session ▶ 1 *office manager* with high school diploma and prior office experience at $450 to $700 per 10 day session ▶ 2 *paramedics* with national or state registration at $600 to $1300 per 10 day session ▶ 1 *products coordinator* with high school diploma at a paid salary per 10 day session ▶ 50–75 *team leaders (peer counselors)* with high school diploma and prior experience with teens at $350 to $600 per 10 day session. Applicants must submit a formal organization application, resume, three letters of recommendation, in-person interview recommended (videotape interview acceptable). International applicants accepted; must obtain own visa, obtain own working papers.

Benefits and Preemployment Training Free housing, free meals, willing to provide letters of recommendation, on-the-job training, willing to complete paperwork for educational credit, and willing to act as a professional reference. Preemployment training is required and includes interpersonal skills, leadership skills.

Contact Jen Myers, Staffing, SuperCamp–Claremont Colleges, 1725 South Coast Highway, Oceanside, California 92054-5319. Telephone: 800-285-3276 Ext. 109. Fax: 760-722-3507. E-mail: staffing@learningforum.com. World Wide Web: http://www.supercamp.com. Contact by e-mail, fax, mail, phone, or through World Wide Web site. Application deadline: continuous.

SUPERCAMP–STANFORD UNIVERSITY
STANFORD UNIVERSITY
PALO ALTO, CALIFORNIA 94305

General Information Residential program for teens designed to build self-confidence and lifelong learning skills through accelerated learning techniques. Established in 1981. 8,200-acre facility located 45 miles from San Francisco. Features: university dormitories; outdoor ropes course.

Profile of Summer Employees Total number: 27–30; typical ages: 18–25. 40% men; 60% women; 80% college students; 10% non-U.S. citizens. Nonsmokers preferred.

Employment Information Openings are from June to August. Jobs available: ▶ 1 *EMT/ wellness person* with national or state registration at $600 to $1300 per 10 day session ▶ 10 *counselors* with college degree and PPS credential, MFCC license, or master's degree in counseling at $900 to $1500 per 10 day session ▶ 4–10 *facilitators* with presentation skills and college degree; teaching credential preferred at $1300 to $2350 per 10 day session ▶ 1 *logistics manager* with excellent organizational skills and high school diploma at $600 to $1100 per 10 day session ▶ 1 *nurse/paramedic* with national or state registration at $600 to $1300 per 10 day session ▶ 1 *office manager* with high school diploma and prior office experience at $450 to $700 per 10 day session ▶ *products coordinator* with high school diploma at a salary paid per 10 day session ▶ 20–25 *team leaders* with high school diploma and prior experience with teens at $350 to $600 per 10 day session. Applicants must submit a formal organization application, resume, three letters of recommendation, in-person interview recommended (videotape interview acceptable). International applicants accepted; must obtain own visa, obtain own working papers.

Benefits and Preemployment Training Free housing, free meals, willing to provide letters of recommendation, on-the-job training, willing to complete paperwork for educational credit, and willing to act as a professional reference. Preemployment training is required and includes interpersonal skills, leadership skills.

Contact Jen Myers, Staffing, SuperCamp–Stanford University, 1725 South Coast Highway, Oceanside, California 92054-5319. Telephone: 800-285-3276 Ext. 109. Fax: 760-722-3507. E-mail: staffing@learningforum.com. World Wide Web: http://www.supercamp.com. Contact by e-mail, fax, mail, phone, or through World Wide Web site. Application deadline: continuous.

THUNDERBIRD RANCH
9455 HIGHWAY 128
HEALDSBURG, CALIFORNIA 95448

General Information Private, independent camp with traditional camp activities and a complete horse mastership program, "Where the fun never sets". Established in 1962. 600-acre facility located 15 miles from Santa Rosa. Features: western theme; pool; Russian River; oak trees; ranch setting; covered wagons/railroad caboose.

Profile of Summer Employees Total number: 16; typical ages: 19–25. 50% men; 50% women; 5% high school students; 45% college students; 45% non-U.S. citizens; 5% local applicants. Nonsmokers required.

Employment Information Openings are from June 9 to August 12. Jobs available: ▶ 3 *Western riding instructors (equine)* (minimum age 18) with experience in riding at $2700 per season ▶ 10–12 *camp counselors* (minimum age 18) with first aid, CPR, lifeguarding, and ability to assist in activities at $2000–$3200 per season. Applicants must submit formal organization application, resume, two personal references, two letters of recommendation. An in-person interview is recommended, but a telephone interview is acceptable. International applicants accepted; must apply through a recognized agency.

Benefits and Preemployment Training Free housing, free meals, on-the-job training, willing to complete paperwork for educational credit, and willing to act as a professional reference. Preemployment training is required and includes accident prevention and safety, interpersonal skills.

Contact Mr. Bruce Johnson, Owner/Director, Thunderbird Ranch. Telephone: 707-433-3729. Fax: 707-433-2960. E-mail: alexvalley@aol.com. Contact by e-mail, fax, mail, or phone. Application deadline: continuous.

WALTON'S GRIZZLY LODGE SUMMER CAMP
PO BOX 519
PORTOLA, CALIFORNIA 96122

General Information Residential, traditional summer camp for children. Established in 1926. 50-acre facility located 45 miles from Reno. Features: private lake; ropes course; historic lodge; horseback riding; arts and crafts; water sports.

Profile of Summer Employees Total number: 50; typical ages: 18–25. 50% men; 50% women; 100% college students. Nonsmokers preferred.

Employment Information Openings are from January 2 to April 15. Jobs available: ▶ 12–20 *general group counselors* (minimum age 18) at $265 per week. Applicants must submit a formal organization application, three personal references. An in-person interview is recommended, but a telephone interview is acceptable.

Benefits and Preemployment Training Free housing, free meals, formal training, willing to provide letters of recommendation, on-the-job training, willing to complete paperwork for educational credit, willing to act as a professional reference, and travel reimbursement. Preemployment training is required and includes accident prevention and safety, interpersonal skills, leadership skills.

Contact Adam Stein, Director, Walton's Grizzly Lodge Summer Camp, 510 West Main Street, Grass Valley, California 95945. Telephone: 530-274-9577. Fax: 530-274-9677. E-mail: wgl4u@aol.com. World Wide Web: http://www.grizzlylodge.com. Contact by phone. Application deadline: April 15.

W.E.T. RIVER TRIPS
PO BOX 160024
SACRAMENTO, CALIFORNIA 95816
General Information Whitewater rafting on Class III to Class V rivers throughout the western United States with majority in California, Oregon, and Arizona. Program emphasizes adventure sports. Established in 1978. 1-acre facility.
Profile of Summer Employees Total number: 20; typical ages: 20–40. 80% men; 20% women; 5% minorities; 100% college students; 80% local applicants. Nonsmokers required.
Employment Information Openings are from March to September. Jobs available: ▶ *bus drivers* (minimum age 25) with California driver's license, DMV records, class B license, medical release, auto mechanic experience, CPR and first aid, and drug test at $300–$3000 per month ▶ 1–10 *whitewater guides* (minimum age 18) with CPR, first aid, EMT, mountain medicine certification (required), and swiftwater rescue (preferred) at $300–$3000 per month.
Benefits and Preemployment Training Willing to provide letters of recommendation, on-the-job training, willing to act as a professional reference, and opportunity to attend seminars/workshops. Preemployment training is required and includes accident prevention and safety, whitewater rescue.
Contact W.E.T., W.E.T. River Trips, PO Box 160024, Sacramento, California 95816. Telephone: 916-451-3241. World Wide Web: http://www.raftwet.com. Contact by phone or through World Wide Web site. Application deadline: February 15.

YES TO JOBS
PO BOX 3390
LOS ANGELES, CALIFORNIA 90078
General Information Organization providing paid internships for minority high school and college students in the entertainment industry for ten weeks. Established in 1987.
Profile of Summer Employees Total number: 150; typical ages: 17–21. 50% men; 50% women; 98% minorities; 80% high school students; 20% college students.
Employment Information Openings are from June 10 to August 31. Jobs available: ▶ 100–150 *YES interns* (minimum age 17) must be a minority high school or college student with interest in entertainment or media. Applicants must submit formal organization application, resume, academic transcripts, letter of recommendation, statement of interest. An in-person interview is recommended, but a telephone interview is acceptable.
Benefits and Preemployment Training Willing to provide letters of recommendation, on-the-job training, willing to act as a professional reference, and opportunity to attend seminars/workshops. Preemployment training is required and includes interpersonal skills, leadership skills.
Contact Program Manager, YES TO JOBS. Telephone: 310-358-4923. Fax: 310-358-4330. E-mail: yestojobs@aol.com. World Wide Web: http://www.yestojobs.org. Contact by e-mail, mail, or through World Wide Web site.

YMCA CAMP SURF
106 CARNATION AVENUE
IMPERIAL BEACH, CALIFORNIA 91932
General Information Residential oceanside camp serving groups and individuals for summer camp, outdoor education, teen leadership, youth retreats, mission projects to Mexico, and beach tent camping. Established in 1969. 40-acre facility located 2 miles from San Diego. Features: beach camping; guarded ocean waterfront; salt marsh reserve; 13 wooden cabins; outdoor dining deck; nearby town pier.
Profile of Summer Employees Total number: 60; typical ages: 19–28. 25% minorities; 5% high school students; 70% college students; 1% retirees; 30% non-U.S. citizens; 20% local applicants. Nonsmokers required.

Employment Information Openings are from June 1 to September 1. Year-round positions also offered. Jobs available: ▶ 30–40 *camp counselors* (minimum age 18) with first aid and CPR certification, (lifeguard training helpful) at $180–$240 per week ▶ 5–6 *coordinators* (minimum age 21) with leadership experience, Class B license, and lifeguard training at $240–$300 per week ▶ 1 *health services coordinator* (minimum age 21) with first aid, CPR, BLS, and EMT certification at $3000–$3600 per season ▶ 8–12 *ocean lifeguards* (minimum age 18) with lifeguarding and Basic Life Support certification at $180–$240 per week ▶ 1 *photographer/ technology support* (minimum age 21) with basic photography and Web design experience at $180–$240 per week. Applicants must submit a formal organization application, letter of interest, resume, personal reference, three letters of recommendation. An in-person interview is recommended, but a telephone interview is acceptable.

Benefits and Preemployment Training Free housing, free meals, willing to provide letters of recommendation, on-the-job training, willing to complete paperwork for educational credit, willing to act as a professional reference, and opportunity to attend seminars/workshops. Preemployment training is required and includes accident prevention and safety, first aid, CPR, interpersonal skills, leadership skills, lifeguard training.

Contact Zayanne Thompson, Senior Program Director, YMCA Camp Surf, 106 Carnation Avenue, Imperial Beach, California 91932. Telephone: 619-423-5850. Fax: 619-423-4141. E-mail: zgardner@ymca.org. World Wide Web: http://camp.ymca.org. Contact by e-mail, fax, mail, phone, or through World Wide Web site. Application deadline: continuous.

YOSEMITE CONCESSION SERVICES CORPORATION
PO BOX 578
YOSEMITE NATIONAL PARK, CALIFORNIA 95389

General Information Main concessionaire for Yosemite National Park, providing all aspects of guest services. 100 miles from Fresno. Features: wooded setting; high sierra lakes; steep granite walls; waterfalls; meadows.

Profile of Summer Employees Total number: 1,800; typical ages: 18–25. 50% men; 50% women; 17% minorities; 1% high school students; 40% college students; 3% retirees; 6% non-U.S. citizens; 50% local applicants.

Employment Information Openings are from March 1 to October 30. Year-round positions also offered. Jobs available: ▶ 3–5 *assistant dining room managers* (minimum age 18) with some restaurant and management experience required at $25,000 to $30,000 per year (full benefits) ▶ 20–30 *buspeople* (minimum age 18) with restaurant experience at $6.75–$7.75 per hour ▶ 10–20 *cooks* (minimum age 18) with experience in the field at $9–$10 per hour ▶ 15–30 *custodians* (minimum age 18) at $6.75–$7.75 per hour ▶ 10–20 *drivers* (minimum age 18) with class A or B license, airbrake, and passenger endorsements at $9–$10 per hour ▶ 75–150 *food service utility staff* (minimum age 18) at $6.75–$7.75 per hour ▶ 10–20 *front desk personnel* (minimum age 18) with cash handling and computer experience at $7–$8 per hour ▶ 10–20 *hosts/hostesses* (minimum age 18) with restaurant experience at $7–$8 per hour ▶ 50–75 *kitchen utility staff* (minimum age 18) at $6.75–$7.75 per hour ▶ 14–15 *lifeguards* (minimum age 18) with CPR for Professional Rescuer, BFA, lifeguard certification, and Title 22 at $7.07–$8.50 per hour ▶ 100–250 *roomkeepers* (minimum age 18) at $6.75–$7.75 per hour ▶ 25–100 *sales clerks* (minimum age 18) with cash handling experience at $7–$8 per hour ▶ 20–30 *waitresses/waiters* (minimum age 18) with restaurant experience at $6.75 per hour. Applicants must submit formal organization application. International applicants accepted; must obtain own visa, obtain own working papers, apply through a recognized agency.

Benefits and Preemployment Training Housing at a cost, meals at a cost, formal training, possible full-time employment, health insurance, on-the-job training, and opportunity to attend seminars/workshops. Preemployment training is required and includes accident prevention and safety, first aid, CPR, interpersonal skills, leadership skills, AHLA certification (American Hotel and Lodging Association).

Contact Debbie Brown, Recruiting Manager, Yosemite Concession Services Corporation. Telephone: 209-372-1236. Fax: 209-372-1050. E-mail: dbrown@dncinc.com. World Wide Web: http://www.yosemitepark.com. Contact by e-mail, fax, mail, phone, or through World Wide Web site. Application deadline: continuous.

COLORADO

A CHRISTIAN MINISTRY IN THE NATIONAL PARKS–COLORADO
See A Christian Ministry in the National Parks–Maine on page 107 for complete description.

ANDERSON WESTERN COLORADO CAMPS, LTD.
7177 COLORADO RIVER ROAD
GYPSUM, COLORADO 81637
General Information Residential coed camp serving 125 campers per session. Children are given daily choices of noncompetitive activities. Wilderness pioneer camp for 14-17 year olds emphasizes out-of-camp trips. Established in 1962. 200-acre facility located 140 miles from Denver. Features: Colorado River; climbing wall; ropes course; cliffs for rappelling; creek; pond.
Profile of Summer Employees Total number: 40; typical ages: 19–22. 50% men; 50% women; 25% minorities; 3% high school students; 60% college students; 5% retirees; 15% non-U.S. citizens; 20% local applicants. Nonsmokers required.
Employment Information Openings are from May 12 to August 20. Year-round positions also offered. Jobs available: ▶ 20 *camp counselors* with two years of college preferred at $975–$1200 per season ▶ 2 *cooks* at $2500–$7000 per season ▶ 4 *lodge/grounds staff members* (minimum age 16) at $975–$1200 per season ▶ *nurse* with RN certification at $200–$400 per week ▶ *program coordinators* (minimum age 21) at $1000–$1300 per season ▶ 1 *rafting director* (minimum age 21) with rafting ability, organizational skills, and teaching skills ▶ 3 *wranglers* with knowledge of horses at $975–$1200 per season. Applicants must submit a formal organization application, writing sample, three personal references. An in-person interview is recommended, but a telephone interview is acceptable. International applicants accepted; must obtain own visa, obtain own working papers.
Benefits and Preemployment Training Free housing, free meals, formal training, possible full-time employment, willing to provide letters of recommendation, names of contacts, on-the-job training, willing to complete paperwork for educational credit, willing to act as a professional reference, and travel reimbursement. Preemployment training is required and includes accident prevention and safety, first aid, CPR, interpersonal skills, leadership skills.
Contact Christopher Porter, Director, Anderson Western Colorado Camps, Ltd., 7177 Colorado River Road, Gypsum, Colorado 81637. Telephone: 970-524-7766. Fax: 970-524-7107. E-mail: andecamp@rof.net. World Wide Web: http://www.andersoncamps.com. Contact by e-mail, fax, mail, phone, or through World Wide Web site. Application deadline: continuous.

BAR LAZY J GUEST RANCH
447 COUNTY ROAD 3, BOX N
PARSHALL, COLORADO 80468
General Information Guest ranch with capacity for 40 people. Established in 1912. 70-acre facility located 110 miles from Denver. Features: 60 horses; 2/3 mile of Colorado River; pool; hot tub; 12 cabins; mountain bikes.

Profile of Summer Employees Total number: 20; typical age: 18. 50% men; 50% women; 82% college students; 18% retirees.

Employment Information Openings are from May 1 to September 30. Jobs available: ▶ 1 *assistant cook* at $550 per month ▶ 2 *counselors* with experience working with children at $450 per month ▶ 1 *head cook* with experience running a kitchen and serving 60 people at $1000 per month ▶ 1 *head wrangler* with experience in the field at $800 per month ▶ 2 *housekeepers* at $450 per month ▶ 1 *kitchen helper* at $450 per month ▶ 2 *waitresses/waiters* at $450 per month ▶ 5 *wranglers* with experience in the field at $500 per month. Applicants must submit a formal organization application, resume, writing sample, three personal references. A telephone interview is required.

Benefits and Preemployment Training Free housing, free meals, formal training, and on-the-job training. Preemployment training is required and includes first aid, CPR, (required for wranglers and children's counselors).

Contact Cheri Amos Helmicki, Owners, Bar Lazy J Guest Ranch, Box N, Parshall, Colorado 80468. Telephone: 970-725-3437. Fax: 970-725-0121. E-mail: barlazyj@rkymtnhi.com. World Wide Web: http://www.barlazyj.com. Contact by e-mail, fax, mail, or phone. Application deadline: April 15.

BAR NI RANCH
6614 HIGHWAY 12, STONEWALL GAP
WESTON, COLORADO 81091

General Information Private guest ranch with 15–35 guests per week; gentle, resistance-free horse training and riding; quarter horse breeding; ranch-style, health conscious, and gourmet meals; hiking, fishing, ninety percent repeat guests, conservation easement, and a fabulous staff. Established in 1946. 36,000-acre facility located 35 miles from Trinidad. Features: Sangre de Cristo Mountain range; 13,000 and 14,000-foot mountain peaks; 36,000 acres of forests, meadows, and alpine basins; environmentally protected setting; 7 streams and 5 ponds; abundant wildlife: elk, deer, wild turkey, bear, eagles.

Profile of Summer Employees Total number: 12–14; typical ages: 18–50. 50% men; 50% women; 10% minorities; 10% high school students; 30% college students; 40% local applicants. Nonsmokers preferred.

Employment Information Openings are from April 15 to November 15. Year-round positions also offered. Jobs available: ▶ 1 *chef/cook* (minimum age 18) with cooking school certification preferred at $1500 per month ▶ 2–4 *cook's helpers/waitstaff/lawn care workers* (minimum age 18) at $900 per month ▶ 2 *housekeepers* (minimum age 18) at $900 per month ▶ 2 *mechanics/general ranch help* (minimum age 18) with large and small engine mechanical skills at $1000 per month ▶ 2 *wranglers/general ranch help* (minimum age 18) with experience and CPR/first aid certification desirable at $1000 per month. Applicants must submit a formal organization application, resume, 3 work references. A telephone interview is required.

Benefits and Preemployment Training Free housing, free meals, possible full-time employment, willing to provide letters of recommendation, on-the-job training, and willing to complete paperwork for educational credit.

Contact Tom Perry, Ranch Manager, Bar NI Ranch, 6614 Highway 12, Weston, Colorado 81091. Fax: 719-868-2708. E-mail: barniranch@aol.com. Contact by e-mail, fax, or mail. No phone calls. Application deadline: continuous.

BLAZING ADVENTURES
BOX 5068, 48 UPPER VILLAGE MALL
SNOWMASS VILLAGE, COLORADO 81615

General Information Organization providing outdoor adventure tours. Established in 1969. Located 10 miles from Aspen. Features: mountains; rivers; national forest; summer resort.

Profile of Summer Employees Total number: 100; typical ages: 22–40. 55% men; 45% women; 15% college students; 80% local applicants.

Employment Information Openings are from May 1 to September 1. Jobs available: ▶ *adventure guides* (minimum age 21) at $9–$11 per hour ▶ 3 *group coordinators* (minimum age 20) at $9–$12 per hour ▶ 10 *office staff* (minimum age 20) at $9–$11 per hour ▶ 10 *sales and marketing coordination reservation interns* (minimum age 20) at $9–$11 per hour. Applicants must submit a formal organization application, 3-4 letters of recommendations, 3-4 personal references. A telephone interview is required.

Benefits and Preemployment Training Formal training, possible full-time employment, willing to provide letters of recommendation, on-the-job training, willing to complete paperwork for educational credit, and willing to act as a professional reference. Preemployment training is required and includes first aid, CPR, interpersonal skills, leadership skills.

Contact Teresa Haller, Controller, Blazing Adventures, Box 5068, Snowmass Village, Colorado 81615. Telephone: 970-923-4544. Fax: 970-923-4994. E-mail: blazing@rof.net. World Wide Web: http://www.blazingadventures.com. Contact by e-mail, fax, mail, or phone. Application deadline: continuous.

CENTRAL CITY OPERA
621 17TH STREET, SUITE 1601
DENVER, COLORADO 80293

General Information Opera house that produces three mainstage productions per summer between late June and early August. Established in 1932. Features: Rocky Mountains.

Profile of Summer Employees Total number: 150; typical ages: 20–25. 50% men; 50% women; 20% minorities; 85% college students; 20% local applicants. Nonsmokers preferred.

Employment Information Openings are from May 24 to August 17. Jobs available: ▶ 1 *assistant house manager* (minimum age 22) with ability to manage people well, previous experience preferred, and maturity at $230 per week ▶ 2–3 *costume shop assistants and dressers* (minimum age 22) with skills in detailed work such as sewing (hand and machine) and dressing performers at $230 per week ▶ 1 *gardener* (minimum age 19) with horticulture background and outdoor enjoyment at $230 per week ▶ 1–2 *gift shop assistants* (minimum age 22) with previous experience in retail, good people and money skills, and good organizational skills at $230 per week ▶ 1–2 *music librarians* (minimum age 21) with ability to read music, a music background, organizational skills, and maturity at $230 per week ▶ 1–2 *office assistants* (minimum age 22) with organizational skills, good people skills, and maturity at $230 per week ▶ 3 *production assistants (stage management)* (minimum age 22) with ability to read music, good organization skills, maturity, and ability to handle stress and deadlines at $230 per week ▶ 1 *properties intern* (minimum age 20) with previous experience (helpful) and skills in construction, building, crafts or sewing at $230 per week ▶ 1 *public relations assistant* (minimum age 22) with good organizational and writing skills, good personality, and maturity at $230 per week ▶ 1 *receptions/events assistant* (minimum age 22) with caterience experience (helpful) and excellent people, planning, and budgeting skills at $230 per week ▶ 1–2 *wigs/ makeup interns* (minimum age 20) with previous experience preferred in wigs and makeup at $230 per week. Applicants must submit a formal organization application, letter of interest, resume, three personal references, three letters of recommendation. A telephone interview is required. International applicants accepted; must obtain own visa, obtain own working papers.

Benefits and Preemployment Training Free housing, willing to provide letters of recommendation, on-the-job training, willing to complete paperwork for educational credit, willing to act as a professional reference, and travel reimbursement.

Contact Karen T. Federing, Festival Manager, Central City Opera, 621 17th Street, Suite 1601, Denver, Colorado 80293. Telephone: 303-292-6500. Fax: 303-292-4958. E-mail: kfedering@ centralcityopera.org. World Wide Web: http://www.centralcityopera.org. Contact by e-mail, fax, mail, phone, or through World Wide Web site. Application deadline: April 1.

CHELEY COLORADO CAMPS
ESTES PARK, COLORADO 80517

General Information Residential camp serving 475 campers ages 9–17 for four-week sessions in a rigorous outdoor western adventure program. Established in 1921. 1,600-acre facility located 75 miles from Denver. Features: wooded setting; mountain streams; 14,000-foot peak; 5 western riding rings; historic log lodges; freshwater lake.

Profile of Summer Employees Total number: 210; typical ages: 19–70. 50% men; 50% women; 1% minorities; 90% college students; 15% retirees; 5% non-U.S. citizens; 20% local applicants. Nonsmokers required.

Employment Information Openings are from May 23 to August 29. Jobs available: ▶ 40 *cooks* (minimum age 19) with experience at $1600–$2200 per season ▶ 100 *counselors* (minimum age 19) with CPR/first aid certification at $1500–$1700 per season ▶ 10–12 *drivers* (minimum age 21) with clean driving record at $1500–$1800 per season ▶ 6 *nurses* (minimum age 24) with RN license at $3200 per season ▶ 4–6 *office staff members* (minimum age 19) with office experience at $1500–$1700 per season. Applicants must submit formal organization application, resume, three personal references, three letters of recommendation. A telephone interview is required. International applicants accepted; must apply through a recognized agency.

Benefits and Preemployment Training Free housing, free meals, formal training, health insurance, willing to provide letters of recommendation, on-the-job training, willing to complete paperwork for educational credit, willing to act as a professional reference, opportunity to attend seminars/workshops, and travel reimbursement. Preemployment training is required and includes accident prevention and safety, first aid, CPR, interpersonal skills, leadership skills, child behavior skills.

Contact Brooke Cheley, Staff Director, Cheley Colorado Camps, PO Box 6525, Denver, Colorado 80206. Telephone: 303-377-3616. Fax: 303-377-3605. E-mail: brooke@cheley.com. World Wide Web: http://www.cheley.com. Contact by e-mail, fax, mail, phone, or through World Wide Web site. Application deadline: continuous.

CHEROKEE PARK RANCH
436 CHEROKEE HILLS DRIVE
LIVERMORE, COLORADO 80536

General Information Summer guest ranch providing fun outdoor activities for the entire family and specializing in Western hospitality. Established in 1886. 300-acre facility located 180 miles from Denver. Features: heated swimming pool; hot tub; horseback riding; lake and river; Rocky Mountain location.

Profile of Summer Employees Total number: 22; typical ages: 20–24. 42% men; 58% women; 11% minorities; 90% college students; 12% local applicants. Nonsmokers preferred.

Employment Information Openings are from May 10 to September 30. Jobs available: ▶ 2 *children's counselors* (minimum age 19) with CPR/first aid and lifesaving certification, experience working with children preferred at $500–$600 per month ▶ 1 *cook* (minimum age 19) with experience cooking for large groups preferred at $1000–$1500 per month ▶ 5 *housekeepers/ waitresses/waiters* (minimum age 19) at $450–$600 per month ▶ 1 *prep cook/dishwasher* (minimum age 19) with kitchen experience preferred at $500–$750 per month ▶ 1 *secretary* (minimum age 19) with office/clerical experience preferred at $500–$700 per month ▶ 1 *wrangler* (minimum age 19) with CPR certification (preferred), experience with horses and tack and Western riding at $500–$650 per month. Applicants must submit a formal organization application, three personal references, photograph. A telephone interview is required. International applicants accepted.

Benefits and Preemployment Training Free housing, free meals, willing to provide letters of recommendation, on-the-job training, willing to act as a professional reference, and gratuity pool. Preemployment training is required and includes first aid, CPR.

Contact Christine Prince, Owner, Cherokee Park Ranch, 436 Cherokee Hills Drive, Livermore, Colorado 80536. Telephone: 800-628-0949. Fax: 970-493-5802. E-mail: ccpranch@aol.com. World Wide Web: http://www.cherokeeparkranch.com. Contact by e-mail, mail, or phone. Application deadline: January 15.

THE COLORADO MOUNTAIN RANCH
10063 GOLD HILL ROAD
BOULDER, COLORADO 80302

General Information Day camp serving approximately 200 boys and girls ages 7-17 and enjoyed by other clientele for mountain events, parties, weddings, horse-drawn rides, company picnics, and retreats. Residential staff. Established in 1947. 200-acre facility. Features: pine and aspen forests and wildflower meadows; snowy peak vistas; lodge and cabins; heated swimming pool; horse and foot trails; dirt basketball and volleyball.

Profile of Summer Employees Total number: 45; typical ages: 19–25. 40% men; 60% women; 10% minorities; 90% college students; 5% non-U.S. citizens. Nonsmokers preferred.

Employment Information Openings are from June 2 to August 15. Jobs available: ▶ 1 *Indian lore instructor* (minimum age 18) at $1650 per season ▶ 1 *administrative assistant* at $1800 per season ▶ 1 *archery instructor* (minimum age 18) with experience in the field at $1650 per season ▶ 1 *arts and crafts instructor* (minimum age 18) at $1650 per season ▶ 3 *bus drivers* (minimum age 21) with commercial driver's license; training and certification given at $1950 per season ▶ 10 *day-camp counselors* (minimum age 18) at $1650 per season ▶ 1 *drama/ creative writing/newspaper instructor* (minimum age 18) at $1650 per season ▶ 2 *gymnastics instructors* (minimum age 18) at $1650 per season ▶ 1 *head cook/kitchen manager* (minimum age 21) with experience in menu planning, food ordering, and staff management at $3500 per season ▶ 2 *kitchen workers* (minimum age 18) at $1950 per season ▶ 2 *maintenance staff* (minimum age 18) at $1950 per season ▶ 1 *office staff* (minimum age 18) at $800–$1950 per season ▶ 2 *outcamp/hiking/backpacking/outdoor living/nature instructors* (minimum age 21) at $1650 per season ▶ 1 *riflery instructor* (minimum age 18) with experience in the field at $1650 per season ▶ 1 *ropes course instructor* (minimum age 18) at $1650 per season ▶ 2 *swimming instructors* (minimum age 18) with one required to have WSI certification and both required to have LGT certification at $1750 per season ▶ 8 *wranglers/western riding instructors* (minimum age 18) with experience with horses at $1650 per season. Applicants must submit a formal organization application, three personal references and/or letters of recommendation. A telephone interview is required. International applicants accepted; must obtain own visa, obtain own working papers.

Benefits and Preemployment Training Free housing, free meals, willing to provide letters of recommendation, on-the-job training, willing to complete paperwork for educational credit, willing to act as a professional reference, and opportunity to attend seminars/workshops. Preemployment training is required and includes accident prevention and safety, first aid, CPR, interpersonal skills, leadership skills.

Contact Lynn Walker, Director, The Colorado Mountain Ranch, 10063 Gold Hill Road, Boulder, Colorado 80302. Telephone: 800-267-9573. E-mail: office@coloradomountainranch.com. World Wide Web: http://www.coloradomountainranch.com. Contact by e-mail, mail, phone, or through World Wide Web site. Application deadline: May 1.

COLORADO TRAILS RANCH
12161 CR 240
DURANGO, COLORADO 81301

General Information Full service, family-oriented guest ranch offering cabin accommodations, meals, and a full activity program including horseback riding, fishing, marksmanship, sports and more. Established in 1960. 500-acre facility. Features: mountain location; heated pool; beautiful lodge; excellent children's program; excellent riding program; excellent fishing program.

Profile of Summer Employees Total number: 30; typical ages: 19–25. 40% men; 60% women; 95% college students; 5% non-U.S. citizens; 5% local applicants. Nonsmokers preferred.

Employment Information Openings are from May to October. Jobs available: ▶ 2 *cooks* with kitchen/cooking experience ▶ 3–4 *counselors* (minimum age 18) with horse experience required, experience with children and teens preferred ▶ 4 *general staff (floaters)* (minimum age 18) with flexible attitude and willingness to help where needed ▶ 8 *housekeepers/waitstaff (rotational)* (minimum age 18) ▶ 3 *maintenance staff* (minimum age 18) with general maintenance experience preferred ▶ 2 *prep cooks* (minimum age 18) with kitchen experience preferred ▶ 7–8 *wranglers* (minimum age 18) with extensive horse experience. Applicants must submit formal organization application, three personal references, three letters of recommendation, optional photograph. An in-person interview is recommended, but a telephone interview is acceptable. International applicants accepted; must obtain own visa, obtain own working papers, apply through a recognized agency.

Benefits and Preemployment Training Free housing, free meals, willing to provide letters of recommendation, on-the-job training, willing to complete paperwork for educational credit, willing to act as a professional reference, and opportunity to participate in ranch activities.

Contact Jane Giese, Assistant Manager, Colorado Trails Ranch, 12161 CR 240, Durango, Colorado 81301. Telephone: 970-247-5055. Fax: 970-385-7372. E-mail: colotrailsjmg@aol.com. World Wide Web: http://www.coloradotrails.com. Contact by e-mail, fax, mail, phone, or through World Wide Web site. Application deadline: continuous.

COLVIG SILVER CAMPS
9665 FLORIDA ROAD
DURANGO, COLORADO 81301

General Information Outdoor adventure camp located in natural surroundings; mix of traditional summer camp activities and wilderness adventure. Established in 1969. 600-acre facility located 250 miles from Albuquerque, New Mexico. Features: rustic setting; creek running through site; Ponderosa Forest; 2 ponds; National Forest access; proximity to high alpine and desert areas.

Profile of Summer Employees Total number: 45–55; typical ages: 18–25. 50% men; 50% women; 90% college students; 5% local applicants. Nonsmokers required.

Employment Information Openings are from June 2 to August 9. Jobs available: ▶ 1 *arts and crafts director* (minimum age 21) with first aid and CPR certification, supervisory experience, and experience with all types of arts and crafts at $1200 per season ▶ 6–10 *assistant counselors/ trip leaders* (minimum age 18) with first aid and CPR certification; additional consideration for lifeguarding and wilderness first aid; should have experience with children and wilderness skills at $1000 per season ▶ 1 *climbing program coordinator* (minimum age 21) with first aid and CPR certification; experience with top rope climbing and anchor systems as well as experience with children at $1200 per season ▶ 20 *head counselors/trip leaders* (minimum age 21) with first aid and CPR certification; additional consideration for lifeguarding and wilderness first aid; should have experience with children and wilderness skills at $1100 per season ▶ 1 *head wrangler* (minimum age 21) with first aid and CPR certification; experience with horses and Western riding instruction at $1400 per season ▶ 1 *nurse* (minimum age 21) with RN license, CPR certification, and pediatric/summer camp experience at $2000–$3000 per season. Applicants must submit formal organization application, three personal references. A telephone interview is required. International applicants accepted; must obtain own visa, obtain own working papers, apply through a recognized agency.

Benefits and Preemployment Training Free housing, free meals, formal training, willing to provide letters of recommendation, on-the-job training, willing to complete paperwork for educational credit, willing to act as a professional reference, and laundry, workmen's compensation insurance. Preemployment training is required and includes accident prevention and safety, interpersonal skills, leadership skills, individual program area and wilderness training, wilderness first aid.

Contact Megan Weidmann, Program Director, Colvig Silver Camps, 9665 Florida Road, Durango, Colorado 81301. Telephone: 970-247-2564. Fax: 970-247-2547. E-mail: colvigsilvercamps@ compuserve.com. World Wide Web: http://www.colvigsilvercamps.com. Contact by e-mail, fax, mail, phone, or through World Wide Web site. Application deadline: continuous.

CROSS BAR X YOUTH RANCH
2111 COUNTY ROAD 222
DURANGO, COLORADO 81303

General Information Christian camp for low income and inner city youth. Established in 1977. 149-acre facility. Features: lake; trails; obstacle course; basketball court; horseback riding; mountain bikes.

Profile of Summer Employees Total number: 12; typical ages: 18–22. 50% men; 50% women; 90% college students. Nonsmokers required.

Employment Information Openings are from May 26 to August 9. Jobs available: ▶ *activities coordinator* (minimum age 18) at $100–$160 per week ▶ 1 *cook* with ability to cook for 50 people ▶ 8 *counselors* (minimum age 18) with general understanding of the Bible and strong Christian commitment at $100–$160 per week. Applicants must submit a formal organization application, five personal references. International applicants accepted; must obtain own visa, obtain own working papers.

Benefits and Preemployment Training Free housing, free meals, formal training, on-the-job training, and willing to complete paperwork for educational credit. Preemployment training is required and includes accident prevention and safety, first aid, CPR, interpersonal skills, leadership skills.

Contact Jeremy Yarbrough, Director, Cross Bar X Youth Ranch, 2111 County Road 222, Durango, Colorado 81303. Telephone: 970-259-2716. Fax: 970-259-8006. E-mail: crossbar@frontier.net. World Wide Web: http://www.crossbarxcamp.org. Contact by e-mail, mail, phone, or through World Wide Web site. Application deadline: May 15.

CYBERCAMPS–UNIVERSITY OF DENVER
DENVER, COLORADO
See Cybercamps–University of Washington on page 326 for complete description.

DROWSY WATER RANCH
PO BOX 147 J
GRANBY, COLORADO 80446

General Information Mountain dude ranch serving 60 guests weekly. Established in 1977. 600-acre facility located 110 miles from Denver. Features: mountains; horses; entertainment; Colorado River.

Profile of Summer Employees Total number: 27; typical ages: 18–50. 48% men; 52% women; 15% high school students; 75% college students; 1% non-U.S. citizens; 5% local applicants. Nonsmokers required.

Employment Information Openings are from May 1 to September 30. Jobs available: ▶ 2 *assistant cooks* with experience in the field at a paid salary plus tips ▶ 2 *counselors* with first aid certification and experience in the field at a paid salary plus tips ▶ 2 *dishwashers* at a paid salary plus tips ▶ 1 *head chef* with experience in the field at a paid salary plus tips ▶ 8 *horse wranglers/trail guides* with first aid certification and experience in the field at a paid salary plus tips ▶ 6 *housekeeping staff members/wait persons* at a paid salary plus tips ▶ 2 *maintenance staff members* at a paid salary plus tips ▶ 1 *office person* with experience in the field at a paid salary plus tips. Applicants must submit formal organization application, letter of interest, resume, personal reference. A telephone interview is required. International applicants accepted; must obtain own visa, obtain own working papers, apply through a recognized agency.

Benefits and Preemployment Training Free housing, free meals, possible full-time employment, on-the-job training, and willing to complete paperwork for educational credit. Preemployment training is optional and includes accident prevention and safety, first aid, CPR, leadership skills.

Contact Randy Sue Fosha, Owner, Drowsy Water Ranch, PO Box 147 J, Granby, Colorado 80446. Telephone: 970-725-3456. Fax: 970-725-3611. E-mail: dwrken@aol.com. World Wide Web: http://www.drowsywater.com. Contact by e-mail, fax, mail, phone, or through World Wide Web site. Application deadline: continuous.

DVORAK'S KAYAKING AND RAFTING EXPEDITIONS
17921 HIGHWAY 285
NATHROP, COLORADO 81236

General Information Outfitters offering whitewater rafting and kayaking expeditions on 10 rivers and in 29 canyons in 5 states of the Southwest. Established in 1984. 10-acre facility located 130 miles from Denver.

Profile of Summer Employees Total number: 40; typical ages: 20–60. 60% men; 40% women; 60% college students; 10% non-U.S. citizens; 30% local applicants. Nonsmokers required.

Employment Information Openings are from April 15 to September 15. Jobs available: ▶ 3 *instructors (multi-day, kayaking, rafting)* (minimum age 18) with instruction skills and guide experience at $575–$2000 per month ▶ 1 *logistics manager* with computer skills and ordering and packing experience at $1200 per month ▶ 2 *reservations/office staff members* with computer and telephone skills and outdoor background for sales and customer service at $650–$1200 per month ▶ 35 *river guides (multi-day)* (minimum age 18) with advanced first aid/CPR valid to season-end at $575–$2000 per month ▶ 1 *transportation manager/mechanic* (minimum age 21) with CDL license/driver and mechanic skills on buses/vans/trucks at $900–$1200 per month. Applicants must submit a formal organization application, resume, three personal references, three letters of recommendation, if hired there is a 14-day training course; the fee is $630 which includes all food and equipment. An in-person interview is recommended, but a telephone interview is acceptable. International applicants accepted; must obtain own visa.

Benefits and Preemployment Training Free housing, free meals, willing to provide letters of recommendation, on-the-job training, willing to complete paperwork for educational credit, willing to act as a professional reference, travel reimbursement, and swift water rescue technician certification. Preemployment training is required and includes accident prevention and safety, first aid, CPR, interpersonal skills, leadership skills, swift water rescue.

Contact Bill Dvorak, President, Dvorak's Kayaking and Rafting Expeditions, 17921 Highway 285, Nathrop, Colorado 81236. Telephone: 719-539-6851. Fax: 719-539-3378. E-mail: dvorakex@amigo.net. World Wide Web: http://www.dvorakexpeditions.com. Contact by e-mail, fax, mail, phone, or through World Wide Web site. Application deadline: April 15.

EAGLE LAKE CAMP–COLORADO
3820 NORTH 30TH STREET
COLORADO SPRINGS, COLORADO 80904

General Information 4 camps including wilderness adventure, horsemanship, mountain and road biking, resident experiences. Serves more than 2000 campers ages 8-18 each summer. Established in 1957. 330-acre facility located 80 miles from Denver. Features: located in Pikes National Forest; 10-acre freshwater lake; zipline; covered basketball courts; cabins and teepees; waterslide.

Profile of Summer Employees Total number: 125; typical ages: 19–28. 50% men; 50% women; 10% minorities; 90% college students; 10% local applicants. Nonsmokers required.

Employment Information Openings are from May 20 to August 15. Jobs available: ▶ 65 *counselors* (minimum age 19) with one year of college and CPR/SFA certification at $1200 per season ▶ 2 *emergency medical technicians* (minimum age 19) with EMT basic training at $1200 per season ▶ 1 *food service staff member* at $1200 per season ▶ 5 *maintenance staff members* (minimum age 19) with experience at $1200 per season ▶ 3 *registered nurses* (minimum age 19) with licenses at $1200–$2500 per season ▶ 1 *transportation director* (minimum age 21) with first aid/CPR certifications, valid driver's license at $1200 per season ▶ 1 *videographer* (minimum age 19) with experience in the field at $1200 per season. Applicants must submit a formal organization application, two personal references. A telephone interview is required. International applicants accepted; must obtain own visa, obtain own working papers.

Benefits and Preemployment Training Free housing, free meals, willing to provide letters of recommendation, on-the-job training, willing to complete paperwork for educational credit, willing to act as a professional reference, and opportunity to attend seminars/workshops. Preemployment training is required and includes accident prevention and safety, first aid, CPR, interpersonal skills, leadership skills.

Contact Adam Sperling, Resident Director, Eagle Lake Camp–Colorado, PO Box 6000, Colorado Springs, Colorado 80934. Telephone: 719-472-1260. Fax: 719-623-0148. E-mail: adam_sperling@navigators.org. World Wide Web: http://www.eaglelake.org. Contact by e-mail or through World Wide Web site. Application deadline: continuous.

ECHO CANYON RIVER EXPEDITIONS
45000 U.S. HIGHWAY 50 WEST
CAÑON CITY, COLORADO 81212

General Information Professional white-water river outfitter offering guided river trips ranging from mild to wild to more than 20,000 guests per year. Established in 1978. 4-acre facility located 8 miles from Canon City.

Profile of Summer Employees Total number: 75; typical age: 24. 60% men; 40% women; 10% minorities; 2% high school students; 65% college students; 4% retirees; 20% local applicants.

Employment Information Openings are from April to September. Jobs available: ▶ 10 *bus drivers* with CDL license for Colorado, pre-employment drug/alcohol test, and physical at $200–$400 per week ▶ 10 *customer service representatives* with guest service experience (preferred) at $200–$400 per week ▶ 15 *river guides* with standard first aid and CPR certification and river guide experience or completion of our training program (fee charged) at $200–$800 per week.

Benefits and Preemployment Training Preemployment training is required and includes accident prevention and safety, interpersonal skills, leadership skills.

Contact Andy Neinas, Owner/Operator, Echo Canyon River Expeditions. Telephone: 719-275-3154. E-mail: echocanyon@amigo.net. World Wide Web: http://www.raftecho.com. Contact by e-mail, mail, phone, or through World Wide Web site. Application deadline: applications by April 1 preferred.

ELK MOUNTAIN RANCH
13300 COUNTY ROAD 185B
BUENA VISTA, COLORADO 81211

General Information Guest ranch serving 35 guests. A true Western vacation experience offering weekly packages from June through the end of September. Established in 1981. 5-acre facility located 90 miles from Colorado Springs. Features: highest elevation in Colorado (9,500 feet); family-oriented; very remote setting; horseback riding through unspoiled wilderness; white-water rafting; hot tub.

Profile of Summer Employees Total number: 14; typical ages: 19–27. 50% men; 50% women; 100% college students. Nonsmokers required.

Employment Information Openings are from May 15 to September 30. Jobs available: ▶ 1 *assistant cook* with service- and quality-oriented personality at $650 per month plus gratuities

▶ 1 *children's counselor* with experience, love of children 4-7, familiarity with horses, and first aid/CPR preferred at $575 per month plus gratuities ▶ 1 *cook* with high-quality service and love of great food at $800 per month plus gratuities ▶ 1 *general maintenance person* with knowledge of minor repairs, groundskeeping, and vehicle maintenance at $575 per month plus gratuities ▶ 5 *waitstaff/housekeeping personnel/dishwashers* with service- and quality-oriented personality at $575 per month plus gratuities ▶ 6 *wranglers* with experience riding and/or instructing horsemanship, basic knowledge of horses (care, feeding, and grooming), good people skills, and first aid/CPR preferred at $575 per month plus gratuities. Applicants must submit a formal organization application, three personal references. A telephone interview is required.

Benefits and Preemployment Training Free housing, free meals, willing to provide letters of recommendation, on-the-job training, willing to complete paperwork for educational credit, willing to act as a professional reference, and gratuities. Preemployment training is required and includes first aid, CPR.

Contact Sue Murphy, Co-Owner, Elk Mountain Ranch, PO Box 910, Buena Vista, Colorado 81211. Telephone: 800-432-8812. Fax: 719-539-4430. E-mail: info@elkmtn.com. World Wide Web: http://www.elkmtn.com. Contact by e-mail, mail, phone, or through World Wide Web site. Application deadline: May 1.

ESTES VALLEY RESORTS
6120 HIGHWAY 7
ESTES PARK, COLORADO 80517

General Information Resort, conference center, and ranch providing lodging, entertainment, and meals. Established in 1947. 85-acre facility located 80 miles from Denver.

Profile of Summer Employees Total number: 150. 50% men; 50% women.

Employment Information Openings are from May 15 to September 15. Year-round positions also offered. Jobs available: ▶ 5 *children's counselors* (minimum age 18) at $6.50 per hour plus bonus ▶ 4–6 *front desk attendants* (minimum age 18) at $6.50 per hour plus bonus ▶ 7 *livery staff/wranglers* (minimum age 18) with experience with horses at $6.50 per hour plus bonus ▶ 5 *recreation staff* (minimum age 18) at $6.50 per hour plus bonus ▶ *various positions* (minimum age 18) ▶ 15 *waitresses* (minimum age 18) at $5 to $6 per hour plus tips. Applicants must submit formal organization application. A telephone interview is required. International applicants accepted; must obtain own visa, obtain own working papers, apply through a recognized agency.

Benefits and Preemployment Training Housing at a cost, meals at a cost, formal training, possible full-time employment, on-the-job training, and willing to complete paperwork for educational credit.

Contact Deborah Vallia, Human Resources Officer, Estes Valley Resorts, 6120 Highway 7, Estes Park, Colorado 80517. Telephone: 970-577-3416. Fax: 970-577-3414. E-mail: humanres@ aspenlodge.net. World Wide Web: http://www.estesvalleyresorts.com. Contact by e-mail, fax, mail, phone, or through World Wide Web site. Application deadline: continuous.

FLYING G RANCH, TOMAHAWK RANCH–GIRL SCOUTS MILE HI COUNCIL
400 SOUTH BROADWAY, PO BOX 9407
DENVER, COLORADO 80209-0407

General Information Traditional overnight camp programs focusing on enhancing self-esteem, social relationships, outdoor skills, and leadership development. Features: mountain setting.

Profile of Summer Employees Total number: 80. Nonsmokers required.

Employment Information Openings are from June 1 to August 15. Jobs available: ▶ 2 *administrative assistants* (minimum age 21) with first aid certification, valid driver's license, business and administrative experience, skill in several program specialties, and college degree or equivalent work experience at $150–$175 per week ▶ 2 *assistant camp directors/program* *directors* (minimum age 21) with first aid certification, administrative and supervisory experience, experience in planning and implementing outdoor programs, skill in several program specialties, college degree or equivalent experience, and valid driver's license at $175–$250 per week ▶ 36 *assistant counselors* (minimum age 18) with experience with children, first aid training, experience as camper or camp leader, and at least one year of college or equivalent post-high school work experience at $140–$155 per week ▶ 2 *backpacking instructors* (minimum age 21) with experience teaching backpacking to children in camp setting, taking children on backpacking trips or equivalent, ability to carry backpack and walk long distances, first aid training, one year of college or equivalent, and wilderness first responder certification at $140–$180 per week ▶ 2 *business managers/assistant day camp directors* (minimum age 21) with administrative experience, valid driver's license, automobile, auto insurance, first aid and CPR training, and one year of college or equivalent at $260–$300 per week ▶ 2 *campcraft instructors* (minimum age 18) with experience teaching campcraft skills, ability to carry a backpack and walk long distances, first aid, and one year or more college experience or equivalent at $145–$160 per week ▶ 2 *challenge course instructors* (minimum age 21) with first aid certification, experience working with children, one year or more college experience or equivalent, ability to teach children in informal resident camp setting, and documented challenge course experience at $145–$180 per week ▶ 12 *counselors* (minimum age 21) with experience in camp counseling, team leader, first aid certification, three years or more college experience or equivalent post-high school work, and organizational skills at $160–$180 per week ▶ 2 *craft instructors* (minimum age 18) with first aid certification and at least one year of college or equivalent work experience at $140–$180 per week ▶ 1 *dance/drama instructor* (minimum age 18) with first aid training and at least one year of college or equivalent work experience at $140–$170 per week ▶ 1 *farm instructor* (minimum age 18) with experience feeding and caring for farm animals, one year or more college experience or equivalent work experience, and first aid training at $145–$160 per week ▶ 2 *handymen* (minimum age 18) with driver's license, acceptable driving record, and strong communication skills at $180–$260 per week ▶ *health supervisor* (minimum age 21) must be registered RN or LPN, first aid training, experience working with children, and valid driver's license at $375–$475 per week ▶ 7 *horseback riding counselors* (minimum age 18) with instructional western riding experience, organized camp experience, experience with horses, first aid training, and one year or more college experience or equivalent work experience at $150–$170 per week ▶ 1 *horseback riding director* (minimum age 21) with western riding skills, ability to teach riding skills to kids, first aid, and CPR training at $185–$225 per week ▶ 2 *nature instructors* (minimum age 18) with experience working with children in outdoor activities, one year or more college experience or equivalent work experience, and first aid skills at $140–$180 per week ▶ 2 *sports instructors* (minimum age 18) with first aid certification, one year or more college experience, certification or training in archery, and experience teaching variety of sports to children at $145–$160 per week. Applicants must submit formal organization application, three personal references. An in-person interview is recommended, but a telephone interview is acceptable. International applicants accepted; must apply through a recognized agency.

Benefits and Preemployment Training Free housing, free meals, health insurance, on-the-job training, willing to complete paperwork for educational credit, opportunity to attend seminars/workshops, and accident insurance, time off, end-of-season bonus, travel allowance. Preemployment training is required and includes accident prevention and safety, interpersonal skills, leadership skills, discipline policies, camp procedures, emergency procedures.

Contact Gretchen Vaughn, Camp Administrator, Flying G Ranch, Tomahawk Ranch–Girl Scouts Mile Hi Council, PO Box 9407, Denver, Colorado 80209-0407. Telephone: 303-778-0109 Ext. 281. Fax: 303-733-6345. E-mail: gretchenv@gsmhc.org. World Wide Web: http://www. girlscoutsmilehi.org. Contact by e-mail or phone. Application deadline: May 15.

GENEVA GLEN CAMP, INC.
PO BOX 248, 5793 SANTA CLARA ROAD
INDIAN HILLS, COLORADO 80454

General Information Private co-ed residence camp offering traditional program activities, rich tradition of THEME programming emphasizing American Heritage, Knighthood, and World Friendship. Established in 1922. 485-acre facility located 25 miles from Denver. Features: heated pool; ropes course; climb wall; horses; perfect climate; social atmosphere.

Profile of Summer Employees Total number: 95; typical ages: 18–23. 50% men; 50% women; 10% minorities; 30% high school students; 45% college students; 25% local applicants. Nonsmokers required.

Employment Information Openings are from June 9 to August 10. Jobs available: ▶ 1 *assistant nurse* (minimum age 21) EMT or nursing student, some medical experience at $2500 per season ▶ 10–20 *counselors* (minimum age 19) with experience (helpful) and sincere desire to live with kids at $1250 per season ▶ 1–2 *registered nurses* (minimum age 21) with Colorado RN license or reciprocity at $3500 per season. Applicants must submit a formal organization application. A telephone interview is required.

Benefits and Preemployment Training Free housing, free meals, formal training, health insurance, willing to provide letters of recommendation, on-the-job training, willing to complete paperwork for educational credit, willing to act as a professional reference, opportunity to attend seminars/workshops, and travel reimbursement. Preemployment training is required and includes accident prevention and safety, first aid, CPR, interpersonal skills, leadership skills.

Contact Ken Atkinson, Director, Geneva Glen Camp, Inc. Telephone: 303-697-4621. E-mail: ggcamp@genevaglen.org. World Wide Web: http://www.genevaglen.org. Contact by e-mail, mail, or phone. Application deadline: April 15.

GORE RANGE NATURAL SCIENCE SCHOOL
PO BOX 250
RED CLIFF, COLORADO 81649

General Information School (GRNSS) seeking to raise environmental awareness and inspire stewardship through natural science learning experiences in the Rocky Mountain ecosystem. Established in 1998. Located 12 miles from Vail. Features: bordered by White River National Forest; near Gore and Sawatch Mountain ranges; remote field sites.

Profile of Summer Employees Total number: 17; typical ages: 20–24. 30% men; 70% women; 40% college students; 20% local applicants.

Employment Information Openings are from June to September 1. Jobs available: ▶ 6 *summer naturalists* with first aid and CPR experience at $150 per week. Applicants must submit a formal organization application, letter of interest, resume, three personal references. A telephone interview is required.

Benefits and Preemployment Training Free housing, formal training, possible full-time employment, willing to provide letters of recommendation, names of contacts, on-the-job training, willing to complete paperwork for educational credit, willing to act as a professional reference, and opportunity to attend seminars/workshops. Preemployment training is required and includes accident prevention and safety, interpersonal skills, leadership skills, interpretive and teaching techniques.

Contact Kim Langmaid, Executive Director, Gore Range Natural Science School. Telephone: 970-827-9725. Fax: 970-827-9730. E-mail: kiml@gorerange.org. World Wide Web: http://www. gorerange.org. Contact by e-mail, phone, or through World Wide Web site. Application deadline: April 1.

HARMEL'S RANCH RESORT
6748 COUNTY ROAD 742
ALMONT, COLORADO 81210

General Information Family-oriented guest ranch with 38 units, stables, dining room, lounge, heated pool, and store situated at the confluence of 3 river canyons, surrounded by the National Forest. Established in 1958. 300-acre facility located 150 miles from Colorado Springs. Features: gold medal fishing; horseback riding; white-water rafting; fine dining; guided wilderness pack trips; nightly entertainment.

Profile of Summer Employees Total number: 60; typical ages: 18–27. 50% men; 50% women; 80% college students; 10% non-U.S. citizens; 10% local applicants. Nonsmokers preferred.

Employment Information Openings are from May 1 to November 7. Jobs available: ▶ 20 *housekeepers/waitpersons* (minimum age 18) at $750 to $1200 per month plus room and board ▶ *kitchen workers* (minimum age 18) at $750 to $1200 per month plus room and board ▶ 5 *ranch hands* (minimum age 18) at $750 to $1200 per month plus room and board ▶ 5 *store and office personnel* (minimum age 18) at $750 to $1200 per month plus room and board ▶ 12 *wranglers* (minimum age 18) at $750 to $1200 per month plus room and board. Applicants must submit formal organization application, letter of interest, resume, two personal references, two letters of recommendation. An in-person interview is recommended, but a telephone interview is acceptable. International applicants accepted; must apply through a recognized agency.

Benefits and Preemployment Training Free housing, free meals, formal training, possible full-time employment, willing to provide letters of recommendation, on-the-job training, willing to complete paperwork for educational credit, willing to act as a professional reference, and opportunity to attend seminars/workshops.

Contact Brad Roberts, Manager, Harmel's Ranch Resort, PO Box 399, Almont, Colorado 81210. Telephone: 970-641-1740. Fax: 970-641-1944. E-mail: stay@harmels.com. World Wide Web: http://www.harmels.com. Contact by e-mail, fax, mail, phone, or through World Wide Web site. Application deadline: continuous.

LONGACRE EXPEDITIONS, COLORADO
TAYLOR PARK, COLORADO

General Information Adventure travel program in Colorado for teenagers, emphasizing group living skills, physical challenges, and fun. Challenging programs place equal emphasis on physical accomplishment and emotional growth. Established in 1981. 60-acre facility located 20 miles from Crested Butte.

Profile of Summer Employees Total number: 20; typical ages: 21–30. 50% men; 50% women; 10% minorities; 40% college students; 30% local applicants. Nonsmokers required.

Employment Information Openings are from June 15 to August 1. Jobs available: ▶ 8 *assistant trip leaders* (minimum age 21) with WFR and CPR certification, and good driving record at $252–$300 per week ▶ 1 *mountaineering instructor* (minimum age 21) with good driving record, WFR, and CPR at $300–$400 per week ▶ 1 *rock climbing instructor* (minimum age 21) with good driving record, WFR, and CPR at $300–$400 per week ▶ 3 *support and logistics staff members* (minimum age 21) with good driving record, CPR, and WFR at $180–$240 per week. Applicants must submit a formal organization application, letter of interest, resume, three personal references. An in-person interview is recommended, but a telephone interview is acceptable. International applicants accepted; must obtain own visa, obtain own working papers.

Benefits and Preemployment Training Free housing, free meals, willing to provide letters of recommendation, on-the-job training, willing to complete paperwork for educational credit, willing to act as a professional reference, and pro-deal purchase program. Preemployment training is required and includes accident prevention and safety, interpersonal skills, leadership skills.

Contact Meredith Schuler, Director, Longacre Expeditions, Colorado, 4030 Middle Ridge Road, Newport, Pennsylvania 17074-8110. Telephone: 717-567-6790. Fax: 717-567-3955. E-mail:

merry@longacreexpeditions.com. World Wide Web: http://www.longacreexpeditions.com. Contact by e-mail, fax, mail, phone, or through World Wide Web site. Application deadline: continuous.

NATIONAL PARK SERVICE BLACK CANYON OF THE GUNNISON NATIONAL PARK AND CURECANTI NATIONAL RECREATION AREA
102 ELK CREEK
GUNNISON, COLORADO 81230

General Information Preserves resources, provides for public enjoyment, and offers educational programs on natural and historic aspects of area. Established in 1916. 75,000-acre facility. Features: river; reservoir; canyon; mesas; mountains; vistas.

Profile of Summer Employees Total number: 100; typical ages: 18–70. 50% men; 50% women; 2% minorities; 50% college students; 25% retirees; 2% local applicants. Nonsmokers preferred.

Employment Information Year-round positions also offered. Jobs available: ▶ 1–3 *interpretation interns* (minimum age 18) with education, life sciences, communications, or history background at $100 per week ▶ 1–5 *outreach education interns* (minimum age 18) with education, life sciences, communications, or history background at $100 per week. Applicants must submit letter of interest, resume, academic transcripts, three personal references, three letters of recommendation, online application. A telephone interview is required. International applicants accepted; must obtain own visa.

Benefits and Preemployment Training Free housing, formal training, willing to provide letters of recommendation, on-the-job training, willing to complete paperwork for educational credit, willing to act as a professional reference, opportunity to attend seminars/workshops, and food stipend. Preemployment training is required and includes accident prevention and safety, leadership skills, resource and agency orientation.

Contact Wm. Johnson, PhD, Supervisory Education Specialist, National Park Service Black Canyon of the Gunnison National Park and Curecanti National Recreation Area, 102 Elk Creek, Gunnison, Colorado 81230. Telephone: 970-641-2337 Ext. 204. Fax: 970-641-3127. E-mail: bj_johnson@nps.gov. World Wide Web: http://www.nps.gov/blca. Contact by e-mail, fax, mail, phone, or through World Wide Web site. Application deadline: continuous.

NORTH FORK GUEST RANCH
55395 HIGHWAY 285, PO BOX B
SHAWNEE, COLORADO 80475

General Information Small ranch offering a weekly family-oriented vacation. All-inclusive package (meals, activities, and lodging) with lots of personal attention and Western fun. Established in 1985. 520-acre facility located 50 miles from Denver. Features: horseback riding; fly fishing; swimming pool; fishing pond and river; mountain setting.

Profile of Summer Employees Total number: 22; typical ages: 19–29. 40% men; 60% women; 90% college students; 10% local applicants. Nonsmokers required.

Employment Information Openings are from April 1 to November 1. Jobs available: ▶ 3 *activity personnel/maintenance/drivers* (minimum age 19) with good driving record and people skills at $600–$700 per month ▶ 3 *cooks* (minimum age 19) must enjoy cooking; no formal training needed at $600–$700 per month ▶ 3 *kids' counselors* (minimum age 19) with WSI/lifeguard certification, CPR and first aid training (preferred), and genuine love for small children at $600–$700 per month ▶ 6 *waitresses/waiters and cabin staff members* (minimum age 19) with food service experience preferred, must have good people skills at $600–$700 per month ▶ 8 *wranglers* (minimum age 19) with CPR/first aid training, experience with horses, and good people skills at $600–$700 per month. Applicants must submit formal organization application, letter of recommendation. A telephone interview is required. International applicants accepted; must obtain own visa, obtain own working papers, apply through a recognized agency.

Benefits and Preemployment Training Free housing, free meals, possible full-time employment, willing to provide letters of recommendation, on-the-job training, willing to complete paperwork for educational credit, and willing to act as a professional reference.

Contact Karen May, Co-Owner/Manager, North Fork Guest Ranch, PO Box B, Shawnee, Colorado 80475. Telephone: 800-843-7895. Fax: 303-838-1549. E-mail: northforkranch@ worldnet.att.net. World Wide Web: http://www.northforkranch.com. Contact by e-mail, fax, mail, phone, or through World Wide Web site. Application deadline: continuous.

POULTER COLORADO CAMPS
STEAMBOAT SPRINGS, COLORADO 80477

General Information Residential camp and adventure programs serving 80 campers (ages 10–18) per session with group dynamics and outdoor education emphasis. There are frequent wilderness excursions. Established in 1966. 180-acre facility located 160 miles from Denver. Features: athletic fields; picturesque wooded setting; natural hot springs; cabins; freshwater lakes.

Profile of Summer Employees Total number: 30; typical ages: 19–34. 43% men; 57% women; 10% minorities; 15% high school students; 71% college students; 5% non-U.S. citizens. Nonsmokers required.

Employment Information Openings are from June 10 to August 20. Jobs available: ▶ 3 *cooks* (minimum age 19) with first aid/CPR and experience cooking for large groups at $1000–$3000 per season ▶ 1 *nurse* (minimum age 21) with RN license, first aid, and CPR required (wilderness first aid preferred); camp experience or work with youth preferred at $2000–$3000 per season ▶ 12 *senior counselors/trip leaders* (minimum age 21) with wilderness first aid/CPR (required), lifeguard training (preferred), and experience working with youth at $1300–$1400 per season ▶ 4–6 *wilderness instructors* (minimum age 21) with Wilderness First Responder/ EMT and CPR, technical skills, and teaching experience at $1600–$2000 per season. Applicants must submit formal organization application, three personal references, three letters of recommendation. An in-person interview is recommended, but a telephone interview is acceptable. International applicants accepted; must apply through a recognized agency.

Benefits and Preemployment Training Free housing, free meals, formal training, willing to provide letters of recommendation, on-the-job training, willing to complete paperwork for educational credit, and willing to act as a professional reference. Preemployment training is required and includes accident prevention and safety, first aid, interpersonal skills, leadership skills, wilderness skills, team building.

Contact Jay B. Poulter, Director, Poulter Colorado Camps, PO Box 772947-P, Steamboat Springs, Colorado 80477. Telephone: 970-879-4816. Fax: 800-860-3587. E-mail: poulter@poultercamps. com. World Wide Web: http://www.poultercamps.com. Contact by e-mail, phone, or through World Wide Web site. Application deadline: continuous.

ROCKY MOUNTAIN VILLAGE
2644 ALVARADO ROAD
EMPIRE, COLORADO 80438

General Information Nonprofit organization that provides camping services for children and adults with physical and/or mental disabilities. Established in 1951. 140-acre facility located 40 miles from Denver. Features: mountains; pond; stream.

Profile of Summer Employees Total number: 60; typical ages: 18–25. 45% men; 55% women; 5% minorities; 15% high school students; 75% college students; 10% non-U.S. citizens; 10% local applicants.

Employment Information Openings are from May 27 to August 13. Year-round positions also offered. Jobs available: ▶ 1 *arts and crafts instructor* (minimum age 18) at $190–$250 per week ▶ 1 *assistant cook* (minimum age 19) at $190–$250 per week ▶ 1 *athletics specialist* (minimum age 18) at $2125 per season ▶ 14 *boys counselors* (minimum age 18) at $190–$250 per week

► 1 *computer specialist* (minimum age 18) with knowledge of Microsoft XP and assistive technology experience preferred at $190–$250 per week ► 1 *digital photography specialist* (minimum age 18) at $190–$250 per week ► 14 *girls counselors* (minimum age 18) at $190–$250 per week ► 1 *head female counselor* (minimum age 18) with prior experience working at a camp for people with disabilities at $215–$250 per week ► 1 *head male counselor* (minimum age 18) with prior experience working at a camp for people with disabilities at $215–$250 per week ► 1 *horseback specialist* (minimum age 18) with therapeutic riding experience at $190–$250 per week ► 3 *kitchen helpers* (minimum age 16) at $190–$250 per week ► 3 *maintenance helpers* (minimum age 16) at $190–$250 per week ► 2 *pool specialists* (minimum age 18) with WSI/advanced lifesaving certification at $2125 per season ► 2 *registered nurses* (minimum age 21) at $700–$900 per week ► 1 *trip specialist* (minimum age 21) with outdoor camping experience and first aid/CPR certification at $190–$250 per week. Applicants must submit formal organization application, three personal references, one writing sample (required for public relations specialist position). An in-person interview is recommended, but a telephone interview is acceptable. International applicants accepted; must apply through a recognized agency.

Benefits and Preemployment Training Free housing, free meals, formal training, willing to provide letters of recommendation, on-the-job training, and willing to complete paperwork for educational credit. Preemployment training is required and includes accident prevention and safety, first aid, CPR, interpersonal skills, leadership skills, providing personal care for people with disabilities.

Contact Ms. Melissa Huber, Assistant Director, Rocky Mountain Village, PO Box 115, Empire, Colorado 80438. Telephone: 303-569-2333. Fax: 303-569-3857. E-mail: huberm@cess.org. World Wide Web: http://www.eastersealsco.org. Contact by e-mail, fax, mail, phone, or through World Wide Web site. Application deadline: before May (preferred).

SANBORN WESTERN CAMPS
PO BOX 167
FLORISSANT, COLORADO 80816

General Information Boys and girls camps serving ages 8-16 in 2 five-week sessions. Established in 1948. 6,000-acre facility located 35 miles from Colorado Springs. Features: 2 riding stables; science interpretive center; 3 ponds; 17½-inch telescope; 2 heated and filtered pools; 4 tennis courts.

Profile of Summer Employees Total number: 120; typical ages: 20–25. 50% men; 50% women; 20% minorities; 100% college students; 5% non-U.S. citizens. Nonsmokers required.

Employment Information Openings are from June 1 to August 25. Jobs available: ► 8 *arts and crafts instructors* (minimum age 20) with experience in the field at $1500 per season ► 20 *backpacking instructors* (minimum age 20) with experience in the field at $1500 per season ► 8 *campcraft instructors* (minimum age 20) with experience in the field at $1500 per season ► 8 *canoeing instructors* (minimum age 20) with experience in the field at $1500 per season ► 4–6 *cooks* (minimum age 18) with experience in the field at $1800–$2000 per season ► 4 *drama instructors* (minimum age 20) with experience in the field at $1500 per season ► 10 *ecology instructors* (minimum age 20) with experience in the field at $1500 per season ► 60 *general counselors* (minimum age 20) with interest and experience in working with children at $1500 per season ► 4 *geology instructors* (minimum age 20) with experience in the field at $1500 per season ► 10 *mountaineering instructors* (minimum age 20) with experience in the field at $1500 per season ► 4 *nurses* (minimum age 22) with RN license and experience at $4000 per season ► 12 *riding instructors* (minimum age 20) with experience in the field at $1500 per season ► 8 *rock climbing instructors* (minimum age 20) with experience in the field at $1500 per season ► 8 *sports instructors* (minimum age 20) with experience in the field at $1500 per season ► 8 *swimming instructors* (minimum age 20) with lifeguard training and experience in the field at $1500 per season ► 8 *tennis instructors* (minimum age 20) with experience in the field at $1500 per season. Applicants must submit a formal organization application, letter of interest, resume, four letters of recommendation, 3 to 4 personal references. An in-person interview is recommended, but a telephone interview is acceptable. International applicants accepted; must obtain own visa.

Benefits and Preemployment Training Free housing, free meals, formal training, willing to provide letters of recommendation, on-the-job training, and willing to complete paperwork for educational credit. Preemployment training is required and includes accident prevention and safety, first aid, CPR, interpersonal skills, leadership skills.

Contact Mike MacDonald, Director, Boys Camp, Sanborn Western Camps, 2000 Old Stage Road, PO Box 167, Florissant, Colorado 80816. Telephone: 719-748-3341. Fax: 719-748-3259. E-mail: info@sanbornwesterncamps.com. World Wide Web: http://www.sanbornwesterncamps. com. Contact by e-mail, mail, phone, or through World Wide Web site. Application deadline: continuous.

THE SOUTHWESTERN COMPANY, COLORADO
See The Southwestern Company on page 297 for complete description.

STIVERS STAFFING SERVICES–COLORADO
See Stivers Staffing Services–Illinois on page 96 for complete description.

STUDENT CONSERVATION ASSOCIATION (SCA), COLORADO
See Student Conservation Association (SCA), New Hampshire on page 200 for complete description.

SUPERCAMP–COLORADO COLLEGE
COLORADO COLLEGE
COLORADO SPRINGS, COLORADO 80903

General Information Residential program for teens designed to build self-confidence and lifelong learning skills through accelerated learning techniques. Established in 1981. 1,227-acre facility. Features: university dormitories; outdoor ropes course.

Profile of Summer Employees Total number: 27–30; typical ages: 18–25. 50% men; 50% women; 80% college students; 10% non-U.S. citizens. Nonsmokers preferred.

Employment Information Openings are from July 3 to August 10. Winter break positions also offered. Jobs available: ▶ 1 *EMT* with national or state registration at $700 to $2800 per 10 day session ▶ 10 *counselors* with college degree and PPS credentials, MFCC license, or master's degree in counseling at $1000 to $4000 per 10 day session ▶ 4–10 *facilitators* with presentation skills and college degree; teaching credentials preferred at $1500 to $6000 per 10 day session ▶ 1 *nurse/paramedic* with national or state registration at $1000 to $4000 per 10 day session ▶ 1 *office manager* with high school diploma at $1000 to $2000 per 10 day session ▶ *products coordinator* with high school diploma at a salary paid per 10 day session ▶ 15 *team leaders* with high school diploma at $350 to $600 per 10 day session. Applicants must submit a formal organization application, three letters of recommendation, in-person interview recommended (videotape interview acceptable). International applicants accepted; must obtain own visa, obtain own working papers.

Benefits and Preemployment Training Free housing, free meals, possible full-time employment, willing to provide letters of recommendation, on-the-job training, willing to complete paperwork for educational credit, and willing to act as a professional reference. Preemployment training is required.

Contact Jen Myers, Staffing, SuperCamp–Colorado College, 1725 South Coast Highway, Oceanside, California 92054. Telephone: 760-722-0072 Ext. 109. Fax: 760-722-3507. E-mail:

staffing@learningforum.com. World Wide Web: http://www.supercamp.com. Contact by e-mail, fax, mail, phone, or through World Wide Web site. Application deadline: continuous.

TOMAHAWK RANCH
DENVER, COLORADO 80209

General Information Residential camp serving approximately 1,500 girls ages 6-17 throughout the summer. Established in 1953. 480-acre facility. Features: Rocky Mountain setting; surrounded by National Forest; cabins and tents.

Profile of Summer Employees Total number: 40; typical ages: 19–23. 1% men; 99% women; 15% minorities; 1% high school students; 90% college students; 1% retirees; 17% non-U.S. citizens; 50% local applicants. Nonsmokers required.

Employment Information Openings are from June 1 to August 8. Jobs available: ▶ 18 *assistant unit leaders* (minimum age 18) with experience working with children and/or camp experience at $140–$150 per week ▶ 1 *dance and drama instructor* (minimum age 18) with ability to teach music, dance, puppetry, or theater to groups of children at $140–$160 per week ▶ 1 *health supervisor* (minimum age 21) with RN or LPN license; recent first aid training; school/camp work with children preferred at $300–$400 per week ▶ 1 *nature instructor* (minimum age 18) with experience working with children in nature awareness and outdoor appreciation activities at $140–$160 per week ▶ 1 *sports/archery instructor* (minimum age 18) with certification in archery instruction or proven teaching experience with children and ability to teach games and non-competitive sports at $140–$160 per week ▶ 6 *unit leaders* (minimum age 21) with supervisory skills, experience working with children including camp counseling or leadership techniques, and first aid and CPR certifications at $160–$180 per week. Applicants must submit formal organization application, three personal references. An in-person interview is recommended, but a telephone interview is acceptable. International applicants accepted; must apply through a recognized agency.

Benefits and Preemployment Training Free housing, free meals, willing to provide letters of recommendation, on-the-job training, willing to complete paperwork for educational credit, willing to act as a professional reference, opportunity to attend seminars/workshops, and health/accident insurance, travel allowance.

Contact Angela Langhus, Camp Administrator, Tomahawk Ranch, PO Box 9407, Denver, Colorado 80209-0407. Telephone: 303-778-8774. Fax: 303-733-6345. E-mail: angelal@gsmhc. org. Contact by e-mail, fax, mail, or phone. Application deadline: continuous.

TUMBLING RIVER RANCH
PO BOX 30
GRANT, COLORADO 80448

General Information Guest ranch serving families. Established in 1940. 200-acre facility located 62 miles from Denver. Features: wilderness area; 9,200-12,000-foot mountains; remote area; rustic and very comfortable; family-oriented atmosphere; fly fishing.

Profile of Summer Employees Total number: 30; typical ages: 19–40. 50% men; 50% women; 75% college students. Nonsmokers preferred.

Employment Information Openings are from May 1 to October 1. Year-round positions also offered. Jobs available: ▶ 2 *assistant cooks* (minimum age 19) ▶ 1 *baker* (minimum age 19) with bed and breakfast experience ▶ 8–12 *cabin staff/waitstaff* (minimum age 19) with willingness to alternate jobs weekly ▶ 3 *children's counselors* (minimum age 19) with horseman skills and first aid certification ▶ 2 *cooks* (minimum age 19) with commercial kitchen experience ▶ 1 *fly-fishing guide* (minimum age 19) with guiding experience necessary ▶ 3 *general maintenance personnel* (minimum age 19) ▶ 1 *secretary* (minimum age 19) ▶ 7 *wranglers* (minimum age 19) with horseman skills and first aid/CPR certification. Applicants must submit formal organization application, letter of interest, resume, writing sample, two personal references, 3-4 work references. International applicants accepted; must obtain own visa, obtain own working papers, apply through a recognized agency.

Benefits and Preemployment Training Free housing, free meals, formal training, possible full-time employment, willing to provide letters of recommendation, on-the-job training, willing to complete paperwork for educational credit, and willing to act as a professional reference.

Contact Megan Dugan, Owner, Tumbling River Ranch, PO Box 30, Grant, Colorado 80448. Telephone: 800-654-8770. Fax: 303-838-5133. E-mail: info@tumblingriver.com. World Wide Web: http://www.tumblingriver.com. Contact by e-mail, fax, mail, phone, or through World Wide Web site. Application deadline: continuous.

VAIL RESORTS
PO BOX 7
VAIL, COLORADO 81658

General Information Owners and operators of Vail, Beaver Creek, Keystone, and Breckenridge ski resorts. near Denver. Features: Rocky Mountains of Colorado; rivers; golf courses; national forests.

Profile of Summer Employees Total number: 2,500; typical ages: 21–25. 60% men; 40% women.

Employment Information Jobs available: ▶ 1 *adventure ridge attraction attendant* at $8.75–$9.50 per hour ▶ *childcare staff members* at $8–$9 per hour ▶ *day camp attendants* at $8–$9 per hour ▶ *food service personnel* at $8–$9 per hour ▶ *golf course staff members* at $8–$9 per hour ▶ *grounds/maintenance persons* at $8–$9 per hour ▶ *hospitality positions* at $8–$9 per hour ▶ *lift-operations personnel* (minimum age 18) at $8.75–$9.50 per hour ▶ *outdoor mountain, indoor hotel, ticket sales, food and beverage* (minimum age 18) with guest service skills at $8.75–$9.50 per hour. Applicants must submit a formal organization application. An in-person interview is recommended, but a telephone interview is acceptable. International applicants accepted; must obtain own visa.

Benefits and Preemployment Training Housing at a cost, meals at a cost, formal training, possible full-time employment, health insurance, on-the-job training, willing to complete paperwork for educational credit, and ski pass in winter, free lift rides in summer. Preemployment training is required and includes accident prevention and safety, interpersonal skills, leadership skills.

Contact Kay Schneider, Recruiting Coordinator, Vail Resorts. Telephone: 970-845-5268. Fax: 970-845-2473. E-mail: beavercreekjobs@vailresorts.com. World Wide Web: http://www.skijob1.com. Contact by e-mail, fax, mail, phone, or through World Wide Web site. Application deadline: continuous.

VISTA VERDE RANCH
PO BOX 465
STEAMBOAT SPRINGS, COLORADO 80477

General Information Upscale dude ranch with a wide variety of activities and adventures in both summer and winter. Established in 1975. 500-acre facility located 150 miles from Denver. Features: secluded setting; surrounded by forest; adjacent to continental divide; elegantly furnished accommodations; on-property streams and ponds; wonderful vistas.

Profile of Summer Employees Total number: 35; typical ages: 20–25. 50% men; 50% women; 95% college students; 5% non-U.S. citizens. Nonsmokers preferred.

Employment Information Openings are from May 1 to October 31. Winter break positions also offered. Jobs available: ▶ 2–4 *fishing/hiking guides* with knowledge of fly-fishing and biology at $400 per month plus tips ▶ 2–4 *housekeepers* with at least one year of college at $400 per month plus tips ▶ 3–4 *kid's wranglers* with one year of college, experience working with children, and horse experience at $400 per month plus tips ▶ 2–3 *ranch hands* with at least one year of college at $400 per month plus tips ▶ 2–4 *waitstaff* with one year of college and previous serving experience at $400 per month plus tips ▶ 3–4 *wranglers* with one year of college and extensive horse experience at $400 per month plus tips. Applicants must submit formal organization application, letter of interest, resume, five personal references, photo. A telephone interview is required. International applicants accepted; must obtain own visa, obtain own working papers, apply through a recognized agency.

Benefits and Preemployment Training Free housing, free meals, possible full-time employment, on-the-job training, willing to complete paperwork for educational credit, and willing to act as a professional reference. Preemployment training is required and includes accident prevention and safety, first aid, CPR, interpersonal skills, outdoor skills, guest relations.

Contact Mark Sortum, Staff Manager, Vista Verde Ranch, PO Box 465, Steamboat Springs, Colorado 80477. Telephone: 800-526-7433. Fax: 970-879-6814. E-mail: vvranch@cs.com. World Wide Web: http://www.vistaverde.com. Contact by e-mail, fax, mail, phone, or through World Wide Web site. Application deadline: continuous.

YMCA OF THE ROCKIES ESTES PARK CENTER
2515 TUNNEL ROAD
ESTES PARK, COLORADO 80511-2550

General Information Large Christian-oriented family resort and conference center offering a day camp and serving an average of 3,500 family and conference guests daily during the summer months. Established in 1907. 850-acre facility located 60 miles from Denver. Features: located next to Rocky Mountain National Park; property surrounded by majestic mountains; variety of recreational activities.

Profile of Summer Employees Total number: 500; typical ages: 18–82. 45% men; 55% women; 8% minorities; 5% high school students; 45% college students; 25% retirees; 17% non-U.S. citizens; 20% local applicants.

Employment Information Openings are from January 1 to December 31. Spring break positions also offered. Jobs available: ▶ *craft shop instructors* (minimum age 18) with artistic talent and/or experience with arts and crafts at $155 per week ▶ *day camp/adventure camp counselors* (minimum age 21) with first aid/CPR and training and/or practical experience in education/day camp work/childcare at $155 per week ▶ *family programmers* (minimum age 18) with first aid/CPR certification preferred and interest in working with families planning activities at $155 per week ▶ *food service workers* (minimum age 18) with ability to carry 40 pounds up to 20 feet at $155 per week ▶ *front desk clerks* (minimum age 18) with computer and public relations skills at $155 per week ▶ *housekeeping staff members* (minimum age 18) with ability to carry up to 30 pounds up/downstairs and to move furniture at $155 per week ▶ *lifeguards* with lifeguard certification (Red Cross or YMCA), first aid, and CPR at $155 per week ▶ *maintenance workers* (minimum age 18) with good driving record at $155 per week ▶ *miniature golf and roller skating rink attendants* (minimum age 18) with ability to lift 60 pounds up to 4 feet at $155 per week ▶ *resident assistants* (minimum age 21) with good driving record and at least one year experience as a college resident assistant at $205 per week. Applicants must submit formal organization application, telephone interview for day camp positions, 3 personal references (forms provided) or 3 letters of recommendation. International applicants accepted; must obtain own visa, obtain own working papers, apply through a recognized agency.

Benefits and Preemployment Training Free housing, free meals, possible full-time employment, on-the-job training, willing to complete paperwork for educational credit, and willing to act as a professional reference. Preemployment training is required.

Contact Stacy Gallagher, Human Resources, YMCA of the Rockies Estes Park Center, 2515 Tunnel Road, Estes Park, Colorado 80511-2550. Telephone: 970-586-3341 Ext. 1018. Fax:

970-577-8322. E-mail: sgallagher@ymcarockies.org. World Wide Web: http://www.ymcarockies. org. Contact by e-mail, fax, mail, phone, or through World Wide Web site. Application deadline: continuous.

CONNECTICUT

AWOSTING AND CHINQUEKA CAMPS
BANTAM, CONNECTICUT 06750

General Information Residential camps serving 150 boys and 150 girls in programs of two to eight weeks. There are two separate campuses 4 miles apart that have daily coed programs as well as coed evening activities. Established in 1900. 200-acre facility located 10 miles from Torrington. Features: large 3½-mile long lake; cabins with facilities; wooded setting; 1,000-foot elevations with great weather; more than 100 watercraft; go-kart and minibike tracks.

Profile of Summer Employees Total number: 85; typical ages: 19–30. 50% men; 50% women; 10% minorities; 80% college students; 5% retirees; 30% non-U.S. citizens; 5% local applicants. Nonsmokers required.

Employment Information Openings are from June 17 to August 18. Jobs available: ▶ 2 *archery instructors* (minimum age 19) with NAA certification (clinic available) at $1500 to $2500 per season plus tips ▶ 3 *arts and crafts instructors* (minimum age 19) with experience teaching or assisting instruction at $1500 to $2500 per season plus tips ▶ 4 *black-and-white photography/ video/filming instructors* (minimum age 19) with knowledge of equipment at $1500 to $2500 per season plus tips ▶ 2 *ceramics/clay instructors* (minimum age 19) with pottery wheel and kiln firing knowledge at $1500 to $2500 per season plus tips ▶ 4 *computers, journalism, and Web master staff members* (minimum age 19) with ability to operate Apple and IBM computers, experience in the field, and experience in Web-strong graphics $1500 to $2500 per season plus tips ▶ 3 *dance/theater/music instructors* (minimum age 19) with some stage and music background at $1500 to $2500 per season plus tips ▶ 2 *fencing instructors* (minimum age 19) with some coaching background at $1500 to $2500 per season plus tips ▶ 2 *go-cart/minibike/and quads personnel* (minimum age 20) with knowledge of equipment and racing at $1500 to $2500 per season plus tips ▶ 2 *golf instructors* (minimum age 19) with experience at $1500 to $2500 per season plus tips ▶ 3 *gymnastics instructors* (minimum age 19) with coach certification and experience in the field at $1500 to $2500 per season plus tips ▶ 6 *kitchen aides* (minimum age 20) with food service experience at $2000–$2500 per season ▶ 2 *laundry workers* with some laundry experience at $2000–$2500 per season ▶ 2 *maintenance personnel* (minimum age 21) with background in painting, carpentry, grounds maintenance, electrical, and plumbing at $2500– $3000 per season ▶ 2 *mountain biking instructors* (minimum age 19) with off-road biking experience at $1500 to $2500 per season plus tips ▶ 2 *nurses or first aid persons* (minimum age 21) with RN, LPN, EMT, or standard first aid and CPR certification at $2500–$4500 per season ▶ 2 *outdoor camping and hiking staff members* (minimum age 21) with first aid/CPR and experience in Outward Bound/scouting at $1500 to $2500 per season plus tips ▶ 2–4 *ropes instructors* (minimum age 20) with certification in ACCT, prior experience with rappelling and zipline (training and certification clinic is available) at $1500 to $2500 per season plus tips ▶ 6 *small-craft instructors* (minimum age 19) with certification in one or more of the following: canoeing, sailing, kayaking, or boating (clinic available) at $1600 to $2600 per season plus tips ▶ 6 *sports instructors* (minimum age 19) with background in one or more of the following: softball, soccer, tennis, or golf (varsity level or coaching) at $1500 to $2500 per season plus tips

▶ 6 *swimming instructors* (minimum age 19) with WSI, LGT, or LGTI certification (clinic available) at $1600 to $2600 per season plus tips ▶ 3 *waterskiing instructors* (minimum age 19) with LGT and CPR certification, teaching experience, and Coast Guard boating license at $1500 to $2500 per season plus tips ▶ 2 *woodworking instructors* (minimum age 20) with teaching or assisting woodworking experience; background in woodworking as a hobby; and ability with wood, tools, and machines at $1500 to $2500 per season plus tips. Applicants must submit formal organization application, personal reference, two letters of recommendation, copies of any certifications. An in-person interview is recommended, but a telephone interview is acceptable. International applicants accepted; must apply through a recognized agency.

Benefits and Preemployment Training Free housing, free meals, willing to provide letters of recommendation, on-the-job training, willing to complete paperwork for educational credit, opportunity to attend seminars/workshops, and travel reimbursement. Preemployment training is required and includes accident prevention and safety, first aid, CPR, interpersonal skills, leadership skills.

Contact Oscar Ebner, Director, Awosting and Chinqueka Camps, 4 Breezy Hill, Harwinton, Connecticut 06791. Telephone: 860-485-9566. Fax: 860-485-1681. E-mail: info@awosting.com. World Wide Web: http://www.awosting.com. Contact by e-mail, fax, mail, phone, or through World Wide Web site. Application deadline: continuous.

BUCK'S ROCK PERFORMING AND CREATIVE ARTS CAMP
59 BUCK'S ROCK ROAD
NEW MILFORD, CONNECTICUT 06776

General Information Creative arts camp primarily devoted to the development of talents and the potential of boys and girls ages 11–16. Established in 1943. 130-acre facility located 75 miles from New York, New York. Features: wooded setting; Olympic-size pool; more than 30 art studios of the highest standard; glass blowing facility; 75 miles from New York City; 5 performance sites.

Profile of Summer Employees Total number: 200–230; typical ages: 21–39. 50% men; 50% women; 10% minorities; 66% college students; 20% non-U.S. citizens; 5% local applicants. Nonsmokers preferred.

Employment Information Openings are from June 19 to August 18. Jobs available: ▶ 2–3 *batik instructors* (minimum age 21) at $1500–$1800 per season ▶ 4–6 *dining room staff members* (minimum age 18) at $1500–$1800 per season ▶ 2–4 *farming instructors* (minimum age 21) at $1500–$1800 per season ▶ 16–26 *guidance counselors* (minimum age 21) at $1500–$1800 per season ▶ 8–15 *kitchen staff members* (minimum age 19) at $1500–$1800 per season ▶ 6–10 *maintenance staff members* (minimum age 19) at $1500–$1800 per season ▶ 8–16 *music instructors* (minimum age 21) at $1500–$1800 per season ▶ 2–4 *office assistants* (minimum age 21) at $1500–$1800 per season ▶ 2–3 *registered nurses* (minimum age 25) with RN or LPN license at $2500–$3500 per season ▶ 2–4 *sculpture instructors* (minimum age 21) at $1500–$1800 per season ▶ 4–8 *sewing instructors* (minimum age 21) at $1500–$1800 per season ▶ 4–8 *silversmithing instructors* (minimum age 21) at $1500–$1800 per season ▶ 1–2 *sports instructors* (minimum age 21) at $1500–$1800 per season ▶ 4–7 *stage design and construction personnel* (minimum age 21) at $1500–$1700 per season ▶ 2–4 *videotaping instructors* (minimum age 21) at $1500–$1800 per season ▶ 2–4 *waterfront staff members* (minimum age 21) with WSI and ARC certifications at $1500–$1850 per season ▶ 3–5 *weaving instructors* (minimum age 21) at $1500–$1800 per season ▶ 5–9 *woodworking instructors* (minimum age 21) at $1500–$1800 per season. Applicants must submit formal organization application, resume, portfolio, three personal references, slides of art work in SASE. An in-person interview is recommended, but a telephone interview is acceptable. International applicants accepted; must apply through a recognized agency.

Benefits and Preemployment Training Free housing, free meals, formal training, health insurance, willing to provide letters of recommendation, on-the-job training, willing to act as a professional reference, and laundry service. Preemployment training is required and includes first aid, general orientation to the program.

Contact Ms. Laura Morris, Director, Buck's Rock Performing and Creative Arts Camp. Telephone: 860-354-5030. Fax: 860-354-1355. E-mail: bucksrock@bucksrockcamp.com. World Wide Web: http://www.bucksrockcamp.com. Contact by e-mail, fax, mail, phone, or through World Wide Web site. Application deadline: continuous.

CAMP JEWELL YMCA
PROCK HILL ROAD
COLEBROOK, CONNECTICUT 06021

General Information Full-featured coeducational residential camp with teen adventure trips, year-round environmental education, and team building. Established in 1901. 540-acre facility located 35 miles from Hartford. Features: located in the Berkshire Mountains; 55 acre private lake; unique and innovated; indoor bouldering room; giant slide; rope swing.

Profile of Summer Employees Total number: 155; typical ages: 16–65. 50% men; 50% women; 10% minorities; 5% high school students; 85% college students; 1% retirees; 10% non-U.S. citizens; 25% local applicants. Nonsmokers required.

Employment Information Openings are from June 14 to August 17. Year-round positions also offered. Jobs available: ▶ 4 *aquatic program specialists* at $1600–$2300 per season ▶ 30 *cabin counselors* with one year of college completed at $1775–$1850 per season ▶ 3 *crafts program specialists* at $1600–$2500 per season ▶ 1 *drama program specialist* at $1600–$2200 per season ▶ 1 *leader-in-training director* at $2400–$2600 per season ▶ 4 *leader-in-training staff* at $2000–$2150 per season ▶ 2 *naturalists* at $1600–$2500 per season ▶ 2 *ropes course directors* with experience in the field at $1750–$2500 per season ▶ 2 *sailing program specialists* at $1600–$2300 per season ▶ 15 *teen trip leaders* at $1700–$2400 per season ▶ 2 *tennis program specialists* at $1600–$2200 per season ▶ 6 *village directors* with experience in the field at $1800–$2500 per season ▶ 1 *waterfront director* with lifeguard/WSI certification and experience in the field at $1700–$3500 per season. Applicants must submit formal organization application, three personal references, drug screening (provided by camp). An in-person interview is recommended, but a telephone interview is acceptable. International applicants accepted; must apply through a recognized agency.

Benefits and Preemployment Training Free housing and free meals.

Contact Vince Pattengale, Camp Director, Camp Jewell YMCA, Prock Hill Road, Colebrook, Connecticut 06021. Telephone: 860-379-2782. Fax: 860-379-8715. E-mail: vince.pattengale@ghymca.org. World Wide Web: http://www.ghymca.org. Contact by e-mail, fax, mail, phone, or through World Wide Web site. Application deadline: continuous.

CAMP SLOANE YMCA, INC.
124 INDIAN MOUNTAIN ROAD, PO BOX 1950
LAKEVILLE, CONNECTICUT 06039-1950

General Information Not-for-profit, independent YMCA camp in northwest Connecticut Berkshire Mountains. Established in 1928. 250-acre facility located 130 miles from New York, New York. Features: lake; pool; high/low ropes; climbing wall; indoor/outdoor stage at Performing Arts Building; tent living.

Profile of Summer Employees Total number: 155; typical ages: 17–25. 45% men; 55% women; 20% minorities; 10% high school students; 85% college students; 30% non-U.S. citizens; 5% local applicants. Nonsmokers required.

Employment Information Openings are from June 14 to August 17. Year-round positions also offered. Jobs available: ▶ 80 *counselors* (minimum age 18) at $1100–$1400 per season ▶ 35

supervisors (minimum age 21) with certifications as needed at $1800–$2000 per season. Applicants must submit formal organization application, writing sample, two personal references. A telephone interview is required. International applicants accepted; must apply through a recognized agency. **Benefits and Preemployment Training** Free housing, free meals, willing to provide letters of recommendation, willing to complete paperwork for educational credit, and willing to act as a professional reference. Preemployment training is required and includes accident prevention and safety, CPR, interpersonal skills, leadership skills.
Contact Kathleen H. Woods, Director of Camping Services, Camp Sloane YMCA, Inc., PO Box 1950, Lakeville, Connecticut 06039. Telephone: 860-435-2557. Fax: 860-435-2599. E-mail: staff@camp-sloane.org. World Wide Web: http://www.camp-sloane.org. Contact by e-mail, fax, mail, or phone. Application deadline: continuous.

CAMP WASHINGTON
190 KENYON ROAD
LAKESIDE, CONNECTICUT 06758

General Information Episcopal, coeducational summer resident and day camp serving a diverse population of campers from Connecticut. Traditional and specialty programs available: tripping program with backpacking, canoeing/kayaking, mountain biking; theater week; choir camp; inner-city day camp; family camps. Established in 1917. 300-acre facility located 25 miles from Waterbury. Features: private pond for swimming; 300 private woodland acres; Adirondack shelter on property for primitive camp set up; 8 dormitory-style cabins (heated with indoor plumbing); easy train access to New York City; located in foothills of Berkshire Mountains in historic Litchfield County.
Profile of Summer Employees Total number: 50–60; typical ages: 18–28. 50% men; 50% women; 15% minorities; 20% high school students; 80% college students; 10% non-U.S. citizens; 90% local applicants. Nonsmokers required.
Employment Information Openings are from June to August. Jobs available: ▶ 1 *counselor-in-training director* (minimum age 21) with experience facilitating young people (ages 16-17) in leadership positions and prior camp work or school equivalent at $2000–$2500 per season ▶ 16–18 *general counselors* (minimum age 18) with experience working with children at $1700–$2100 per season ▶ 2 *head counselors* (minimum age 21) with ability to work with staff, campers, and community in a conflict and behavior management position; ability to conduct staff meetings at $2000–$2500 per season ▶ 1 *nurse* (minimum age 21) with RN or LPN license (valid in Connecticut) at $800 per week ▶ 5–6 *program coordinators* (minimum age 19) with ability to teach a specific activity, facilitate program area, supervise staff, program inventory and order, and evaluate program at $2300–$2700 per season ▶ 1 *waterfront director* (minimum age 18) with WSI certification and lifeguard training at $3000 per season ▶ 4 *wilderness challenge staff* (minimum age 21) with ability to lead 10-14 day primitive camping trips in the areas of backpacking, canoeing, kayaking, and mountain biking; good communication skills are a must at $2000–$3000 per season. Applicants must submit formal organization application, three personal references, criminal record background check. An in-person interview is recommended, but a telephone interview is acceptable. International applicants accepted; must apply through a recognized agency.
Benefits and Preemployment Training Free housing, free meals, formal training, possible full-time employment, willing to provide letters of recommendation, on-the-job training, willing to complete paperwork for educational credit, willing to act as a professional reference, and opportunity to attend seminars/workshops.
Contact LéAnn Cassidy, Camp Director, Camp Washington, 190 Kenyon Road, Lakeside, Connecticut 06758. Telephone: 860-567-9623. Fax: 860-567-3037. E-mail: leanncassidy@mailcity.com. World Wide Web: http://www.campwashington.org. Contact by e-mail, fax, mail, or phone. Application deadline: continuous.

CHANNEL 3 KIDS CAMP
73 TIMES FARM ROAD
ANDOVER, CONNECTICUT 06232

General Information Camp for underprivileged children. Established in 1910. 365-acre facility located 18 miles from Hartford. Features: woods; cabins; river; swimming pools; trails; campsites.

Profile of Summer Employees Total number: 50; typical ages: 18–30. 50% men; 50% women; 35% minorities; 75% college students; 15% non-U.S. citizens; 60% local applicants.

Employment Information Openings are from June 15 to August 18. Jobs available: ▶ 1 *archery instructor* with archery safety course certification at $2000–$2800 per season ▶ 2 *athletics instructors* (minimum age 18) with ability to work well with children at $1700–$2500 per season ▶ 8 *counselors* with two years of organizational camp experience and college junior or senior status at $1500–$2000 per season ▶ 1 *creative crafts instructor* (minimum age 18) with child-handicraft experience and college junior or senior status at $2000–$2800 per season ▶ 1 *environmental education instructor* (minimum age 18) with interest and experience in nature, and college junior or senior status at $1700–$2500 per season ▶ 1 *health care director* with American Red Cross first aid, BLS, and CPR certification at $2800–$3300 per season ▶ 1 *swimming director* with lifeguard training and WSI, American Red Cross BLS, and CPR certification at $2700–$2900 per season ▶ 2 *swimming instructors* (minimum age 18) with LG/CPR, WSI, and American Red Cross ALS certification (preferred) at $2000–$2500 per season. Applicants must submit formal organization application, three personal references. An in-person interview is recommended, but a telephone interview is acceptable. International applicants accepted; must obtain own visa, apply through a recognized agency.

Benefits and Preemployment Training Free housing, free meals, health insurance, willing to provide letters of recommendation, on-the-job training, and willing to complete paperwork for educational credit. Preemployment training is required and includes accident prevention and safety, first aid, CPR, interpersonal skills, leadership skills.

Contact David Meizels, Director, Channel 3 Kids Camp, 73 Times Farm Road, Andover, Connecticut 06232. Telephone: 860-742-2267. Fax: 860-742-3298. E-mail: ch3cc@aol.com. World Wide Web: http://www.channel3kidscamp.org. Contact by e-mail, fax, mail, phone, or through World Wide Web site. Application deadline: continuous.

CHOATE ROSEMARY HALL
333 CHRISTIAN STREET
WALLINGFORD, CONNECTICUT 06492

General Information Secondary school with summer enrichment programs. Established in 1916. 400-acre facility located 15 miles from Hartford. Features: small college-like campus; air-conditioned classrooms; air-conditioned dining hall; 24 tennis courts and pool; close to major cities and attractions; 56,000-volume library.

Profile of Summer Employees Total number: 100. 50% men; 50% women; 100% college students. Nonsmokers preferred.

Employment Information Openings are from June 27 to August 1. Jobs available: ▶ 25–30 *teaching interns* at $2,400 to $2,500 per 5-week session. Applicants must submit formal organization application, letter of interest, resume, academic transcripts, two letters of recommendation. An in-person interview is recommended, but a telephone interview is acceptable. International applicants accepted; must obtain own visa, obtain own working papers.

Benefits and Preemployment Training Free housing, free meals, willing to provide letters of recommendation, and on-the-job training. Preemployment training is required.

Contact Jim Irzyk, Director of Summer Program, Choate Rosemary Hall, 333 Christian Street, Wallingford, Connecticut 06492. Telephone: 203-697-2365. Fax: 203-697-2519. E-mail: jirzyk@choate.edu. World Wide Web: http://www.choate.edu/summer. Contact by e-mail or through World Wide Web site. Application deadline: February 31.

CYBERCAMPS–UNIVERSITY OF HARTFORD
HARTFORD, CONNECTICUT
See Cybercamps–University of Washington on page 326 for complete description.

NATIONAL GUITAR WORKSHOP
PO BOX 222
LAKESIDE, CONNECTICUT 06758
General Information Workshop designed to provide its participants with an individualized program of study in a non-competitive atmosphere with small class sizes, exceptional teachers, and hands-on learning.

Employment Information Openings are from June to August. Jobs available: ▶ *music teachers.* Applicants must submit resume. An in-person interview is recommended, but a telephone interview is acceptable.

Contact Paula Abate, National Guitar Workshop. Telephone: 860-567-3736. Fax: 860-567-0374. World Wide Web: http://www.guitarworkshop.com. Contact by fax or phone. Application deadline: continuous.

SJ RANCH, INC.
130 SANDY BEACH ROAD
ELLINGTON, CONNECTICUT 06029
General Information Residential camp offering extensive riding and horse care programs for 48 girls ages 7–15. Established in 1956. 100-acre facility located 20 miles from Hartford. Features: 3 riding rings; cross-country course; lake; tennis and basketball courts; rustic cedar cabins; dining hall and recreation hall.

Profile of Summer Employees Total number: 15; typical ages: 18–35. 1% men; 99% women; 10% high school students; 90% college students; 5% non-U.S. citizens; 10% local applicants. Nonsmokers required.

Employment Information Openings are from June 15 to August 23. Jobs available: ▶ *crafts, kitchen, general, and sports staff members* (minimum age 18) at $1700–$1900 per season ▶ *kitchen and general counselors* (minimum age 18) at $1700–$1900 per season ▶ 4–5 *riding counselors* (minimum age 18) with one year of college completed, teaching experience helpful; should be experienced riders at $1700–$2600 per season ▶ *swimming counselor* (minimum age 20) with lifeguard training and FPR/CPR certification at $2100–$2400 per season ▶ 2 *swimming instructors* (minimum age 18) with WSI certification at $1700–$1900 per season. Applicants must submit formal organization application, three personal references. An in-person interview is recommended, but a telephone interview is acceptable. International applicants accepted; must obtain own visa, obtain own working papers, apply through a recognized agency.

Benefits and Preemployment Training Free housing, free meals, formal training, willing to provide letters of recommendation, on-the-job training, willing to complete paperwork for educational credit, willing to act as a professional reference, and riding instructors may attend seminars/workshops. Preemployment training is required and includes accident prevention and safety, interpersonal skills, leadership skills, working with children, teaching skills.

Contact Pat Haines, Director, SJ Ranch, Inc., 130 Sandy Beach Road, Ellington, Connecticut 06029. Telephone: 860-872-4742. Fax: 860-870-4914. E-mail: sjranch@erols.com. Contact by e-mail, mail, or phone. Application deadline: continuous.

THE SOUTHWESTERN COMPANY, CONNECTICUT
See The Southwestern Company on page 297 for complete description.

STUDENT CONSERVATION ASSOCIATION (SCA), CONNECTICUT

See Student Conservation Association (SCA), New Hampshire on page 200 for complete description.

SUNRISE RESORT
ROUTE 151, PO BOX 415
MOODUS, CONNECTICUT 06469

General Information Summer resort catering to families, day outing groups, music festivals, and weddings. Established in 1916. 140-acre facility located 20 miles from Hartford. Features: 50 x 100- foot pool; Salmon River; mountain biking; horseback riding; rural setting.

Profile of Summer Employees Total number: 125; typical ages: 17–24. 40% men; 60% women; 5% minorities; 40% high school students; 20% college students; 5% retirees; 28% non-U.S. citizens; 75% local applicants.

Employment Information Openings are from May 15 to October 15. Jobs available: ▶ 3–5 *housekeeping staff* (minimum age 19) at $3500–$4500 per season ▶ 2–3 *kitchen helpers* (minimum age 19) at $3500–$4500 per season ▶ 2–3 *lifeguards* (minimum age 19) with lifesaving and CPR; WSI certification preferred at $3500–$4500 per season ▶ 1–3 *office personnel* (minimum age 19) with typing ability at $3500–$4500 per season ▶ 1 *tennis instructor* (minimum age 19) at $3500–$4500 per season ▶ 10–12 *waiters/waitresses* (minimum age 19) at $3500–$4500 per season. Applicants must submit a formal organization application. A telephone interview is required. International applicants accepted; must obtain own visa.

Benefits and Preemployment Training Housing at a cost, possible full-time employment, willing to provide letters of recommendation, on-the-job training, willing to complete paperwork for educational credit, willing to act as a professional reference, and room and board at $40 per week. Preemployment training is optional.

Contact Jim Johnson, Director, Sunrise Resort, PO Box 415, Moodus, Connecticut 06469. Telephone: 860-873-8681. Fax: 860-873-8681. E-mail: suntimes@connix.com. World Wide Web: http://www.sunriseresort.com. Contact by e-mail, fax, mail, phone, or through World Wide Web site. Application deadline: April 15.

TENNIS: EUROPE
73 ROCKRIDGE LANE
STAMFORD, CONNECTICUT 06903

General Information Takes teams of junior players to international tennis tournaments, allowing them to gain valuable experience in match play and providing them with intercultural educational experiences. There are 10 teams in Europe and 5 teams in North America. Established in 1973.

Profile of Summer Employees Typical ages: 21–45. 50% men; 50% women; 5% minorities; 33% college students; 5% non-U.S. citizens. Nonsmokers required.

Employment Information Openings are from June 23 to August 13. Jobs available: ▶ 22 *tennis coaches/chaperones* (minimum age 21) with ability to coach tennis at high school varsity or ranked players' levels and must serve as chaperone to students during travel; all positions require extensive travel and no positions are in Connecticut; 20 positions for Europe and 10 in North America at $400 to $550 per trip. Applicants must submit a formal organization application, letter of interest, resume, four personal references. An in-person interview is recommended, but a telephone interview is acceptable. International applicants accepted; must obtain own visa.

Benefits and Preemployment Training Free housing, free meals, possible full-time employment, willing to provide letters of recommendation, names of contacts, on-the-job training, willing to complete paperwork for educational credit, willing to act as a professional reference, and domestic travel reimbursement ($100); while on trip, organization pays all airfare and other travel expenses. Preemployment training is required and includes accident prevention and safety, interpersonal skills, leadership skills.

Contact Dr. Martin Vinokur, Director, TENNIS: EUROPE, 73 Rockridge Lane, Stamford, Connecticut 06903. Telephone: 203-322-9803. Fax: 203-322-0089. E-mail: tenniseuro@aol.com. World Wide Web: http://www.tenniseurope.com. Contact by e-mail, fax, mail, phone, or through World Wide Web site. Application deadline: preferred deadline March 15, later applications accepted.

UNITED CEREBRAL PALSY ASSOCIATION OF GREATER HARTFORD
301 GREAT NECK ROAD
WATERFORD, CONNECTICUT 06385

General Information Residential camping program serving individuals with physical disabilities, ages 8-adult, during a nine-week summer program. Established in 1957. 5-acre facility located 5 miles from New London. Features: beachfront facility; community outings; basketball courts; heated, fully equipped cabins; horseback riding; gardens and horticulture.

Profile of Summer Employees Total number: 12; typical ages: 18–35. 30% men; 70% women; 20% minorities; 1% high school students; 60% college students; 1% non-U.S. citizens; 40% local applicants.

Employment Information Openings are from June 17 to August 17. Jobs available: ▶ 1 *assistant director* with some college required ▶ 12 *general counselors* (minimum age 18) with high school diploma, dedication and maturity, willingness to learn, and experience working with disabled persons (preferred) at $2400–$2700 per season. Applicants must submit a formal organization application, two personal references, two letters of recommendation, physical, background check, drug test, copy of high school diploma or GED. An in-person interview is recommended, but a telephone interview is acceptable. International applicants accepted.

Benefits and Preemployment Training Free housing, free meals, formal training, names of contacts, on-the-job training, and willing to complete paperwork for educational credit. Preemployment training is required and includes accident prevention and safety, first aid, CPR, interpersonal skills, leadership skills, bloodborne pathogens information, abuse and neglect prevention, lifting and transferring, disability sensitivity.

Contact Shannon Credit, Program Coordinator, United Cerebral Palsy Association of Greater Hartford, 80 Whitney Street, Hartford, Connecticut 06105. Telephone: 860-236-6201. Fax: 860-236-6205. Contact by fax, mail, or phone. Application deadline: continuous.

DELAWARE

CHESAPEAKE BAY GIRL SCOUT COUNCIL
501 SOUTH COLLEGE AVENUE
NEWARK, DELAWARE 19713

General Information Residential and day camps serving girls ages 5–17 during June, July, and August. 265-acre facility located 60 miles from Wilmington. Features: swimming pool; waterfront (river); wooded property; tennis courts; nature trails.

Profile of Summer Employees Total number: 30; typical ages: 18–23. 5% men; 95% women; 10% minorities; 80% college students; 20% non-U.S. citizens; 50% local applicants. Nonsmokers preferred.

Employment Information Openings are from June 12 to August 10. Jobs available: ▶ 7 *aquatics assistants* (minimum age 18) with lifeguard certification; Red Cross waterfront module; certification in advanced lifesaving or WSI, first aid, CPR, and windsurfing/sailing/canoeing experience preferred (one or all) at $1200–$1350 per season ▶ 1 *pool director* (minimum age 21) with WSI (preferred), Red Cross Advanced Lifesaving, first aid/CPR certification, and experience working in a camp setting at $1500–$1650 per season ▶ *registered nurse/camp nurse* with RN required at $300 per week ▶ 10 *unit counselors* (minimum age 18) with children/camp experience preferred at $1100–$1300 per season ▶ 6 *unit leaders* (minimum age 21) with training in Girl Scout program or camp counseling and experience preferred at $1300–$1500 per season. Applicants must submit formal organization application, three personal references, three letters of recommendation, criminal history check (fingerprinting). An in-person interview is recommended, but a telephone interview is acceptable. International applicants accepted; must apply through a recognized agency.

Benefits and Preemployment Training Free housing, free meals, formal training, willing to provide letters of recommendation, on-the-job training, willing to complete paperwork for educational credit, willing to act as a professional reference, and first aid and CPR training provided. Preemployment training is required and includes accident prevention and safety, first aid, CPR, interpersonal skills, leadership skills, Girl Scout outdoor skills.

Contact Mrs. Peg Reynolds, Director of Outdoor Programs, Chesapeake Bay Girl Scout Council, 501 South College Avenue, Newark, Delaware 19713. Telephone: 302-456-7150. Fax: 302-456-7188. E-mail: preynolds@cbgsc.org. World Wide Web: http://www.cbgsc.org. Contact by e-mail, fax, or phone. Application deadline: continuous.

THE SOUTHWESTERN COMPANY, DELAWARE
See The Southwestern Company on page 297 for complete description.

STUDENT CONSERVATION ASSOCIATION (SCA), DELAWARE
See Student Conservation Association (SCA), New Hampshire on page 200 for complete description.

VIKING GOLF THEME & WATERPARK
CORNER OF ROUTE 1 AND ROUTE 54
FENWICK ISLAND, DELAWARE 19944

General Information Amusement/theme park with mini-golf, go-kart track, waterslides, activity pools, and food shops. Established in 1984. 2-acre facility located 120 miles from Washington, DC. Features: one block from beach; bayside; located on 10-mile island; new 2800-square-foot themed activity pool; 6 waterslides; boardwalk concessions.

Profile of Summer Employees Total number: 40–50; typical ages: 15–29. 50% men; 50% women; 30% high school students; 40% college students; 10% non-U.S. citizens; 30% local applicants. Nonsmokers preferred.

Employment Information Openings are from May 14 to September 30. Jobs available: ▶ 10 *amusement ride attendants/GoKart operators* (minimum age 16) with English fluency at $7 to $9 per hour; bonus at end of season if work performance meets requirements ▶ 15–25 *food shop attendants* (minimum age 15) with short order cooking skills (a plus but not required for all shops) at $6.15 to $9 per hour; bonus at end of season if work performance meets requirements ▶ 6 *miniature golf attendants* (minimum age 16) with English fluency at $6.25 to $9 per hour; bonus at end of season if work performance meets requirements ▶ 20–30 *waterpark lifeguards* (minimum age 16) with CPR and lifeguard certification preferred at $7 to $9 per hour; bonus at end of season if work performance meets requirements. Applicants must submit a formal organization application. An in-person interview is recommended, but a telephone interview is acceptable. International applicants accepted; must obtain own visa, obtain own working papers.

Benefits and Preemployment Training Meals at a cost, willing to provide letters of recommendation, names of contacts, on-the-job training, and willing to act as a professional reference. Preemployment training is optional and includes interpersonal skills, job-specific training.

Contact Jon Andersen, Vice President, Viking Golf Theme & Waterpark, 11004 Trappe Creek Road, Berlin, Maryland 21811. Telephone: 302-539-1644. Fax: 302-537-1551. Contact by fax, mail, or phone. Application deadline: continuous.

DISTRICT OF COLUMBIA

AMERICAN RED CROSS NATIONAL HEADQUARTERS
2025 E STREET, NW
WASHINGTON, DISTRICT OF COLUMBIA 20006

General Information A humanitarian organization that provides relief to victims of disasters and helps people prevent, prepare for, and respond to emergencies. Established in 1881.

Profile of Summer Employees Typical ages: 18–25. 100% college students.

Employment Information Openings are from June 1 to August 30. Jobs available: ▶ 10–30 *Presidential Interns for undergraduate and graduate students* with enrollment in undergraduate or graduate program required at $9.40 per hour. Applicants must submit a letter of interest, resume. A telephone interview is required. International applicants accepted.

Benefits and Preemployment Training Formal training, possible full-time employment, willing to provide letters of recommendation, on-the-job training, willing to complete paperwork for educational credit, willing to act as a professional reference, and opportunity to attend seminars/workshops.

Contact Jennifer Carino, Diversity Associate, American Red Cross National Headquarters. E-mail: carinoj@usa.redcross.org. World Wide Web: http://www.redcross.org. Contact by e-mail or through World Wide Web site. Application deadline: March 1.

CENTER FOR STUDENT MISSIONS–DC
WASHINGTON, DISTRICT OF COLUMBIA
See Center for Student Missions on page 37 for complete description.

CYBERCAMPS–GEORGE WASHINGTON UNIVERSITY
WASHINGTON, DISTRICT OF COLUMBIA
See Cybercamps–University of Washington on page 326 for complete description.

THE SOUTHWESTERN COMPANY, DISTRICT OF COLUMBIA
See The Southwestern Company on page 297 for complete description.

STUDENT CONSERVATION ASSOCIATION (SCA), DISTRICT OF COLUMBIA
See Student Conservation Association (SCA), New Hampshire on page 200 for complete description.

SUMMER DISCOVERY AT GEORGETOWN
GEORGETOWN UNIVERSITY
WASHINGTON, DISTRICT OF COLUMBIA 20057
General Information Precollege enrichment program for high school students at Georgetown University. Established in 1994. Features: sport facilities; beaches; mountains; lakes; major cities nearby; college towns.
Profile of Summer Employees Total number: 20; typical ages: 21–35. 10% minorities; 60% college students; 2% non-U.S. citizens. Nonsmokers required.
Employment Information Openings are from June to August. Jobs available: ▶ 20 *resident counselors* (minimum age 21) with experience working with high school students/children at $200 per week. Applicants must submit a formal organization application, resume, personal reference. An in-person interview is required. International applicants accepted; must obtain own visa, obtain own working papers.
Benefits and Preemployment Training Free housing, free meals, and on-the-job training. Preemployment training is required and includes accident prevention and safety, CPR, leadership skills.
Contact Rouel Belleza, Operations, Summer Discovery at Georgetown, 1326 Old Northern Boulevard, Roslyn, New York 11576, United States. Telephone: 516-621-3939. Fax: 516-625-3438. E-mail: staff@summerfun.com. World Wide Web: http://www.summerfun.com. Contact by e-mail or phone. Application deadline: continuous.

FLORIDA

A CHRISTIAN MINISTRY IN THE NATIONAL PARKS– FLORIDA
See A Christian Ministry in the National Parks–Maine on page 107 for complete description.

ACTIONQUEST
PO BOX 5517
SARASOTA, FLORIDA 34277
General Information Worldwide, live-aboard sailing and diving certification voyages for 13-19 year olds with waterskiing, windsurfing, and marine biology. No experience necessary. Established in 1986. Features: locations in British Virgin Islands, Mediterranean, Leeward Islands, Galapagos, Australia, and South Pacific; 12 50-foot sailing yachts.
Profile of Summer Employees Total number: 40; typical age: 28. 60% men; 40% women; 50% college students; 10% non-U.S. citizens. Nonsmokers required.
Employment Information Openings are from June 10 to August 20. Year-round positions also offered. Jobs available: ▶ 12 *PADI diving instructors* with PADI instructor-level certification and/or USCG license at $2200 per season ▶ *emergency medical technician* with PADI instructor certification, USCG license, or windsurfing/sailing/waterski instruction skills at $1000 per season ▶ *marine science instructors* with PADI scuba instructor-level certification at $2200 per season ▶ 12 *sailing instructors* should be United States Coast Guard licensed or British Yachtmasters at $3000 per season ▶ *windsurfing instructors* with certification in field at $1000 per season. Applicants must submit a formal organization application, letter of interest, resume, two personal references. A telephone interview is required. International applicants accepted.

Benefits and Preemployment Training Free housing, free meals, willing to provide letters of recommendation, opportunity to attend seminars/workshops, and travel reimbursement. Preemployment training is required and includes accident prevention and safety, first aid, CPR, interpersonal skills, leadership skills.

Contact James Stoll, Director, ActionQuest, PO Box 5517, Sarasota, Florida 34277. Telephone: 941-924-2115. Fax: 941-924-6075. E-mail: info@actionquest.com. World Wide Web: http://www. actionquest.com. Contact by e-mail, fax, mail, phone, or through World Wide Web site. Application deadline: continuous.

CAMP THUNDERBIRD
909 EAST WELCH ROAD
APOPKA, FLORIDA 32712

General Information Residential camp designed exclusively to benefit children and adults who have a developmental disability. Campers participate in traditional camping activities which help increase the camper's level of independence and self-esteem. 20-acre facility located 15 miles from Orlando. Features: freshwater lake; wooded setting; air-conditioned dorms; ropes challenge course; private staff recreation room; close to local attractions and beaches.

Profile of Summer Employees Total number: 70; typical ages: 18–40. 25% men; 75% women; 17% minorities; 60% college students; 50% non-U.S. citizens; 35% local applicants.

Employment Information Openings are from June 14 to August 14. Jobs available: ▶ 6 *activity leaders* (minimum age 18) with experience leading a specific activity ▶ 30 *cabin counselors* with experience working with the mentally retarded ▶ 2–3 *camp nurses* with Florida nursing license (1 RN, 2 LPNs) ▶ 4 *head counselors* (minimum age 21) with experience working at summer camps; supervisory experience preferred ▶ 2 *kitchen staff members* with experience ▶ 3 *swimming pool staff members* (minimum age 18) with WSI and lifeguard certification. Applicants must submit formal organization application, three personal references, three letters of recommendation. An in-person interview is recommended, but a telephone interview is acceptable. International applicants accepted; must obtain own visa, obtain own working papers, apply through a recognized agency.

Benefits and Preemployment Training Free housing, free meals, willing to provide letters of recommendation, on-the-job training, willing to complete paperwork for educational credit, and possible free admission to local attractions (Disney, Universal Studios, Sea World, and more). Preemployment training is required and includes accident prevention and safety, first aid, CPR, interpersonal skills, leadership skills.

Contact Greg Giraulo, Program Director, Camp Thunderbird, 909 East Welch Road, Apopka, Florida 32712. Telephone: 407-889-8088. Fax: 407-889-8072. E-mail: ggiraulo@questinc.org. World Wide Web: http://www.questinc.org. Contact by e-mail, fax, mail, phone, or through World Wide Web site. Application deadline: continuous.

CORKSCREW SWAMP SANCTUARY
375 SANCTUARY ROAD
NAPLES, FLORIDA 34120

General Information 10,560-acre wilderness area in southwest Florida providing preservation, protection, and public education; home to old-growth bald cypress forest and Florida's largest nesting colony of endangered wood storks. Management goals are preservation of natural ecosystems and public education through extensive visitor programs. Established in 1954. 10,560-acre facility. Features: 2.25-mile boardwalk trail; 500- to 600-year-old cypress forest; wood stork colony; nature store; environmental resource library.

Profile of Summer Employees Total number: 17; typical ages: 22–30. 50% men; 50% women; 100% college students.

Employment Information Year-round positions also offered. Jobs available: ▶ 2–4 *seasonal naturalists* (minimum age 18) with some background in resource management and environmental education at $150 per week. Applicants must submit a letter of interest, resume, three personal references. A telephone interview is required. International applicants accepted; must obtain own visa, obtain own working papers.

Benefits and Preemployment Training Free housing, formal training, willing to provide letters of recommendation, on-the-job training, willing to complete paperwork for educational credit, willing to act as a professional reference, and opportunity to attend seminars/workshops.

Contact Lori Piper, Office Manager, Corkscrew Swamp Sanctuary, 375 Sanctuary Road, Naples, Florida 34120, United States. Telephone: 239-348-9151. Fax: 239-348-1522. E-mail: lpiper@ audubon.org. World Wide Web: http://www.audubon.org/local/sanctuary/corkscrew. Contact by e-mail, fax, or mail. Application deadline: continuous.

CYBERCAMPS–ROLLINS COLLEGE
WINTER PARK, FLORIDA
See Cybercamps–University of Washington on page 326 for complete description.

PINE TREE CAMPS AT LYNN UNIVERSITY
3601 NORTH MILITARY TRAIL
BOCA RATON, FLORIDA 33431
General Information Day camp serving campers ages 3-14; overnight camp serving campers ages 6-13. Established in 1978. 123-acre facility located 15 miles from West Palm Beach. Features: 6 small lakes; 6 tennis courts; 2 pools; soccer and baseball fields; gym; fitness center.

Profile of Summer Employees Total number: 200; typical ages: 18–50. 40% men; 60% women; 10% minorities; 20% high school students; 80% college students; 20% non-U.S. citizens; 80% local applicants. Nonsmokers preferred.

Employment Information Openings are from June 2 to August 8. Jobs available: ▶ 10–20 *general counselors* (minimum age 18) with experience working with children at $180–$210 per week ▶ 30–40 *overnight counselors* (minimum age 19) at $250–$300 per week ▶ 5–10 *preschool teachers* (minimum age 22) with health and rehabilitative services clearance and education certification at $250–$275 per week ▶ 10–15 *swim instructors* (minimum age 18) with lifeguard training and/or WSI certification preferred at $180–$250 per week. Applicants must submit formal organization application, resume, two personal references, two letters of recommendation. An in-person interview is recommended, but a telephone interview is acceptable. International applicants accepted; must apply through a recognized agency.

Benefits and Preemployment Training Free meals, willing to provide letters of recommendation, on-the-job training, willing to complete paperwork for educational credit, willing to act as a professional reference, and free housing (overnight camp only). Preemployment training is required and includes accident prevention and safety, first aid, CPR, interpersonal skills, leadership skills.

Contact Diane DiCerbo, Director, Pine Tree Camps at Lynn University, 3601 North Military Terrace, Boca Raton, Florida 33431. Telephone: 561-237-7310. Fax: 561-237-7962. E-mail: ddicerbo@lynn.edu. World Wide Web: http://www.pinetreecamp.com. Contact by e-mail, fax, mail, phone, or through World Wide Web site. Application deadline: continuous.

SEA WORLD OF FLORIDA
7007 SEA HARBOR DRIVE
ORLANDO, FLORIDA 32821
General Information Marine life theme park, open year-round, designed to entertain and educate guests offers employees an enthusiastic, imaginative, and intellectually stimulating atmosphere. Established in 1973. Features: roller coasters; water park; themed rides; animal attractions.

Profile of Summer Employees Total number: 1,500; typical ages: 16–24. 50% men; 50% women; 30% high school students; 20% college students; 10% retirees; 40% non-U.S. citizens.

Florida –Georgia

Employment Information Openings are from May 15 to September 5. Spring break, winter break, and year-round positions also offered. Jobs available: ▶ *buspersons* at $6.65 per hour ▶ *counter persons* at $6.65 per hour ▶ *dishwashers* at $6.65 per hour ▶ *gift shop personnel* with ability to operate cash register, assist guests, and stock shelves at $6.65 per hour ▶ *kitchen staff* at $6.65 per hour ▶ *landscape personnel* with ability to work with a wide variety of plant material and design beds, plus maintain drainage and irrigation (some experience preferred) at $6.90–$7.70 per hour ▶ *lifeguards* at $7–$7.95 per hour ▶ *operations, crowd and traffic control personnel* with desire to maintain park cleanliness and assist at information center at $6.65 per hour ▶ *prep cooks* at $6.65–$7.50 per hour ▶ *swim gear staff* at $6.65 per hour ▶ *ticket sellers* with cash handling experience at $6.65 per hour ▶ *tour guides* (minimum age 18) with ability to narrate at animal exhibits throughout the park and conduct educational tours at $6–$7 per hour ▶ *waiters/waitresses* at $4.70 per hour plus gratuity ▶ *warehouse personnel* at $7.10–$7.50 per hour. Applicants must submit formal organization application. An in-person interview is required. International applicants accepted; must obtain own visa, obtain own working papers, apply through a recognized agency.

Benefits and Preemployment Training Meals at a cost, formal training, possible full-time employment, on-the-job training, opportunity to attend seminars/workshops, and opportunity to purchase health insurance, free meals for food service employees. Preemployment training is required and includes accident prevention and safety, CPR, interpersonal skills, leadership skills.

Contact Laura Schmidt, Manager of Employment, Sea World of Florida, 7007 Sea Harbor Drive, Orlando, Florida 32821. Fax: 407-363-2615. Contact by fax. No phone calls. Application deadline: continuous.

THE SOUTHWESTERN COMPANY, FLORIDA
See The Southwestern Company on page 297 for complete description.

SPORTS INTERNATIONAL–KEENAN MCCARDELL AND JIMMY SMITH FOOTBALL CAMP
JACKSONVILLE, FLORIDA
See Sports International, Inc. on page 134 for complete description.

STUDENT CONSERVATION ASSOCIATION (SCA), FLORIDA
See Student Conservation Association (SCA), New Hampshire on page 200 for complete description.

GEORGIA

CAMP FIRE USA–GEORGIA COUNCIL/CAMP TOCCOA
ROUTE 3, BOX 3026
TOCCOA, GEORGIA 30577
General Information Traditional, coeducational camp serving youth, 2nd grade through high school; located in the beautiful Northeast Georgia council. Established in 1910. 176-acre facility located 89 miles from Atlanta. Features: freshwater lake; equestrian center; high ropes course; swimming pool; 176 acres of hiking trails; year-round winterized cabins.

Profile of Summer Employees Total number: 30; typical ages: 18–22. 50% men; 50% women; 90% college students; 2% local applicants.

Employment Information Openings are from June 5 to July 31. Jobs available: ▶ 20 *counselors* (minimum age 18) must be high school graduate at $1000–$1100 per season ▶ 1 *horseback director* (minimum age 21) must be high school graduate at $1200–$1400 per season ▶ 1 *nurse* must be registered nurse with Georgia license and certified in American Red Cross CPR and first aid at $300 per week ▶ 1 *photographer/Web site manager* at $1200 for 8-week session ▶ *ropes course staff* (minimum age 21) must be high school graduate and highly experienced with adventure/ropes programs at $1200 for 8-week session ▶ 1 *trading post manager* at $1000 for 8-week session ▶ 5 *unit directors* (minimum age 21) must be high school graduate at $1200 for 8-week session ▶ *waterfront director* (minimum age 21) must be high school graduate and water safety instructor at $1200 for 8-week session. Applicants must submit a formal organization application, letter of interest, three personal references. An in-person interview is recommended, but a telephone interview is acceptable.

Benefits and Preemployment Training Free housing, free meals, health insurance, and worker's compensation. Preemployment training is required and includes accident prevention and safety, first aid, CPR, interpersonal skills, leadership skills.

Contact Sue K. Edwards, Director, Camp Fire USA–Georgia Council/Camp Toccoa. Telephone: 706-886-2457. Fax: 706-886-5123. E-mail: toccoa@campfireusaga.org. World Wide Web: http://www.campfireusaga.org. Contact by e-mail, fax, mail, or phone. Application deadline: continuous.

CAMP WOODMONT FOR BOYS AND GIRLS ON LOOKOUT MOUNTAIN
1339 YANKEE ROAD
CLOUDLAND, GEORGIA 30731

General Information Residential summer camp serving up to 100 boys and girls ages 6–14 for one- to two-week sessions; wholesome, fun activities emphasizing nature. Established in 1981. 170-acre facility located 28 miles from Chattanooga, Tennessee. Features: stables/horseback; swimming pool/lake; challenge trail, climbing tower, and high ropes; recreation/dining hall; cabins with central bathhouses; beaver lodge/gym.

Profile of Summer Employees Total number: 15–20; typical ages: 18–35. 50% men; 50% women; 2% minorities; 2% high school students; 96% college students. Nonsmokers required.

Employment Information Openings are from June 4 to August 10. Jobs available: ▶ 10 *counselors* (minimum age 18) with current CPR/FA certification required, LGT and experience preferred at $1000–$2200 per season ▶ 2 *swimming instructors* (minimum age 18) with LGT/WSI certification at $950–$2000 per season. Applicants must submit a formal organization application, resume, two writing samples, three personal references, letter of recommendation, background search. An in-person interview is recommended, but a telephone interview is acceptable. International applicants accepted; must obtain own visa, obtain own working papers.

Benefits and Preemployment Training Free housing, free meals, formal training, possible full-time employment, willing to provide letters of recommendation, on-the-job training, willing to complete paperwork for educational credit, willing to act as a professional reference, and opportunity to attend seminars/workshops. Preemployment training is required and includes accident prevention and safety, interpersonal skills, leadership skills.

Contact Jane Bennett, Camp Director, Camp Woodmont for Boys and Girls on Lookout Mountain, 2339 Welton Place, Dunwoody, Georgia 30338. Telephone: 770-457-0862. E-mail: campdirector@campwoodmont.com. World Wide Web: http://www.campwoodmont.com. Contact by e-mail, mail, phone, or through World Wide Web site. Application deadline: continuous.

THE SOUTHWESTERN COMPANY, GEORGIA
See The Southwestern Company on page 297 for complete description.

STUDENT CONSERVATION ASSOCIATION (SCA), GEORGIA
See Student Conservation Association (SCA), New Hampshire on page 200 for complete description.

HAWAII

CENTER FOR TALENTED YOUTH/JOHNS HOPKINS UNIVERSITY–HAWAII PACIFIC UNIVERSITY
KANEOHE, HAWAII
See Center for Talented Youth/Johns Hopkins University on page 131 for complete description.

LONGACRE EXPEDITIONS, HAWAII
HAWAII
General Information Adventure travel program in Hawaii for teenagers, emphasizing group living skills and physical challenges. Established in 1981.
Profile of Summer Employees Total number: 6; typical ages: 23–30. 50% men; 50% women; 100% college students. Nonsmokers required.
Employment Information Openings are from June 30 to July 30. Jobs available: ▶ 4 *assistant leaders* (minimum age 21) with scuba certification, WFR, CPR, and lifeguard training at $252–$300 per week. Applicants must submit a formal organization application, letter of interest, resume, three personal references. An in-person interview is recommended, but a telephone interview is acceptable. International applicants accepted; must obtain own visa, obtain own working papers.
Benefits and Preemployment Training Free housing, free meals, willing to provide letters of recommendation, on-the-job training, willing to complete paperwork for educational credit, willing to act as a professional reference, and pro-deal purchase program. Preemployment training is required and includes accident prevention and safety, interpersonal skills, leadership skills.
Contact Meredith Schuler, Director, Longacre Expeditions, Hawaii, 4030 Middle Ridge Road, Newport, Pennsylvania 17074-8110. Telephone: 717-567-6790. Fax: 717-567-3955. E-mail: longacre@longacreexpeditions.com. World Wide Web: http://www.longacreexpeditions.com. Contact by e-mail, fax, mail, phone, or through World Wide Web site. Application deadline: continuous.

THE SOUTHWESTERN COMPANY, HAWAII
See The Southwestern Company on page 297 for complete description.

STUDENT CONSERVATION ASSOCIATION (SCA), HAWAII
See Student Conservation Association (SCA), New Hampshire on page 200 for complete description.

IDAHO

EPLEY'S WHITEWATER ADVENTURES
BOX 987
MCCALL, IDAHO 83638

General Information River rafting on Salmon River offering adventures to groups of up to 100 people on short trips. Also offers overnight trips for 2–24 people. Established in 1962. 1-acre facility located 150 miles from Boise. Features: River of No Return; free flowing river with no dams; wildlife; very deep canyon; large sandy beaches; Class III river run.

Profile of Summer Employees Total number: 18; typical ages: 18–28. 80% men; 20% women; 75% college students; 25% local applicants. Nonsmokers required.

Employment Information Openings are from May 1 to September 15. Jobs available: ▶ 4–6 *food service, laundry and office staff, and shuttle drivers* (minimum age 18) with Red Cross, first aid, and CPR (training provided); experience preferred at $750–$1000 per month ▶ 12–15 *river guides* (minimum age 18) with Red Cross, first aid, and CPR; training provided for license at $750–$1200 per month. Applicants must submit formal organization application, letter of interest, resume, portfolio, three personal references, letter of recommendation. An in-person interview is recommended, but a telephone interview is acceptable. International applicants accepted; must obtain own visa, obtain own working papers, apply through a recognized agency.

Benefits and Preemployment Training Free housing, free meals, formal training, willing to provide letters of recommendation, on-the-job training, willing to complete paperwork for educational credit, and laundry service. Preemployment training is required and includes accident prevention and safety, first aid, CPR, leadership skills.

Contact Ted Epley, Owner, Epley's Whitewater Adventures, Box 987, McCall, Idaho 83638. Telephone: 208-634-5173. Fax: 208-634-5270. World Wide Web: http://www.epleys.com. Contact by fax, mail, or phone. Application deadline: applications accepted December 1 through March 31.

REDFISH LAKE LODGE
BOX 9
STANLEY, IDAHO 83278

General Information Family-oriented rustic lodge on a lake in the Sawtooth Mountains with restaurant, marina, and general store. Established in 1930. 20-acre facility located 150 miles from Boise. Features: freshwater lake; Sawtooth Mountains; white-water rafting; mountain biking; hiking; Salmon River.

Profile of Summer Employees Total number: 60; typical ages: 18–28. 50% men; 50% women; 1% minorities; 10% high school students; 85% college students; 5% retirees; 50% local applicants. Nonsmokers preferred.

Employment Information Openings are from May 1 to October 10. Jobs available: ▶ 1 *bartender* (minimum age 19) at $700 to $900 per month plus room and board ▶ 4 *buspersons* (minimum age 16) at $5.50 per hour ▶ 8 *cooks* with one year of restaurant line experience at $7–$9 per hour ▶ 3 *dishwashers* at $5.50 per hour ▶ 4 *front desk personnel* (minimum age 18) at $5.50 per hour ▶ 8 *housekeepers* (minimum age 17) at $5.50 per hour ▶ 3 *maintenance personnel* (minimum age 18) at $5.50 per hour ▶ 5 *marina personnel* (minimum age 20) at $5.50 per hour ▶ 2 *service station personnel* (minimum age 50) with maintenance experience (helpful); retired couple (preferred) at $5.50 per hour ▶ 4 *store personnel* (minimum age 19) at $5.50 per hour ▶ 7 *waitresses/waiters* (minimum age 19) with 2 to 3 years serving experience at $3.69 per hour.

Applicants must submit a formal organization application, three personal references. An in-person interview is recommended, but a telephone interview is acceptable. International applicants accepted; must obtain own visa, obtain own working papers.

Benefits and Preemployment Training Housing at a cost, meals at a cost, willing to provide letters of recommendation, on-the-job training, willing to complete paperwork for educational credit, willing to act as a professional reference, and end-of-job bonus, possible internships.

Contact Jeff Clegg, Manager, Redfish Lake Lodge, Box 43, Jerome, Idaho 83338. Telephone: 208-774-3536. Fax: 208-774-3546. E-mail: hr@redfishlake.com. World Wide Web: http://www.redfishlake.com. Contact by e-mail, mail, or through World Wide Web site. Application deadline: continuous.

THE SOUTHWESTERN COMPANY, IDAHO
See The Southwestern Company on page 297 for complete description.

STUDENT CONSERVATION ASSOCIATION (SCA), IDAHO
See Student Conservation Association (SCA), New Hampshire on page 200 for complete description.

ILLINOIS

CAMP ALGONQUIN
1889 CARY ROAD
ALGONQUIN, ILLINOIS 60102

General Information A nonprofit retreat and educational facility offering a variety of programs designed to serve adults, youth and families, providing summer residential camp sessions to youth, mothers and children and senior adults experiencing financial hardship.

Employment Information Openings are from June to August. Jobs available: ▶ 1 *aquatics director* (minimum age 18) with supervisory skills, American Red Cross lifeguard certification, and four-year degree (desirable) at $1900–$2200 per season ▶ 1 *arts and crafts director* with skills in arts and crafts, group leadership and/or teaching experience with groups, ability to work with others to plan activities, and two-year degree at $1700 per season ▶ 20 *cabin counselors* (minimum age 18) with high school diploma required at $1550–$1950 per season ▶ 1 *camp nurse* (minimum age 21) with RN at $2160–$5200 per season ▶ 6 *food service assistants* with high school diploma and work or volunteer experience at $1450–$1700 per season ▶ 3 *lifeguards* (minimum age 18) with high school diploma and experience in canoeing and boating at $1600–$1940 per season ▶ 2 *medical aides* (minimum age 18) with two-year degree at $1600–$1925 per season ▶ 1 *outdoor education specialist* (minimum age 18) with group leadership and/or teaching experience with groups and two-year degree at $1640–$1975 per season ▶ 1 *outdoor living skills instructor* with two-year degree or 2 years of college experience at $1640–$1975 per season ▶ 1 *sports and game specialist* (minimum age 18) with group leadership and teaching skills at $1640–$1975 per season. Applicants must submit formal organization application, resume. International applicants accepted; must apply through a recognized agency.

Benefits and Preemployment Training Housing at a cost and career development opportunities, staff lounge, paid time-off after each session, paid internship and field placement. Preemployment training is required and includes accident prevention and safety, first aid, CPR, interpersonal skills, leadership skills.

Contact Richard Morris, Director, Camp Algonquin. Telephone: 847-658-8212. Fax: 847-658-8431. World Wide Web: http://www.campalgonquin.org. Contact by fax, phone, or through World Wide Web site. Application deadline: continuous.

CAMP CEDAR POINT
1327 CAMP CEDAR POINT LANE
MAKANDA, ILLINOIS 62958

General Information Girl Scout residential camp serving 150 girls weekly for both Girl Scouts and nonmembers ages 6–17. Established in 1953. 250-acre facility located 115 miles from St. Louis, Missouri. Features: freshwater lake; wooded setting; platform tents/hogans; located within National Wildlife Refuge; rolling hills; sandstone rock formations.

Profile of Summer Employees Total number: 45; typical ages: 18–25. 5% men; 95% women; 10% minorities; 9% high school students; 90% college students; 5% non-U.S. citizens; 40% local applicants. Nonsmokers required.

Employment Information Openings are from June 1 to August 1. Jobs available: ▶ 1 *arts/crafts instructor* (minimum age 18) with experience in the field at $200 per week ▶ 15 *assistant unit leaders/counselors* (minimum age 18) with experience working with children at $200 per week ▶ 1 *environmental education instructor* (minimum age 18) with experience in the field at $200 per week ▶ 1 *junior lifeguard* (minimum age 16) with lifeguard certification at $90 per week ▶ 5 *lifeguards* (minimum age 18) with lifeguarding certification at $200 per week ▶ 8 *unit leaders/counselors* (minimum age 21) with experience working with children at $215 per week ▶ 1 *waterfront coordinator* (minimum age 21) with lifeguarding certification, supervisory experience preferred at $250 per week. Applicants must submit a formal organization application, three personal references. An in-person interview is recommended, but a telephone interview is acceptable. International applicants accepted; must obtain own visa, obtain own working papers.

Benefits and Preemployment Training Free housing, free meals, formal training, willing to provide letters of recommendation, on-the-job training, willing to complete paperwork for educational credit, willing to act as a professional reference, and CPR/first aid certification. Preemployment training is required and includes accident prevention and safety, first aid, CPR, interpersonal skills, leadership skills.

Contact Kristi Hettenhausen, Camp Director, Camp Cedar Point, Girl Scouts of Shagbark Council, 304 North 14th Street, Herrin, Illinois 62948. Telephone: 618-942-3164. Fax: 618-942-7153. E-mail: khettenhausen@shagbark.org. World Wide Web: http://www.shagbark.org. Contact by e-mail, fax, mail, or phone. Application deadline: continuous.

CAMP LITTLE GIANT AT TOUCH OF NATURE ENVIRONMENTAL CENTER
MAILCODE 6888, SOUTHERN ILLINOIS UNIVERSITY
CARBONDALE, ILLINOIS 62901-6888

General Information Residential camping program for persons of varying ability levels and medical conditions with a focus on success-building therapeutic recreation activities. Established in 1951. 3,200-acre facility located 100 miles from St. Louis. Features: freshwater lake; rich, wooded grounds; high and low ropes courses; swimming area; dining lodge; pontoon and other watercraft.

Profile of Summer Employees Total number: 45; typical ages: 18–50. 40% men; 60% women; 25% minorities; 2% high school students; 90% college students; 2% non-U.S. citizens; 60% local applicants. Nonsmokers preferred.

Employment Information Openings are from May 30 to July 31. Jobs available: ▶ 1–2 *activity coordinators* (minimum age 21) with two years of leadership experience with special populations and CPR/first aid certifications at $840 per month ▶ 1 *adventure specialist* with two years of experience in camping/adventure programs, lifeguard, and CPR/first aid certifications at $625 per month ▶ 1–3 *aquatics assistants* with one or two years of experience, lifeguard, CPR/first aid, and WSI training at $625 per month ▶ 1 *aquatics specialist* with two years experience with special populations, lifeguarding, CPR/first aid, and WSI training at $680 per month ▶ 1 *arts and crafts specialist* with 2 years of camp experience, art background, and first aid/CPR certifications at $625 per month ▶ 1 *boating specialist* with lifeguarding, CPR/first aid, and small craft certifications at $625 per month ▶ 1–5 *camp nurses* with RN or LPN license and CPR/first aid certifications at $1857–$2097 per month ▶ 10–15 *general counselors* (minimum age 16) with experience or interest in working with special populations and CPR/first aid certifications at $600–$650 per month ▶ *head counselor* (minimum age 21) with one or two years of leadership, counseling, and group process experience; CPR/first aid certifications at $840 per month ▶ *music/drama specialist* with one or two years of experience in camping; knowledge of drama, music, and dance; CPR/first aid certifications at $625 per month ▶ 1 *naturalist* with 2 years of camping experience, training in nature lore/outdoor education, and CPR/first aid certifications at $625 per month ▶ 1–4 *recreation specialists* with two years leadership experience in new games/sports and adapting at $625 per month. Applicants must submit formal organization application, two personal references, background check. An in-person interview is recommended, but a telephone interview is acceptable. International applicants accepted; must obtain own visa, obtain own working papers, apply through a recognized agency.

Benefits and Preemployment Training Free housing, free meals, formal training, willing to provide letters of recommendation, on-the-job training, willing to complete paperwork for educational credit, willing to act as a professional reference, and opportunity to attend seminars/workshops. Preemployment training is required and includes accident prevention and safety, first aid, CPR, interpersonal skills, leadership skills, information on disabilities and related issues.

Contact Randy Osborn, Director, Camp Little Giant at Touch of Nature Environmental Center, Mailcode 6888-Touch of Nature, Carbondale, Illinois 62901-6888. Telephone: 618-453-1121 Ext. 231. Fax: 618-453-1188. E-mail: randyo@pso.siu.edu. World Wide Web: http://www.pso.siu. edu/tonec/?littlegiant. Contact by e-mail, fax, mail, phone, or through World Wide Web site. Application deadline: applications accepted until full, usually by May 1.

CAMP TAPAWINGO
ROUTE 5, BOX 15
METAMORA, ILLINOIS 61548

General Information Residential camp serving 120 Girl Scouts and non-Girl Scouts per week. Established in 1951. 640-acre facility located 15 miles from Peoria. Features: pool; lake; wooded setting.

Profile of Summer Employees Total number: 20–25; typical ages: 18–26. 100% women; 1% minorities; 98% college students; 5% non-U.S. citizens; 15% local applicants. Nonsmokers preferred.

Employment Information Openings are from June 2 to August 15. Jobs available: ▶ 3 *canoe instructors* (minimum age 18) with canoe experience and lifeguard certification at $160–$180 per week ▶ 1 *health supervisor* (minimum age 21) with RN, LPN, or EMT license at $200–$220 per week ▶ 12–15 *unit counselors* (minimum age 18) at $160–$180 per week ▶ 5 *unit leaders* (minimum age 21) at $175–$195 per week ▶ 1 *waterfront supervisor* (minimum age 21) with lifeguard certification and canoeing background at $180–$200 per week. Applicants must submit formal organization application, 2-3 personal references, 2-3 letters of recommendation. A telephone interview is required. International applicants accepted; must apply through a recognized agency.

Benefits and Preemployment Training Free housing, free meals, health insurance, willing to provide letters of recommendation, on-the-job training, willing to complete paperwork for educational credit, and willing to act as a professional reference. Preemployment training is required and includes accident prevention and safety, first aid, CPR, leadership skills, skills for working with girls, Girl Scouts orientation.

Contact Lara Campbell, Director of Program, Camp Tapawingo, 1103 West Lake, Peoria, Illinois 61614. Telephone: 309-688-8671 Ext. 24. Fax: 309-688-7358. E-mail: campbell@girlscouts-kickapoocouncil.org. World Wide Web: http://girlscouts-kickapoocouncil.org. Contact by e-mail, fax, mail, or phone. Application deadline: continuous.

CATERING BY MICHAEL'S
6203 PARK AVENUE
MORTON GROVE, ILLINOIS 60053

General Information Off-premises catering. From summer picnic/April parties to very elegant and sophisticated "black tie" parties. Catering events for 10 to 10,000 people; fun, outdoor work. Much of it is on weekends. Established in 1983. Located 7 miles from Chicago.

Profile of Summer Employees Total number: 125–150; typical ages: 15–30. 65% men; 35% women; 10% minorities; 15% high school students; 20% college students; 10% non-U.S. citizens; 55% local applicants. Nonsmokers preferred.

Employment Information Spring break, winter break, and year-round positions also offered. Jobs available: ▶ 10–20 *part-time waiters* (minimum age 18) with good manners, pleasant disposition, and good appearance at $10–$13 per hour ▶ 40–50 *summer picnic staff* (minimum age 15) with good manners, pleasant disposition, and good appearance at $7.50 per hour. Applicants must submit a formal organization application, 2-3 personal references. An in-person interview is required.

Benefits and Preemployment Training Free meals, possible full-time employment, willing to provide letters of recommendation, on-the-job training, and willing to act as a professional reference. Preemployment training is required and includes general meeting with hand-outs and discussions as well as demonstrations.

Contact Veronique Sigre, Staffing Director, Catering by Michael's, 6203 Park Avenue, Morton Grove, Illinois 60053. Telephone: 847-966-8950. Fax: 847-966-6626. E-mail: vsigre@cateringbymichaels.com. World Wide Web: http://www.cateringbymichaels.com. Contact by e-mail, fax, mail, phone, or through World Wide Web site. Application deadline: continuous.

CENTER FOR STUDENT MISSIONS–CHICAGO
CHICAGO, ILLINOIS
See Center for Student Missions on page 37 for complete description.

CYBERCAMPS–BENEDICTINE UNIVERSITY
LISLE, ILLINOIS
See Cybercamps–University of Washington on page 326 for complete description.

RGIS INVENTORY SPECIALISTS
2604 EAST DEMPSTER, SUITE 208
PARK RIDGE, ILLINOIS 60068

General Information Inventory service that goes to different retail locations and counts inventory using a hand held computer similar to a calculator. Established in 1959. Located 10 miles from Chicago.

Profile of Summer Employees Total number: 175–200; typical ages: 18–70. 50% men; 50% women; 20% minorities; 20% college students; 5% retirees; 10% non-U.S. citizens; 45% local applicants.

Employment Information Year-round positions also offered. Jobs available: ▶ 30 *inventory counters* (minimum age 18) at $8 per hour. An in-person interview is required. International applicants accepted; must obtain own visa, obtain own working papers.

Benefits and Preemployment Training Possible full-time employment and on-the-job training. Preemployment training is required and includes introduction to our system and equipment.

Contact Marie Nonato-Zuniga, District Manager, RGIS Inventory Specialists. Telephone: 847-296-3031. Fax: 847-296-3226. E-mail: dist074@rgis.com. World Wide Web: http://www.rgisinv. com. Contact by fax, mail, phone, or through World Wide Web site. Application deadline: continuous.

THE SOUTHWESTERN COMPANY, ILLINOIS
See The Southwestern Company on page 297 for complete description.

SPORTS INTERNATIONAL FOOTBALL CAMP
EDWARDSVILLE, ILLINOIS
See Sports International, Inc. on page 134 for complete description.

SPORTS INTERNATIONAL–JIM MILLER AND BOBBY ENGRAM FOOTBALL CAMP
DEERFIELD, ILLINOIS
See Sports International, Inc. on page 134 for complete description.

STIVERS STAFFING SERVICES–ILLINOIS
200 WEST MONROE
CHICAGO, ILLINOIS 60606

General Information National staffing service that places people in office support positions throughout the United States. Locations include: Arizona (Phoenix, Scottsdale, Temple); Colorado (Aurora, Denver); Indiana (Indianapolis); Kansas (Overland Park); Missouri (Des Peres, Kansas City, St. Ann, St. Louis, North Kansas City); Wisconsin (Milwaukee); California (Encino, Westwood, Los Angeles, Pasadena, San Diego, San Francisco); Illinois (Chicago, Deerfield, Des Plaines, Evanston, Oak Brook, Schaumburg, Fox Valley, Niles); Pennsylvania (Philadelphia, Pittsburgh, King of Prussia); Canada (Toronto). Established in 1945. Features: office settings; professional environments.

Profile of Summer Employees Total number: 2,000. 5% high school students; 60% college students; 10% retirees; 20% local applicants.

Employment Information Openings are from January to December. Year-round positions also offered. Jobs available: ▶ *clerk/typist* with six months office experience at $7–$10 per hour ▶ *customer service representative* with six months relevant experience at $8–$12 per hour ▶ *receptionist* with six months office experience at $7–$10 per hour. Applicants must submit a formal organization application, testing. An in-person interview is required.

Benefits and Preemployment Training Possible full-time employment, health insurance, willing to provide letters of recommendation, on-the-job training, and willing to act as a professional reference.

Contact Chris Goodfarb, Internet Manager, Stivers Staffing Services–Illinois, 1717 West Northern, #117, Phoenix, Arizona 85021. Telephone: 602-264-4580. Fax: 602-678-5649. E-mail: chrisg@ stivers.com. World Wide Web: http://www.stivers.com. Contact by e-mail, fax, mail, phone, or through World Wide Web site. Application deadline: continuous.

STUDENT CONSERVATION ASSOCIATION (SCA), ILLINOIS
See Student Conservation Association (SCA), New Hampshire on page 200 for complete description.

INDIANA

CAMP LOGAN
203 EMS LANE D14
SYRACUSE, INDIANA 46567

General Information Residential camp serving girls ages 7-17. Established in 1928. 200-acre facility located 50 miles from Fort Wayne. Features: freshwater lake; wooded setting; rustic dining lodge; natural wetland area; wetland observation platform; tent-cabin units.

Profile of Summer Employees Total number: 35; typical ages: 18–26. 5% men; 95% women; 5% minorities; 10% high school students; 75% college students; 15% non-U.S. citizens; 40% local applicants. Nonsmokers preferred.

Employment Information Openings are from June 6 to August 12. Jobs available: ▶ 3–4 *aquatic assistants* (minimum age 18) with lifeguard training, CPR/first aid certification, and experience with children or teaching at $1620 per season ▶ 1 *aquatic manager* (minimum age 21) with CPR/first aid/lifeguard training/WSI certifications, aquatic facility or program management experience, teaching and supervisory experience, and certification or experience in canoeing, sailing, kayaking, rowing, or other boating activities at $1920 per season ▶ 1 *assistant director* (minimum age 25) with three years experience in camp setting, one year administration experience, and strong organizational, supervisory, and communication skills at $2100 per season ▶ 1 *business manager* (minimum age 21) with excellent organizational and communication skills and experience in bookkeeping or accounting at $1920 per season ▶ 8–12 *counselors* (minimum age 18) with ability to work as part of a team and experience or background with children, camping, or girl scouting at $1620 per season ▶ 1 *environmental education director* (minimum age 21) with leadership, organization, and communication skills, teaching experience, and environmental education/nature study knowledge at $1920 per season ▶ 3–4 *equestrian assistants* (minimum age 18) with ability to work as part of a team, knowledge of horse care and western horseback riding, and experience with children or teaching at $1620 per season ▶ 1 *equestrian manager* (minimum age 21) with CHA/AAHS certification or extensive background in western horseback riding, strong organizational skills, and strong supervisory skills at $1920 per season ▶ 2–4 *food service assistants* (minimum age 18) with food service experience and excellent organizational skills at $1620 per season ▶ 1–2 *food service managers* (minimum age 21) with food service experience, excellent organizational skills, and supervisory skills at $1920 per season ▶ 1 *health manager* (minimum age 21) with CPR and advanced first aid certifications, LPN/RN/EMT, and strong organizational and people skills at $1920 per season ▶ 1–2 *program coordinators* (minimum age 21) with first aid/CPR certifications, three years experience in camp setting or programming, strong organizational and communication skills, certification or experience in ropes course, teambuilding, primitive camping, tripping, environmental education, arts and crafts or other specialty area at $1920 per season ▶ 8–10 *senior counselors* (minimum age 21) with strong organizational and communication skills, background in leadership and supervision, experience in teaching and working with children, and camping and girl scout experience preferred at $1820 per season ▶ 1–2 *support services coordinators* (minimum age 18) with excellent organizational skills and ability to work with minimal supervision at $1620 per season. Applicants must submit formal organization application, three personal references, copies of certifications. A telephone interview is required. International applicants accepted; must apply through a recognized agency.

Benefits and Preemployment Training Free housing, free meals, formal training, willing to provide letters of recommendation, on-the-job training, willing to complete paperwork for

educational credit, willing to act as a professional reference, and opportunity to attend seminars/ workshops. Preemployment training is required and includes accident prevention and safety, first aid, CPR, interpersonal skills, leadership skills, child development, program skills.

Contact Sandy Kohne, Director, Camp Logan, 203 EMS Lane D14, Syracuse, Indiana 46567. Telephone: 574-457-2841. Fax: 574-457-3021. E-mail: camplogan@hotmail.com. World Wide Web: http://www.girlscouts-limberlost.org. Contact by e-mail, fax, mail, phone, or through World Wide Web site. Application deadline: continuous.

CULVER SUMMER CAMPS
1300 ACADEMY ROAD, #138
CULVER, INDIANA 46511

General Information Six-week all-activity program followed by a two-week session of ten specialty camps. Established in 1902. 1,800-acre facility located 50 miles from South Bend. Features: Indiana's 2nd largest natural lake; 120 sail and power boats; hockey and ice skating facilities; 6 Piper Cherokee "140" aircraft; more than 100 horses; ropes/initiatives challenge courses.

Profile of Summer Employees Total number: 325; typical ages: 19–25. 60% men; 40% women; 5% minorities; 2% high school students; 40% college students; 5% retirees; 1% non-U.S. citizens; 10% local applicants. Nonsmokers preferred.

Employment Information Openings are from June 16 to August 23. Jobs available: ▶ 1 *English instructor* with at least one year of experience and English teaching certification at a competitive salary ▶ 3 *administrative assistants* (minimum age 19) with good typing, computer, phone, and organizational skills at a competitive salary ▶ 1 *aerobics instructor* (minimum age 19) with knowledge and experience in area, and ability to work with children at a competitive salary ▶ 4 *aquatics instructors* (minimum age 19) with certificate in lifeguarding, CPR, first aid preferred; WSI certification desirable; may obtain certifications prior to camp paid at a competitive salary ▶ 1 *art instructor* with knowledge and teaching experience in the area at a competitive salary ▶ 20 *assistant counselors* (minimum age 19) with one year of college, experience working with children, and a sense of responsibility and maturity at a competitive salary ▶ 2 *athletic instructors* with knowledge and experience in the field and one year of teaching experience at a competitive salary ▶ 7 *aviation flight instructors* (minimum age 19) with certification by FAA to give flying instruction and experience teaching children at a competitive salary ▶ 1 *computer instructor* with knowledge and experience teaching children in related area at a competitive salary ▶ 35 *counselors* (minimum age 19) with at least one year of college and experience working with children at a competitive salary ▶ 10 *dining hall assistants* (minimum age 17) with one year of college experience, responsibility, and maturity at a competitive salary ▶ 1 *driver's training experience instructor* with certification and at least one year teaching experience at a competitive salary ▶ 5 *equitation instructors* (minimum age 19) with knowledge and experience teaching children equitation skills, basic care for animals at a competitive salary ▶ 1 *fencing instructor* (minimum age 19) with teaching experience and skills in epee, foil, and saber at a competitive salary ▶ 2 *golf instructors* with knowledge and teaching experience with children a plus at a competitive salary ▶ 1 *hockey instructor* with adequate knowledge and teaching experience in the field at a competitive salary ▶ 1 *ice skating instructor* with adequate knowledge and teaching experience in the area at a competitive salary ▶ 1 *math instructor* with at least one year experience and must be a certified math teacher at a competitive salary ▶ 1 *music instructor* (minimum age 19) with music/band teaching experience preferred at a competitive salary ▶ 1 *nurse assistant* (minimum age 19) with one year of college, responsibility, and maturity at a competitive salary ▶ 1 *photography instructor* with adequate knowledge, skills, and teaching experience in area at a competitive salary ▶ 1 *reading instructor* with teacher certification in related field and at least one year of experience at a competitive salary ▶ 1 *rifle instructor* with adequate knowledge and teaching experience in the field at a competitive salary

▶ 1–5 *sailing instructors* (minimum age 19) with knowledge and experience teaching sailing in a variety of craft at a competitive salary ▶ 2 *soccer instructors* (minimum age 19) with knowledge and experience in coaching at a competitive salary ▶ 2 *tennis instructors* (minimum age 19) with knowledge and coaching experience in tennis at a competitive salary ▶ 1 *theater instructor* with adequate knowledge, skills, and teaching experience at a competitive salary ▶ 3 *waterski instructors* (minimum age 19) with proficiency in teaching waterskiing and working with children at a competitive salary. Applicants must submit formal organization application, three personal references. An in-person interview is recommended, but a telephone interview is acceptable. International applicants accepted; must obtain own working papers, apply through a recognized agency.

Benefits and Preemployment Training Free housing, free meals, willing to provide letters of recommendation, on-the-job training, willing to complete paperwork for educational credit, willing to act as a professional reference, and uniforms provided.

Contact Marc T. Read, Assistant Director, Culver Summer Camps, 1300 Academy Road, #138, Culver, Indiana 46511. Telephone: 800-221-2020. Fax: 574-842-8462. E-mail: summer@culver. org. World Wide Web: http://www.culver.org. Contact by e-mail, fax, mail, phone, or through World Wide Web site. Application deadline: continuous.

DUDLEY GALLAHUE VALLEY CAMPS
MORGANTOWN, INDIANA 46160

General Information Residential camp serving 128–140 campers weekly and biweekly. Established in 1912. 800-acre facility located 50 miles from Indianapolis. Features: freshwater lake; wooded setting; platform tents; hills.

Profile of Summer Employees Total number: 40; typical age: 18. 2% men; 98% women; 5% minorities; 5% high school students; 80% college students; 10% local applicants. Nonsmokers preferred.

Employment Information Openings are from June 1 to August 15. Jobs available: ▶ 24 *assistant unit leaders* with completion of group leadership, counselor-in-training, or leader-in-training course and experience in the field at $1400–$1700 per season ▶ 4 *cooks* with ability to provide records of necessary health exams required by Department of Health ▶ 1 *health supervisor* with state license or registration as a physician, physician's assistant, RN, LPN, paramedic, camp health director, or EMT; advanced first aid and/or CPR certification; emotional stability to meet emergencies; and knowledge of medicine and pesticide storage and use at $2000–$2500 per season ▶ 1 *horseback unit leader* with experience in leadership, outdoor, and program specialty training at $1600 per season ▶ 1 *trip unit leader* with leadership, outdoor, and program specialty training and work experience as a teacher or counselor of children at $1600 per season ▶ 8 *unit leaders* with experience in the field, first aid and lifesaving training, training in Girl Scout program, and management and organizational skills at $1600–$1900 per season ▶ 4 *waterfront assistants, canoe/sailing assistants* with current basic swimming instructor certification issued by the American Red Cross or equivalent from the YMCA at $1400 per season. Applicants must submit formal organization application, resume, two personal references, three letters of recommendation. An in-person interview is recommended, but a telephone interview is acceptable. International applicants accepted; must apply through a recognized agency.

Benefits and Preemployment Training Free housing, free meals, formal training, on-the-job training, and willing to complete paperwork for educational credit. Preemployment training is required and includes accident prevention and safety, first aid, CPR, interpersonal skills, leadership skills.

Contact Diana Keely, Outdoor Program Specialist, Dudley Gallahue Valley Camps, Hoosier Capital Girl Scout Council, 1800 North Meridian Street, Indianapolis, Indiana 46202-1433. Telephone: 317-924-3450 Ext. 155. Fax: 317-924-2976. E-mail: dkeely@gshcc.org. World Wide Web: http://www.gshcc.org. Contact by e-mail, fax, mail, phone, or through World Wide Web site. Application deadline: continuous.

HOLIDAY WORLD & SPLASHIN' SAFARI
452 EAST CHRISTMAS BOULEVARD
SANTA CLAUS, INDIANA 47579

General Information Theme and water park. Established in 1946. 100-acre facility located 60 miles from Louisville, Kentucky. Features: two of world's top 5 wooden roller coasters; Indiana's largest waterpark; voted world's friendliest park employees for last 5 years; voted cleanest park for last 3 years; offers free parking, soft drinks, and sunscreen to park guests.

Profile of Summer Employees Total number: 1,050; typical ages: 14–22. 40% men; 60% women; 1% minorities; 50% high school students; 31% college students; 7% retirees; 99% local applicants.

Employment Information Openings are from May to October. Jobs available: ▶ 40 *admissions staff* (minimum age 16) at $5–$6 per hour ▶ 25 *entertainment staff* (minimum age 16) with audition required at $200–$300 per week ▶ 55 *facilities maintenance staff* (minimum age 18) with some age requirements for using equipment at $5–$6 per hour ▶ 250 *food service staff* (minimum age 14) at $5–$6 per hour ▶ 80 *games staff* (minimum age 14) at $5–$6 per hour ▶ 65 *gift shop clerks* (minimum age 14) at $5–$6 per hour ▶ 125 *lifeguards* (minimum age 16) must pass minimal swim requirements; paid at $5–$6 per hour ▶ 15 *office and security staff* (minimum age 18) at $5–$6 per hour ▶ 120 *ride operators* (minimum age 16) with some age requirements for using equipment at $5–$6 per hour. Applicants must submit a formal organization application, three personal references. An in-person interview is recommended, but a telephone interview is acceptable.

Benefits and Preemployment Training Formal training, willing to provide letters of recommendation, on-the-job training, and willing to act as a professional reference. Preemployment training is required and includes accident prevention and safety, first aid, CPR, leadership skills.

Contact Brandon Berg, Human Resources, Holiday World & Splashin' Safari, PO Box 179, Santa Claus, Indiana 47579, United States. Telephone: 812-937-5217. Fax: 812-489-5771. E-mail: bberg@holidayworld.com. World Wide Web: http://www.holidayworld.com. Contact by e-mail. Application deadline: continuous.

HOWE MILITARY SCHOOL SUMMER CAMP
PO BOX 191
HOWE, INDIANA 46746

General Information A residential camp serving boys ages 9-15 in a modified military setting, emphasizing leadership, sports and academics. Established in 1932. 50-acre facility located 30 miles from South Bend. Features: freshwater lake; wooded setting; cabins; basketball courts and baseball fields; full waterfront; tennis courts.

Profile of Summer Employees Total number: 40; typical ages: 18–55. 80% men; 20% women; 20% minorities; 50% high school students; 30% college students; 20% local applicants. Nonsmokers preferred.

Employment Information Openings are from June 23 to August 2. Jobs available: ▶ 2 *English instructors* (minimum age 19) with a major in teaching at $1800–$2000 per season ▶ 8–12 *cabin counselors* (minimum age 19) with one year of college completed at $1800–$2000 per season ▶ 2 *math instructors* (minimum age 19) with a major in teaching at $1800–$2000 per season ▶ 3–5 *waterfront staff members* (minimum age 18) with WSI or lifeguard certifications at $1600–$1800 per season. Applicants must submit a formal organization application, three personal references, three letters of recommendation. An in-person interview is required.

Benefits and Preemployment Training Free housing, free meals, formal training, possible full-time employment, willing to provide letters of recommendation, on-the-job training, willing to complete paperwork for educational credit, and willing to act as a professional reference. Preemployment training is required and includes accident prevention and safety, first aid, CPR, interpersonal skills, leadership skills.

Contact William McClish, Camp Director, Howe Military School Summer Camp, Howe Military School, Howe, Indiana 46746. Fax: 219-562-3678. Contact by fax or mail. No phone calls. Application deadline: May 15.

THE SOUTHWESTERN COMPANY, INDIANA
See The Southwestern Company on page 297 for complete description.

STIVERS STAFFING SERVICES–INDIANA
See Stivers Staffing Services–Illinois on page 96 for complete description.

STUDENT CONSERVATION ASSOCIATION (SCA), INDIANA
See Student Conservation Association (SCA), New Hampshire on page 200 for complete description.

IOWA

CAMP COURAGEOUS OF IOWA
12007 190TH STREET
MONTICELLO, IOWA 52310-0418

General Information Year-round camp for children and adults with disabilities. Traditional camp activities such as swimming, canoeing, nature activities, and crafts are offered. Also adventure activities such as rock climbing, high ropes, and caving are available. Established in 1972. 80-acre facility located 35 miles from Cedar Rapids. Features: wooded setting; caves; bluffs; indoor pool; air conditioned buildings.

Profile of Summer Employees Total number: 50; typical ages: 18–30. 30% men; 70% women; 3% minorities; 70% college students; 1% retirees; 10% non-U.S. citizens; 5% local applicants. Nonsmokers required.

Employment Information Openings are from May 18 to August 15. Year-round positions also offered. Jobs available: ▶ 2 *adventure specialists* (minimum age 18) with belaying training and experience leading rock climbing, rappelling, and high/low ropes; training can be provided at $240–$340 per week ▶ 15–20 *camp counselors* (minimum age 18) with a sincere desire to work with people with disabilities at $240–$340 per week ▶ 1 *canoeing specialist* with current lifeguard training certification and experience leading canoeing at $240–$340 per week ▶ 1 *crafts specialist* (minimum age 18) with experience with projects for people with disabilities at $240–$340 per week ▶ 1 *health staff assistant* (minimum age 18) with CPR and first aid training at $240 per week ▶ 1 *nature specialist* (minimum age 18) with experience leading nature activities and working with small farm animals at $240–$340 per week ▶ 1 *outdoor living skills specialist* (minimum age 18) with experience teaching outdoor living skills for people with disabilities at $240–$340 per week ▶ 1 *recreation specialist* (minimum age 18) with experience with recreational activities for people with disabilities at $240–$340 per week ▶ 1 *swimming specialist* (minimum age 18) with current lifeguard training certification at $240–$340 per week. Applicants must submit formal organization application, resume, three letters of recommendation, in-person interview (for year-round jobs), telephone interview acceptable for seasonal jobs; online applications available on Web site. International applicants accepted; must obtain own visa, obtain own working papers, apply through a recognized agency.

Benefits and Preemployment Training Free housing, free meals, formal training, possible full-time employment, willing to provide letters of recommendation, on-the-job training, willing to complete paperwork for educational credit, willing to act as a professional reference, and first aid/CPR training, restricted medical plan. Preemployment training is required and includes accident prevention and safety, first aid, CPR, interpersonal skills, leadership skills, behavior management, child and dependant adult abuse awareness.

Contact Jeanne Muellerleile, Camp Director, Camp Courageous of Iowa, 12007 190th Street, PO Box 418, Monticello, Iowa 52310-0418. Telephone: 319-465-5916 Ext. 206. Fax: 319-465-5919. E-mail: jmuellerleile@campcourageous.org. World Wide Web: http://www.campcourageous. org. Contact by e-mail, fax, mail, phone, or through World Wide Web site. Application deadline: continuous.

CAMP HANTESA
1450 ORIOLE ROAD
BOONE, IOWA 50036

General Information Residential and day camp serving boys and girls ages 5–18 with small group activities in noncompetitive atmosphere. Established in 1919. 144-acre facility located 40 miles from Des Moines. Features: hills; woods; hiking trails; lodges and cabins.

Profile of Summer Employees Total number: 50; typical ages: 18–22. 50% men; 50% women; 1% minorities; 99% college students; 10% non-U.S. citizens; 50% local applicants. Nonsmokers preferred.

Employment Information Openings are from May 27 to August 10. Spring break and winter break positions also offered. Jobs available: ▶ 1 *arts and crafts instructor* (minimum age 18) at $1500 per season ▶ 5 *cooks* (minimum age 18) at $1500 per season ▶ 20 *general counselors* (minimum age 18) with interest in children at $1500 per season ▶ 3 *riding instructors* (minimum age 18) with riding skills (English or Western style) and AAHS (clinic provided) at $1500 per season ▶ 1 *swimming guard* (minimum age 18) with ARC lifeguard certification at $1500 per season ▶ 1 *swimming instructor* (minimum age 18) with Red Cross WSI certification at $1500 per season ▶ 6 *unit directors* (minimum age 20) with management skills at $1500 per season. Applicants must submit formal organization application, three personal references. An in-person interview is recommended, but a telephone interview is acceptable. International applicants accepted; must apply through a recognized agency.

Benefits and Preemployment Training Free housing, free meals, health insurance, willing to provide letters of recommendation, on-the-job training, willing to complete paperwork for educational credit, and willing to act as a professional reference. Preemployment training is required and includes accident prevention and safety, first aid, CPR, interpersonal skills, leadership skills.

Contact Suz Welch, Director, Camp Hantesa, 1450 Oriole Road, Boone, Iowa 50036. Telephone: 515-432-1417. Fax: 515-432-1294. E-mail: hantesa@hantesa.com. World Wide Web: http://www. hantesa.com. Contact by e-mail, fax, mail, or phone. Application deadline: continuous.

CAMP HITAGA
5551 HITAGA ROAD
WALKER, IOWA 52352

General Information Day camp serving boys and girls from kindergarten through fifth grade. Residential camp serving boys and girls from first to ninth grade. Conference center serving community groups. Established in 1931. 240-acre facility located 20 miles from Cedar Rapids.

Profile of Summer Employees 25% men; 75% women; 100% college students; 25% local applicants.

Employment Information Openings are from June 6 to August 7. Jobs available: ▶ 1 *assistant director* at $1400–$1700 per season ▶ *general counselors* at $1100–$1500 per season ▶ *riding, aquatic, arts and crafts, and nature staff heads* at $1200–$1450 per season.

Benefits and Preemployment Training Free housing, free meals, and on-the-job training. Preemployment training is required and includes accident prevention and safety, first aid, CPR, interpersonal skills, leadership skills.

Contact Emily Evers, Camp Director, Camp Hitaga, 6300 Rockwell Drive NE, PO Box 10075, Cedar Rapids, Iowa 52410. Telephone: 319-294-2411. Fax: 319-294-2413. World Wide Web: http://www.iowanacouncil.org. Contact by fax, mail, or phone. Application deadline: applications in by April 15 (preferred).

THE SOUTHWESTERN COMPANY, IOWA
See The Southwestern Company on page 297 for complete description.

STUDENT CONSERVATION ASSOCIATION (SCA), IOWA
See Student Conservation Association (SCA), New Hampshire on page 200 for complete description.

KANSAS

THE SOUTHWESTERN COMPANY, KANSAS
See The Southwestern Company on page 297 for complete description.

STIVERS STAFFING SERVICES–KANSAS
See Stivers Staffing Services–Illinois on page 96 for complete description.

STUDENT CONSERVATION ASSOCIATION (SCA), KANSAS
See Student Conservation Association (SCA), New Hampshire on page 200 for complete description.

KENTUCKY

A CHRISTIAN MINISTRY IN THE NATIONAL PARKS–KENTUCKY
See A Christian Ministry in the National Parks–Maine on page 107 for complete description.

CAMP WOODMEN OF THE WORLD
93 SCHWARTZ ROAD
MURRAY, KENTUCKY 42071

General Information Residential camp serving Woodmen of the World members ages 8–15; also a senior program serving adults ages 60 and over with a general camp program that provides transportation Monday and Friday. Established in 1983. 14-acre facility located 117 miles from Nashville. Features: junior olympic swimming pool; 45-foot rappelling tower; 24-foot pool slide; 2 tennis courts; 6 cabins; outdoor stage.

Profile of Summer Employees Total number: 25–30; typical ages: 18–25. 50% men; 50% women; 2% minorities; 30% high school students; 70% college students; 2% non-U.S. citizens; 40% local applicants.

Employment Information Openings are from May to August. Jobs available: ▶ 1 *archery instructor* (minimum age 18) with certification in field at $130 per week ▶ 1 *arts and crafts instructor* (minimum age 18) with experience in the field at $130 per week ▶ 1 *assistant cook* (minimum age 21) with quantity cooking skills at $150 per week ▶ 1 *food service staff–head cook* (minimum age 21) with quantity cooking skills at $175 per week ▶ 8–12 *general counselors* (minimum age 18) with experience in the field at $120 per week ▶ 2 *kitchen helpers* (minimum age 15) with basic kitchen assistance skills at $90 per week ▶ 1 *rifle instructor* (minimum age 21) with experience or NRA certification at $130 per week ▶ 2 *ropes course instructors* (minimum age 18) with certification or documented experience at $130 per week ▶ 1 *water safety instructor/ pool manager* (minimum age 21) with WSI certification (preferred) at $130 per week. Applicants must submit formal organization application, three personal references. An in-person interview is recommended, but a telephone interview is acceptable. International applicants accepted; must obtain own visa, obtain own working papers, apply through a recognized agency.

Benefits and Preemployment Training Free housing, free meals, health insurance, willing to provide letters of recommendation, names of contacts, on-the-job training, willing to complete paperwork for educational credit, and willing to act as a professional reference. Preemployment training is required and includes accident prevention and safety, first aid, CPR, leadership skills, lifeguard certification.

Contact Colleen Anderson, Camp Director, Camp Woodmen of the World, 401-A Maple Street, Murray, Kentucky 42071. Telephone: 270-753-4382. Fax: 270-753-4396. E-mail: campwow@ theedgepc.net. World Wide Web: http://www.campwow.net. Contact by e-mail, fax, phone, or through World Wide Web site. Application deadline: April 1.

LIFE ADVENTURE CAMP
140 PARK STREET
VERSAILLES, KENTUCKY 40383

General Information Primitive wilderness camp with weekly programs that serve 32–40 campers per session (ages 9–18) who are either emotionally or behaviorally challenged, or who are in need of enhanced self-esteem, cooperation, and team-building skills. Established in 1977. 600-acre facility located 60 miles from Lexington. Features: wooded setting; 6 caves on site; large creek; primitive camping (no facilities).

Profile of Summer Employees Total number: 15; typical ages: 19–30. 31% men; 69% women; 5% high school students; 75% college students; 20% local applicants. Nonsmokers required.

Employment Information Openings are from May 28 to July 30. Jobs available: ▶ 10–15 *counselors* (minimum age 19) with first aid/CPR certification, one year of college or related work experience, some camping or outdoor experience, ability to live and work comfortably in a primitive outdoor setting, and some experience in a leadership role with children, preferably with children who have emotional and/or behavioral problems at $1600–$1800 per season ▶ 1 *food director* (minimum age 21) with experience with food management and valid driver's license at $1000–$1200 per season ▶ 1 *health supervisor* (minimum age 19) with first aid/CPR certification, valid driver's license, and experience administering first aid and medications in a wilderness setting at $1600–$1900 per season. Applicants must submit a formal organization application, three personal references, background check. An in-person interview is recommended, but a telephone interview is acceptable. International applicants accepted; must obtain own visa, obtain own working papers.

Benefits and Preemployment Training Free housing, free meals, formal training, willing to provide letters of recommendation, on-the-job training, willing to complete paperwork for educational credit, and willing to act as a professional reference. Preemployment training is required and includes accident prevention and safety, first aid, CPR, interpersonal skills, leadership skills, behavior management, crisis management (SCM), wilderness programming.

Contact Jill Braun, Assistant Program Director, Life Adventure Camp. Telephone: 859-879-0331. Fax: 859-873-2410. E-mail: jbraun@clevelandhome.org. World Wide Web: http://www.lifeadventurecamp.org. Contact by e-mail, fax, mail, phone, or through World Wide Web site. Application deadline: April 30.

THE SOUTHWESTERN COMPANY, KENTUCKY
See The Southwestern Company on page 297 for complete description.

STUDENT CONSERVATION ASSOCIATION (SCA), KENTUCKY
See Student Conservation Association (SCA), New Hampshire on page 200 for complete description.

LOUISIANA

MARYDALE RESIDENT CAMP
10317 MARYDALE ROAD
ST. FRANCISVILLE, LOUISIANA 70775

General Information Residential camp serving girls ages 7 –17 with a general outdoor program and specialty programs in horseback riding and swimming. Established in 1948. 400-acre facility located 40 miles from Baton Rouge. Features: lake; 2 outdoor horse arenas; pool; challenge course; several hiking trails; new multi-purpose facility.

Profile of Summer Employees Total number: 40; typical age: 20. 1% men; 99% women; 25% minorities; 5% high school students; 95% college students; 90% local applicants.

Employment Information Openings are from June 1 to July 31. Jobs available: ► 1 *arts and crafts director* (minimum age 18) at $150–$225 per week ► 1 *business manager* (minimum age 21) with some type of accounting or bookkeeping experience at $200–$250 per week ► 16–20 *counselors* (minimum age 18) with leadership experience at $150–$200 per week ► 2 *health supervisors* (minimum age 21) with RN, LPN, or physician's license at $225–$275 per week ► 4 *lifeguards* (minimum age 18) with American Red Cross certification and swimming experience, will train at $150–$200 per week ► 1 *naturalist* (minimum age 18) with experience in wildlife education at $150–$200 per week ► 1 *program director/assistant director* (minimum age 21) with camp experience preferably in Girl Scout programming, documented experience in leadership and activity organization, and recreation background at $225–$275 per week ► 2 *riding directors* (minimum age 21) with CHA certification or documented experience (possible nine-week contract) at $175–$225 per week ► 4 *riding instructors* (minimum age 18) with Camp Horsemanship Association certification or documented experience at $175–$225 per week

▶ 5 *unit leaders* (minimum age 21) with camp and documented leadership experience at $175–$225 per week ▶ 1 *waterfront director* (minimum age 21) with lifeguard, CPR, first aid, and WSI certification recommended (possible nine-week contract and weekend employment) at $200–$250 per week. Applicants must submit a formal organization application, two personal references. An in-person interview is recommended, but a telephone interview is acceptable.

Benefits and Preemployment Training Free housing, free meals, formal training, willing to provide letters of recommendation, on-the-job training, willing to complete paperwork for educational credit, and willing to act as a professional reference. Preemployment training is required and includes accident prevention and safety, first aid, CPR, interpersonal skills, leadership skills, child abuse prevention, conflict resolution, outdoor living skills.

Contact Jill Pollard, Camp Director, Marydale Resident Camp, 545 Colonial Drive, Baton Rouge, Louisiana 70806-6520. Telephone: 800-852-8421. Fax: 225-927-8402. E-mail: info@ girlscoutsaudubon.org. Contact by e-mail or phone. Application deadline: continuous.

THE SOUTHWESTERN COMPANY, LOUISIANA
See The Southwestern Company on page 297 for complete description.

STUDENT CONSERVATION ASSOCIATION (SCA), LOUISIANA
See Student Conservation Association (SCA), New Hampshire on page 200 for complete description.

MAINE

ACADIA CORPORATION
85 MAIN STREET, BOX 24
BAR HARBOR, MAINE 04609

General Information National park concessioner operating a restaurant and three gift shops in Acadia National Park and several shops in the town of Bar Harbor. Established in 1932. Located 18 miles from Ellsworth. Features: national park setting; near Atlantic Ocean; hiking, biking, and sailing activities available; busy resort community; tea and popovers on the lawn.

Profile of Summer Employees Total number: 150–175; typical ages: 18–70. 44% men; 56% women; 4% minorities; 1% high school students; 50% college students; 10% retirees; 15% non-U.S. citizens; 20% local applicants.

Employment Information Openings are from May 15 to October 26. Jobs available: ▶ 1 *bartender* (minimum age 18) with ability to operate service bar and cash register per hour at $5.75 per hour plus tips ▶ 5 *buspersons* (minimum age 18) with ability to lift and carry more than 25 pounds up to 100 times per day at $5.75 per hour plus tips ▶ 6 *hosts* (minimum age 18) with pleasant personality and calm demeanor to greet and seat customers and take reservations at $5.75 per hour plus tips ▶ 1–2 *housekeepers* (minimum age 18) with willingness to clean housing, offices, and restrooms at $9 per hour ▶ 15 *kitchen workers* (minimum age 18) with ability to run cold food line and bakery and to perform food prep work, dishwashing, cleaning and lifting, and carrying more than 25 pounds up to 100 times per day at $8.50 per hour plus bonus ▶ 3 *lead cooks* (minimum age 18) with strong creative cooking skills including sauté and sauces and two years of supervisory experience or equivalent at $9.50 per hour ▶ 2 *office clerks* (minimum age 18) with valid driver's license, ability to perform work accurately, pay attention to detail, and type at $8 per hour ▶ 32 *shop clerks* (minimum age 18) with ability to perform various duties, including operating cash register, assisting with purchases, stocking and ordering merchandise, and orienting park visitors at $8 per hour ▶ 36 *waiters/waitresses* (minimum age 18) with pleasant personality, calm demeanor, and ability to lift and carry more than 25 pounds up to 100 times per day at $3.13 per hour plus tips ▶ 4 *warehouse clerks* (minimum age 18) with ability to maintain accurate records and pay attention to detail, clean driving record, valid driver's license, and ability to frequently lift and carry up to 50 pounds at $8 per hour. Applicants must submit formal organization application, two personal references, letter of recommendation. A telephone interview is required. International applicants accepted; must obtain own visa, obtain own working papers, apply through a recognized agency.

Benefits and Preemployment Training Housing at a cost, meals at a cost, willing to provide letters of recommendation, and on-the-job training. Preemployment training is required and includes accident prevention and safety, interpersonal skills, information about camping policies, information about Acadia National Park and surrounding area.

Contact Leisa Litvay, Personnel, Acadia Corporation, PO Box 24, Bar Harbor, Maine 04609. Telephone: 207-276-3610. Fax: 207-288-2420. E-mail: llitvay@acadia.net. World Wide Web: http://www.jordanpond.com. Contact by e-mail, fax, mail, phone, or through World Wide Web site. Application deadline: continuous.

A CHRISTIAN MINISTRY IN THE NATIONAL PARKS–MAINE
10 JUSTIN'S WAY
FREEPORT, MAINE 04032

General Information Nonprofit interdenominational Christian ministry that places individuals in the national parks to work, witness, and conduct worship services and activities. Established in 1952. Features: National Parks; mountains; water; lakes; hiking opportunities.

Profile of Summer Employees Total number: 200–250; typical ages: 19–25. 40% men; 60% women; 10% minorities; 80% college students; 5% retirees; 5% local applicants.

Employment Information Openings are from January 1 to December 31. Year-round positions also offered. Jobs available: ▶ 20–30 *ministry staff leaders* (minimum age 18) with willingness to learn the following: leading worship, preaching, providing pastoral care, teaching, administration, and music at $1200 to $2000 per three months ▶ 220–250 *ministry staff members* (minimum age 18) with abilities in leading bible studies, Christian education, drama, music, leading discussion groups, and offering recreation ideas at $1200 to $2000 per three months ▶ 20–30 *ministry staff musicians* (minimum age 18) to provide music for weekly services of worship, lead choirs, and organize special musical events at $1200 to $2000 per three months. Applicants must submit a formal organization application, three letters of recommendation. International applicants accepted; must obtain own visa, obtain own working papers.

Benefits and Preemployment Training Housing at a cost, meals at a cost, willing to provide letters of recommendation, and on-the-job training. Preemployment training is optional and includes interpersonal skills, leadership skills, ministry preparation.

Contact Rev. Richard P. Camp, Jr., Director, A Christian Ministry in the National Parks–Maine. Telephone: 207-865-6436. Fax: 207-865-6852. E-mail: info@acmnp.com. World Wide Web: http://www.acmnp.com. Contact by e-mail, fax, mail, phone, or through World Wide Web site. Application deadline: continuous.

AIMHI LODGE
14 AIMHI WOODS ROAD
NORTH WINDHAM, MAINE 04062

General Information Family owned summer resort; American plan including meals, cottages, and sports facilities. Established in 1919. 30-acre facility located 20 miles from Portland. Features: lake; quiet, wooded setting; 2 tennis courts; kayaks and canoes; individual cottages.

Profile of Summer Employees Total number: 20; typical ages: 19–25. 25% men; 75% women; 1% high school students; 95% college students; 1% non-U.S. citizens; 1% local applicants. Nonsmokers required.

Employment Information Openings are from June 26 to August 28. Jobs available: ▶ 1 *activities director* (minimum age 21) with experience and elementary education courses helpful at $190 per week plus tips ▶ 1 *housekeeper* (minimum age 20) with neatness, organizational skills, and fast work habits at $265 per week plus tips and possible bonus at end of season ▶ 1–2 *maintenance workers* (minimum age 21) with minor carpentry, electrical, and plumbing experience helpful at $8 to $9.50 per hour with possible bonus and raise at end of season for exceptional work ▶ 1 *office worker/receptionist* (minimum age 21) with attentiveness and bookkeeping experience or courses helpful at $375 to $425 per week with possible end of season raise ▶ 6–8 *waitstaff* (minimum age 19) with easy going personality, quickness, attentiveness, and experience (helpful) at $4.14 per hour plus tips. Applicants must submit online application. An in-person interview is recommended, but a telephone interview is acceptable. International applicants accepted; must obtain own visa, obtain own working papers, apply through a recognized agency.

Benefits and Preemployment Training Willing to provide letters of recommendation, on-the-job training, willing to complete paperwork for educational credit, willing to act as a professional reference, and room and board available (depending on position). Preemployment training is required and includes job training (waitstaff).

Contact Susan Bennett, Owner/Manager, Aimhi Lodge. E-mail: aimhilodge@aol.com. World Wide Web: http://www.aimhilodge.com. Contact by e-mail or through World Wide Web site. No phone calls. Application deadline: continuous.

ALFORD LAKE CAMP
258 ALFORD LAKE ROAD
HOPE, MAINE 04847

General Information Residential camp offering a multiactivity program for 175 girls ages 8–15. Extensive trip programs for girls and/or boys on the Appalachian Trail and in Great Britain offered, as well as exchange programs in Mexico, Japan, and Nova Scotia. Established in 1907. 416-acre facility located 10 miles from Camden. Features: freshwater lake; wooded setting; 4 tennis courts; library; stables and riding rings; climbing wall/high and low cable courses.

Profile of Summer Employees Total number: 90; typical ages: 17–25. 2% men; 98% women; 60% college students; 6% non-U.S. citizens. Nonsmokers required.

Employment Information Openings are from June 12 to August 18. Jobs available: ▶ 1 *archery instructor* (minimum age 18) with National Archery Association Level 1 certification at $1800–$2200 per season ▶ 1–3 *canoeing instructors* (minimum age 18) with Red Cross canoeing (or equivalent) and American Red Cross lifeguard certification at $1800–$2200 per season ▶ 2 *climbing wall and high/low cable course instructors* (minimum age 18) with climbing experience at $1800–$2200 per season ▶ 1 *community service worker* (minimum age 21) with valid driver's license and clean driving record at $1800–$2200 per season ▶ 1–2 *drama instructors* (minimum age 18) with teaching and production experience at $1800–$2200 per season ▶ 1–2 *gymnastics instructors* (minimum age 18) with teaching experience and certification or documentation at $1800–$2200 per season ▶ 2 *office personnel* (minimum age 20) with knowledge of computers, attention to detail, and telephone skills (essential) at $1500–$2000 per season ▶ 1–3 *outdoor explorations (campcraft and nature)* (minimum age 18) with Maine trip-leading certification, Wilderness First Aid and ARS Lifeguard Training Certification at $1800–$2200 per season

▶ 5 *riding instructors* (minimum age 18) with British Horse Society, Pony Club certification, or equivalent at $1800–$2200 per season ▶ 1–2 *sailboarding instructors* (minimum age 18) with sailboarding experience documentation and American Red Cross lifeguard training certification at $1800–$2200 per season ▶ 3–5 *sailing instructors* (minimum age 18) with Red Cross lifeguard training and sailing experience at $1800–$2200 per season ▶ 5–9 *swimming instructors* (minimum age 18) with WSI and American Red Cross lifeguard certification at $1800–$2200 per season ▶ 4 *tennis counselors* (minimum age 18) with teaching experience at $1800–$2200 per season ▶ 4 *trip leaders* (minimum age 21) with Maine Trip Leading Certification, Wilderness First Aid, LGT, CPR, first aid, and experience leading 2- to 3-day trips at $1800–$2200 per season. Applicants must submit formal organization application, three personal references. A telephone interview is required. International applicants accepted; must apply through a recognized agency.

Benefits and Preemployment Training Free housing, free meals, formal training, willing to provide letters of recommendation, on-the-job training, willing to complete paperwork for educational credit, and possible internship. Preemployment training is required and includes accident prevention and safety, interpersonal skills, leadership skills.

Contact Ms. Betsy Brayley, Assistant Director, Alford Lake Camp, 5 Salt Marsh Way, Cape Elizabeth, Maine 04107. Telephone: 207-799-3005. Fax: 207-799-5044. E-mail: alc@alfordlake. com. Contact by e-mail, fax, mail, or phone. Application deadline: continuous.

CAMP AGAWAM
CRESCENT LAKE, 54 AGAWAM ROAD
RAYMOND, MAINE 04071

General Information Residential camp serving 125 boys ages 8–15 in a single 7-week session. There is also a 1-week session for 85 disadvantaged boys. Established in 1919. 115-acre facility located 35 miles from Portland. Features: freshwater lake; wooded setting; renovated screened cabins and bathrooms; new dining hall and main lodge; 4 new tennis courts; new basketball court; 2 new soccer fields; well-maintained facility.

Profile of Summer Employees Total number: 65; typical ages: 18–70. 90% men; 10% women; 5% minorities; 20% high school students; 80% college students; 10% non-U.S. citizens; 10% local applicants. Nonsmokers required.

Employment Information Openings are from June 9 to August 14. Jobs available: ▶ 1 *counselor/ crafts instructor* (minimum age 18) with experience preferred at $1350–$1600 per season ▶ 1 *counselor/dramatics instructor* (minimum age 18) with acting classes, directing, and performing experience at $1350–$1600 per season ▶ 1 *counselor/woodworking instructor* (minimum age 19) at $1350–$2000 per season ▶ 2 *counselors/archery and riflery instructors* (minimum age 19) with NAA or NRA certification or equivalent at $1350–$1800 per season ▶ 4 *counselors/ campcraft and trip leaders* with LGT, CPR/first aid, Maine Trip Leader certification, and Wilderness First Aid at $1350–$1600 per season ▶ 15 *counselors/sports instructors/coaches* with experience, including attending clinics at $1350–$1600 per season ▶ 4 *counselors/water sports instructors* (minimum age 18) with CPR, first aid, and WSI or LGT certification at $1350–$1750 per season ▶ 1 *health care assistant* (minimum age 21) with LPN, CNA, or EMT at $3000 and up per season ▶ *ropes course facilitator* (minimum age 19) with ropes course facilitator certification at $1350–$1750 per season ▶ *watercraft counselor (sailboards, sailboats, canoes, rowboats)* (minimum age 18) at $1350–$1600 per season. Applicants must submit formal organization application, three personal references. An in-person interview is recommended, but a telephone interview is acceptable. International applicants accepted; must apply through a recognized agency.

Benefits and Preemployment Training Free housing, free meals, formal training, willing to provide letters of recommendation, on-the-job training, willing to complete paperwork for educational credit, willing to act as a professional reference, and opportunity to attend seminars/ workshops. Preemployment training is required and includes accident prevention and safety, first aid, CPR, interpersonal skills, leadership skills, child development.

Contact Scott Malm, Program Director, Camp Agawam, 30 Fieldstone Lane, Hanover, Massachusetts 02339. Telephone: 781-826-5913. Fax: 781-829-0208. E-mail: bowman@campagawam. org. World Wide Web: http://www.campagawam.org. Contact by e-mail, fax, mail, phone, or through World Wide Web site. Application deadline: continuous.

CAMP ANDROSCOGGIN
WAYNE, MAINE 04284
General Information Private residential camp serving 250 boys from the United States and abroad in one 8-week session. Established in 1907. 125-acre facility located 15 miles from Augusta. Features: freshwater lake; wooded setting; 12 tennis courts; 4 sports fields; 30 watercraft; indoor gymnasium.

Profile of Summer Employees Total number: 100; typical ages: 19–25. 90% men; 10% women; 80% college students; 10% non-U.S. citizens; 10% local applicants. Nonsmokers preferred.

Employment Information Openings are from June 17 to August 17. Jobs available: ▶ 1 *animation/video instructor* at $1250–$1750 per season ▶ 1 *archery instructor* at $1250–$1750 per season ▶ 4 *baseball instructors* at $1250–$1750 per season ▶ 4 *basketball instructors* at $1250–$1750 per season ▶ 1 *bicycling instructor* at $1250–$1750 per season ▶ 2 *canoeing instructors* at $1250–$1750 per season ▶ 1 *ceramics instructor* at $1250–$1750 per season ▶ 1 *crafts instructor* at $1250–$1750 per season ▶ 2 *drama instructors* at $1250–$1750 per season ▶ 1 *kayaking instructor* at $1250–$1750 per season ▶ 2 *lacrosse instructors* at $1250–$1750 per season ▶ 1 *nature instructor* at $1250–$1750 per season ▶ 2 *nurses* at $3000–$4000 per season ▶ 1 *photography instructor* at $1250–$1750 per season ▶ 1 *radio broadcasting instructor* at $1250–$1750 per season ▶ 1 *riflery instructor* at $1250–$1750 per season ▶ 4 *ropes course instructors* at $1250–$1750 per season ▶ 3 *sailing instructors* at $1250–$1750 per season ▶ 2 *secretaries* at $1750–$2250 per season ▶ 4 *soccer instructors* at $1250–$1750 per season ▶ 10 *swimming instructors* with WSI certification or lifeguard training at $1250–$1750 per season ▶ 10 *tennis instructors* at $1250–$1750 per season ▶ 4 *waterskiing instructors* at $1250–$1750 per season ▶ 1 *windsurfing instructor* at $1250–$1750 per season ▶ 1 *woodworking instructor* at $1250–$1750 per season. Applicants must submit formal organization application, letter of interest, three personal references. An in-person interview is recommended, but a telephone interview is acceptable. International applicants accepted; must apply through a recognized agency.

Benefits and Preemployment Training Free housing, free meals, willing to provide letters of recommendation, on-the-job training, willing to complete paperwork for educational credit, willing to act as a professional reference, and travel reimbursement. Preemployment training is required and includes accident prevention and safety, first aid, CPR, interpersonal skills, leadership skills.

Contact Peter Hirsch, Director, Camp Androscoggin, 601 West Street, Harrison, New York 10528. Telephone: 914-835-5800. Fax: 914-777-2718. E-mail: staff@campandro.com. World Wide Web: http://www.campandro.com. Contact by e-mail, fax, mail, phone, or through World Wide Web site. Application deadline: continuous.

CAMP ARCADIA
ROUTE 121
CASCO, MAINE 04015
General Information Residential camp for girls serving 160 campers for part of the season or seven full weeks concentrating on individual camper growth and development in a warm, family atmosphere. Established in 1916. 365-acre facility located 35 miles from Portland. Features: extensive freshwater lake frontage; 2 natural sandy beaches; sunny fields and pine woods; tennis courts; riding ring and stables.

Profile of Summer Employees Total number: 80; typical ages: 19–23. 10% men; 90% women; 5% minorities; 75% college students; 10% non-U.S. citizens. Nonsmokers preferred.

Employment Information Openings are from June 13 to August 19. Jobs available: ▶ 1 *archery instructor* at $1100–$1300 per season ▶ 2 *arts and crafts instructors* with silk-screening, block-printing, batik, drawing, and painting experience at $1500–$2200 per season ▶ 4 *canoeing instructors* (minimum age 19) with lifeguard training certification at $1500–$2000 per season ▶ 1 *ceramics instructor* with electric kiln and potter's wheel experience at $1500–$2000 per season ▶ *chef/baker* at a negotiable salary ▶ 2 *drama instructors* with driver's license and experience in children's drama, directing, lighting, and sets at $1500–$2200 per season ▶ 1 *environmental (nature) instructor* at $1500–$2500 per season ▶ 1 *gymnastics instructor* with rhythmic, floor, and low beam gymnastics experience at $1500–$2000 per season ▶ 1 *music instructor* with piano playing and camp song leadership ability at $1500–$2200 per season ▶ 2 *nurses* with RN license at a negotiable salary ▶ 2 *office workers* with 50 wpm typing and knowledge of computers at $1500–$2000 per season ▶ 1 *photography instructor* with black-and-white darkroom experience at $1500–$2000 per season ▶ 2 *riding instructors* with English balance seat-riding and stable management ability at $1500–$2000 per season ▶ 4 *sailing instructors* with lifeguard training and knowledge of racing at $1300–$2000 per season ▶ *swimming instructors* with WSI and lifeguard training certification at $1200–$1600 per season ▶ 4 *tennis instructors* with tennis team background at $1500–$2200 per season ▶ 3 *trip instructors* (minimum age 21) with driver's license at $1500–$2500 per season ▶ 2 *weaving instructors* with knowledge of floor, table, and hand looms at $1500–$1800 per season. Applicants must submit formal organization application, personal reference, letter of recommendation. An in-person interview is recommended, but a telephone interview is acceptable. International applicants accepted; must obtain own visa, obtain own working papers, apply through a recognized agency.

Benefits and Preemployment Training Free housing, free meals, formal training, health insurance, willing to provide letters of recommendation, names of contacts, on-the-job training, willing to complete paperwork for educational credit, willing to act as a professional reference, travel reimbursement, and free uniforms. Preemployment training is required and includes accident prevention and safety, first aid, CPR, leadership skills.

Contact Anne Henderson Fritts, Director, Camp Arcadia, PO Box 225, Pleasantville Road, New Vernon, New Jersey 07976. Telephone: 973-538-5409. Fax: 973-540-1555. World Wide Web: http://www.camparcadia.com. Contact by fax, mail, or phone. Application deadline: continuous.

CAMP CEDAR
PO BOX 240
CASCO, MAINE 04015-0240

General Information Residential private camp for 250 boys offering one 8-week session including land sports, water sports, adventure activities and creative arts in a warm, nurturing environment. Established in 1954. 150-acre facility located 30 miles from Portland. Features: freshwater spring-fed lake; wooded setting; great facilities; close to mountains and ocean; modern cabins; great food.

Profile of Summer Employees Total number: 110; typical ages: 19–26. 75% men; 25% women; 10% minorities; 5% high school students; 80% college students; 10% non-U.S. citizens; 5% local applicants. Nonsmokers preferred.

Employment Information Openings are from June 20 to August 20. Jobs available: ▶ 75 *counselors* with ability to teach an activity at $1000–$1500 per season ▶ 5 *rock climbers* with experience in technical rock climbing, top roping, and belaying at $1000–$1500 per season ▶ 10 *swimming instructors* with WSI and/or lifeguard certification at $1000–$1500 per season ▶ 10 *tennis instructors* with high school or college varsity experience at $1000–$1500 per season. Applicants must submit formal organization application, three personal references, three letters of recommendation. An in-person interview is recommended, but a telephone interview is acceptable. International applicants accepted; must apply through a recognized agency.

Benefits and Preemployment Training Free housing, free meals, formal training, health insurance, willing to provide letters of recommendation, on-the-job training, willing to complete paperwork for educational credit, and travel reimbursement. Preemployment training is required and includes accident prevention and safety, first aid, CPR, interpersonal skills, leadership skills. **Contact** Jeff Hacker, Director, Camp Cedar, 1758 Beacon Street, Brookline, Massachusetts 02445. Telephone: 617-277-8080. Fax: 617-277-1488. E-mail: campcedar@aol.com. World Wide Web: http://www.campcedar.com/cedar. Contact by e-mail, fax, mail, phone, or through World Wide Web site. Application deadline: continuous.

CAMP COBBOSSEE
PO BOX 575, ROUTE 135
WINTHROP, MAINE 04364

General Information Residential competitive and instructionally-oriented sports camp serving 200 boys. Established in 1902. 150-acre facility located 15 miles from Augusta. Features: climbing wall and zip line; location on 11-mile lake; extensive waterfront area; ball fields and courts; clay and all-weather tennis courts; regulation-size roller-hockey court.

Profile of Summer Employees Total number: 100; typical ages: 19–25. 90% men; 10% women; 5% minorities; 90% college students; 10% non-U.S. citizens. Nonsmokers required.

Employment Information Openings are from June 14 to August 20. Jobs available: ▶ *activity heads* (minimum age 19) with teaching and/or coaching experience (preference for high school or college coaches or teachers) at $1500–$4500 per season ▶ 1 *chef* with cooking experience at a negotiable salary ▶ *hiking/camping/rock climbing staff members* (minimum age 19) with experience in working with children and rock climbing/ropes certification (training available) at $1250–$3000 per season ▶ *nurses* with RN license at a negotiable salary ▶ *swimming instructors* (minimum age 19) with LGT and WSI certification (training available) at $1250–$3000 per season ▶ *team sports staff members* (minimum age 19) with experience in coaching or working with children and ability to instruct one or more of the following: baseball, basketball, soccer, lacrosse, street hockey, ice hockey, or team handball at $1250–$3000 per season ▶ *tennis staff members* (minimum age 19) with high school and/or college varsity or tournament competition experience preferred at $1250–$3000 per season ▶ *waterfront staff members* (minimum age 19) with sailing, waterskiing, or scuba experience; WSI and lifeguard certification (training available) at $1250–$3000 per season. Applicants must submit formal organization application, letter of interest, resume, three personal references. An in-person interview is recommended, but a telephone interview is acceptable. International applicants accepted; must obtain own visa, obtain own working papers, apply through a recognized agency.

Benefits and Preemployment Training Free housing, free meals, willing to provide letters of recommendation, on-the-job training, willing to complete paperwork for educational credit, willing to act as a professional reference, travel reimbursement, and laundry service. Preemployment training is required and includes accident prevention and safety, first aid, CPR, interpersonal skills, leadership skills, lifeguard training, ropes/climbing certification, WSI. **Contact** Steven Rubin, Owner, Camp Cobbossee, 10 Silvermine Drive, South Salem, New York 10590. Telephone: 914-533-6104. Fax: 914-533-6069. E-mail: cobbachief@aol.com. Contact by e-mail, fax, mail, or phone. Application deadline: continuous.

CAMP ENCORE-CODA FOR A GREAT SUMMER OF MUSIC, SPORTS, AND FRIENDS
50 ENCORE/CODA LANE
SWEDEN, MAINE 04040

General Information Residential coed music and sports camp. Ensembles and private instruction in the areas of classical, jazz, and rock music as well as musical theater are featured.

Established in 1950. 80-acre facility located 40 miles from Portland. Features: freshwater lake; wooded setting; 2 tennis courts; cabins; 28 pianos.

Profile of Summer Employees Total number: 75; typical ages: 17–60. 50% men; 50% women; 5% minorities; 10% high school students; 50% college students; 5% non-U.S. citizens; 5% local applicants. Nonsmokers required.

Employment Information Openings are from June 16 to August 15. Jobs available: ▶ 1 *arts and crafts counselor* (minimum age 19) at $1200–$1600 per season ▶ *assistant head counselor* (minimum age 21) with camp leadership experience, good organizational skills, and a college degree at $2000–$2500 per season ▶ *boating counselor* (minimum age 19) with LGT certification (ARC, Boy Scouts, Y, Ellis all acceptable) at $1400–$1800 per season ▶ *head counselor* with camp leadership experience, good organizational skills, and a college degree at $2500–$3000 per season ▶ 4 *land sports counselors* with CPR and first aid at $1200–$1600 per season ▶ 10 *music counselors* (minimum age 21) with solid performing skills on your instrument or voice, ability to teach these skills to students aged 7-17, and prior teaching experience desired at $1400–$1700 per season ▶ 3 *piano accompanists* (minimum age 19) with excellent sight reading skills at $1200–$1700 per season ▶ 1–2 *sailing counselors* (minimum age 19) with LGT certification (ARC, Boy Scouts, Y, Ellis all acceptable) at $1400–$1800 per season ▶ 7 *swimming instructors* (minimum age 19) with LGT certification at $1300–$1800 per season ▶ 2 *tennis counselors* (minimum age 19) with CPR and first aid at $1100–$1600 per season ▶ 1 *waterfront director* (minimum age 21) with LGT/WSI certification, CPR, first aid, and LGI preferred at $2300–$3000 per season. Applicants must submit formal organization application, three personal references, three letters of recommendation. An in-person interview is recommended, but a telephone interview is acceptable. International applicants accepted; must apply through a recognized agency.

Benefits and Preemployment Training Free housing, free meals, formal training, willing to provide letters of recommendation, names of contacts, on-the-job training, willing to complete paperwork for educational credit, willing to act as a professional reference, and opportunity to attend seminars/workshops. Preemployment training is required and includes accident prevention and safety, interpersonal skills, leadership skills.

Contact Ellen Donohue-Saltman, Director, Camp Encore-Coda for a Great Summer of Music, Sports, and Friends, 32 Grassmere Road, Brookline, Massachusetts 02467. Telephone: 617-325-1541. Fax: 617-325-7278. E-mail: ellen@encore-coda.com. World Wide Web: http://www.encore-coda.com. Contact by e-mail, fax, mail, phone, or through World Wide Web site. Application deadline: continuous.

CAMP HAWTHORNE
PLUMMER ROAD, PANTHER POND
RAYMOND, MAINE 04071

General Information Coed residential camp with visual and performing arts programs and noncompetitive sports. Established in 1919. 140-acre facility located 20 miles from Portland. Features: 2½ miles of shorefront; pristine lake; professional staff for theater, art, and moviemaking; great sailing instruction.

Profile of Summer Employees Total number: 45; typical ages: 19–26. 50% men; 50% women; 15% minorities; 5% high school students; 80% college students; 5% non-U.S. citizens. Nonsmokers preferred.

Employment Information Openings are from June 18 to August 12. Jobs available: ▶ 2 *archery/riflery instructors* (minimum age 18) ▶ 2 *canoeing/boating instructors* (minimum age 18) with knowledge of canoeing, waterskiing, and small kayaks at $1300–$1600 per season ▶ 4 *creative arts teachers* (minimum age 18) ▶ 2 *drama instructors* (minimum age 18) at $1300–$1700 per season ▶ 6 *sailing instructors* (minimum age 18) with ability to rig a sail (14- to 18-foot sailboat with 2 sails) at $1300–$1700 per season ▶ 6 *sports instructors* at $1400–$1700 per season ▶ 5 *swimming instructors* with lifeguard training or WSI certification at $1300–$1800 per season. Applicants must submit a formal organization application, letter of interest, resume. International applicants accepted; must obtain own visa.

Benefits and Preemployment Training Free housing, free meals, on-the-job training, travel reimbursement, and leadership skills, accident prevention and safety, first aid, and CPR training available.

Contact Ronald Furst, Owner, Camp Hawthorne, 10 Scotland Bridge Road, York, Maine 03909. Telephone: 207-363-1773. Fax: 207-363-1773. Contact by mail or phone. Application deadline: May 30.

CAMP LAUREL
ROUTE 41
READFIELD, MAINE 04355

General Information Camp welcoming 235 boys and 235 girls ages 8-15 from all over the United States as well as several other countries. Established in 1949. 150-acre facility located 15 miles from Augusta. Features: 4-mile lake; 15 tennis courts; 4000-square foot gymnastics building; 18 horses; cabins; 55-foot climbing tower.

Profile of Summer Employees Total number: 280; typical ages: 20–45. 50% men; 50% women; 75% college students; 3% non-U.S. citizens; 3% local applicants. Nonsmokers required.

Employment Information Openings are from June 1 to August 30. Jobs available: ▶ 2 *AM radio personalities* (minimum age 19) at $1600–$2200 per season ▶ 2 *archery instructors* (minimum age 19) at $1600–$2200 per season ▶ 2 *arts and crafts instructors* (minimum age 19) at $1600–$2200 per season ▶ 15 *athletics counselors* (minimum age 18) at $1600–$2200 per season ▶ 5 *ceramics instructors* (minimum age 18) at $1600–$2200 per season ▶ 3 *climbing and ropes course staff* (minimum age 18) at $1600–$2200 per season ▶ 3 *dance counselors* (minimum age 18) at $1600–$2200 per season ▶ 5 *fitness counselors* (minimum age 19) at $1600–$2200 per season ▶ 6 *gymnastics instructors* (minimum age 18) at $1600–$2200 per season ▶ 2 *ice hockey counselors* (minimum age 18) at $1600–$2200 per season ▶ 2 *lacrosse counselors* (minimum age 19) at $1600–$2200 per season ▶ 7 *nurses* (minimum age 22) at $3500 per season ▶ 2 *paddling counselors* (minimum age 18) at $1600–$2200 per season ▶ 3 *photography instructors* (minimum age 18) at $1600–$2200 per season ▶ 2 *piano/music instructors* (minimum age 19) at $1600–$2200 per season ▶ 6 *riding (English) counselors* (minimum age 19) at $1600–$2200 per season ▶ 2 *roller hockey counselors* (minimum age 18) at $1600–$2200 per season ▶ 3 *sailboarding counselors* (minimum age 18) at $1600–$2200 per season ▶ 7 *sailing counselors* (minimum age 18) at $1600–$2200 per season ▶ 12 *swimming counselors* (minimum age 18) at $1600–$2200 per season ▶ 18 *tennis counselors* (minimum age 18) at $2200 per season ▶ 10 *waterskiing counselors* (minimum age 18) at $1600–$2200 per season. Applicants must submit formal organization application. International applicants accepted; must apply through a recognized agency.

Benefits and Preemployment Training Free housing, free meals, formal training, willing to provide letters of recommendation, on-the-job training, willing to complete paperwork for educational credit, willing to act as a professional reference, and travel reimbursement. Preemployment training is required and includes accident prevention and safety, first aid, CPR, interpersonal skills, leadership skills.

Contact Jeremy Sollinger, Associate Director, Camp Laurel, Box 661, Alpine, New Jersey 07620. Telephone: 800-327-3509. Fax: 201-750-0665. E-mail: summer@camplaurel.com. World Wide Web: http://www.camplaurel.com. Contact by e-mail, fax, mail, phone, or through World Wide Web site. Application deadline: continuous.

CAMP LAUREL SOUTH
48 LAUREL ROAD
CASCO, MAINE 04015

General Information Family-oriented, coed, residential camp in Maine. Operates two 4-week sessions offering a variety of land and water sports, theater, arts, adventure, riding, and much more. Established in 1921. 120-acre facility located 24 miles from Portland. Features: freshwater, sandy-bottom lake; 8 hardcourt tennis courts; extensive staff lounge/cafe; wooded setting; top-notch program facilities; family atmosphere.

Profile of Summer Employees Total number: 185; typical ages: 19–50. 50% men; 50% women; 2% high school students; 85% college students; 8% non-U.S. citizens; 5% local applicants. Nonsmokers preferred.

Employment Information Openings are from June 17 to August 18. Jobs available: ▶ *adventure/ ropes course instructors* at $1500 and up per season ▶ *aerobics instructor* at $1500 and up per season ▶ *archery instructors* at $1500 and up per season ▶ *arts and crafts instructors* at $1500 and up per season ▶ *baseball instructors* at $1500 and up per season ▶ *basketball instructors* at $1500 and up per season ▶ *campus leaders* at $2500 and up per season ▶ *ceramics instructors* at $1500 and up per season ▶ *dance instructors* at $1500 and up per season ▶ *field hockey instructor* at $1500 and up per season ▶ *fishing instructor* at $1500 and up per season ▶ *fitness instructors* at $1500 and up per season ▶ *football instructors* at $1500 and up per season ▶ *golf instructor* at $1500 and up per season ▶ *gymnastics instructors* at $1500 and up per season ▶ *horseback riding (English) instructors* at $1500 and up per season ▶ *lacrosse instructor* at $1500 and up per season ▶ *maintenance staff* at $1500 and up per season ▶ *nature counselor* at $1500 and up per season ▶ *nurses* at $3000 and up per season ▶ *office staff* at $1500 and up per season ▶ *photography instructors* at $1500 and up per season ▶ *piano player* at $1500 and up per season ▶ *program heads* at $2000 and up per season ▶ *riflery instructor* at $1500 and up per season ▶ *rocketry instructor* at $1500 and up per season ▶ *sailing instructors* at $1500 and up per season ▶ *soccer instructors* at $1500 and up per season ▶ *special programs coordinator* at $2000 and up per season ▶ *street/roller hockey instructors* at $1500 and up per season ▶ *swimming instructors* at $1500 and up per season ▶ *tennis instructors* at $1500 and up per season ▶ *theater staff* at $1500 and up per season ▶ *volleyball instructor* at $1500 and up per season ▶ *waterski instructors* at $1500 and up per season ▶ *windsurfing instructors* at $1500 and up per season. Applicants must submit formal organization application, three personal references. An in-person interview is recommended, but a telephone interview is acceptable. International applicants accepted; must apply through a recognized agency.

Benefits and Preemployment Training Free housing, free meals, formal training, willing to provide letters of recommendation, on-the-job training, willing to complete paperwork for educational credit, willing to act as a professional reference, travel reimbursement, and laundry service. Preemployment training is required and includes accident prevention and safety, interpersonal skills, leadership skills, teamwork training.

Contact Roger Christian, Director, Camp Laurel South, PO Box 14130, Gainesville, Florida 32604. Telephone: 888-528-7357. Fax: 352-331-0014. E-mail: fun@camplaurelsouth.com. World Wide Web: http://www.camplaurelsouth.com. Contact by e-mail, fax, mail, phone, or through World Wide Web site. Application deadline: applications are accepted September 15 to June 15.

CAMP MATOAKA FOR GIRLS
1 GREAT PLACE
SMITHFIELD, MAINE 04978-1288

General Information Residential camp serving 275 girls with a variety of activities. Established in 1951. 150-acre facility located 9 miles from Waterville. Features: 1½ miles of shore frontage; large gymnasium; heated 25-meter swimming pool; 3 waterslides 200 feet each; professional waterski program; full bathrooms in cabins.

Profile of Summer Employees Total number: 150; typical ages: 20–24. 20% men; 80% women; 3% minorities; 10% high school students; 45% college students; 2% retirees; 30% non-U.S. citizens; 10% local applicants. Nonsmokers required.

Employment Information Openings are from June 1 to August 18. Jobs available: ▶ 3 *English equitation instructors* (minimum age 19) with high skill level and horsemanship certification at $1100–$2000 per season ▶ 6 *arts and crafts instructors* (minimum age 19) with a major in fine arts at $1000–$1200 per season ▶ 2 *dance instructors* (minimum age 19) with a major in dance/movement and aerobics instructor experience at $1100–$1200 per season ▶ 3 *drama/ music instructors* (minimum age 19) with a major in theater/drama at $1100–$1300 per season ▶ 3 *gymnastics instructors* (minimum age 19) with previous coaching/instructing and college team experience at $1200–$1400 per season ▶ 4 *land sports instructors* (minimum age 19) with a major in physical education or health/recreation at $1000–$1300 per season ▶ 5–10 *office administration workers* (minimum age 20) with organizational skills and computer skills at $2500–$3500 per season ▶ 2 *photographers* (minimum age 19) with major in photography at $1100–$1300 per season ▶ 1 *pianist/accompanist* (minimum age 19) with ability to sight read at $1100–$1600 per season ▶ 2 *ropes course instructors* (minimum age 23) with Project Adventure or Outward Bound certification at $1500–$2500 per season ▶ 2 *sewing instructors* (minimum age 19) with a major in home economics at $1200 per season ▶ 6 *ski instructors* (minimum age 19) with high skill level at $1100–$1500 per season ▶ 6 *small craft instructors* (minimum age 19) with Red Cross, CPR, and lifeguard certification at $1200–$1400 per season ▶ 6 *swimming instructors* (minimum age 19) with WSI certification at $1100–$1300 per season ▶ 6 *tennis instructors* (minimum age 19) with teaching and college team experience at $1000–$1400 per season ▶ 4 *trip instructors* (minimum age 21) with valid driver's license and experience in the field at $1200–$1400 per season ▶ 7 *video/radio personnel* (minimum age 19) with major in video/radio/communication at $1150–$1400 per season. Applicants must submit formal organization application, resume, two personal references, two letters of recommendation. An in-person interview is recommended, but a telephone interview is acceptable. International applicants accepted; must apply through a recognized agency.

Benefits and Preemployment Training Free housing, free meals, possible full-time employment, willing to provide letters of recommendation, willing to complete paperwork for educational credit, willing to act as a professional reference, and travel reimbursement. Preemployment training is required and includes accident prevention and safety, first aid, CPR, interpersonal skills, leadership skills.

Contact Abigail Tatel, Assistant Director, Camp Matoaka for Girls, 8751 Horseshoe Lane, Boca Raton, Florida 33496. Telephone: 800-MATOAKA. Fax: 561-488-6386. E-mail: abby@matoaka. com. World Wide Web: http://www.matoaka.com. Contact by e-mail, fax, mail, phone, or through World Wide Web site. Application deadline: continuous.

CAMP MICAH
11 MOOSE COVE LODGE ROAD
BRIDGTON, MAINE 04009

General Information A coed Jewish, overnight summer camp offering a full range of camp activities including team, individual, and waterfront sports, arts, multimedia, ropes, wilderness, hiking, and more. Established in 2001. 253-acre facility located 25 miles from Portland. Features: freshwater lake; wooded setting in mountains; 7 tennis courts, hockey court; 3 basketball courts; skate park; brand new facility in 2001.

Profile of Summer Employees Total number: 100; typical ages: 18–30. 50% men; 50% women; 1% minorities; 3% high school students; 70% college students; 4% non-U.S. citizens; 15% local applicants. Nonsmokers preferred.

Employment Information Openings are from June 18 to August 16. Jobs available: ▶ 10–70 *cabin counselors with particular specialties* (minimum age 18) with experience working with children and teaching an activity at a salary based on experience. Applicants must submit formal organization application, 2 to 3 personal references. An in-person interview is recommended, but a telephone interview is acceptable. International applicants accepted; must apply through a recognized agency.

Benefits and Preemployment Training Free housing, free meals, willing to provide letters of recommendation, on-the-job training, willing to complete paperwork for educational credit, and willing to act as a professional reference. Preemployment training is required and includes accident prevention and safety, interpersonal skills, leadership skills, one week of staff training prior to summer employment.

Contact Mark Lipof, Director, Camp Micah, 11 Hammond Pond Parkway #2, Chestnut Hill, Massachusetts 02467. Telephone: 617-244-6540. Fax: 617-277-7108. E-mail: markl@campmicah. com. World Wide Web: http://www.campmicah.com. Contact by e-mail, fax, mail, phone, or through World Wide Web site. Application deadline: continuous.

CAMP MODIN
MODIN WAY
BELGRADE, MAINE 04917

General Information Privately owned Jewish camp in New England serving 325 international campers. Established in 1922. 50-acre facility located 60 miles from Portland. Features: 13,000-square foot indoor recreation center; gymnastics and fitness center; climbing tower and zip line; state-of-the art waterfront; overnight camping trips; specialized program for teens.

Profile of Summer Employees Total number: 150; typical ages: 18–28. 50% men; 50% women; 100% college students; 30% non-U.S. citizens. Nonsmokers required.

Employment Information Openings are from June 20 to August 15. Jobs available: ▶ 3–4 *arts and crafts instructors* with teaching experience in numerous areas at $1500–$2500 per season ▶ 20–30 *athletics instructors* with experience in field at $1500–$2500 per season ▶ 2–3 *fitness instructors* with experience in field at $1500–$2500 per season ▶ 40–50 *general counselors* with experience at $1300–$2500 per season ▶ 2–3 *gymnastics instructors* with experience in field at $1500–$2500 per season ▶ 4–5 *music, theater, and dance instructors* with experience in the field at $1500–$2500 per season ▶ 2 *photography instructors* with experience in the field at $1500–$2500 per season ▶ 4 *registered nurses* with RN or LPN and experience in the field at $3000–$4000 per season ▶ 2–3 *riflery/archery instructors* with experience and/or certification at $1500 $2500 per season ▶ 8–10 *swimming instructors* with WSI certification (minimum) and experience in the field at $1300–$2500 per season ▶ 4–6 *tennis instructors* with coaching experience at $1500–$2500 per season ▶ 10–15 *tripping/ropes/outdoor pursuits instructors* with certification and/or experience at $1500–$2500 per season ▶ 10–12 *waterskiing/sailing instructors* with experience in the field at $1500–$2500 per season. Applicants must submit formal organization application, three letters of recommendation. A telephone interview is required. International applicants accepted; must apply through a recognized agency.

Benefits and Preemployment Training Free housing, free meals, formal training, willing to provide letters of recommendation, on-the-job training, willing to complete paperwork for educational credit, willing to act as a professional reference, and travel reimbursement. Preemployment training is required and includes accident prevention and safety, interpersonal skills, leadership skills.

Contact Howard Salzberg, Director, Camp Modin, 401 East 80th Street, Suite 28EF, New York, New York 10021. Telephone: 212-570-1600. Fax: 212-570-1677. E-mail: modin@modin.com. World Wide Web: http://www.modin.com. Contact by e-mail, fax, mail, phone, or through World Wide Web site. Application deadline: continuous.

CAMP PINECLIFFE
HARRISON, MAINE 04040

General Information Traditional residential camp offering instruction at all levels. Established in 1917. 75-acre facility located 40 miles from Portland.

Profile of Summer Employees Total number: 90. 25% men; 75% women; 10% minorities; 60% college students; 25% non-U.S. citizens; 15% local applicants. Nonsmokers preferred.

Employment Information Openings are from June 18 to August 21. Jobs available: ▶ 1 *archery instructor* at $1500–$2500 per season ▶ *boating/sailing instructors* with Red Cross lifesaving certification or equivalent at $1500–$2500 per season ▶ *ceramics instructors* at $1500–$2500 per season ▶ 1 *dance instructor* at $1500–$2500 per season ▶ 1 *drama instructor* with experience in the field at $1500–$2500 per season ▶ *highly skilled arts and crafts instructors* at $1500–$2500 per season ▶ 1 *highly skilled gymnastics instructor* at $1500–$2500 per season ▶ *highly skilled waterskiing instructors* with lifesaving certification at $1500–$2500 per season ▶ *land sports instructors* at $1500–$2500 per season ▶ 1 *music instructor* with ability to play piano by ear at $1500–$2500 per season ▶ 4 *nurses* with RN license at a negotiable salary ▶ *riding instructor* with Pony Club experience at $1500–$2500 per season ▶ 1 *silversmithing instructor* at $1500–$2500 per season ▶ *swimming instructors* with WSI/lifeguard certification at $1500–$2500 per season ▶ *tennis instructors* with high school or college team experience at $1500–$2500 per season ▶ *trip leaders* at $1500–$2500 per season. Applicants must submit formal organization application, resume, three personal references, three letters of recommendation. An in-person interview is recommended, but a telephone interview is acceptable. International applicants accepted; must apply through a recognized agency.

Benefits and Preemployment Training Free housing, free meals, formal training, willing to provide letters of recommendation, on-the-job training, willing to complete paperwork for educational credit, willing to act as a professional reference, and travel reimbursement. Preemployment training is required and includes accident prevention and safety, first aid, CPR, interpersonal skills, leadership skills.

Contact Susan R. Lifter, Director, Camp Pinecliffe, 277 South Cassingham Road, Columbus, Ohio 43209. Telephone: 614-236-5698. Fax: 614-235-2267. E-mail: pinecliff@msn.com. World Wide Web: http://www.pinecliffe.com. Contact by e-mail, fax, mail, phone, or through World Wide Web site. Application deadline: continuous.

CAMP PONDICHERRY
RR 2, BOX 588
BRIDGTON, MAINE 04009

General Information Residential camp serving 144 girls ages 7–17 per session; season includes three 2-week sessions and one week of pre-camp. Established in 1971. 700-acre facility located 45 miles from Portland. Features: freshwater lake; platform tents; wooded setting; view of White Mountains; food service; program center.

Profile of Summer Employees Total number: 40; typical ages: 18–42. 1% men; 99% women; 5% minorities; 1% high school students; 90% college students; 30% non-U.S. citizens; 50% local applicants. Nonsmokers preferred.

Employment Information Openings are from June 20 to August 16. Spring break, winter break, and year-round positions also offered. Jobs available: ▶ 1 *assistant camp director* (minimum age 21) with degree, administrative experience, and valid driver's license at $2800–$3000 per season ▶ 12 *assistant unit leaders* (minimum age 18) with experience working with children at $1785–$1850 per season ▶ 1 *business manager* (minimum age 21) with skills in money management and valid driver's license at $1800–$2000 per season ▶ 1 *camp steward* (minimum age 18) at $6–$8 per hour ▶ 1 *counselor-in-training director* (minimum age 21) with experience working with older girls at $2000–$2800 per season ▶ 1 *health supervisor* (minimum age 21) with RN, LPN, or EMT license at $2520–$3000 per season ▶ 3 *kitchen helpers* (minimum age 16) with a positive attitude and team-orientation at $1600–$1700 per season ▶ 1 *kitchen steward* (minimum age 21) with ability to supervise kitchen helpers and packout at $1800–$2100 per season ▶ 4 *program consultants* (minimum age 21) with experience in designated field (dance, arts and crafts, sports, games, and nature) at $1840–$2300 per season ▶ 6 *unit leaders* (minimum age 21) with leadership ability and experience working with children at $1850–$2200 per season ▶ 6 *waterfront assistants* (minimum age 18) with current lifeguard, first aid, and CPR certification at $1800–$2100 per season ▶ 1 *waterfront director* (minimum age 21) with certification in first aid, CPR, lifeguard training, and waterfront administration experience at $2420–$2900 per season. Applicants must submit formal organization application, three personal references. An in-person interview is recommended, but a telephone interview is acceptable. International applicants accepted; must apply through a recognized agency.

Benefits and Preemployment Training Free housing, free meals, formal training, health insurance, willing to provide letters of recommendation, on-the-job training, willing to complete paperwork for educational credit, willing to act as a professional reference, and opportunity to attend seminars/workshops. Preemployment training is required and includes accident prevention and safety, first aid, CPR, interpersonal skills, leadership skills, lifeguard instruction, small craft safety (if applicable).

Contact Daisy Wilson, Camp Director/Program Manager, Camp Pondicherry, PO Box 9421, South Portland, Maine 04116-9421. Telephone: 207-772-1177. Fax: 207-874-2646. E-mail: daisyw@kgsc.org. World Wide Web: http://www.kgsc.org. Contact by e-mail, fax, mail, or phone. Application deadline: continuous.

CAMP RUNOIA
POINT ROAD
BELGRADE LAKES, MAINE 04918

General Information Residential camp for girls ages 7–17. Traditional program offering waterfront, riding, outdoor living skills, and more. Established in 1907. 88-acre facility located 12 miles from Augusta. Features: location at the end of a rural road; 128-square mile freshwater lake; clear lake water; mixture of woods and fields; clay tennis courts; stables.

Profile of Summer Employees Total number: 43; typical ages: 20–28. 5% men; 95% women; 5% minorities; 65% college students; 5% retirees; 15% non-U.S. citizens; 25% local applicants. Nonsmokers required.

Employment Information Openings are from June 18 to August 18. Jobs available: ▶ 1 *canoeing instructor* (minimum age 19) with lifeguard (or equivalent), first aid, CPR, and/or small watercraft certification at $1400–$2300 per season ▶ 1 *photography instructor* (minimum age 19) with basic darkroom skills and composition theory at $1400–$2300 per season ▶ 2 *riding instructors* (minimum age 21) with CHA certification or BHS 1 and/or 2, or documented experience in teaching at $1800–$2300 per season ▶ 1 *ropes course instructor* (minimum age 19) with certification as a ropes course leader at $1600–$2300 per season ▶ 2 *sailing instructors* (minimum age 19) with lifeguard (or equivalent), first aid, CPR, and/or small watercraft certification at $1400–$2300 per season ▶ 2 *target sports (archery and riflery) instructors* (minimum age 19) with American Archery Association and National Riflery Association certification (or equivalent) at $1400–$2300 per season ▶ 1 *tennis instructor* (minimum age 19) with documented experience at $1400–$2300 per season ▶ 3–4 *trip leaders* (minimum age 21) with lifeguard training, prefer wilderness first aid at $1600–$2300 per season. Applicants must submit formal organization application, three personal references. An in-person interview is recommended, but a telephone interview is acceptable. International applicants accepted; must apply through a recognized agency.

Benefits and Preemployment Training Free housing, free meals, formal training, willing to provide letters of recommendation, names of contacts, on-the-job training, willing to complete paperwork for educational credit, willing to act as a professional reference, opportunity to attend seminars/workshops, and travel allowance. Preemployment training is required and includes accident prevention and safety, first aid, CPR, interpersonal skills, leadership skills.

Contact Pamela N. Cobb, Director, Camp Runoia, 56 Jackson Street, Cambridge, Massachusetts 02140. Telephone: 617-547-4676. Fax: 617-661-1964. E-mail: info@runoia.com. World Wide Web: http://www.runoia.com. Contact by e-mail, fax, mail, phone, or through World Wide Web site. Application deadline: continuous.

CAMP TAKAJO
NAPLES, MAINE 04055
General Information Residential boys camp offering an eight-week session to 395 campers ages 7-16. Established in 1947. 100-acre facility located 28 miles from Portland. Features: 11-mile freshwater lake; 17 tennis courts; indoor basketball gym; 50 cabins/bunks; 3 soccer/baseball fields; 4 basketball courts.

Profile of Summer Employees Total number: 180; typical ages: 19–30. 90% men; 10% women; 5% minorities; 1% high school students; 90% college students; 1% retirees; 25% non-U.S. citizens; 1% local applicants. Nonsmokers required.

Employment Information Openings are from June 18 to August 18. Jobs available: ▶ 2 *archery instructors* ▶ 6 *arts and crafts instructors* with appropriate schooling ▶ 6 *baseball instructors* with playing experience in high school or college ▶ 6 *basketball instructors* with playing experience in high school or college ▶ 6 *general counselors* ▶ 1 *journalism instructor* ▶ 2 *nature study instructors* ▶ 1 *photography instructor* ▶ 15 *pioneering/trip instructors* with Boy Scout, Eagle Scout, Outward Bound, or similar experience ▶ 2 *riflery instructors* ▶ 8 *sailing instructors* with Red Cross certification ▶ 6 *soccer instructors* with playing experience in high school or college ▶ 15 *swimming instructors* with WSI certification (training provided) at $800–$1500 per season ▶ 20 *tennis instructors* with playing experience in high school or college ▶ 4 *waterskiing instructors*. Applicants must submit formal organization application, letter of interest, three personal references, online application. An in-person interview is recommended, but a telephone interview is acceptable. International applicants accepted; must apply through a recognized agency.

Benefits and Preemployment Training Free housing, free meals, willing to provide letters of recommendation, on-the-job training, willing to complete paperwork for educational credit, willing to act as a professional reference, and travel reimbursement. Preemployment training is required and includes accident prevention and safety, interpersonal skills, leadership skills.

Contact Bob Lewis, Staffing Coordinator, Camp Takajo, 118 Julian Place, Suite 311, Syracuse, New York 13210. Telephone: 800-250-8252. Fax: 315-478-7687. Contact by fax, mail, or phone. Application deadline: continuous.

CAMP TAPAWINGO
166 TAPAWINGO ROAD
SWEDEN, MAINE 04040
General Information Residential private girls camp offering a 7½-week program to 170 campers with a focus on developing self-confidence and independence in a caring environment. Established in 1919. 200-acre facility located 50 miles from Portland. Features: private lake; foothills of the White Mountains; 8 tennis courts; sports fields and courts; bunks with running water and electricity; main lodge and dining room.

Profile of Summer Employees Total number: 70; typical ages: 19–30. 10% men; 90% women; 1% minorities; 80% college students; 8% non-U.S. citizens; 1% local applicants. Nonsmokers required.

Employment Information Openings are from June 15 to August 14. Jobs available: ▶ 2 *art instructors* at $1750–$1900 per season ▶ 2 *canoeing instructors* (minimum age 19) with lifeguard certification and instructor rating at $1750–$1900 per season ▶ 1 *ceramics instructor* with teaching experience (preferred) at $1750–$1900 per season ▶ 2 *dramatics instructors* (minimum age 19) at $1750–$1900 per season ▶ 2 *gymnastics instructors* (minimum age 19) with experience in the field at $1750–$2000 per season ▶ 5–8 *landsports instructors* (minimum age 19) with college-level experience and ability to teach one or more of the following: softball, lacrosse, field hockey, basketball, volleyball, soccer at $1750–$1900 per season ▶ 1 *photography instructor* (minimum age 19) with knowledge of black-and-white photography and developing at $1750–$1900 per season ▶ 1 *piano accompanist* with sight-reading and transposing ability at $1800 per season ▶ 2 *ropes instructors* (minimum age 19) with first aid, CPR, and instructor certification at $1750–$1900 per season ▶ 2 *sailboard/sailing instructors* (minimum age 19) with lifeguard certification and instructor rating at $1750–$1900 per season ▶ 1 *stained glass instructor* at $1750–$1900 per season ▶ 8 *swimming instructors* (minimum age 19) with WSI and lifeguard certification at $1750–$1900 per season ▶ 5 *tennis instructors* (minimum age 19) with college-level experience at $1750–$1900 per season ▶ 6 *trip leaders* (minimum age 21) with lifeguard certification at $1750–$1900 per season ▶ 1 *waterskiing instructor* (minimum age 19) with lifeguard certification and instructor rating at $1750–$1900 per season. Applicants must submit formal organization application, three personal references. A telephone interview is required. International applicants accepted; must apply through a recognized agency.

Benefits and Preemployment Training Free housing, free meals, willing to provide letters of recommendation, on-the-job training, willing to complete paperwork for educational credit, willing to act as a professional reference, and laundry service. Preemployment training is required and includes accident prevention and safety, CPR, interpersonal skills, leadership skills, child development.

Contact Ms. Jane Lichtman, Director, Camp Tapawingo, PO Box 248, Maplewood, New Jersey 07040. Telephone: 973-275-1139. Fax: 973-275-1182. E-mail: camptap@aol.com. World Wide Web: http://www.camptapawingo.com. Contact by e-mail, fax, mail, phone, or through World Wide Web site. Application deadline: continuous.

CAMP WAWENOCK
33 CAMP WAWENOCK ROAD
RAYMOND, MAINE 04071-6824

General Information Residential camp serving 110 campers ages 8–16, all of whom attend for the full 7-week season. Features traditional camp experience with emphasis on human relationships and personal development. Established in 1910. 100-acre facility located 26 miles from Portland. Features: natural sand beach; freshwater lake; cabins; stables and paddocks; 4 tennis courts; wooded setting.

Profile of Summer Employees Total number: 50; typical ages: 18–21. 5% men; 95% women; 3% minorities; 5% high school students; 95% college students; 1% retirees; 10% non-U.S. citizens; 3% local applicants. Nonsmokers required.

Employment Information Openings are from June 15 to August 15. Jobs available: ▶ 1 *riding instructor* (minimum age 19) with certification or documented experience at $1000–$1400 per season ▶ 1 *riflery instructor* (minimum age 19) with instructor certification at $1000–$1400 per season ▶ 2 *swimming instructors* (minimum age 19) with WSI certification at $900–$1300 per season. Applicants must submit formal organization application, resume, three personal references. An in-person interview is recommended, but a telephone interview is acceptable. International applicants accepted; must apply through a recognized agency.

Benefits and Preemployment Training Free housing, free meals, willing to provide letters of recommendation, on-the-job training, willing to complete paperwork for educational credit, willing to act as a professional reference, opportunity to attend seminars/workshops, travel reimbursement, and laundry service. Preemployment training is required and includes accident prevention and safety, first aid, CPR, interpersonal skills, leadership skills.

Contact June W. Gray, Director/Owner, Camp Wawenock, 33 Camp Wawenock Road, Raymond, Maine 04071-6824. Telephone: 207-655-4657. Contact by mail or phone. Application deadline: June 15.

CAMP WEKEELA
RFD 1, BOX 275, ROUTE 219
CANTON, MAINE 04221

General Information Residential traditional coeducational camp serving 290 campers with an emphasis on sports, water sports, and arts. Established in 1922. 150-acre facility located 20 miles from Lewiston. Features: freshwater lake; wooded setting; 10 tennis courts; multiple athletic fields; gymnasium; extensive waterfront.

Profile of Summer Employees Total number: 120; typical ages: 20–65. 50% men; 50% women; 84% college students; 1% retirees; 10% non-U.S. citizens; 5% local applicants. Nonsmokers required.

Employment Information Openings are from June 15 to August 22. Jobs available: ▶ *ceramics staff members* (minimum age 20) at $1200–$1600 per season ▶ *creative arts staff members* (minimum age 20) at $1200–$1600 per season ▶ 1 *department program head* (minimum age 24) with management skills as well as knowledge of program area at $2300–$3000 per season ▶ 3 *group leaders* (minimum age 23) with college degree; must oversee counselors and campers at $2000–$2500 per season ▶ *guitar instructors* (minimum age 20) at $1200–$1600 per season ▶ *gymnastics staff members* (minimum age 20) at $1200–$1600 per season ▶ *land sports staff members (tennis)* (minimum age 20) at $1200–$1600 per season ▶ *piano/music staff members* (minimum age 20) at $1200–$1600 per season ▶ *pioneering staff members* (minimum age 20) at $1200–$1600 per season ▶ *radio staff members* (minimum age 20) at $1200–$1500 per season ▶ *ropes instructors* (minimum age 20) at $1200–$1600 per season ▶ *tennis staff members* (minimum age 20) at $1200–$1600 per season ▶ *theatrical arts staff members* (minimum age 20) at $1200–$1500 per season ▶ *video/photo staff members* (minimum age 20) at $1200–$1500 per season ▶ *waterfront staff members* (minimum age 20) at $1200–$1600 per season ▶ *waterskiing staff members* (minimum age 20) at $1200–$1800 per season ▶ *woodworking staff members* (minimum age 20) at $1200–$1600 per season. Applicants must submit formal organization application, resume, portfolio, three personal references, three letters of recommendation. An in-person interview is recommended, but a telephone interview is acceptable. International applicants accepted; must apply through a recognized agency.

Benefits and Preemployment Training Free housing, free meals, formal training, on-the-job training, willing to complete paperwork for educational credit, and travel reimbursement. Preemployment training is required and includes accident prevention and safety, first aid, CPR, interpersonal skills, leadership skills.

Contact Eric Scoblionko, Director, Camp Wekeela, 2807C Delmar Drive, Columbus, Ohio 43209. Telephone: 614-253-3177. Fax: 614-253-3661. E-mail: wekeela1@aol.com. World Wide Web: http://www.campwekeela.com. Contact by e-mail, fax, mail, phone, or through World Wide Web site. Application deadline: continuous.

CAMP WINNEBAGO
17 ECHO LAKE ROAD
FAYETTE, MAINE 04349

General Information Residential camp serving 155 boys for four- and eight-week sessions. Established in 1919. 350-acre facility located 17 miles from Augusta. Features: 6 mile freshwater lake; wooded setting; 7 tennis courts; extensive waterfront program; campers from 7 countries and 20 states.

Profile of Summer Employees Total number: 75; typical ages: 19–60. 90% men; 10% women; 10% minorities; 60% college students; 15% non-U.S. citizens; 15% local applicants. Nonsmokers required.

Employment Information Openings are from June 17 to August 19. Jobs available: ▶ 2 *archery instructors* with certification in field experience instructing archery preferred at $1200–$2500 per season ▶ 2 *arts and crafts instructors* (minimum age 19) with experience in clay, woodwork, weaving, or other crafts; teaching experience preferred at $1200–$2500 per season ▶ 4 *athletics instructors* (minimum age 19) with coaching experience preferred, competitive experience acceptable at $1200–$2500 per season ▶ 3 *camping skills instructors* (minimum age 19) with outdoor camping skills at $1200–$2500 per season ▶ 1 *nature instructor* (minimum age 19) with ability to relate the natural environment to children at $1200–$2500 per season ▶ 1 *newspaper instructor* (minimum age 19) with college or high school newspaper experience preferred at $1200–$2500 per season ▶ 2 *photography instructors* (minimum age 19) with experience in photography or teaching at $1200–$2500 per season ▶ 1 *piano accompanist* (minimum age 19) with knowledge of show music at $1200–$2500 per season ▶ 2 *riflery instructors* with certification in field, experience instructing riflery preferred at $1200–$2500 per season ▶ 4 *swimming instructors* (minimum age 19) with WSI or lifeguard certification at $1200–$2500 per season ▶ 4 *tennis instructors* (minimum age 19) with coaching experience preferred, competitive playing experience acceptable at $1200–$2500 per season ▶ 2 *theater instructors* (minimum age 19) with theater experience, experience directing children preferred at $1200–$2500 per season ▶ 1 *videography instructor* (minimum age 19) with facility in use of video camera and ability to script shows at $1200–$2500 per season ▶ 2 *waterskiing instructors* (minimum age 19) with waterskiing and boat driving experience, teaching experience preferred at $1200–$2500 per season ▶ 1 *windsurfing instructor* (minimum age 19) with ability to windsurf and experience working with children preferred at $1200–$2500 per season. Applicants must submit formal organization application, two personal references, two letters of recommendation. An in-person interview is recommended, but a telephone interview is acceptable. International applicants accepted; must apply through a recognized agency.

Benefits and Preemployment Training Free housing, free meals, willing to provide letters of recommendation, willing to complete paperwork for educational credit, willing to act as a professional reference, travel reimbursement, and health insurance at cost. Preemployment training is required and includes accident prevention and safety, first aid, interpersonal skills, leadership skills.

Contact Andy Lilienthal, Director, Camp Winnebago, 3357 36th Avenue South, Minneapolis, Minnesota 55406. Telephone: 612-721-9500. Fax: 612-721-3144. E-mail: unkandycw@aol.com. World Wide Web: http://www.campwinnebago.com. Contact by e-mail, fax, mail, phone, or through World Wide Web site. Application deadline: continuous.

HIDDEN VALLEY CAMP
161 HIDDEN VALLEY CAMP ROAD
FREEDOM, MAINE 04941

General Information Residential, international, noncompetitive camp offering two 4-week sessions to 270 campers. Established in 1948. 350-acre facility located 80 miles from Portland. Features: spring-fed private lake; miles of wooded trails; modern, fully equipped art studios; adventure ropes course; heated pool.

Profile of Summer Employees Total number: 90; typical age: 23. 40% men; 60% women; 10% minorities; 5% high school students; 40% college students; 3% retirees; 20% non-U.S. citizens; 10% local applicants. Nonsmokers required.

Employment Information Openings are from June 1 to August 25. Jobs available: ▶ 10 *English riding instructors* with experience in the field at $1000–$1400 per season ▶ 4 *animal care personnel* with experience in the field at $1000–$1400 per season ▶ 5 *dance instructors* with experience in the field at $1000–$1400 per season ▶ 3 *guitar/music staff* at $1000–$1400 per season ▶ 2 *gymnastics instructors* at $1000–$1400 per season ▶ 2 *outdoor living staff* with experience in the field at $1000–$1500 per season ▶ 2 *outdoor travel leaders* with experience in the field at $1000–$1500 per season ▶ 2 *pottery instructors* at $1000–$1400 per season ▶ 6 *ropes instructors* with experience in the field at $1000–$1400 per season ▶ 2 *soccer instructors* at $1000–$1400 per season ▶ 3 *stained glass instructors* at $1000–$1400 per season ▶ 10 *swimming instructors* with WSI/lifeguard certification at $1000–$1400 per season. Applicants must submit formal organization application, letter of interest, resume, three personal references, letter of recommendation. An in-person interview is recommended, but a telephone interview is acceptable. International applicants accepted; must apply through a recognized agency.

Benefits and Preemployment Training Free housing, free meals, formal training, willing to provide letters of recommendation, on-the-job training, willing to complete paperwork for educational credit, and willing to act as a professional reference. Preemployment training is required and includes accident prevention and safety, interpersonal skills, leadership skills.

Contact Meg Kassen, Co-Director/Owner, Hidden Valley Camp. Telephone: 207-342-5177. Fax: 207-342-5685. E-mail: summer@hiddenvalleycamp.com. World Wide Web: http://www. hiddenvalleycamp.com. Contact by e-mail, fax, mail, phone, or through World Wide Web site. Application deadline: continuous.

IDLEASE AND SHORELANDS GUEST RESORT
PO BOX 3035
KENNEBUNK, MAINE 04043

General Information Resort serving visitors to scenic Kennebunkport. Established in 1967. 4-acre facility located 2 miles from Kennebunkport. Features: wooded country setting; close to sandy beach; near fishing river; family-oriented.

Profile of Summer Employees Total number: 8; typical ages: 20–25. 100% women; 30% high school students; 60% college students; 50% non-U.S. citizens; 50% local applicants. Nonsmokers required.

Employment Information Openings are from May 1 to October 31. Jobs available: ▶ 4 *housekeeping associates (females only)* with ability to stay from June to October (should be college or high school student or teacher) at $150–$200 per week. Applicants must submit letter of interest, resume. International applicants accepted; must obtain own visa, obtain own working papers, apply through a recognized agency.

Benefits and Preemployment Training Free housing, willing to provide letters of recommendation, on-the-job training, and willing to complete paperwork for educational credit.

Contact Sonja Haag-Ducharme, Owner, Idlease and Shorelands Guest Resort, PO Box 3035, Kennebunk, Maine 04043. E-mail: info@idlease.com. World Wide Web: http://www.idlease. com. Contact by e-mail or through World Wide Web site. No phone calls. Application deadline: April 15.

KAMP KOHUT
151 KOHUT ROAD
OXFORD, MAINE 04270

General Information Private, residential camp serving 175 boys and girls with traditional activities in 2 four-week sessions. Focuses on single-gender classes at one campus facility. Established in 1907. 115-acre facility located 38 miles from Portland. Features: large freshwater lake; beautiful wooded setting; top-notch facilities; excellent waterfront program; large adventure and tripping program; 1 hour from Maine coast and White Mountains.

Profile of Summer Employees Total number: 100; typical ages: 20–24. 50% men; 50% women; 1% minorities; 73% college students; 2% retirees; 25% non-U.S. citizens; 5% local applicants. Nonsmokers required.

Employment Information Openings are from June 10 to August 18. Jobs available: ▶ 90 *activity specialists* (minimum age 19) with enthusiasm, friendliness, energy, and reliability at $1500–$3000 per season. Applicants must submit formal organization application, three personal references. An in-person interview is recommended, but a telephone interview is acceptable. International applicants accepted; must apply through a recognized agency.

Benefits and Preemployment Training Free housing, free meals, formal training, health insurance, willing to provide letters of recommendation, on-the-job training, willing to complete paperwork for educational credit, willing to act as a professional reference, opportunity to attend seminars/workshops, and travel reimbursement. Preemployment training is required and includes accident prevention and safety, interpersonal skills, leadership skills.

Contact Lisa Tripler, Director, Kamp Kohut, Two Tall Pine Road, Cape Elizabeth, Maine 04107. Telephone: 207-767-2406. Fax: 207-767-0604. E-mail: kampkohut@aol.com. World Wide Web: http://www.kampkohut.com. Contact by e-mail, fax, mail, phone, or through World Wide Web site. Application deadline: continuous.

LONGACRE EXPEDITIONS, MAINE
UNITY, MAINE 04988

General Information Adventure travel program throughout Maine, New Hampshire, and into Canada, emphasizing group living skills, physical challenges, and fun. Longacre's challenging programs place equal emphasis on physical accomplishment and emotional growth. Established in 1981. Located 20 miles from Waterville.

Profile of Summer Employees Total number: 30; typical ages: 21–32. 50% men; 50% women; 10% minorities; 40% college students; 10% local applicants. Nonsmokers required.

Employment Information Openings are from June 15 to August 15. Jobs available: ▶ 20 *assistant trip leaders* (minimum age 21) with wilderness first aid, CPR, and good driving record at $150–$175 per week ▶ 1 *rock climbing instructor* (minimum age 21) with good driving record, wilderness first aid or WFR training, and CPR certification at $300–$450 per week ▶ 4 *support and logistics staff members* (minimum age 21) with good driving record and wilderness first aid and CPR certifications at $180–$240 per week. Applicants must submit a formal organization application, letter of interest, resume, three personal references. An in-person interview is recommended, but a telephone interview is acceptable. International applicants accepted; must obtain own visa, obtain own working papers.

Benefits and Preemployment Training Free housing, free meals, willing to provide letters of recommendation, on-the-job training, willing to complete paperwork for educational credit, willing to act as a professional reference, and pro-deal purchase program. Preemployment training is required and includes accident prevention and safety, interpersonal skills, leadership skills.

Contact Meredith Schuler, Director, Longacre Expeditions, Maine, 4030 Middle Ridge Road, Newport, Pennsylvania 17074-8110. Telephone: 717-567-6790. Fax: 717-567-3955. E-mail: merry@longacreexpeditions.com. World Wide Web: http://www.longacreexpeditions.com. Contact by e-mail, fax, mail, phone, or through World Wide Web site. Application deadline: continuous.

MAINE TEEN CAMP
481 BROWNFIELD ROAD
PORTER, MAINE 04068

General Information Residential coed camp for teenagers offering two sessions with 300 campers participating in each session. Established in 1985. 55-acre facility located 45 miles from Portland. Features: freshwater lake; wooded setting; 5 tennis courts; cabins; large main lodge; large ropes course.

Profile of Summer Employees Total number: 130; typical ages: 21–40. 47% men; 53% women; 10% minorities; 50% college students; 2% retirees; 30% non-U.S. citizens; 2% local applicants.

Employment Information Openings are from June 12 to August 16. Jobs available: ▶ 1 *ESL/ academics head coordinator* (minimum age 21) with teacher certification and an ESL course ▶ 1 *MIDI instructor* (minimum age 21) with experience and/or certification at $1300 per season ▶ 1–3 *arts instructors* (minimum age 21) with experience and/or certification at $1300 per season ▶ 2 *dance instructors* (minimum age 21) with experience and/or certification at $1300 per season ▶ 1 *drum instructor* (minimum age 21) with experience and/or certification at $1300 per season ▶ 1 *head of ropes* (minimum age 22) with relevant certifications at $1800–$2500 per season ▶ 1 *jewelry-crafting instructor* (minimum age 21) with experience and/or certification at $1300 per season ▶ 1 *keyboard instructor* (minimum age 21) with experience and/or certification at $1300 per season ▶ 1–5 *land sports instructors* (minimum age 21) with experience and/or certification and ability to teach one or more of the following: soccer, basketball, baseball, field hockey, lacrosse, golf, volleyball, or badminton at $1300 per season ▶ 2–3 *mountain biking instructors* (minimum age 21) with experience and/or certification at $1300 per season ▶ 2 *nurses* (minimum age 21) with RN or LPN preferred at $2000–$4000 per season ▶ 1 *photography head* (minimum age 21) with specific training and high level experience ▶ 4–10 *ropes instructors* (minimum age 21) with experience and/or certification at $1300 per season ▶ 2 *sailing/ windsurfing instructors* (minimum age 21) with experience and/or certification at $1300 per season ▶ 1 *stained glass instructor* (minimum age 21) with skill and experience ▶ 1 *voice instructor* (minimum age 21) with experience and/or certification at $1300 per season ▶ 2 *waterskiing instructors* (minimum age 21) with experience and/or certification at $1300 per season. Applicants must submit formal organization application, 2-3 personal references or letters of recommendation. A telephone interview is required. International applicants accepted; must apply through a recognized agency.

Benefits and Preemployment Training Free housing, free meals, formal training, willing to provide letters of recommendation, names of contacts, on-the-job training, and staff cabin facility, staff lounge, and email access. Preemployment training is required and includes accident prevention and safety, first aid, CPR, interpersonal skills, leadership skills, lifeguard training, ropes course training.

Contact Ms. Monique Rafuse, Assistant Director, Maine Teen Camp, 190 Upper Gulph Road, Radnor, Pennsylvania 19087. Telephone: 610-527-6759. Fax: 610-520-0182. E-mail: mtc@ teencamp.com. World Wide Web: http://www.teencamp.com. Contact by e-mail, fax, phone, or through World Wide Web site. Application deadline: continuous.

NEW ENGLAND CAMPING ADVENTURES
PANTHER POND, PO BOX 160
RAYMOND, MAINE 04071

General Information Coed wilderness rafting and sailing programs for 120 campers that include backpacking, white-water canoe trips, rock climbing, ocean kayaking, mountain biking, ocean sailing, and wilderness adventure trips. 140-acre facility located 25 miles from Portland. Features: 2½ miles of shoreline; freshwater lake; acres of pine woods; small camp with family atmosphere.

Profile of Summer Employees Total number: 40. 50% men; 50% women; 15% minorities; 5% high school students; 80% college students; 5% non-U.S. citizens; 20% local applicants. Nonsmokers preferred.

Employment Information Openings are from June 15 to August 11. Jobs available: ▶ 4 *backpacking leaders* at $1400–$1800 per season ▶ 15–20 *camp counselors (crafts, sports, waterfront)* (minimum age 18) at $1200–$1650 per season ▶ 5 *canoe trip leaders* at $1400– $1800 per season ▶ 2 *rock climbing leaders* at $1300–$1800 per season ▶ 6 *sailing instructors* (minimum age 18) with ability to sail a 14-foot boat with 2 sails (FJ's) at $1250–$1800 per season. Applicants must submit a formal organization application, resume. International applicants accepted.

Benefits and Preemployment Training Free housing, free meals, formal training, willing to provide letters of recommendation, on-the-job training, willing to complete paperwork for educational credit, willing to act as a professional reference, and travel reimbursement.

Contact Ronald Furst, Director, New England Camping Adventures, 10 Scotland Bridge Road, York, Maine 03909. Telephone: 207-363-1773. Fax: 207-363-1773. E-mail: camphaw@nh.ultranet. com. Contact by e-mail, fax, mail, or phone. Application deadline: May 10.

OAKLAND HOUSE SEASIDE RESORT
435 HERRICK ROAD
BROOKSVILLE, MAINE 04617

General Information Rural, low-key family vacation resort and adults-only inn accommodating a combined total of approximately 75 guests. Established in 1889. 50-acre facility located 50 miles from Bangor. Features: 1/2-mile of ocean front with beach; freshwater lake; rowboats; hiking trails; 1 hour from Acadia National Park; recreation hall.

Profile of Summer Employees Total number: 35; typical ages: 18–50. 48% men; 52% women; 5% minorities; 52% college students; 22% non-U.S. citizens; 35% local applicants. Nonsmokers preferred.

Employment Information Openings are from May 15 to October 31. Jobs available: ▶ 4 *culinary staff members* at $250–$340 per week ▶ 1 *gardener* at $250–$340 per week ▶ 1 *host/hostess* at $4000–$6000 per season ▶ 4 *housekeepers* at $200–$400 per week ▶ 3 *maintenance/cabin attendants/boat stewards* at $250–$340 per week ▶ 1 *office receptionist* at $250–$340 per week ▶ 1–2 *sous chefs* (minimum age 21) at a negotiable salary with benefits ▶ 6 *waiters/waitresses* (minimum age 18) at $250–$475 per week. Applicants must submit formal organization application, letter of interest, resume, three personal references. A telephone interview is required. International applicants accepted; must apply through a recognized agency.

Benefits and Preemployment Training Housing at a cost, meals at a cost, on-the-job training, willing to complete paperwork for educational credit, willing to act as a professional reference, and beautiful location, multi-talented and multi-national staff. Preemployment training is required and includes accident prevention and safety, first aid, interpersonal skills, leadership skills, hospitality training, maintenance, skill development, culinary internships.

Contact James Littlefield, Owner, Oakland House Seaside Resort, 435 Herrick Road, Brooksville, Maine 04617. Fax: 207-359-9865. E-mail: jim@oaklandhouse.com. World Wide Web: http://www. oaklandhouse.com. Contact by e-mail, fax, mail, or through World Wide Web site. No phone calls. Application deadline: continuous.

THE SOUTHWESTERN COMPANY, MAINE
See The Southwestern Company on page 297 for complete description.

STUDENT CONSERVATION ASSOCIATION (SCA), MAINE
See Student Conservation Association (SCA), New Hampshire on page 200 for complete description.

MARYLAND

BLACKWATER NATIONAL WILDLIFE REFUGE
2145 KEY WALLACE DRIVE
CAMBRIDGE, MARYLAND 21613
General Information Nonprofit government National Wildlife Refuge with visitor center and public use program. Established in 1933. 26,000-acre facility. Features: visitor center/exhibits; Wildlife Drive; 2 hiking trails; photoblind; 26,000 acres wildlife habitat; fresh water impoundment, Blackwater River.
Profile of Summer Employees Total number: 1–2; typical ages: 20–25. 50% men; 50% women; 100% college students. Nonsmokers preferred.
Employment Information Openings are from May 1 to September 30. Jobs available: ▶ 1–2 *interns-public use* with knowledge of wildlife (preferred), people skills, computer skills, and a valid driver's license. Applicants must submit resume, three personal references. An in-person interview is recommended, but a telephone interview is acceptable. International applicants accepted; must obtain own visa, obtain own working papers.
Benefits and Preemployment Training Free housing, willing to provide letters of recommendation, on-the-job training, willing to complete paperwork for educational credit, and willing to act as a professional reference.
Contact Maggie Briggs, Outdoor Recreation Planner, Blackwater National Wildlife Refuge. Telephone: 410-228-2677. Fax: 410-228-3261. E-mail: maggie_briggs@fws.gov. World Wide Web: http://www.blackwater.fws.gov/. Contact by e-mail, fax, mail, or phone. Application deadline: continuous.

CAMP AIRY FOR BOYS
14938 OLD CAMP AIRY ROAD
THURMONT, MARYLAND 21788
General Information Nonprofit residential camp serving 400 boys in each of four 2-week sessions or two 4-week sessions. Established in 1924. 450-acre facility located 50 miles from Washington, DC. Features: numerous ball fields; several craft facilities; outdoor living area with high and low element ropes courses; tennis courts and gym; theaters; comfortable bunk with counselor rooms.
Profile of Summer Employees Total number: 150; typical ages: 18–23. 95% men; 5% women; 5% minorities; 95% college students; 3% retirees; 20% non-U.S. citizens; 10% local applicants. Nonsmokers preferred.
Employment Information Openings are from June 15 to August 16. Jobs available: ▶ 2–4 *archery instructors (counselors)* (minimum age 18) with formal training and at least one year of college completed; NAA instructor certification preferred (we will locate classes and provide $400 bonus for successful completion) at $1,150 minimum per season with annual increments for returning staff ▶ 3–6 *arts and crafts instructors(counselors)* (minimum age 18) with formal training and at least one year of college completed; teaching experience preferred at $1,150 minimum per season with annual increments for returning staff ▶ 30 *athletics instructors (counselors)* (minimum age 18) with at least one year of college completed at $1,150 minimum per season with annual increments for returning staff ▶ 3–6 *ceramics instructors (counselors)* (minimum age 18) with formal training and at least one year of college completed; teaching experience preferred at $1,150 minimum per season with annual increments for returning staff

► 4 *drama instructors (counselors)* (minimum age 18) with at least one year of college completed at $1,150 minimum per season with annual increments for returning staff ► 1–2 *fencing instructors (counselors)* (minimum age 18) with formal training and at least one year of college completed; teaching experience preferred at $1,150 minimum per season with annual increments for returning staff ► 30 *general counselors* (minimum age 18) with at least one year of college completed at $1,150 minimum per season with annual increments for returning staff ► 5 *music instructors (counselors)* (minimum age 18) with one year of college completed and ability to teach one or more instruments (all types) at $1,150 minimum per season with annual increments for returning staff ► 2 *nature instructors (counselors)* (minimum age 18) with formal training and at least one year of college completed; teaching experience preferred at $1,150 minimum per season with annual increments for returning staff ► 12–15 *nurses* (minimum age 18) with RN (Maryland); flexible commitment of one to eight weeks at $250 per week or generous tuition discount for staff with children ► 10 *outdoor living instructors (counselors)* (minimum age 18) with one year of college completed and ability to teach rock climbing, rappelling, caving, survival training, and backpacking at $1,550 minimum per season with annual increments for returning staff ► 3–6 *photography instructors (counselors)* (minimum age 18) with formal training and at least one year of college completed; teaching experience preferred at $1,150 minimum per season with annual increments for returning staff ► 15 *swimming instructors (counselors)* (minimum age 18) with lifeguard training and one year of college completed; $400 bonus for WSI or LGI certification at $1,150 minimum per season with annual increments for returning staff. Applicants must submit formal organization application, two personal references, fingerprinting/background check to complete hiring process; international applicants apply through BUNAC. An in-person interview is recommended, but a telephone interview is acceptable. International applicants accepted; must apply through a recognized agency.

Benefits and Preemployment Training Free housing, free meals, formal training, willing to provide letters of recommendation, on-the-job training, willing to complete paperwork for educational credit, willing to act as a professional reference, travel reimbursement, and worker's compensation. Preemployment training is required and includes accident prevention and safety, first aid, CPR, interpersonal skills, leadership skills.

Contact Steve Goldklang, Assistant Director, Camp Airy for Boys, 5750 Park Heights Avenue, Baltimore, Maryland 21215. Telephone: 410-466-9010. Fax: 410-466-0560. E-mail: steve@ airylouise.org. World Wide Web: http://www.airylouise.org. Contact by e-mail, fax, mail, phone, or through World Wide Web site. Application deadline: applications before April 15 are preferred.

CAMP LOUISE
24959 PEN MAR ROAD
CASCADE, MARYLAND 21719

General Information Nonprofit residential camp serving 400 Jewish girls in each of four 2-week sessions or two 4-week sessions. Established in 1922. 400-acre facility located 50 miles from Washington, DC. Features: athletic fields; arts and crafts facilities; ropes course; tennis courts; theater/dance studio; comfortable bunk with counselor rooms.

Profile of Summer Employees Total number: 150; typical ages: 18–23. 2% men; 98% women; 5% minorities; 95% college students; 3% retirees; 20% non-U.S. citizens; 30% local applicants. Nonsmokers preferred.

Employment Information Openings are from June 15 to August 16. Jobs available: ► 2–4 *archery instructors* (minimum age 18) with formal training and at least one year of college completed; NAA instructor certification preferred (we will locate classes and provide $400 bonus for successful completion) at $1150 per season with annual increments for returning staff ► 3–6 *arts and crafts instructors (counselors)* (minimum age 18) with relevant experience and at least one year of college completed; teaching experience preferred at $1150 per season with annual increments for returning staff ► 30 *athletics instructors* (minimum age 18) with at least one year of college completed; relevant experience in team and individual sports at $1150 per season with annual increments for returning staff ▶ 3–6 *ceramics instructors (counselors)* (minimum age 18) with experience and at least one year of college completed; teaching experience preferred at $1150 per season with annual increments for returning staff ▶ 6–10 *dance instructors (counselors)* (minimum age 18) with formal training and at least one year of college completed; teaching experience preferred at $1150 per season with annual increments for returning staff ▶ 4 *drama instructors (counselors)* (minimum age 18) with at least one year of college completed and relevant experience at $1150 per season plus annual increments for returning staff ▶ 1–2 *fencing instructors (counselors)* (minimum age 18) with formal training and at least one year of college completed; teaching experience preferred at $1150 per season with annual increments for returning staff ▶ 2 *karate instructors (counselors)* (minimum age 18) with formal training and at least one year of college completed; teaching experience preferred at $1150 per season with annual increments for returning staff ▶ 5 *music instructors (counselors)* (minimum age 18) with one year of college completed and ability to teach one or more instruments (all types) at $1150 per season plus annual increments for returning staff ▶ 2 *nature instructors (counselors)* (minimum age 18) with relevant experience and at least one year of college completed; teaching experience preferred at $1150 per season with annual increments for returning staff ▶ 12–15 *nurses* (minimum age 18) with RN (Maryland); flexible commitment of one to eight weeks at $250 per week or generous tuition discount for staff with children ▶ 3–6 *photography instructors (counselors)* (minimum age 18) with relevant experience and at least one year of college; teaching experience preferred at $1150 per season with annual increments for returning staff ▶ 15 *swimming instructors (counselors)* (minimum age 18) with lifeguard training and one year of college completed; $400 bonus for WSI or LGI certification at $1150 per season with annual increments for returning staff. Applicants must submit formal organization application, two personal references, fingerprinting/background check to complete the hiring process; international applicants apply through BUNAC. An in-person interview is recommended, but a telephone interview is acceptable. International applicants accepted; must apply through a recognized agency.

Benefits and Preemployment Training Free housing, free meals, formal training, willing to provide letters of recommendation, on-the-job training, willing to complete paperwork for educational credit, willing to act as a professional reference, travel reimbursement, and worker's compensation. Preemployment training is required and includes accident prevention and safety, first aid, CPR, interpersonal skills, leadership skills.

Contact Roberta Miller, Associate Director, Camp Louise, 5750 Park Heights Avenue, Baltimore, Maryland 21215, United States. Telephone: 410-466-9010. Fax: 410-466-0560. E-mail: airlou@airylouise.org. World Wide Web: http://www.airylouise.org. Contact by e-mail, fax, mail, phone, or through World Wide Web site. Application deadline: before April 15 (preferred).

CAMP SONSHINE
16819 NEW HAMPSHIRE AVENUE
SILVER SPRING, MARYLAND 20905

General Information Nonprofit Christian day camp for kids 4-16 years old. Activities include go-karts, paddleboats, crafts, nature, drama, swimming, and much more. Established in 1981. 60-acre facility located 10 miles from Washington, DC. Features: pond; woods; go-karts; paddleboats; ropes/climbing wall; sports.

Profile of Summer Employees Total number: 250; typical ages: 18–34. 30% men; 70% women; 80% college students; 13% non-U.S. citizens; 7% local applicants. Nonsmokers required.

Employment Information Openings are from June 16 to August 16. Jobs available: ▶ 40 *activity counselors (lifeguards, archery, drama, crafts, and go-karts)* (minimum age 18) at $1200 per season ▶ 50–100 *group counselors* (minimum age 18) at $1240 per season. Applicants must submit formal organization application, three personal references. A telephone interview is required. International applicants accepted; must apply through a recognized agency.

Benefits and Preemployment Training Free housing, free meals, willing to provide letters of recommendation, willing to complete paperwork for educational credit, willing to act as a professional reference, and travel reimbursement. Preemployment training is required and includes accident prevention and safety, interpersonal skills, leadership skills.

Contact William Tibbetts, Director of Recruiting, Camp Sonshine. Telephone: 888-883-2285. Fax: 301-989-7116. E-mail: staff@campsonshine.org. World Wide Web: http://www.campsonshine. org/campstaff.html. Contact by e-mail, mail, phone, or through World Wide Web site. Application deadline: continuous.

CAPITAL CAMPS
133 ROLLINS ROAD, UNIT 4
ROCKVILLE, MARYLAND 20852

General Information Residential kosher Jewish camp serving young teens. Established in 1990. 230-acre facility located 65 miles from Washington, DC. Features: tennis courts; lake; 2 Olympic-size swimming pools; wooded environment; ropes course; numerous sports facilities.

Profile of Summer Employees Total number: 150; typical ages: 17–30. 50% men; 50% women; 2% minorities; 10% high school students; 75% college students; 20% non-U.S. citizens; 10% local applicants. Nonsmokers preferred.

Employment Information Openings are from June 15 to August 20. Jobs available: ▶ *arts and crafts director* with art teaching background at $1200–$1500 per season ▶ *counselors* (minimum age 18) at $1100–$1500 per season ▶ *drama specialist* with ability to direct and produce a play at $1200–$1500 per season ▶ *nature specialist* with ropes course certification and outdoor living skills at $1200–$1500 per season ▶ *swimming instructors* with lifeguard training and WSI certification at $1100–$1600 per season ▶ *video specialist* with ability to produce camp videos at $1200–$1500 per season ▶ *waterfront director* with WSI certification and lifeguard training; pool operator preferred at $2000–$3500 per season. Applicants must submit formal organization application, three personal references, three letters of recommendation. An in-person interview is recommended, but a telephone interview is acceptable. International applicants accepted; must apply through a recognized agency.

Benefits and Preemployment Training Free housing, free meals, formal training, willing to provide letters of recommendation, on-the-job training, willing to complete paperwork for educational credit, willing to act as a professional reference, opportunity to attend seminars/workshops, and travel reimbursement. Preemployment training is required and includes accident prevention and safety, CPR, interpersonal skills, leadership skills, child development.

Contact Joe Finkelstein, Associate Director, Capital Camps, 133 Rollins Avenue, Unit 4, Rockville, Maryland 20852. Telephone: 301-468-2267. Fax: 301-468-1719. E-mail: joe@capitalcamps.org. World Wide Web: http://www.capitalcamps.org. Contact by e-mail, mail, phone, or through World Wide Web site. Application deadline: continuous.

CENTER FOR TALENTED YOUTH/JOHNS HOPKINS UNIVERSITY
2701 NORTH CHARLES STREET
BALTIMORE, MARYLAND 21218

General Information Organization that provides academically talented pre-college students the opportunity to take rigorous courses in mathematics, science, computer science, humanities, and writing at college campuses in the United States. Established in 1980. Features: university dormitories; libraries; athletic facilities; playing fields; small, quiet campuses.

Profile of Summer Employees Total number: 150; typical ages: 18–50. 50% men; 50% women; 10% minorities; 60% college students; 2% non-U.S. citizens; 10% local applicants.

Employment Information Openings are from June to August. Jobs available: ▶ 8 *academic counselors* with graduate training in counseling with 2 years counseling experience, familiarity with Attention Deficit Disorder, and experience in a boarding school or residential camp environment at $5000–$5400 per season ▶ 8 *academic deans* with graduate training in an academic discipline and teaching experience at $4400–$5400 per season ▶ 8 *deans of residential life* with master's degree preferred, 2 years residential administrative experience in a school or college, and counseling experience at $4400–$5400 per season ▶ 36 *health assistants* (minimum age 21) with junior or senior status in college or medical student, interest in medicine and health issues, certification in CPR and first aid, and a valid driver's license at $2200 per season ▶ 100–120 *instructors* with BA or BS (master's degree preferred), experience with students in this age group, and leadership skills at $1800–$2700 per season ▶ 8 *office managers* with excellent office skills, bookkeeping experience, at least junior status in college, and 3.2 GPA or higher at $3400–$3600 per season ▶ 36 *office/general assistants* with office experience, at least one year of college, and 3.2 GPA at $2200 per season ▶ 400–450 *resident assistants* with experience as a college RA or as a camp counselor, GPA of 3.2 or higher, and experience in events planning at $2000 per season ▶ 8 *site directors* with master's degree preferred, teaching and administrative background, and leadership in an educational environment at $5400–$7400 per season ▶ 200–250 *teaching/laboratory assistants* with GPA of 3.2 or higher, strong interest in teaching, and experience with young people at $1800 per season. Applicants must submit formal organization application, letter of interest, resume, academic transcripts, letter of recommendation. A telephone interview is required. International applicants accepted; must obtain own working papers.

Benefits and Preemployment Training Free housing, free meals, willing to provide letters of recommendation, on-the-job training, willing to complete paperwork for educational credit, and willing to act as a professional reference. Preemployment training is required and includes accident prevention and safety, first aid, interpersonal skills, leadership skills, diversity training.

Contact Dawn Butler, Senior Coordinator for Academic Programs, Center for Talented Youth/Johns Hopkins University, 2701 North Charles Street, Baltimore, Maryland 21218. Telephone: 410-516-0053. Fax: 410-516-0093. E-mail: ctysummer@jhu.edu. World Wide Web: http://www.cty.jhu.edu/summer/employment. Contact by e-mail, fax, mail, phone, or through World Wide Web site. Application deadline: printed deadline is January 30 but it is flexible; applications are accepted through June 1.

CENTER FOR TALENTED YOUTH/JOHNS HOPKINS UNIVERSITY–GARRISON FOREST SCHOOL
OWINGS MILLS, MARYLAND

See Center for Talented Youth/Johns Hopkins University on page 131 for complete description.

CENTER FOR TALENTED YOUTH/JOHNS HOPKINS UNIVERSITY–MARINE SCIENCES PROGRAM
BALTIMORE, MARYLAND

See Center for Talented Youth/Johns Hopkins University on page 131 for complete description.

CENTER FOR TALENTED YOUTH/JOHNS HOPKINS UNIVERSITY–SANDY SPRING FRIENDS SCHOOL
SANDY SPRING, MARYLAND

See Center for Talented Youth/Johns Hopkins University on page 131 for complete description.

CENTER FOR TALENTED YOUTH/JOHNS HOPKINS UNIVERSITY–ST. MARY'S COLLEGE
ST. MARY'S CITY, MARYLAND
See Center for Talented Youth/Johns Hopkins University on page 131 for complete description.

CENTER FOR TALENTED YOUTH/JOHNS HOPKINS UNIVERSITY–WASHINGTON COLLEGE
CHESTERTOWN, MARYLAND
See Center for Talented Youth/Johns Hopkins University on page 131 for complete description.

CYBERCAMPS–JOHNS HOPKINS UNIVERSITY
BALTIMORE, MARYLAND
See Cybercamps–University of Washington on page 326 for complete description.

CYBERCAMPS–UNIVERSITY OF MARYLAND
COLLEGE PARK, MARYLAND
See Cybercamps–University of Washington on page 326 for complete description.

ECHO HILL CAMP
13655 BLOOMINGNECK ROAD
WORTON, MARYLAND 21678
General Information Coeducational residential camp serving 140 campers per session in two-, four-, and eight-week sessions along with one-week post-camp sail and ski and fishing and crabbing camps. Established in 1915. 350-acre facility located 90 miles from Washington, DC. Features: Chesapeake Bay location.

Profile of Summer Employees Total number: 50; typical ages: 18–24. 55% men; 45% women; 2% minorities; 10% high school students; 70% college students; 10% non-U.S. citizens; 2% local applicants.

Employment Information Openings are from June 10 to August 30. Jobs available: ▶ *general counselors* (minimum age 18). Applicants must submit formal organization application. An in-person interview is recommended, but a telephone interview is acceptable. International applicants accepted; must apply through a recognized agency.

Benefits and Preemployment Training Free housing, free meals, formal training, willing to provide letters of recommendation, on-the-job training, and willing to act as a professional reference. Preemployment training is required and includes accident prevention and safety, first aid, CPR, interpersonal skills, leadership skills.

Contact Peter Rice, Director, Echo Hill Camp, 13655 Bloomingneck Road, Worton, Maryland 21678. Telephone: 410-348-5303. Fax: 410-348-2010. E-mail: info@echohillcamp.com. World Wide Web: http://www.echohillcamp.com. Contact by e-mail, mail, or phone. Application deadline: continuous.

MANIDOKAN OUTDOOR MINISTRY CENTER
1600 HARPERS FERRY ROAD
KNOXVILLE, MARYLAND 21758
General Information Residential camp with a variety of accommodations and programs for all ages. Established in 1949. 426-acre facility located 70 miles from Washington, DC. Features: ropes and initiatives course; on the Potomac River; historic sites close by Harper's Ferry and Antietam Battlefield; 10 miles of hiking trails; climbing wall; canoeing, rafting, and kayaking.

Profile of Summer Employees Total number: 20; typical ages: 16–25. 50% men; 50% women; 7% minorities; 7% high school students; 73% college students; 20% retirees; 35% local applicants. Nonsmokers preferred.

Employment Information Openings are from June 1 to August 25. Year-round positions also offered. Jobs available: ▶ 4–6 *kitchen aides* at $190 per week ▶ 1 *maintenance person* at $6.50–$7.50 per hour ▶ 12 *program resource personnel* (minimum age 18) with lifeguard training (preferred), CPR, and first aid certification at $200–$250 per week. Applicants must submit formal organization application, three personal references, letter of recommendation. An in-person interview is required. International applicants accepted; must obtain own visa, obtain own working papers, apply through a recognized agency.

Benefits and Preemployment Training Free housing, free meals, willing to provide letters of recommendation, on-the-job training, and willing to complete paperwork for educational credit. Preemployment training is required and includes accident prevention and safety, interpersonal skills, leadership skills, ropes course, canoeing, rafting, kayaking.

Contact Rev. Bill Herche, Manager/Director, Manidokan Outdoor Ministry Center. Telephone: 301-834-7244. Fax: 301-834-8096. E-mail: manidokan@earthlink.net. World Wide Web: http://www.bwconf.org/camping. Contact by e-mail, fax, mail, or phone. Application deadline: most hiring complete by April 30.

THE SOUTHWESTERN COMPANY, MARYLAND
See The Southwestern Company on page 297 for complete description.

SPORTS INTERNATIONAL–CHARLES MANN FOOTBALL CAMP
WESTMINSTER, MARYLAND
See Sports International, Inc. below for complete description.

SPORTS INTERNATIONAL, INC.
12061 TECH ROAD
SILVER SPRING, MARYLAND 20904

General Information Privately owned company, organizing and running youth football camps hosted by professional football players. Established in 1983. Located 15 miles from Washington, DC. Features: easy access to public transportation; beltway accessible.

Profile of Summer Employees Total number: 15; typical ages: 30–50. 95% men; 5% women; 1% high school students; 9% college students; 90% local applicants. Nonsmokers preferred.

Employment Information Openings are from June to July. Jobs available: ▶ *various positions* (minimum age 18) paid at a stipend dependent on position. Applicants must submit a formal organization application, resume, personal reference. An in-person interview is recommended, but a telephone interview is acceptable.

Benefits and Preemployment Training Formal training, possible full-time employment, willing to provide letters of recommendation, on-the-job training, and willing to complete paperwork for educational credit.

Contact Brian Kenney, Camp Director, Sports International, Inc. Telephone: 301-625-7713. Fax: 301-625-7723. E-mail: briank@footballcamps.com. World Wide Web: http://www. footballcamps.com. Contact by e-mail, fax, mail, phone, or through World Wide Web site. Application deadline: applications accepted from January to March.

SPORTS INTERNATIONAL–JOE KRIVAK QUARTERBACK CAMP
WESTMINSTER, MARYLAND
See Sports International, Inc. above for complete description.

STUDENT CONSERVATION ASSOCIATION (SCA), MARYLAND

See Student Conservation Association (SCA), New Hampshire on page 200 for complete description.

WEST RIVER UNITED METHODIST CENTER
5100 CHALK POINT ROAD
CHURCHTON, MARYLAND 20733

General Information Residential camp on a mile-long waterfront near the Chesapeake Bay. Established in 1951. 45-acre facility located 15 miles from Annapolis. Features: diverse program; wooded setting; sailing and boating; lodges; one mile of waterfront; near Chesapeake Bay.

Profile of Summer Employees Total number: 25; typical ages: 17–24. 40% men; 60% women; 18% minorities; 12% high school students; 62% college students; 37% local applicants. Nonsmokers preferred.

Employment Information Openings are from June 1 to August 20. Jobs available: ▶ 2 *cooks* at $300–$400 per week ▶ 1 *head lifeguard* (minimum age 18) with WSI certification at $200–$250 per week ▶ 4 *kitchen aides* (minimum age 18) at $175–$200 per week ▶ 5 *lifeguards* (minimum age 18) with Red Cross lifeguard training at $200–$250 per week ▶ 2 *maintenance personnel* (minimum age 18) at $175–$200 per week ▶ 1 *nurse* (minimum age 20) with state RN license at $300–$400 per week ▶ 7 *program resource persons* (minimum age 18) with lifesaving training (preferred) at $200–$250 per week ▶ 1 *sailing instructor* (minimum age 18) with US Coast Guard or Red Cross sailing instructor certification or equivalent at $200–$250 per week. Applicants must submit formal organization application, letter of interest, resume, three personal references, criminal background check. An in-person interview is recommended, but a telephone interview is acceptable. International applicants accepted; must apply through a recognized agency.

Benefits and Preemployment Training Free housing, free meals, willing to provide letters of recommendation, on-the-job training, willing to complete paperwork for educational credit, and willing to act as a professional reference. Preemployment training is required and includes accident prevention and safety, first aid, CPR, interpersonal skills, leadership skills.

Contact Andrew Thornton, Manager, West River United Methodist Center, PO Box 429, Churchton, Maryland 20733. Telephone: 410-867-0991. Fax: 410-867-3741. E-mail: westriver. center@verizon.net. World Wide Web: http://www.bwconf.org/camping. Contact by e-mail, fax, mail, or phone. Application deadline: continuous.

MASSACHUSETTS

ASPEN OUTDOOR ADVENTURE PROGRAM
PO BOX 540484
WALTHAM, MASSACHUSETTS 02454

General Information Campus- and travel-based outdoor adventure program for boys and girls ages 10 to 13. Established in 1995. 35-acre facility located 10 miles from Boston. Features: high ropes; low ropes; swimming pool; day trips; overnight trips.

Profile of Summer Employees Total number: 6; typical ages: 18–25. 40% men; 60% women; 100% college students; 100% local applicants. Nonsmokers required.

Employment Information Openings are from June 20 to August 20. Jobs available: ▶ 2–6 *adventure counselors* (minimum age 18) with first aid/CPR certifications and wilderness/

camping experience at $400–$600 per week. Applicants must submit a formal organization application, resume, three personal references. An in-person interview is recommended, but a telephone interview is acceptable.

Benefits and Preemployment Training Willing to provide letters of recommendation, on-the-job training, willing to complete paperwork for educational credit, and willing to act as a professional reference. Preemployment training is required and includes accident prevention and safety, interpersonal skills, leadership skills.

Contact John Cloninger, Owner, Aspen Outdoor Adventure Program. E-mail: runningbrook@rcn. com. World Wide Web: http://www.aspencamp.com. Contact by e-mail, mail, or through World Wide Web site. No phone calls. Application deadline: continuous.

BELVOIR TERRACE
80 CLIFFWOOD STREET
LENOX, MASSACHUSETTS 01240

General Information Residential camp serving 180 girls with a focus on fine and performing arts. The program provides specific services for the academically talented and the gifted. Established in 1954. 48-acre facility located 4 miles from Pittsfield. Features: mansion; 2 pools; 6 tennis courts; 5 modern dorms; 5 theaters; 4 dance studios; 16 art studios.

Profile of Summer Employees Total number: 90; typical ages: 25–40. 10% men; 90% women; 5% minorities; 10% college students; 5% non-U.S. citizens. Nonsmokers required.

Employment Information Openings are from June 16 to August 24. Jobs available: ▶ *voice or piano teacher* (minimum age 21) with BM or MM at $1800–$2600 per season. Applicants must submit formal organization application, letter of interest, resume, portfolio, three personal references, letter of recommendation. An in-person interview is recommended, but a telephone interview is acceptable. International applicants accepted; must apply through a recognized agency.

Benefits and Preemployment Training Free housing, free meals, willing to provide letters of recommendation, on-the-job training, willing to complete paperwork for educational credit, willing to act as a professional reference, opportunity to attend seminars/workshops, and travel reimbursement. Preemployment training is required and includes accident prevention and safety, first aid, CPR, interpersonal skills, leadership skills.

Contact Ms. Nancy S. Goldberg, Director, Belvoir Terrace, 101 West 79th Street, New York, New York 10024. Fax: 212-579-7282. E-mail: info@belvoirterrace.com. World Wide Web: http://www.belvoirterrace.com. Contact by e-mail, mail, or through World Wide Web site. No phone calls. Application deadline: continuous.

BONNIE CASTLE RIDING CAMP
574 BERNARDSTON ROAD
GREENFIELD, MASSACHUSETTS 01301

General Information Residential camp for girls ages 9-16 with three 2-week sessions. Established in 1982. 100-acre facility located 50 miles from Hartford, Connecticut. Features: swimming pool; 5 tennis courts; boarding school facilities; gymnasium; dance studio; ceramics studio.

Profile of Summer Employees Total number: 18; typical ages: 18–30. 100% women; 10% minorities; 10% high school students; 90% college students; 60% local applicants. Nonsmokers preferred.

Employment Information Openings are from June 25 to August 19. Jobs available: ▶ 1 *arts and crafts instructor* (minimum age 20) with specific art media experience at $1100–$1800 per season ▶ 1 *camp nurse* with RN license and current CPR certification at $2700 per season ▶ 1 *dance instructor* (minimum age 20) at $1100–$1800 per season ▶ 1 *lifeguard* at $1500–$1800 per season ▶ 1–3 *riding instructors* (minimum age 20) with extensive Hunt Seat riding and showing experience at $1100–$1800 per season. Applicants must submit a formal organization application, letter of interest, resume, three personal references. An in-person interview is required. International applicants accepted.

Benefits and Preemployment Training Free housing, free meals, and willing to provide letters of recommendation. Preemployment training is required and includes accident prevention and safety, leadership skills.

Contact Karen E. Bertin, Associate Director of Summer Programs, Bonnie Castle Riding Camp, 574 Bernardston Road, Greenfield, Massachusetts 01301. Telephone: 413-774-2711 Ext. 306. Fax: 413-772-2602. E-mail: summer@sbschool.org. World Wide Web: http://www.sbschool.org. Contact by e-mail, fax, mail, or phone. Application deadline: May 15.

BREWSTER DAY CAMP
3570 MAIN STREET
BREWSTER, MASSACHUSETTS 02631

General Information Fully inclusive day camp whose mission is to challenge, nurture, and support children and their families on Cape Cod. Established in 1981. 5-acre facility located 90 miles from Boston. Features: olympic pool; wooded 4.5 acres; sailing ponds; pavilions; playgrounds.

Profile of Summer Employees Total number: 95; typical ages: 17–64. 50% men; 50% women; 10% high school students; 40% college students; 5% non-U.S. citizens; 25% local applicants. Nonsmokers required.

Employment Information Openings are from June 15 to August 20. Jobs available: ▶ 4 *water safety instructors* (minimum age 17) with Red Cross certification at $2900–$4000 per season. Applicants must submit a formal organization application, letter of interest, resume, three personal references. An in-person interview is recommended, but a telephone interview is acceptable.

Benefits and Preemployment Training Formal training, possible full-time employment, willing to provide letters of recommendation, on-the-job training, willing to complete paperwork for educational credit, willing to act as a professional reference, and opportunity to attend seminars/workshops. Preemployment training is required and includes accident prevention and safety, first aid, interpersonal skills, leadership skills.

Contact Milisa Galazzi, Director, Brewster Day Camp, 1406 Narragansett Boulevard, Cranston, Rhode Island 02905. Telephone: 888-396-CAMP. Fax: 401-461-4647. World Wide Web: http://www.brewsterdaycamp.com. Contact by fax, mail, phone, or through World Wide Web site. Application deadline: continuous.

CAMP GOOD NEWS
ROUTE 130
FORESTDALE, MASSACHUSETTS 02644

General Information Coeducational, residential, and day camp serving 220 children ages 6–16. Established in 1935. 214-acre facility located 10 miles from Hyannis. Features: freshwater lake with sandy beach; wooded setting; 6 miles from ocean; 3 tennis courts; tutoring center.

Profile of Summer Employees Total number: 80; typical ages: 18–45. 45% men; 55% women; 3% minorities; 1% high school students; 58% college students; 1% retirees; 2% non-U.S. citizens; 5% local applicants. Nonsmokers required.

Employment Information Openings are from June 19 to August 17. Jobs available: ▶ 2 *arts and crafts instructors* (minimum age 25) with experience in the field at $1200–$1400 per season ▶ 35 *counselors* (minimum age 18) should be college student at $1500–$1800 per season ▶ 10 *kitchen staff members* (minimum age 18) at $1200 per season ▶ 2 *nurses* (minimum age 25) with RN of LPN at $1500 per season ▶ 1 *sports expert* (minimum age 19) at $1200–$1500 per season ▶ 1 *store manager* (minimum age 18) with driver's license at $1000–$1200 per season

▶ 1 *waterfront director* (minimum age 21) at $1500–$1800 per season. Applicants must submit a formal organization application, three personal references, $100-$200 application fee applied toward total fee. An in-person interview is recommended, but a telephone interview is acceptable. International applicants accepted; must obtain own visa, obtain own working papers.

Benefits and Preemployment Training Free housing, free meals, on-the-job training, tuition assistance, and full campership in lieu of or with salary in some cases. Preemployment training is required and includes first aid, CPR, leadership skills, LGT, WSI.

Contact Faith Willard, Director, Camp Good News, PO Box 1295, Forestdale, Massachusetts 02644. Telephone: 508-477-9731. Fax: 508-477-8016. E-mail: office@campgoodnews.org. World Wide Web: http://www.campgoodnews.org. Contact by e-mail, fax, or mail. Application deadline: continuous.

CAMP NAWAKA
622 RESERVOIR ROAD
EAST OTIS, MASSACHUSETTS 01029

General Information Small, non-profit resident camp located in Berkshires of Western Massachusetts. Traditional summer camp with swimming, boating, arts, athletics, and outdoor activities. Established in 1967. 130-acre facility located 25 miles from Springfield. Features: 20-acre freshwater pond; 180 forested acres; 2 tennis courts; archery range.

Profile of Summer Employees Total number: 45; typical ages: 17–25. 40% men; 60% women; 10% minorities; 10% high school students; 80% college students; 5% retirees; 50% local applicants. Nonsmokers required.

Employment Information Openings are from June 23 to August 19. Jobs available: ▶ 1 *CIT/LT director* (minimum age 21) with experience in camp setting and working with teens at $2500–$3000 per season ▶ 1 *business manager* (minimum age 21) with basic experience with accounting at $2500–$3000 per season ▶ 1–3 *camp nurses* (minimum age 21) with RN license at $2500–$3000 per season ▶ 20–30 *counselors* (minimum age 18) with teaching skills in camp activities at $1600 per season ▶ 4 *department heads/area directors* (minimum age 21) with experience running camp activities at $2500–$3000 per season ▶ 1 *head cook/food service manager* (minimum age 21) with experience cooking, ordering, and menu planning at $4500–$5000 per season ▶ 1 *head counselor* (minimum age 21) with experience supervising in a camp setting at $2500–$3000 per season ▶ 1 *program director/assistant director* (minimum age 25) with experience planning and running programs at $3000–$3500 per season ▶ 1 *senior camp director* (minimum age 21) with experience working with teens at $2500–$3000 per season. Applicants must submit formal organization application, three writing samples, three personal references. An in-person interview is recommended, but a telephone interview is acceptable. International applicants accepted; must apply through a recognized agency.

Benefits and Preemployment Training Free housing, free meals, formal training, willing to provide letters of recommendation, on-the-job training, willing to complete paperwork for educational credit, willing to act as a professional reference, and opportunity to attend seminars/workshops. Preemployment training is required and includes accident prevention and safety, first aid, CPR, interpersonal skills, leadership skills.

Contact Christopher Egan, Camp Director, Camp Nawaka, 108 Union Wharf, Boston, Massachusetts 02109. Telephone: 617-523-6006 Ext. 41. Fax: 617-523-6290. E-mail: egan@nawaka.org. World Wide Web: http://www.nawaka.org. Contact by e-mail. Application deadline: continuous.

CAMP PEMBROKE OF THE ELI AND BESSIE COHEN FOUNDATION
LAKE OLDHAM
PEMBROKE, MASSACHUSETTS 02359

General Information Residential Jewish cultural and kosher camp serving 300 girls. Established in 1930. 68-acre facility located 23 miles from Boston. Features: lake and pool; 8 tennis courts; new arts and crafts building; newly renovated dining hall; new volleyball and basketball courts.

Profile of Summer Employees Total number: 100; typical ages: 16–50. 10% men; 90% women; 18% high school students; 80% college students; 5% non-U.S. citizens. Nonsmokers preferred.

Employment Information Openings are from June 20 to August 22. Jobs available: ► *archery instructors* at $1350–$2000 per season ► 1 *arts and crafts director* (minimum age 21) at $2000 and up per season ► *arts and crafts instructors* at $1350–$2000 per season ► 1 *athletics director* (minimum age 21) at $2000 and up per season ► *athletics instructors* at $1350–$2000 per season ► *canoeing instructors* with lifeguard certification and at least 1 year of college completed at $1350–$2000 per season ► 1 *drama director* (minimum age 21) at $2000 and up per season ► *drama instructors* at $1350–$2000 per season ► *horseback riding instructors* at $1350–$2000 per season ► *ice skating instructors* at $1350–$2000 per season ► 3 *nurses* (minimum age 21) with RN license at $5000 per season ► *sailing instructors* with lifeguard certification and at least 1 year of college completed at $1350–$2000 per season ► 1 *swimming director* (minimum age 21) with WSI and lifeguard certification at $2000 and up per season ► *swimming instructors* with lifeguard, WSI certification, and at least 1 year of college completed at $1350–$2000 per season ► 1 *tennis director* (minimum age 21) at $2000 and up per season ► *tennis instructors* at $1350–$2000 per season ► 1–2 *waterski boat drivers* (minimum age 21) with lifeguard certification and at least 1 year of college completed at $2000 and up per season ► 1 *waterskiing director* (minimum age 21) at $2000 and up per season ► 1 *windsurfing instructor* with LGT certification at $1350–$2000 per season. Applicants must submit formal organization application, three personal references. An in-person interview is recommended, but a telephone interview is acceptable. International applicants accepted; must obtain own visa, obtain own working papers, apply through a recognized agency.

Benefits and Preemployment Training Free housing, free meals, formal training, willing to provide letters of recommendation, on-the-job training, willing to complete paperwork for educational credit, and laundry service. Preemployment training is required and includes accident prevention and safety, first aid, CPR, interpersonal skills, leadership skills, aquatics school, archery certification.

Contact Pearl Lourie, Co-Director, Camp Pembroke of the Eli and Bessie Cohen Foundation, 42 McAdams Road, Framingham, Massachusetts 01701. Telephone: 800-375-8444. Fax: 508-881-1006. E-mail: director_pembroke@cohencamps.org. World Wide Web: http://www.cohencamps. org. Contact by e-mail, fax, mail, phone, or through World Wide Web site. Application deadline: continuous.

CAMP TACONIC
770 NEW WINDSOR ROAD
HINSDALE, MASSACHUSETTS 01235

General Information Residential 7-week coed camp for 280 children offering top instruction in a wide range of program areas. Established in 1932. 250-acre facility located 10 miles from Pittsfield. Features: beautiful Berkshire Mountains; 2 heated swimming pools; 10 tennis courts; golf driving range; freshwater lake; ball fields and courts.

Profile of Summer Employees Total number: 140; typical ages: 19–25. 50% men; 50% women; 85% college students. Nonsmokers required.

Employment Information Openings are from June 16 to August 16. Jobs available: ► 16 *aquatics staff members (swimming, sailing, waterskiing, windsurfing, and boating)* with WSI certification for swimming at $1400–$2000 per season ▶ 10 *arts and crafts staff members (fine arts, ceramics, crafts, and silver jewelry)* at $1400–$4000 per season ▶ 14 *athletics staff members (team and individual sports)* at $1400–$2000 per season ▶ 2 *cooking instructors* with ability to teach cooking to campers at $1400–$2000 per season ▶ 12 *general counselors for 7-10 year olds* (must be a college sophomore) at $1400–$2000 per season ▶ 6 *media arts staff members (newspaper, photography, and video)* at $1400–$2000 per season ▶ 5 *outdoor adventure staff members (pioneering, climbing wall, and ropes course)* at $1400–$2000 per season ▶ 12 *tennis staff members* at $1400–$2000 per season ▶ 12 *theater arts staff members (dance, costume making, musical theater, and stagecraft)* at $1400–$2000 per season. Applicants must submit a formal organization application, three personal references. A telephone interview is required. International applicants accepted.

Benefits and Preemployment Training Free housing, free meals, formal training, willing to provide letters of recommendation, on-the-job training, willing to complete paperwork for educational credit, willing to act as a professional reference, and travel reimbursement. Preemployment training is required and includes accident prevention and safety, first aid, CPR, interpersonal skills, leadership skills, low ropes/zipline, archery, lifeguard, WSI.

Contact Barbara Ezrol, Co-Director, Camp Taconic, 66 Chestnut Hill Lane, Briarcliff Manor, New York 10510. Telephone: 914-762-2820. Fax: 914-762-4437. E-mail: ctaconic@aol.com. World Wide Web: http://www.camptaconic.com. Contact by e-mail, fax, mail, phone, or through World Wide Web site. Application deadline: continuous.

CAMP WATITOH
CENTER LAKE
BECKET, MASSACHUSETTS 01223

General Information Residential summer camp serving 200 children with a wide variety of land and water sports activities, including drama, nature, and trips to all Berkshire area attractions. Established in 1937. 85-acre facility located 130 miles from Boston. Features: mountain-top setting; attractive lakefront; noted cultural arts region; cabins with bathrooms; wide variety of athletic facilities.

Profile of Summer Employees Total number: 75; typical ages: 19–28. 50% men; 50% women; 85% college students; 10% non-U.S. citizens. Nonsmokers preferred.

Employment Information Openings are from June 25 to August 21. Jobs available: ▶ 3 *arts and crafts instructors* (minimum age 20) with experience preferred at $1500–$2500 per season ▶ *general sports instructor* (minimum age 19) must be completing first year of college and have some experience with sports at $1300–$1800 per season ▶ 2 *sailing instructors* (minimum age 20) with experience in open water sailing, competitive experience is helpful at $1400–$1800 per season ▶ 6 *swimming instructors* (minimum age 20) with WSI or LGT certification at $1400–$1800 per season ▶ 2 *waterskiing instructors* (minimum age 21) with teaching experience and ability to slalom and trick ski at $1400–$1800 per season. Applicants must submit formal organization application, two letters of recommendation. International applicants accepted; must apply through a recognized agency.

Benefits and Preemployment Training Free housing, free meals, willing to provide letters of recommendation, on-the-job training, willing to complete paperwork for educational credit, willing to act as a professional reference, and travel reimbursement.

Contact William Hoch, Director, Camp Watitoh, 28 Sammis Lane, White Plains, New York 10605. Telephone: 914-428-1894. Fax: 914-428-1648. E-mail: watitoh@msn.com. World Wide Web: http://www.campwatitoh.com. Contact by mail, phone, or through World Wide Web site. Application deadline: continuous.

CAPE COD SEA CAMPS
PO BOX 1880
BREWSTER, MASSACHUSETTS 02631

General Information Residential camp serving 380 campers for 3½ or 7 weeks and a day camp serving 280 campers weekly. Established in 1922. 125-acre facility located 90 miles from Boston. Features: Cape Cod Bay; site on Cape's largest lake; 9 tennis courts; more than 50 sailboats; outdoor theater; photography lab.

Profile of Summer Employees Total number: 200; typical ages: 20–40. 50% men; 50% women; 5% minorities; 80% college students; 5% non-U.S. citizens; 10% local applicants. Nonsmokers preferred.

Employment Information Openings are from June 20 to August 17. Jobs available: ▶ 3–6 *activity department heads* (minimum age 21) with CPR, first aid, and teaching certification at $2500–$3500 per season ▶ 10–40 *general counselors* (minimum age 19) with documented experience in camp activities, CPR, and first aid certification at $1900–$2400 per season ▶ 2–5 *photography counselors* (minimum age 19) with CPR/first aid; should have taken photography courses and have experience developing pictures at $2100–$2500 per season ▶ 5–16 *sailing staff members* (minimum age 19) with instruction and racing experience, CPR, first aid, small boat sailing, and small craft safety certification at $2000–$2400 per season ▶ 4–10 *swimming instructors* (minimum age 19) with WSI and LG certification at $2000–$2400 per season ▶ 6–10 *tennis counselors* (minimum age 19) at $2000–$2500 per season ▶ 4–8 *windsurfing counselors* (minimum age 19) at $2000–$2500 per season. Applicants must submit formal organization application, either three personal references or three letters of recommendation. An in-person interview is recommended, but a telephone interview is acceptable. International applicants accepted; must apply through a recognized agency.

Benefits and Preemployment Training Free housing, free meals, willing to provide letters of recommendation, on-the-job training, willing to complete paperwork for educational credit, and willing to act as a professional reference. Preemployment training is required and includes accident prevention and safety, first aid, CPR, interpersonal skills, leadership skills, certification courses: small boat sailing, lifeguard training, small craft water safety, archery and riflery instructor training, kayak clinic.

Contact Sherry Mernick, Associate Director, Cape Cod Sea Camps, PO Box 1880, Brewster, Massachusetts 02631. Telephone: 508-896-3451. Fax: 508-896-8272. E-mail: sherry@ capecodseacamps.com. Contact by e-mail, fax, mail, or phone. Application deadline: continuous.

CENTER FOR TALENTED YOUTH/JOHNS HOPKINS UNIVERSITY–MOUNT HOLYOKE COLLEGE
SOUTH HADLEY, MASSACHUSETTS
See Center for Talented Youth/Johns Hopkins University on page 131 for complete description.

CLARA BARTON CAMP
30 ENNIS ROAD
NORTH OXFORD, MASSACHUSETTS 01537

General Information The Barton Center for Diabetes Education (Clara Barton Camp). Established in 1932. 208-acre facility located 50 miles from Boston. Features: modern log cabins; challenge course; pool and pond; tennis courts; hiking trails; conference center.

Profile of Summer Employees Total number: 75; typical ages: 17–25. 5% men; 95% women; 15% minorities; 15% high school students; 75% college students; 20% non-U.S. citizens; 20% local applicants. Nonsmokers preferred.

Employment Information Openings are from June 1 to August 31. Year-round positions also offered. Jobs available: ▶ 30 *cabin counselors* (minimum age 18) with leadership in program activities and enthusiasm at $1440–$2350 per season ▶ 10 *camp nurses* with Massachusetts RN license, national board certification, experience with diabetes, and CPR and first aid certificate at $2500–$5000 per season ▶ 1–5 *challenge course staff* (minimum age 18) with documented challenge course experience at $2000–$3000 per season ▶ 5 *kitchen staff* (minimum age 18) with kitchen experience at $2500–$6000 per season ▶ 5 *travelling day camp staff* (minimum age 18) at $1440–$2000 per season ▶ 2 *waterfront directors* (minimum age 18) with lifeguarding, WSI, CPR, and first aid training; waterfront experience at $2000–$2800 per season. Applicants must submit formal organization application, resume, criminal background check, activity reference forms, 3 personal references/letters of recommendation. An in-person interview is recommended, but a telephone interview is acceptable. International applicants accepted; must apply through a recognized agency.

Benefits and Preemployment Training Free housing, free meals, health insurance, willing to provide letters of recommendation, willing to complete paperwork for educational credit, and willing to act as a professional reference. Preemployment training is required and includes accident prevention and safety, first aid, CPR, interpersonal skills, leadership skills, lifeguarding, ropes course.

Contact Gaylen McCann, Resident Camps Director, Clara Barton Camp, 30 Ennis Road, PO Box 356, North Oxford, Massachusetts 01537. Telephone: 508-987-3856. Fax: 508-987-2002. E-mail: gaylen.mccann@bartoncenter.org. World Wide Web: http://www.bartoncenter.org. Contact by e-mail, fax, mail, phone, or through World Wide Web site. Application deadline: continuous.

COLLEGE GIFTED PROGRAMS
AMHERST COLLEGE
AMHERST, MASSACHUSETTS 01002-5000

General Information Residential educational academic summer camp for gifted and talented students in grades 4–11. Program blends in-depth academics with recreational and cultural activities. Established in 1984. 1,000-acre facility located 45 miles from Springfield. Features: dormitories; campus classroom facilities; campus recreational facilities include pool, tennis courts, and gym; campus library; beautiful campus setting.

Profile of Summer Employees Total number: 65; typical ages: 19–70. 50% men; 50% women; 30% minorities; 50% college students; 10% retirees; 10% non-U.S. citizens; 25% local applicants. Nonsmokers required.

Employment Information Openings are from July 25 to August 14. Jobs available: ▶ 30 *counselors* with two years of college completed and experience working with children at $1000 to $1300 per 3-week session ▶ 4 *directors* with at least 5 years teaching/supervisory experience; master's degree required, doctorate preferred at $4500–$7000 per year ▶ 8 *housemasters/ instructors (residential)* with master's degree, teaching, and supervisory experience at $2500 to $3500 per 3-week session ▶ 20 *instructors (non-residential)* with master's degree and teaching experience at $720 to $2900 per 3-week session ▶ 2 *nurses* with RN license, school experience preferred at $260–$300 per day. Applicants must submit formal organization application, resume, academic transcripts, two personal references, two letters of recommendation. An in-person interview is recommended, but a telephone interview is acceptable. International applicants accepted; must apply through a recognized agency.

Benefits and Preemployment Training Free housing, free meals, willing to provide letters of recommendation, willing to complete paperwork for educational credit, and willing to act as a professional reference. Preemployment training is required and includes accident prevention and safety, interpersonal skills, leadership skills, instructional strategies for gifted students.

Contact Charles Zeichner, Director, College Gifted Programs, 120 Littleton Road, Suite 201, Parsippany, New Jersey 07054-1803. Telephone: 973-334-6991. Fax: 973-334-9756. E-mail: info@cgp-sig.com. World Wide Web: http://www.cgp-sig.com. Contact by e-mail, fax, mail, phone, or through World Wide Web site. Application deadline: continuous.

COLLEGE LIGHT OPERA COMPANY
HIGHFIELD THEATRE, PO DRAWER 906
FALMOUTH, MASSACHUSETTS 02541

General Information Residential summer-stock music theater for training undergraduate and graduate students. Established in 1969. 6-acre facility located 70 miles from Boston. Features: wooded setting on salt water; 100 yards from salt water beach; Cape Cod resort area.

Profile of Summer Employees Total number: 80; typical ages: 17–23. 50% men; 50% women; 5% minorities; 2% high school students; 80% college students; 2% local applicants. Nonsmokers preferred.

Employment Information Openings are from June 5 to August 30. Jobs available: ▶ 1 *assistant business manager* with word processing skills, driver's license, and experience in the field at $2000 per season ▶ 2 *box office treasurers* with outgoing, friendly personality and driver's license at $2000 per season ▶ 1 *choreographer* with experience in the field at $2700 per season ▶ 2 *chorus masters* with piano experience at $2000 per season ▶ 1 *co-op work director* with driver's license and experience in the field of student co-op management at $3000–$4000 per season ▶ 1 *cook* with driver's license and experience in the field at $5000–$6000 per season ▶ 5 *costume crew* with experience in the field at $2000 per season ▶ 1 *costume designer* with driver's license and experience in the field at $4000 per season ▶ 18 *orchestra staff* with experience in the field at $1500 per season ▶ 2 *piano accompanists* with experience in the field at $2000 per season ▶ 1 *publicity director* with driver's license and car, word processing skills, and experience in the field at $2000 per season ▶ 1 *set designer/technical director* with driver's license and experience in the field at $4000 per season ▶ 6 *stage crew* with experience in the field at $2000 per season ▶ 32 *vocalists* with experience in the field; salary is room and board. Applicants must submit a formal organization application, resume, two letters of recommendation, mandatory audio tape or CD audition for vocal and orchestra candidates. International applicants accepted; must obtain own visa, obtain own working papers.

Benefits and Preemployment Training Free housing, free meals, willing to provide letters of recommendation, on-the-job training, willing to complete paperwork for educational credit, and willing to act as a professional reference.

Contact Ursula P. Haslun, Producer, College Light Opera Company, 162 South Cedar Street, Oberlin, Ohio 44074. Telephone: 440-774-8485. Fax: 440-775-8642. E-mail: ursula.haslun@oberlin.edu. World Wide Web: http://www.collegelightopera.com. Contact by e-mail, fax, mail, phone, or through World Wide Web site. Application deadline: rolling admissions begin March 15 and continue until all positions are filled.

CRANE LAKE CAMP
STATE LINE ROAD
WEST STOCKBRIDGE, MASSACHUSETTS 01266

General Information Reform Jewish coeducational camp serving children ages 6–15 with traditional sports and a full cultural program. Established in 1890. 120-acre facility located 15 miles from Pittsfield. Features: springfed lake; all water sports; all land sports; in the Berkshires.

Profile of Summer Employees Total number: 130; typical ages: 18–24. 50% men; 50% women; 75% college students; 5% retirees; 25% non-U.S. citizens; 5% local applicants. Nonsmokers preferred.

Employment Information Openings are from June 15 to August 28. Jobs available: ▶ 2–4 *arts and crafts instructors* at $1200–$2000 per season ▶ 10–15 *athletics counselors* (minimum age 18) with a major in physical education or varsity athletics experience at $1200–$2000 per season ▶ 1–2 *dance staff* (minimum age 18) with teaching experience at $1200–$2000 per season ▶ 4 *doctors* must be a physician ▶ 40–60 *general counselors* (minimum age 18) with high school diploma at $1200–$2500 per season ▶ 2–4 *guitar instructors* (minimum age 18) at $1200–$2000 per season ▶ 2–4 *gymnastics instructors* with experience in the field at $1200–$2000 per season ▶ 1–2 *nature instructors* (minimum age 18) at $1200–$2000 per season ▶ 3–4 *nurses* with Massachusetts RN license at $3000–$5000 per season ▶ 3–4 *painting/sketching/crafts/ pottery instructors* (minimum age 18) at $1200–$2000 per season ▶ 1 *piano player* (minimum age 18) with ability to play by ear at $1200–$2000 per season ▶ 2–3 *pioneering/hiking instructors* (minimum age 18) at $1200–$2000 per season ▶ 6–9 *tennis instructors* (minimum age 18) with teaching experience at $1200–$2500 per season ▶ 6–12 *waterfront instructors* (minimum age 18) with small crafts certification and waterskiing, sailing, or canoeing experience at $1200–$2000 per season. Applicants must submit formal organization application, three personal references. An in-person interview is recommended, but a telephone interview is acceptable. International applicants accepted; must apply through a recognized agency.

Benefits and Preemployment Training Free housing, free meals, formal training, health insurance, willing to provide letters of recommendation, on-the-job training, willing to complete paperwork for educational credit, willing to act as a professional reference, and travel reimbursement.

Contact Herb May, Site Director, Crane Lake Camp, 633 3rd Avenue, New York, New York 10017. Telephone: 212-650-4208. Fax: 212-650-4139. E-mail: iluvcamp@aol.com. World Wide Web: http://www.cranelakecamp.com. Contact by e-mail, fax, mail, phone, or through World Wide Web site. Application deadline: continuous.

CYBERCAMPS–AMHERST COLLEGE
AMHERST, MASSACHUSETTS
See Cybercamps–University of Washington on page 326 for complete description.

CYBERCAMPS–BABSON COLLEGE
BABSON PARK, MASSACHUSETTS
See Cybercamps–University of Washington on page 326 for complete description.

CYBERCAMPS–BENTLEY COLLEGE
WALTHAM, MASSACHUSETTS
See Cybercamps–University of Washington on page 326 for complete description.

CYBERCAMPS–MERRIMACK COLLEGE
NORTH ANDOVER, MASSACHUSETTS
See Cybercamps–University of Washington on page 326 for complete description.

CYBERCAMPS–MIT
CAMBRIDGE, MASSACHUSETTS
See Cybercamps–University of Washington on page 326 for complete description.

GOLD MEDAL BAKERY
21 PENN STREET
FALL RIVER, MASSACHUSETTS 02724
General Information Ultra modern, highly automated, family owned manufacturing facility that produces bakery products for supermarkets throughout New England. Established in 1912. Located 20 miles from Providence. Features: on waterfront property; outside picnic tables; well maintained facility.

Profile of Summer Employees Total number: 325; typical ages: 19–25. 90% college students; 10% local applicants.

Employment Information Openings are from April 1 to September 1. Jobs available: ▶ 5–10 *machine operators* (minimum age 18) at $12.20–$14 per hour ▶ 7–15 *shippers* (minimum age 18) at $12.20–$14 per hour. Applicants must submit a formal organization application, pre-

employment drug test. An in-person interview is recommended, but a telephone interview is acceptable. International applicants accepted; must obtain own visa, obtain own working papers.
Benefits and Preemployment Training Possible full-time employment, on-the-job training, willing to complete paperwork for educational credit, and end of summer bonus. Preemployment training is required and includes accident prevention and safety, sanitation, food safety practices, ergonomics, security and evacuation procedures, hearing protection.
Contact Debra Parent, Vice President, Human Resources, Gold Medal Bakery. Telephone: 800-642-7568 Ext. 310. Fax: 508-673-3041. E-mail: dparent@goldmedalbakery.com. World Wide Web: http://www.goldmedalbakery.com. Contact by e-mail, fax, mail, or phone. Application deadline: continuous.

HORIZONS FOR YOUTH
121 LAKEVIEW STREET
SHARON, MASSACHUSETTS 02067

General Information Residential environmental education center/summer camp that works with children from low-income families. Established in 1938. 161-acre facility located 25 miles from Boston. Features: lake; ecology center; wooded setting; hiking trails; pond; hills.
Profile of Summer Employees Total number: 70; typical ages: 18–28. 40% men; 60% women; 20% minorities; 85% college students; 1% retirees; 20% non-U.S. citizens; 20% local applicants. Nonsmokers required.
Employment Information Openings are from June 14 to August 23. Year-round positions also offered. Jobs available: ► 1 *CIT director* (minimum age 21) with significant experience in working with disadvantaged teens; first aid/CPR certification preferred at $2200 per season ► 4 *activity specialists* (minimum age 21) with experience with disadvantaged children and in activity area; supervisory experience and first aid/CPR certification preferred at $2300 per season ► 1 *assistant cook* (minimum age 21 preferred) with cooking experience (quantity cooking experience preferred) at $275 per week ► 1 *cook* (minimum age 21 preferred) with supervisory and cooking experience; quantity cooking experience preferred at $350 per week ► 36 *counselors* (minimum age 18) with experience working with disadvantaged children; first aid/CPR certification preferred, American Red Cross certification required for lifeguards at $1700 per season ► 4 *kitchen staff* (minimum age 20 preferred) with experience preferred in general kitchen skills; first aid/CPR certification preferred at $2700 per season ► 3 *maintenance staff members* (minimum age 20 preferred) with general skills including carpentry, painting, and landscaping; first aid/CPR certification preferred at $2700 per season ► 2 *nurses* (minimum age 21 preferred) with RN or LPN license or EMT, WFR, or WRA certification, current first aid/CPR certification, and relevant experience at a negotiable salary ► 4 *unit leaders* (minimum age 21) with supervisory and extensive experience with disadvantaged children; first aid/CPR certification preferred at $2300 per season ► 2 *waterfront directors* (minimum age 21) with American Red Cross CPR, LGT, WSI, and first aid certification, experience with disadvantaged children and supervisory experience at $2300 per season. Applicants must submit formal organization application, resume, two personal references, three letters of recommendation, criminal background check. An in-person interview is recommended, but a telephone interview is acceptable. International applicants accepted; must apply through a recognized agency.
Benefits and Preemployment Training Housing at a cost, meals at a cost, formal training, willing to provide letters of recommendation, on-the-job training, willing to complete paperwork for educational credit, willing to act as a professional reference, and opportunity to attend seminars/workshops. Preemployment training is required and includes accident prevention and safety, first aid, CPR, interpersonal skills, leadership skills, wilderness first aid, lifeguarding, preventing disease transmission, behavior management.
Contact Rebecca O. Lopez, Summer Program Director, Horizons for Youth, 121 Lakeview Street, Sharon, Massachusetts 02067. Telephone: 781-828-7550. Fax: 781-784-1287. E-mail:

camp@hfy.org. World Wide Web: http://www.hfy.org. Contact by e-mail, fax, mail, phone, or through World Wide Web site. Application deadline: continuous.

LIGHTHOUSE INN, INC.
1 LIGHTHOUSE INN ROAD, PO BOX 128
WEST DENNIS, MASSACHUSETTS 02670
General Information Seasonal, oceanfront resort specializing in banquets, weddings, and group conferences in May, June, September, and October. July and August cater to social guests vacationing. Established in 1938. 9-acre facility located 80 miles from Boston. Features: oceanfront; swimming pool; tennis court; restaurant; private beach; children's program.
Profile of Summer Employees Total number: 90; typical ages: 19–28. 50% men; 50% women; 1% high school students; 15% college students; 10% local applicants.
Employment Information Openings are from May 15 to October 20. Jobs available: ▶ 5–10 *dining room staff* (minimum age 18) at $2.63 per hour plus tips. Applicants must submit formal organization application, resume, three personal references, two letters of recommendation, photograph. An in-person interview is recommended, but a telephone interview is acceptable. International applicants accepted; must obtain own visa, obtain own working papers, apply through a recognized agency.
Benefits and Preemployment Training Housing at a cost, meals at a cost, willing to provide letters of recommendation, and willing to complete paperwork for educational credit.
Contact Bill Sherman, Food and Beverage Manager, Lighthouse Inn, Inc., 1 Lighthouse Inn Road, PO Box 128, West Dennis, Massachusetts 02670. Telephone: 508-398-2244. Fax: 508-398-5658. E-mail: shoe@lighthouseinn.com. World Wide Web: http://www.lighthouseinn.com. Contact by e-mail, fax, mail, phone, or through World Wide Web site. Application deadline: continuous.

MAZEMAKERS
31 CONCORD ROAD
WAYLAND, MASSACHUSETTS 01778
General Information Daytime summer program for young people entering grades three through eight; offering courses based in the arts, technology, and group problem solving. Established in 1976. Located 15 miles from Boston. Features: beautiful high school campus setting; auditorium; athletic fields; pond and creek; darkroom.
Profile of Summer Employees Total number: 28; typical ages: 16–33. 50% men; 50% women; 10% minorities; 25% high school students; 50% college students; 85% local applicants. Nonsmokers preferred.
Employment Information Openings are from June 21 to August 20. Jobs available: ▶ 15–20 *counselors* (minimum age 17) with ability to teach one or more courses at $300–$375 per week ▶ 1 *program administrator* (minimum age 19) with administrative, organizational, and interpersonal skills at $200 to $250 per week (15 to 20 hours per week). Applicants must submit a formal organization application, resume, portfolio, three personal references. An in-person interview is recommended, but a telephone interview is acceptable.
Benefits and Preemployment Training Meals at a cost, willing to provide letters of recommendation, on-the-job training, and willing to act as a professional reference. Preemployment training is required and includes accident prevention and safety, interpersonal skills, leadership skills, curriculum design.
Contact Matthew Boulton, Executive Director, Mazemakers. E-mail: mboulton@ants.edu. World Wide Web: http://www.mazemakers.com. Contact by e-mail or through World Wide Web site. No phone calls. Application deadline: continuous.

NORTH SHORE MUSIC THEATRE
62 DUNHAM ROAD, PO BOX 62
BEVERLY, MASSACHUSETTS 01915–0062

General Information Musical theater with a six-show season of Broadway musicals as well as children's shows, concerts, and special events. Professional theater dedicated to the American musical and programs for young audiences, serving more than 300,000 patrons from March through December. Established in 1955. Located 20 miles from Boston. Features: 1800-seat arena theatre; celebrity concert series; on-site shop facilities; half hour north of Boston; on-site rehearsal studios.

Profile of Summer Employees Total number: 133; typical ages: 18–25. 40% men; 60% women; 10% minorities; 70% college students; 20% local applicants.

Employment Information Openings are from February to December 23. Year-round positions also offered. Jobs available: ▶ 20 *technical theater interns* (minimum age 18) with college or summer stock experience in the field at $270 per week. Applicants must submit a letter of interest, resume. An in-person interview is required. International applicants accepted; must obtain own visa, obtain own working papers.

Benefits and Preemployment Training Housing at a cost, possible full-time employment, on-the-job training, willing to complete paperwork for educational credit, willing to act as a professional reference, and opportunity to attend seminars/workshops.

Contact Ali Sheehan Mignone, Associate Production Manager, North Shore Music Theatre, PO Box 62, Beverly, Massachusetts 01915–0062. Fax: 978-922-0768. E-mail: internship@nsmt.org. World Wide Web: http://www.nsmt.org. Contact by e-mail, fax, or mail. No phone calls. Application deadline: continuous.

OFFENSE-DEFENSE GOLF CAMP, MASSACHUSETTS
THE WINCHENDON SCHOOL AND GOLF FACILITY
WINCHENDON, MASSACHUSETTS 01475

General Information Residential and day camp teaching golf to boys and girls ages 10–18. Established in 1992. 1,000-acre facility located 28 miles from Boston. Features: prep school dorms and cafeteria; putting green; 18-hole regulation golf course; golf range; 4 tennis courts; outdoor swimming pool; gymnasium.

Profile of Summer Employees Total number: 40; typical ages: 19–50. 80% men; 20% women; 10% minorities; 80% college students. Nonsmokers preferred.

Employment Information Openings are from July 1 to July 30. Jobs available: ▶ 1 *bus driver* (minimum age 21) with license to drive yellow school bus and CDL at $300–$350 per week ▶ 10 *general (non-golf) counselors* (minimum age 19) with interest in working with children at $275–$300 per week ▶ 10 *golf instructors* with college varsity, college coaching, PGA Pro (very low handicap players) status, or USGTF certification at $250–$350 per week ▶ *swimming counselors* (minimum age 19) with WSI certification at $300–$350 per week. A telephone interview is required. International applicants accepted; must obtain own visa.

Benefits and Preemployment Training Free housing, free meals, formal training, on-the-job training, and willing to complete paperwork for educational credit. Preemployment training is required and includes accident prevention and safety, first aid, CPR, interpersonal skills, leadership skills.

Contact Mr. Mike Meshken, President, Offense-Defense Golf Camp, Massachusetts, PO Box 6, Easton, Connecticut 06612. Telephone: 800-824-7336. Fax: 203-255-5666. World Wide Web: http://www.offensedefensegolf.com. Contact by phone. Application deadline: May 30.

SIX FLAGS NEW ENGLAND
PO BOX 307
AGAWAM, MASSACHUSETTS 01001

General Information Theme park featuring more than 100 rides, shows, major concerts, games, and restaurants. Established in 2000. 150-acre facility located 7 miles from Springfield. Features: Hurricane Harbor; Superman, Scream, and Batman rides; sky coaster; Batman show.

Profile of Summer Employees Total number: 1,500–2,000; typical ages: 16–30. 55% men; 45% women; 25% minorities; 25% high school students; 45% college students; 30% retirees; 10% non-U.S. citizens; 50% local applicants.

Employment Information Openings are from April 20 to November 2. Jobs available: ▶ 30–50 *cash control staff members* (minimum age 18) at $7–$9 per hour ▶ 5 *first aid staff members* (minimum age 18) with Massachusetts EMT certification at $8–$15 per hour ▶ 200–300 *food service attendants* (minimum age 16) at $6.85 per hour ▶ 100–200 *games attendants* (minimum age 16) at $6.85 per hour ▶ 80–125 *lifeguards* (minimum age 16) with Ellis certification (training available), experience preferred at $8–$10 per hour ▶ 60–100 *merchandise sales team members* (minimum age 16) at $6.85–$7.50 per hour ▶ 350 *ride operators* (minimum age 16) at $6.85 per hour ▶ 50–125 *security team members* (minimum age 16) at $6.85 per hour ▶ 40–60 *waterpark attendants* (minimum age 16) will receive CPR/first aid training when hired at $6.85 per hour. Applicants must submit formal organization application, three personal references. An in-person interview is required. International applicants accepted; must apply through a recognized agency.

Benefits and Preemployment Training Meals at a cost, health insurance, and on-the-job training. Preemployment training is required and includes accident prevention and safety, customer service. **Contact** Renee Detura, Recruiting and Staffing Supervisor, Six Flags New England, PO Box 307, Agawam, Massachusetts 01001. Telephone: 413-789-9998. Fax: 413-821-0038. E-mail: sfnehr@sftp.com. World Wide Web: http://www.sixflags.com. Contact by e-mail, fax, mail, or phone. Application deadline: continuous.

SOUTH SHORE YMCA CAMPS
75 STOWE ROAD
SANDWICH, MASSACHUSETTS 02563

General Information Brother/sister residential camps on Cape Cod. Nonprofit, YMCA traditional camps. Established in 1928. 400-acre facility located 65 miles from Boston. Features: freshwater lake; wooded setting; high/low ropes; horseback riding; tennis courts; basketball courts.

Profile of Summer Employees Total number: 165; typical ages: 18–28. 40% men; 60% women; 2% minorities; 10% high school students; 90% college students; 40% non-U.S. citizens; 5% local applicants.

Employment Information Openings are from June 20 to August 23. Jobs available: ▶ 76 *cabin counselors* (minimum age 18) at $160 per week ▶ 2 *cooks* (minimum age 21) at $300–$400 per week ▶ 3 *nurses* (minimum age 21) with RN and experience in the field at $400 per week ▶ 3 *office staff* (minimum age 18) with office experience at $175 per week ▶ 14 *specialists* (minimum age 21) with any appropriate specialized skills such as WSI, CPR, first aid certification, or ropes course certification at $175 per week ▶ 16 *support staff (in kitchen, maintenance, and bathroom)* (minimum age 18) at $160 per week ▶ 8 *unit leaders* (minimum age 21) with leadership qualities at $175 per week ▶ 2 *van drivers/security staff* (minimum age 21) with driver's license for at least two years, first aid and CPR certification, and clean driving record at $175 per week. Applicants must submit formal organization application, three personal references. An in-person interview is recommended, but a telephone interview is acceptable. International applicants accepted; must apply through a recognized agency.

Benefits and Preemployment Training Free housing, free meals, formal training, willing to provide letters of recommendation, on-the-job training, willing to complete paperwork for

educational credit, and willing to act as a professional reference. Preemployment training is required and includes accident prevention and safety, first aid, interpersonal skills, leadership skills.

Contact Casey Tucci, Camp Director, South Shore YMCA Camps, 75 Stowe Road, Sandwich, Massachusetts 02563. Telephone: 508-428-2571. Fax: 508-420-3545. E-mail: camp@ssymca. org. World Wide Web: http://www.ssymca.org. Contact by e-mail, fax, mail, phone, or through World Wide Web site. Application deadline: continuous.

THE SOUTHWESTERN COMPANY, MASSACHUSETTS
See The Southwestern Company on page 297 for complete description.

STUDENT CONSERVATION ASSOCIATION (SCA), MASSACHUSETTS
See Student Conservation Association (SCA), New Hampshire on page 200 for complete description.

STUDENT HOSTELING PROGRAM
1356 ASHFIELD ROAD, PO BOX 419
CONWAY, MASSACHUSETTS 01341

General Information Organization offering 1-8 week teenage bicycle touring trips through the countrysides and cultural centers of the US, Canada, and Europe. Established in 1970. 60-acre facility located 25 miles from Northampton. Features: rural; wooded setting; camping; wildlife; very scenic.

Profile of Summer Employees Total number: 55; typical ages: 19–30. 50% men; 50% women; 100% college students. Nonsmokers preferred.

Employment Information Openings are from June 25 to August 25. Jobs available: ▶ 1 *assistant director* (minimum age 25) at $4000–$5000 per season ▶ 25–30 *assistant leaders* (minimum age 18) at $840–$2010 per season ▶ 25–30 *senior leaders* (minimum age 21) at $1120–$2680 per season. Applicants must submit a formal organization application, letter of interest, three personal references, three letters of recommendation. An in-person interview is required. International applicants accepted; must obtain own visa.

Benefits and Preemployment Training Free housing, free meals, formal training, willing to provide letters of recommendation, on-the-job training, willing to act as a professional reference, and travel reimbursement. Preemployment training is required and includes accident prevention and safety, leadership skills.

Contact Ted Lefkowitz, Director, Student Hosteling Program. Telephone: 800-343-6132. Fax: 413-369-4257. E-mail: shpbike@aol.com. World Wide Web: http://www.bicycletrips.com. Contact by e-mail, fax, mail, phone, or through World Wide Web site. Application deadline: May 12.

SUPERCAMP–HAMPSHIRE COLLEGE
HAMPSHIRE COLLEGE
AMHERST, MASSACHUSETTS

General Information Residential program for teens designed to build self-confidence and lifelong learning skills through accelerated learning techniques. Established in 1981. near Hartford, Connecticut. Features: university dormitories; outdoor ropes course.

Profile of Summer Employees Total number: 27–30; typical ages: 18–25. 40% men; 60% women; 80% college students; 10% non-U.S. citizens. Nonsmokers preferred.

Employment Information Openings are from July 9 to August 4. Winter break positions also offered. Jobs available: ▶ 10 *counselors* with college degree and PPS credential, MFCC license, or master's degree in counseling at $900 to $1500 per 10 day session ▶ 4–10 *facilitators* with presentation skills and college degree; teaching credentials preferred at $1300 to $2350 per 10 day session ▶ 1 *logistics manager* with excellent organizational skills and a high school diploma at $600 to $1100 per 10 day session ▶ 1 *nurse* with national or state registration at $600 to $1300 per 10 day session ▶ 1 *office manager* with high school diploma and prior office experience at $450 to $700 per 10 day session ▶ 1 *paramedic* with national or state registration at $600 to $1300 per 10 day session ▶ 1 *products coordinator* with high school diploma at a salary paid per 10 day session ▶ 20–25 *team leaders* with high school diploma and prior experience with teens at $350 to $600 per 10 day session. Applicants must submit a formal organization application, resume, three letters of recommendation, in-person interview recommended (videotape interview acceptable). International applicants accepted; must obtain own visa, obtain own working papers.

Benefits and Preemployment Training Free housing, free meals, willing to provide letters of recommendation, on-the-job training, willing to complete paperwork for educational credit, and willing to act as a professional reference. Preemployment training is required and includes interpersonal skills, leadership skills.

Contact Jen Myers, Staffing, SuperCamp–Hampshire College, 1725 South Coast Highway, Oceanside, California 92054. Telephone: 760-722-0072 Ext. 109. Fax: 760-722-3507. E-mail: staffing@learningforum.com. World Wide Web: http://www.supercamp.com. Contact by e-mail, fax, mail, phone, or through World Wide Web site. Application deadline: continuous.

WILDERNESS EXPERIENCES UNLIMITED, INC.
499 LOOMIS STREET
WESTFIELD, MASSACHUSETTS 01085

General Information Residential program which ranges from five days to two weeks. It serves approximately 30–40 campers ages 8–17 per week, and it offers general outdoor activities through high adventure. Established in 1981. 125-acre facility located 25 miles from Springfield. Features: wooded setting; ropes course; lake; lodges/cabins.

Profile of Summer Employees Total number: 18; typical ages: 16–28. 60% men; 40% women; 50% high school students; 50% college students. Nonsmokers required.

Employment Information Openings are from July 1 to September 31. Jobs available: ▶ 1 *aquatic director* (minimum age 20) with WSI, first aid, LGT certification, canoeing experience, lifeguard instructor (helpful), and extensive experience in kayaking at $200–$325 per week ▶ 2–3 *senior counselors* (minimum age 18) with first aid/CPR certification and LGT; should be outdoor-loving and fun at $150–$300 per week ▶ 2–3 *trip leaders* (minimum age 18) with outdoor and leadership skills, climbing and mountain biking experience, first aid/CPR, kayak instructors certification, and LGT at $150–$300 per week. Applicants must submit a formal organization application, letter of interest, resume, three personal references, photo of applicant on a trip/adventure. International applicants accepted; must obtain own visa.

Benefits and Preemployment Training Free housing, free meals, possible full-time employment, willing to provide letters of recommendation, on-the-job training, willing to complete paperwork for educational credit, willing to act as a professional reference, and opportunity to attend seminars/workshops.

Contact T. Scott Cook, Executive Director, Wilderness Experiences Unlimited, Inc., 499 Loomis Street, Westfield, Massachusetts 01085. Telephone: 413-562-7431. Fax: 413-569-6445. E-mail: adventures@weu.com. World Wide Web: http://www.weu.com. Contact by e-mail, mail, phone, or through World Wide Web site. Application deadline: May 15.

WILLIAMSTOWN THEATER FESTIVAL
PO BOX 517
WILLIAMSTOWN, MASSACHUSETTS 01267

General Information Summer theater festival presenting productions of revivals of classics and new works by new and established playwrights. Established in 1953. Located 40 miles from

Albany, New York. Features: Williams College campus; culturally rich area; idyllic New England town; 3 hours to New York City and Boston; fully equipped theater facility; beautiful Berkshires.
Profile of Summer Employees Total number: 70; typical ages: 17–35. 50% men; 50% women; 10% minorities; 1% high school students; 50% college students; 1% retirees; 1% non-U.S. citizens; 5% local applicants.
Employment Information Openings are from June 1 to September 1. Year-round positions also offered. Jobs available: ▶ 70 *acting apprentices* (minimum age 17) who pay fee for room, board, and tuition ▶ 50–70 *administrative and technical interns* with some experience in chosen field ▶ 100 *equity actors* at salary as per AEA contract ▶ 20 *non-equity actors* with advanced educational and/or professional acting experience (no salary) ▶ 60–70 *staff members* with advanced educational and/or professional experience at $50–$400 per week. Applicants must submit 2-3 personal references or 2-3 letters of recommendation, $30 processing fee (for apprentice applicants only). International applicants accepted; must obtain own visa, obtain own working papers.
Benefits and Preemployment Training Meals at a cost, willing to provide letters of recommendation, names of contacts, on-the-job training, willing to complete paperwork for educational credit, willing to act as a professional reference, opportunity to attend seminars/workshops, and housing free for staff, housing at a cost for interns.
Contact Michael Coglan, Company Manager, Williamstown Theater Festival, 229 West 42nd Street, #801, New York, New York 10036. Telephone: 212-395-9090. Fax: 212-395-9099. E-mail: mcoglan@wtfestival.org. World Wide Web: http://www.wtfestival.org. Contact by e-mail, fax, mail, phone, or through World Wide Web site. Application deadline: February 1 for apprentice workshop; continuous for staff and interns.

YMCA CAMP HI-ROCK
162 EAST STREET
MT. WASHINGTON, MASSACHUSETTS 01258
General Information Year-round YMCA camp and conference center offering residential and day camp, teen adventure trips, leader-in-training program, and experiential and environmental activities for all groups. Established in 1947. 1,000-acre facility located 70 miles from Albany, New York. Features: high ropes course; climbing wall; private lake; 1000 mountain acres; 3 waterskiing boats; year-round facilities and programs.
Profile of Summer Employees Total number: 120; typical ages: 17–24. 45% men; 55% women; 10% minorities; 25% high school students; 70% college students; 33% non-U.S. citizens; 5% local applicants. Nonsmokers required.
Employment Information Openings are from June 8 to August 18. Year-round positions also offered. Jobs available: ▶ 4 *adventure leaders* (minimum age 21) with first aid/CPR certifications and lifeguard training at $210 per week ▶ 1 *arts and crafts director* with first aid/CPR certifications, arts and crafts background, and must be at least a college sophomore at $200 per week ▶ 1 *assistant camp director* with first aid/CPR certifications, 2 years administrative experience, and must be a college graduate at $400 per week ▶ 1 *assistant day camp director* with first aid/CPR certifications, camp experience, and must be a college sophomore at $200 per week ▶ 1 *assistant nurse/medic* (minimum age 21) must be a RN, LPN, or EMT at $550 per week ▶ 26 *counselors* with first aid/CPR certifications and must be at least a high school senior at $170 per week ▶ 1 *head nurse* (minimum age 21) must be a Massachusetts RN or MD at $650 per week ▶ 1 *intervention specialist* (minimum age 21) with first aid/CPR certifications and experience dealing with troubled youth at $200 per week ▶ 3 *program directors* with first aid/CPR certifications, program staff experience, and must be at least a college sophomore at $250 per week ▶ 1 *ropes course director* (minimum age 21) with first aid/CPR certifications and ropes training and experience at $210 per week ▶ 32 *senior counselors* (minimum age 18) with first aid/CPR certifications and must be at least a college freshman at $190 per week ▶ 1 *store manager* (minimum age 21) with first aid/CPR certifications and organizational skills at $200 per week

▶ 14 *support staff-kitchen, maintenance, office* with first aid/CPR certifications and must be a college sophomore at $175 per week ▶ 1 *transportation director* (minimum age 21) with first aid/CPR certifications and a clean driving record at $200 per week ▶ *unit director* (minimum age 19) with first aid/CPR certifications, camp experience, and must be at least a college sophomore at $200 per week ▶ 2 *waterfront directors* (minimum age 21) with lifeguard and WSI certifications and administrative experience at $250 per week ▶ 2 *waterski directors* (minimum age 21) with lifeguard certification and waterski experience at $210 per week ▶ 1 *wrangler* (minimum age 21) with first aid/CPR certifications and horseback riding experience at $200 per week. Applicants must submit formal organization application, three personal references. A telephone interview is required. International applicants accepted; must apply through a recognized agency.

Benefits and Preemployment Training Free housing, free meals, formal training, willing to provide letters of recommendation, on-the-job training, willing to complete paperwork for educational credit, and willing to act as a professional reference. Preemployment training is required and includes accident prevention and safety, interpersonal skills, leadership skills.

Contact Scott Elliott, Camping Director, YMCA Camp Hi-Rock. Telephone: 413-528-1227 Ext. 14. Fax: 413-528-4234. E-mail: summer@camphirock.com. World Wide Web: http://www. camphirock.com. Contact by e-mail, fax, mail, phone, or through World Wide Web site. Application deadline: continuous.

MICHIGAN

A CHRISTIAN MINISTRY IN THE NATIONAL PARKS– MICHIGAN
See A Christian Ministry in the National Parks–Maine on page 107 for complete description.

AMERICAN YOUTH FOUNDATION–CAMP MINIWANCA
8845 WEST GARFIELD ROAD
SHELBY, MICHIGAN 49455

General Information Camp focusing on developing the leadership capacities of young people by helping them achieve their personal best, lead balanced lives, and serve others. Established in 1925. 360-acre facility located 80 miles from Grand Rapids. Features: 1 mile of Lake Michigan beach; Stoney Lake; wooded dunes; sand dunes; council circle at base of 2 dunes; open-air cabins and dormitories.

Profile of Summer Employees Total number: 200; typical ages: 18–60. 40% men; 60% women; 3% minorities; 10% high school students; 55% college students; 5% retirees; 8% non-U.S. citizens; 10% local applicants. Nonsmokers preferred.

Employment Information Openings are from January 1 to December 1. Spring break and year-round positions also offered. Jobs available: ▶ 1 *Four Trails program coordinator (year-round)* (minimum age 21) with WFR, CPR, first aid, lifeguard certifications, current physical, TB test, and police background check at $2000–$3000 per month ▶ 1 *bike mechanic* (minimum age 18) with a current physical, TB test, and police background check at $300 per week ▶ 5 *building/grounds personnel* (minimum age 18) with some skill with tools and power equipment at $300 per week ▶ 90 *cabin leaders* (minimum age 18) should be college student or teacher at

$175–$220 per week ▶ 6 *camp cleaning personnel* (minimum age 18) should be college student or retired person at $300 per week ▶ 4 *camp store staff members* (minimum age 18) should be college student or retired person at $275 per week ▶ 20 *central summer staff members* (minimum age 18) should be teachers or instructors at $200–$500 per week ▶ 2–4 *craft house staff members* (minimum age 18) should be college student or retired person at $250–$300 per week ▶ 2 *drivers* (minimum age 21) with a current physical, police background check, TB test, and a valid driver's license at $8.10 per hour ▶ *food/equipment manager* (minimum age 18) with CPR and first aid certifications, TB test, current physical, and police background checks at $250 per week ▶ 2–4 *health center staff* with EMT, RN, LPN, or 2nd year RN students (BSN) at $500 per week ▶ 1 *logistics coordinator* (minimum age 18) with CPR and first aid certifications, TB test, current physical, and police background checks at $350 per week ▶ 1 *logistics specialist category A* (minimum age 21) with first aid and CPR certifications, current physical, TB test, police background check, and a valid driver's license at $270 per week ▶ 1 *logistics specialist category B* (minimum age 21) with CPR and first aid certifications, current physical, TB test, police background check, and a valid driver's license at $270 per week ▶ *logistics specialist category C* (minimum age 21) with CPR and first aid certifications, current physical, TB test, police background check, and a valid driver's license at $270 per week ▶ 2 *office staff members* (minimum age 18) should be college student or retired person at $250–$300 per week ▶ *secretary (Four Trails)* with a current physical, TB test, and police background check at $250 per week ▶ 2 *security personnel* (minimum age 21) at $300 per week ▶ 2 *trip coordinators categories A and B* (minimum age 21) with first aid and CPR certifications, current physical, TB test, and police background check at $350 per week ▶ 12 *trip leaders category A* (minimum age 18) with wilderness first aid, lifeguarding and CPR certifications, current physical, TB test, and police background check at $305–$350 per week ▶ 5–10 *trip leaders category B* (minimum age 18) with wilderness first aid, and lifeguarding/CPR certifications, current physical, TB test, and police background check at $295 per week ▶ 7 *trip leaders category C* (minimum age 18) with a current physical, CPR and first aid certifications, TB test, and police background check at $270 per week ▶ 1 *waterfront management* (minimum age 21) with LS/LGT/WSI, sailing, and canoeing experience at $350 per week ▶ 2 *wood shop staff members* (minimum age 18) should be college student or retired person at $250–$300 per week ▶ 6 *year-round interns* (minimum age 20) with junior/senior status in college or college degree at $500 per month. Applicants must submit a formal organization application, letter of interest, resume, three personal references, three letters of recommendation. An in-person interview is recommended, but a telephone interview is acceptable. International applicants accepted.

Benefits and Preemployment Training Free housing, free meals, formal training, possible full-time employment, willing to provide letters of recommendation, on-the-job training, willing to complete paperwork for educational credit, willing to act as a professional reference, opportunity to attend seminars/workshops, travel reimbursement, and health insurance for interns. Preemployment training is required and includes accident prevention and safety, first aid, CPR, interpersonal skills, leadership skills, Wilderness First Responder, lifeguarding, WSI, high/low ropes challenge course/climbing tower.

Contact Jonathan Gilburg, Assistant to the Director, American Youth Foundation–Camp Miniwanca, 8845 West Garfield Road, Shelby, Michigan 49455. Telephone: 231-861-2262. Fax: 231-861-5244. E-mail: jon.gilburg@ayf.com. World Wide Web: http://www.ayf.com. Contact by e-mail, fax, mail, phone, or through World Wide Web site. Application deadline: May 31.

BAY CLIFF HEALTH CAMP
BIG BAY, MICHIGAN 49808
General Information Residential therapy camp serving 180 children with disabilities ages 3–17 during one 8-week session. Established in 1934. 170-acre facility located 323 miles from Milwaukee, Wisconsin. Features: outdoor setting; pool and beachfront.

Profile of Summer Employees Total number: 147; typical ages: 19–25. 30% men; 70% women; 5% minorities; 10% high school students; 50% college students; 2% retirees; 15% local applicants. Nonsmokers preferred.

Employment Information Openings are from June 13 to August 14. Jobs available: ▶ *arts and crafts aide* (minimum age 18) with interest in the field at $1200 per season ▶ 1 *arts and crafts instructor* with ability to plan and implement classes for all camp units, experience preferred at $2000 per season ▶ 1 *assistant cook* with experience in the field at $250–$300 per week ▶ 1 *baker* with experience at $2000 per season ▶ 50 *counselors* (minimum age 18) with one year of college completed (preferably in the study of special education, therapy, nursing, or human services) at $1600 per season ▶ 1 *dental assistant* with license at $1600 per season ▶ 1 *dental hygienist* with license at $2000 per season ▶ 12 *dining room aides* (minimum age 16) at $1000 per season ▶ *dining room supervisor* (minimum age 21) with experience in food management and supervision at $2000 per season ▶ 1 *head cook* at $350–$400 per week ▶ 3 *instructors for hearing impaired* with certification in field at $3000 per season ▶ 2 *instructors for visually impaired* with certification in the field at $3000 per season ▶ 3 *laundry/housekeeping personnel* (minimum age 18) at $1500 per season ▶ 2 *linen room personnel* (minimum age 18) at $1500 per season ▶ 4 *maintenance personnel* (minimum age 18) with experience at $1500–$2000 per season ▶ 1–2 *music therapists* with certification in field at $2600 per season ▶ 1 *nature instructor* with ability to plan and implement classes for all camp units, experience preferred at $2000 per season ▶ 3 *nurses* with RN or LPN license at $3000–$3500 per season ▶ 6 *occupational therapists* with certification in field at $3000 per season ▶ 5 *physical therapists* with certification in field at $3000 per season ▶ 1 *recreation instructor* with ability to plan and implement classes for all camp units, experience preferred at $2000 per season ▶ 8 *roving counselors* (minimum age 18) with one year of college completed (preferably in the study of special education, therapy, nursing, or human services) at $1600 per season ▶ 2 *secretaries* with good clerical skills and a pleasant, enthusiastic personality at $1600 per season ▶ 10 *speech therapists* with certification in field at $3000 per season ▶ 6 *student therapists* with formal school affiliation and ability to work with a supervising therapist at $600 per season ▶ 5 *unit leaders* (minimum age 22) with teaching experience and special education degree (preferred) at $2400 per season ▶ 4 *waterfront staff members* (minimum age 18) with WSI or lifeguard certification at $1600–$2000 per season ▶ *waterfront/pool supervisor* (minimum age 21) with certification, pool management, and leadership experience at $2000 per season. Applicants must submit a formal organization application, 3-6 personal references. An in-person interview is recommended, but a telephone interview is acceptable.

Benefits and Preemployment Training Free housing, free meals, on-the-job training, willing to complete paperwork for educational credit, and travel reimbursement. Preemployment training is required and includes accident prevention and safety, first aid, interpersonal skills, camp policies. **Contact** Tim Bennett, Camp Director, Bay Cliff Health Camp, 310 West Washington Street, Suite 300, Marquette, Michigan 49855. Telephone: 906-228-5770. Fax: 906-228-5769. E-mail: baycliffhc@aol.com. World Wide Web: http://www.baycliff.org. Contact by e-mail, mail, or phone. Application deadline: continuous.

BLUE LAKE FINE ARTS CAMP
300 EAST CRYSTAL LAKE ROAD
TWIN LAKE, MICHIGAN 49457

General Information Summer school of the arts serving over 4,700 junior high and high school students over an eight-week season. Established in 1966. 1,400-acre facility located 45 miles from Grand Rapids. Features: wooded setting; on small lake; music shell seats 5,000; 3 athletic fields; 2 pools; in Manistee National Forest; over 270 cabins, structures, buildings, and facilities.
Profile of Summer Employees Total number: 650; typical ages: 19–45. 45% men; 55% women; 20% minorities; 60% college students; 5% retirees; 5% non-U.S. citizens; 15% local applicants. Nonsmokers preferred.

Employment Information Openings are from June 15 to August 30. Jobs available: ▶ 105 *cabin counselors* (minimum age 18) with one year of college and interest and/or experience in the fine arts at $1200–$2200 per season ▶ 4 *camp nurses* with RN or LPN license at $950 per 12-day session ▶ 1 *health lodge director* (minimum age 21) with First Responder or EMT certification; camp and administrative experience at $3000–$4000 per season ▶ 10 *health lodge staff members* (minimum age 19) with Red Cross Response to Emergencies, EMT, or First Responder certification at $1600–$2200 per season ▶ 4 *music library staff members* (minimum age 18) with clerical and/or music library experience at $8 per hour ▶ 3 *production assistants* (minimum age 18) with interest in gaining experience in backstage/arts production at $1500–$1700 per season ▶ 1 *production manager* (minimum age 21) with backstage, arts production, and supervisory experience at $3000–$4000 per season ▶ 1 *waterfront director* (minimum age 21) with WSI certification, American Red Cross lifeguard instructor certification, managerial, and supervisory experience at $3500–$4300 per season. Applicants must submit a formal organization application, three personal references, audition cassette for musical openings. A telephone interview is required. International applicants accepted; must obtain own visa, obtain own working papers.

Benefits and Preemployment Training Free housing, free meals, formal training, willing to provide letters of recommendation, on-the-job training, willing to complete paperwork for educational credit, willing to act as a professional reference, opportunity to attend seminars/workshops, and opportunities to perform in summer arts festival. Preemployment training is required and includes accident prevention and safety, first aid, CPR, interpersonal skills, leadership skills.

Contact Heidi Stansell, Camp Director, Blue Lake Fine Arts Camp, 300 East Crystal Lake Road, Twin Lake, Michigan 49457. Telephone: 231-894-1966. Fax: 231-893-5120. World Wide Web: http://www.bluelake.org. Contact by fax, mail, or phone. Application deadline: continuous.

CAMP FOWLER AT THE FOWLER CENTER
2315 HARMON LAKE ROAD
MAYVILLE, MICHIGAN 48744-9737

General Information Accessible outdoor recreation camp for children and adults with developmental disabilities promoting personal growth in those with special needs. Established in 1957. 202-acre facility located 90 miles from Detroit. Features: spring-fed lake; organic garden; equestrian stables; wheelchair-accessible nature trails; climbing wall and tree house; sports fields.

Profile of Summer Employees Total number: 75; typical ages: 18–30. 45% men; 55% women; 12% minorities; 3% high school students; 85% college students; 5% retirees; 5% non-U.S. citizens; 15% local applicants. Nonsmokers preferred.

Employment Information Openings are from May 15 to October 31. Spring break, winter break, and year-round positions also offered. Jobs available: ▶ 15–20 *counselors* (minimum age 18) with high motivation to work with special needs campers (will train) at $1900–$2300 per season ▶ 1 *creative arts instructor* (minimum age 18) with experience or desire to work with special needs campers at $1900–$2300 per season ▶ 2 *health officers* (minimum age 21) with RN certification at $8500 per season ▶ *horseback riding instructors* (minimum age 18) with NARHA or CHA certification and experience or desire to work with special needs campers at $1900–$2300 per season ▶ 1 *organic garden and barn instructor* (minimum age 18) with gardening experience and desire to work with special needs campers at $1900–$2300 per season ▶ 1 *outdoor education instructor* (minimum age 18) with camping experience and desire to work with special needs campers at $1900–$2300 per season ▶ 1 *sports and recreation instructor* (minimum age 18) with experience or desire to work with special needs campers at $1900–$2300 per season ▶ *waterfront staff members* (minimum age 18) with lifeguard and WSI certification and experience or desire to work with special needs campers at $1900–$2300 per season. Applicants must submit formal organization application, three letters of recommendation, criminal background check. An in-person interview is recommended, but a telephone interview is acceptable. International applicants accepted; must apply through a recognized agency.

Benefits and Preemployment Training Free housing, free meals, formal training, possible full-time employment, willing to provide letters of recommendation, on-the-job training, willing to complete paperwork for educational credit, willing to act as a professional reference, and opportunity to attend seminars/workshops. Preemployment training is required and includes accident prevention and safety, first aid, CPR, interpersonal skills, leadership skills, direct care.

Contact Charles Morrison, Assistant Camp Director, Camp Fowler at The Fowler Center, 2315 Harmon Lake Road, Mayville, Michigan 48744-9737. Telephone: 989-673-2050. Fax: 989-673-6355. E-mail: camp@thefowlercenter.org. World Wide Web: http://www.thefowlercenter.org. Contact by e-mail, fax, mail, phone, or through World Wide Web site. Application deadline: continuous.

CAMP LOOKOUT
4410 LOOKOUT ROAD
FRANKFORT, MICHIGAN 49635

General Information Small, coeducational, loosely-structured residential camp that is noncompetitive and nonsectarian, emphasizing individual growth. Established in 1930. 10-acre facility located 30 miles from Traverse City. Features: large inland lake; proximity to National Lakeshore; Lake Michigan (sand dunes and a beach accessible only by boat); 10-acre island.

Profile of Summer Employees Total number: 15; typical ages: 17–35. 5% minorities; 20% high school students; 65% college students; 5% retirees; 15% non-U.S. citizens; 5% local applicants. Nonsmokers required.

Employment Information Openings are from June 15 to August 18. Jobs available: ▶ 1 *art specialist* (minimum age 19) with ability to organize art program (teacher preferred) at $1000–$2000 per season ▶ 1 *assistant director/program director* with ability to conduct programs for small and large groups at $1700–$4000 per season ▶ 1–2 *cooks* with experience at $1200–$3000 per season ▶ 8 *counselors* (minimum age 19) with lifesaving training and art, sailing, trip, or sports skills at $1100–$1700 per season ▶ 3 *junior counselors (high school students)* (minimum age 17) at $500–$700 per season ▶ 2 *nurses* with RN, LPN, or EMT license at $1200–$2500 per season ▶ *waterfront directors* with current LGT and WSI certification and experience at $1200–$2700 per season ▶ 3 *windsurfing instructors* (minimum age 19) with lifesaving training and experience in the field at $1100–$1700 per season. Applicants must submit formal organization application, resume. An in-person interview is recommended, but a telephone interview is acceptable. International applicants accepted; must obtain own visa, apply through a recognized agency.

Benefits and Preemployment Training Free housing, free meals, formal training, willing to provide letters of recommendation, on-the-job training, willing to complete paperwork for educational credit, and opportunity to attend seminars/workshops. Preemployment training is required and includes accident prevention and safety, first aid, CPR, interpersonal skills, leadership skills.

Contact David B. Reid, Director, Camp Lookout, 2768 South Shore Road East, Frankfort, Michigan 49635. Telephone: 231-352-7589. Fax: 231-352-6609. E-mail: camp_info@ crystalairecamp.com. World Wide Web: http://www.crystalairecamp.com. Contact by e-mail, fax, mail, phone, or through World Wide Web site. Application deadline: continuous.

CAMP MAPLEHURST
12055 WARING ROAD
KEWADIN, MICHIGAN 49648

General Information Residential camp serving 120 campers per session. Wide variety of activities offered. Community spirit and development of decision-making abilities is encouraged among campers. Established in 1955. 400-acre facility located 18 miles from Traverse City. Features: private, freshwater lake; views of 7 lakes; wooded setting with open fields; 3 tennis courts; 2 waterfronts; cabins and main lodge.

Profile of Summer Employees Total number: 40; typical ages: 18–50. 50% men; 50% women; 5% high school students; 70% college students; 5% retirees; 10% non-U.S. citizens. Nonsmokers preferred.

Employment Information Openings are from June 15 to August 18. Jobs available: ▶ 2 *cooks* (minimum age 18) with food handler's card at $200–$400 per week ▶ 1 *housekeeping staff member* at a negotiable salary ▶ 4 *kitchen aides* at a negotiable salary ▶ 1–2 *maintenance staff members* at a negotiable salary ▶ 1 *nurse* (minimum age 21) with RN and experience with children preferred at a negotiable salary ▶ 1 *sailing instructor* (minimum age 19) at $1300–$1600 per season ▶ 1 *scuba instructor* (minimum age 21) with teaching experience and instructor certification preferred at $1300–$1600 per season ▶ 4 *sports instructors* (minimum age 18) at $1300–$1600 per season ▶ 2 *swimming instructors* (minimum age 19) with WSI and lifeguard certification at $1300–$1600 per season ▶ 1 *tennis instructor* (minimum age 19) at $1300–$1600 per season. Applicants must submit formal organization application, three letters of recommendation. An in-person interview is recommended, but a telephone interview is acceptable. International applicants accepted; must apply through a recognized agency.

Benefits and Preemployment Training Free housing, free meals, formal training, willing to provide letters of recommendation, on-the-job training, willing to complete paperwork for educational credit, and willing to act as a professional reference. Preemployment training is required and includes accident prevention and safety, first aid, CPR, interpersonal skills, leadership skills.

Contact Laurence Cohn, Director, Camp Maplehurst, 1455 Quarton Road, Birmingham, Michigan 48009. Telephone: 248-647-2646. Fax: 248-647-6716. E-mail: campmaple@aol.com. World Wide Web: http://www.campmaplehurst.com. Contact by e-mail, fax, mail, or phone. Application deadline: continuous.

CAMP O'FAIR WINDS
3235 MCKEEN LAKE ROAD
COLUMBIAVILLE, MICHIGAN 48421

General Information Nonprofit organization dedicated to providing girls with challenging outdoor programs; emphasis is placed on helping girls develop self-confidence, group communication skills, and independence. Established in 1930. 465-acre facility located 40 miles from Flint. Features: wooded setting; aquatic center with waterslide; low initiatives and high ropes course; freshwater lake; archery field; arts and crafts center.

Profile of Summer Employees Total number: 40; typical ages: 18–25. 1% men; 99% women; 10% minorities; 90% college students; 1% retirees; 30% non-U.S. citizens; 50% local applicants.

Employment Information Openings are from June 1 to August 15. Year-round positions also offered. Jobs available: ▶ 1 *aquatic director* (minimum age 18) with strong communication skills, supervisory experience, lifeguard training, willingness to be a team player, and experience working with children at $235 per week ▶ 1 *arts and craft director* (minimum age 18) with good teaching ability, strong leadership skills, and experience teaching creative art projects to children at $220 per week ▶ 1 *assistant director* (minimum age 18) with supervisory experience, strong communication skills, team skills, and experience working at camps at $250 per week ▶ 1 *business manager* (minimum age 18) with good leadership skills, experience handling cash, good organization skills, and valid driver's license at $220 per week ▶ 1 *head cook* (minimum age 21) with experience in food preparation, menu planning, food safety, certification/degree preferred, supervisory experience, and a flexible attitude at $280 per week ▶ 1 *health supervisor* (minimum age 18) with RN or EMT certification and experience working with children at $225 per week ▶ 4 *kitchen aides* (minimum age 18) with experience in food handling, good team skills, and a positive attitude at $170 per week ▶ 4 *lifeguards* (minimum age 18) with lifeguard, first aid, CPR training, experience working with children, and good leadership skills at $200 per week ▶ 1 *packout supervisor* (minimum age 18) with good communication skills and knowledge of food handling procedures; must be licensed driver and team player at $190 per week ▶ 1 *program director* (minimum age 18) with strong communication skills, camp experience, driver's license, and supervisory experience at $220 per week ▶ 1 *ropes/initiative director* (minimum age 18) with experience working with children, willingness to be a team player, strong leadership skills, moderate athletic ability, and comfort with heights at $225 per week ▶ 1 *small craft instructor* (minimum age 18) with lifeguard training, smallcraft experience, willingness to be a team player, and experience working with children at $225 per week ▶ 1 *trip/overnight director* (minimum age 18) with good leadership skills, strong camping/outdoor skills, experience working with children, and good organizational skills at $220 per week ▶ 20 *unit assistants* (minimum age 18) with experience with children and a high comfort level outdoors at $190 per week ▶ 8 *unit leaders* (minimum age 18) with strong communication skills, leadership ability, and experience working with children at $210 per week. Applicants must submit formal organization application, three personal references, physical exam and TB test. An in-person interview is recommended, but a telephone interview is acceptable. International applicants accepted; must apply through a recognized agency.

Benefits and Preemployment Training Free housing, free meals, health insurance, on-the-job training, and willing to complete paperwork for educational credit. Preemployment training is required and includes accident prevention and safety, first aid, CPR, interpersonal skills, leadership skills, lifeguard training, archery instructor training, high ropes training.

Contact Therese Plotz, Camp Director, Camp O'Fair Winds, 2029-C South Elms Road, PO Box 349, Swartz Creek, Michigan 48473. Telephone: 800-482-6734. Fax: 810-230-0955. E-mail: tplotz@fwgsc.org. World Wide Web: http://www.fwgsc.org/campjobs.htm. Contact by e-mail, fax, phone, or through World Wide Web site. Application deadline: May 31.

CAMP WESTMINSTER ON HIGGINS LAKE
116 WESTMINSTER DRIVE
ROSCOMMON, MICHIGAN 48653

General Information Residential camp offering a unique combination of activities designed to promote a sense of responsibility and self-worth in a Christian community. Established in 1925. 40-acre facility located 200 miles from Detroit. Features: freshwater lake; wooded setting; climbing tower; high ropes course; 2 tennis courts; sailboat and canoe fleets.

Profile of Summer Employees Total number: 30; typical ages: 16–55. 50% men; 50% women; 30% minorities; 5% high school students; 90% college students; 5% retirees; 25% non-U.S. citizens; 5% local applicants. Nonsmokers required.

Employment Information Openings are from June 1 to August 15. Jobs available: ▶ 20 *counselors/program specialists* (minimum age 19) with specialized training at $175–$300 per week ▶ *kitchen staff* (minimum age 18) at $125–$500 per week ▶ 6 *lifeguards* (minimum age 19) with lifeguard training and CPR/first aid certification at $175–$300 per week ▶ 2 *program directors* (minimum age 21) at $250–$500 per week ▶ 1 *registered nurse* (minimum age 21) at $200–$400 per week ▶ 6 *ropes course facilitators* (minimum age 19) with certification in field at $200–$350 per week ▶ 1 *waterfront director* (minimum age 21) with WSI certification at $200–$350 per week. Applicants must submit formal organization application, three personal references. An in-person interview is recommended, but a telephone interview is acceptable. International applicants accepted; must apply through a recognized agency.

Benefits and Preemployment Training Free housing, free meals, formal training, willing to provide letters of recommendation, on-the-job training, willing to complete paperwork for educational credit, willing to act as a professional reference, opportunity to attend seminars/workshops, and travel reimbursement. Preemployment training is required and includes accident prevention and safety, first aid, CPR, interpersonal skills, leadership skills, lifeguard training, ropes course facilitation, health officer training, sailing instruction.

Contact Suzanne Getz Bates, Executive Director, Camp Westminster on Higgins Lake, 17567 Hubbell Avenue, Detroit, Michigan 48235. Telephone: 313-341-8969. Fax: 313-341-1514. E-mail: suzanne@campwestminster.com. World Wide Web: http://www.campwestminster.com. Contact by e-mail, fax, mail, phone, or through World Wide Web site. Application deadline: continuous.

CEDAR LODGE
47000 52ND STREET
LAWRENCE, MICHIGAN 49064

General Information Residential coeducational camp serving 60 campers in a relaxed, loosely structured program with a special emphasis on horsemanship from the beginner to the show jumper. Established in 1964. 160-acre facility located 105 miles from Chicago, Illinois. Features: full riding stables; indoor arena; private lake.

Profile of Summer Employees Typical ages: 23–53. 25% men; 75% women; 95% college students; 5% retirees; 60% non-U.S. citizens; 5% local applicants. Nonsmokers required.

Employment Information Openings are from June 15 to August 20. Jobs available: ▶ 1 *arts and crafts instructor* (minimum age 19) at $1000–$1200 per season ▶ 1 *biking/trip instructor* (minimum age 19) at $1000–$1200 per season ▶ 2 *kitchen assistants* (minimum age 18) at $1200–$1500 per season ▶ 1 *music/dance/drama instructor* (minimum age 19) at $1000–$1200 per season ▶ 2 *riding instructors* (minimum age 19) with English riding experience at $1000–$1500 per season ▶ 1 *sports instructor* (minimum age 19) at $1000–$1200 per season ▶ 2 *swimming instructors* (minimum age 21) with swimming experience at $1000–$1500 per season. Applicants must submit formal organization application, resume, three personal references. A telephone interview is required. International applicants accepted; must apply through a recognized agency.

Benefits and Preemployment Training Free housing, free meals, formal training, willing to provide letters of recommendation, on-the-job training, and willing to complete paperwork for educational credit. Preemployment training is required and includes accident prevention and safety, first aid, CPR, leadership skills.

Contact Amy Edwards, Program Director, Cedar Lodge, PO Box 218, Lawrence, Michigan 49064. Telephone: 616-674-8071. Fax: 616-674-3143. E-mail: info@cedarlodge.com. World Wide Web: http://www.cedarlodge.com. Contact by e-mail, fax, mail, or phone. Application deadline: continuous.

CIRCLE PINES CENTER SUMMER CAMP
8650 MULLEN ROAD
DELTON, MICHIGAN 49046

General Information Small, cooperatively owned and run residential camp for children ages 7–17 teaching peace, social justice, ecology, and cooperation. Established in 1938. 294-acre facility located 30 miles from Kalamazoo. Features: springfed lake; woodlands; meadows; organic garden; pre-Civil War farmhouse.

Profile of Summer Employees Total number: 24; typical ages: 19–22. 45% men; 55% women; 5% minorities; 40% college students; 5% local applicants. Nonsmokers required.

Employment Information Openings are from June 15 to August 10. Jobs available: ▶ 4 *cooks* (minimum age 18) with experience working with whole foods, large groups, and children at $1090 per season ▶ 11 *counselors* (minimum age 18) with experience with children and skills in leading activities at $1090 per season ▶ 1 *health officer* (minimum age 21) with RN, LPN, or EMT license or camp health officer training and experience at $1200–$1500 per season ▶ 1 *housekeeper* (minimum age 18) with cleaning skills and ability to work with children at $1090 per season ▶ 1 *kitchen manager* (minimum age 18) with menu planning, supervisory, inventory, and purchasing experience at $1210 per season ▶ 1 *volunteer coordinator* (minimum age 18) with volunteer coordination background at $1090 per season ▶ 1 *waterfront assistant* with CPR certificate plus lifeguard and first aid training at $1090 per season ▶ 1 *waterfront director* (minimum age 21) with CPR and lifeguard training/certification at $1000–$1200 per season. Applicants must submit a formal organization application, three personal references. An in-person interview is recommended, but a telephone interview is acceptable.

Benefits and Preemployment Training Free housing, free meals, on-the-job training, and willing to complete paperwork for educational credit.

Contact Traci Furman, Camp Director, Circle Pines Center Summer Camp, 8650 Mullen Road, Delton, Michigan 49046. Telephone: 269-623-5555. Fax: 269-623-9054. E-mail: circle@net-link. net. World Wide Web: http://www.circlepinescenter.org. Contact by e-mail, fax, mail, phone, or through World Wide Web site. Application deadline: continuous.

CRYSTALAIRE CAMP
2768 SOUTH SHORE ROAD EAST
FRANKFORT, MICHIGAN 49635

General Information Small, coeducational, loosely-structured residential camp that is noncompetitive and nonsectarian, emphasizing individual growth. Established in 1924. 145-acre facility located 30 miles from Traverse City. Features: large inland lake; proximity to National Lakeshore; Lake Michigan (sand dunes and beach accessible only by boat).

Profile of Summer Employees Total number: 45; typical ages: 17–28. 50% men; 50% women; 5% minorities; 20% high school students; 65% college students; 5% retirees; 15% non-U.S. citizens; 5% local applicants. Nonsmokers required.

Employment Information Openings are from June 15 to August 20. Jobs available: ▶ 1 *art specialist* (minimum age 19) with ability to organize art program (teacher preferred) at $1000–$2000 per season ▶ 1 *assistant director/program director* with ability to conduct programs for small and large groups at $1500–$4000 per season ▶ 2–3 *cooks* with experience at $1200–$3000 per season ▶ 14 *counselors* (minimum age 19) with lifesaving training, and art, sailing, trip, or sports skills at $1100–$1700 per season ▶ 5 *junior counselors (high school students)* (minimum age 17) at $500–$900 per season ▶ 2 *nurses* with RN, LPN, or EMT license; will consider partial summer availability at $1200–$2200 per season ▶ 1 *riding instructor* (minimum age 19) with experience and ability to manage Western-style riding program at $1000–$1600 per season ▶ 3 *sailing/windsurfing instructors* (minimum age 19) with lifesaving training and experience in the field at $1000–$1800 per season ▶ *sports specialists* with experience in competitive and noncompetitive sports and games at $1000–$1500 per season ▶ 1 *stable helper* (minimum age 19) at $60–$150 per week ▶ 1 *trip coordinator* (minimum age 19) with ability to organize wilderness camping trips, train staff, and maintain bicycles, tents, and camping equipment at $1200–$2300 per season ▶ 2 *waterfront directors* with current LGT and WSI certification and experience at $1200–$2700 per season. Applicants must submit formal organization application, resume. An in-person interview is recommended, but a telephone interview is acceptable. International applicants accepted; must obtain own visa, apply through a recognized agency.

Benefits and Preemployment Training Free housing, free meals, formal training, willing to provide letters of recommendation, willing to complete paperwork for educational credit, opportunity to attend seminars/workshops, and travel reimbursement. Preemployment training is required and includes accident prevention and safety, first aid, CPR, interpersonal skills, leadership skills.

Contact David B. Reid, Director, Crystalaire Camp, 2768 South Shore Road East, Frankfort, Michigan 49635. Telephone: 231-352-7589. Fax: 231-352-6609. E-mail: camp_info@ crystalairecamp.com. World Wide Web: http://www.crystalairecamp.com. Contact by e-mail, fax, mail, phone, or through World Wide Web site. Application deadline: continuous.

CYBERCAMPS–UNIVERSITY OF MICHIGAN
ANN ARBOR, MICHIGAN
See Cybercamps–University of Washington on page 326 for complete description.

CYO BOYS CAMP
1295 LAKESHORE ROAD
CARSONVILLE, MICHIGAN 48419

General Information CYO summer camps are open to boys ages 7½–16. The Pioneer Program is especially designed to meet the needs of experienced campers ages 14–16. Established in 1946. 70-acre facility located 90 miles from Detroit. Features: climbing wall; ropes course; lakeside setting; acres of woods and nature trails.

Profile of Summer Employees Total number: 40; typical ages: 17–25. 90% men; 10% women; 25% minorities; 20% high school students; 75% college students; 5% retirees.

Employment Information Openings are from June 16 to August 2. Jobs available: ▶ 1 *archery director* (minimum age 18) at $900–$1000 per season ▶ 1 *arts and crafts director* (minimum age 18) at $900–$1000 per season ▶ 10–15 *counselors-in-training* (minimum age 17) at $800 per season ▶ *group counselors/assistants* (minimum age 18) at $1000–$1200 per season ▶ *nurse or health officer* (minimum age 21) with RN, LPN, or EMT with CPR training at $1400–$1600 per season ▶ 2 *waterfront directors/assistants* (minimum age 18) with WSI certification at $1100–$1400 per season. Applicants must submit formal organization application, three personal references. An in-person interview is recommended, but a telephone interview is acceptable. International applicants accepted; must obtain own visa, obtain own working papers, apply through a recognized agency.

Benefits and Preemployment Training Free housing, free meals, on-the-job training, and opportunity to attend seminars/workshops. Preemployment training is required and includes accident prevention and safety, interpersonal skills, leadership skills.

Contact Caroline Krucker, Parish Services and Camps Director, CYO Boys Camp, 305 Michigan Avenue, 9th Floor, Detroit, Michigan 48266. Telephone: 313-963-7172. Fax: 313-963-7179. E-mail: ckrucker@cyodetroit.org. World Wide Web: http://www.cyocamps.org. Contact by e-mail, fax, mail, phone, or through World Wide Web site. Application deadline: continuous.

CYO GIRLS CAMP
1564 LAKESHORE ROAD
PORT SANILAC, MICHIGAN 48469

General Information CYO summer camps are open to girls ages 7½–16. The Pioneer Program is especially designed to meet the needs of experienced campers ages 14–16. Established in 1946. 30-acre facility located 90 miles from Detroit. Features: location on the shore of Lake Huron; with long sandy beaches; acres of woods and nature trails; climbing wall; high ropes course.

Profile of Summer Employees Total number: 40; typical ages: 17–25. 10% men; 90% women; 25% minorities; 20% high school students; 75% college students; 10% local applicants.

Employment Information Openings are from June 16 to August 2. Jobs available: ▶ 1 *archery director* (minimum age 21) at $900–$1100 per season ▶ 1 *arts and crafts director* (minimum age 18) at $900–$1100 per season ▶ 10–15 *counselors-in-training* (minimum age 17) at $800 per season ▶ 10 *group counselors/assistants* (minimum age 18) at $1000–$1200 per season ▶ *nurse or health officer* (minimum age 21) with RN, LPN, EMT, or advanced first aid with CPR at $1400–$1600 per season ▶ 2 *waterfront directors/assistants* (minimum age 18) with WSI certification at $1000–$1200 per season. Applicants must submit a formal organization application, three personal references. An in-person interview is recommended, but a telephone interview is acceptable. International applicants accepted; must obtain own visa, obtain own working papers.

Benefits and Preemployment Training Free housing, free meals, on-the-job training, and opportunity to attend seminars/workshops. Preemployment training is required and includes accident prevention and safety, interpersonal skills, leadership skills.

Contact Caroline Krucker, Parish Services and Camps Director, CYO Girls Camp, 305 Michigan Avenue, 9th Floor, Detroit, Michigan 48226. Telephone: 313-963-7172. Fax: 313-963-7179.

E-mail: ckrucker@cyodetroit.org. World Wide Web: http://www.cyocamps.org. Contact by e-mail, fax, mail, phone, or through World Wide Web site. Application deadline: continuous.

DOUBLE JJ RESORT
PO BOX 94
ROTHBURY, MICHIGAN 49452

General Information Full service resort ranch with exclusive programming for adults, families, and children. Established in 1937. 1,500-acre facility located 20 miles from Muskegon. Features: horseback riding; championship 18-hole golf course; year-round activities; pools, spas, water slide; cabins, hotel and condominiums; snow tubing/dogsledding.

Profile of Summer Employees Total number: 300; typical ages: 18–30. 50% men; 50% women; 2% minorities; 5% high school students; 50% college students; 5% retirees; 8% non-U.S. citizens; 30% local applicants.

Employment Information Openings are from January 1 to December 31. Year-round positions also offered. Jobs available: ▶ 15 *children's counselors* (minimum age 18) at $150 per week ▶ 6 *cooks* (minimum age 18) with experience in the field at $200–$350 per week ▶ 10 *day care staff* (minimum age 18) at $150 per week ▶ 3 *dining room managers* (minimum age 18) with waiter/waitressing experience at $150–$220 per week ▶ 1 *disc jockey* (minimum age 18) with experience at $150–$200 per week ▶ 4 *dishwashers* (minimum age 18) at $150 per week ▶ 10 *golf course groundskeepers* (minimum age 18) at $150–$200 per week ▶ 10 *golf course personnel* (minimum age 18) with golfing knowledge and ability at $150 per week ▶ 15 *housekeepers* (minimum age 18) at $150–$200 per week ▶ 20 *lawn maintenance personnel* (minimum age 18) at $130–$200 per week ▶ 12 *lifeguards* (minimum age 18) with American Red Cross or Ellis lifeguard certification at $150–$200 per week ▶ 15 *office staff members* (minimum age 18) with computer experience and ability to answer phones and make reservations at $150 per week ▶ 10 *prep cooks/bakers* (minimum age 18) with experience at $150–$200 per week ▶ 12 *pro shop/gift shop staff members* (minimum age 18) at $150 per week ▶ 10 *snack bar/bar staff members* (minimum age 18) at $130 per week ▶ 9 *talented entertainers (guitarists, singers, pianists, and musicians)* (minimum age 18) with outgoing personality at $150–$200 per week ▶ 20 *waiters/waitresses* (minimum age 18) at $130 per week ▶ 10 *wranglers* (minimum age 18) with experience at $150–$220 per week. Applicants must submit formal organization application. An in-person interview is recommended, but a telephone interview is acceptable. International applicants accepted; must obtain own visa, obtain own working papers, apply through a recognized agency.

Benefits and Preemployment Training Free housing, free meals, possible full-time employment, willing to provide letters of recommendation, on-the-job training, willing to complete paperwork for educational credit, willing to act as a professional reference, and use of all resort amenities. Preemployment training is required and includes resort-wide orientation to familiarize employees with facility, procedures, and job description.

Contact Densie Angell, Human Resources, Double JJ Resort, PO Box 94, Rothbury, Michigan 49452. Telephone: 231-894-4444. Fax: 231-893-5355. E-mail: jobs@doublejj.com. World Wide Web: http://www.doublejj.com. Contact by e-mail, fax, mail, phone, or through World Wide Web site. Application deadline: continuous.

INTERLOCHEN ARTS CAMP
4000 HIGHWAY M-137
INTERLOCHEN, MICHIGAN 49643

General Information America's first and foremost summer arts program for students age 8–18, offering instruction in creative writing, dance, music, theatre arts, and visual arts. Established in 1928. 1,200-acre facility located 16 miles from Traverse City. Features: freshwater lakes; wooded setting; performance venues; ropes course; tennis court; basketball court.

Profile of Summer Employees Total number: 1,500; typical ages: 18–40. 40% men; 60% women; 20% minorities; 12% high school students; 70% college students; 12% retirees; 1% non-U.S. citizens; 5% local applicants.

Employment Information Openings are from June 8 to August 11. Jobs available: ▶ 16 *accompanists* with BA degree (required) at $1000–$1300 per season ▶ 13 *art assistants* (minimum age 18) with a major in art at $900 per season ▶ 10 *audio services staff* (minimum age 18) at $900 per season ▶ 8 *box office staff* (minimum age 18) at $1000 per season ▶ 250 *cabin counselors* (minimum age 18) at $950–$1100 per season ▶ 6 *clerical staff* at $800 per season ▶ 12 *concert office staff* (minimum age 18) at $800 per season ▶ 5 *crafts instructors* (minimum age 18) at $800 per season ▶ 16 *music library staff* (minimum age 18) at $800 per season ▶ 25 *nurses* with Michigan license, RN, LPN at $13–$16 per hour ▶ 8 *physicians* preferably primary care physicians at $450 per week ▶ 6 *piano technicians* (minimum age 18) ▶ 14 *practice supervisors* (minimum age 18) at $1000 per season ▶ 8 *security staff* (minimum age 21) ▶ 3 *staff hall counselors* (minimum age 21) at $900 per season ▶ 36 *stage services staff* (minimum age 18) at $900 per season ▶ 2 *stage technicians/master electricians* with stage lighting and production experience at $900–$1500 per season ▶ 26 *theatre production staff* (minimum age 18) at $900–$1800 per season ▶ 8 *transportation drivers* (minimum age 21) at $900 per season ▶ 8 *waterfront staff* (minimum age 18) with current Red Cross lifeguard training at $950 per season. Applicants must submit a formal organization application, three letters of recommendation. International applicants accepted; must obtain own visa, obtain own working papers.

Benefits and Preemployment Training Free housing, free meals, willing to provide letters of recommendation, names of contacts, on-the-job training, willing to complete paperwork for educational credit, opportunity to attend seminars/workshops, and private lessons, playing in ensembles. Preemployment training is required and includes first aid, CPR, leadership skills.

Contact Grimaldo D. Robles, Coordinator, Seasonal Employment, Interlochen Arts Camp, Human Resources, PO Box 199, Interlochen, Michigan 49643. Telephone: 231-276-7337. Fax: 231-276-7850. E-mail: roblesgd@interlochen.org. World Wide Web: http://www.interlochen.org/. Contact by e-mail, fax, mail, phone, or through World Wide Web site. Application deadline: continuous.

MCGAW YMCA CAMP ECHO AND THE OUTDOOR DISCOVERY CENTER
3782 SOUTH TRIANGLE TRAIL
FREMONT, MICHIGAN 49412

General Information Residential coeducational camp serving 250 youngsters in two-week sessions. Emphasis is on building self-esteem through YMCA principles. Outdoor education center operates during non-summer months for Michigan schools and interest groups. Established in 1902. 472-acre facility located 60 miles from Grand Rapids. Features: freshwater lake; wooded setting; low and high ropes course; numerous water sports; numerous land sports.

Profile of Summer Employees Total number: 60; typical ages: 18–60. 45% men; 55% women; 10% minorities; 25% high school students; 75% college students; 10% non-U.S. citizens; 80% local applicants. Nonsmokers required.

Employment Information Openings are from April 15 to September 15. Jobs available: ▶ 10 *adventure trip leaders* (minimum age 21) with lifeguard, wilderness first responder, and CPR certification at $175–$225 per week ▶ 1 *aquatic director* with first aid, CPR, and lifeguard instructor certification, or WSI and LG at $150–$250 per week ▶ 1 *assistant wrangler* (minimum age 18) with standard first aid and CPR certification at $150–$200 per week ▶ 3 *cooks* (minimum age 18) with CPR certification and experience with large groups at $100–$300 per week ▶ 5 *health officers* (minimum age 21) with MD, RN, EMT or paramedic license, CPR and standard first aid certification at $250–$275 per week ▶ 18 *outdoor education staff members* (minimum age 18) with CPR/first aid at $120–$150 per week ▶ 1 *ropes course director* (minimum age 21) with CPR, first aid, and extensive experience in supervising high and low ropes course at $175–$250 per week ▶ 3 *sailing/canoeing/waterskiing directors* (minimum age 18) with standard first aid, CPR, and lifeguard certification at $150–$200 per week ▶ 18 *senior counselors* with standard first aid, LG, and CPR certification at $125–$155 per week ▶ 1 *social worker* (minimum age 21) with MSW, CPR, and first aid certifications at $200–$275 per week ▶ 2 *wilderness site leaders* (minimum age 21) with lifeguard, first aid, and CPR certification at $150–$200 per week ▶ 1 *wrangler* (minimum age 21) with first aid and CPR certification at $175–$275 per week. Applicants must submit formal organization application, three personal references. An in-person interview is recommended, but a telephone interview is acceptable. International applicants accepted; must apply through a recognized agency.

Benefits and Preemployment Training Free housing, free meals, willing to provide letters of recommendation, on-the-job training, and willing to complete paperwork for educational credit. Preemployment training is required and includes accident prevention and safety, first aid, CPR, interpersonal skills, leadership skills.

Contact Rob Grierson, Director, McGaw YMCA Camp Echo and the Outdoor Discovery Center. E-mail: rg@mcgawymca.org. World Wide Web: http://www.ymcacampecho.org. Contact by e-mail. No phone calls. Application deadline: continuous.

MICHIGAN TECHNOLOGICAL UNIVERSITY SUMMER YOUTH PROGRAM
1400 TOWNSEND DRIVE
HOUGHTON, MICHIGAN 49931

General Information Summer program for students ages 12-18 in 70 explorations designed to introduce students to careers and knowledge (theater, engineering, pottery, and more), and give them a taste of residential college dorm life. Established in 1973. 120-acre facility located 250 miles from Green Bay, Wisconsin. Features: Lake Superior location; waterfalls; old growth forests; biking/hiking paths; Isle Royale; all university facilities.

Profile of Summer Employees Total number: 250; typical ages: 18–28. 50% men; 50% women; 20% minorities; 97% college students; 1% retirees; 30% non-U.S. citizens; 10% local applicants. Nonsmokers preferred.

Employment Information Openings are from June 8 to August 31. Jobs available: ▶ *counselors* (minimum age 18) with one semester of college completed at $220 per week plus room and board ▶ *teaching assistants* (minimum age 18) with one year of college completed at $200 per week. Applicants must submit formal organization application, two personal references. An in-person interview is recommended, but a telephone interview is acceptable. International applicants accepted; must obtain own visa, obtain own working papers, apply through a recognized agency.

Benefits and Preemployment Training Free housing, free meals, and on-the-job training. Preemployment training is required and includes accident prevention and safety, first aid, interpersonal skills, leadership skills.

Contact Cheryl Gherna, Youth Programs Secretary, Michigan Technological University Summer Youth Program, 1400 Townsend Drive, Houghton, Michigan 49931. Telephone: 906-487-2219. Fax: 906-487-3101. E-mail: yp@mtu.edu. World Wide Web: http://www.youthprograms.mtu. edu. Contact by e-mail, mail, or phone. Application deadline: applications are accepted December through April; most hiring complete by end of March.

THE SOUTHWESTERN COMPANY, MICHIGAN
See The Southwestern Company on page 297 for complete description.

STUDENT CONSERVATION ASSOCIATION (SCA), MICHIGAN
See Student Conservation Association (SCA), New Hampshire on page 200 for complete description.

SUMMER DISCOVERY AT MICHIGAN
UNIVERSITY OF MICHIGAN
ANN ARBOR, MICHIGAN 48109

General Information Precollege enrichment program for high school students at University of Michigan. Established in 1991. near Detroit. Features: sport facilities; beaches; mountains; lakes; major cities nearby; college towns.

Profile of Summer Employees Total number: 40; typical ages: 21–35. 45% men; 55% women; 10% minorities; 60% college students; 2% non-U.S. citizens. Nonsmokers required.

Employment Information Openings are from June to August. Jobs available: ▶ 30 *resident counselors* (minimum age 21) with experience working with high school students/children at $200 per week. Applicants must submit a formal organization application, resume, three personal references. An in-person interview is required. International applicants accepted; must obtain own visa, obtain own working papers.

Benefits and Preemployment Training Free housing, free meals, possible full-time employment, on-the-job training, willing to complete paperwork for educational credit, and willing to act as a professional reference. Preemployment training is required and includes accident prevention and safety, CPR, leadership skills.

Contact Rouel Belleza, Operations, Summer Discovery at Michigan, 1326 Old Northern Boulevard, Roslyn, New York 11576, United States. Telephone: 516-621-3939. Fax: 516-625-3438. E-mail: staff@summerfun.com. World Wide Web: http://www.summerfun.com. Contact by e-mail, fax, mail, phone, or through World Wide Web site. Application deadline: continuous.

MINNESOTA

CAMP BUCKSKIN
9830 FREDRICKSON LANE
ELY, MINNESOTA 55731

General Information Residential camp offering two 30-day sessions for youths with academic and/or social skills difficulties (learning disabilities, Attention Deficit Disorder, and related difficulties). Established in 1959. 165-acre facility located 80 miles from Duluth. Features: freshwater lake; wooded setting; library; hiking trails; cabins; dining hall.

Profile of Summer Employees Total number: 70; typical ages: 19–25. 50% men; 50% women; 5% minorities; 10% high school students; 80% college students; 10% non-U.S. citizens; 10% local applicants. Nonsmokers preferred.

Employment Information Openings are from June 1 to August 25. Jobs available: ▶ 3 *counselors/archery instructors* (minimum age 18) with experience and certification from such organizations as the National Archery Association at $1750–$2750 per season ▶ 6 *counselors/arts and crafts instructors* (minimum age 18) with creativity and ability to teach at $1750–$2750 per season ▶ 10 *counselors/canoeing instructors* (minimum age 18) with lifeguard training, standard first aid, and CPR (preferred) at $1750–$2750 per season ▶ 6 *counselors/nature and environment instructors* (minimum age 18) with experience and certification in programs such as NOLS and Nature Quest (preferred) at $1750–$2750 per season ▶ 3 *counselors/riflery instructors* (minimum age 18) with gun and range safety training with the National Rifle Association, military, or similar agency (preferred) at $1750–$2750 per season ▶ 8 *counselors/swimming instructors* (minimum age 19) with WSI certification, lifeguard training, standard first aid, and CPR (preferred) at $1750–$2750 per season ▶ 5 *kitchen assistants* (minimum age 16) with positive attitude and ability to work with others at $1500–$2100 per season ▶ 2 *nurses* with RN license (preferred), or LPN license at a negotiable salary ▶ 2 *office assistants* (minimum age 16) with good typing and phone skills (computer experience a plus) at $1500–$2300 per season ▶ 8 *reading teachers* with license in elementary or secondary education or special education certification (preferred) at $1900–$3000 per season ▶ 8 *trip counselors* with lifeguard, CPR, and standard first aid training at $1800–$3000 per season. Applicants must submit formal organization application, writing sample, three personal references. An in-person interview is recommended, but a telephone interview is acceptable. International applicants accepted; must apply through a recognized agency.

Benefits and Preemployment Training Free housing, free meals, formal training, possible full-time employment, willing to provide letters of recommendation, names of contacts, on-the-job training, willing to complete paperwork for educational credit, willing to act as a professional reference, opportunity to attend seminars/workshops, and travel reimbursement. Preemployment training is required and includes accident prevention and safety, interpersonal skills, leadership skills, seminars relate to ADHD/learning disabilities, behavior management, teaching methodologies, social skills goal setting, certification in Crisis Prevention Institute's Non-violent Physical Crisis Intervention.

Contact Thomas Bauer, Director, Camp Buckskin, 8700 West 36th Street, Suite 6W, St. Louis Park, Minnesota 55426-3936. Telephone: 952-930-3544. Fax: 952-938-6996. E-mail: buckskin@spacestar.net. World Wide Web: http://www.campbuckskin.com. Contact by e-mail, fax, mail, phone, or through World Wide Web site. Application deadline: continuous.

CAMP CHIPPEWA FOUNDATION
CASS LAKE, MINNESOTA 56633

General Information Residential camp for 60 boys offering land and water activities including extensive Canadian fishing, canoe, and kayak tripping. Established in 1935. 88-acre facility located 250 miles from Minneapolis. Features: isthmus between 2 lakes; one mile of shoreline; island fishing lodge in Ontario; location in Chippewa National Forest; 3 tennis courts.

Profile of Summer Employees Total number: 30; typical ages: 19–45. 95% men; 5% women; 5% minorities; 5% high school students; 65% college students; 10% non-U.S. citizens; 5% local applicants. Nonsmokers required.

Employment Information Openings are from June 10 to August 12. Jobs available: ▶ *NRA rifle instructor* (minimum age 19) with NRA certification at $1200–$1400 per season ▶ *archery instructor* (minimum age 19) at $1200–$1400 per season ▶ *general cabin counselors* (minimum age 19) at $1100–$1500 per season ▶ *sailing instructor* (minimum age 19) at $1200–$2200 per season ▶ *swimming instructor* (minimum age 19) with Red Cross WSI certification at $1200–$1800 per season. Applicants must submit formal organization application, three personal references. An in-person interview is recommended, but a telephone interview is acceptable. International applicants accepted; must apply through a recognized agency.

Benefits and Preemployment Training Free housing, free meals, formal training, health insurance, names of contacts, on-the-job training, and travel reimbursement. Preemployment training is required and includes accident prevention and safety, interpersonal skills, leadership skills.

Contact Michael Thompson, Director, Camp Chippewa Foundation, 15 East 5th Street, Suite 4022, Tulsa, Oklahoma 74103. Telephone: 800-262-1544. Fax: 918-582-7896. E-mail: mike@campchippewa.com. World Wide Web: http://www.campchippewa.com. Contact by e-mail, fax, mail, phone, or through World Wide Web site. Application deadline: continuous.

CAMP COURAGE
8046 83RD STREET, NW
MAPLE LAKE, MINNESOTA 55358

General Information Programs offered for physically disabled children and adults, including adventure camping for the deaf and speech therapy for speech/language-impaired children. Established in 1955. 300-acre facility located 50 miles from Minneapolis. Features: pool; gymnasium; tennis courts; lake; horses; accessible site.

Profile of Summer Employees Total number: 120; typical ages: 18–50. 50% men; 50% women; 8% minorities; 10% high school students; 80% college students; 1% retirees; 8% non-U.S. citizens; 60% local applicants.

Employment Information Openings are from June 1 to August 20. Year-round positions also offered. Jobs available: ▶ 6 *cooks* at $9 per hour ▶ 36 *counselors* at $165–$200 per week ▶ 3 *nurses* with RN, LPN, or GN license at $500–$600 per week ▶ 20 *program specialists* with appropriate certification for area at $160–$185 per week ▶ 3 *program specialists (crafts)* with certification or experience in the field at $165–$200 per week ▶ 3 *program specialists (photography)* with certification or experience in the field at $165–$225 per week ▶ 14 *speech clinicians* with MS in speech pathology/communications disorders (BA acceptable at lower pay rate) at $335–$455 per week ▶ 6 *waterfront personnel* with lifeguard certification at $165–$210 per week. Applicants must submit formal organization application, two personal references or two letters of recommendation. An in-person interview is recommended, but a telephone interview is acceptable. International applicants accepted; must obtain own visa, obtain own working papers, apply through a recognized agency.

Benefits and Preemployment Training Free housing, free meals, formal training, health insurance, willing to provide letters of recommendation, on-the-job training, willing to complete paperwork for educational credit, willing to act as a professional reference, opportunity to attend seminars/workshops, travel reimbursement, and tuition assistance. Preemployment training is required and includes accident prevention and safety, first aid, CPR, interpersonal skills, leadership skills, camp skills.

Contact Roger Upcraft, Program Manager, Camp Courage, 8046 83rd Street, NW, Maple Lake, Minnesota 55358. Telephone: 320-963-3121. Fax: 320-963-3698. E-mail: camping@mtn.org. World Wide Web: http://www.couragecamps.org. Contact by e-mail, fax, mail, phone, or through World Wide Web site. Application deadline: continuous.

CAMP LINCOLN FOR BOYS/CAMP LAKE HUBERT FOR GIRLS
LAKE HUBERT, MINNESOTA 56459

General Information Separate boys and girls camps offering 30 land and water activities, staff from around the world, one- to four-week sessions for ages 8 to 17. Established in 1909. 800-acre facility located 140 miles from Minneapolis. Features: 800 acres; boys and girls camps; mile of lakeshore; 30 land water activities; log cabins; 150 fun staff.

Profile of Summer Employees Total number: 155; typical ages: 19–30. 50% men; 50% women; 10% minorities; 80% college students; 2% retirees; 15% non-U.S. citizens; 15% local applicants. Nonsmokers required.

Employment Information Openings are from June 3 to August 29. Jobs available: ▶ 8–12 *activity directors* (minimum age 20) with experience and ability to teach one or more of the following: sports, riflery, archery, campcraft, riding, windsurfing, arts and crafts, karate, sailing, high ropes, climbing wall at $1700–$3000 per season ▶ 4–8 *cooks/bakers* (minimum age 21) with food service experience at $1800–$3200 per season ▶ 80–120 *counselors* (minimum age 19) with some experience working with young people at $1600–$2500 per season ▶ 1–2 *drivers* (minimum age 21) with Class B driver's license, clean driving record, and ability to complete training course at $1700–$2500 per season ▶ 12–20 *general food service staff members* (minimum age 19) at $1600–$3000 per season ▶ 20–30 *head counselors* (minimum age 21) with leadership experience at $1750–$2700 per season ▶ 2–4 *nurses* (minimum age 21) with LPN, RN at $250–$375 per week ▶ 3–5 *office staff members* with computer experience at $1700–$2900 per season ▶ 6–10 *trip leaders* (minimum age 21) with lifeguard training, CPR, first aid, canoe and pack experience at $1700–$2500 per season. Applicants must submit formal organization application, three personal references. An in-person interview is recommended, but a telephone interview is acceptable. International applicants accepted; must apply through a recognized agency.

Benefits and Preemployment Training Free housing, free meals, formal training, willing to provide letters of recommendation, on-the-job training, willing to complete paperwork for educational credit, and travel reimbursement. Preemployment training is required and includes accident prevention and safety, interpersonal skills, leadership skills, lifeguard training.

Contact Ruggs Cote, Director, Camp Lincoln for Boys/Camp Lake Hubert for Girls, 10179 Crosstown Circle, Eden Prairie, Minnesota 55344. Telephone: 800-242-1909. Fax: 952-922-7149. E-mail: home@lincoln-lakehubert.com. World Wide Web: http://www.lincoln-lakehubert. com. Contact by e-mail, fax, mail, phone, or through World Wide Web site. Application deadline: continuous.

CAMP NEW HOPE
53035 LAKE AVENUE
MCGREGOR, MINNESOTA 55760

General Information Nonprofit organization that provides recreation and leisure opportunities to individuals with developmental disabilities. Established in 1968. 40-acre facility located 70 miles from Duluth. Features: freshwater lake; wooded setting; peaceful; modern and rustic facilities.

Profile of Summer Employees Total number: 40; typical ages: 16–26. 20% men; 80% women; 6% high school students; 60% college students; 15% non-U.S. citizens; 16% local applicants.

Employment Information Openings are from May 20 to August 25. Jobs available: ▶ 1 *arts and crafts specialist* (minimum age 18) at $195–$215 per week ▶ 2 *camp nurses* (minimum age 21) with current LPN or RN license in Minnesota at $350–$600 per week ▶ 18 *counselors* (minimum age 16) at $195–$205 per week ▶ 1 *music specialist* (minimum age 18) with experience in music therapy at $195–$215 per week ▶ 1 *nature specialist* with interest in nature and/or environmental education at $195–$215 per week ▶ 1 *nurse* with RN certification ▶ 1 *recreation specialist* (minimum age 18) at $195–$215 per week ▶ 2 *waterfront lifeguards* (minimum age 18) with current lifeguard certification at $215–$230 per week ▶ 1 *waterfront specialist* with WSI, lifeguard, CPR, and first aid training. Applicants must submit formal organization application, three personal references. An in-person interview is recommended, but a telephone interview is acceptable. International applicants accepted; must apply through a recognized agency.

Benefits and Preemployment Training Free housing, free meals, willing to provide letters of recommendation, names of contacts, on-the-job training, willing to complete paperwork for educational credit, willing to act as a professional reference, and tuition assistance. Preemployment training is required and includes accident prevention and safety, first aid, CPR, interpersonal skills, leadership skills, therapeutic intervention, disability awareness.

Contact Lori Czarneski, Director, Camp New Hope. Telephone: 218-426-3560. Fax: 218-426-3560. E-mail: cnewhope@lcp2.net. World Wide Web: http://www.campnewhopemn.org. Contact by e-mail, fax, mail, phone, or through World Wide Web site. Application deadline: continuous.

CAMP THUNDERBIRD FOR GIRLS
49491 219 AVENUE
BEMIDJI, MINNESOTA 56601

General Information Residential camp serving 150 girls from forty U.S. cities and five other countries. Established in 1970. 250-acre facility. Features: 1½ miles of sand beach shoreline;

700 pristine acres of property; extensive waterfront program and equipment; English riding program; gymnastic program; tennis courts.

Profile of Summer Employees Total number: 100; typical ages: 19–70. 10% men; 90% women; 2% minorities; 12% high school students; 60% college students; 1% retirees; 20% non-U.S. citizens; 5% local applicants. Nonsmokers preferred.

Employment Information Openings are from June 1 to August 21. Jobs available: ► 1 *arts and crafts specialist* with experience as an art teacher or art student preferred, completion of junior year in college required at a negotiable salary ► 2 *horseback specialists* with experience in English Hunt Seat specialty; junior year of college completed; CHA or HSA certification preferred, but will send to clinic for certification at a negotiable salary ► 10 *kitchen personnel* (minimum age 19) with ability to assist with kitchen operations, food preparation, dishwashing, and cleanup; one year of college completed at a negotiable salary ► 2 *nurses* with RN or LPN at $400 and up per week ► 2 *office personnel* (minimum age 19) with bookkeeping and computer knowledge, ability to handle camper/staff cash accounts, average or above-average typing skills, and sophomore year of college completed at a negotiable salary ► 1 *program director* with experience encompassing staff supervision and direct leadership of children in outdoor recreation/camp activities, college graduate at a negotiable salary ► 1 *sailing instructor* with sailing and lifeguard certification at a negotiable salary ► 6 *swimming instructors* with WSI, lifeguard, and CPR certifications; teaching experience (preferred) at a negotiable salary ► 1 *trip director* with experience in diverse kinds of wilderness trips and equipment use, college graduate at a negotiable salary ► 3 *unit directors* (minimum age 23) with experience encompassing staff supervision and direct leadership of children in outdoor recreation/camp activities, college graduate at a negotiable salary ► 1 *waterfront director* with WSI, first aid, lifeguard, and CPR certification, college degree, and knowledge of various water sports at a negotiable salary ► 10 *wilderness and trip leaders* (minimum age 21) with certifications in CPR, AWFA, WFR, and lifeguard (must be comfortable and confident living in the wilderness) at $1200–$1800 per season. Applicants must submit formal organization application, resume, three personal references. An in-person interview is recommended, but a telephone interview is acceptable. International applicants accepted; must apply through a recognized agency.

Benefits and Preemployment Training Free housing, free meals, willing to provide letters of recommendation, on-the-job training, willing to complete paperwork for educational credit, willing to act as a professional reference, opportunity to attend seminars/workshops, and travel reimbursement. Preemployment training is required and includes accident prevention and safety, first aid, CPR, interpersonal skills, leadership skills, WSI, lifeguard training, WFA.

Contact Carol A. Sigoloff, Director, Camp Thunderbird for Girls, 10420 Old Olive Street Road, Suite 202, St. Louis, Missouri 63141. Telephone: 314-567-3167. Fax: 314-567-7218. E-mail: tbirdcamp@primary.net. World Wide Web: http://www.camptbird.com. Contact by e-mail, fax, mail, phone, or through World Wide Web site. Application deadline: continuous.

CYBERCAMPS–UNIVERSITY OF MINNESOTA
MINNEAPOLIS, MINNESOTA
See Cybercamps–University of Washington on page 326 for complete description.

DEEP PORTAGE CONSERVATION RESERVE
2197 NATURE CENTER DRIVE, NW
HACKENSACK, MINNESOTA 56452

General Information 6000-acre forest and conservation education center that conducts programs in environmental education. Established in 1973. 6,307-acre facility located 50 miles from Brainerd. Features: rolling, wooded glacial hills; 10 lakes; bogs; streams; large modern dormitory.

Profile of Summer Employees Total number: 16; typical ages: 18–25. 50% men; 50% women; 10% minorities; 10% high school students; 70% college students; 10% non-U.S. citizens.

Employment Information Openings are from June 5 to August 25. Jobs available: ▶ 10 *instructors/camp counselors* with college training in related fields at $175–$225 per week. Applicants must submit a letter of interest, resume, three personal references. A telephone interview is required. International applicants accepted; must obtain own visa, obtain own working papers.

Benefits and Preemployment Training Free housing, free meals, formal training, and on-the-job training.

Contact Dale Yerger, Executive Director, Deep Portage Conservation Reserve, 2197 Nature Center Drive, NW, Hackensack, Minnesota 56452. Telephone: 218-682-2325. Fax: 218-682-3121. E-mail: portage@uslink.net. World Wide Web: http://www.deep-portage.org. Contact by e-mail, fax, mail, phone, or through World Wide Web site. Application deadline: continuous.

DRIFTWOOD FAMILY RESORT & GOLF
6020 DRIFTWOOD LANE
PINE RIVER, MINNESOTA 56474

General Information Resort specializing in family vacations with an emphasis on many different types of recreation. Established in 1902. 44-acre facility located 30 miles from Brainerd. Features: freshwater lakes; wooded setting; tennis court; 9-hole golf course; authentic Norwegian smorgasbord; family resort.

Profile of Summer Employees Total number: 14; typical ages: 16–65. 50% men; 50% women; 50% high school students; 50% college students; 10% retirees; 50% non-U.S. citizens; 50% local applicants. Nonsmokers preferred.

Employment Information Openings are from May 1 to October 1. Jobs available: ▶ 2–4 *cabin maids* (minimum age 16) at $7–$8 per hour ▶ 4 *cooks or cook's helpers* (minimum age 18) with chef's certificate preferred at $7–$8 per hour ▶ 1 *dining room host/hostess* (minimum age 20) at $7 and up per hour ▶ 2 *front desk/office staff members* (minimum age 16) at $7 and up per hour ▶ 2 *lawn/golf maintenance staff members/gardeners* (minimum age 16) at $7–$8 per hour ▶ 2 *recreation directors* (minimum age 18) at $7–$8 per hour ▶ 8–10 *waiters/waitresses* (minimum age 17) at $800–$1000 per month. Applicants must submit writing sample, two personal references, two letters of recommendation. An in-person interview is recommended, but a telephone interview is acceptable. International applicants accepted; must obtain own visa, obtain own working papers, apply through a recognized agency.

Benefits and Preemployment Training Housing at a cost, meals at a cost, willing to provide letters of recommendation, willing to act as a professional reference, and contract completion bonus. Preemployment training is optional and includes accident prevention and safety, interpersonal skills, leadership skills.

Contact Dan Leagjeld, Owner, Driftwood Family Resort & Golf, 6020 Driftwood Lane, Pine River, Minnesota 56474. Telephone: 218-568-4221. Fax: 218-568-4222. E-mail: ponyride@uslink. net. World Wide Web: http://www.driftwoodresort.com. Contact by e-mail, fax, mail, phone, or through World Wide Web site. Application deadline: May 15.

FRIENDSHIP VENTURES/CAMP FRIENDSHIP
10509 108TH STREET, NW
ANNANDALE, MINNESOTA 55302

General Information Residential camp serving children and adults with developmental disabilities. Established in 1964. 115-acre facility located 60 miles from Minneapolis. Features: wooded setting; large waterfront; challenge course; cabins.

Profile of Summer Employees Total number: 150; typical ages: 16–25. 25% men; 75% women; 5% minorities; 15% high school students; 85% college students; 10% non-U.S. citizens; 20% local applicants.

Employment Information Openings are from May 29 to September 1. Year-round positions also offered. Jobs available: ▶ 5 *adventure/recreation specialists* with preference for current major in recreation, physical education, or adaptive physical recreation and leadership skills involving group activities at $125–$180 per week ▶ 2 *arts and crafts specialists* with preference for current major in therapeutic recreation, occupational therapy, or art education/therapy or experience planning and implementing arts and crafts activities/projects at $125–$180 per week ▶ 1 *camping specialist* with tent camping and outdoor experience and environmental education knowledge at $125–$180 per week ▶ 1 *canteen/camp store manager* with record-keeping skills at $125–$180 per week ▶ 60 *counselors* at $165–$180 per week ▶ 1 *dietary specialist* with experience in food service area with an emphasis on special diets at $125–$180 per week ▶ 2 *dining hall workers* with experience working in food service or dining hall areas at a negotiable salary ▶ 12 *junior counselors* (minimum age 16) with physical and emotional strength, mental alertness, creativity, flexibility, and high school student status (successful volunteer experience may be substituted for the age requirement) at $90–$110 per week ▶ 2 *laundry/housekeeping staff members* at a negotiable salary ▶ 2 *music specialists* with preference for current major in music, music therapy, or special education and experience planning and implementing activities at $125–$180 per week ▶ 4 *nurses* with RN, LPN, or GN license or BSN degree at a negotiable salary ▶ 2 *office support staff* with computer, typing, phone, and filing experience at $125–$180 per week ▶ 1 *outdoor specialist* with preference for current major in an environmental, outdoor, or education field at $125–$180 per week ▶ 1 *public relations assistant* with current major in journalism, photography, or related field and experience with a 35mm camera at $125–$180 per week ▶ 1 *respite specialist* with experience working with people with developmental disabilities in a camp setting at $200–$250 per week ▶ 1 *waterfront director* with WSI and lifeguard certification, experience working on waterfront helpful at $180–$250 per week ▶ 4 *waterfront lifeguards* with WSI and lifeguard certification (preferred) at $125–$180 per week ▶ 3 *weekend counselors* with physical strength, mental alertness, and at least one year of college completed at $185 per weekend. Applicants must submit formal organization application, 2 personal references or 2 letters of recommendation. An in-person interview is recommended, but a telephone interview is acceptable. International applicants accepted; must apply through a recognized agency.

Benefits and Preemployment Training Free housing, free meals, formal training, willing to provide letters of recommendation, on-the-job training, willing to complete paperwork for educational credit, willing to act as a professional reference, and scholarships available. Preemployment training is required and includes accident prevention and safety, first aid, CPR, interpersonal skills, leadership skills.

Contact Maria Schugel, Program Manager, Friendship Ventures/Camp Friendship, 10509 108th Street, NW, Annandale, Minnesota 55302. Telephone: 952-852-0101. Fax: 952-852-0123. E-mail: jobs@friendshipventures.org. World Wide Web: http://www.friendshipventures.org. Contact by e-mail, fax, mail, or phone. Application deadline: continuous.

FRIENDSHIP VENTURES/EDEN WOOD CAMP
10509 108TH STREET, NW
ANNANDALE, MINNESOTA 55302

General Information Residential and day camp serving children and adults with developmental disabilities. Established in 1958. 12-acre facility located 15 miles from Minneapolis. Features: wooded setting; walking trails; cabins/dormitory; close to lakes area; challenge course.

Profile of Summer Employees Total number: 35; typical ages: 16–25. 25% men; 75% women; 5% minorities; 15% high school students; 85% college students; 10% non-U.S. citizens; 20% local applicants.

Employment Information Openings are from May 26 to September 1. Year-round positions also offered. Jobs available: ▶ 1 *arts and crafts specialist* with preference for current major in therapeutic recreation, occupational therapy, or art education/therapy or experience planning and implementing arts and crafts activities/projects at $165–$225 per week ▶ 30 *counselors* (minimum age 16) at $165–$225 per week ▶ 1 *creative movement/drama specialist* with experience in the performing arts field at $165–$200 per week ▶ 1 *dining hall staff worker* with experience in food service/dining hall area at a negotiable salary ▶ 6 *junior counselors* (minimum age 16) with physical and emotional strength, mental alertness, creativity, flexibility, and high school student status (successful volunteer experience may be substituted for the age requirement) at $100 per week ▶ 2 *laundry/housekeeping staff members* (minimum age 18) at $165–$200 per week ▶ 2 *lifeguards* with WSI and lifeguard certification (preferred) at $165–$225 per week ▶ 1 *music specialist* with preference for major in music, music therapy, or special education and experience planning and implementing activities at $165–$200 per week ▶ 2 *nurses* with RN, LPN, GN license or BSN degree at a negotiable salary ▶ 1 *office support staff* with computer, typing, phone, and filing experience at $165–$200 per week ▶ 1 *outdoor specialist* with preference for current major in environmental, outdoor, or education field at $165–$200 per week ▶ 1 *recreation specialist* with preference for current major in recreation, physical education, or adaptive physical recreation and leadership skills involving group activities at $165–$200 per week ▶ 6 *travel leaders* (minimum age 21) with leadership skills and valid driver's license at $20–$35 per day ▶ 10 *weekend counselors* with physical strength, mental alertness, and at least one year of college completed at $165 to $200 per weekend. Applicants must submit formal organization application, two personal references, letter of recommendation. An in-person interview is recommended, but a telephone interview is acceptable. International applicants accepted; must apply through a recognized agency.

Benefits and Preemployment Training Free housing, free meals, formal training, willing to provide letters of recommendation, on-the-job training, willing to complete paperwork for educational credit, willing to act as a professional reference, and academic scholarship. Preemployment training is required and includes accident prevention and safety, first aid, CPR, interpersonal skills, leadership skills.

Contact Maria Schugel, Program Manager, Friendship Ventures/Eden Wood Camp, 10509 108th Street, NW, Annandale, Minnesota 55302. Telephone: 952-852-0101. Fax: 952-852-0123. E-mail: jobs@friendshipventures.org. World Wide Web: http://www.friendshipventures.org. Contact by e-mail, fax, mail, phone, or through World Wide Web site. Application deadline: continuous.

GRAND VIEW LODGE GOLF AND TENNIS CLUB
23521 NOKOMIS AVENUE
NISSWA, MINNESOTA 56468

General Information Resort that caters to families and business conventions and operates public golf courses in Minnesota. Established in 1914. 1,300-acre facility located 150 miles from Minneapolis. Features: tennis courts; golf; beautiful lake for swimming, fishing, and waterskiing; wooded areas; indoor pool.

Profile of Summer Employees Total number: 500; typical ages: 16–25. 45% men; 55% women; 10% minorities; 20% high school students; 50% college students; 10% retirees; 20% non-U.S. citizens; 20% local applicants.

Employment Information Openings are from April 15 to November 1. Jobs available: ▶ 5 *bartenders* (minimum age 18) with experience in the field at $175–$220 per week ▶ 5 *beach staff members* (minimum age 16) with knowledge of boats and motors at $190–$240 per week ▶ 3 *children's program instructors* (minimum age 17) with CPR certification at $190–$240 per week ▶ 25 *dining room wait staff* (minimum age 18) at $200–$260 per week ▶ 10 *golf course maintenance staff* with knowledge of equipment at $225–$280 per week ▶ 5 *golf shop staff* with golf background and merchandise skills at $225–$280 per week ▶ 15 *housekeepers* (minimum age 15) at $210–$260 per week ▶ 3 *skilled front desk staff* (minimum age 18) at $185–$240 per week. Applicants must submit resume. An in-person interview is recommended, but a telephone interview is acceptable. International applicants accepted; must obtain own visa.

Benefits and Preemployment Training Housing at a cost, meals at a cost, formal training, willing to provide letters of recommendation, on-the-job training, and willing to complete paperwork for educational credit. Preemployment training is required and includes accident prevention and safety, leadership skills.

Contact Jan Kummet, Human Resources, Grand View Lodge Golf and Tennis Club, 23521 Nokomis Avenue, Nisswa, Minnesota 56468. Telephone: 218-963-2234. Fax: 218-963-0261. E-mail: work@grandviewlodge.com. World Wide Web: http://www.grandviewlodge.com. Contact by e-mail, fax, mail, phone, or through World Wide Web site. Application deadline: continuous.

GUNFLINT LODGE AND OUTFITTERS
143 SOUTH GUNFLINT LAKE
GRAND MARAIS, MINNESOTA 55604

General Information Family and fishing resort offering cabin accommodations with modified or full American plan packages. Guide services, naturalist activities, and access to Boundary Waters Canoe Area. Established in 1927. 100-acre facility located 150 miles from Duluth. Features: freshwater lake for fishing; BWCA wilderness for camping; Superior National Forest; canoeing; hiking; horse stable.

Profile of Summer Employees Total number: 65; typical ages: 20–40. 55% men; 45% women; 1% minorities; 5% high school students; 60% college students; 8% retirees; 20% non-U.S. citizens; 5% local applicants. Nonsmokers preferred.

Employment Information Openings are from May 1 to November 1. Winter break and year-round positions also offered. Jobs available: ▶ 1–2 *activity leaders/naturalists* (minimum age 18) with driver's license, good driving record, training in biology/forestry/geography, and experience (preferred) at $1065 per month ▶ 1 *baker* (minimum age 18) with great desire to learn, experience preferred at $1065–$1300 per month ▶ 1 *breakfast and lunch cook* (minimum age 18) with great desire to learn, experience preferred at $1065–$1400 per month ▶ 3 *dishwasher/housekeepers* (minimum age 17) at $1065 per month ▶ 2 *dock staff* (minimum age 18) with ability to lift and carry 75 pounds, knowledge of outboard motors, driver's license, and good driving record at $1150 per month ▶ 3 *front desk/guest services staff* at $1200 per month ▶ 3 *kitchen assistants/bartenders* (minimum age 18) with previous bartending experience preferred at $1065 per month ▶ 3–6 *outfitters* (minimum age 18) with driver's license, good driving record, and ability to lift and carry 75 pounds at $1065–$1200 per month ▶ 1 *prep cook* (minimum age 18) with great desire to learn, experience preferred at $1065–$1400 per month ▶ 1–2 *stable hands* (minimum age 18) with experience handling horses, riding, and grooming at $1065 per month ▶ 5–10 *waitresses* (minimum age 18) with experience preferred at $1150 per month. Applicants must submit a formal organization application. A telephone interview is required. International applicants accepted; must obtain own visa, obtain own working papers.

Benefits and Preemployment Training Housing at a cost, possible full-time employment, willing to provide letters of recommendation, on-the-job training, willing to complete paperwork for educational credit, willing to act as a professional reference, and discounted equipment rental rates. Preemployment training is required and includes accident prevention and safety, CPR.

Contact Miranda Kerfoot, Assistant Manager, Gunflint Lodge and Outfitters, 143 South Gunflint Lake, Grand Marais, Minnesota 55604. Telephone: 800-328-3325. Fax: 218-388-9429. E-mail: gunflint@gunflint.com. World Wide Web: http://www.gunflint.com. Contact by e-mail, fax, mail, phone, or through World Wide Web site. Application deadline: continuous.

LAKE HUBERT TENNIS CAMP
BOX 1308
LAKE HUBERT, MINNESOTA 56459

General Information Six or seven-day tennis camps featuring five hours of court time instruction daily for all skill levels; 12 courts for 36 campers. Established in 1973. 750-acre facility located 15 miles from Brainerd. Features: 12 outdoor courts; true camp setting; waterfront.

Profile of Summer Employees Total number: 15; typical ages: 19–45. 50% men; 50% women; 75% college students. Nonsmokers required.

Employment Information Openings are from June 6 to August 28. Jobs available: ▶ 6 *cabin counselors* (minimum age 19) at $175–$200 per week ▶ 10 *tennis instructors* (minimum age 19) with experience in the field at $200–$350 per week ▶ 2 *waterfront staff* (minimum age 21) with lifeguard training at $200–$250 per week. Applicants must submit formal organization application, three personal references. An in-person interview is recommended, but a telephone interview is acceptable. International applicants accepted; must apply through a recognized agency.

Benefits and Preemployment Training Free housing, free meals, formal training, willing to provide letters of recommendation, and travel reimbursement.

Contact Sam Cote, Director, Lake Hubert Tennis Camp, 10179 Crosstown Circle, Eden Prairie, Minnesota 55344. Telephone: 800-242-1909. Fax: 952-922-7149. E-mail: home@lincoln-lakehubert.com. World Wide Web: http://www.lincoln-lakehubert.com. Contact by e-mail, mail, phone, or through World Wide Web site. Application deadline: continuous.

LONG LAKE CONSERVATION CENTER
28952 438TH LANE
PALISADE, MINNESOTA 56469

General Information Residential environmental learning center. Established in 1960. 760-acre facility located 135 miles from Minneapolis/St. Paul. Features: lake; bogs; forested areas; natural setting.

Profile of Summer Employees Total number: 19; typical ages: 19–25. 30% men; 70% women; 100% college students. Nonsmokers preferred.

Employment Information Openings are from June 20 to August 21. Jobs available: ▶ 4–5 *counselors* (minimum age 18) with ability to work with children ages 6 to 16 in an outdoor setting at $180 per week ▶ 2–3 *naturalist interns* (minimum age 18) with ability to work with children ages 6 to 16 in an outdoor setting at $180 per week ▶ 1 *summer program coordinator* (minimum age 23) with B.S. or B.A. degree and experience in supervision of seasonal staff and campers at $280 per week. Applicants must submit a formal organization application, letter of recommendation.

Benefits and Preemployment Training Free housing, free meals, willing to provide letters of recommendation, willing to complete paperwork for educational credit, and willing to act as a professional reference. Preemployment training is required and includes accident prevention and safety, first aid, CPR, interpersonal skills, leadership skills.

Contact Pam Carlson, Administrative Coordinator, Long Lake Conservation Center. Telephone: 800-450-5522. Fax: 218-768-2309. E-mail: llcc@mlecmn.net. World Wide Web: http://www.llcc.org. Contact by e-mail. Application deadline: March 1.

MENOGYN–YMCA WILDERNESS ADVENTURES
55 MENOGYN TRAIL
GRAND MARAIS, MINNESOTA 55604

General Information Wilderness camp specializing in canoeing, backpacking, and rock-climbing trips in wilderness areas of North America. Established in 1922. 80-acre facility located 180 miles from Duluth. Features: 2,000,000 acres of wilderness; freshwater lakes; mountain hiking; rustic wilderness base camp; rock climbing; boundary waters canoe area.

Profile of Summer Employees Total number: 56; typical ages: 20–35. 50% men; 50% women; 5% minorities; 90% college students; 5% non-U.S. citizens; 75% local applicants. Nonsmokers required.

Employment Information Openings are from June 6 to August 30. Jobs available: ▶ 1 *cook* (minimum age 20) with experience in the field and references at $6–$9 per hour ▶ 3–120 *in-camp staff members* with CPR, first aid, and lifeguard training at $140–$203 per week ▶ 1 *nurse* with current Minnesota license at $1200–$2000 per season ▶ 24–36 *trail counselors* (minimum age 19) with CPR, first aid, and lifeguard training at $140–$189 per week. Applicants must submit formal organization application, three personal references. An in-person interview is recommended, but a telephone interview is acceptable. International applicants accepted; must apply through a recognized agency.

Benefits and Preemployment Training Free housing, free meals, formal training, willing to provide letters of recommendation, on-the-job training, willing to complete paperwork for educational credit, and willing to act as a professional reference. Preemployment training is required and includes accident prevention and safety, first aid, CPR, interpersonal skills, leadership skills.

Contact Paul Danicic, Camp Director, Menogyn–YMCA Wilderness Adventures, 4 West Rustic Lodge Avenue, Minneapolis, Minnesota 55409. Telephone: 612-821-2905. Fax: 612-823-2482. E-mail: info@campmenogyn.org. World Wide Web: http://www.campmenogyn.org. Contact by e-mail, fax, mail, phone, or through World Wide Web site. Application deadline: April 30.

NELSON'S RESORT
7632 NELSON ROAD
CRANE LAKE, MINNESOTA 55725

General Information Family resort with conventions in the fall. Established in 1931. 84-acre facility located 70 miles from Virginia. Features: freshwater lake; wooded setting; proximity to Voyageurs National Park; near Boundary Water Canoe Area; Canadian Border Waters.

Profile of Summer Employees Total number: 30; typical ages: 18–40. 44% men; 56% women; 25% college students; 2% retirees; 1% non-U.S. citizens; 6% local applicants.

Employment Information Openings are from May 1 to October 15. Jobs available: ▶ 1–2 *bartenders* at $800–$1000 per month ▶ 1 *bellperson* at $800–$900 per month ▶ 5 *cabin staff members* at $800–$900 per month ▶ 3 *dock attendants* at $800–$900 per month ▶ 3 *kitchen helpers* at $800–$900 per month ▶ 1 *store clerk* at $800–$900 per month ▶ 6 *waiters/waitresses* at $800–$900 per month. Applicants must submit a formal organization application. International applicants accepted; must obtain own visa, obtain own working papers.

Benefits and Preemployment Training Meals at a cost, free housing, willing to provide letters of recommendation, and on-the-job training.

Contact Jerry Pohlman, Co-Owner, Nelson's Resort, 7632 Nelson Road, Crane Lake, Minnesota 55725. Telephone: 218-993-2295. Fax: 218-993-2242. E-mail: nelsons@citlink.net. World Wide Web: http://www.nelsonresort.com. Contact by e-mail, fax, mail, phone, or through World Wide Web site. Application deadline: continuous.

SINGING HILLS GIRL SCOUT CAMP AND CANNON VALLEY DAY CAMPS
49496 193RD AVENUE
WATERVILLE, MINNESOTA 56096

General Information Residential camp serving 88 girls (grades 4–12) weekly, and day camp serving 60–100 girls (grades 2–5) weekly; day camps held at several sites. Established in 1967. 160-acre facility located 30 miles from Minneapolis/St. Paul. Features: rustic setting; clean and clear lake; wooded area.

Profile of Summer Employees Total number: 20; typical ages: 16–65. 100% women; 10% high school students; 70% college students; 10% retirees; 10% non-U.S. citizens; 90% local applicants.

Employment Information Openings are from June 4 to August 10. Jobs available: ▶ 2 *cooks* (minimum age 16) with experience in group cooking and menu planning at $1750 per season ▶ 12 *general counselors* (minimum age 18) with love of working with kids and love of the outdoors at $1500–$2100 per season ▶ 1 *health supervisor* (minimum age 18) with CPR/first aid/EMT, Registered Nurse/Physician, or Nursing student at $3000–$4000 per season ▶ 1 *waterfront director* with lifeguard training at $1800 per season. Applicants must submit formal organization application, three personal references. An in-person interview is recommended, but a telephone interview is acceptable. International applicants accepted; must apply through a recognized agency.

Benefits and Preemployment Training Free housing, free meals, formal training, health insurance, and on-the-job training. Preemployment training is required and includes accident prevention and safety, first aid, CPR, interpersonal skills, leadership skills.

Contact Jennifer Tschida, Camp Director, Singing Hills Girl Scout Camp and Cannon Valley Day Camps, PO Box 61, Northfield, Minnesota 55057. Telephone: 507-645-6603. Fax: 507-645-6605. E-mail: jennifert@gsccv.org. World Wide Web: http://www.gsccv.org. Contact by e-mail, fax, mail, phone, or through World Wide Web site. Application deadline: continuous.

THE SOUTHWESTERN COMPANY, MINNESOTA
See The Southwestern Company on page 297 for complete description.

SPORTS INTERNATIONAL–TICE BROTHERS FOOTBALL CAMP
ST. PAUL, MINNESOTA
See Sports International, Inc. on page 134 for complete description.

STRAW HAT PLAYERS
CENTER FOR THE ARTS–MINNESOTA STATE UNIVERSITY MOORHEAD
MOORHEAD, MINNESOTA 56563
General Information Summer stock theater producing four shows in a nine-week season. Established in 1963. 20-acre facility located near Fargo, North Dakota. Features: 870-seat proscenium theater; 321-seat thrust theater; scene shops, costume shops, and dance studio; access to library, pool, athletic center; largest metropolitan area between Minneapolis and Seattle.

Profile of Summer Employees Total number: 60; typical ages: 22–50. 40% men; 60% women; 5% minorities; 10% high school students; 80% college students; 40% local applicants.

Employment Information Openings are from May 26 to July 26. Jobs available: ▶ 40 *acting company members* (minimum age 17) must be high school junior or senior (minimum) at $100–$180 per week ▶ 3 *costume stitchers* at $100–$250 per week. Applicants must submit formal organization application, letter of interest, resume, videotape. An in-person interview is required. International applicants accepted; must obtain own visa, obtain own working papers, apply through a recognized agency.

Benefits and Preemployment Training Free housing, formal training, on-the-job training, willing to complete paperwork for educational credit, and tuition assistance.

Contact Jim Bartruff, Director of Theater, Straw Hat Players, Minnesota State University Moorhead, Moorhead, Minnesota 56563. Telephone: 218-236-4616. Fax: 218-236-4612. E-mail: bartruff@mnstate.edu. World Wide Web: http://www.mnstate.edu. Contact by e-mail, fax, mail, or through World Wide Web site. Application deadline: April 15.

STUDENT CONSERVATION ASSOCIATION (SCA), MINNESOTA
See Student Conservation Association (SCA), New Hampshire on page 200 for complete description.

WILDERNESS DANCE CAMP
10251 LYNDALE AVENUE SOUTH
BLOOMINGTON, MINNESOTA 55420

General Information Resident camp teaching ballet, tap, jazz, modern, and musical theatre. Established in 1997. Located 1 mile from Bemidji. Features: wooded setting; freshwater lake; swimming pool; recreation center; dormitories.

Profile of Summer Employees Total number: 15; typical age: 21. 10% men; 90% women; 15% minorities; 15% high school students; 25% college students; 15% retirees; 15% non-U.S. citizens; 15% local applicants. Nonsmokers required.

Employment Information Openings are from June 1 to August 31. Jobs available: ▶ 1–4 *camp nurses* (minimum age 22) with nursing experience and additional knowledge of sports injuries at a salary varying upon qualifications ▶ 10–40 *counselors* (minimum age 19) with an interest in kids and enjoyment of dance at $100–$200 per week. Applicants must submit letter of interest, resume, academic transcripts, three personal references, three letters of recommendation, criminal background check. An in-person interview is recommended, but a telephone interview is acceptable. International applicants accepted; must obtain own visa, obtain own working papers, apply through a recognized agency.

Benefits and Preemployment Training Free housing, free meals, willing to provide letters of recommendation, willing to complete paperwork for educational credit, willing to act as a professional reference, and opportunity to attend seminars/workshops. Preemployment training is required.

Contact Chandra Saign, Director, Wilderness Dance Camp. Telephone: 952-884-6009. E-mail: info@dancecamp.org. World Wide Web: http://www.dancecamp.org. Contact by e-mail, mail, or phone. Application deadline: continuous.

YMCA CAMP PEPIN
434 MAIN STREET
RED WING, MINNESOTA 55066

General Information Youth camp serving over 800 campers; specialty programs include riding camp, adventure camp, theater camp, and CIT and LIT training sessions. Established in 1935. 40-acre facility located 60 miles from Minneapolis. Features: freshwater lake; bluff setting; canoe trips; camping/hiking; rock climbing; ropes course.

Profile of Summer Employees Total number: 35; typical ages: 18–24. 45% men; 55% women; 15% minorities; 90% college students; 15% non-U.S. citizens; 20% local applicants. Nonsmokers preferred.

Employment Information Openings are from June 12 to August 14. Year-round positions also offered. Jobs available: ▶ 1 *CIT/LDP counselor* (minimum age 19) with experience in teen programming at $155–$185 per week ▶ *adventure director* (minimum age 21) with wilderness skills at $150–$185 per week ▶ 1 *arts and crafts instructor* (minimum age 19) at $155–$185 per week ▶ 1–5 *counselors* (minimum age 19) at $145–$175 per week ▶ *health director* (minimum age 21) with RN or EMT license at $195–$245 per week ▶ 1 *program director* (minimum age 21) with previous program experience at $195–$235 per week ▶ 1 *ropes/trips director* (minimum age 21) with previous ropes course work at $155–$175 per week ▶ 2 *unit leaders/senior counselors* (minimum age 21) at $155–$185 per week ▶ *waterfront director* (minimum age 21) with CPR, LGT, and WSI certifications at $160–$195 per week. Applicants must submit formal organization application, three personal references. An in-person interview is recommended, but a telephone interview is acceptable. International applicants accepted; must apply through a recognized agency.

Benefits and Preemployment Training Free housing, free meals, formal training, willing to provide letters of recommendation, on-the-job training, willing to complete paperwork for

educational credit, willing to act as a professional reference, and opportunity to attend seminars/ workshops. Preemployment training is required and includes accident prevention and safety, interpersonal skills, leadership skills.

Contact Clint Knox, Camp Director, YMCA Camp Pepin, 434 Main Street, Red Wing, Minnesota 55066. Telephone: 651-388-4724. Fax: 651-388-5340. E-mail: camppepin@hotmail.com. World Wide Web: http://www.redwingymca.org. Contact by e-mail, fax, mail, phone, or through World Wide Web site. Application deadline: April 15.

MISSISSIPPI

CAMP STANISLAUS
304 SOUTH BEACH BOULEVARD
BAY ST. LOUIS, MISSISSIPPI 39520

General Information Camp Stanislaus is a traditional camp for boys with a carefully supervised and structured environment which enables a boy to succeed daily in a variety of recreational and learning pursuits. Established in 1928. 33-acre facility located 60 miles from New Orleans, Louisiana. Features: 1000 foot pier; white, sandy beaches; Gulf of Mexico; Jouron River; air conditioned dormitory; 3 tennis courts.

Profile of Summer Employees Total number: 80; typical ages: 16–75. 90% men; 10% women; 5% minorities; 15% high school students; 40% college students; 1% retirees; 50% local applicants. Nonsmokers preferred.

Employment Information Openings are from May 20 to July 28. Jobs available: ▶ 1–2 *archery instructor* (minimum age 20) with leadership ability, self-motivation, and ability to instruct boys in the fundamentals of archery at $1300–$3000 per season ▶ *computer staff* (minimum age 18) with Web design, e-mail, PageMaker, and Microsoft Word experience; must be a positive role model, leader, and self-motivated at $1500–$2500 per season ▶ 1–30 *counselors* (minimum age 18) with ability to be a positive role model and a self-motivated leader at $1300–$3000 per season ▶ 1–16 *counselors in training (CIT)* (minimum age 16) self-motivated leader and positive role model at $800–$1000 per season ▶ 1–12 *sailing instructors* (minimum age 16) with ability to teach sailing on sunfish, catamarans, and harpoons; must be a self-motivated leader at $800–$3000 per season ▶ 1–8 *skiing instructors* (minimum age 18) with ability to be a self-motivated leader and role model and instruct water skiing, wake boarding, knee boarding at $1300–$3000 per season. Applicants must submit formal organization application, two personal references. An in-person interview is recommended, but a telephone interview is acceptable. International applicants accepted; must apply through a recognized agency.

Benefits and Preemployment Training Free housing, free meals, formal training, possible full-time employment, willing to provide letters of recommendation, names of contacts, on-the-job training, willing to complete paperwork for educational credit, willing to act as a professional reference, opportunity to attend seminars/workshops, and access to weight room and other facilities including water skiing. Preemployment training is required and includes accident prevention and safety, first aid, CPR, interpersonal skills, leadership skills, lifeguard training, dealing with undesirable behaviors, sailing, skiing, and communication.

Contact Michael J. Reso, Camp Director, Camp Stanislaus. Telephone: 228-467-9057 Ext. 235. Fax: 228-466-2972. E-mail: mreso@ststan.com. World Wide Web: http://www.campstanislaus. com. Contact by e-mail, fax, mail, or phone. Application deadline: continuous.

MARINE LIFE OCEANARIUM
JOSEPH T. JONES PARK, HIGHWAY 90
GULFPORT, MISSISSIPPI 39501

General Information Oceanarium with dolphins, sea lions, sharks, rays, giant sea turtles, exotic birds, and more. Established in 1956. 25-acre facility located 60 miles from New Orleans, Louisiana. Features: location on Gulf Coast; diving; boating; gift shop; snack bar; gravity ship.

Profile of Summer Employees Total number: 50; typical ages: 15–20. 66% men; 34% women; 40% high school students; 10% college students; 50% local applicants.

Employment Information Openings are from May 20 to September 20. Jobs available: ▶ *operations department staff, divers* (minimum age 18) with scuba certification at $150 per week ▶ 2–5 *operations department staff, fish sellers* (minimum age 15) at $150 per week. Applicants must submit a formal organization application, letter of interest. An in-person interview is recommended, but a telephone interview is acceptable.

Benefits and Preemployment Training Formal training, possible full-time employment, willing to provide letters of recommendation, names of contacts, on-the-job training, willing to complete paperwork for educational credit, and willing to act as a professional reference.

Contact Jeffrey Siegel, Operations Manager/Education Director, Marine Life Oceanarium, PO Box 4078, Gulfport, Mississippi 39502. Fax: 228-575-8899. E-mail: dolfin@cableone.net. World Wide Web: http://www.dolphinsrus.com. Contact by e-mail, mail, or through World Wide Web site. No phone calls. Application deadline: continuous.

THE SOUTHWESTERN COMPANY, MISSISSIPPI
See The Southwestern Company on page 297 for complete description.

STUDENT CONSERVATION ASSOCIATION (SCA), MISSISSIPPI
See Student Conservation Association (SCA), New Hampshire on page 200 for complete description.

MISSOURI

CAMP SABRA
30750 CAMP SABRA ROAD
ROCKY MOUNT, MISSOURI 65072

General Information Residential coed summer camping facility of St. Louis Jewish Community Center serving boys, girls, and teens entering grades 3-10 with complete waterfront and land activity program. Established in 1938. 960-acre facility located 10 miles from Eldon. Features: 3½ miles of private shoreline; large fleet of ski and sailboats; 12 miles of horseback riding trails; 3 lighted tennis courts; summer theater; 960 tree-shaded acres.

Profile of Summer Employees Total number: 130; typical ages: 18–22. 50% men; 50% women; 20% high school students; 75% college students; 10% non-U.S. citizens; 5% local applicants. Nonsmokers preferred.

Employment Information Openings are from June 2 to August 5. Jobs available: ▶ 10–20 *counselors* (minimum age 17) with experience preferred at $1000–$2000 per season ▶ *ropes course director* (minimum age 21) with experience with climbing tower, low ropes course, and high ropes course at $2000 and up per season ► 4–5 *ropes course specialists* (minimum age 17) with experience with climbing tower, low ropes courses, and high ropes courses at $1000–$2000 per season ► 1 *songleader* with experience with singing and musical instrument at $2000 and up per season ► 20–30 *specialists* (minimum age 17) with LGT for waterfront staff and experience in specialty required at $1000–$2000 per season ► 1–3 *unit head programmers* (minimum age 21) with experience with 3rd-8th grade children and supervision at $2000 and up per season. Applicants must submit formal organization application, three personal references. An in-person interview is recommended, but a telephone interview is acceptable. International applicants accepted; must apply through a recognized agency.

Benefits and Preemployment Training Free housing, free meals, formal training, on-the-job training, and willing to complete paperwork for educational credit. Preemployment training is required and includes accident prevention and safety, first aid, CPR, interpersonal skills, leadership skills.

Contact Mr. Randy Comensky, Director, Camp Sabra, 16801 Baxter Road, Chesterfield, Missouri 63005. Telephone: 314-442-3426. Fax: 314-442-3404. E-mail: rcomensky@jccstl.org. World Wide Web: http://www.campsabra.com. Contact by e-mail, fax, mail, phone, or through World Wide Web site. Application deadline: continuous.

CYBERCAMPS–WASHINGTON UNIVERSITY
ST. LOUIS, MISSOURI
See Cybercamps–University of Washington on page 326 for complete description.

THE SOUTHWESTERN COMPANY, MISSOURI
See The Southwestern Company on page 297 for complete description.

STIVERS STAFFING SERVICES–MISSOURI
See Stivers Staffing Services–Illinois on page 96 for complete description.

STUDENT CONSERVATION ASSOCIATION (SCA), MISSOURI
See Student Conservation Association (SCA), New Hampshire on page 200 for complete description.

TRAILS WILDERNESS SCHOOL
5 WHITE GATE LANE
ST. LOUIS, MISSOURI 63124-1905
General Information Wilderness adventure summer program for grades 5 and up; campers learn outdoor skills in WY, AK, Pacific NW, MO, Europe, and Mexico; activities include backpacking, rock climbing, kayaking, canoeing, surfing, skiing and snowboarding. Established in 1994. Located 15 miles from Jackson, Wyoming. Features: base camp in Jackson Hole, WY; Grand Teton National Park; scenic views; wilderness setting; evening campfires; 10 minutes from airport.

Profile of Summer Employees Total number: 30; typical age: 29. 50% men; 50% women; 10% college students; 5% non-U.S. citizens; 10% local applicants. Nonsmokers required.

Employment Information Openings are from May 15 to August 31. Jobs available: ► 1–2 *drovers* (minimum age 21) with a clean driving record at $180–$250 per week ► 8–20 *instructors* (minimum age 25) with backpacking, surfing, and rock climbing experience at $180–$350 per week ► 1–2 *wizards* (minimum age 21) with a clean driving record at $180–$300 per week.

Applicants must submit formal organization application, letter of interest, resume, three letters of recommendation, five personal references. International applicants accepted; must apply through a recognized agency.

Benefits and Preemployment Training Free housing, free meals, possible full-time employment, willing to provide letters of recommendation, names of contacts, willing to complete paperwork for educational credit, and willing to act as a professional reference. Preemployment training is required and includes accident prevention and safety, interpersonal skills, leadership skills, wilderness specific travel.

Contact Whigger Mullins, Director, Trails Wilderness School. Telephone: 314-994-9308. Fax: 314-994-9307. E-mail: info@trailsws.com. World Wide Web: http://www.trailsws.com. Contact by e-mail, mail, phone, or through World Wide Web site. Application deadline: continuous.

WORLDS OF FUN/OCEANS OF FUN
4545 WORLD OF FUN AVENUE
KANSAS CITY, MISSOURI 64161

General Information Amusement park. Established in 1973. 170-acre facility. Features: Mamba-roller coaster; 4 roller coasters; 5 restaurants; 6 live entertainment shows; water rides; rip cord.

Profile of Summer Employees Total number: 2,000; typical age: 14. 40% men; 60% women; 60% high school students; 25% college students; 15% retirees.

Employment Information Openings are from February 28 to October 31. Spring break positions also offered. Jobs available: ▶ 400–450 *food operations staff* (minimum age 14) at $5.15 to $7.00 per hour plus bonus ▶ 125–175 *games staff* (minimum age 14) at $5.15 to $7.00 per hour plus bonus ▶ 25–50 *grounds personnel* (minimum age 14) at $5.15 to $7.00 per hour plus bonus ▶ *lifeguards* (minimum age 16) at $6.50 to $7.00 per hour plus bonus ▶ 125–175 *merchandise staff* (minimum age 14) at $5.15 to $7.00 per hour plus bonus ▶ 300–350 *ride operations staff* (minimum age 16) at $6.50 to $7.00 per hour plus bonus ▶ *ticket sellers* (minimum age 16) at $6.50 to $7.00 per hour plus bonus. Applicants must submit a formal organization application, three personal references, resume for internships. An in-person interview is required.

Benefits and Preemployment Training On-the-job training and discounted meals, housing allowance. Preemployment training is required and includes accident prevention and safety, first aid, interpersonal skills.

Contact Brent A. Barr, Employment Manager, Worlds of Fun/Oceans of Fun. Telephone: 816-454-4545. Fax: 816-303-5012. E-mail: wofhr@worldsoffun.com. World Wide Web: http://www.worldsoffun.com. Contact by fax, mail, phone, or through World Wide Web site. Application deadline: continuous.

MONTANA

A CHRISTIAN MINISTRY IN THE NATIONAL PARKS– MONTANA
See A Christian Ministry in the National Parks–Maine on page 107 for complete description.

BEST WESTERN BUCKS T-4 LODGE OF BIG SKY
PO BOX 160279
BIG SKY, MONTANA 59716

General Information 74-unit Best Western Lodge serving skiers, outdoor enthusiasts, and visitors to Yellowstone National Park. Established in 1972. 20-acre facility located 40 miles from

Bozeman. Features: Yellowstone National Park; Big Sky Resort; Gallatin River; mountain setting; whitewater rafting; horseback riding.

Profile of Summer Employees Total number: 60; typical ages: 19–25. 50% men; 50% women; 10% minorities; 5% high school students; 20% college students; 5% retirees; 60% non-U.S. citizens; 20% local applicants.

Employment Information Openings are from May 21 to November 1. Year-round positions also offered. Jobs available: ▶ 10 *cooks* at $5–$8 per hour ▶ 8 *dishwashers* at $6.50–$7 per hour ▶ 5 *front desk staff* with computer and typing skills at $7–$10 per hour ▶ 10 *housekeeping staff* at $6–$7 per hour ▶ 25 *waitstaff* at $5.15 per hour. Applicants must submit formal organization application. An in-person interview is recommended, but a telephone interview is acceptable. International applicants accepted; must obtain own visa, obtain own working papers, apply through a recognized agency.

Benefits and Preemployment Training Housing at a cost, meals at a cost, possible full-time employment, willing to provide letters of recommendation, on-the-job training, and willing to act as a professional reference.

Contact Jayne Menzel, Hotel Manager, Best Western Bucks T-4 Lodge of Big Sky, PO Box 160279, Big Sky, Montana 59716. Telephone: 406-993-5321. Fax: 406-995-2191. E-mail: jmenzel@buckst4.com. World Wide Web: http://www.buckst4.com. Contact by e-mail, fax, mail, phone, or through World Wide Web site. Application deadline: continuous.

BIG SKY RESORT
PO BOX 160001
BIG SKY, MONTANA 59716

General Information Winter and summer resort attracting both families and conventions. Established in 1976. 10,000-acre facility located 45 miles from Bozeman. Features: full-service resort facilities; Rocky Mountain setting; golf course; mountain biking.

Profile of Summer Employees Total number: 400; typical ages: 19–27. 70% men; 30% women; 5% minorities; 5% high school students; 40% college students; 20% non-U.S. citizens; 30% local applicants.

Employment Information Openings are from June 1 to October 7. Year-round positions also offered. Jobs available: ▶ 1–3 *bartenders* (minimum age 18) with previous bartending experience at $5.40 per hour plus tips ▶ 5–10 *bell porters* (minimum age 18) with good customer service skills at $5.15 per hour plus tips ▶ 5–10 *bussers* (minimum age 18) at $5.55 per hour plus tips ▶ 5–10 *concierge staff* (minimum age 18) with strong customer service skills at $6.75 per hour ▶ 10–20 *cooks* (minimum age 18) with cooking experience preferred at $7.50–$10 per hour ▶ 10–20 *dishwashers* (minimum age 18) at $7 per hour ▶ 10–20 *food and beverage positions* (minimum age 18) ▶ 5–10 *front desk personnel* (minimum age 18) with good customer service skills at $7.50 per hour ▶ 5–10 *golf pro-shop staff/starters (summer season)* (minimum age 18) at $6.75 per hour ▶ *hosts/hostesses* (minimum age 18) at $6 per hour ▶ 10–20 *housekeepers* (minimum age 18) at a piecework salary ▶ *laundry staff* (minimum age 18) at $7 per hour ▶ *public area/janitorial attendants* (minimum age 18) at $7 per hour ▶ 5–10 *retail sales personnel* (minimum age 18) with retail experience (preferred) at $6.75 per hour ▶ 1–5 *room inspectors* (minimum age 18) with supervisory skills and an eye for detail at $8.15 per hour ▶ 100 *ticket sales/lift operators (winter season)* (minimum age 18) at $7 per hour ▶ 20–30 *waitstaff* (minimum age 18) with food service experience required at $5.15 per hour plus tips. Applicants must submit formal organization application, two letters of recommendation. A telephone interview is required. International applicants accepted; must apply through a recognized agency.

Benefits and Preemployment Training Housing at a cost, meals at a cost, possible full-time employment, on-the-job training, and lodging discounts for family. Preemployment training is required and includes accident prevention and safety.

Contact Velvet Williams, Human Resources, Big Sky Resort, c/o Human Resources, PO Box 160001, Big Sky, Montana 59716. Telephone: 406-995-5812. Fax: 406-995-5001. E-mail: vwilliams@bigskyresort.com. World Wide Web: http://www.bigskyresort.com. Contact by e-mail, fax, mail, phone, or through World Wide Web site. Application deadline: continuous.

CHRISTIKON
1108 24TH STREET WEST
BILLINGS, MONTANA 59102-3810

General Information Serving all on behalf of area ELCA Lutherans. Christikon offers residential, backpack, and Creation Care programs in the Rocky Mountains near Yellowstone National Park. Established in 1951. 67-acre facility. Features: mountain wilderness setting.

Profile of Summer Employees Total number: 32; typical ages: 19–29. 50% men; 50% women; 4% minorities; 85% college students; 20% local applicants. Nonsmokers preferred.

Employment Information Openings are from June 1 to August 15. Jobs available: ▶ 21 *counselors* (minimum age 19) at $2100 per season ▶ 2 *forestry stewards* (minimum age 19) at $2100 per season ▶ 1 *head cook* (minimum age 19) at $2100 per season ▶ 1 *health care manager* (minimum age 19) at $2100 per season ▶ 1 *maintenance supervisor* (minimum age 21) at $2100 per season ▶ 1 *secretary* (minimum age 19) at $2100 per season ▶ 1 *trails room coordinator* (minimum age 19) at $2100 per season. Applicants must submit a formal organization application, three personal references. An in-person interview is recommended, but a telephone interview is acceptable.

Benefits and Preemployment Training Free housing, free meals, formal training, health insurance, willing to provide letters of recommendation, on-the-job training, willing to complete paperwork for educational credit, and willing to act as a professional reference. Preemployment training is required and includes accident prevention and safety, first aid, CPR, interpersonal skills, leadership skills, program development skills.

Contact Bob Quam, Pastor/Director, Christikon. Telephone: 406-656-1969. Fax: 406-656-1969. E-mail: christikon@aol.com. World Wide Web: http://www.christikon.org. Contact by e-mail, mail, phone, or through World Wide Web site. Application deadline: continuous.

LAZY K BAR RANCH
PO BOX 1550
BIG TIMBER, MONTANA 59011

General Information One-hundred-seventeen-year-old operating cattle and horse ranch that has welcomed selected guests for 82 summers. Established in 1887. 22,000-acre facility located 107 miles from Billings-Bozeman. Features: river; hot tub; mountains; lakes; timber; seclusion.

Profile of Summer Employees Total number: 15–18; typical ages: 16–25. 40% men; 60% women; 1% minorities; 40% high school students; 60% college students; 5% retirees; 5% non-U.S. citizens; 5% local applicants. Nonsmokers preferred.

Employment Information Openings are from June 10 to September 10. Jobs available: ▶ 1 *children's wrangler (female)* with extensive childcare experience and horse expertise at $600 per month ▶ 1 *chore person* (minimum age 16) with experience with milk cows at $600 per month ▶ 1 *dishwasher* (minimum age 17) at $575 per month ▶ 1 *head cook* (minimum age 20) with ability to cook for 40-45 people and experience in the field at $1500–$2000 per month ▶ 3 *housekeepers/laundry workers* (minimum age 16) with housekeeping and laundry experience at $575 per month ▶ 1 *second cook/baker* (minimum age 18) with baking experience at $650–$800 per month ▶ 1 *split-shift worker* (minimum age 20) with experience in cooking, baking, cleaning, waiting tables, and laundry at $600 per month ▶ 1 *storekeeper* (minimum age 18) with attention to detail at $550 per month ▶ 3 *waiters/waitresses* (minimum age 16) with serving experience at $575 per month ▶ 1 *winter caretaker* with desire for solitude and experience with chainsaws and other tools (position available from September 12 to June 12) at $600 per month

▶ 3 *wranglers* (minimum age 17) with extensive experience in the field at $600 per month. Applicants must submit formal organization application, resume, three letters of recommendation, photo. An in-person interview is recommended, but a telephone interview is acceptable. International applicants accepted; must obtain own visa, obtain own working papers, apply through a recognized agency.

Benefits and Preemployment Training Free housing, free meals, willing to provide letters of recommendation, on-the-job training, willing to complete paperwork for educational credit, and willing to act as a professional reference.

Contact Carol Kirby, Partner, Lazy K Bar Ranch, Box 1181, Big Timber, Montana 59011. Telephone: 406-932-4449. Fax: 406-932-4844. E-mail: kirby@mcn.net. World Wide Web: http://www.lazykbar.net. Contact by e-mail, mail, or through World Wide Web site. Application deadline: May 1.

NINE QUARTER CIRCLE RANCH
5000 TAYLOR FORK ROAD
GALLATIN GATEWAY, MONTANA 59730

General Information Family-oriented dude ranch hosting 75 guests weekly. Established in 1946. 1,000-acre facility located 60 miles from Bozeman. Features: mountain valley setting; stream-side location; fishing pond.

Profile of Summer Employees Total number: 25. 40% men; 60% women; 90% college students; 10% retirees. Nonsmokers preferred.

Employment Information Openings are from May 15 to September 15. Jobs available: ▶ 2 *baby sitters* (minimum age 18) with first aid and adult, child, and infant CPR certification at $800–$900 per month ▶ 4 *cabin cleaners/servers* (minimum age 18) at $800–$900 per month ▶ 1 *fishing guide* (minimum age 18) at $800–$900 per month ▶ *kiddie wrangler* (minimum age 18) at $800–$900 per month ▶ 2 *kitchen helpers/dishwashers* (minimum age 18) at $800–$900 per month ▶ 1 *laundry worker* (minimum age 18) at $800–$900 per month ▶ *maintenance workers* (minimum age 18) with ability to make minor repairs and knowledge of carpentry at $800–$900 per month ▶ 4 *ranch hands* (minimum age 18) with first aid and adult, child, and infant CPR certification at $800–$900 per month ▶ 1 *second cook* (minimum age 18) at $800–$900 per month. A telephone interview is required.

Benefits and Preemployment Training Free housing, free meals, on-the-job training, and willing to complete paperwork for educational credit.

Contact Kelly Kelsey, Owner, Nine Quarter Circle Ranch, 5000 Taylor Fork Road, Gallatin Gateway, Montana 59730. Telephone: 406-995-4276. E-mail: nineqtrcircle@mcn.net. World Wide Web: http://www.ninequartercircle.com. Contact by mail or phone. Application deadline: continuous.

THE RESORT AT GLACIER, ST. MARY LODGE
GLACIER NATIONAL PARK
ST. MARY, MONTANA 59417

General Information One of Montana's noted full-service high country resorts. Established in 1932. 100-acre facility located 90 miles from Kalispell. Features: mountain setting; updated rustic physical setting; small town atmosphere; 900 miles of hiking trails; exceptional staff.

Profile of Summer Employees Total number: 180; typical ages: 19–24. 40% men; 60% women; 2% minorities; 3% high school students; 80% college students; 3% retirees; 2% non-U.S. citizens; 10% local applicants. Nonsmokers preferred.

Employment Information Openings are from May 1 to October 15. Jobs available: ▶ 4 *accounting/secretarial staff members* with experience in the field at $996 per month ▶ 6 *bartenders/cocktail servers* with experience at $918 per month ▶ 5 *clerical staff members* at $996 per month ▶ 11 *deli cooks* at $996 per month ▶ 14 *dishwashing/kitchen personnel* at $996 per month ▶ 4 *front desk clerks* at $996 per month ▶ 5 *gas station attendants* at $996 per month ▶ 10 *gift shop clerks* with experience at $996 per month ▶ 6 *hosts/buspersons* at $918 per month ▶ 15 *housekeepers* at $996 per month ▶ 10 *maintenance personnel* at $996 per month ▶ 12 *pantry/fry cooks* with experience at $996 per month ▶ 4 *pizza parlor staff members* at $996 per month ▶ 3 *sporting-goods clerks* at $996 per month ▶ 9 *supermarket staff members* at $996 per month ▶ 26 *waiters/waitresses* with experience at $893 per month. Applicants must submit formal organization application, three personal references. An in-person interview is recommended, but a telephone interview is acceptable. International applicants accepted; must obtain own visa, obtain own working papers, apply through a recognized agency.

Benefits and Preemployment Training Housing at a cost, meals at a cost, on-the-job training, willing to complete paperwork for educational credit, willing to act as a professional reference, and employee discounts. Preemployment training is required and includes accident prevention and safety, interpersonal skills, leadership skills.

Contact Rocky Black, Resort Manager, The Resort at Glacier, St. Mary Lodge, PO Box 1808, Sun Valley, Idaho 83353. Telephone: 208-726-6279. Fax: 208-726-6282. E-mail: jobs@glcpark. com. World Wide Web: http://www.glcpark.com. Contact by e-mail, fax, mail, phone, or through World Wide Web site. Application deadline: continuous.

63 RANCH
PO BOX 979
LIVINGSTON, MONTANA 59047

General Information Working cattle and dude ranch operating from June through September with capacity for 30 guests. Ranch specializes in teaching horseback riding on all levels. Established in 1929. 2,000-acre facility located 50 miles from Bozeman. Features: Gallatin National Forest; Absaroka—Bear Tooth Wilderness; Yellowstone National Park; Yellowstone River; 5 mountain ranges; where the mountains meet the prairie.

Profile of Summer Employees Total number: 20; typical ages: 18–70. 47% men; 53% women; 5% high school students; 1% college students; 45% retirees; 19% non-U.S. citizens; 10% local applicants. Nonsmokers required.

Employment Information Openings are from June 1 to September 15. Jobs available: ▶ 6–8 *cabin cleaners, dishwashers, and dining room servers* (minimum age 18) with first aid and CPR certifications at $800–$1000 per month ▶ 1 *head cook* (minimum age 18) with health certificate, first aid, CPR, and ability to run a kitchen and cook for 50 people at $1700–$2200 per month ▶ 1 *kitchen helper* (minimum age 18) with first aid, CPR, and health certificate at $800 per month ▶ 1 *second cook* (minimum age 18) with first aid, CPR, health certificate, and experience at $1000–$1500 per month. Applicants must submit formal organization application, letter of interest, three work references with phone numbers. An in-person interview is recommended, but a telephone interview is acceptable. International applicants accepted; must obtain own visa, obtain own working papers, apply through a recognized agency.

Benefits and Preemployment Training Free housing, free meals, willing to provide letters of recommendation, on-the-job training, and opportunity to attend seminars/workshops. Preemployment training is required and includes accident prevention and safety, first aid, CPR, job skills.

Contact Sandra C. Cahill, President, 63 Ranch, PO Box 979-P, Livingston, Montana 59047. Telephone: 406-222-0570. Fax: 406-222-9446. E-mail: sixty3ranch@mcn.net. World Wide Web: http://www.63ranch.com. Contact by e-mail, fax, mail, phone, or through World Wide Web site. Application deadline: continuous.

THE SOUTHWESTERN COMPANY, MONTANA
See The Southwestern Company on page 297 for complete description.

STUDENT CONSERVATION ASSOCIATION (SCA), MONTANA

See Student Conservation Association (SCA), New Hampshire on page 200 for complete description.

SWEET GRASS RANCH
460 REIN LANE
BIG TIMBER, MONTANA 59011

General Information Working cattle ranch that accepts 20 guests to live ranch life. Established in 1965. 20,000-acre facility located 120 miles from Billings. Features: mountains; stream for fishing; horseback riding; working ranch experience; guests from around the world.

Profile of Summer Employees Total number: 10; typical ages: 20–30. 50% men; 50% women; 100% college students; 25% local applicants. Nonsmokers preferred.

Employment Information Openings are from June 1 to September 10. Jobs available: ▶ 2 *cabin staff members* (minimum age 19) with organizational and interpersonal skills, and attention to cleanliness and detail at $850 per month plus room, board, and tips ▶ 2 *cooks* (minimum age 19) with group cooking experience, love of cooking, experience or training as a baker/cook, attention to detail, and ability to work well with others at $1000-$1500 per month plus room, board, and tips. Applicants must submit a formal organization application, resume, personal reference, two letters of recommendation. A telephone interview is required. International applicants accepted; must obtain own visa, obtain own working papers.

Benefits and Preemployment Training Free housing, free meals, willing to provide letters of recommendation, on-the-job training, willing to complete paperwork for educational credit, and willing to act as a professional reference.

Contact Shelly Carroccia, Owner, Sweet Grass Ranch. Telephone: 406-537-4477. Fax: 406-537-4477. E-mail: sweetgrass@mcn.net. World Wide Web: http://www.sweetgrassranch.com. Contact by e-mail, mail, or phone. Application deadline: April 30.

YELLOWSTONE GENERAL STORES
707 BRIDGER DRIVE, SUITE C
BOZEMAN, MONTANA 59718

General Information Twelve general stores located throughout Yellowstone National Park with a general office and a warehouse in West Yellowstone, Montana. Established in 2003. Features: National Park; thermal features; fishing; hiking; white-water rafting; canoeing.

Profile of Summer Employees Total number: 1,000; typical ages: 18–82. 49% men; 51% women; 12% minorities; 30% college students; 70% retirees; 3% non-U.S. citizens; 1% local applicants.

Employment Information Openings are from March 23 to October 20. Jobs available: ▶ 20–25 *auditors* (minimum age 18) with background in 10-key and money handling, computer experience, and ability to lift 20 pounds at $6 to $7.25 per hour plus $.45 per hour incentive completion bonus ▶ 10–15 *custodians* (minimum age 18) with ability to lift 50 pounds at $6.10 per hour plus $.45 per hour incentive completion bonus ▶ 20–25 *dining room assistants* (minimum age 18) at $5.60 per hour plus $.45 per hour incentive completion bonus ▶ 10 *dishwashers* (minimum age 18) at $5.60 per hour plus $.45 per hour incentive completion bonus ▶ 10–12 *dormitory manager leads* (minimum age 18) with ability to lift 50 pounds; must work May through September at $6.10 per hour plus $.45 per hour incentive completion bonus ▶ 20–30 *employee dining room cooks* (minimum age 18) with experience in large volume food preparation at $6 to $10 per hour plus $.45 per hour incentive completion bonus ▶ 40–100 *food service clerks* (minimum age 18) at $3.60 to $5.60 per hour plus $.45 per hour incentive completion bonus plus gratuities for some jobs ▶ 30–50 *fry cooks* (minimum age 18) with prior experience helpful, but not necessary at $6.60 per hour plus $.45 per hour incentive completion bonus ▶ 50–100 *grocery clerks* (minimum age 21) with ability to lift 50 pounds and willingness to sell alcohol and tobacco at $5.60 per hour plus $.45 per hour incentive completion bonus ▶ 8 *maintenance workers* (minimum age 18) with ability to lift 70 pounds and general maintenance experience in plumbing, electrical work, and other areas at $7 to $13 per hour plus $.45 per hour bonus (season is March through November) ▶ 100–200 *sales associates* (minimum age 18) with cash register experience preferred at $5.60 per hour plus $.45 per hour incentive completion bonus ▶ 50 *warehouse workers* (minimum age 19) with ability to lift 70 pounds at $5.60 to $6.55 per hour plus $.45 per hour incentive completion bonus. Applicants must submit formal organization application. A telephone interview is required. International applicants accepted; must obtain own visa, obtain own working papers, apply through a recognized agency.

Benefits and Preemployment Training Housing at a cost, meals at a cost, health insurance, on-the-job training, willing to complete paperwork for educational credit, and opportunity to attend seminars/workshops. Preemployment training is required.

Contact Charlene Owens, Human Resources Generalist, Yellowstone General Stores. Telephone: 406-586-7593. Fax: 406-586-7592. World Wide Web: http://www.hamiltonstores.com. Contact by mail, phone, or through World Wide Web site. Application deadline: August 30.

NEBRASKA

THE SOUTHWESTERN COMPANY, NEBRASKA
See The Southwestern Company on page 297 for complete description.

STUDENT CONSERVATION ASSOCIATION (SCA), NEBRASKA
See Student Conservation Association (SCA), New Hampshire on page 200 for complete description.

NEVADA

CAMP WASIU II
605 WASHINGTON STREET
RENO, NEVADA 89503

General Information Resident camp of the Girl Scouts of the Sierra Nevada. Established in 1912. 40-acre facility. Features: wooded Sierra Nevada mountains; platform tents; pool; canoeing; horseback riding; dining hall.

Profile of Summer Employees Total number: 40; typical ages: 18–30. 100% women; 5% minorities; 80% college students; 10% non-U.S. citizens; 30% local applicants.

Employment Information Openings are from January 1 to June 1. Jobs available: ▶ 1 *assistant cook* (minimum age 18) with some kitchen experience and organization at $60–$70 per day ▶ 1 *business manager* (minimum age 21) with leadership skills, business procedures, and valid

California or Nevada driver's license at $40–$50 per day ▶ 1 *canoe instructor* (minimum age 18) with experience working with children, prior canoeing experience, and canoeing certificate at $35–$40 per day ▶ 1 *counselor-in-training director* (minimum age 21) with leadership skills, supervisory experience, prior camp experience, experience working with children, and communication skills at $40 per day ▶ 1 *environmental education/archery instructor* (minimum age 18) with experience working with children and communication and organization skills at $35 per day ▶ 1 *head caretaker* (minimum age 21) with experience in plumbing, electrical, carpentry, vehicle maintenance, and pool maintenance at $80–$90 per day ▶ 1 *head cook* (minimum age 21) with experience in kitchen supervision, menu prep, prep for 100 or more people, and food handler's certificate at $80–$90 per day ▶ 1 *health supervisor* (minimum age 21) with California state license as a physician or registered nurse and communication skills at $80–$90 per day ▶ 3 *lifeguards* (minimum age 18) with teamwork skills, American Red Cross Lifeguard Training, first aid, and CPR certification at $35–$45 per day ▶ 1 *maintenance assistant* (minimum age 18) with valid driver's license and ability to work hard at $35–$40 per day ▶ 1 *program director* (minimum age 21) with camp experience, leadership skills, California or Nevada driver's license, and communication skills at $40–$50 per day ▶ 15 *unit counselors* (minimum age 18) with experience working with children at $30–$40 per day ▶ 6 *unit leaders* (minimum age 21) with leadership skills and supervisory experience at $35–$45 per day ▶ 1 *waterfront director* (minimum age 21) with lifeguarding and supervisory experience, Red Cross Advanced Lifeguard Training, first aid, and CPR certification at $40–$50 per day. Applicants must submit formal organization application, three personal references. An in-person interview is recommended, but a telephone interview is acceptable. International applicants accepted; must apply through a recognized agency.

Benefits and Preemployment Training Free housing, free meals, health insurance, willing to provide letters of recommendation, on-the-job training, willing to complete paperwork for educational credit, and willing to act as a professional reference. Preemployment training is required and includes accident prevention and safety, interpersonal skills, leadership skills.

Contact Frances Brown, Camp Director, Camp Wasiu II, 605 Washington Street, Reno, Nevada 89503. Telephone: 775-322-0642. Fax: 775-322-0701. E-mail: fbrown@gssn.org. World Wide Web: http://www.gssn.org. Contact by e-mail, fax, mail, phone, or through World Wide Web site. Application deadline: continuous.

THE SOUTHWESTERN COMPANY, NEVADA
See The Southwestern Company on page 297 for complete description.

STUDENT CONSERVATION ASSOCIATION (SCA), NEVADA
See Student Conservation Association (SCA), New Hampshire on page 200 for complete description.

WILD ISLAND FAMILY ADVENTURE PARK
250 WILD ISLAND COURT
SPARKS, NEVADA 89434

General Information Amusement park with miniature golf course, go-kart track, indoor arcade, and waterpark. Established in 1988. 11-acre facility located 5 miles from Reno. Features: wave pool; 2 speed slides; 36-hole mini golf course; 3 family slides; interactive water play area; go-kart racetrack.

Profile of Summer Employees Total number: 250; typical ages: 14–20. 60% men; 40% women; 20% minorities; 80% high school students; 10% college students; 3% retirees; 100% local applicants. Nonsmokers preferred.

Employment Information Openings are from May 1 to September 30. Year-round positions also offered. Jobs available: ▶ 12–16 *admissions attendants* (minimum age 14) at $4.50–$5.50 per hour ▶ 4–6 *admissions cashiers* (minimum age 15) at $5–$6 per hour ▶ 4–6 *golf course cashiers* (minimum age 16) at $5–$7 per hour ▶ 6–10 *kitchen cashiers* (minimum age 15) at $4.50–$7 per hour ▶ 20–30 *kitchen runners* (minimum age 14) at $4.50–$5 per hour ▶ 75–90 *lifeguards* (minimum age 15) with Ellis and Associates certification at $4.50–$6.50 per hour ▶ 15–20 *park services attendants* (minimum age 14) at $4.50–$6 per hour ▶ 6–10 *raceway attendants* (minimum age 16) with small engine repair experience preferred at $5.50–$7 per hour. Applicants must submit a formal organization application. An in-person interview is required.

Benefits and Preemployment Training Meals at a cost, possible full-time employment, willing to provide letters of recommendation, names of contacts, on-the-job training, and willing to complete paperwork for educational credit. Preemployment training is required and includes accident prevention and safety, first aid, CPR, interpersonal skills, leadership skills, customer service (job specific).

Contact Pat Morandi, General Manager, Wild Island Family Adventure Park, 250 Wild Island Court, Sparks, Nevada 89434, United States. Telephone: 702-359-2927 Ext. 101. Fax: 702-359-5942. World Wide Web: http://www.wildisland.com. Contact by fax, mail, or phone. Application deadline: continuous.

NEW HAMPSHIRE

AMERICAN YOUTH FOUNDATION–CAMP MERROWVISTA
147 CANAAN ROAD
CENTER TUFTONBORO, NEW HAMPSHIRE 03816

General Information Coed residential program for students ages 8–16. The focus is on leadership development and includes general program activities for students ages 8–12 and extended backpacking, canoeing, and cycling for students ages 13–16. Established in 1925. 600-acre facility located 140 miles from Boston, Massachusetts. Features: freshwater lake; beautiful mountains; trails leave right from camp into mountains; rustic, wooded setting.

Profile of Summer Employees Total number: 85; typical ages: 18–65. 50% men; 50% women; 2% minorities; 5% high school students; 60% college students; 3% non-U.S. citizens. Nonsmokers required.

Employment Information Openings are from June 10 to August 17. Winter break and year-round positions also offered. Jobs available: ▶ 1 *arts and crafts coordinator* (minimum age 18, 21 preferred) with crafts knowledge at $1800–$2000 per season ▶ 1 *bike mechanic* (minimum age 18, 21 preferred) with experience repairing and assembling touring bicycles, instruction of touring road safety, and bike maintenance at $2000–$2500 per season ▶ 1–4 *kitchen staff members* (minimum age 18, 21 preferred) with desire to pursue culinary arts as a career at $1800–$3000 per season ▶ 1 *naturalist* (minimum age 18, 21 preferred) with experience teaching environmental activities and live animal experience preferred at $1800–$2000 per season ▶ 1 *nurse* (minimum age 21) with RN eligibility for New Hampshire license at $400–$550 per week ▶ 1 *office staff member* (minimum age 18, 21 preferred) with computer skills at $1800–$2200 per season ▶ 1 *outcamping equipment coordinator* (minimum age 18, 21 preferred) with some driving of passenger vans required and ability to perform repair, inventory, check-out/check-in of backpacking and canoeing equipment at $1800–$2000 per season ▶ 1 *outcamping* *food coordinator* (minimum age 18, 21 preferred) with an interest in outdoor education at $1800–$2000 per season ▶ *program directors* (minimum age 21) with supervisory experience at $3000–$4000 per season ▶ 1–3 *sailing instructors* (minimum age 18) with experience sailing Laser I and Laser II boats and lifeguard certification at $1800–$2000 per season ▶ 12 *trip leaders* (minimum age 21) with experience leading trips, WFR, lifeguard, and CPR/first aid training preferred at $215–$315 per week ▶ 20 *village leaders* (minimum age 18) with WSI and lifeguard certification, CPR/first aid training preferred at $180–$280 per week ▶ 2 *waterfront staff members* (minimum age 21) with WSI and lifeguard certification required at $1800–$3000 per season. Applicants must submit formal organization application, three personal references, trip resume outlining outdoor experiences for trip leading. A telephone interview is required. International applicants accepted; must apply through a recognized agency.

Benefits and Preemployment Training Free housing, free meals, formal training, willing to provide letters of recommendation, on-the-job training, willing to complete paperwork for educational credit, willing to act as a professional reference, and WFA and LGT courses. Preemployment training is required and includes accident prevention and safety, first aid, interpersonal skills, leadership skills, Wilderness First Responder training.

Contact Heather R. Kiley, Director of Camp Programs, American Youth Foundation–Camp Merrowvista, 147 Canaan Road, Center Tuftonboro, New Hampshire 03816. Telephone: 603-539-6607. Fax: 603-539-7504. E-mail: heather.kiley@ayf.com. World Wide Web: http://www.ayf.com. Contact by e-mail, fax, mail, phone, or through World Wide Web site. Application deadline: continuous.

THE BALSAMS GRAND RESORT HOTEL
ROUTE 26
DIXVILLE NOTCH, NEW HAMPSHIRE 03576-9710

General Information Facility catering to vacationers (July, August, and winter) as well as convention groups (spring and fall). Established in 1866. 15,000-acre facility located 200 miles from Boston, MA. Features: lake; mountains; hiking trails; 2 golf courses; 2 tennis courts; mountain biking trails.

Profile of Summer Employees Total number: 400; typical ages: 18–30. 50% men; 50% women; 11% minorities; 4% high school students; 22% college students; 6% retirees; 6% non-U.S. citizens; 53% local applicants.

Employment Information Openings are from June 15 to October 18. Spring break and winter break positions also offered. Jobs available: ▶ 5 *bellpersons* (minimum age 18) at $5.25 per hour ▶ 5 *beverage servers* (minimum age 18) at $200 to $300 per week plus gratuities ▶ 30 *dining room waitstaff members* at $200 to $400 per week plus gratuities ▶ 10 *housekeeping staff members* (minimum age 18) at $200 to $300 per week plus gratuities ▶ 5 *kitchen staff members* (minimum age 18) at $7 per hour ▶ 5 *laundry staff members* (minimum age 18) at $6.50 per hour ▶ 3 *lifeguards* (minimum age 18) with lifeguard certification at $720–$840 per month. Applicants must submit a formal organization application, resume, writing sample. International applicants accepted; must obtain own visa, obtain own working papers.

Benefits and Preemployment Training Housing at a cost, meals at a cost, formal training, on-the-job training, and free tennis, golf, hiking (winter: skiing, ice skating, snow shoeing).

Contact Suzanne Ingram, Director of Personnel, The BALSAMS Grand Resort Hotel, Route 26, Dixville Notch, New Hampshire 03576. Telephone: 603-255-3400 Ext. 2666. Fax: 603-255-4670. World Wide Web: http://www.thebalsams.com. Contact by mail or phone. Application deadline: continuous.

BROOKWOODS FOR BOYS/DEER RUN FOR GIRLS
CHESTNUT COVE ROAD
ALTON, NEW HAMPSHIRE 03809

General Information Residential religious camps serving 300 campers in two- and four-week sessions. Established in 1944. 320-acre facility located 100 miles from Boston, Massachusetts. Features: freshwater lake (26 miles across).

Profile of Summer Employees Total number: 105; typical ages: 18–55. 50% men; 50% women; 10% minorities; 10% high school students; 90% college students; 10% non-U.S. citizens; 20% local applicants. Nonsmokers required.

Employment Information Openings are from June 18 to August 22. Winter break and year-round positions also offered. Jobs available: ▶ 20 *general counselors* with minimum one year of college completed at $2000 per season ▶ 3 *riding instructors* with CHA certification at $1750 per season ▶ 2 *riflery instructors* with NRA certification at $2000 per season ▶ 4 *trip staff members* (minimum age 21) with CPR and first aid certification; must be over 21 to drive 15-passenger van at $1900 per season. Applicants must submit formal organization application, three personal references. An in-person interview is recommended, but a telephone interview is acceptable. International applicants accepted; must apply through a recognized agency.

Benefits and Preemployment Training Free housing, free meals, formal training, willing to provide letters of recommendation, on-the-job training, willing to complete paperwork for educational credit, and willing to act as a professional reference. Preemployment training is required and includes accident prevention and safety, interpersonal skills, leadership skills.

Contact Bob Strodel, Executive Director, Brookwoods for Boys/Deer Run for Girls, Chestnut Cove Road, Alton, New Hampshire 03809. Telephone: 603-875-3600. Fax: 603-875-4606. E-mail: bob@brookwoods.org. World Wide Web: http://www.brookwoods.org. Contact by e-mail, fax, mail, phone, or through World Wide Web site. Application deadline: continuous.

CAMP DEERWOOD
HOLDERNESS, NEW HAMPSHIRE 03245

General Information Residential camp serving 130 boys for seven weeks. Established in 1945. 88-acre facility located 100 miles from Boston, Massachusetts. Features: freshwater lake; woods; 4 tennis courts; blacksmith shop.

Profile of Summer Employees Total number: 50; typical ages: 17–30. 96% men; 4% women; 3% minorities; 20% high school students; 60% college students; 5% retirees; 8% non-U.S. citizens; 5% local applicants. Nonsmokers required.

Employment Information Openings are from June 20 to August 15. Jobs available: ▶ 1 *ceramics instructor* at $1600–$3000 per season ▶ *general counselors* with WSI/lifeguard certification preferred (waterfront staff only) at $1200–$2500 per season ▶ *swimming instructors* with WSI/lifeguard certification at $1200–$2500 per season ▶ 2 *trip leaders* (minimum age 21) at $2000–$3000 per season. Applicants must submit formal organization application, letter of interest, resume, two letters of recommendation or personal references. An in-person interview is recommended, but a telephone interview is acceptable. International applicants accepted; must apply through a recognized agency.

Benefits and Preemployment Training Free housing, free meals, willing to provide letters of recommendation, on-the-job training, willing to complete paperwork for educational credit, willing to act as a professional reference, opportunity to attend seminars/workshops, and tuition assistance. Preemployment training is required and includes accident prevention and safety, first aid, CPR, interpersonal skills, leadership skills.

Contact Tommy Thomsen, Director, Camp Deerwood, Box 188, Holderness, New Hampshire 03245. Telephone: 603-279-4237. Contact by mail or phone. Application deadline: March 1.

CAMP PEMIGEWASSETT
ROUTE 25A
WENTWORTH, NEW HAMPSHIRE 03282

General Information Traditional residential camp for 170 boys ages 8–15. A broad range of activities including sports, hiking, nature study, dramatics, and art in a 7-week session. Established in 1908. 600-acre facility located 75 miles from Manchester. Features: private lake; 7 tennis courts; 3 baseball fields; 2 soccer/lacrosse fields; fully equipped woodshop; superb nature facility.

Profile of Summer Employees Total number: 75; typical ages: 17–60. 90% men; 10% women; 5% minorities; 20% high school students; 40% college students; 8% retirees; 8% non-U.S. citizens; 10% local applicants. Nonsmokers required.

Employment Information Openings are from June 21 to August 16. Jobs available: ▶ *assistant counselors* (minimum age 17) with Red Cross CPR certification preferred at $1100–$1200 per season ▶ *cabin counselors/instructors* (minimum age 18) with Red Cross first aid and CPR certification preferred, minimum of one year of college completed at $1400–$1800 per season ▶ *cabin counselors/swimming instructors* (minimum age 18) with Red Cross WSI certification and minimum of one year of college completed at $1400–$1800 per season ▶ *kitchen workers* (minimum age 16) at $1100–$1400 per season. Applicants must submit formal organization application, letter of interest, three personal references. An in-person interview is required. International applicants accepted; must apply through a recognized agency.

Benefits and Preemployment Training Free housing, free meals, formal training, and on-the-job training. Preemployment training is required and includes accident prevention and safety, interpersonal skills, leadership skills.

Contact Robert Grabill, Director, Camp Pemigewassett, 25 Rayton Road, Hanover, New Hampshire 03755. Telephone: 603-643-8055. Fax: 603-643-9601. E-mail: robert.grabill@valley. net. World Wide Web: http://www.camppemi.com. Contact by e-mail, fax, mail, or phone. Application deadline: continuous.

CAMP ROBIN HOOD FOR BOYS AND GIRLS
65 ROBIN HOOD LANE
FREEDOM, NEW HAMPSHIRE 03836

General Information Residential camp serving 280 boys and girls ages 7–16 for 4-, 6-, and 8-week sessions. Established in 1927. 210-acre facility located 60 miles from Portland, Maine. Features: freshwater lake; wooded setting; extensive athletic fields; cabins with electricity and bathrooms; beautiful stables and riding facilities; lighted tennis, basketball, and volleyball courts.

Profile of Summer Employees Total number: 140; typical ages: 18–60. 60% men; 40% women; 3% minorities; 15% high school students; 70% college students; 20% non-U.S. citizens. Nonsmokers preferred.

Employment Information Openings are from June 19 to August 16. Jobs available: ▶ 2 *archery instructors* (minimum age 19) with experience in the field at $1000–$1500 per season ▶ 2 *ceramics instructors* (minimum age 19) with experience with wheel and kiln at $1000–$1800 per season ▶ 2 *crafts instructors* (minimum age 19) with experience in the field at $1000–$1800 per season ▶ 1 *dance instructor* (minimum age 19) at $1000–$1200 per season ▶ 10 *general counselors* (minimum age 19) at $900–$1200 per season ▶ 1 *gymnastics instructor* (minimum age 19) with experience in the field at $1000–$1500 per season ▶ 10 *kitchen/pantry staff* (minimum age 17) at $800–$1500 per season ▶ 2 *maintenance staff* (minimum age 19) with general carpentry skills at $1000–$1500 per season ▶ 2 *nurses* with RN certification at $3000–$3500 per season ▶ 3 *riding instructors* (minimum age 19) with English riding/teaching experience at $1000–$1500 per season ▶ 1 *riflery assistant* (minimum age 19) with experience at $1000–$1400 per season ▶ 3 *sailing and canoeing instructors* (minimum age 19) with experience in the field at $1000–$1500 per season ▶ 2 *secretaries* (minimum age 18) with computer skills at $900–$1500 per season ▶ 8 *sports coaches* (minimum age 19) with experience in the field at $1000–$1500 per season ▶ 4 *swimming instructors* (minimum age 19) with WSI certification, lifeguard training, or Bronze Medallion at $1000–$1600 per season ▶ 1 *tennis director* (minimum age 20) with teaching and program directing experience at $2500–$3500 per season ▶ 5 *tennis instructors* (minimum age 18) with playing and/or teaching experience at $1000–$1800 per season ▶ 1 *waterfront director* (minimum age 21) with Red Cross certifications at $2000–$3000 per season ▶ 3 *waterskiing instructors/boat drivers* (minimum age 19) with experience in the field at $1000–$1500 per season ▶ 1 *woodworking instructor* (minimum age 19) with skills with power tools at $1000–$1800 per season. Applicants must submit formal organization application, three personal references. An in-person interview is recommended, but a telephone interview is acceptable. International applicants accepted; must apply through a recognized agency.

Benefits and Preemployment Training Free housing, free meals, formal training, willing to provide letters of recommendation, on-the-job training, and willing to complete paperwork for educational credit. Preemployment training is required and includes accident prevention and safety, first aid, CPR, interpersonal skills, leadership skills, group dynamics.

Contact John Klein, Director, Camp Robin Hood for Boys and Girls, 344 Thistle Trail, Mayfield Heights, Ohio 44124. Telephone: 440-646-1911. Fax: 440-646-1972. E-mail: robinhdnh@aol. com. World Wide Web: http://www.camprobinhood.com. Contact by e-mail, fax, mail, phone, or through World Wide Web site. Application deadline: continuous.

CAMP TEL NOAR OF THE ELI AND BESSIE COHEN FOUNDATION
167 MAIN STREET
HAMPSTEAD, NEW HAMPSHIRE 03841

General Information Jewish coeducational cultural and kosher residential camp serving 265 children. Established in 1945. 60-acre facility located 50 miles from Boston, Massachusetts. Features: freshwater lake; 8 tennis courts; staff lounge; gymnasium; bunks with full bathroom facilities.

Profile of Summer Employees Total number: 90; typical ages: 18–25. 50% men; 50% women; 16% high school students; 82% college students; 2% non-U.S. citizens. Nonsmokers required.

Employment Information Openings are from June 1 to August 23. Jobs available: ▶ 1 *archery instructor* (minimum age 18) at $1350–$2000 per season ▶ 1 *arts and crafts director* (minimum age 21) at $2000 and up per season ▶ *arts and crafts instructors* (minimum age 18) at $1350–$2000 per season ▶ 1 *athletics director* (minimum age 21) at $2000 and up per season ▶ *athletics instructors* at $1350–$2000 per season ▶ 2 *canoe instructors* (minimum age 18) with lifeguard training certification at $1350–$2000 per season ▶ 1 *drama director* (minimum age 21) at $2000 and up per season ▶ *drama instructors* at $1350–$2000 per season ▶ 3 *nurses* (minimum age 21) with RN at $5000 per season ▶ 2 *sailing instructors* (minimum age 18) with lifeguard training certification at $1350–$2000 per season ▶ 3 *swimming instructors* (minimum age 18) with WSI and lifeguard training certification at $1350–$2000 per season ▶ 1 *swimming program director* (minimum age 21) with WSI, lifeguard training certification, and experience teaching swimming at $2000 and up per season ▶ 1 *tennis director* (minimum age 21) at $2000 and up per season ▶ *tennis instructors* at $1350–$2000 per season ▶ 1–2 *waterski boat drivers* (minimum age 21) at $2000 and up per season ▶ 1 *waterskiing director* (minimum age 21) at $2000 and up per season ▶ 1 *windsurf instructor* (minimum age 18) with lifeguard training certification at $1350–$2000 per season. Applicants must submit formal organization application, resume, two personal references, two letters of recommendation, 2 work references. An in-person interview is recommended, but a telephone interview is acceptable. International applicants accepted; must obtain own visa, obtain own working papers, apply through a recognized agency.

Benefits and Preemployment Training Free housing, free meals, formal training, willing to provide letters of recommendation, on-the-job training, willing to complete paperwork for

educational credit, and willing to act as a professional reference. Preemployment training is required and includes accident prevention and safety, interpersonal skills, leadership skills.

Contact Pearl Lourie, Director, Camp Tel Noar of the Eli and Bessie Cohen Foundation, 30 Main Street, Ashland, Massachusetts 01701. Telephone: 800-375-8444. Fax: 508-881-1006. E-mail: director_telnoar@cohencamps.org. World Wide Web: http://www.cohencamps.org. Contact by e-mail, fax, mail, phone, or through World Wide Web site. Application deadline: continuous.

CAMP TEVYA OF THE ELI AND BESSIE COHEN FOUNDATION
BROOKLINE, NEW HAMPSHIRE 03033

General Information Jewish coeducational cultural and kosher camp serving 325 campers. Established in 1940. 650-acre facility located 50 miles from Boston, Massachusetts. Features: freshwater lake; 8 tennis courts; wooded setting.

Profile of Summer Employees Total number: 85–100; typical ages: 18–23. 50% men; 50% women; 16% high school students; 82% college students; 2% non-U.S. citizens. Nonsmokers preferred.

Employment Information Openings are from June 19 to August 16. Jobs available: ▶ *archery instructors* at $1350–$2000 per season ▶ 1 *arts and crafts director* (minimum age 21) at $2000 and up per season ▶ 2–5 *arts and crafts instructors* at $1350–$2000 per season ▶ 1 *athletics director* (minimum age 21) at $2000 and up per season ▶ *athletics instructors* at $1350–$2000 per season ▶ *canoe instructors* at $1350–$2000 per season ▶ 1 *drama director* at $2000 and up per season ▶ *drama instructors* at $1350–$2000 per season ▶ 3 *nurses* (minimum age 21) with RN at $5000 per season ▶ *sailing instructors* at $1350–$2000 per season ▶ 1 *swimming director* (minimum age 21) at $2000 and up per season ▶ *swimming instructors* at $1350–$2000 per season ▶ 1 *tennis director* (minimum age 21) at $2000 and up per season ▶ *tennis instructors* at $1350–$2000 per season ▶ 1–2 *waterskiing boat drivers* (minimum age 21) with lifeguard certification at $2000 and up per season ▶ 1 *waterskiing director* (minimum age 21) at $2000 and up per season ▶ 1 *windsurfing instructor* with LGT certification at $1350–$2000 per season. Applicants must submit formal organization application, personal reference, three letters of recommendation. An in-person interview is recommended, but a telephone interview is acceptable. International applicants accepted; must obtain own visa, obtain own working papers, apply through a recognized agency.

Benefits and Preemployment Training Free housing, free meals, formal training, on-the-job training, and willing to complete paperwork for educational credit. Preemployment training is required and includes accident prevention and safety, CPR, interpersonal skills, leadership skills.

Contact Ed Pletman, Director, Camp Tevya of the Eli and Bessie Cohen Foundation, 30 Main Street, Ashland, Massachusetts 01701. Telephone: 800-375-8444. Fax: 508-881-1006. E-mail: director_tevya@cohencamps.org. World Wide Web: http://www.cohencamps.org. Contact by e-mail, fax, mail, phone, or through World Wide Web site. Application deadline: continuous.

CAMP TOHKOMEUPOG
EAST MADISON ROAD
EAST MADISON, NEW HAMPSHIRE 03849

General Information Residential camp accommodating 120 boys ages 6–16 and featuring sports, mountain and canoe camping trips, and adventure program including ropes course and rock climbing. Established in 1932. 1,000-acre facility located 50 miles from Portland, Maine. Features: freshwater lake; 5 tennis courts; near White Mountain National Forest; 1000 acres; climbing wall- ropes course; street hockey rink.

Profile of Summer Employees Total number: 35; typical ages: 17–65. 95% men; 5% women; 5% minorities; 10% high school students; 50% college students; 5% retirees; 10% non-U.S. citizens; 85% local applicants. Nonsmokers preferred.

Employment Information Openings are from June 21 to August 17. Jobs available: ▶ 1 *archery instructor* (minimum age 20) at $1300–$1800 per season ▶ 4 *cabin counselors* (minimum age 20) with CPR, lifeguard, and first aid training at $700–$1400 per season ▶ 1 *registered nurse* (minimum age 25) with RN license at $400 per week ▶ 1 *rock climbing instructor and trip leader* (minimum age 22) at $250–$275 per week. Applicants must submit formal organization application, resume, three personal references, two letters of recommendation. An in-person interview is recommended, but a telephone interview is acceptable. International applicants accepted; must obtain own visa, obtain own working papers, apply through a recognized agency.

Benefits and Preemployment Training Free housing, free meals, formal training, willing to provide letters of recommendation, on-the-job training, and opportunity to attend seminars/ workshops. Preemployment training is required and includes accident prevention and safety, first aid, CPR, interpersonal skills, leadership skills.

Contact Andrew Mahoney, Director, Camp Tohkomeupog, HC 63, Box 40, East Madison, New Hampshire 03849. Telephone: 603-367-8362. Fax: 603-367-8664. E-mail: tohko@tohko.com. World Wide Web: http://www.tohko.com. Contact by e-mail, fax, mail, or phone. Application deadline: continuous.

CAMP WALT WHITMAN
1000 CAPE MOONSHINE ROAD
PIERMONT, NEW HAMPSHIRE 03779

General Information Coeducational residential camp serving 390 campers and offering a strong general program. Established in 1948. 300-acre facility located 110 miles from Boston, Massachusetts. Features: freshwater lake; heated swimming pool; 11 clay tennis courts; multi sports complex; 3 arts studios; wooded, mountain setting.

Profile of Summer Employees Total number: 220; typical ages: 18–30. 50% men; 50% women; 75% college students; 2% retirees; 10% non-U.S. citizens. Nonsmokers required.

Employment Information Openings are from June 18 to August 17. Jobs available: ▶ 3 *art/ woodshop instructors* (minimum age 20) with experience at $1300–$2500 per season ▶ 1 *arts and crafts staff* (minimum age 19) with experience at $1500–$3000 per season ▶ 2 *dance/ gymnastics instructors* (minimum age 19) with experience at $1200–$1800 per season ▶ 20–30 *general counselors* (minimum age 19) with experience at $1100–$1600 per season ▶ 3 *hiking and camping specialists* (minimum age 20) with experience at $1300–$1800 per season ▶ 6 *kitchen and maintenance personnel* (minimum age 20) with experience at $1200–$2500 per season ▶ 1 *radio station manager* (minimum age 19) with experience at $1200–$1500 per season ▶ 3 *sailing, canoeing, and windsurfing instructors* (minimum age 19) with experience at $1300–$2000 per season ▶ 6 *sports coaches* (minimum age 20) with experience in the field at $1400–$2000 per season ▶ 6 *swimming instructors* (minimum age 19) with WSI and LG certification at $1300–$2000 per season ▶ 6 *tennis instructors* (minimum age 19) with experience at $1300–$2000 per season ▶ 2 *water skiing instructors* (minimum age 19) with experience at $1300–$2000 per season. Applicants must submit formal organization application, three personal references. A telephone interview is required. International applicants accepted; must apply through a recognized agency.

Benefits and Preemployment Training Free housing, free meals, formal training, willing to provide letters of recommendation, on-the-job training, willing to complete paperwork for educational credit, willing to act as a professional reference, opportunity to attend seminars/ workshops, travel reimbursement, and leadership and management training. Preemployment training is required and includes accident prevention and safety, first aid, CPR, interpersonal skills, leadership skills.

Contact Jancy Dorfman, Director, Camp Walt Whitman, PO Box 938, Bedford, New York 10506. Telephone: 800-657-8282. Fax: 914-234-5487. E-mail: staff@campwalt.com. World Wide Web: http://www.campwalt.com. Contact by e-mail, fax, mail, phone, or through World Wide Web site. Application deadline: continuous.

CHENOA
BRIMSTONE CORNER ROAD
ANTRIM, NEW HAMPSHIRE 03440

General Information Girl Scout residential camp serving 175 girls ages 6–16 in one- and two-week sessions, emphasizing girl decision-making and leadership development. Established in 1994. 300-acre facility located 80 miles from Boston, Massachusetts. Features: freshwater lake; wooded area; all new buildings; beaver pond.

Profile of Summer Employees Total number: 70; typical ages: 18–35. 1% men; 99% women; 2% minorities; 50% college students; 25% non-U.S. citizens; 15% local applicants. Nonsmokers preferred.

Employment Information Openings are from June 11 to August 24. Spring break, winter break, and year-round positions also offered. Jobs available: ▶ 2–4 *administrators* (minimum age 21) with experience supervising staff and kids at $2800–$4800 per season ▶ 4 *cooks* (minimum age 18) with experience in quantity cooking at $2400–$4000 per season ▶ 2 *nurses* (minimum age 21) with RN, LPN, or EMT at $3500–$7000 per season ▶ 2–3 *program specialists* (minimum age 18) with experience teaching groups of children and ability to lead programs in science, math, diversity, and gender issues at $1500–$3200 per season ▶ 20 *unit counselors* (minimum age 18) with high school diploma and experience working with groups of children at $1500– $2800 per season ▶ 4–6 *waterfront assistants* (minimum age 18) with WSI and LGT certification at $1500–$2400 per season ▶ 1 *waterfront director* (minimum age 21) with WSI and LGT certification at $2500–$3500 per season. Applicants must submit formal organization application, resume, three personal references. An in-person interview is recommended, but a telephone interview is acceptable. International applicants accepted; must apply through a recognized agency.

Benefits and Preemployment Training Free housing, free meals, formal training, health insurance, willing to provide letters of recommendation, on-the-job training, willing to complete paperwork for educational credit, willing to act as a professional reference, and opportunity to attend seminars/workshops. Preemployment training is required and includes accident prevention and safety, first aid, CPR, interpersonal skills, leadership skills, program skills.

Contact Missy Long, Camp Director, Chenoa, SWGSC, One Commerce Drive, Bedford, New Hampshire 03110. Telephone: 800-654-1270. Fax: 603-627-4169. E-mail: mlong@swgirlscouts. org. World Wide Web: http://www.swgirlscouts.org. Contact by e-mail, fax, mail, phone, or through World Wide Web site. Application deadline: continuous.

COLD RIVER CAMP, A.M.C.
HCR BOX 221
CENTER CONWAY, NEW HAMPSHIRE 03813

General Information Family camp for hiking and outdoor activities in White Mountain National Forest owned by Appalachian Mountain Club. Established in 1919. 135-acre facility located 65 miles from Portland, Maine. Features: mountain setting; rustic setting; individual cabins; excellent meals; organized hikes; mountain streams.

Profile of Summer Employees Total number: 14; typical ages: 18–23. 50% men; 50% women; 20% high school students; 80% college students; 10% retirees; 30% non-U.S. citizens; 10% local applicants. Nonsmokers preferred.

Employment Information Openings are from June 22 to August 31. Jobs available: ▶ 8 *crew members* (minimum age 18) at $2300 per season ▶ 2 *kitchen positions* (minimum age 18) with food preparation experience at $2800–$3800 per season. Applicants must submit formal organization application, letter of interest, three personal references, three letters of recommendation. An in-person interview is recommended, but a telephone interview is acceptable. International applicants accepted; must apply through a recognized agency.

Benefits and Preemployment Training Free housing, free meals, willing to provide letters of recommendation, and willing to act as a professional reference.

Contact Bill Waste, Manager, Cold River Camp, A.M.C., 69 Washburn Hill Road, Lyme, New Hampshire 03768. Telephone: 603-795-4440. E-mail: bill.waste@valley.net. World Wide Web: http://www.outdoors.org. Contact by e-mail, mail, phone, or through World Wide Web site. Application deadline: January 31.

GENEVA POINT CENTER
MOULTONBORO, NEW HAMPSHIRE 03254
General Information Ecumenical conference center hosting groups and Elderhostel. Established in 1919. 200-acre facility located 40 miles from Concord. Features: freshwater lake; 200 acres; located in lakes region of New Hampshire; near White Mountains.

Profile of Summer Employees Total number: 30–40; typical ages: 18–24. 50% men; 50% women; 5% minorities; 20% college students; 25% retirees; 45% non-U.S. citizens; 5% local applicants. Nonsmokers required.

Employment Information Openings are from May 13 to October 19. Jobs available: ▶ 4–6 *dining room staff* at $170–$206 per week ▶ 6–8 *general kitchen staff* at $170–$206 per week ▶ 3–6 *housekeepers* at $170–$206 per week ▶ 5–6 *lifeguards* at $200–$220 per week. Applicants must submit formal organization application, three personal references, three letters of recommendation. A telephone interview is required. International applicants accepted; must apply through a recognized agency.

Benefits and Preemployment Training Free housing, free meals, on-the-job training, and opportunity to attend seminars/workshops. Preemployment training is required and includes accident prevention and safety.

Contact Jess Schlood, Executive Director, Geneva Point Center, HCR 62, Box 469, Center Harbor, New Hampshire 03226. Telephone: 603-253-4366. Fax: 603-253-4883. E-mail: geneva@genevapoint.org. Contact by e-mail or phone. Application deadline: continuous.

INTERLOCKEN INTERNATIONAL SUMMER CAMP
19 INTERLOCKEN WAY
HILLSBORO, NEW HAMPSHIRE 03244
General Information Creative, noncompetitive international summer camp offering a wide range of activities to 180 campers per session from the United States and around the world. Established in 1961. 1,000-acre facility located 100 miles from Boston, Massachusetts. Features: several freshwater lakes; theatre/dance/art facilities; architect-designed buildings; rope swing and lake launch; ropes course and climbing wall; comprehensive sports facilities.

Profile of Summer Employees Total number: 60; typical ages: 19–28. 50% men; 50% women; 20% minorities; 50% college students; 20% non-U.S. citizens. Nonsmokers required.

Employment Information Openings are from June 1 to September 30. Spring break, winter break, and year-round positions also offered. Jobs available: ▶ 4 *applied arts staff members* (minimum age 19) with experience in the field at $200–$450 per week ▶ 2 *environmental education staff members* (minimum age 19) with experience in the field at $200–$450 per week ▶ 4 *music staff members* (minimum age 19) with experience in the field at $200–$450 per week ▶ 4 *performing arts staff members* (minimum age 19) with experience in the field at $200–$450 per week ▶ 4 *sports staff members* (minimum age 19) with experience in the field at $200–$450 per week ▶ 4 *waterfront instructors* (minimum age 19) with experience in the field at $200–$450 per week ▶ 6 *wilderness staff members* (minimum age 19) with experience in the field at $200–$450 per week. Applicants must submit formal organization application, letter of interest, resume, three personal references. An in-person interview is recommended, but a telephone interview is acceptable. International applicants accepted; must apply through a recognized agency.

Benefits and Preemployment Training Free housing, free meals, willing to provide letters of recommendation, on-the-job training, and willing to act as a professional reference. Preemployment training is required and includes accident prevention and safety, first aid, CPR, interpersonal skills, leadership skills, lifeguard training.

Contact Tom Herman, Staffing Director, Interlocken International Summer Camp. Telephone: 603-478-3166. Fax: 603-478-5260. E-mail: jobs@interlocken.org. World Wide Web: http://www. interlocken.org. Contact by e-mail, fax, mail, or through World Wide Web site. Application deadline: continuous (best if received prior to January 31st).

INTERLOCKEN TRAVEL PROGRAMS
19 INTERLOCKEN WAY
HILLSBORO, NEW HAMPSHIRE 03244

General Information Experientially-based domestic and international small group travel programs that focus on performing arts, adventure/wilderness, community service, language, leadership training, adventure cycling, and environment. Travel programs are an outgrowth of the Interlocken International Summer Camp. Established in 1967. 1,000-acre facility located 100 miles from Boston, Massachusetts.

Profile of Summer Employees Total number: 30; typical ages: 24–35. 50% men; 50% women; 20% minorities; 20% non-U.S. citizens. Nonsmokers required.

Employment Information Openings are from June 1 to August 22. Spring break, winter break, and year-round positions also offered. Jobs available: ▶ 12 *adventure/wilderness leaders* (minimum age 24) with WFR certification and experience leading high school students at $275–$400 per week ▶ 6 *cycling leaders* (minimum age 24) with experience working with high school age students at $275–$400 per week ▶ 4 *leadership training leaders* (minimum age 24) with residential camp background and experience teaching leadership training at $275–$400 per week ▶ 6 *performing arts leaders* (minimum age 24) with background in physical theatre and experience teaching teenagers at $275–$400 per week ▶ 35 *travel leaders* (minimum age 24) with experience working with high school age students at $275–$400 per week. Applicants must submit formal organization application, letter of interest, resume, three letters of recommendation. An in-person interview is recommended, but a telephone interview is acceptable. International applicants accepted; must apply through a recognized agency.

Benefits and Preemployment Training Free housing, free meals, formal training, willing to provide letters of recommendation, willing to complete paperwork for educational credit, willing to act as a professional reference, opportunity to attend seminars/workshops, and travel reimbursement. Preemployment training is required and includes accident prevention and safety, first aid, CPR, interpersonal skills, leadership skills, lifeguard training.

Contact Tom Herman, Staffing Director, Interlocken Travel Programs. Telephone: 603-478-3166. Fax: 603-478-5260. E-mail: jobs@interlocken.org. World Wide Web: http://www. interlocken.org. Contact by e-mail, fax, mail, or through World Wide Web site. Application deadline: continuous (best chance if submitted before February 31st).

KINYON/JONES TENNIS CAMP AT DARTMOUTH COLLEGE
6083 ALUMNI GYM
HANOVER, NEW HAMPSHIRE 03755-3512

General Information Tennis camp for boys and girls age 10–17. Established in 1988. Located 120 miles from Boston, Massachusetts. Features: 6 outdoor courts; 6 indoor courts; college dorms; college dining hall.

Profile of Summer Employees Total number: 10; typical ages: 19–50. 50% men; 50% women; 90% college students. Nonsmokers required.

Employment Information Openings are from June 16 to July 27. Jobs available: ▶ 8–10 *tennis instructors* (minimum age 19) with experience in tennis instruction at $300 per week. Applicants must submit a formal organization application, resume. A telephone interview is required.

Benefits and Preemployment Training Free housing, free meals, and on-the-job training.

Contact David Jones, Co-Director, Kinyon/Jones Tennis Camp at Dartmouth College, 24 College Hill, Hanover, New Hampshire 03755. Telephone: 603-646-3819. Fax: 603-646-0757. E-mail: chuck.kinyon@dartmouth.edu. World Wide Web: http://www.dartmouth.edu/~mten/camp.html. Contact by e-mail, mail, or phone. Application deadline: continuous.

ROAD'S END FARM HORSEMANSHIP CAMP
JACKSON HILL ROAD
CHESTERFIELD, NEW HAMPSHIRE 03443-0197

General Information Residential camp program serving 60 girls ages 8–16 who love horses, English pleasure riding, and the noncompetitive atmosphere of a family-owned horse farm at the end of a quiet dirt road. Sessions vary from 2 to 8 weeks in length. Established in 1958. 505-acre facility located 95 miles from Boston, Massachusetts. Features: family atmosphere; noncompetitive philosophy; 50 saddle horses; scenic and secluded setting; freshwater lake; 20 miles of private bridlepaths.

Profile of Summer Employees Total number: 26; typical ages: 19–40. 100% women; 10% minorities; 80% college students; 10% non-U.S. citizens. Nonsmokers required.

Employment Information Openings are from June 1 to August 17. Jobs available: ▶ 1 *camp nurse* (minimum age 22) with LPN or RN license at $4000–$5000 per season ▶ 1 *canoeing instructor* (minimum age 19) with Red Cross credentials and experience in the field at $3000–$3500 per season ▶ 4–6 *lead riders* (minimum age 19) with English-style equestrian competence and experience at $3000–$3500 per season ▶ 4 *lifeguards* (minimum age 19) with Red Cross credentials and experience in the field at $3000–$3500 per season ▶ 4–6 *riding instructors* (minimum age 19) with Pony Club, CHA, or BHS credentials or some very good experience at $3000–$3500 per season ▶ 3 *swimming instructors* (minimum age 19) with WSI certification and experience in the field at $3000–$3500 per season. Applicants must submit formal organization application, three personal references. An in-person interview is recommended, but a telephone interview is acceptable. International applicants accepted; must apply through a recognized agency.

Benefits and Preemployment Training Free housing, free meals, willing to provide letters of recommendation, on-the-job training, and willing to act as a professional reference. Preemployment training is required and includes accident prevention and safety, interpersonal skills, leadership skills.

Contact Tom Woodman, Director, Road's End Farm Horsemanship Camp, PO Box 197, Chesterfield, New Hampshire 03443-0197. Telephone: 603-363-4900. Fax: 603-363-4949. World Wide Web: http://www.roadsendfarm.com. Contact by fax, mail, or phone. Application deadline: continuous.

ROCKYWOLD–DEEPHAVEN CAMPS, INC. (RDC)
PINEHURST ROAD, PO BOX B
HOLDERNESS, NEW HAMPSHIRE 03245

General Information Family vacation camp providing guests with a unique family living experience offering rustic simplicity, high-quality services, and a natural setting. Established in 1897. 115-acre facility located 50 miles from Concord. Features: Squam Lake; location on the southern edge of White Mountain National Forest; 8 clay tennis courts; hiking and mountain bike trails leading from the property; old-fashioned ice boxes and fire places in each cottage; ballfield and basketball courts.

Profile of Summer Employees Total number: 90–100; typical ages: 18–25. 50% men; 50% women; 5% minorities; 4% high school students; 70% college students; 1% retirees; 45% non-U.S. citizens; 10% local applicants. Nonsmokers required.

Employment Information Openings are from May 15 to October 7. Jobs available: ▶ 20–25 *food service personnel* (minimum age 18) with a positive and flexible attitude and high work standards at $6–$9 per hour ▶ 10–12 *grounds/maintenance personnel* (minimum age 18) with experience in soft-surface tennis court maintenance and carpentry at $6–$6.50 per hour ▶ 22–24 *housekeeping personnel* (minimum age 18) with a positive and flexible attitude and high work standards at $6–$6.50 per hour ▶ 6–8 *office staff members* (minimum age 18) with word-processing and money handling skills and experience working with the public at $6.20–$6.50 per hour ▶ 5–7 *recreation staff members* (minimum age 18) with experience in tennis, water sports, outdoor recreation, crafts, and working with various age groups at $235–$260 per week. Applicants must submit formal organization application, three personal references, 3 recommendation forms. An in-person interview is recommended, but a telephone interview is acceptable. International applicants accepted; must apply through a recognized agency.

Benefits and Preemployment Training Free housing, free meals, willing to provide letters of recommendation, on-the-job training, willing to complete paperwork for educational credit, willing to act as a professional reference, and opportunity to attend seminars/workshops.

Contact Ann Rampulla, General Manager, Rockywold–Deephaven Camps, Inc. (RDC), PO Box B, Holderness, New Hampshire 03245. Telephone: 603-968-3313. Fax: 603-968-3438. E-mail: rdc@lr.net. World Wide Web: http://www.rdcsquam.com. Contact by e-mail, fax, mail, phone, or through World Wide Web site. Application deadline: February 15.

THE SOUTHWESTERN COMPANY, NEW HAMPSHIRE
See The Southwestern Company on page 297 for complete description.

STUDENT CONSERVATION ASSOCIATION (SCA), NEW HAMPSHIRE
689 RIVER ROAD, PO BOX 550
CHARLESTOWN, NEW HAMPSHIRE 03603

General Information Nonprofit organization that places interns year-round in expense-paid conservation projects in national parks, forests, and wildlife refuges nationwide. Established in 1957. 20-acre facility located 120 miles from Hartford, Connecticut. Features: national parks; mountains; lakes and rivers; wooded setting/forests; historic sites; national landmarks.

Profile of Summer Employees Total number: 100; typical ages: 16–30. 45% men; 55% women; 15% minorities; 30% high school students; 70% college students; 5% retirees; 5% non-U.S. citizens; 5% local applicants.

Employment Information Openings are from January to December. Year-round positions also offered. Jobs available: ▶ 1200–1600 *conservation interns* (minimum age 18) with high school diploma and valid driver's license; housing, travel, insurance, and AmeriCorps education awards available at $50–$160 per week ▶ 150–200 *high school crew leaders* (minimum age 21) with experience working with high school students; travel, training, and room and board included at $1360–$2360 per season ▶ 650 *high school trail crew members-volunteer* (must be 15 to 19 years of age) with an interest in outdoors and service ▶ 100–150 *residential trails/education interns* (must be 18 to 25 years of age) with an interest in outdoors and working with children at $60 per week. Applicants must submit formal organization application, academic transcripts, two personal references or two letters of recommendation, $20 processing fee ($40 for international applicants); additional requirements on searchable database at Web site. A telephone interview is required. International applicants accepted; must obtain own visa.

Benefits and Preemployment Training Free housing, free meals, formal training, possible full-time employment, health insurance, names of contacts, on-the-job training, willing to complete

paperwork for educational credit, opportunity to attend seminars/workshops, and travel reimbursement. Preemployment training is required and includes accident prevention and safety, first aid, CPR, interpersonal skills, leadership skills, wilderness work skills, WFA, WFR.
Contact Recruitment Department, Student Conservation Association (SCA), New Hampshire. Telephone: 603-543-1700. Fax: 603-543-1828. E-mail: internships@sca-inc.org. World Wide Web: http://www.thesca.org. Contact by e-mail, fax, mail, phone, or through World Wide Web site. Application deadline: continuous.

THE WHALE'S TALE WATER PARK
ROUTE 3 NORTH
LINCOLN, NEW HAMPSHIRE 03251
General Information Water park with more than 10 wet and dry attractions. Established in 1985. 17-acre facility located 100 miles from Boston, Massachusetts. Features: 7 water slides; wave pool; children's play area; lazy river; volleyball courts; great mountain views.
Profile of Summer Employees Total number: 80; typical ages: 16–25. 48% men; 52% women; 60% high school students; 10% college students; 30% local applicants.
Employment Information Openings are from June 1 to September 1. Jobs available: ▶ 10–20 *food service staff* (minimum age 16) at $6–$10 per hour ▶ 10–20 *lifeguards* (minimum age 16) with ARC certification at $6–$10 per hour ▶ 5–10 *sales staff* (minimum age 16) with money handling and customer service skills at $6–$8 per hour. Applicants must submit a formal organization application, online application. An in-person interview is recommended, but a telephone interview is acceptable.
Benefits and Preemployment Training Meals at a cost, willing to provide letters of recommendation, on-the-job training, willing to complete paperwork for educational credit, and willing to act as a professional reference. Preemployment training is required and includes accident prevention and safety, first aid, interpersonal skills, leadership skills.
Contact Jeb Boyd, General Manager, The Whale's Tale Water Park, PO Box 67, Lincoln, New Hampshire 03251. Telephone: 603-745-8810. Fax: 603-745-6958. E-mail: wtwp@together.net. World Wide Web: http://www.getsettogetwet.com. Contact by e-mail, fax, or mail. Application deadline: continuous.

YMCA CAMP LINCOLN
PO BOX 729, 67 BALL ROAD
KINGSTON, NEW HAMPSHIRE 03848
General Information YMCA Camp Lincoln is a year-round coed camp that offers girls and boys the opportunity to grow through engaging programs involving travel, nature, community development, and fun. Established in 1926. 75-acre facility located 40 miles from Boston, Massachusetts. Features: freshwater lake; beautiful cabins; close to ocean; close to mountains; excellent climbing wall/high ropes; great sports fields.
Profile of Summer Employees Total number: 120; typical ages: 16–26. 40% men; 60% women; 5% minorities; 50% high school students; 40% college students; 2% retirees; 5% non-U.S. citizens; 90% local applicants. Nonsmokers required.
Employment Information Openings are from June 1 to August 31. Spring break, winter break, and year-round positions also offered. Jobs available: ▶ 1–4 *adventure trip leaders* (minimum age 21) at $3000–$4000 per season ▶ 1 *camp nurse* (minimum age 25) with RN certification at $5000–$8000 per season ▶ 1–30 *general counselors* (minimum age 16) at $2000–$3000 per season ▶ 1–15 *program specialists* (minimum age 18) at $2500–$3500 per season. Applicants must submit formal organization application, two personal references. A telephone interview is required. International applicants accepted; must obtain own visa, obtain own working papers, apply through a recognized agency.
Benefits and Preemployment Training Free housing, free meals, possible full-time employment, willing to provide letters of recommendation, on-the-job training, willing to complete

paperwork for educational credit, willing to act as a professional reference, and opportunity to attend seminars/workshops. Preemployment training is required and includes accident prevention and safety, first aid, CPR, interpersonal skills, leadership skills, lifeguard training, archery. **Contact** Eric Tucker, Director, YMCA Camp Lincoln, PO Box 729, Kingston, New Hampshire 03848, United States. Telephone: 603-642-3361. Fax: 603-642-4340. E-mail: eric@ymcacamplincoln. org. World Wide Web: http://www.ymcacamplincoln.org. Contact by e-mail or through World Wide Web site. Application deadline: continuous.

YOGI BEAR'S JELLYSTONE PARK
ROUTE 132N, PO BOX 1926
ASHLAND, NEW HAMPSHIRE 03217

General Information Family fun resort and campground offering day trips, overnights, and weekend vacations in a trailer, log cabin rental, or campsite. Theme park with planned daily activities for all ages. Established in 1978. 40-acre facility located 30 miles from Concord. Features: sandy-bottomed river; pool and hot tub; hayrides; movies and planned activities; snack bar; mini golf; large general store.

Profile of Summer Employees Total number: 50; typical ages: 17–69. 50% men; 50% women; 10% minorities; 5% high school students; 5% college students; 20% retirees; 40% non-U.S. citizens; 20% local applicants. Nonsmokers preferred.

Employment Information Openings are from April to October. Year-round positions also offered. Jobs available: ▶ 3 *food service staff* (minimum age 18) at a salary starting at minimum wage ▶ 10 *general operations and maintenance staff* (minimum age 16) at a salary starting at minimum wage ▶ 14 *housekeepers* (minimum age 16) at a salary starting at minimum wage ▶ 3–4 *recreation directors* (minimum age 16) at a salary starting at minimum wage ▶ 2–3 *reservationists* (minimum age 16) with computer experience preferred at a salary starting at minimum wage ▶ 2–3 *store clerks* (minimum age 16) at a salary starting at minimum wage. Applicants must submit formal organization application, letter of interest, resume, three personal references, two letters of recommendation. An in-person interview is recommended, but a telephone interview is acceptable. International applicants accepted; must obtain own visa, obtain own working papers, apply through a recognized agency.

Benefits and Preemployment Training Housing at a cost, possible full-time employment, willing to provide letters of recommendation, on-the-job training, willing to complete paperwork for educational credit, willing to act as a professional reference, and discounts at store and snack bar, use of amenities.

Contact Rachel Capps, Personnel Director, Yogi Bear's Jellystone Park, PO Box 1926, Ashland, New Hampshire 03217. Fax: 603-968-7349. E-mail: yogi@jellystonenh.com. World Wide Web: http://www.jellystonenh.com. Contact by e-mail, fax, or mail. No phone calls. Application deadline: continuous.

NEW JERSEY

APPEL FARM ARTS AND MUSIC CENTER
457 SHIRLEY ROAD
ELMER, NEW JERSEY 08318

General Information Fine and performing arts center concentrating on 3 areas: presenting arts (music, dance, theater) to the local community, providing affordable meeting and work space for artists and art organizations, and offering arts education for children through a summer camp. Established in 1960. 170-acre facility located 25 miles from Philadelphia, Pennsylvania. Features: tennis courts; swimming pool; new dining hall, fine arts building, and teaching spaces; rural setting near a major metropolitan area; beach 50 minutes away.

Profile of Summer Employees Total number: 80; typical ages: 20–35. 40% men; 60% women; 20% minorities; 15% college students; 20% non-U.S. citizens; 10% local applicants. Nonsmokers required.

Employment Information Openings are from June 16 to August 23. Jobs available: ▶ 10 *art instructors* (minimum age 20) with extensive experience in painting, drawing, printmaking, sculpture, weaving, and ceramics at $1600–$2000 per season ▶ 1 *community-outreach coordinator* (minimum age 20) with organizational ability and office work experience at $1600–$2000 per season ▶ 3 *dance instructors* (minimum age 20) with experience and expert knowledge of modern, jazz, and ballet dancing at $1600–$2000 per season ▶ 10 *music instructors* (minimum age 20) with extensive experience in woodwinds, piano, strings, percussion, voice, brass, electronic music, and rock at $1600–$2000 per season ▶ 5 *photography instructors* (minimum age 20) with experience in the field at $1600–$2000 per season ▶ 2 *registered nurses* (minimum age 20) with RN license, NJ certification preferred ▶ 3 *sports staff members* (minimum age 20) with experience in tennis and noncompetitive sports at $1600–$2000 per season ▶ 4 *swimming instructors* (minimum age 20) with Red Cross lifeguard training or WSI certification and Bronze Medallion at $1600–$2000 per season ▶ 5 *technical theater personnel* (minimum age 20) with experience in stagecraft, set design, costumes, and lighting at $1600–$2200 per season ▶ 10 *theater instructors* (minimum age 20) with directing experience at $1600–$2000 per season ▶ 3 *video instructors* (minimum age 20) with experience in the field at $1600–$2000 per season. Applicants must submit resume, three personal references, performance audio tapes, slides of present work. An in-person interview is recommended, but a telephone interview is acceptable. International applicants accepted.

Benefits and Preemployment Training Free housing, free meals, formal training, willing to provide letters of recommendation, on-the-job training, willing to complete paperwork for educational credit, willing to act as a professional reference, and opportunity to attend seminars/workshops.

Contact Matt Sisson, Camp Director, Appel Farm Arts and Music Center, PO Box 888, Elmer, New Jersey 08318. Telephone: 856-358-2472. Fax: 856-358-6513. E-mail: appelcamp@aol. com. World Wide Web: http://www.appelfarm.org. Contact through World Wide Web site. Application deadline: continuous.

CAMP LOUEMMA
43 LOUEMMA LANE
SUSSEX, NEW JERSEY 07461

General Information Nonprofit traditional, general interest sleepaway camp for girls and boys ages 7-15. Established in 1941. 152-acre facility located 30 miles from Newark. Features: private lake; pool; hockey rink (roller); beach volleyball; athletic fields; climbing wall.

Profile of Summer Employees Total number: 80; typical ages: 16–60. 50% men; 50% women; 20% high school students; 75% college students. Nonsmokers preferred.

Employment Information Openings are from June 20 to August 15. Jobs available: ▶ 4–8 *male and female counselors* (minimum age 18) must enjoy working with children at $750–$1500 per season ▶ 1 *nurse* with RN or LPN at a negotiable salary (season or session) ▶ 1 *waterfront director* (minimum age 21) with WSI and/or LGTI certification at $3000–$3500 per season. Applicants must submit formal organization application, two personal references. An in-person interview is recommended, but a telephone interview is acceptable. International applicants accepted; must obtain own visa, apply through a recognized agency.

Benefits and Preemployment Training Free housing, free meals, willing to provide letters of recommendation, on-the-job training, and willing to complete paperwork for educational credit.

Preemployment training is required and includes accident prevention and safety, interpersonal skills, leadership skills, role playing.

Contact Hal Pugach, Director, Camp Louemma, 214-45 42nd Avenue, Bayside, New York 11361. Telephone: 973-316-0362. Fax: 973-316-0980. E-mail: camplouemma@aol.com. Contact by e-mail, fax, mail, or phone. Application deadline: continuous.

CAMP LOU HENRY HOOVER
961 WEST SHORE DRIVE
MIDDLEVILLE, NEW JERSEY 07855

General Information Nonprofit girl scout camp that focuses on providing girls with a wide range of activities. Established in 1953. 328-acre facility located 15 miles from Newton. Features: waterfront; wooded area; tents facilities; multipurpose building; canoe/hike trips.

Profile of Summer Employees Total number: 60; typical ages: 16–32. 2% men; 98% women; 10% minorities; 30% high school students; 40% college students; 20% non-U.S. citizens; 10% local applicants. Nonsmokers preferred.

Employment Information Openings are from June 30 to August 20. Jobs available: ▶ 20–30 *counselors* (minimum age 18) at $1000–$3000 per season ▶ 2–4 *head cook/kitchen staff* (minimum age 18) at $800–$3000 per season ▶ 2–6 *waterfront staff* (minimum age 18) at $800–$2000 per season. Applicants must submit formal organization application, three personal references. An in-person interview is recommended, but a telephone interview is acceptable. International applicants accepted; must apply through a recognized agency.

Benefits and Preemployment Training Free housing, free meals, formal training, willing to provide letters of recommendation, on-the-job training, willing to complete paperwork for educational credit, and willing to act as a professional reference. Preemployment training is required and includes accident prevention and safety, first aid, CPR, interpersonal skills, leadership skills.

Contact Deborah Hooker, Director, Camp Lou Henry Hoover, 201 Grove Street East, Westfield, New Jersey 07090. Telephone: 908-232-3236 Ext. 1226. Fax: 908-232-2140. E-mail: hookie@ix. netcom.com. Contact by e-mail or phone. Application deadline: continuous.

COLLEGE GIFTED PROGRAMS
DREW UNIVERSITY
MADISON, NEW JERSEY 07940

General Information Residential educational academic summer camp for gifted and talented students in grades 4-11. Program blends in-depth academics with recreational and cultural activities. Established in 1984. 186-acre facility located 20 miles from New York, New York. Features: dormitories; campus classroom facilities; campus recreational facilities include pool, tennis courts, and gym; campus library; beautiful college setting.

Profile of Summer Employees Total number: 65; typical ages: 19–70. 50% men; 50% women; 30% minorities; 50% college students; 10% retirees; 10% non-U.S. citizens; 25% local applicants. Nonsmokers required.

Employment Information Openings are from June 27 to July 17. Jobs available: ▶ *administrative assistant* with computer skills and ability to work effectively with other individuals at $2000 per 3-week session ▶ 30 *counselors* with two years of college completed and experience working with children at $1000 to $1200 per 3-week session ▶ 4 *directors* with at least 5 years teaching/supervisory experience; master's degree required, doctorate preferred at $4500–$7000 per year ▶ 6 *housemasters/instructors (residential)* with master's degree, teaching, and supervisory experience at $2500 to $3500 per 3-week session ▶ 20 *instructors (non-residential)* with master's degree and teaching experience at $725 to $2900 per 3-week session ▶ 2 *nurses* with RN license, school experience preferred at $260–$300 per day. Applicants must submit formal organization application, resume, academic transcripts, two personal references, two letters of recommendation. An in-person interview is recommended, but a telephone interview is acceptable. International applicants accepted; must apply through a recognized agency.

Benefits and Preemployment Training Free housing, free meals, willing to provide letters of recommendation, willing to complete paperwork for educational credit, and willing to act as a professional reference. Preemployment training is required and includes accident prevention and safety, interpersonal skills, leadership skills, instructional strategies for gifted students.

Contact Charles Zeichner, Director, College Gifted Programs, 120 Littleton Road, Suite 201, Parsippany, New Jersey 07054-1803. Telephone: 973-334-6991. Fax: 973-334-9756. E-mail: info@cgp-sig.com. World Wide Web: http://www.cgp-sig.com. Contact by e-mail, fax, mail, phone, or through World Wide Web site. Application deadline: continuous.

CYBERCAMPS–FDU MADISON
MADISON, NEW JERSEY
See Cybercamps–University of Washington on page 326 for complete description.

CYBERCAMPS–FDU TEANECK
TEANECK, NEW JERSEY
See Cybercamps–University of Washington on page 326 for complete description.

CYBERCAMPS–PRINCETON UNIVERSITY
PRINCETON, NEW JERSEY
See Cybercamps–University of Washington on page 326 for complete description.

DWIGHT-ENGLEWOOD SCHOOL
315 EAST PALISADE AVENUE
ENGLEWOOD, NEW JERSEY 07631-0489

General Information Summer school providing a variety of opportunities for students from public, parochial and independent schools through a combination of advancement, introduction, and enrichment courses in all academic disciplines, in the arts, and in sports, allowing for diversity of study. Established in 1889. Affiliated with National Association of Independent Schools, Secondary School Admission Test Board. 34-acre facility located 3 miles from New York, New York. Features: 5 tennis courts; nature sanctuary; theatre; state-of-the-art lower school; library; state-of-the-art fitness room.

Profile of Summer Employees Total number: 120; typical ages: 16–24. 50% men; 50% women; 50% minorities; 65% high school students; 25% college students; 10% local applicants.

Employment Information Openings are from June 23 to August 1. Jobs available: ▶ 10–15 *counselors* (minimum age 16) at $1600–$2100 per season ▶ 2–3 *science lab assistants* (minimum age 16) with knowledge of science at $1400–$1600 per season ▶ 4–8 *sports clinicians* (minimum age 16) with knowledge of a variety of sports at $1300–$1800 per season. Applicants must submit a formal organization application, resume, three personal references, letter of recommendation. An in-person interview is required. International applicants accepted; must obtain own visa, obtain own working papers.

Benefits and Preemployment Training Possible full-time employment, willing to provide letters of recommendation, on-the-job training, willing to complete paperwork for educational credit, willing to act as a professional reference, and free or discounted meals possible. Preemployment training is required and includes accident prevention and safety, interpersonal skills, leadership skills.

Contact Mark A. Schultz, Summer School Principal, Dwight-Englewood School, 25 East Broadway, Hackensack, New Jersey 07601. Telephone: 201-569-9500 Ext. 3501. Fax: 201-568-5018. E-mail: schultm@d-e.org. World Wide Web: http://www.d-e.org. Contact by e-mail. Application deadline: continuous.

EASTER SEALS CAMP MERRY HEART
21 O'BRIAN ROAD
HACKETTSTOWN, NEW JERSEY 07840

General Information Residential camp for persons with a disability ages 5–60, day camp for nondisabled children ages 5–12, and Travel Recreation Experiences in Camping (TREC) program for persons with a disability, ages 18-35. Established in 1949. 121-acre facility located 50 miles from New York, New York. Features: woodlands; freshwater lake; cabins; pool; tennis court/ volleyball court; accessible facility.

Profile of Summer Employees Total number: 55; typical ages: 16–60. 50% men; 50% women; 25% minorities; 10% high school students; 75% college students; 25% non-U.S. citizens; 10% local applicants. Nonsmokers preferred.

Employment Information Openings are from June 9 to August 28. Jobs available: ▶ 2 *cooks* (minimum age 21) with knowledge of cooking for groups at $3600–$4800 per season ▶ 20 *counselors (female)* (minimum age 18) should be college students with education backgrounds at $2000 per season ▶ 20 *counselors (male)* (minimum age 18) should be college students with education backgrounds at $2000 per season ▶ 2 *lifeguards* at $3000 per season ▶ 2 *nurses* with experience and NJ state RN license, first aid, and CPR certification at $12000 per season ▶ 1 *program specialist* (minimum age 19) with experience in the field at $3900 per season ▶ 1 *recreation specialist* (minimum age 21) with therapeutic background at $2500 per season. Applicants must submit formal organization application, three personal references, three letters of recommendation. An in-person interview is recommended, but a telephone interview is acceptable. International applicants accepted; must apply through a recognized agency.

Benefits and Preemployment Training Free housing, free meals, formal training, willing to provide letters of recommendation, on-the-job training, and willing to complete paperwork for educational credit. Preemployment training is required and includes accident prevention and safety, interpersonal skills, leadership skills, skills for working with people with disabilities.

Contact Alex Humanick, Director, Easter Seals Camp Merry Heart, 21 O'Brien Road, Hackettstown, New Jersey 07840. Telephone: 908-852-3896. Fax: 908-852-9263. E-mail: ahumanick@nj.easter-seals.org. World Wide Web: http://www.eastersealsnj.org. Contact by fax, mail, or phone. Application deadline: continuous.

FAIRVIEW LAKE ENVIRONMENTAL TRIP
1035 FAIRVIEW LAKE ROAD
NEWTON, NEW JERSEY 07860

General Information Facility offering traditional camping program plus discovery and challenge trips to enhance an appreciation of the natural environment while fostering skills in communication, cooperation, and trust through physical challenges. Established in 1915. 600-acre facility located 60 miles from New York, New York. Features: 110-acre glacial lake; 20 minute walk to the Appalachian Trail; 500 acres of woods; adjoined to Delaware Water Gap National Recreation Area; camp dormitory housing; many species of endangered wildlife.

Profile of Summer Employees Total number: 110; typical ages: 17–28. 50% men; 50% women; 10% minorities; 50% college students; 10% non-U.S. citizens; 30% local applicants. Nonsmokers required.

Employment Information Openings are from June 15 to August 15. Year-round positions also offered. Jobs available: ▶ 25 *general counselors* (minimum age 18) with love of children and the outdoors, excellent character references, and interpersonal skills at $125–$175 per week ▶ 3 *trip counselors* (minimum age 21) with lifeguard training, first aid, CPR certification, and love of nature and adventure at $180–$275 per week ▶ 3 *unit leaders* (minimum age 21) with same skills and requirements as counselors plus maturity, leadership, and supervisory skills at $200–$250 per week. Applicants must submit formal organization application, three personal references. An in-person interview is recommended, but a telephone interview is acceptable. International applicants accepted; must apply through a recognized agency.

Benefits and Preemployment Training Free housing, free meals, possible full-time employment, on-the-job training, willing to complete paperwork for educational credit, and willing to act as a professional reference. Preemployment training is required and includes accident prevention and safety, first aid, CPR, interpersonal skills, leadership skills, child abuse prevention, sexual harassment prevention, YMCA orientation, conflict management.

Contact Marc Koch, Director, Fairview Lake Environmental Trip, 1035 Fairview Lake Road, Newton, New Jersey 07860. Telephone: 973-383-9282. Fax: 973-383-6386. E-mail: mkoch@ metroymcas.org. World Wide Web: http://www.fairviewlake.org. Contact by e-mail or phone. Application deadline: continuous.

FAIRVIEW LAKE YMCA CAMP
1035 FAIRVIEW LAKE ROAD
NEWTON, NEW JERSEY 07860

General Information Coed residential camp serving 275 campers. Emphasis is on improving self-esteem through creativity and/or physical challenges. Large sports, drama, and outdoor adventure programs offered. Established in 1915. 600-acre facility located 65 miles from New York, New York. Features: mile long freshwater lake; Appalachian Trail borders camp; climbing tower; 2 waterfronts; modern cabins; fine arts programs.

Profile of Summer Employees Total number: 75; typical ages: 18–35. 40% men; 60% women; 25% minorities; 10% high school students; 85% college students; 5% retirees; 10% non-U.S. citizens; 5% local applicants. Nonsmokers preferred.

Employment Information Openings are from June 15 to August 9. Year-round positions also offered. Jobs available: ▶ 60 *counselors* (minimum age 18) with experience working with children, program skills, and EMT licensure highly valued but not required at $1000–$1700 per season ▶ 1 *drama director* (minimum age 18) at $1400–$1800 per season ▶ 1–4 *nurses* with RN and NJ state license at $250–$650 per week ▶ 1–3 *support staff* (minimum age 20) with maintenance/housekeeping skills at $1000–$2000 per season ▶ 1–2 *teen leadership directors* (minimum age 21) with relative experience at $1800–$2500 per season ▶ 1–3 *trip leaders* (minimum age 21) with lifeguard certification and experience working with children at $1200–$1800 per season ▶ 1–2 *waterfront directors* (minimum age 21) with lifeguard certification, first aid/CPR, and management experience at $1800–$2500 per season. Applicants must submit formal organization application, three personal references. An in-person interview is recommended, but a telephone interview is acceptable. International applicants accepted; must obtain own visa, obtain own working papers, apply through a recognized agency.

Benefits and Preemployment Training Free housing, free meals, formal training, possible full-time employment, willing to provide letters of recommendation, on-the-job training, willing to complete paperwork for educational credit, willing to act as a professional reference, opportunity to attend seminars/workshops, and travel reimbursement. Preemployment training is required and includes accident prevention and safety, interpersonal skills, leadership skills, lifeguard training.

Contact Marc Koch, Summer Camp Director, Fairview Lake YMCA Camp, 1035 Fairview Lake Road, Newton, New Jersey 07860. Telephone: 973-383-9282. Fax: 973-383-6386. E-mail: mkoch@metroymcas.org. World Wide Web: http://www.fairviewlake.org. Contact by e-mail, fax, mail, phone, or through World Wide Web site. Application deadline: continuous.

FELLOWSHIP DEACONRY, INC. (DAY CAMP SUNSHINE AND FELLOWSHIP CONFERENCE CENTER)
3575 VALLEY ROAD
LIBERTY CORNER, NEW JERSEY 07938

General Information Children's day camp and adult conference center that provides a program to meet the spiritual and physical needs of all participants by providing the study of God's word, rest, and recreation in a Christian community. Established in 1933. 50-acre facility located 40 miles from New York, New York. Features: location surrounded by beautiful Watchung Mountains; well-stocked Christian bookstore/gift shop; 2 swimming pools; pond for canoeing; historic areas with sightseeing attractions; miniature golf course; tennis courts.

Profile of Summer Employees Total number: 60–100; typical age: 20. 45% men; 55% women; 10% minorities; 20% high school students; 60% college students; 10% non-U.S. citizens; 25% local applicants. Nonsmokers required.

Employment Information Openings are from June 15 to September 10. Year-round positions also offered. Jobs available: ▶ 20–30 *counselors* (minimum age 18) at $250–$350 per week ▶ 10 *counselors-in-training* (minimum age 16) at $140–$200 per week ▶ 2–4 *housekeeping staff* (minimum age 16) at $140–$270 per week ▶ 2–4 *kitchen crew* at $140–$200 per week ▶ 8–10 *lifeguards* with Red Cross advanced lifesaving and CPR/first aid certifications at $160–$350 per week ▶ 1–2 *pantry person* (minimum age 16) at $200–$280 per week ▶ 4–6 *waitresses* (minimum age 15) at $90–$280 per week. Applicants must submit formal organization application, letter of interest, resume, two personal references, letter of recommendation. An in-person interview is recommended, but a telephone interview is acceptable. International applicants accepted; must apply through a recognized agency.

Benefits and Preemployment Training Free housing, free meals, possible full-time employment, on-the-job training, and laundry facilities. Preemployment training is required and includes interpersonal skills, general Christian living.

Contact Rita Krohn, Directing Deaconess, Fellowship Deaconry, Inc. (Day Camp Sunshine and Fellowship Conference Center), PO Box 204, Liberty Corner, New Jersey 07938-0204. Telephone: 908-647-1777. Fax: 908-647-4117. E-mail: deaconry@fellowshipdeaconry.org. World Wide Web: http://www.fellowshipdeaconry.org. Contact by e-mail, fax, mail, or phone. Application deadline: May 15.

LINDLEY G. COOK 4-H CAMP
100A STRUBLE ROAD
BRANCHVILLE, NEW JERSEY 07826

General Information Residential camp facility with a weekly capacity of 150 campers ages 9–16. Established in 1951. 108-acre facility located 65 miles from New York, New York. Features: freshwater lake; located in a state forest; cabins; shooting sports areas; indoor teaching areas; mountain setting.

Profile of Summer Employees Total number: 30; typical ages: 18–60. 40% men; 60% women; 10% minorities; 5% high school students; 95% college students; 1% retirees; 10% non-U.S. citizens; 10% local applicants. Nonsmokers preferred.

Employment Information Openings are from June 18 to August 12. Winter break positions also offered. Jobs available: ▶ 1 *CIT director* (minimum age 21) with camp experience at $300–$400 per week ▶ 1 *arts and crafts director* (minimum age 21) with experience at $250–$350 per week ▶ 2 *assistant cooks* (minimum age 18) with food preparation experience at $220–$300 per week ▶ 2 *boating/canoeing instructors/counselors* (minimum age 18) with lifeguard certification and experience in the field at $225–$270 per week ▶ 6 *cabin counselors* (minimum age 18) at $200–$270 per week ▶ 1 *chef* (minimum age 21) with kitchen, ordering, and supervisory experience at $300–$400 per week ▶ 1 *cook* (minimum age 18) with experience in the field at $275–$350 per week ▶ 2 *health directors* (minimum age 21) with EMT or RN at $360–$450 per week ▶ 2 *lifeguards/counselors* (minimum age 18) with certification in field at $225–$270 per week ▶ 1 *outdoor education director* (minimum age 21) with experience working with youth at $250–$350 per week ▶ 1 *outdoor living skills director* (minimum age 21) with experience in field at $250–$350 per week ▶ 1 *shooting sports director* (minimum age 21) at $270–$350 per week ▶ 1 *waterfront supervisor* (minimum age 21) with lifeguard certification at $280–$350 per week. Applicants must submit formal organization application, three personal references. An in-person interview is recommended, but a telephone interview is acceptable. International applicants accepted; must obtain own visa, obtain own working papers, apply through a recognized agency.

Benefits and Preemployment Training Free housing, free meals, formal training, willing to provide letters of recommendation, on-the-job training, willing to complete paperwork for educational credit, and willing to act as a professional reference. Preemployment training is required and includes accident prevention and safety, first aid, CPR, interpersonal skills, leadership skills, conflict resolution.

Contact James Tavares, Director, Lindley G. Cook 4-H Camp, 100A Struble Road, Branchville, New Jersey 07826. Telephone: 973-948-3550. Fax: 973-948-0735. E-mail: 4hcamp@aesop.rutgers. edu. World Wide Web: http://www.nj4hcamp.rutgers.edu. Contact by e-mail, fax, mail, phone, or through World Wide Web site. Application deadline: continuous.

PALISADES INTERSTATE PARK COMMISSION
PO BOX 155
ALPINE, NEW JERSEY 07620

General Information State park serving the cultural, historical, environmental, and recreational needs of the general public. Established in 1900. 2,500-acre facility located 10 miles from New York, New York. Features: 3 picnic areas; 2 boat basins; 2 historic sites; 30 miles of hiking trails; scenic overlook; cross-country ski trails.

Profile of Summer Employees Total number: 40; typical ages: 18–65. 60% men; 40% women; 20% minorities; 49% high school students; 50% college students; 1% retirees; 100% local applicants. Nonsmokers preferred.

Employment Information Openings are from April 1 to November 1. Year-round positions also offered. Jobs available: ▶ 1 *administrative assistant* (minimum age 18) with flexibility, judgement, calm manner and ability to work for Operations Supervisor at $9–$10 per hour ▶ 4 *boat basin stewards* (minimum age 19) with knowledge of the Hudson River and boating experience preferred at $9 per hour ▶ 4–8 *concession stand operators* (minimum age 16) with valid, current driver's license and the use of a car at $6–$7 per hour ▶ 12–20 *fee collectors/parking attendants* (minimum age 17) with driver's license and own reliable transportation at $5.50–$6.50 per hour ▶ 1 *historic site assistant* (minimum age 18) with strong interest in history, research, giving tours, and related activities; driver's license and access to a car; must be a self-starter at $8 per hour ▶ 10–15 *maintenance workers* (minimum age 16) with interest in learning grounds maintenance, recycling, and trail maintenance at $7–$8 per hour ▶ 1 *money manager* (minimum age 18) must be organized, responsible, self-possessed individual with ability to handle money at $9–$10 per hour ▶ 4–8 *trail crew* (minimum age 17) with trail clearing, hand tools, and general maintenance experience; with driver's license and reliable transportation at $7–$8.50 per hour. Applicants must submit a formal organization application, resume, three personal references. An in-person interview is recommended, but a telephone interview is acceptable.

Benefits and Preemployment Training Willing to provide letters of recommendation, on-the-job training, willing to complete paperwork for educational credit, and willing to act as a professional reference.

Contact Linn Pierson, Supervisor of Operations, Palisades Interstate Park Commission, PO Box 155, Alpine, New Jersey 07620. Fax: 201-767-3842. World Wide Web: http://www.njpalisades. org. Contact by fax, mail, or through World Wide Web site. No phone calls. Application deadline: continuous.

PRESBYTERIAN CAMP JOHNSONBURG
PO BOX 475
JOHNSONBURG, NEW JERSEY 07046

General Information Presbyterian camp that runs a seven week summer program focusing on faith development in a small group coed setting. Established in 1948. 400-acre facility located 50 miles from New York, New York. Features: springfed lake; swimming pool; high ropes course; team building course; archery range; recreation center.

Profile of Summer Employees Total number: 120; typical ages: 16–24. 50% men; 50% women; 10% minorities; 20% high school students; 70% college students; 10% non-U.S. citizens. Nonsmokers preferred.

Employment Information Openings are from June 14 to August 24. Jobs available: ▶ 1 *adventure director* (minimum age 21) with WFA and lifeguard certification at $250 per week ▶ 10 *kitchen workers* (minimum age 16) at $130 per week ▶ 50 *summer counselors* (minimum age 18) at $165–$195 per week ▶ 4 *summer directors* must be college graduates at $250 per week ▶ 1 *waterfront director* (minimum age 21) with lifeguard certification and waterfront experience at $250 per week. Applicants must submit formal organization application, personal reference. An in-person interview is recommended, but a telephone interview is acceptable. International applicants accepted; must apply through a recognized agency.

Benefits and Preemployment Training Free housing, free meals, formal training, willing to provide letters of recommendation, on-the-job training, and willing to act as a professional reference. Preemployment training is required and includes accident prevention and safety, interpersonal skills, leadership skills.

Contact Harry Zweckbronner, Program Director, Presbyterian Camp Johnsonburg. Telephone: 908-852-2349. Fax: 908-852-0045. E-mail: campjburg@campjburg.org. World Wide Web: http://www.camjburg.org. Contact by e-mail or phone. Application deadline: May 1.

REIN TEEN TOURS
30 GALESI DRIVE
WAYNE, NEW JERSEY 07470

General Information Company specializing in teen travel during the summer. Established in 1985. Located 18 miles from New York, New York.

Profile of Summer Employees Total number: 6; typical ages: 21–35. 40% men; 60% women; 80% college students; 20% local applicants. Nonsmokers required.

Employment Information Openings are from June 3 to August 1. Jobs available: ▶ 60 *counselors* (minimum age 21) at $100 per week ▶ *counselors/cooks* (minimum age 21) with some cooking skills at $225 per week. Applicants must submit a formal organization application, two personal references. An in-person interview is required.

Benefits and Preemployment Training Free housing, free meals, formal training, willing to provide letters of recommendation, on-the-job training, willing to complete paperwork for educational credit, and willing to act as a professional reference. Preemployment training is required and includes accident prevention and safety, interpersonal skills, leadership skills.

Contact Chris Vicari, Director, Rein Teen Tours. Telephone: 800-831-1313. Fax: 973-785-4268. E-mail: staff@reinteentours.com. World Wide Web: http://www.reinteentours.com. Contact by e-mail, phone, or through World Wide Web site. Application deadline: May 31.

SOMERSET COUNTY PARK COMMISSION ENVIRONMENTAL EDUCATION CENTER
190 LORD STIRLING ROAD
BASKING RIDGE, NEW JERSEY 07920

General Information Environmental education center/park providing leisure and learning opportunities for the public, schools, and scouting groups. Established in 1971. 430-acre facility located 15 miles from Morristown. Features: ponds; forests; fields; hiking trails; observation blinds; observation towers.

Profile of Summer Employees Total number: 14; typical ages: 19–24. 50% men; 50% women; 10% high school students; 90% college students. Nonsmokers preferred.

Employment Information Openings are from June 7 to August 27. Jobs available: ▶ 3–4 *maintenance crew* (minimum age 19) with CPR/first aid preferred; college graduate or upperclassman with outdoor skills, trail and general maintenance skills, and ability to use hand tools at $8.25 per hour ▶ 8 *seasonal naturalist assistants* (minimum age 19) with CPR, first aid, and LGT preferred; college graduate or upperclassman with summer camp, student teaching, or similar volunteer experience at $9 per hour. Applicants must submit a formal organization application, letter of interest, resume, driver's license. An in-person interview is required.

Benefits and Preemployment Training Possible full-time employment, willing to provide letters of recommendation, names of contacts, on-the-job training, willing to complete paperwork for educational credit, and willing to act as a professional reference. Preemployment training is required and includes first aid, CPR, interpersonal skills, educational program delivery, park property orientation.

Contact Kurt Bender, Environmental Science Supervisor, Somerset County Park Commission Environmental Education Center. Telephone: 908-766-2489 Ext. 332. Fax: 908-766-2687. E-mail: kbbender@parks.co.somerset.nj.us. World Wide Web: http://www.park.co.somerset.nj.us. Contact by e-mail, fax, mail, phone, or through World Wide Web site. Application deadline: May 15.

THE SOUTHWESTERN COMPANY, NEW JERSEY
See The Southwestern Company on page 297 for complete description.

STONY BROOK-MILLSTONE WATERSHED ASSOCIATION-ENVIRONMENTAL EDUCATION DAY CAMP
31 TITUS MILL ROAD
PENNINGTON, NEW JERSEY 08534

General Information Environmental education day camp conducting one- and two-week programs. Established in 1949. 785-acre facility located 9 miles from Trenton. Features: nature center; butterfly house; woodlands and rolling fields; 8 miles of trails; freshwater pond.

Profile of Summer Employees Total number: 21; typical ages: 16–36. 40% men; 60% women; 10% minorities; 10% high school students; 50% college students; 100% local applicants. Nonsmokers preferred.

Employment Information Openings are from June 24 to August 16. Year-round positions also offered. Jobs available: ▶ 2 *camp group leaders* with experience in camp setting, teaching, and ecology ▶ 4 *camp interns* with experience or interest in camps, teaching, and ecology ▶ 2 *camp naturalists* with extensive knowledge of local ecology. Applicants must submit a letter of interest, resume, two personal references, letter of recommendation. An in-person interview is recommended, but a telephone interview is acceptable. International applicants accepted.

Benefits and Preemployment Training Formal training, willing to provide letters of recommendation, on-the-job training, willing to complete paperwork for educational credit, and willing to act as a professional reference. Preemployment training is required and includes accident prevention and safety, first aid, CPR, interpersonal skills, leadership skills.

Contact Rick Lear, Program Coordinator, Stony Brook-Millstone Watershed Association-Environmental Education Day Camp, 31 Titus Mill Road, Pennington, New Jersey 08534. Telephone: 609-737-7592. Fax: 609-737-3075. E-mail: rlear@thewatershed.org. World Wide Web: http://www.thewatershed.org. Contact by e-mail, fax, mail, or phone. Application deadline: April 15.

STUDENT CONSERVATION ASSOCIATION (SCA), NEW JERSEY
See Student Conservation Association (SCA), New Hampshire on page 200 for complete description.

TOMAHAWK LAKE WATER PARK
TOMAHAWK TRAIL, PO BOX 109
SPARTA, NEW JERSEY 07871-0109

General Information Swimming and picnicking park with water rides, boating, mini-golf, ball fields, arcade, snackbar, and a beer garden; open to the public between Memorial Day weekend and Labor Day weekend. Established in 1952. 150-acre facility located 50 miles from New York, New York. Features: freshwater lake for swimming; large white sand beach; shaded picnic groves; 7 water slides; boat rides; catered picnic facilities.

Profile of Summer Employees Total number: 80–100; typical ages: 16–45. 50% men; 50% women; 2% minorities; 30% high school students; 30% college students; 15% retirees; 4% non-U.S. citizens; 80% local applicants. Nonsmokers preferred.

Employment Information Openings are from May 28 to September 12. Jobs available: ▶ 1–2 *arcade attendants* (minimim age 55) with CPR and first aid training on-site at $7.25–$7.50 per hour ▶ 2–3 *bartenders* (minimum age 18) with food handler training preferred at $5.15 per hour; tips are additional income ▶ 9–12 *food service staff (snack bars)* (minimum age 16) with food handler training preferred at $5.50–$6.50 per hour ▶ 4–5 *front office assistants* (minimum age 19) with first aid/CPR training on-site required; college degree or full-time, year-round work experience preferred at $7.75–$10 per hour ▶ 5–6 *front office attendants* (minimum age 19) with on-site training in first aid/CPR; paid at $7.50–$7.75 per hour ▶ 10–20 *junior waterpark attendants* (minimum age 14) with working papers at $5.25–$5.75 per hour ▶ 10–20 *lifeguards (shallow water)* (minimum age 15) with national pool and waterpark lifeguard license (training available) at $6.25–$6.75 per hour ▶ 15–25 *lifeguards (special facilities)* (minimum age 16) with completion of on-site national pool and waterpark lifeguard training at $7.25–$7.75 per hour ▶ 10–20 *parking attendants* (minimum age 16) with first aid/CPR training on-site at $5.75–$6.50 per hour ▶ *retail sales attendant* (minimum age 19) with CPR and first aid training on-site at $7.50 per hour ▶ 15–17 *ride dispatchers (water and boat rides)* (minimum age 17) with on-site training in first aid and CPR; National Pool and Waterpark lifeguard license offered; paid at $6–$6.75 per hour ▶ 2–3 *rides supervisors* (minimum age 24) with lifeguarding training preferred; CPR/first aid required (classes on-site) at $9–$11 per hour. Applicants must submit formal organization application, letter of interest, resume, working papers if under 18. An in-person interview is recommended, but a telephone interview is acceptable. International applicants accepted; must obtain own visa, apply through a recognized agency.

Benefits and Preemployment Training Housing at a cost, meals at a cost, formal training, willing to provide letters of recommendation, on-the-job training, willing to complete paperwork for educational credit, willing to act as a professional reference, and use of facility, complimentary iced water and lemonade. Preemployment training is required and includes accident prevention and safety, first aid, CPR, interpersonal skills, leadership skills, lifeguard training.

Contact June Wallace, General Manager, Tomahawk Lake Water Park, PO Box 109, Sparta, New Jersey 07871. Telephone: 973-398-7785. Fax: 973-398-5056. World Wide Web: http://www. tomahawklake.com. Contact by fax, mail, or phone. Application deadline: applications accepted beginning in March for upcoming summer season.

YMCA CAMPS OCKANICKON AND MATOLLIONEQUAY
1303 STOKES ROAD
MEDFORD, NEW JERSEY 08055

General Information YMCA brother/sister summer resident camp with traditional activities, high ropes, low ropes, climbing wall, and multiple lakes in the scenic pine barrens of New Jersey. Established in 1906. 560-acre facility located 20 miles from Philadelphia, Pennsylvania. Features: aquatics; horsemanship; challenge course; creative arts; freshwater lakes; outdoor education.

Profile of Summer Employees Total number: 200; typical ages: 19–29. 50% men; 50% women; 15% minorities; 15% high school students; 65% college students; 20% non-U.S. citizens; 5% local applicants. Nonsmokers preferred.

Employment Information Openings are from May 1 to October 30. Spring break, winter break, and year-round positions also offered. Jobs available: ▶ 1–10 *activity directors* (minimum age 21) with experience in nature, sports, arts and crafts, or boating at $1400–$1700 per season ▶ 1–60 *cabin counselors* (minimum age 19) with willingness to live in cabin with campers at $1300–$1500 per season ▶ 1–15 *lifeguard counselors* (minimum age 18) with current certifications at $1400–$1700 per season ▶ 1–2 *nurses* with RN or LPN registered with State of New Jersey at $3000–$4000 per season ▶ 1–5 *ropes instructors* (minimum age 19) with experience or training at $1500–$1800 per season ▶ 2–3 *trip and travel leaders* (minimum age 21) with lifeguard, wilderness, and first responder certification at $1500–$2000 per season. Applicants must submit formal organization application, three personal references. An in-person interview is recommended, but a telephone interview is acceptable. International applicants accepted; must apply through a recognized agency.

Benefits and Preemployment Training Free housing, free meals, formal training, possible full-time employment, willing to provide letters of recommendation, names of contacts, on-the-job training, willing to complete paperwork for educational credit, willing to act as a professional reference, and travel reimbursement. Preemployment training is required and includes accident prevention and safety, first aid, CPR, interpersonal skills, leadership skills, asset-based training.

Contact Mr. Tom Rapine, Associate Executive Director, YMCA Camps Ockanickon and Matollionequay, 1303 Stokes Road, Medford, New Jersey 08055. Telephone: 609-654-8225. Fax: 609-654-8895. E-mail: tom@ycamp.org. World Wide Web: http://www.ycamp.org. Contact by e-mail, fax, mail, phone, or through World Wide Web site. Application deadline: continuous.

NEW MEXICO

LIFEWAY GLORIETA CONFERENCE CENTER
EXIT 299, I-25
GLORIETA, NEW MEXICO 87535

General Information Support facilities and services for approximately 28,000 guests attending summer conferences. Established in 1952. 2,271-acre facility located 18 miles from Santa Fe. Features: mountain setting; arid climate.

Profile of Summer Employees Total number: 350; typical ages: 19–25. 40% men; 60% women; 15% minorities; 13% high school students; 78% college students; 5% retirees; 20% local applicants. Nonsmokers preferred.

Employment Information Openings are from May 15 to September 15. Year-round positions also offered. Jobs available: ▶ 21 *chuckwagon workers/recreation* (minimum age 17) at $6–$9 per hour ▶ 11 *conference service workers* (minimum age 17) at $6–$6.50 per hour ▶ 14 *day-camp workers* (minimum age 17) with Southern Baptist (required for some) at $6–$7.24 per hour ▶ 30 *food service workers* (minimum age 17) at $6 per hour ▶ 32 *housekeepers* (minimum age 17) at $6 per hour ▶ 26 *preschool workers* (minimum age 17) with Southern Baptist (required for some) at $6–$7.24 per hour ▶ 4 *residence hall/campus ministry coordinators* (minimum age 17) with preference to seminarians at $2200 per season ▶ 9 *sound and lighting technicians* (minimum age 17) at $6–$9.11 per hour. Applicants must submit a formal organization application, three personal references. International applicants accepted; must obtain own visa, obtain own working papers.

Benefits and Preemployment Training Housing at a cost, meals at a cost, on-the-job training, willing to complete paperwork for educational credit, and opportunity to attend seminars/ workshops. Preemployment training is required and includes accident prevention and safety, leadership skills.

Contact Sixta Varela, Administrative Coordinator, Lifeway Glorieta Conference Center, PO Box 8, Glorieta, New Mexico 87535. Telephone: 505-757-4265. Fax: 505-757-4386. E-mail: svarela@ lifeway.com. World Wide Web: http://www.lifeway.com/glorieta. Contact by e-mail, fax, mail, phone, or through World Wide Web site. Application deadline: continuous.

PHILMONT SCOUT RANCH
RR 1, PO BOX 35
CIMARRON, NEW MEXICO 87714

General Information Camp and family conference center offering mountain backpacking with a wide variety of outdoor and historical experiences. Established in 1938. 137,493-acre facility located 200 miles from Albuquerque. Features: mountain backpacking-12,440 feet; 3 horseback riding camps; 3 rock climbing camps; over 220 miles of hiking trails; 32 staffed backcountry camps; exceptional wildlife and fishing.

Profile of Summer Employees Total number: 950; typical ages: 18–25. 70% men; 30% women; 9% minorities; 1% high school students; 95% college students; 1% retirees; 3% local applicants.
Employment Information Openings are from May 15 to August 22. Jobs available: ▶ 4 *backcountry managers* (minimum age 21) at $1076–$1500 per month ▶ 4–8 *bookkeeping clerk and clerks/typists* (minimum age 18) with clerical, typing, and computer skills at $800–$1000 per month ▶ 30–35 *camp directors* (minimum age 21) at $1000–$1500 per month ▶ 7 *commissary staff members (clerks)* (minimum age 18) at $800–$1000 per month ▶ 70–75 *conservation staff members* (minimum age 18) at $800–$1000 per month ▶ 10 *crafts lodge manager and staff members* (minimum age 18) at $800–$1000 per month ▶ 30–40 *custodial staff members (custodian, housekeeper, and lawn maintenance personnel)* (minimum age 18) at $800–$1000 per month ▶ 40 *family programs staff members* (minimum age 18) including manager, assistant manager, nursery leader, and leaders for activities for various age groups at $800–$1000 per month ▶ 60 *food services staff members* (minimum age 18) including dining hall manager, backcountry cook, assistant dining hall manager, dining hall staff, and snack bar clerks at $800–$1076 per month ▶ 20 *headquarters activities manager and staff members* (minimum age 18) at $800–$1500 per month ▶ 13–15 *headquarters maintenance staff members* (minimum age 18) at $800–$1000 per month ▶ 20 *headquarters services manager, assistant manager, and staff members* (minimum age 18) at $800–$1000 per month ▶ 30–35 *horse department staff members (supervisors and wranglers)* (minimum age 18) must be an experienced horseman at $1000– $1500 per month ▶ 20 *logistic services manager, assistant manager, and staff members* (minimum age 18) at $800–$1500 per month ▶ 25–30 *medical/health lodge staff members* (minimum age 18) including administrator, medics, medical secretary, nurse, and health lodge drivers at $800– $1500 per month ▶ 4 *museum shop clerks and guides* (minimum age 18) at $800–$1000 per month ▶ 20 *news and photo service members* (minimum age 18) including manager, assistant manager, photo lab manager, and photographers at $800–$1000 per month ▶ 1 *postmaster* (minimum age 21) at $1000–$1500 per month ▶ 200 *program counselors* (minimum age 18) with knowledge of and experience in one or more of the following: adobe construction, archaeology, black powder weapons, blacksmithing, burro packing and racing, challenge events, environmental ecology and nature studies, fishing and fly tying, gold mining and panning, mountain technology, rock climbing at $800–$1000 per month ▶ 6 *quartermaster staff members* (minimum age 18) including equipment and tent repair manager, tent repair helper, and warehouse

clerk at $800–$1000 per month ▶ 220 *rangers* (minimum age 18) including chief ranger, associate chief ranger, Rayado trek coordinator, mountain trek coordinator, and training rangers at $800–$1000 per month ▶ 5 *seasonal registrars* (minimum age 18) at $800–$1000 per month ▶ 13–15 *security staff members* (minimum age 21) at $837–$1000 per month ▶ 5 *support services manager and staff members* (minimum age 18) at $800–$1000 per month ▶ 6 *tent city managers and assistant managers* (minimum age 21) at $1000–$1500 per month ▶ 40 *trading post managers and clerks for headquarters, craft lodge, and backcountry* (minimum age 18) at $800–$1000 per month ▶ 5 *training center office staff members* (minimum age 18) at $800–$1000 per month ▶ 3 *transportation managers* (minimum age 21) at $800–$1000 per month ▶ 5 *truck drivers* (minimum age 21) with experience driving a two-ton truck over dirt roads at $837–$1000 per month. Applicants must submit a formal organization application, resume, two personal references.

Benefits and Preemployment Training Free housing, free meals, formal training, health insurance, willing to provide letters of recommendation, on-the-job training, willing to complete paperwork for educational credit, and willing to act as a professional reference. Preemployment training is required and includes accident prevention and safety, first aid, CPR, interpersonal skills, leadership skills.

Contact Richard A. Mahalik, Associate Director of Program, Philmont Scout Ranch. Telephone: 505-376-2281. Fax: 505-376-2636. Contact by fax, mail, or phone. Application deadline: applications by April 1 are preferred.

THE SOUTHWESTERN COMPANY, NEW MEXICO
See The Southwestern Company on page 297 for complete description.

STUDENT CONSERVATION ASSOCIATION (SCA), NEW MEXICO
See Student Conservation Association (SCA), New Hampshire on page 200 for complete description.

NEW YORK

ADIRONDACK MOUNTAIN CLUB
PO BOX 867
LAKE PLACID, NEW YORK 12946
General Information Nonprofit conservation organization. Established in 1922. 640-acre facility located 125 miles from Albany. Features: lake; campground; information center; lodge; wooded; cabins.

Profile of Summer Employees Total number: 40; typical ages: 18–30. 50% men; 50% women; 5% minorities; 5% high school students; 80% college students; 5% non-U.S. citizens; 5% local applicants. Nonsmokers preferred.

Employment Information Openings are from June to September. Year-round positions also offered. Jobs available: ▶ 4 *HPIC crew* (minimum age 16) at $6 per hour ▶ 10 *LOJ crew* (minimum age 16) at $6 per hour. Applicants must submit formal organization application, resume, three personal references. An in-person interview is recommended, but a telephone interview is acceptable. International applicants accepted; must obtain own visa, obtain own working papers, apply through a recognized agency.

Benefits and Preemployment Training Housing at a cost, meals at a cost, possible full-time employment, willing to provide letters of recommendation, on-the-job training, willing to act as a professional reference, opportunity to attend seminars/workshops, and merchandise and lodging discounts. Preemployment training is required and includes interpersonal skills, leadership skills.

Contact Janet Morgan, Administrative Assistant, Adirondack Mountain Club. Telephone: 518-523-3480. Fax: 518-523-3518. E-mail: adkinfo@northnet.org. World Wide Web: http://www.adk. org. Contact by e-mail, fax, mail, or through World Wide Web site. Application deadline: continuous.

AMERICAN CAMPING ASSOCIATION–NEW YORK SECTION
1375 BROADWAY, 4TH FLOOR
NEW YORK, NEW YORK 10018

General Information Community of camping professionals dedicated to enriching the lives of children and adults through the camp experience. The New York Section of the American Camping Association assists member camps in finding qualified staff. Overnight camps are located in New York, New Jersey, Connecticut, Pennsylvania, Massachusetts, New Hampshire, Maine, and Vermont. Established in 1954. Features: freshwater lake; ropes course; climbing wall; tennis courts; arts/fine arts; horseback riding.

Profile of Summer Employees Total number: 10; typical ages: 17–30. 50% men; 50% women; 5% high school students; 85% college students. Nonsmokers preferred.

Employment Information Openings are from June 15 to August 25. Jobs available: ▶ *EMT staff members* with EMT certification ▶ *general counselors/group leaders* with a love of working with children and enjoyment of outdoor life ▶ *horseback riding instructors* ▶ *kitchen staff members* with chef/cook experience with large organizations ▶ *land sports instructors* with a love of working with children and enjoyment of outdoor life. Positions are available in tennis, golf, team sports, archery, and/or gymnastics ▶ *maintenance staff members* ▶ *office/administrative staff members* ▶ *outdoor adventure instructors* with experience in ropes course, rock climbing, and climbing wall ▶ *outdoor education instructors* ▶ *visual and performing arts staff members* with a love of working with children and enjoyment of outdoor life; skills related to position are required ▶ *water sports instructors* with a love of working with children and enjoyment of outdoor life along with training and skills in water sports ▶ *waterfront staff (lifeguards and WSI)* with lifeguarding, water safety instruction, CPR, and first aid certifications. Applicants must submit online application at www.acampjob4u.org. International applicants accepted; must apply through a recognized agency.

Benefits and Preemployment Training Free housing, free meals, willing to provide letters of recommendation, on-the-job training, willing to complete paperwork for educational credit, willing to act as a professional reference, and travel reimbursement. Preemployment training is required and includes accident prevention and safety, first aid, CPR, interpersonal skills, leadership skills.

Contact Robin Katz Wenczl, Director, Camp Staffing Services, American Camping Association–New York Section. Fax: 212-391-5207. E-mail: robin@aca-ny.org. World Wide Web: http://www. aca-ny.org. Contact through World Wide Web site. Application deadline: before mid-June is recommended.

BRANT LAKE CAMP
7586 STATE ROUTE 8
BRANT LAKE, NEW YORK 12815

General Information Eight-week high-tuition private residential camp for boys ages 7–15 with a capacity of 330 campers. Also 2 three-week sessions for 60 teenage girls in dance, arts, and sports, particularly tennis. Established in 1917. 95-acre facility located 70 miles from Albany. Features: 6 mile long freshwater lake; 16 tennis courts; 7 basketball courts; 4 baseball fields.

Profile of Summer Employees Total number: 150; typical ages: 19–40. 85% men; 15% women; 10% minorities; 5% high school students; 70% college students; 2% retirees; 20% non-U.S. citizens; 5% local applicants. Nonsmokers required.

Employment Information Openings are from June 5 to August 20. Jobs available: ▶ 9 *athletics specialists* must be college-age at $1400–$1800 per season ▶ 15 *general staff members* must be college-age at $1400–$1600 per season ▶ 2 *group heads/athletics directors* (minimum age 25) with experience teaching/coaching at $2000–$3200 per season ▶ 2 *swimming instructors* with lifeguard certification at $1400–$1800 per season ▶ 6 *waterfront staff members* with WSI certification/lifeguard training; must be college age at $1600–$2000 per season. Applicants must submit formal organization application, resume, three personal references, three letters of recommendation. A telephone interview is required. International applicants accepted; must apply through a recognized agency.

Benefits and Preemployment Training Free housing, free meals, willing to provide letters of recommendation, on-the-job training, willing to complete paperwork for educational credit, willing to act as a professional reference, and travel reimbursement. Preemployment training is required and includes accident prevention and safety, first aid, CPR, leadership skills.

Contact Richard Gersten, Director, Brant Lake Camp, 8 Colonial Court, Armonk, New York 10504. Telephone: 914-273-5401. Fax: 914-273-1587. E-mail: brantlakec@aol.com. World Wide Web: http://www.brantlake.com. Contact by e-mail, fax, mail, phone, or through World Wide Web site. Application deadline: continuous.

BROOKLYN BOTANIC GARDEN
1000 WASHINGTON AVENUE
BROOKLYN, NEW YORK 11225

General Information Nonprofit, botanic cultural institution serving the community and the world with horticultural display, education, science research, community outreach and conservation. Established in 1910. 52-acre facility. Features: 10 "Gardens within the Garden"; conservatory for plants; gift shop; outdoor cafe; library.

Profile of Summer Employees Total number: 250; typical ages: 16–24. 35% men; 65% women; 60% high school students; 40% college students; 10% non-U.S. citizens.

Employment Information Openings are from June 1 to August 31. Jobs available: ▶ 10 *children's garden interns* (minimum age 19) with horticulture, agriculture education, biology background at $7 per hour ▶ 3 *junior botanist summer adventures interns* (minimum age 19) must be college student with science education at $7 per hour ▶ 12 *junior instructors* (minimum age 15) with initial 100 hours unpaid. Applicants must submit formal organization application, letter of interest, resume. An in-person interview is recommended, but a telephone interview is acceptable. International applicants accepted; must obtain own visa, obtain own working papers, apply through a recognized agency.

Benefits and Preemployment Training Willing to provide letters of recommendation, on-the-job training, and opportunity to attend seminars/workshops. Preemployment training is required and includes accident prevention and safety, interpersonal skills, leadership skills, gardening, lesson planning, botany.

Contact Romi Ige, Coordinator of Interpretation and Internships, Brooklyn Botanic Garden. Telephone: 718-623-7298. Fax: 718-622-7839. E-mail: romiige@bbg.org. World Wide Web: http://www.bbg.org. Contact by e-mail, phone, or through World Wide Web site. Application deadline: April 1.

CAMP HILLCROFT
BOX 5
BILLINGS, NEW YORK 12510
General Information Day camp serving 400 children ages 4–14 for 4–8 weeks. Established in 1950. 185-acre facility located 11 miles from Poughkeepsie. Features: 3 pools and a lake; creative workshops and studios; dance studio, theater, and music barn; outdoor adventure facilities; fields and courts for sports; farm and vegetable garden.
Profile of Summer Employees Total number: 170; typical ages: 20–35. 50% men; 50% women; 1% high school students; 50% college students; 25% non-U.S. citizens; 70% local applicants. Nonsmokers preferred.
Employment Information Openings are from June 30 to August 23. Jobs available: ▶ 1–2 *art and ceramics instructors* (minimum age 20) with BFA or MFA preferred and teaching experience at $1400–$1600 per season ▶ 2–4 *group leaders* (minimum age 22) with at least 2 years of college completed and leadership experience with children at $1400–$1800 per season ▶ 1–2 *tennis instructors* (minimum age 20) with experience with children at $1400–$1600 per season. Applicants must submit formal organization application, resume, three work-related references, personal interview with selected staff member in applicant's location. International applicants accepted; must apply through a recognized agency.
Benefits and Preemployment Training Free housing, free meals, formal training, willing to provide letters of recommendation, on-the-job training, willing to complete paperwork for educational credit, and willing to act as a professional reference. Preemployment training is required and includes accident prevention and safety, first aid, CPR, interpersonal skills, leadership skills, lifeguard training.
Contact Sally Buttinger, Director, Camp Hillcroft. Telephone: 845-223-5826. Fax: 845-223-5280. E-mail: fun@camphillcroft.com. World Wide Web: http://www.camphillcroft.com. Contact by e-mail, fax, mail, phone, or through World Wide Web site. Application deadline: continuous.

CAMP HILLTOP
7825 COUNTY HIGHWAY 67
HANCOCK, NEW YORK 13783
General Information Traditional residential coed camp for campers ages 7-15. Established in 1924. 400-acre facility located 40 miles from Binghamton. Features: lake; pool; lighted tennis courts; beautiful wooded setting; 300-foot zip line; well-equipped horse barn.
Profile of Summer Employees Total number: 80; typical ages: 19–28. 50% men; 50% women; 5% minorities; 60% college students; 30% non-U.S. citizens. Nonsmokers required.
Employment Information Openings are from June 20 to August 20. Jobs available: ▶ 3 *archery staff members* (minimum age 20) with archery certification at $1400–$2000 per season ▶ 5 *arts and crafts staff members* (minimum age 19) at $1400–$2000 per season ▶ 2 *computer staff members* (minimum age 19) at $1400–$2000 per season ▶ 12–14 *high/low ropes staff* (minimum age 19) with willingness to become certified at $1400–$2000 per season ▶ 3 *horseback riding staff members* (minimum age 20) at $1400–$2000 per season ▶ *lifeguards* with WSI certification at $1400–$2000 per season ▶ 4 *sports staff members* (minimum age 19) at $1400–$2000 per season ▶ 2 *tennis staff members* (minimum age 19) at $1400–$2000 per season ▶ 7 *waterfront staff members* (minimum age 19) with ARC lifeguard or WSI certification at $1400–$2000 per season. Applicants must submit formal organization application, three personal references, two

letters of recommendation. An in-person interview is recommended, but a telephone interview is acceptable. International applicants accepted; must obtain own visa, apply through a recognized agency.

Benefits and Preemployment Training Free housing, free meals, willing to provide letters of recommendation, on-the-job training, willing to complete paperwork for educational credit, willing to act as a professional reference, opportunity to attend seminars/workshops, and travel reimbursement. Preemployment training is required and includes accident prevention and safety, first aid, CPR, interpersonal skills, leadership skills.

Contact William H. Young, Director, Camp Hilltop. Telephone: 607-637-5201. Fax: 607-637-2389. E-mail: hilltop@hancock.net. World Wide Web: http://www.camphilltop.com. Contact by e-mail, fax, mail, phone, or through World Wide Web site. Application deadline: continuous.

CAMP JEANNE D'ARC
154 GADWAY ROAD
MERRILL, NEW YORK 12955

General Information Residential camp for 120 girls ages 6–17 focusing on individual activities and personal achievement. Established in 1922. 230-acre facility located 30 miles from Plattsburgh. Features: location on 14-mile lake in Adirondack State Park; surrounded by woodlands; Swiss chalet-type cabins with fireplaces and indoor baths; mile-long 28-station fitness trail; 3 tennis courts.

Profile of Summer Employees Total number: 50; typical ages: 19–23. 5% men; 95% women; 10% minorities; 10% high school students; 75% college students; 20% non-U.S. citizens; 15% local applicants. Nonsmokers required.

Employment Information Openings are from June 24 to August 18. Jobs available: ► 1 *administrative assistant* (minimum age 19) with computer, organizational, and writing skills at $2000–$2500 per season ► 2 *arts and crafts instructors* (minimum age 19) at $1000–$1500 per season ► 1 *canoeing instructor* (minimum age 19) with current CPR (preferred) and LGT (training available) at $1000–$1500 per season ► 1 *dance instructor* (minimum age 19) at $1000–$1500 per season ► 1 *drama instructor* (minimum age 19) at $1000–$1500 per season ► 1 *music/guitar instructor* (minimum age 19) at $1000–$1500 per season ► 2 *nurses* with RN, EMT, or LPN at a negotiable salary ► 5 *other land sports instructors* (minimum age 19) at $1000–$1500 per season ► 5 *other water sports instructors* (minimum age 19) with current CPR (preferred) and LGT (training available) at $1000–$1500 per season ► 2 *outdoor camping counselors* (minimum age 19) with current CPR (preferred) and RTE (training available) at $1000–$1500 per season ► 3 *riding instructors* (minimum age 19) with CHA certification and RTE (training available) at $1000–$2000 per season ► 1 *riflery instructor* (minimum age 19) with NRA rifle instructor certification at $1000–$1500 per season ► 1 *sailing instructor* (minimum age 19) with current CPR (preferred) and LGT (training available) at $1000–$1500 per season ► 3 *swimming instructors* (minimum age 19) with WSI and American Red Cross lifeguard certification and current CPR (preferred) at $1000–$1500 per season ► 2 *tennis instructors* (minimum age 19) at $1000–$1500 per season ► 2 *waterskiing instructors* (minimum age 19) with LGT (training available) and boat driving experience at $1000–$1500 per season. Applicants must submit formal organization application, three personal references, three letters of recommendation. An in-person interview is recommended, but a telephone interview is acceptable. International applicants accepted; must apply through a recognized agency.

Benefits and Preemployment Training Free housing, free meals, willing to provide letters of recommendation, on-the-job training, willing to complete paperwork for educational credit, willing to act as a professional reference, opportunity to attend seminars/workshops, and travel reimbursement. Preemployment training is required and includes accident prevention and safety, first aid, CPR, interpersonal skills, leadership skills, RTE (responding to emergencies).

Contact Fran Bisselle, Director, Camp Jeanne d'Arc, 154 Gadway Road, Merrill, New York 12955, United States. Telephone: 518-425-3311. Fax: 518-425-6673. E-mail: franb@campjeannedarc.

com. World Wide Web: http://www.campjeannedarc.com. Contact by e-mail, fax, mail, phone, or through World Wide Web site. Application deadline: continuous.

CAMP JENED–A FACILITY OF THE UNITED CEREBRAL PALSY ASSOCIATION OF NEW YORK STATE
ADAMS ROAD
ROCK HILL, NEW YORK 12775

General Information Nonprofit residential vacationing facility for adults who have physical, intellectual and/or behavioral disabilities. Established in 1978. 150-acre facility located 90 miles from New York. Features: located in the Catskill Mountains; wheelchair accessible buildings; freshwater, well stocked lake; wheelchair accessible swimming pool; wheelchair accessible cooking and camping out facilities; 2 hours from New York City.

Profile of Summer Employees Total number: 165; typical ages: 21–23. 35% men; 65% women; 23% minorities; 90% college students; 61% non-U.S. citizens; 1% local applicants.

Employment Information Openings are from June 1 to August 26. Jobs available: ▶ 3 *cooks* (minimum age 18) with ability to prepare meals for large groups at a negotiable salary ▶ 20 *counselors* (minimum age 18) at $1900 per season, plus room and board. Applicants must submit formal organization application, two letters of recommendation. A telephone interview is required. International applicants accepted; must apply through a recognized agency.

Benefits and Preemployment Training Free housing, free meals, willing to provide letters of recommendation, willing to complete paperwork for educational credit, willing to act as a professional reference, and partial travel reimbursement. Preemployment training is required and includes accident prevention and safety, interpersonal skills, leadership skills, skills to provide personal care.

Contact Michael Branam, Camp Director, Camp Jened–A Facility of the United Cerebral Palsy Association of New York State, PO Box 483, Rock Hull, New York 12775. Telephone: 914-434-2220. Fax: 914-434-2253. E-mail: jened@catskill.net. World Wide Web: http://www.campjened. org. Contact by e-mail, fax, mail, phone, or through World Wide Web site. Application deadline: continuous.

CAMP LAKELAND/JEWISH COMMUNITY CENTER OF GREATER BUFFALO, INC.
787 DELAWARE AVENUE
BUFFALO, NEW YORK 14209

General Information Summer camp located on 733 acres of forested hills and meadows, bringing campers together in a magical setting, creating special friendships and living Jewish experiences to last a lifetime. Established in 1910. 733-acre facility located 2 miles from Franklinville. Features: canoeing, boating, kayaking; water skiing; climbing wall; in-ground pool; mountain boarding; mountain bikes.

Profile of Summer Employees Total number: 100; typical ages: 17–26. 50% men; 50% women; 30% non-U.S. citizens. Nonsmokers preferred.

Employment Information Openings are from June 15 to September 1. Jobs available: ▶ 75–100 *camp counselors* (minimum age 17) at $900–$4000 per season. Applicants must submit formal organization application, resume, letter of recommendation. A telephone interview is required. International applicants accepted; must apply through a recognized agency.

Benefits and Preemployment Training Free housing, free meals, willing to provide letters of recommendation, on-the-job training, and willing to complete paperwork for educational credit. Preemployment training is required and includes accident prevention and safety, first aid, CPR, interpersonal skills, leadership skills.

Contact David Miller, Camp Director, Camp Lakeland/Jewish Community Center of Greater Buffalo, Inc. Telephone: 716-886-3145. Fax: 716-961-0863. E-mail: summer@camplakeland. com. World Wide Web: http://www.camplakeland.com. Contact through World Wide Web site. Application deadline: continuous.

CAMP MICHIKAMAU–YMCA OF GREATER BERGEN COUNTY
BEAR MOUNTAIN, NEW YORK 10911

General Information Coed residential YMCA camp in rustic setting serving 110 campers ages 8–15. Features traditional camping, waterfront activities, arts and crafts, and outdoor activities. Established in 1927. 20-acre facility located 30 miles from New York. Features: freshwater lakes; wooded setting; rustic cabins; miles of hiking trails; basketball courts/low ropes; location in a state park.

Profile of Summer Employees Total number: 35; typical ages: 18–26. 60% men; 40% women; 20% high school students; 80% college students; 20% non-U.S. citizens; 80% local applicants. Nonsmokers preferred.

Employment Information Openings are from June 22 to August 22. Jobs available: ▶ 1 *arts and crafts director* (minimum age 20) at $1600–$2000 per season ▶ 20 *counselors* (minimum age 18) at $900–$1600 per season ▶ 5 *lifeguards/counselors* (minimum age 17) with American Red Cross lifeguard training at $900–$2000 per season ▶ 2 *nurses* (minimum age 20) with LPN, RN, or EMT license at $2000–$2800 per season ▶ 1–2 *waterfront directors* (minimum age 21) with WSI certification/lifeguard training at $2000–$2800 per season. Applicants must submit formal organization application, letter of interest, two letters of recommendation. An in-person interview is recommended, but a telephone interview is acceptable. International applicants accepted; must obtain own visa, apply through a recognized agency.

Benefits and Preemployment Training Free housing, free meals, willing to provide letters of recommendation, on-the-job training, willing to complete paperwork for educational credit, and willing to act as a professional reference. Preemployment training is required and includes accident prevention and safety, first aid, CPR, interpersonal skills, leadership skills.

Contact Ken Riscinti, Camping Director, Camp Michikamau–YMCA of Greater Bergen County, 360 Main Street, Hackensack, New Jersey 07601. Telephone: 201-487-6600. Fax: 201-487-4539. World Wide Web: http://www.ymcagbc.org. Contact by mail or phone. Application deadline: continuous.

CAMP MONROE
MONROE, NEW YORK 10950

General Information A well-structured, coed camp meeting the needs and interests of today's youth in a traditional Jewish camp setting. Established in 1941. 192-acre facility located 60 miles from New York. Features: swimming pool; freshwater lake; horseback riding trails and ring; 5 tennis courts; 2 hockey rinks; 2 indoor gyms.

Profile of Summer Employees Total number: 150; typical ages: 20–24. 50% men; 50% women; 10% high school students; 60% college students; 1% retirees; 30% non-U.S. citizens; 10% local applicants. Nonsmokers required.

Employment Information Openings are from June 20 to August 22. Jobs available: ▶ 2 *aerobics/ dance instructors* (minimum age 21) with related teaching experience at $450–$1200 per season ▶ 1 *archery instructor* (minimum age 21) with experience in archery instruction at $450–$1200 per season ▶ 2 *boating lifeguards* (minimum age 21) with lifeguard certification at $450–$1200 per season ▶ 2–10 *general counselors* (minimum age 20) with experience working with children at $450–$1200 per season ▶ 1 *piano player* (minimum age 21) with ability to play for musical shows, sight read, and change keys easily in order to play with children as they sing at $450–

$1200 per season ▶ 1 *tennis instructor* (minimum age 21) with relevant teaching experience at $450–$1200 per season ▶ 1 *videographer* (minimum age 21) with experience in the field at $450–$1200 per season. Applicants must submit formal organization application, letter of interest, three personal references, three letters of recommendation. An in-person interview is required. International applicants accepted; must apply through a recognized agency.

Benefits and Preemployment Training Free housing, free meals, formal training, willing to provide letters of recommendation, on-the-job training, willing to complete paperwork for educational credit, and willing to act as a professional reference. Preemployment training is required and includes accident prevention and safety, first aid, CPR, interpersonal skills, leadership skills.

Contact Stanley Felsinger, Director, Camp Monroe, PO Box 475, Monroe, New York 10950. Telephone: 845-782-8695. Fax: 845-782-2247. Contact by fax, mail, or phone. Application deadline: continuous.

CAMP OF THE WOODS
ROUTE 30
SPECULATOR, NEW YORK 12164

General Information Nonprofit Christian family resort serving over 1000 people each week and Christian girls camp, Tapawingo, serving 72 girls ages 9-17 per week, both in a mountain setting. Established in 1900. 120-acre facility located 80 miles from Albany. Features: 1500-foot beach; 1400-seat auditorium; 16-element challenge course; fantastic Chapel speakers and concerts; Adirondack Mountains; 2 gyms, 6 tennis courts, climbing wall.

Profile of Summer Employees Total number: 300; typical ages: 16–24. 45% men; 55% women; 5% minorities; 15% high school students; 75% college students; 2% retirees; 8% non-U.S. citizens; 2% local applicants. Nonsmokers required.

Employment Information Openings are from May 15 to September 7. Winter break and year-round positions also offered. Jobs available: ▶ 50 *counselors/teachers* (minimum age 17) with ability to provide leadership and programming for children in preschool through high school at $1250–$1800 per season ▶ 45 *food service personnel* (minimum age 18) at $1250–$2000 per season ▶ 10 *maintenance personnel* (minimum age 16) at $1400–$1600 per season ▶ 45 *musical performance staff members (instrumental/vocal; double as waitstaff)* (minimum age 17) at $2000–$2500 per season ▶ 3 *nurses* (minimum age 21) with RN, LPN, or EMT license at $2000–$2500 per season ▶ 10 *office/clerical staff members* (minimum age 18) at $1400–$1500 per season ▶ 50 *operational personnel (dishwashers, maintenance staff, and housekeepers)* (minimum age 16) at $1250–$3000 per season ▶ 12–15 *recreation leaders* (minimum age 17) with tennis, hiking, rafting, and team sports experience at $1500–$1800 per season ▶ 4 *soundroom technicians* (minimum age 18) with experience running sound at $1500–$2000 per season ▶ 15 *supervisors (all departments)* (minimum age 21) at $1750–$2100 per season ▶ 10 *waterfront staff members* (minimum age 17) with WSI certification (director), lifeguard training, and CPR training (staff) at $1400–$1600 per season. Applicants must submit formal organization application, three writing samples, two personal references, $5 processing fee (waived for international applicants). An in-person interview is recommended, but a telephone interview is acceptable. International applicants accepted; must obtain own visa, obtain own working papers, apply through a recognized agency.

Benefits and Preemployment Training Free housing, free meals, formal training, possible full-time employment, willing to provide letters of recommendation, on-the-job training, willing to complete paperwork for educational credit, willing to act as a professional reference, opportunity to attend seminars/workshops, and tuition assistance. Preemployment training is required and includes first aid, CPR, leadership skills, lifeguarding, RTE, climbing wall, challenge course.

Contact Andrew Mather, Personnel Director, Camp of the Woods, Route 30, Speculator, New York 12164. Telephone: 518-548-4311. Fax: 518-548-9751. E-mail: andym@camp-of-the-woods.

org. World Wide Web: http://www.camp-of-the-woods.org. Contact by e-mail, fax, mail, phone, or through World Wide Web site. Application deadline: March 1.

CAMP TEL YEHUDAH
BARRYVILLE, NEW YORK 12719

General Information Residential, kosher Zionist camp serving teens ages 14–17. Established in 1948. 12,500-acre facility located near Port Jervis.

Profile of Summer Employees Total number: 120.

Employment Information Openings are from June to August. Jobs available: ▶ *arts and crafts specialists* with experience and skill with a variety of crafts ▶ *drama specialists* with experience in play directing and education background ▶ *drivers* with CDL training and experience with 15-passenger vans ▶ *general counselors* with experience working with teens and group leadership skills ▶ *hiking and outdoor specialists* with personal and group hiking experience ▶ *kitchen workers* ▶ *lifeguards* with BLS and WSI certification ▶ *ropes course specialists* with experience. Applicants must submit formal organization application, three personal references. An in-person interview is recommended, but a telephone interview is acceptable. International applicants accepted; must apply through a recognized agency.

Benefits and Preemployment Training Free housing, free meals, on-the-job training, and travel reimbursement.

Contact Noah Gallagher, Head of Camp, Camp Tel Yehudah, 50 West 58th Street, New York, New York 10019. Telephone: 800-970-CAMP. Fax: 212-303-4572. E-mail: telyehudah@ youngjudaea.org. World Wide Web: http://www.youngjudaea.org. Contact by e-mail, fax, mail, or phone. Application deadline: continuous.

CAMP WALDEN NY
429 TROUT LAKE ROAD
DIAMOND POINT, NEW YORK 12824

General Information Co-ed residential camp for children 6–16 located in the Adirondacks of New York. Established in 1931. 100-acre facility located 50 miles from Albany. Features: lake; swimming pool; ropes challenge course; 2 roller hockey rinks; 5 new, lit tennis courts; wonderful and caring staff.

Profile of Summer Employees Total number: 100; typical ages: 17–35. 50% men; 50% women; 10% high school students; 90% college students; 30% non-U.S. citizens. Nonsmokers required.

Employment Information Openings are from June 18 to August 17. Jobs available: ▶ *activity specialists* (minimum age 17) at a negotiable salary ▶ *counselors* (minimum age 17) at a negotiable salary ▶ 1–4 *drivers* (minimum age 21) at a negotiable salary ▶ *head chef* (minimum age 25) with experience as a chef at a negotiable salary ▶ 1–4 *kitchen staff* at a negotiable salary ▶ 1–4 *office staff* at a negotiable salary ▶ 1 *registered nurse* (minimum age 25) with RN experience at a negotiable salary. Applicants must submit formal organization application, resume, three personal references. An in-person interview is recommended, but a telephone interview is acceptable. International applicants accepted; must apply through a recognized agency.

Benefits and Preemployment Training Free housing, free meals, willing to provide letters of recommendation, on-the-job training, willing to complete paperwork for educational credit, and willing to act as a professional reference. Preemployment training is required and includes leadership skills.

Contact Robyn Spector, Director/Head Counselor, Camp Walden NY, 61 Peter Andrew Crescent, Thornhill, Ontario L4J 3E2, Canada. Fax: 905-771-1971. E-mail: spector@rogers.com. World Wide Web: http://www.campwalden.org. Contact by e-mail. No phone calls. Application deadline: continuous.

CAMP WENDY
151 SAINT ELMO ROAD
WALLKILL, NEW YORK 12589

General Information Combination three-week residential camp and three-week day camp. Activities offered cover badge work for the Girl Scouts. Well-rounded program of outdoor activities. Established in 1926. 54-acre facility located 75 miles from New York. Features: wooded setting; pool; lake.

Profile of Summer Employees Total number: 25–30; typical ages: 18–45. 2% men; 98% women; 20% minorities; 10% high school students; 35% college students; 10% non-U.S. citizens; 25% local applicants. Nonsmokers preferred.

Employment Information Openings are from June 30 to August 23. Jobs available: ▶ 1 *arts and crafts director* (minimum age 19) at $1200–$1600 per season ▶ 1 *head cook* (minimum age 21) with food service experience or quantity cooking and ordering at $2000–$3000 per season ▶ 1 *health director* (minimum age 21) must be RN or EMT with first aid and CPR certification at $1900–$2400 per season ▶ 2 *kitchen helpers* (minimum age 16) with interest in food preparation at $100–$125 per week ▶ 10 *unit counselors* (minimum age 18) with desire to work with children in the out-of-doors at $1000–$1400 per season ▶ 4 *unit directors* (minimum age 21) with desire to work with children in the out-of-doors at $1400–$1800 per season ▶ 1 *waterfront director* (minimum age 21) with ARC lifeguard and/or WSI; pool and supervisory experience at $2000–$2400 per season ▶ 4 *waterfront staff* (minimum age 18) with ARC lifeguard or small craft certification or equivalent at $1200–$1600 per season. Applicants must submit formal organization application, resume, three personal references. An in-person interview is recommended, but a telephone interview is acceptable. International applicants accepted; must apply through a recognized agency.

Benefits and Preemployment Training Free housing, free meals, formal training, willing to provide letters of recommendation, on-the-job training, willing to complete paperwork for educational credit, and willing to act as a professional reference. Preemployment training is required and includes accident prevention and safety, first aid, CPR, interpersonal skills, leadership skills.

Contact Mrs. Karen Daughtrey, Camp Director, Camp Wendy, 65 St. James Street, PO Box 3039, Kingston, New York 12402. Telephone: 914-338-5367 Ext. 17. Fax: 914-338-6802. Contact by mail or phone. Application deadline: hiring season from January 1 to July 1.

CAROUSEL DAY SCHOOL
9 WEST AVENUE
HICKSVILLE, NEW YORK 11801

General Information Summer day camp for children ages 3–15. Established in 1956. 5-acre facility located 25 miles from New York. Features: deck hockey; 3 pools; archery range; beach volleyball; adventure ropes course; all sports.

Profile of Summer Employees Total number: 100; typical ages: 18–55. 20% high school students; 50% college students; 30% local applicants. Nonsmokers preferred.

Employment Information Openings are from June to August. Year-round positions also offered. Jobs available: ▶ 35 *general counselors* (minimum age 18) with ability to relate to children at $900–$1300 per season ▶ 25 *group leaders* (minimum age 21) ▶ 7 *lifeguards* with certification in Nassau County at $1800–$2200 per season ▶ 2 *ropes/challenge course instructors* (minimum age 18) at $1800 per season plus tips ▶ 5 *specialists (sports)* (minimum age 18) with ability to teach at $1000–$2000 per season ▶ 5 *sports instructors/counselors* with knowledge of coaching and skills in sports at $1225–$1450 per season ▶ 7 *swimming instructors and lifeguards* with WSI, Nassau County, and CPR/BLS certification at $8.50–$10 per hour. Applicants must submit a formal organization application, resume, three personal references. An in-person interview is required. International applicants accepted.

Benefits and Preemployment Training Formal training, possible full-time employment, willing to provide letters of recommendation, on-the-job training, and willing to complete paperwork for educational credit. Preemployment training is required and includes accident prevention and safety, first aid, CPR, interpersonal skills, leadership skills.

Contact Gene Formica, Director, Carousel Day School, 9 West Avenue, Hicksville, New York 11801. Telephone: 516-938-1137. Fax: 516-822-9269. World Wide Web: http://www. carouseldayschool.com. Contact by fax, mail, or phone. Application deadline: continuous.

CENTER FOR TALENTED YOUTH/JOHNS HOPKINS UNIVERSITY–SIENA COLLEGE
LOUDONVILLE, NEW YORK
See Center for Talented Youth/Johns Hopkins University on page 131 for complete description.

CENTER FOR TALENTED YOUTH/JOHNS HOPKINS UNIVERSITY–SKIDMORE COLLEGE
SARATOGA SPRINGS, NEW YORK
See Center for Talented Youth/Johns Hopkins University on page 131 for complete description.

CHAUTAUQUA INSTITUTION
CHAUTAUQUA, NEW YORK 14722
General Information Residential summer school focusing on orchestra, piano, drama, voice, fine arts, and ballet. Established in 1874. 751-acre facility located 90 miles from Buffalo. Features: lake; concert/lecture programs; golf course; tennis courts; library; summer resort.
Profile of Summer Employees Total number: 1,800; typical ages: 20–50. 70% men; 30% women; 20% minorities; 3% high school students; 50% college students; 20% retirees; 1% non-U.S. citizens; 40% local applicants.
Employment Information Openings are from June 23 to August 26. Jobs available: ▶ *carpenter intern* ▶ *costume designers (theater interns)* ▶ *lighting designers (theater)* ▶ *lighting intern* ▶ *scenic designers (theater)* ▶ *stage managers (theater)* ▶ *technical director (theater)*. Applicants must submit a formal organization application, letter of interest, resume. International applicants accepted; must obtain own visa, obtain own working papers.
Benefits and Preemployment Training Formal training and on-the-job training. Preemployment training is required and includes accident prevention and safety, first aid, CPR.
Contact Richard R. Redington, Vice President, Chautauqua Institution, PO Box 1098, Chautauqua, New York 14722. Telephone: 716-357-6232. Fax: 716-357-9014. World Wide Web: http://www. chautauqua-inst.org. Contact by fax, mail, phone, or through World Wide Web site.

COLLEGE GIFTED PROGRAMS
VASSAR COLLEGE
POUGHKEEPSIE, NEW YORK 12601
General Information Residential educational academic summer camp for gifted and talented students in grades 4-11. Program blends in-depth academics with recreational and cultural activities. Established in 1984. 1,000-acre facility located 70 miles from New York. Features: dormitories; campus classroom facilities; campus recreational facilities include pool, tennis courts, and gym; campus library; beautiful college setting.
Profile of Summer Employees Typical ages: 19–70. 40% men; 60% women; 30% minorities; 50% college students; 10% retirees; 10% non-U.S. citizens; 25% local applicants. Nonsmokers required.

Employment Information Openings are from June 26 to August 7. Jobs available: ▶ 45 *counselors* with two years of college completed and experience working with children at $1000 to $1300 per 3-week session ▶ 4 *directors* with at least 5 years teaching/supervisory experience; master's degree required, doctorate preferred at $4500–$7000 per year ▶ 9 *housemasters/ instructors (residential)* with master's degree, teaching, and supervisory experience at $2500 to $3500 per 3-week session ▶ 20 *instructors (non-residential)* with master's degree and teaching experience at $725 to $2900 per 3-week session ▶ 2 *nurses* with RN license, school experience preferred at $260–$300 per day. Applicants must submit formal organization application, resume, academic transcripts, two personal references, two letters of recommendation. An in-person interview is recommended, but a telephone interview is acceptable. International applicants accepted; must apply through a recognized agency.

Benefits and Preemployment Training Free housing, free meals, willing to provide letters of recommendation, willing to complete paperwork for educational credit, and willing to act as a professional reference. Preemployment training is required and includes accident prevention and safety, interpersonal skills, leadership skills, instructional strategies for gifted students.

Contact Charles Zeichner, Director, College Gifted Programs, 120 Littleton Road, Suite 201, Parsippany, New Jersey 07054-1803. Telephone: 973-334-6991. Fax: 973-334-9756. E-mail: info@cgp-sig.com. World Wide Web: http://www.cgp-sig.com. Contact by e-mail, fax, mail, phone, or through World Wide Web site. Application deadline: continuous.

CYBERCAMPS–ADELPHI UNIVERSITY
GARDEN CITY, NEW YORK
See Cybercamps–University of Washington on page 326 for complete description.

CYBERCAMPS–LONG ISLAND UNIVERSITY, CW POST CAMPUS
BROOKVILLE, NEW YORK
See Cybercamps–University of Washington on page 326 for complete description.

CYBERCAMPS–MANHATTANVILLE COLLEGE
PURCHASE, NEW YORK
See Cybercamps–University of Washington on page 326 for complete description.

EASTERN EXCEL TENNIS
SUNY–OLD WESTBURY
OLD WESTBURY, NEW YORK 11568
General Information Camp that trains children in playing all aspects of tennis, including competition and match play. Established in 1991. Located 25 miles from New York. Features: 37 tennis courts; olympic size pool.

Profile of Summer Employees Total number: 28; typical ages: 18–35. 75% men; 25% women; 10% high school students; 60% college students; 5% non-U.S. citizens. Nonsmokers required.

Employment Information Openings are from June 23 to August 22. Jobs available: ▶ 5–15 *tennis instructors* (minimum age 18) with some teaching experience at $150–$350 per week. Applicants must submit a formal organization application, resume, three personal references. An in-person interview is recommended, but a telephone interview is acceptable. International applicants accepted; must obtain own visa.

Benefits and Preemployment Training Willing to provide letters of recommendation and on-the-job training. Preemployment training is required and includes accident prevention and safety, interpersonal skills.

Contact Lawrence Kleger, Owner, Eastern Excel Tennis, 38 Club Drive North, Jericho, New York 11753. Telephone: 516-938-6076. Fax: 516-827-0981. E-mail: lkleger@optonline.net. Contact by e-mail, mail, or phone. Application deadline: June 1.

ENCHANTED FOREST/WATER SAFARI AND OLD FORGE
3183 STATE ROUTE 38
OLD FORGE, NEW YORK 13420

General Information Amusement/theme/water park, campground, and family entertainment center. Established in 1956. 200-acre facility located 50 miles from Utica. Features: water rides; amusement park rides; circus shows; campground; camping cabins; go-carts.

Profile of Summer Employees Total number: 350; typical ages: 14–20. 50% men; 50% women; 5% minorities; 70% high school students; 30% college students; 5% retirees; 1% non-U.S. citizens; 10% local applicants. Nonsmokers preferred.

Employment Information Openings are from May to October. Jobs available: ▶ 10 *admissions staff* (minimum age 16) at $5.15 per hour ▶ 30 *food service personnel* (minimum age 14) at $5.15 per hour ▶ 10 *games attendants* (minimum age 14) at $5.15 per hour ▶ 20 *grounds crew/housekeeping staff* (minimum age 16) at $5.15 per hour ▶ 20 *lifeguards* (minimum age 15) with CPR/lifeguard certification at $6.50 per hour ▶ 10 *registration/reservations* (minimum age 16) at $6 per hour ▶ 20 *retail personnel* (minimum age 14) at $5.15 per hour ▶ 30 *ride operators* (minimum age 18) at $5.15 per hour ▶ 75 *water/amusement ride operators* (minimum age 14) at $5.15 per hour. Applicants must submit a formal organization application, two personal references. An in-person interview is required. International applicants accepted; must obtain own visa, obtain own working papers.

Benefits and Preemployment Training Housing at a cost, meals at a cost, formal training, willing to provide letters of recommendation, on-the-job training, willing to complete paperwork for educational credit, willing to act as a professional reference, and scholarships, parties, discounts. Preemployment training is required and includes first aid, CPR, interpersonal skills, leadership skills, training for lifeguards, guest relations.

Contact Peter Pepper, Human Resources Manager, Enchanted Forest/Water Safari and Old Forge, 3183 State Route 28, Old Forge, New York 13420. Telephone: 315-369-6145. Fax: 315-369-6400. E-mail: safari@telenet.net. World Wide Web: http://www.watersafari.com. Contact by e-mail, fax, mail, phone, or through World Wide Web site. Application deadline: continuous.

FIVE RIVERS CENTER
GAME FARM ROAD
DELMAR, NEW YORK 12054

General Information Environmental education center serving schools and families. Established in 1973. 330-acre facility located 10 miles from Albany. Features: natural setting; many ponds; wooded areas; open meadows; visitor center; picnic area.

Profile of Summer Employees Total number: 6–8; typical ages: 18–65. 50% men; 50% women; 10% minorities; 10% high school students; 30% college students; 30% retirees; 20% local applicants. Nonsmokers required.

Employment Information Openings are from January 1 to December 31. Year-round positions also offered. Jobs available: ▶ 2 *naturalist interns* (minimum age 18) with college-level study in natural sciences preferred at $200 per week. Applicants must submit formal organization application, resume, academic transcripts, three personal references. An in-person interview is recommended, but a telephone interview is acceptable. International applicants accepted; must obtain own visa, obtain own working papers.

Benefits and Preemployment Training Free housing, formal training, willing to provide letters of recommendation, on-the-job training, willing to complete paperwork for educational credit, willing to act as a professional reference, and opportunity to attend seminars/workshops.

Contact A. Sanchez, Senior Educator, Five Rivers Center, 56 Game Farm Road, Delmar, New York 12054. Telephone: 518-475-0291. Contact by mail or phone. Application deadline: continuous.

FORRESTEL FARM CAMP
4536 SOUTH GRAVEL ROAD
MEDINA, NEW YORK 14103

General Information Coed residential camp serving 60 children ages 7–16 for four 2-week sessions. Established in 1981. 1,000-acre facility located 40 miles from Buffalo. Features: 800-acre working farm; freshwater pond; 3 miles of Oak Orchard Creek; elaborate stable; tennis court; wooded setting.

Profile of Summer Employees Total number: 20; typical ages: 19–25. 30% men; 70% women; 100% college students; 80% non-U.S. citizens; 20% local applicants. Nonsmokers required.

Employment Information Openings are from June 20 to August 20. Jobs available: ▶ 1 *arts and crafts instructor* (minimum age 19) with some experience in the field ▶ 4 *athletics instructors* (minimum age 19) with coaching and teaching experience in one of the following: soccer, volleyball, basketball, softball, lacrosse ▶ 2 *cooks* (minimum age 19) with experience in the field ▶ 4 *lifeguards* (minimum age 19) with Red Cross lifeguard or WSI certification ▶ 1 *naturalist/conservationist* (minimum age 19) with experience in the field at a salary commensurate with experience ▶ 3 *outdoor adventure instructors (canoeing, hiking, mountain biking, fishing, archery, riflery, wall climbing, and orienteering)* (minimum age 19) with experience in the field ▶ 8–10 *riding instructors* (minimum age 19) with previous teaching experience recommended per season ▶ 2 *tennis instructors* (minimum age 19) with USTA coaching or teaching experience recommended. Applicants must submit formal organization application, letter of interest, resume, two personal references, two letters of recommendation. An in-person interview is recommended, but a telephone interview is acceptable. International applicants accepted; must apply through a recognized agency.

Benefits and Preemployment Training Free housing, free meals, willing to provide letters of recommendation, on-the-job training, willing to complete paperwork for educational credit, willing to act as a professional reference, and travel reimbursement. Preemployment training is required and includes accident prevention and safety, first aid, CPR, interpersonal skills, leadership skills.

Contact Mary Herbert, Camp Owner/Director, Forrestel Farm Camp, 4536 South Gravel Road, Medina, New York 14103. Telephone: 585-798-2222. Fax: 585-798-2222. E-mail: camp@ forrestelfarmcamp.com. World Wide Web: http://www.forrestelfarmcamp.com. Contact by e-mail, fax, mail, phone, or through World Wide Web site. Application deadline: application by March 1 is preferred.

FRENCH WOODS FESTIVAL OF THE PERFORMING ARTS
350 BOUCHOUX BROOK ROAD
HANCOCK, NEW YORK 13783

General Information Private children's summer camp with individualized programming in performing and visual arts, sports, and more. Established in 1970. 600-acre facility located 40 miles from Binghamton. Features: private lake; heated pool; five theatres; large circus building; air conditioned dining room; ample recreational facilities.

Profile of Summer Employees Total number: 350; typical ages: 19–25. 45% men; 55% women; 5% minorities; 70% college students; 5% retirees; 50% non-U.S. citizens; 50% local applicants. Nonsmokers required.

Employment Information Openings are from June 20 to August 25. Jobs available: ▶ 8–10 *head counselors* (minimum age 23) with ability to supervise group of counselors and campers at $3000–$6000 per season ▶ 10–20 *program heads* (minimum age 25) with extensive background in program area at $2500–$5000 per season ▶ 175–225 *specialist counselors* (minimum age 18) with skill in a program area and ability to teach at $1400–$2400 per season. Applicants must submit formal organization application, resume, two personal references, two letters of recommendation. An in-person interview is recommended, but a telephone interview is acceptable. International applicants accepted; must apply through a recognized agency.

Benefits and Preemployment Training Free housing, free meals, willing to provide letters of recommendation, on-the-job training, willing to complete paperwork for educational credit, willing to act as a professional reference, and travel reimbursement. Preemployment training is required and includes accident prevention and safety, CPR, interpersonal skills, leadership skills.

Contact Beth Schaefer, Director, French Woods Festival of the Performing Arts, PO Box 770100, Coral Springs, Florida 33077. Telephone: 800-634-1703. Fax: 954-346-7564. E-mail: beth_s@ frenchwoodscamp.com. World Wide Web: http://www.frenchwoods.com. Contact by e-mail, fax, mail, or phone. Application deadline: continuous.

THE FRESH AIR FUND
SHARPE RESERVATION, VAN WYCK LAKE ROAD
FISHKILL, NEW YORK 12524

General Information Five residential camps serving 3,000 inner-city children each summer. Established in 1877. 3,000-acre facility located 65 miles from New York.

Profile of Summer Employees Total number: 400; typical ages: 18–23. 55% men; 45% women; 35% minorities; 3% high school students; 90% college students; 25% non-U.S. citizens; 30% local applicants. Nonsmokers preferred.

Employment Information Openings are from June 15 to August 24. Jobs available: ▶ 5 *farmers* (minimum age 18) with course work in animal biology or experience working with livestock at $1700–$2100 per season ▶ 200 *general counselors* (minimum age 18) with some college and experience with children at $1700–$2100 per season ▶ 9 *nurses* with RN license and one year of nursing experience required at $7000–$8000 per season ▶ 2 *nutritionists* (minimum age 18) with cooking experience and course work in nutrition at $1700–$2100 per season ▶ 35 *program specialists* (minimum age 18) with ability to teach in one of the following specialties: photography, video, music, sewing, pioneering, nature, or arts and crafts at $1700–$2200 per season ▶ 6 *ropes course facilitators* (minimum age 19) with experience as an instructor or participant on high and/or low ropes course programs; facilitators will be trained and certified during orientation at $1700–$2100 per season ▶ 22 *village leaders* (minimum age 20) with residential camp employment experience required at $2100–$2600 per season ▶ 20 *waterfront assistants* (minimum age 18) with lifeguard training and CPR for the professional rescuer at $2100–$2400 per season ▶ 5 *waterfront directors* (minimum age 21) with lifeguard training, CPR for the professional rescuer, three years of waterfront experience required, and WSI preferred at $2500–$3000 per season. Applicants must submit formal organization application, three personal references. An in-person interview is recommended, but a telephone interview is acceptable. International applicants accepted; must apply through a recognized agency.

Benefits and Preemployment Training Free housing, free meals, formal training, willing to provide letters of recommendation, on-the-job training, willing to complete paperwork for educational credit, and travel reimbursement. Preemployment training is required and includes accident prevention and safety, first aid, CPR, leadership skills, lifeguard training.

Contact Thomas S. Karger, Deputy Executive Director, The Fresh Air Fund, 633 Third Avenue, New York, New York 10017. Telephone: 800-367-0003. Fax: 212-681-0147. E-mail: freshair@ freshair.org. World Wide Web: http://www.freshair.org. Contact by e-mail, fax, mail, phone, or through World Wide Web site. Application deadline: continuous.

GIRL SCOUTS–INDIAN HILLS COUNCIL, INC.
32 WEST STATE STREET
BINGHAMTON, NEW YORK 13902-2145

General Information Residential camp program at the Amahami Outdoor Center set on 450 acres and serving girls ages 6 to 18. Specialty programs include: swimming, arts and crafts, nature activities, leadership training, and outdoor adventure activities. Established in 1929. 450-acre facility. Features: freshwater lake; staff housing with kitchen; low ropes/high ropes course; wooded setting; kayaks.

Profile of Summer Employees Total number: 30–35; typical ages: 16–40. 20% men; 80% women; 5% minorities; 10% high school students; 50% college students; 35% local applicants. Nonsmokers required.

Employment Information Openings are from June 24 to August 24. Jobs available: ▶ 1 *English riding director* (minimum age 21) with experience instructing English horseback riding at $3000–$3500 per season ▶ 1 *business manager* (minimum age 21) with driver's license and business training at $2400–$2500 per season ▶ 1–2 *camp director/assistant director* (minimum age 21) with Bachelor's Degree or 24 weeks of administrative/supervisory experience at $4200–$5500 per season ▶ 1–2 *cooks* at $2800–$3500 per season ▶ 1 *health supervisor* (minimum age 21) with MD, RN, EMT, NP, or LPN and current first aid/CPR certification at $3000–$4000 per season ▶ 1–3 *kitchen assistants* (minimum age 16) with willingness to assist cooks at $1500–$2000 per season ▶ 3–5 *lifeguards* (minimum age 16) with lifeguard certification/waterfront lifeguard certification at $1800–$2100 per season ▶ 10–20 *unit assistants* (minimum age 17) with a love of working with children, previous work with kids preferred, and a love of being outdoors at $1800–$2100 per season ▶ 1 *western riding director* (minimum age 21) with experience instructing western horseback riding at $3000–$3500 per season. Applicants must submit formal organization application, resume, three personal references. An in-person interview is recommended, but a telephone interview is acceptable. International applicants accepted; must apply through a recognized agency.

Benefits and Preemployment Training Free housing, free meals, formal training, possible full-time employment, willing to provide letters of recommendation, on-the-job training, willing to complete paperwork for educational credit, willing to act as a professional reference, and opportunity to attend seminars/workshops. Preemployment training is required and includes accident prevention and safety, first aid, CPR, interpersonal skills, leadership skills, child abuse recognition.

Contact Eileen Andrews, Program and Adult Development Director, Girl Scouts–Indian Hills Council, Inc. Telephone: 607-724-6572. Fax: 607-724-6575. E-mail: eandrews@gsihc.org. World Wide Web: http://www.gsihc.org. Contact by e-mail, fax, mail, or phone. Application deadline: applications accepted January 1 to May 1.

GIRLS' VACATION FUND, INC.
, NEW YORK

General Information A charitable organization with the mission to help less privileged girls discover their own self worth and grow through caring, educational camp experience. Established in 1935. 500-acre facility located 40 miles from Albany. Features: lake; wooded Catskill Mountains setting; learning center; challenge course; basketball court; Adirondack cabins.

Profile of Summer Employees Total number: 50; typical ages: 19–30. 5% men; 95% women; 25% minorities; 5% high school students; 80% college students; 30% non-U.S. citizens; 5% local applicants. Nonsmokers required.

Employment Information Openings are from June 15 to August 25. Jobs available: ▶ 2 *chefs* (minimum age 21) must have institutional cooking experience at $600 per week ▶ 25 *counselors* (minimum age 19) must be able to live in cabins with girls, early education majors preferred at $200–$250 per week ▶ 2 *crafts and ceramics directors* (minimum age 21) must have ceramics teaching or youth group experience at $250 per week ▶ 2 *hiking directors* (minimum age 21) must have RTE certification and be able to take youth groups on hiking trips out of camp at $250–$300 per week ▶ 4 *lifeguards* (minimum age 19) with current WSI, lifeguard training, and CPR certifications (training available) at $250–$350 per week ▶ 2 *literacy teachers* (minimum age 21) must have teaching experience at $400 per week ▶ 2 *naturalists* (minimum age 20) must be able to teach environmental concepts to children ages 8-15 at $200–$250 per week ▶ 2 *program directors* (minimum age 21) must have extensive organized camp experience at $300–$400 per week ▶ 3 *registered nurses* (minimum age 21) must be able to legally act as a registered nurse in New York state at $400–$600 per week ▶ 2 *sports directors* (minimum age 21) must have teaching experience with emphasis on non-competitive sports and physical education at $250 per week. Applicants must submit formal organization application, three personal references. An in-person interview is recommended, but a telephone interview is acceptable. International applicants accepted; must apply through a recognized agency.

Benefits and Preemployment Training Free housing, free meals, formal training, possible full-time employment, willing to provide letters of recommendation, on-the-job training, willing to complete paperwork for educational credit, and willing to act as a professional reference. Preemployment training is required and includes accident prevention and safety, first aid, CPR, interpersonal skills, leadership skills, lifeguarding.

Contact Ms. Eva Lewandowski, Executive Director, Girls' Vacation Fund, Inc., 370 Lexington Avenue #913, New York, New York 10017. Telephone: 212-532-7050. Fax: 212-532-7061. E-mail: gvfnyc@aol.com. World Wide Web: http://www.girlsvacationfund.org. Contact by e-mail, fax, mail, phone, or through World Wide Web site. Application deadline: continuous.

GOLDEN ACRES FARM AND RANCH RESORT
COUNTY ROAD 14
GILBOA, NEW YORK 12076

General Information Kosher family farm and ranch resort catering to young professional families with children. Established in 1950. 600-acre facility located 60 miles from Albany. Features: horseback riding stable; indoor and outdoor pools; Catskill Mountain location; tennis, volleyball, and paddleball courts; children's day camp; theater productions.

Profile of Summer Employees Total number: 100; typical age: 22. 40% men; 60% women; 10% minorities; 51% college students; 2% retirees; 30% non-U.S. citizens; 10% local applicants.

Employment Information Openings are from June 20 to September 7. Jobs available: ▶ 1 *baker* with experience at $700–$900 per week ▶ 1 *bartender/barmaid* (minimum age 21) with cash-handling references and experience at $6.50 per hour ▶ 3 *bellhops/maintenance personnel* with mechanical abilities and driver's license at $6.50 per hour ▶ 11 *chamber staff members* (minimum age 19) with clean and neat appearance at $6.50 per hour ▶ 1–2 *chefs* (minimum age 25) with experience in banquet cooking; kosher and banquet experience preferred at $800–$1200 per week ▶ 13 *counselors* (minimum age 19) with experience at $6.50 per hour ▶ 1–2 *dining room managers* (minimum age 25) with supervisory and serving experience at $400–$550 per week ▶ 20 *food service assistants* (minimum age 19) with experience at $6.50 per hour ▶ 4 *front desk clerks* with computer, cash, and credit card experience at $6.50 per hour ▶ 1 *head housekeeper* (minimum age 20) with supervisory skills at $350–$450 per week ▶ 3 *nursery counselors* with experience at $6.50 per hour ▶ 1 *social director* (minimum age 21) with driver's license and experience in the field at $300–$400 per week ▶ 2 *swimming instructors* with American Red Cross lifesaving certification at $6.50 per hour ▶ 8 *wranglers* with experience at $6.50 per hour. Applicants must submit formal organization application, resume, two letters of recommendation, two employment references. International applicants accepted; must obtain own visa, obtain own working papers, apply through a recognized agency.

Benefits and Preemployment Training Housing at a cost, meals at a cost, willing to provide letters of recommendation, names of contacts, on-the-job training, willing to complete paperwork for educational credit, willing to act as a professional reference, and end of season bonuses. Preemployment training is required and includes food safety training.

Contact Patricia Gauthier, Golden Acres Farm and Ranch Resort, HCR 1, Box 53, Gilboa, New York 12076. Telephone: 607-588-7329. Fax: 607-588-6911. E-mail: goldenacresfarm@aol.com. World Wide Web: http://www.goldenacres.com. Contact by e-mail, mail, or phone. Application deadline: continuous.

GORDON KENT'S NEW ENGLAND TENNIS CAMP AT TRINITY-PAWLING SCHOOL
300 ROUTE 22
PAWLING, NEW YORK 12564

General Information Tennis camp located at Trinity-Pawling School in Pawling, New York, for 80 campers ages 9–17. Established in 1965. 150-acre facility located 20 miles from Danbury, Connecticut. Features: 12 tennis courts; school dorms; many athletic fields; beautiful campus; gymnasium.

Profile of Summer Employees Total number: 20; typical ages: 18–25. 60% men; 40% women; 10% minorities; 5% high school students; 90% college students; 20% non-U.S. citizens. Nonsmokers required.

Employment Information Openings are from June 29 to August 22. Jobs available: ▶ 5–10 *counselors/tennis instructors* with experience playing tennis (on school team), outgoing personality, and patience; at least one year of college completed at $1450–$2000 per season. Applicants must submit formal organization application, three personal references, three letters of recommendation. An in-person interview is recommended, but a telephone interview is acceptable. International applicants accepted; must apply through a recognized agency.

Benefits and Preemployment Training Free housing, free meals, possible full-time employment, willing to provide letters of recommendation, on-the-job training, willing to complete paperwork for educational credit, willing to act as a professional reference, and opportunity to attend seminars/workshops. Preemployment training is required and includes accident prevention and safety, interpersonal skills, leadership skills, tennis teaching skills.

Contact Gordon Kent, Owner/Director, Gordon Kent's New England Tennis Camp at Trinity-Pawling School, PO Box 143, Riverdale, New York 10471. Telephone: 800-528-2752. Fax: 212-750-3704. E-mail: netennis@aol.com. Contact by e-mail, fax, mail, or phone. Application deadline: continuous.

HILLSIDE OUTDOOR EDUCATION CENTER DAY AND TRIPPING CAMP
400 DOANSBURG ROAD
BREWSTER, NEW YORK 10509-0719

General Information Coed day and tripping camp serving approximately 225 children ages 5-15. Established in 1972. 150-acre facility located 60 miles from New York. Features: farm; high and low ropes course; climbing tower; natural playground; Croton River for canoeing; rural setting.

Profile of Summer Employees Total number: 40–50; typical ages: 15–35. 30% men; 70% women; 2% minorities; 1% high school students; 80% college students; 50% non-U.S. citizens; 25% local applicants. Nonsmokers required.

Employment Information Openings are from June 20 to August 29. Year-round positions also offered. Jobs available: ▶ 2–4 *adventure specialists* (minimum age 21) with experience leading ropes courses, climbing tower, caving, and canoeing at $250 per week ▶ 1 *archery instructor* (minimum age 21) with archery instructor certification at $250 per week ▶ 1 *arts and crafts instructor* (minimum age 20) with experience in the field at $250 per week ▶ 10–20 *general counselors* (minimum age 20) with experience teaching children at $175–$200 per week ▶ 8 *horseback riding instructors* (minimum age 20) with experience teaching riding and children at $175–$250 per week ▶ 2 *swimming instructors* (minimum age 20) with WSI certification and experience as pool director at $500–$650 per month. Applicants must submit formal organization application, letter of interest, resume, three letters of recommendation. An in-person interview is recommended, but a telephone interview is acceptable. International applicants accepted; must obtain own visa, apply through a recognized agency.

Benefits and Preemployment Training Free housing, free meals, formal training, possible full-time employment, and on-the-job training.

Contact Duncan Lester, Director, Hillside Outdoor Education Center Day and Tripping Camp. Telephone: 845-279-2995 Ext. 325. Fax: 845-279-3077. E-mail: hillside@greenchimneys.org. World Wide Web: http://www.greenchimneys.org. Contact by e-mail, fax, mail, phone, or through World Wide Web site. Application deadline: applications by May 1 are preferred.

INTRODUCTION TO INDEPENDENCE
NEW YORK INSTITUTE OF TECHNOLOGY
CENTRAL ISLIP, NEW YORK 11722

General Information Residential pre-college/independent living experience serving 30–45 moderately to severely learning disabled young adults ages 16–20. 600-acre facility located 40 miles from New York. Features: golf course; gymnasium; fitness center; bowling alley; university dormitories; library.

Profile of Summer Employees Total number: 25; typical ages: 21–50. 33% men; 67% women; 15% minorities; 15% college students. Nonsmokers preferred.

Employment Information Openings are from June 21 to August 15. Year-round positions also offered. Jobs available: ▶ *resident advisors* with special education, psychology, or social work background (graduate students) at $1100–$1300 per season. Applicants must submit a letter of interest, resume. An in-person interview is required.

Benefits and Preemployment Training Free housing, free meals, and on-the-job training. Preemployment training is required and includes interpersonal skills, leadership skills, discussion about learning disabilities.

Contact Lauri Alpern, Director, Introduction to Independence, PO Box 730, Central Islip, New York 11722. Telephone: 631-348-3354. Fax: 631-348-0437. Contact by fax, mail, or phone. Application deadline: continuous.

KUTSHER'S SPORTS ACADEMY
ANAWANA LAKE ROAD
MONTICELLO, NEW YORK 12701

General Information Residential coeducational sports camp featuring an elective instructional sports program for 500 campers, as well as arts and crafts, woodworking, dance, drama, computers, and photography programs. Established in 1968. 100-acre facility located 90 miles from New York. Features: extensive athletic facilities; scenic Catskill Mountain setting; location on beautiful private lake; fitness center.

Profile of Summer Employees Total number: 220; typical ages: 19–60. 69% men; 31% women; 20% minorities; 100% college students; 25% non-U.S. citizens. Nonsmokers required.

Employment Information Openings are from June 23 to August 21. Jobs available: ▶ *athletic trainer* with certification in field at $2000–$2500 per season ▶ *coaches* (minimum age 24) with experience in the field at $1800–$3000 per season ▶ *counselors* (minimum age 19) with specialty in at least one sport or college/high school athletics experience at $950–$1450 per season ▶ *nurses* with RN at $3000–$4500 per season. Applicants must submit formal organization application, two personal references. A telephone interview is required. International applicants accepted; must apply through a recognized agency.

Benefits and Preemployment Training Free housing, free meals, formal training, on-the-job training, and willing to complete paperwork for educational credit. Preemployment training is required and includes accident prevention and safety, first aid, interpersonal skills, leadership skills.

Contact Marc White, Executive Director, Kutsher's Sports Academy, 7 Mine Hill Road, Bridgewater, Connecticut 06752. Telephone: 860-350-3819. Fax: 860-350-3819. E-mail: ksamsw@earthlink.net. World Wide Web: http://www.ksacad.com. Contact by e-mail, fax, phone, or through World Wide Web site. Application deadline: continuous.

L.I. ADVENTURELAND
2245 ROUTE 110
EAST FARMINGDALE, NEW YORK 11735

General Information Amusement park with rides, games, and restaurant facilities. Caters to a wide age range between April and October. Established in 1962. 10-acre facility located 35 miles from New York. Features: roller coaster; ferris wheel; merry-go-round; restaurant; arcade; log flume.

Profile of Summer Employees Total number: 500; typical ages: 14–24. 40% men; 60% women; 50% minorities; 65% high school students; 35% college students; 5% retirees; 5% non-U.S. citizens; 95% local applicants.

Employment Information Openings are from April 1 to October 31. Spring break positions also offered. Jobs available: ▶ 50–100 *concession stand staff* (minimum age 14) with good math skills at $5.15–$6.50 per hour ▶ 60–80 *game attendants* (minimum age 14) at $5.50–$6.50 per hour ▶ 150–225 *ride operators* (minimum age 16) at $5.50–$6.50 per hour. Applicants must submit formal organization application. An in-person interview is required. International applicants accepted; must obtain own visa, apply through a recognized agency.

Benefits and Preemployment Training Housing at a cost, meals at a cost, willing to provide letters of recommendation, and willing to complete paperwork for educational credit. Preemployment training is required and includes accident prevention and safety, interpersonal skills.

Contact Paul Gentile, Personnel Manager, L.I. Adventureland, 2245 Route 110, East Farmingdale, New York 11735. Telephone: 631-694-6868. Fax: 631-694-6816. E-mail: paul@adventureland. us. World Wide Web: http://www.adventureland.us. Contact by e-mail, mail, phone, or through World Wide Web site. Application deadline: continuous.

MARTIN'S FANTASY ISLAND
2400 GRAND ISLAND BOULEVARD
GRAND ISLAND, NEW YORK 14072

General Information Amusement park offering rides, shows, waterpark, miniature golf, western shoot-out, pony rides, petting zoo, group outings, and school days. Established in 1961. 80-acre facility located 8 miles from Buffalo. Features: 2 roller coasters; 1 new drop ride; water park; 3 live shows; canoeing; petting zoo.

Profile of Summer Employees Total number: 350; typical ages: 16–20. 50% men; 50% women; 60% high school students; 20% college students; 5% retirees; 15% local applicants.

Employment Information Openings are from May 1 to September 30. Jobs available: ▶ 10–30 *food service/catering staff* with food service experience and ability to operate a cash register at $5.15–$6 per hour ▶ 10–20 *front gate staff/cashiers* (minimum age 16) with ability to operate a cash register at $5.15–$6 per hour ▶ 5–15 *games staff* (minimum age 16) at $5.15–$6 per hour ▶ 10–15 *grounds staff* (minimum age 14) at $5.15–$6 per hour ▶ 25 *lifeguards* (minimum age 16) with Red Cross/lifesaving and CPR certification at $5.40–$6 per hour ▶ 3 *restroom staff* (minimum age 16) at $5.85–$6.15 per hour ▶ *ride operators* (minimum age 16) at $5.15–$6 per hour ▶ 5–15 *shops/retail staff* (minimum age 16) with ability to operate a cash register at $5.15–$6 per hour. An in-person interview is required. International applicants accepted; must apply through a recognized agency.

Benefits and Preemployment Training On-the-job training and willing to complete paperwork for educational credit.

Contact Cindy Williams, Administrative Assistant, Martin's Fantasy Island, 2400 Grand Island Boulevard, Grand Island, New York 14072. Telephone: 716-773-7591. Fax: 716-773-7043. E-mail: martinsfantasyisland@juno.com. World Wide Web: http://www.martinsfantasyisland. com. Contact by e-mail, mail, phone, or through World Wide Web site. Application deadline: continuous.

MIDWAY PARK, INC.
ROUTE 430, PO BOX E
MAPLE SPRINGS, NEW YORK 14756

General Information Amusement kiddie park located on Chautauqua Lake with rides, go-karts, mini-golf, bumper boats, food, and arcade. Established in 1898. 26-acre facility located 12 miles from Jamestown. Features: on Chautauqua Lake; picnic grove; ride area; roller rink.

Profile of Summer Employees Total number: 100; typical ages: 16–25. 50% men; 50% women; 5% minorities; 30% high school students; 60% college students; 10% retirees; 95% local applicants. Nonsmokers preferred.

Employment Information Openings are from May 25 to September 8. Jobs available: ▶ 10 *arcade attendants* (minimum age 16) at $5.15 per hour ▶ 10 *food concession staff* (minimum age 16) at $5.15 per hour ▶ 30 *ride attendants* (minimum age 16) at $5.15 per hour. Applicants must submit a formal organization application, three personal references. An in-person interview is required.

Benefits and Preemployment Training Willing to provide letters of recommendation and on-the-job training. Preemployment training is required and includes accident prevention and safety.

Contact Robin DeLong, Office Manager, Midway Park, Inc., PO Box E, Maple Springs, New York 14756. Fax: 716-386-4700. World Wide Web: http://www.midway-park.com. Contact by mail. No phone calls. Application deadline: continuous.

MUSIKER TOURS
1326 OLD NORTHERN BOULEVARD
ROSLYN, NEW YORK 11576

General Information Active tours and adventure travel for students ages 13–18. Travel through the United States, Canada, and Europe, staying in campgrounds, dormitories, and hotels. Established in 1967. Features: national parks; university dorms; whitewater rafting; mountain biking.

Profile of Summer Employees Total number: 100; typical ages: 21–34. 50% men; 50% women; 10% minorities; 40% college students. Nonsmokers required.

Employment Information Openings are from June 20 to August 20. Jobs available: ▶ 100–200 *summer counselors* (minimum age 21) with valid driver's license, experience in summer camp and with junior and senior high school students, and first aid/CPR certification preferred at $50–$150 per week. Applicants must submit a formal organization application, three personal references. An in-person interview is recommended, but a telephone interview is acceptable.

Benefits and Preemployment Training Free housing, free meals, willing to provide letters of recommendation, willing to complete paperwork for educational credit, and travel reimbursement. Preemployment training is required and includes accident prevention and safety, interpersonal skills, leadership skills.

Contact Jen Strauss, Director of Personnel, Musiker Tours, 1326 Old Northern Boulevard, Roslyn, New York 11576. Telephone: 516-621-3939. Fax: 516-625-3438. E-mail: jen@summerfun. com. World Wide Web: http://www.summerfun.com. Contact by e-mail, fax, mail, or phone. Application deadline: continuous.

92ND STREET Y CAMPS
1395 LEXINGTON AVENUE
NEW YORK, NEW YORK 10128

General Information Summer camps for children ages 5 to 15 that focus on building self-esteem and exposing children to the outdoors in a safe, comfortable environment. Established in 1880. 100-acre facility. Features: rope challenge course; athletic fields; art and ceramic centers; nature center; basketball courts; swimming pools.

New York

Profile of Summer Employees Total number: 300; typical ages: 17–30. 50% men; 50% women; 20% minorities; 35% high school students; 50% college students; 5% non-U.S. citizens; 90% local applicants. Nonsmokers preferred.

Employment Information Openings are from June 18 to August 22. Jobs available: ▶ 25 *activity specialists (arts, sports, ropes, nature, music, karate)* (minimum age 19) at $2000–$4000 per season ▶ 5 *assistant directors* (minimum age 22) with supervisory and camp experience at $3000–$5500 per season ▶ 100 *camp counselors* (minimum age 17) at $1200–$2300 per season ▶ 20 *special needs camp counselors* (minimum age 18) at $1700–$2300 per season. Applicants must submit formal organization application, resume, two personal references. An in-person interview is required. International applicants accepted; must obtain own visa, apply through a recognized agency.

Benefits and Preemployment Training Willing to provide letters of recommendation, names of contacts, on-the-job training, willing to complete paperwork for educational credit, and willing to act as a professional reference. Preemployment training is required and includes accident prevention and safety, first aid, CPR, interpersonal skills, leadership skills.

Contact Steve Levin, Associate Director, Camp Programs, 92nd Street Y Camps, 1395 Lexington Avenue, New York, New York 10128. Telephone: 212-415-5641. Fax: 212-415-5637. E-mail: slevin@92y.org. World Wide Web: http://www.92y.org/camps. Contact by e-mail, fax, mail, phone, or through World Wide Web site. Application deadline: June 15.

PARK SHORE COUNTRY DAY CAMP
450 DEER PARK ROAD
DIX HILLS, NEW YORK 11746

General Information Day camp whose staff focuses on the growth, happiness, and building the self-esteem and confidence of each camper. Established in 1959. 15-acre facility located 30 miles from New York.

Profile of Summer Employees Total number: 200; typical ages: 18–45. 40% men; 60% women; 20% high school students; 50% college students. Nonsmokers preferred.

Employment Information Openings are from June 28 to August 22. Jobs available: ▶ 7 *athletic specialists* (minimum age 18) with experience with children and experience instructing variety of sports at $1200–$2000 per season ▶ 100 *counselors* (minimum age 17) with sensitivity and understanding; must be college student or graduate at $1200–$1500 per season ▶ 50 *group leaders* with college degree and/or teacher certification at $1600–$2200 per season ▶ 20 *swim staff* (minimum age 16) with WSI, CPR, first aid, and lifeguard certifications at $1200–$2000 per season. Applicants must submit a formal organization application, personal reference, 1-3 letters of recommendation. An in-person interview is required.

Benefits and Preemployment Training Free meals, willing to provide letters of recommendation, willing to act as a professional reference, and opportunity to attend seminars/workshops. Preemployment training is required and includes accident prevention and safety, first aid, CPR, leadership skills.

Contact Chuck Budah, Owner, Park Shore Country Day Camp, 450 Deer Park Road, Dix Hills, New York 11746. Telephone: 631-499-8580. Fax: 631-499-6917. E-mail: parkshorekids@aol.com. Contact by e-mail or phone. Application deadline: continuous.

POINT O' PINES CAMP
7201 STATE ROUTE 8
BRANT LAKE, NEW YORK 12815-2236

General Information Eight-week traditional residential girls camp with professional sports instruction as well as arts, performing arts, and horsemanship for 300 campers; winter restaurant and wedding caterers. Established in 1957. 523-acre facility located 90 miles from Albany. Features: peninsula location; freshwater lake; surrounded by wooded mountains; 12 tennis courts (4 with lights); winterized bunks with full bathrooms; winterized dining room with fireplace.

Profile of Summer Employees Total number: 160; typical ages: 18–55. 10% men; 90% women; 10% minorities; 80% college students; 10% non-U.S. citizens; 5% local applicants. Nonsmokers preferred.

Employment Information Openings are from June 16 to August 17. Year-round positions also offered. Jobs available: ▶ 4 *English horseback riding instructors* with at least two years of teaching experience at $1200–$2500 per season ▶ 6 *arts and crafts staff members* with professional teaching experience and/or a major in art at $1000–$1500 per season ▶ 6 *athletics staff members* with experience as college team player or professional instructor at $1000–$1500 per season ▶ 2 *boating instructors* with experience in the field at $1000–$1500 per season ▶ *cleaning and kitchen help* with references and experience ▶ 1 *drama director* with experience in the field at $2500–$3000 per season ▶ 1 *drama technical person* with at least two years of experience in college or community theater at $1500–$2000 per season ▶ *drama-costume director* with sewing ability at $1000–$1600 per season ▶ *fitness and conditioning instructors* with extensive training, certification, and experience in the field at $1500–$2300 per season ▶ 6 *gymnastics/dance staff members* with experience as college team player or instructor at $1000–$1500 per season ▶ 1 *music director* with experience as piano accompanist for theater (must be able to transpose) at $1400–$2000 per season ▶ 3 *nurses* with RN certification and clinical experience at $3500–$4500 per season ▶ 4 *outdoor adventure staff members* with extensive training in safety and experience in the field at $1200–$1600 per season ▶ 2 *photography staff members* with college or professional experience at $1000–$1500 per season ▶ 3 *sailing instructors* with experience in the field at $1000–$1500 per season ▶ 14 *tennis staff members* with experience as college team player or professional instructor at $1000–$1500 per season ▶ 2 *video instructors* with at least two years of experience in operating equipment at $1500–$2000 per season ▶ 23 *waterfront staff members* with extensive water sports experience at $1100–$1600 per season ▶ 8 *waterskiing instructors* with experience in the field at $1000–$1500 per season ▶ 1 *year-round dining room manager for restaurant* (minimum age 22) with college degree and experience in business management or hotel and resort management at $23000–$33000 per year. Applicants must submit formal organization application, resume, three personal references. An in-person interview is recommended, but a telephone interview is acceptable. International applicants accepted; must apply through a recognized agency.

Benefits and Preemployment Training Free housing, free meals, formal training, willing to provide letters of recommendation, on-the-job training, willing to complete paperwork for educational credit, willing to act as a professional reference, travel reimbursement, and free laundry service. Preemployment training is required and includes accident prevention and safety, first aid, CPR, leadership skills.

Contact Sherie Alden, Associate Director, Point O' Pines Camp, 7201 State Route 8, Brant Lake, New York 12815-2236. Telephone: 888-726-9908. Fax: 518-494-3489. E-mail: info@ pointopines.com. World Wide Web: http://www.pointopines.com. Contact by e-mail, fax, mail, phone, or through World Wide Web site. Application deadline: continuous.

SAGAMORE INSTITUTE OF THE ADIRONDACKS
SAGAMORE ROAD, PO BOX 40
RAQUETTE LAKE, NEW YORK 13436-0040

General Information Sagamore Institute is a nonprofit steward of a National Historic Landmark that offers residential programs and public tours promoting culture, nature, and their critical interdependence. Established in 1972. 19-acre facility located 50 miles from Utica. Features: freshwater lake; wooded, wilderness setting; National Historic Landmark of 27 buildings; wide range outdoor programs; history, culture, artisan crafts.

Profile of Summer Employees Total number: 26; typical ages: 20–25. 20% men; 80% women; 100% college students. Nonsmokers preferred.

Employment Information Openings are from June 10 to October 20. Jobs available: ▶ 3 *environmental outdoor education staff* (minimum age 19) with various outdoor skills, environmental interpretation, and teaching experience at $150 per week ▶ 2–5 *historic interpretation staff* (minimum age 19) with American History background and strong communication skills at $150 per week ▶ 1 *manager* (minimum age 19) with retail sales and food preparation experience at $150 per week. Applicants must submit a letter of interest, resume, three personal references, 1 expository writing sample. An in-person interview is recommended, but a telephone interview is acceptable. International applicants accepted; must obtain own visa, obtain own working papers.

Benefits and Preemployment Training Free housing, free meals, willing to provide letters of recommendation, on-the-job training, willing to complete paperwork for educational credit, willing to act as a professional reference, and opportunity to attend seminars/workshops.

Contact Dr. Michael Wilson, Associate Director, Sagamore Institute of the Adirondacks, 9 Kiwassa Road, Saranoe Lake, New York 12983. Telephone: 518-891-1718. Fax: 518-891-2561. E-mail: mwilson@northnet.org. World Wide Web: http://www.sagamore.org. Contact by e-mail. Application deadline: April 15.

SAIL CARIBBEAN
79 CHURCH STREET
NORTHPORT, NEW YORK 11768

General Information Summer sailing and scuba diving program in the Caribbean for teens. Extensive water sports, island exploration, marine sciences, and cultural activities. Established in 1979. Located 60 miles from San Juan. Features: Caribbean Sea; island exploration; 51' yachts; windsurfers; kayaks; waterskiing; scuba diving; beach sports.

Profile of Summer Employees Total number: 50; typical ages: 20–30. 66% men; 34% women; 60% college students. Nonsmokers required.

Employment Information Openings are from June to August. Jobs available: ▶ 2 *ARC lifeguard instructors* (minimum age 20) with CPR/first aid ▶ 6 *PADI scuba instructors* (minimum age 20) with CPR/first aid ▶ 6 *assistant skippers* (minimum age 20) with CPR/first aid ▶ 2 *food supervisors* (minimum age 20) with CPR/first aid ▶ 4 *marine biology teachers* (minimum age 20) with CPR/first aid ▶ 6 *skippers* (minimum age 20) with CPR/first aid; (US Sailing basic keelboat instructor for one position). Applicants must submit a letter of interest, resume, 3-5 personal references, an in-person interview is highly recommended. International applicants accepted; must obtain own visa.

Benefits and Preemployment Training Free housing, free meals, possible full-time employment, willing to provide letters of recommendation, on-the-job training, willing to act as a professional reference, and travel reimbursement. Preemployment training is required and includes accident prevention and safety, interpersonal skills, leadership skills.

Contact Michael D. Liese, Founder/Director, Sail Caribbean, 79 Church Street, Northport, New York 11768. Telephone: 800-321-0994. Fax: 516-754-3362. E-mail: info@sailcaribbean.com. World Wide Web: http://www.sailcaribbean.com. Contact by e-mail, fax, mail, phone, or through World Wide Web site. Application deadline: continuous.

THE SOUTHWESTERN COMPANY, NEW YORK
See The Southwestern Company on page 297 for complete description.

STAGEDOOR MANOR THEATRE AND DANCE CAMP
KARMEL ROAD
LOCH SHELDRAKE, NEW YORK 12759

General Information Residential coeducational camp serving 240 campers in performing arts. Established in 1974. 25-acre facility located 95 miles from New York. Features: dormitory style hotel; indoor-outdoor pools; 7 on-campus theatres; rural setting by lake; two and a half hours from New York City; excellent technical facilities.

Profile of Summer Employees Total number: 127; typical ages: 24–35. 40% men; 60% women; 5% minorities; 25% college students; 50% non-U.S. citizens; 20% local applicants. Nonsmokers preferred.

Employment Information Openings are from June 18 to August 27. Jobs available: ▶ 3 *lifeguards* (minimum age 21) with ARC certification (will provide) at $2000 per season ▶ 2 *modeling instructors* (minimum age 21) with runway experience at $2000–$2500 per season ▶ 3 *nurses* (minimum age 21) with RN or LPN license at $3500–$4500 per season ▶ 6 *scenic designers* (minimum age 21) with theater experience at $2000–$2500 per season ▶ 10 *technicians* (minimum age 21) with theater experience at $1800–$2000 per season ▶ 2 *tennis counselors* (minimum age 21) with coaching experience at $1500–$1800 per season ▶ 4 *video counselors* (minimum age 21) with video experience at $1800–$2000 per season. Applicants must submit a letter of interest, resume, personal reference. A telephone interview is required. International applicants accepted.

Benefits and Preemployment Training Free housing, free meals, formal training, willing to provide letters of recommendation, names of contacts, on-the-job training, willing to complete paperwork for educational credit, willing to act as a professional reference, and opportunity to attend seminars/workshops. Preemployment training is required and includes accident prevention and safety, first aid, CPR, interpersonal skills, leadership skills.

Contact Konnie Kittrell, Production Director, Stagedoor Manor Theatre and Dance Camp, 651 Skyline Drive, Gatlinburg, Tennessee 37738. Fax: 865-436-3030. World Wide Web: http://www. stagedoormanor.com. Contact by fax or mail. No phone calls. Application deadline: May 15.

STUDENT CONSERVATION ASSOCIATION (SCA), NEW YORK

See Student Conservation Association (SCA), New Hampshire on page 200 for complete description.

SUMMER AT HAWTHORNE VALLEY FARM CAMP
327 CR 21C
GHENT, NEW YORK 12075

General Information A farm and nature camp experience for children ages 9 to 15 on a commercial biodynamic dairy farm. Established in 1972. 450-acre facility located 30 miles from Albany. Features: 450 acre working biodynamic dairy farm; market vegetable garden; wooded hiking trails; fresh water pond; health food store on premises.

Profile of Summer Employees Total number: 50; typical ages: 21–30. 25% men; 75% women; 1% minorities; 1% high school students; 97% college students; 1% local applicants. Nonsmokers required.

Employment Information Openings are from June 23 to August 17. Year-round positions also offered. Jobs available: ▶ 4 *boys dorm counselors* (minimum age 18) with interpersonal skills and experience working with groups of children at $1500 per season ▶ 2 *camp assistant cooks* with experience cooking with whole grains for at least 75 people at $2000–$2250 per season ▶ 4 *counselors in training* (minimum age 17) who enjoy outdoor activities and working with children at $750 per season ▶ 4 *field camp counselors* (minimum age 21) with interpersonal skills and experience working with groups of children at $1700 per season ▶ 4 *girls dorm counselors* (minimum age 18) with interpersonal skills and experience working with groups of children at $1500 per season ▶ 3 *specialty counselors in arts and crafts, archery, games* (minimum age 18) with interpersonal skills and experience working with groups of children at $1500 per season. Applicants must submit a formal organization application, letter of interest, resume, three personal references. An in-person interview is recommended, but a telephone interview is acceptable.

Benefits and Preemployment Training Free housing, free meals, willing to provide letters of recommendation, willing to complete paperwork for educational credit, and willing to act as a professional reference.

Contact Nick Franceschelli, Director, Summer at Hawthorne Valley Farm Camp. Telephone: 518-672-4790. Fax: 518-672-7608. E-mail: vsp@taconic.net. Contact by e-mail, fax, mail, or phone. Application deadline: continuous.

TIMBER LAKE WEST
BURNT HILL ROAD
ROSCOE, NEW YORK 12776
General Information Residential camp serving 320 campers in a traditional four-week program. Established in 1988. 320-acre facility located 120 miles from New York. Features: lake; 2 heated pools; main lodge; 6 tennis courts; movie theater; indoor gym.

Profile of Summer Employees Total number: 180; typical ages: 18–23. 50% men; 50% women; 4% high school students; 75% college students; 15% non-U.S. citizens; 1% local applicants. Nonsmokers preferred.

Employment Information Openings are from June 23 to August 24. Jobs available: ▶ 15 *arts and crafts instructors* (minimum age 18) at $1600 to $2000 per season plus $200 for travel over 350 miles ▶ 3 *boating instructors* (minimum age 18) with lifeguard certification at $1600 to $2000 per season plus $200 for travel over 350 miles ▶ 70 *general counselors* (minimum age 18) at $1600 to $2000 per season plus $200 for travel over 350 miles ▶ 8 *housekeeping/maintenance staff members* (minimum age 18) at $2000 per season ▶ 14 *kitchen staff members* (minimum age 18) at $2000 per season ▶ 6 *tennis instructors* (minimum age 18) at $1600 to $2000 per season plus $200 for travel over 350 miles ▶ 6 *water safety instructors* (minimum age 18) with WSI, first aid, lifeguard, and CPR certification at $1850 to $2250 per season plus $200 for travel over 350 miles. Applicants must submit formal organization application, two personal references, two letters of recommendation. An in-person interview is recommended, but a telephone interview is acceptable. International applicants accepted; must apply through a recognized agency.

Benefits and Preemployment Training Free housing, free meals, willing to provide letters of recommendation, names of contacts, on-the-job training, willing to complete paperwork for educational credit, willing to act as a professional reference, and travel reimbursement.

Contact Ms. Jennifer Despagna, Associate Director, Timber Lake West, 85 Crescent Beach Road, Glen Cove, New York 11542, United States. Telephone: 516-656-4210. Fax: 516-656-4215. E-mail: west@camptlc.com. World Wide Web: http://www.timberlakewest.com. Contact by e-mail, fax, mail, phone, or through World Wide Web site. Application deadline: continuous.

TIMBERLOCK VOYAGEURS
ROUTE 30
SABAEL, NEW YORK 12864
General Information Rustic family resort hosting 65 guests weekly in lakeside cabins. Also adventure camp for 9 boys and 9 girls in three-week sessions each. Established in 1964. 66-acre facility located 150 miles from Albany. Features: 15-mile long freshwater lake; wilderness setting; 4 tennis courts; canoes, sailboats, kayaks; 3900-foot mountain climb adjacent to property.

Profile of Summer Employees Total number: 16. 50% men; 50% women; 100% college students. Nonsmokers required.

Employment Information Openings are from June 16 to September 1. Jobs available: ▶ *guest services* at $300–$400 per week ▶ 2 *voyageur leaders* with first aid certification, backcountry experience, and children's camping experience at $350–$450 per week. Applicants must submit formal organization application, two personal references. An in-person interview is required. International applicants accepted; must obtain own visa, obtain own working papers, apply through a recognized agency.

Benefits and Preemployment Training Free housing, free meals, willing to provide letters of recommendation, and on-the-job training. Preemployment training is required and includes accident prevention and safety, interpersonal skills, leadership skills.

Contact Bruce Catlin, Director, Timberlock Voyageurs, 1735 Quaker Street, Lincoln, Vermont 05443. Telephone: 802-453-2540. Fax: 802-453-2548. E-mail: bruce@timberlock.com. World Wide Web: http://www.timberlock.com. Contact by e-mail, fax, mail, phone, or through World Wide Web site. Application deadline: continuous.

TRAILMARK OUTDOOR ADVENTURES
16 SCHUYLER ROAD
NYACK, NEW YORK 10960

General Information Travel adventure program in New England, the Northern Rockies, the Pacific Northwest, Southwest Colorado, and the Mid-Atlantic. Established in 1985.

Profile of Summer Employees Total number: 50; typical ages: 21–32. 50% men; 50% women; 30% college students. Nonsmokers required.

Employment Information Openings are from June 17 to August 20. Jobs available: ▶ 50 *trip leaders* (minimum age 21) with first aid/CPR, lifeguarding preferred; good interpersonal skills and experience working with children at $225–$300 per week. Applicants must submit a formal organization application, letter of interest, resume, three personal references. A telephone interview is required.

Benefits and Preemployment Training Free housing, free meals, health insurance, willing to provide letters of recommendation, on-the-job training, willing to complete paperwork for educational credit, and willing to act as a professional reference. Preemployment training is required and includes accident prevention and safety, first aid, CPR, interpersonal skills, leadership skills, lifeguarding.

Contact Rusty Pedersen, Director, Trailmark Outdoor Adventures, 16 Schuyler Road, Nyack, New York 10960. Telephone: 800-229-0262. Fax: 845-348-0437. E-mail: staff@trailmark.com. World Wide Web: http://www.trailmark.com. Contact by e-mail, fax, phone, or through World Wide Web site. Application deadline: continuous.

WEISSMAN TEEN TOURS
517 ALMENA AVENUE
ARDSLEY, NEW YORK 10502-2127

General Information Owner-operated and escorted personalized activity oriented student travel program in the United States, Western Canada, Hawaii, and Europe. All deluxe and first class hotels and resorts. Established in 1974.

Profile of Summer Employees Total number: 14; typical ages: 21–29. 50% men; 50% women; 50% local applicants. Nonsmokers required.

Employment Information Openings are from June 29 to August 23. Year-round positions also offered. Jobs available: ▶ 3 *tour leaders—Hawaii/LA/cruise to Mexico* (minimum age 21) with experience working with teenagers, CPR, and first aid at $100 per week ▶ 7 *tour leaders-Europe* (minimum age 21) with proficiency in French and/or Italian, background in art history (preferred), experience working with teenagers, CPR, and first aid at $100 per week ▶ 7 *tour leaders-U.S./Western Canada* (minimum age 21) with experience working with teenagers, CPR, and first aid at $100 per week. Applicants must submit a formal organization application, letter of interest, resume, three personal references, three letters of recommendation. An in-person interview is required. International applicants accepted; must obtain own visa, obtain own working papers.

Benefits and Preemployment Training Free housing, free meals, formal training, possible full-time employment, on-the-job training, willing to act as a professional reference, and first class travel. Preemployment training is required and includes accident prevention and safety, interpersonal skills, leadership skills.

Contact Ronee Weissman, Owner/Director, Weissman Teen Tours, 517 Almena Avenue, Ardsley, New York 10502. Telephone: 914-693-7575. Fax: 914-693-4807. E-mail: wtt@cloud9.net. World

Wide Web: http://www.weissmantours.com. Contact by e-mail, fax, mail, phone, or through World Wide Web site. Application deadline: continuous.

WESTCOAST CONNECTION TRAVEL CAMP
154 EAST BOSTON POST ROAD
MAMARONECK, NEW YORK 10543

General Information Travel programs in the United States, western Canada, Europe, Australia, and Israel for students ages 13–19, including active teen tours and outdoor adventure trips. Established in 1982.

Profile of Summer Employees Total number: 160; typical ages: 21–35. 50% men; 50% women; 80% college students. Nonsmokers required.

Employment Information Openings are from June 20 to August 25. Jobs available: ▶ *tour staff members/leaders* (minimum age 20) with experience working with teens; driver's license (CDL for some trips); CPR, lifeguard, first aid, WSI, and lifeguard certification preferred at $75–$600 per week. Applicants must submit a formal organization application, three personal references. An in-person interview is required. International applicants accepted; must obtain own visa, obtain own working papers.

Benefits and Preemployment Training Free housing, free meals, formal training, possible full-time employment, willing to provide letters of recommendation, on-the-job training, willing to complete paperwork for educational credit, willing to act as a professional reference, opportunity to attend seminars/workshops, and travel reimbursement. Preemployment training is required and includes accident prevention and safety, first aid, interpersonal skills, leadership skills, organizational skills.

Contact Jason Tanner, Director, Westcoast Connection Travel Camp, 154 East Boston Post Road, Mamaroneck, New York 10543. Telephone: 914-835-0699. Fax: 914-835-0798. E-mail: usa@westcoastconnection.com. World Wide Web: http://www.westcoastconnection.com. Contact by e-mail, fax, mail, phone, or through World Wide Web site. Application deadline: continuous.

YMCA CAMPING SERVICES–CAMPS GREENKILL/ MCALISTER/TALCOTT
300 BIG POND ROAD
HUGUENOT, NEW YORK 12746

General Information Two traditional residential summer camps and one year-round facility serving general population. Camp McAlister serves ages 6–11, Camp Talcott serves ages 11–15, and Camp Greenkill is home to specialized programs. Established in 1924. 1,000-acre facility located 90 miles from New York. Features: 3 freshwater lakes; 7 tennis courts; 5 basketball courts; new environmental education building and auditorium; wooded setting; 5 miles of hiking trails through all types of terrain.

Profile of Summer Employees Total number: 140; typical ages: 18–25. 50% men; 50% women; 30% minorities; 8% high school students; 60% college students; 35% non-U.S. citizens; 10% local applicants.

Employment Information Openings are from June 15 to August 23. Winter break and year-round positions also offered. Jobs available: ▶ *athletic, arts and crafts, and nature specialists* with experience working with children and supervising staff in a camping or residential environment required at $190 per week ▶ *cabin counselors* (minimum age 18) at $170 per week ▶ *maintenance workers* with experience in light maintenance work required and experience working with children preferred at $180 per week ▶ 2 *nurses* with RN, LPN, or EMT with CPR and first aid certification at $700 per week ▶ *secretary* with experience working with children preferred, basic knowledge of MS Word and Excel required at $170 per week ▶ *village director* with experience working with children and supervising staff, preferably in a camping or residential environment at $210 per week ▶ *waterfront director* (minimum age 21) with WSI, PSI, LGT, and CPR/FPR; experience working in an aquatic program or facility at $250 per week. Applicants must submit formal organization application, three personal references, (cover letter and resume not required but recommended). A telephone interview is required. International applicants accepted; must apply through a recognized agency.

Benefits and Preemployment Training Free housing, free meals, formal training, possible full-time employment, on-the-job training, willing to complete paperwork for educational credit, opportunity to attend seminars/workshops, and possible partial travel reimbursement; children of camp nurses may attend overnight programs for free. Preemployment training is required and includes accident prevention and safety, first aid, CPR, interpersonal skills, leadership skills, lifeguarding, high ropes.

Contact Chris Scheuer, Director of Camping, YMCA Camping Services–Camps Greenkill/McAlister/Talcott, 300 Big Pond Road, Huguenot, New York 12746. Telephone: 845-858-2200. Fax: 845-858-7823. E-mail: cscheuer@ymcanyc.org. World Wide Web: http://www.ymcanyc.org/camps. Contact by e-mail, fax, mail, phone, or through World Wide Web site. Application deadline: continuous.

NORTH CAROLINA

A CHRISTIAN MINISTRY IN THE NATIONAL PARKS– NORTH CAROLINA
See A Christian Ministry in the National Parks–Maine on page 107 for complete description.

BIKINGX
1410 TUNNEL ROAD, PO BOX 9913
ASHEVILLE, NORTH CAROLINA 28815
General Information Mountain biking and touring programs for 12 to 16 year-old students divided by age and ability; multi-adventure programs also offered.

Profile of Summer Employees Total number: 20; typical ages: 25–27. 60% men; 40% women; 60% college students; 10% local applicants. Nonsmokers required.

Employment Information Openings are from June 18 to August 18. Jobs available: ▶ 10–15 *trip leaders–mountain biking or touring* (minimum age 21) with a love of biking and working with students at $50–$60 per day. Applicants must submit a formal organization application, letter of interest, resume. A telephone interview is required.

Benefits and Preemployment Training Free housing, free meals, formal training, willing to provide letters of recommendation, willing to complete paperwork for educational credit, and willing to act as a professional reference. Preemployment training is required and includes accident prevention and safety, first aid, interpersonal skills, leadership skills, biking policy and procedures, lifeguard training.

Contact Fiona McColley, Director, BikingX; PO Box 9913, Asheville, North Carolina 28815. Fax: 828-296-9960. E-mail: info@bikingx.com. World Wide Web: http://www.bikingx.com. Contact by e-mail or through World Wide Web site. No phone calls. Application deadline: continuous.

CAMP CHOSATONGA FOR BOYS
2500 MORGAN MILL ROAD
BREVARD, NORTH CAROLINA 28712

General Information Traditional residential summer camp in the Blue Ridge Mountains of North Carolina with wholesome, dedicated, trained staff which helps to develop lifetime friendships and skills, and a sister camp, Camp Kahdalea for Girls. Established in 1977. 210-acre facility located 25 miles from Asheville. Features: strong in-camp and wilderness programs; only 2 sessions per summer; lake; Christian ideals; 3:1 camper to staff ratio; surrounded on 3 sides by Pisgah National Forest.

Profile of Summer Employees Total number: 30; typical ages: 18–25. 100% men; 1% minorities; 100% college students. Nonsmokers preferred.

Employment Information Openings are from May 24 to August 15. Jobs available: ▶ 15–30 *counselors* (minimum age 18) with at least one year of college completed at $1000–$1300 per season. Applicants must submit a formal organization application, letter of interest, three personal references. A telephone interview is required. International applicants accepted; must obtain own visa, obtain own working papers.

Benefits and Preemployment Training Free housing, free meals, formal training, possible full-time employment, willing to provide letters of recommendation, on-the-job training, willing to complete paperwork for educational credit, and willing to act as a professional reference. Preemployment training is required and includes accident prevention and safety, first aid, CPR, interpersonal skills, leadership skills, wilderness first aid.

Contact Mr. David Trufant, Owner/Director, Camp Chosatonga for Boys. Telephone: 828-884-6834. Fax: 828-884-6834. E-mail: office@kahdalea.com. World Wide Web: http://www.chosatonga.com. Contact by e-mail, fax, mail, phone, or through World Wide Web site. Application deadline: continuous.

CAMP HIGH ROCKS
GREENVILLE HIGHWAY
CEDAR MOUNTAIN, NORTH CAROLINA 28718

General Information Small residential boys camp focusing on development of skills in a non-competitive environment. There is a strong emphasis on outdoor adventure programming with many off-site trips. Established in 1958. 1,100-acre facility located 8 miles from Brevard. Features: freshwater lake; 50-foot climbing tower; 3 tennis courts; 2 activity fields; 29-stall barn facility; wooded mountainous setting.

Profile of Summer Employees Total number: 65; typical ages: 19–26. 67% men; 33% women; 80% college students. Nonsmokers required.

Employment Information Openings are from June 4 to August 12. Jobs available: ▶ 2 *athletics/ tennis instructors* at $220–$280 per week ▶ 6 *backpacking instructors* at $220–$280 per week ▶ 23 *cabin counselor/skill instructors* at $220–$280 per week ▶ 3 *crafts instructors* at $220–$280 per week ▶ 8 *horseback riding instructors* at $220–$280 per week ▶ 4 *mountain biking instructors* at $220–$280 per week ▶ 2 *pottery instructors* at $220–$280 per week ▶ 7 *rock climbing instructors* at $220–$280 per week ▶ 3 *ropes course facilitators* at $220–$280 per week ▶ 3 *swimming instructors* with WSI certification or lifeguard certification at $220–$280 per week ▶ 7 *white-water canoeing instructors* at $220–$280 per week. Applicants must submit formal organization application, three personal references. An in-person interview is recommended, but a telephone interview is acceptable. International applicants accepted; must apply through a recognized agency.

Benefits and Preemployment Training Free housing, free meals, willing to complete paperwork for educational credit, and opportunity to attend seminars/workshops. Preemployment training is required and includes accident prevention and safety, first aid, interpersonal skills, leadership skills, wilderness first aid, rock rescue, and white-water instructor.

Contact Henry Birdsong, Camp Director, Camp High Rocks, PO Box 210, Cedar Mountain, North Carolina 28718. Telephone: 828-885-2153. Fax: 828-884-4612. E-mail: mail@highrocks. com. World Wide Web: http://www.highrocks.com. Contact by e-mail, fax, mail, phone, or through World Wide Web site. Application deadline: continuous.

CAMP KAHDALEA FOR GIRLS
2500 MORGAN MILL ROAD
BREVARD, NORTH CAROLINA 28712

General Information Traditional residential summer camp in the Blue Ridge Mountains of North Carolina, with a wholesome, dedicated, trained staff that helps develop lifetime friend-ships and skills; brother camp is Camp Chosatonga (for boys). Established in 1962. 210-acre facility located 25 miles from Asheville. Features: strong in-camp and wilderness programs; only 2 sessions per summer; lake; Christian ideals; 3:1 camper to staff ratio; surrounded on 3 sides by Pisgah National Forest.

Profile of Summer Employees Total number: 55; typical ages: 18–25. 1% men; 99% women; 1% minorities; 100% college students. Nonsmokers preferred.

Employment Information Openings are from May 24 to August 15. Jobs available: ► 1–3 *barn management* (minimum age 20) with previous barn management and horseback riding teaching experience per season at $1,500 to $2,500 per season, negotiable based on experience ► 30–50 *counselors* (minimum age 18) with at least one year of college completed at $1000–$1300 per season ► 1–5 *kitchen helpers* (minimum age 18) with previous cooking experience at $1000–$1600 per month. Applicants must submit a formal organization application, letter of interest, three personal references. A telephone interview is required. International applicants accepted; must obtain own visa, obtain own working papers.

Benefits and Preemployment Training Free housing, free meals, formal training, possible full-time employment, willing to provide letters of recommendation, on-the-job training, willing to complete paperwork for educational credit, and willing to act as a professional reference. Preemployment training is required and includes accident prevention and safety, first aid, CPR, interpersonal skills, leadership skills, wilderness first aid.

Contact Anne Trufant, Owner/Director, Camp Kahdalea for Girls. Telephone: 828-884-6834. Fax: 828-884-6834. E-mail: office@kahdalea.com. World Wide Web: http://www.kahdalea.com. Contact by e-mail, fax, mail, phone, or through World Wide Web site. Application deadline: continuous.

CAMP MERRIE-WOODE
100 MERRIE-WOODE ROAD
SAPPHIRE, NORTH CAROLINA 28774

General Information A residential girls summer camp dedicated to building self-esteem and confidence through traditional camp and high adventure activities. Established in 1919. 250-acre facility located 60 miles from Asheville. Features: location in mountains of Western North Carolina, 3500-foot elevation; 1-mile-long freshwater lake; covered riding arena; 3 tennis courts; gym; indoor climbing wall; rustic cabins.

Profile of Summer Employees Total number: 80; typical ages: 19–25. 10% men; 90% women; 90% college students. Nonsmokers preferred.

Employment Information Openings are from May 31 to August 11. Jobs available: ► *archery staff members* (minimum age 19) at a salary commensurate with age and experience beginning at $235 per week; all wages paid at the end of the season, but weekly advances may be drawn on request ► *arts/crafts staff members* (minimum age 19) at a salary commensurate with age and experience beginning at $235 per week; all wages paid at the end of the season, but weekly advances may be drawn on request ► *canoeing and kayaking staff members* (minimum age 19) with lifeguard/river rescue/first aid certification and experience at a salary commensurate with age and experience beginning at $235 per week; all wages paid at the end of the season, but weekly advances may be drawn on request ▶ *ceramics staff members* (minimum age 19) with experience in the field at a salary commensurate with age and experience beginning at $235 per week; all wages paid at the end of the season, but weekly advances may be drawn on request ▶ *land sports staff members* (minimum age 19) at a salary commensurate with age and experience beginning at $235 per week; all wages paid at the end of the season, but weekly advances may be drawn on request ▶ *mountaineering staff members* (minimum age 20) with experience in the field, WFR, and WFA at a salary commensurate with age and experience beginning at $235 per week; all wages paid at the end of the season, but weekly advances may be drawn on request ▶ *nature staff members* (minimum age 19) at a salary commensurate with age and experience beginning at $235 per week; all wages paid at the end of the season, but weekly advances may be drawn on request ▶ *performing arts staff members* (minimum age 19) with experience in the field at a salary commensurate with age and experience beginning at $235 per week; all wages paid at the end of the season, but weekly advances may be drawn on request ▶ *photography staff members* (minimum age 19) with black and white dark room experience at a salary commensurate with age and experience beginning at $235 per week; all wages paid at the end of the season, but weekly advances may be drawn on request ▶ *riding staff members* (minimum age 19) with strong riding skills and technique; some barn work and grooming required at a salary commensurate with age and experience beginning at $235 per week; all wages paid at the end of the season, but weekly advances may be drawn on request ▶ *rock climbing staff members* (minimum age 21) with strong leadership and organizational skills; orienteering, first aid, strong climbing and backpacking skills; college degree preferred for head position; WFR, WFA at a salary commensurate with age and experience beginning at $235 per week; all wages paid at the end of the season, but weekly advances may be drawn on request ▶ *sailing staff members* (minimum age 19) with lifeguard certification and experience at a salary commensurate with age and experience beginning at $235 per week; all wages paid at the end of the season, but weekly advances may be drawn on request ▶ *swimming staff members* (minimum age 19) with lifeguard and WSI certification at a salary commensurate with age and experience beginning at $235 per week; all wages paid at the end of the season, but weekly advances may be drawn on request ▶ *tennis staff members* (minimum age 19) with experience at a salary commensurate with age and experience beginning at $235 per week; all wages paid at the end of the season, but weekly advances may be drawn on request ▶ *weaving staff members* (minimum age 19) with experience weaving on floor looms at a salary commensurate with age and experience beginning at $235 per week; all wages paid at the end of the season, but weekly advances may be drawn on request ▶ *woodworking staff members* (minimum age 21) with experience in the field at a salary commensurate with age and experience beginning at $235 per week; all wages paid at the end of the season, but weekly advances may be drawn on request. Applicants must submit formal organization application, three writing samples, three personal references. An in-person interview is recommended, but a telephone interview is acceptable. International applicants accepted; must apply through a recognized agency.

Benefits and Preemployment Training Free housing, free meals, willing to provide letters of recommendation, willing to complete paperwork for educational credit, willing to act as a professional reference, opportunity to attend seminars/workshops, and free laundry service. Preemployment training is required and includes accident prevention and safety, first aid, interpersonal skills, leadership skills.

Contact Ms. Denice Dunn, Director, Camp Merrie-Woode, 100 Merrie-Woode Road, Sapphire, North Carolina 28774. Telephone: 828-743-3300. Fax: 828-743-5846. E-mail: denice@ merriewoode.com. World Wide Web: http://www.merriewoode.com. Contact by e-mail, mail, phone, or through World Wide Web site. Application deadline: continuous.

CAMP SKY RANCH, INC.
634 SKY RANCH ROAD
BLOWING ROCK, NORTH CAROLINA 28605-9738

General Information Coed private residential camp serving 100 mentally disabled children and adults in three 2-week sessions. Campers must be able to walk, dress, and feed themselves, as well as take care of their toilet needs. Established in 1948. 145-acre facility located 100 miles from Charlotte. Features: freshwater lake; mountain setting; heated swimming pool; cool nights; creeks.

Profile of Summer Employees Total number: 20; typical ages: 18–25. 45% men; 55% women; 10% minorities; 20% high school students; 80% college students; 15% local applicants. Nonsmokers preferred.

Employment Information Openings are from June 10 to July 26. Jobs available: ▶ 22 *counselors/ activity leaders* (minimum age 19) at $120–$170 per week ▶ 2 *lifeguards* (minimum age 19) with lifeguard training at $120–$180 per week ▶ 1 *waterfront director* with Red Cross certification at $130–$180 per week. Applicants must submit a formal organization application, three personal references. An in-person interview is recommended, but a telephone interview is acceptable.

Benefits and Preemployment Training Free housing, free meals, willing to provide letters of recommendation, and willing to complete paperwork for educational credit. Preemployment training is required and includes accident prevention and safety, interpersonal skills, working with special children.

Contact Jack L. Sharp, Director, Camp Sky Ranch, Inc., 634 Sky Ranch Road, Blowing Rock, North Carolina 28605-9738. Telephone: 828-264-8600. Fax: 828-265-2339. E-mail: jsharpl@ triad.rr.com. World Wide Web: http://www.campskyranch.com. Contact by e-mail, fax, mail, or phone. Application deadline: continuous.

CAMPS MONDAMIN AND GREEN COVE
1 MONDAMIN ROAD
TUXEDO, NORTH CAROLINA 28784

General Information Residential camps focusing on noncompetitive, lifetime, and outdoor skills with an emphasis on extended trips. Established in 1922. 800-acre facility located 6 miles from Hendersonville. Features: freshwater lake; location in mountains; 800 acres of trails; near Smoky Mountains; tennis courts; climbing tower; horseback riding facilities.

Profile of Summer Employees Total number: 175; typical ages: 19–30. 50% men; 50% women; 2% minorities; 60% college students; 5% retirees; 2% non-U.S. citizens; 5% local applicants. Nonsmokers required.

Employment Information Openings are from June 1 to August 18. Jobs available: ▶ 2 *crafts and games instructors* (minimum age 18) with archery and riflery experience at $2000–$2500 per season ▶ 4 *horseback riding instructors* (minimum age 18) with hunter-style riding and barn experience at $2000–$2500 per season ▶ 2 *mountain biking instructors* (minimum age 18) with camping experience and mechanical expertise at $2000–$2500 per season ▶ 6 *mountaineering instructors (hiking, rock climbing)* (minimum age 21) at $2000–$2600 per season ▶ 2 *sailing instructors* (minimum age 18) with experience at $2000–$2500 per season ▶ 4 *swimming instructors* (minimum age 18) with ARC lifeguard and WSI at $2000–$2500 per season ▶ 2 *tennis instructors* (minimum age 18) with experience at $2000–$2500 per season. Applicants must submit formal organization application, five personal references. An in-person interview is recommended, but a telephone interview is acceptable. International applicants accepted; must apply through a recognized agency.

Benefits and Preemployment Training Free housing, free meals, willing to provide letters of recommendation, on-the-job training, willing to complete paperwork for educational credit, willing to act as a professional reference, and opportunity to attend seminars/workshops.

Preemployment training is required and includes accident prevention and safety, first aid, CPR, interpersonal skills, leadership skills, ARC lifeguard, WSI, WMA wilderness advanced first aid, ARC first aid.

Contact Frank Bell, Director, Camps Mondamin and Green Cove, PO Box 8, Tuxedo, North Carolina 28784. Telephone: 828-693-7446. Fax: 828-696-8895. E-mail: mondamin@mondamin. com. World Wide Web: http://www.mondamin.com. Contact by e-mail, fax, mail, or phone. Application deadline: continuous.

CYBERCAMPS–NORTH CAROLINA STATE
RALEIGH, NORTH CAROLINA
See Cybercamps–University of Washington on page 326 for complete description.

CYBERCAMPS–UNC, CHAPEL HILL
CHAPEL HILL, NORTH CAROLINA
See Cybercamps–University of Washington on page 326 for complete description.

DUKE YOUTH PROGRAMS–DUKE UNIVERSITY CONTINUING EDUCATION
203 BISHOP'S HOUSE, BOX 90702
DURHAM, NORTH CAROLINA 27708
General Information Summer academic enrichment programs serving approximately 650 middle and high school students. Established in 1982. 20 miles from Raleigh. Features: university campus.

Profile of Summer Employees Total number: 50; typical ages: 19–24. 40% men; 60% women; 50% college students. Nonsmokers preferred.

Employment Information Openings are from June 5 to August 5. Jobs available: ▶ 14–16 *residential counselors* (minimum age 19) with good driving records at $2000–$2400 per season. Applicants must submit a formal organization application, letter of interest, resume, two personal references, two letters of recommendation. An in-person interview is recommended, but a telephone interview is acceptable.

Benefits and Preemployment Training Free housing, free meals, formal training, willing to provide letters of recommendation, on-the-job training, and willing to act as a professional reference. Preemployment training is required and includes accident prevention and safety, first aid, interpersonal skills, leadership skills, van driving, programming.

Contact Dr. Sarah Collie, Director, Youth Program, Duke Youth Programs–Duke University Continuing Education, Box 90702, Durham, North Carolina 27708. Telephone: 919-684-6259. Fax: 919-681-8235. E-mail: scollie@duke.edu. World Wide Web: http://www.learnmore.duke. edu/youth. Contact by e-mail, mail, or phone. Application deadline: February 15.

EAGLE'S NEST CAMP
43 HART ROAD
PISGAH FOREST, NORTH CAROLINA 28768
General Information Residential camp serving 185 campers in three 3-week sessions. Experiential education for young people, promoting the natural world and the betterment of human character. Specializes in wilderness adventure and the arts. Established in 1927. 175-acre facility located 30 miles from Asheville. Features: freshwater lakes; tennis courts; open air cabins with hot and cold running water; climbing tower; wooded setting; 12-stall barn and horses.

Profile of Summer Employees Total number: 80; typical ages: 19–26. 50% men; 50% women; 1% minorities; 80% college students; 3% non-U.S. citizens; 1% local applicants. Nonsmokers required.

Employment Information Openings are from May 15 to August 11. Year-round positions also offered. Jobs available: ▶ 5–8 *arts instructors* (minimum age 19) with creativity, teaching experience, CPR, and basic first aid certification at $160–$250 per week ▶ 5–8 *athletics instructors* (minimum age 19) with CPR, first aid, and experience working with children at $160–$250 per week ▶ 6–8 *canoeing instructors* (minimum age 19) with experience or American Canoe Association Instructor, CPR, and basic first aid certification at $160–$250 per week ▶ 4 *horseback instructors* (minimum age 19) with CPR and basic first aid certification and experience in the field at $160–$250 per week ▶ *kitchen staff* (minimum age 18) with experience in whole foods cooking at $160–$250 per week ▶ *medical staff members* should be RN, NP, PA, or MD with CPR certification at $200 to $300 per week or tuition exchange for camper ▶ 6–10 *rock climbing instructors* (minimum age 19) with CPR and basic first aid (minimum) and experience in the field at $160–$300 per week ▶ 4–6 *swimming instructors* (minimum age 19) with WSI, LGT, CPR, and basic first aid certification; teaching and/or lifeguarding experience at $160–$250 per week ▶ 10 *wilderness instructors* (minimum age 19) with wilderness first aid, CPR, basic first aid certification, and experience leading groups in the field at $160–$300 per week. Applicants must submit formal organization application, two personal references, personal statement (with application). A telephone interview is required. International applicants accepted; must apply through a recognized agency.

Benefits and Preemployment Training Free housing, free meals, formal training, possible full-time employment, willing to provide letters of recommendation, on-the-job training, willing to complete paperwork for educational credit, willing to act as a professional reference, opportunity to attend seminars/workshops, and limited health coverage. Preemployment training is required and includes accident prevention and safety, interpersonal skills, leadership skills.

Contact Ms. Paige Lester-Niles, Associate Director, Eagle's Nest Camp, 633 Summit Street, Winston-Salem, North Carolina 27101. Telephone: 336-761-1040. Fax: 336-727-0030. E-mail: paige@enf.org. World Wide Web: http://www.enf.org. Contact by e-mail, mail, phone, or through World Wide Web site. Application deadline: continuous.

FALLING CREEK CAMP FOR BOYS
PO BOX 98
TUXEDO, NORTH CAROLINA 28784

General Information Privately owned camp in the western North Carolina mountains providing boys ages 7–16 with opportunity for growth and fun. Established in 1969. 1,000-acre facility located 12 miles from Hendersonville. Features: dining hall; lodge; 34 camper cabins; athletic field; tennis courts; secluded mountain setting.

Profile of Summer Employees Total number: 100; typical ages: 19–25. 90% men; 10% women; 90% college students; 10% non-U.S. citizens. Nonsmokers preferred.

Employment Information Openings are from May 30 to August 16. Jobs available: ▶ 2 *Indian lore counselors* (minimum age 19) with knowledge of Indian lore at $2100–$2300 per season ▶ 2 *archery instructors* (minimum age 19) with experience in the field and archery instructor certification (on-site certification available) at $2100–$2300 per season ▶ 3–4 *arts and crafts instructors* (minimum age 19) at $2100–$2300 per season ▶ 4 *camp nurses* (minimum age 21) with RN (North Carolina) at $3500–$4500 per season ▶ 4–5 *canoeing staff members* (minimum age 19) with experience in white water in closed and open boats; American Canoeing Association whitewater instructor certification at $2100–$2300 per season ▶ 2 *horseback riding staff members* (minimum age 19) with experience in English-saddle instruction at $2100–$2300 per season ▶ 4 *land sports counselors* (minimum age 19) with experience in soccer, lacrosse, or basketball at $2100–$2300 per season ▶ 2–4 *mountain biking instructors* (minimum age 20) with mountain biking and bike maintenance experience at $2100–$2300 per season ▶ 4–6 *mountaineering staff members* (minimum age 19) with experience in rock climbing and backpacking trips at $2100–$2300 per season ▶ 2 *nature counselors* (minimum age 19) with background in biology, zoology, or ecology at $2100–$2300 per season ▶ 2 *riflery instructors* (minimum age

19) with experience in the field and riflery instructor certification (on-site certification available) at $2100–$2300 per season ▶ 2–3 *sailing instructors* (minimum age 19) with sailing experience and lifeguard certification at $2100–$2300 per season ▶ 5 *swimming instructors* (minimum age 19) with WSI and lifeguard certification at $2100–$2300 per season ▶ 4–6 *tennis instructors* (minimum age 19) with experience at $2100–$2300 per season. Applicants must submit formal organization application, three personal references. An in-person interview is required. International applicants accepted; must apply through a recognized agency.

Benefits and Preemployment Training Free housing, free meals, willing to provide letters of recommendation, on-the-job training, willing to complete paperwork for educational credit, willing to act as a professional reference, and opportunity to attend seminars/workshops. Preemployment training is required and includes accident prevention and safety, first aid, CPR, interpersonal skills, leadership skills.

Contact Donnie Bain, Director, Falling Creek Camp for Boys, PO Box 98, Tuxedo, North Carolina 28784. Telephone: 704-692-0262. Fax: 704-696-1616. E-mail: mail@fallingcreek.com. World Wide Web: http://www.fallingcreek.com. Contact by e-mail, fax, mail, phone, or through World Wide Web site. Application deadline: continuous.

GRANDY FARM MARKET
PO BOX 673
GRANDY, NORTH CAROLINA 27939

General Information Retail fresh fruits and vegetables, bakery goods, and frozen yogurt in an open farm market on a farm setting catering to the tourists on their way to the beaches of the Outerbanks of North Carolina. Established in 1987. Located 50 miles from Norfolk,Virginia. Features: near the beach; farm setting; frozen yogurt stand.

Profile of Summer Employees Total number: 30; typical ages: 16–24. 25% men; 75% women; 30% high school students; 25% college students; 10% retirees; 35% non-U.S. citizens. Nonsmokers required.

Employment Information Openings are from April 1 to October 31. Jobs available: ▶ 4 *general staff positions* (minimum age 18) with supermarket experience at $5.15–$5.50 per hour. International applicants accepted; must obtain own visa, apply through a recognized agency.

Benefits and Preemployment Training Meals at a cost, free housing, willing to provide letters of recommendation, on-the-job training, willing to complete paperwork for educational credit, and willing to act as a professional reference.

Contact Colon Grandy, Jr., Owner, Grandy Farm Market, PO Box 673, Grandy, North Carolina 27939. Telephone: 252-453-2658. Application deadline: continuous.

KEYSTONE CAMP
CASHIERS VALLEY ROAD
BREVARD, NORTH CAROLINA 28712

General Information A camp for girls (ages 7–17) offering programs in horsemanship, daily horseback riding, tennis, land sports, water sports on two lakes, gymnastics, rock climbing, and hiking in Pisgah National Forest. Established in 1916. 80-acre facility located 30 miles from Asheville. Features: 2 lakes; climbing wall; 4 tennis courts; low ropes course; 3 riding rings; beautiful wooded setting.

Profile of Summer Employees Total number: 40; typical ages: 18–30. 10% men; 90% women; 20% minorities; 100% college students; 30% non-U.S. citizens. Nonsmokers preferred.

Employment Information Openings are from June 1 to August 8. Jobs available: ▶ 1 *adventure programs director* (minimum age 18) at $2500–$4000 per season ▶ 1 *aerobics instructor* (minimum age 18) at $1800–$3000 per season ▶ 1 *archery instructor* (minimum age 18) at $1800–$3000 per season ▶ 3 *art instructors* (minimum age 18) at $1800–$3000 per season ▶ 1 *badminton instructor* (minimum age 18) at $1800–$3000 per season ▶ 2 *canoeing instructors* (minimum age 18) with lifeguard certification at $1800–$3000 per season ▶ 1 *dance instructor* (minimum age 18) at $1800–$3000 per season ▶ *dramatics instructor* (minimum age 18) at $1800–$3000 per season ▶ 3 *hiking and camping instructors* (minimum age 18) at $1800–$3000 per season ▶ *nature instructor* (minimum age 18) at $1800–$3000 per season ▶ *riding instructor* (minimum age 18) at $1800–$3000 per season ▶ 1 *riflery instructor* (minimum age 18) at $1800–$3000 per season ▶ 2 *rock climbing instructors* (minimum age 18) with belay skills at $1800–$3000 per season ▶ *stable helper* (minimum age 18) at $1800–$3000 per season ▶ *swimming instructor* (minimum age 18) with WSI and/or lifeguard certification at $1800–$3000 per season ▶ *team instructors* (minimum age 18) at $1800–$3000 per season ▶ 3 *tennis instructors* (minimum age 18) at $1800–$3000 per season. Applicants must submit formal organization application, three personal references, personal essay. An in-person interview is recommended, but a telephone interview is acceptable. International applicants accepted; must apply through a recognized agency.

Benefits and Preemployment Training Free housing, free meals, formal training, willing to provide letters of recommendation, on-the-job training, willing to complete paperwork for educational credit, willing to act as a professional reference, and opportunity to attend seminars/workshops. Preemployment training is required and includes accident prevention and safety, first aid, CPR, interpersonal skills, leadership skills, other certification training (as necessary and available).

Contact Ms. Amy N. Lindsay, Staff Director, Keystone Camp, PO Box 829, Brevard, North Carolina 28712. Telephone: 828-884-9125. Fax: 828-883-8234. E-mail: amy@keystonecamp. com. World Wide Web: http://www.keystonecamp.com. Contact by e-mail, fax, mail, phone, or through World Wide Web site. Application deadline: continuous.

NANTAHALA OUTDOOR CENTER
13077 HIGHWAY 19 WEST
BRYSON CITY, NORTH CAROLINA 28713

General Information One of the nation's largest outdoor recreation outfitters which rafts six white-water rivers, offers canoe and kayak instruction, adventure travel programs, ropes course, outfitter's store, and two restaurants. Established in 1972. Located 75 miles from Asheville. Features: whitewater rivers; Great Smoky Mountains National Park; mountain and road biking; outfitter's store; 2 restaurants; staff housing.

Profile of Summer Employees Total number: 550; typical ages: 20–45. 55% men; 45% women. Nonsmokers preferred.

Employment Information Openings are from April 15 to October 31. Jobs available: ▶ 4–7 *bike shop sales/mechanics* (minimum age 18) with previous work experience and extensive product knowledge at $5.50–$6.50 per hour ▶ 18–40 *guest relations sales agents* (minimum age 18) with exceptional communications skills and basic computer knowledge at $5.15–$6 per hour ▶ 4–7 *housekeepers* (minimum age 18) at $5.50–$7 per hour ▶ 12–26 *outfitter's store/retail sales people* (minimum age 18) with previous related work experience and extensive product knowledge at $5.15–$6 per hour ▶ 1–4 *outpost cooks* (minimum age 18) with previous related work experience and valid driver's license at $5.50–$7 per hour ▶ 8–16 *photographers/photo sales* (minimum age 18) with basic computer skills and solid camera skills at $5.15–$6 per hour ▶ 6–12 *prep/line cooks* (minimum age 18) with previous related work experience and solid knife skills at $5.50–$7 per hour ▶ 50–100 *raft guides* (minimum age 18) with previous experience and current CPR and first aid at $5.15–$6 per hour ▶ 16–40 *servers* (minimum age 18) with previous related work experience at $2.13 per hour plus tips. Applicants must submit formal organization application. A telephone interview is required. International applicants accepted; must obtain own visa, obtain own working papers, apply through a recognized agency.

Benefits and Preemployment Training Housing at a cost, meals at a cost, health insurance, on-the-job training, willing to act as a professional reference, opportunity to attend seminars/

workshops, and 401K available after career level of service reached. Preemployment training is required and includes accident prevention and safety, interpersonal skills, guest service excellence training.

Contact Recruiter, Nantahala Outdoor Center. Fax: 828-488-2498. E-mail: work@noc.com. World Wide Web: http://www.noc.com. Contact by e-mail or through World Wide Web site. No phone calls. Application deadline: continuous (application processing begins in January, hiring between March and May).

NORTH BEACH SAILING/BARRIER ISLAND SAILING CENTER
BOX 8279
DUCK, NORTH CAROLINA 27949

General Information Sailing center specializing in rental and sale of windsurfing, sailing, and jet ski equipment and teaching proper use of this equipment. Offers a line of clothing for enthusiasts. Also offers parasailing and kayak eco-tours. Established in 1984. 75 miles from Virginia Beach, Virginia. Features: ocean beaches; flat water sailing on Currituck Sound.

Profile of Summer Employees Total number: 20; typical ages: 20–25. 50% men; 50% women; 10% minorities; 5% high school students; 40% college students; 40% non-U.S. citizens; 5% local applicants. Nonsmokers required.

Employment Information Openings are from May 15 to October 15. Jobs available: ▶ 4–6 *parasail mates* with boating experience at $300–$400 per week ▶ 4–5 *parasailing instructors/captains* with Coast Guard Master license at $750–$950 per week ▶ 6 *pool and spa service technicians* with CPO, will train at $250–$350 per week ▶ 8 *rental/desk persons* with knowledge of parasailing, will train at $250–$350 per week. Applicants must submit resume, two personal references. A telephone interview is required. International applicants accepted; must obtain own visa, obtain own working papers.

Benefits and Preemployment Training Housing at a cost, on-the-job training, willing to complete paperwork for educational credit, and willing to act as a professional reference.

Contact Secretary, North Beach Sailing/Barrier Island Sailing Center, Box 8279, Duck, North Carolina 27949. Telephone: 252-261-1499. Fax: 252-261-1499. E-mail: nbsail@mindspring. com. World Wide Web: http://www.islandwatersportsinc.com. Contact by e-mail, fax, mail, phone, or through World Wide Web site. Application deadline: applications by March 1 are preferred.

PARAMOUNT'S CAROWINDS
14523 CAROWINDS BOULEVARD
CHARLOTTE, NORTH CAROLINA 28273

General Information Theme park entertaining close to 2 million guests each season with rides, shows, concerts, food, and games. Seasonal operation March through October. Established in 1972. 360-acre facility. Features: Top Gun Steel roller coaster; division of Viacom International; newly expanded waterpark; 10 roller coasters; 3-D action adventure; haunted mansion.

Profile of Summer Employees Total number: 2,000; typical ages: 15–80. 49% men; 51% women; 50% minorities; 35% high school students; 27% college students; 9% retirees; 1% non-U.S. citizens; 28% local applicants.

Employment Information Openings are from March 1 to October 31. Jobs available: ▶ 300–500 *food and beverage associates* (minimum age 16) with neat appearance and outgoing personality at $6–$8 per hour ▶ 50–150 *lifeguards* (minimum age 18) with free training and certification provided at $7–$9 per hour ▶ 500–600 *merchandise, games, and admissions associates* (minimum age 16) with neat appearance and outgoing personality at $6–$7 per hour ▶ 300–500 *ride operators* (minimum age 18) with neat appearance and outgoing personality at $6–$8 per hour. Applicants must submit a formal organization application. An in-person interview is required.

Benefits and Preemployment Training Health insurance, on-the-job training, willing to complete paperwork for educational credit, opportunity to attend seminars/workshops, travel reimbursement, and internships and cooperative education programs available.

Contact Human Resources, Paramount's Carowinds. World Wide Web: http://www.carowinds. com. Contact through World Wide Web site. Application deadline: continuous.

ROCKBROOK CAMP
HIGHWAY 276
BREVARD, NORTH CAROLINA 28712

General Information Residential camp serving girls ages 6–16, promoting independence in a non-competitive environment. Camp has two-, three-, and four-week sessions. Established in 1921. 185-acre facility located 30 miles from Asheville. Features: 1 freshwater lake; wooded setting; 6 tennis courts; climbing wall; Alpine Tower; on-site pottery studio.

Profile of Summer Employees Total number: 70; typical ages: 20–30. 8% men; 92% women; 8% minorities; 3% high school students; 75% college students; 2% retirees; 8% non-U.S. citizens; 8% local applicants. Nonsmokers required.

Employment Information Openings are from May 27 to August 12. Jobs available: ▶ 50 *cabin counselors (women only)* (minimum age 19) with CPR/first aid certification at $200 and up per week ▶ 2–4 *raft and canoeing guides* at $200 and up per week ▶ 6 *registered nurses (women only)* with RN license at $450 per week ▶ 2 *riding instructors (women only)* at $200 per week ▶ 2 *rock climbers* at $150–$200 per week. Applicants must submit formal organization application, three personal references. An in-person interview is recommended, but a telephone interview is acceptable. International applicants accepted; must obtain own visa, obtain own working papers, apply through a recognized agency.

Benefits and Preemployment Training Free housing, free meals, willing to provide letters of recommendation, on-the-job training, willing to act as a professional reference, and laundry. Preemployment training is required and includes accident prevention and safety, interpersonal skills, leadership skills.

Contact Charlotte Page, Associate Director, Rockbrook Camp, PO Box 792, Brevard, North Carolina 28712. Telephone: 828-884-6151. Fax: 828-884-6459. E-mail: rockbrook@citcom.net. World Wide Web: http://www.rockbrookcamp.com. Contact by e-mail, fax, mail, phone, or through World Wide Web site. Application deadline: continuous.

RUBIN'S OSCEOLA LAKE INN
PO BOX 2258
HENDERSONVILLE, NORTH CAROLINA 28793

General Information Summer resort hotel with 80 rooms, serving 3 meals daily. Established in 1941. 12-acre facility. Features: lake; wooded setting; tennis; shuffleboard; putting green; ping-pong.

Profile of Summer Employees Total number: 30; typical ages: 18–50. 50% men; 50% women; 25% minorities; 25% college students; 25% non-U.S. citizens; 25% local applicants. Nonsmokers preferred.

Employment Information Openings are from June to October. Jobs available: ▶ 3 *bellhops* (minimum age 18) ▶ 6 *buspersons* (minimum age 18) ▶ 1 *chauffeur* (minimum age 20) ▶ 4 *desk clerks* (minimum age 18) ▶ 6 *housekeeping personnel* (minimum age 18) ▶ 3 *kitchen aides* (minimum age 18) ▶ 1 *secretary* (minimum age 18) with typing and computer skills ▶ 6 *waiters/waitresses* (minimum age 18). Applicants must submit resume, two personal references, two letters of recommendation. International applicants accepted; must obtain own visa, obtain own working papers, apply through a recognized agency.

Benefits and Preemployment Training Housing at a cost, meals at a cost, possible full-time employment, and on-the-job training.

Contact Stuart Rubin, Owner/Manager, Rubin's Osceola Lake Inn, 5005 Collins Avenue, PH7, Miami Beach, Florida 33140. Telephone: 305-865-6015. Contact by mail or phone. Application deadline: continuous.

THE SOUTHWESTERN COMPANY, NORTH CAROLINA
See The Southwestern Company on page 297 for complete description.

SPORTS INTERNATIONAL–BRAD HOOVER FOOTBALL CAMP
SALISBURY, NORTH CAROLINA
See Sports International, Inc. on page 134 for complete description.

SPORTS INTERNATIONAL–JOE KRIVAK QUARTERBACK CAMP
SALISBURY, NORTH CAROLINA
See Sports International, Inc. on page 134 for complete description.

STUDENT CONSERVATION ASSOCIATION (SCA), NORTH CAROLINA
See Student Conservation Association (SCA), New Hampshire on page 200 for complete description.

SUPERCAMP–WAKE FOREST UNIVERSITY
WAKE FOREST UNIVERSITY
WINSTON-SALEM, NORTH CAROLINA 27106

General Information Residential program for teens designed to build self-confidence and lifelong learning skills through accelerated learning techniques. Established in 1981. Features: university dormitories; outdoor ropes course.

Profile of Summer Employees Total number: 28; typical ages: 18–25. 40% men; 60% women; 5% minorities; 80% college students; 10% non-U.S. citizens; 5% local applicants. Nonsmokers preferred.

Employment Information Openings are from June 30 to August 1. Winter break positions also offered. Jobs available: ▶ 1 *EMT/wellness person* with national or state registration at $600 to $1300 per 10 day session ▶ 1 *counselor* with college degree and PPS credential, MFCC license, or master's degree in counseling at $900 to $1500 per 10 day session ▶ 1–4 *facilitators* with presentation skills and college degree; teaching credential preferred at $1300 to $2350 per 10 day session ▶ 1 *logistics manager* with excellent organizational skills and high school diploma at $600 to $1100 per 10 day session ▶ 1 *nurse/paramedic* with national or state registration at $600 to $1300 per 10 day session ▶ 1 *office manager* with high school diploma and prior office experience at $450 to $700 per 10 day session ▶ *products coordinator* with high school diploma at a salary paid per 10 day session ▶ 1–18 *team leaders* with high school diploma and prior experience with teens at $325 to $600 per 10 day session. Applicants must submit a formal organization application, resume, three letters of recommendation, in-person interview recommended (videotape interview acceptable). International applicants accepted; must obtain own visa, obtain own working papers.

Benefits and Preemployment Training Free housing, free meals, willing to provide letters of recommendation, on-the-job training, willing to complete paperwork for educational credit, and willing to act as a professional reference. Preemployment training is required and includes interpersonal skills, leadership skills, life changing experiences.

Contact Jen Myers, Programs Support, SuperCamp–Wake Forest University, 1725 South Coast Highway, Oceanside, California 92054. Telephone: 760-722-0072 Ext. 109. Fax: 760-722-3507. E-mail: staffing@learningforum.com. World Wide Web: http://www.supercamp.com. Contact by e-mail, fax, mail, phone, or through World Wide Web site. Application deadline: continuous.

YMCA BLUE RIDGE ASSEMBLY
84 BLUE RIDGE CIRCLE
BLACK MOUNTAIN, NORTH CAROLINA 28711

General Information Conference center serving families, teenagers, adults, church groups, and other not-for-profit groups. Established in 1906. 1,200-acre facility located 15 miles from Asheville. Features: hiking and biking trails; 4 tennis courts; swimming pool; ropes course; historical buildings; freshwater lake.

Profile of Summer Employees Total number: 120; typical ages: 18–25. 40% men; 60% women; 11% minorities; 5% high school students; 85% college students; 3% retirees; 14% non-U.S. citizens; 5% local applicants.

Employment Information Openings are from May 15 to August 8. Year-round positions also offered. Jobs available: ▶ 1 *chaplain* with at least one year of divinity (seminary) school at $1500–$2000 per season ▶ 85 *collegiate staff members* with at least six months of work or volunteer experience at $850–$1100 per season ▶ 90–110 *conference support staff* (minimum age 18) at $132 per week ▶ 1 *crafts and child care director* with at least one year experience in field at $1000–$2000 per season ▶ 30 *department supervisors* with at least one year work experience at $1000–$1200 per season ▶ 1 *pool director* with WSI, lifeguard, CPR, and first aid certification at $1000–$1200 per season ▶ 1 *staff program director* with work or school experience in recreation with adults at $1000–$1200 per season. Applicants must submit formal organization application, three personal references. A telephone interview is required. International applicants accepted; must apply through a recognized agency.

Benefits and Preemployment Training Free housing, free meals, formal training, health insurance, willing to provide letters of recommendation, on-the-job training, willing to complete paperwork for educational credit, travel reimbursement, and tuition assistance. Preemployment training is required and includes accident prevention and safety, interpersonal skills, leadership skills.

Contact Elaine Godfrey, Staff Development Director, YMCA Blue Ridge Assembly, 84 Blue Ridge Circle, YMCA Blue Ridge Assembly, Black Mountain, North Carolina 28711. Telephone: 828-669-8422. Fax: 828-669-8497. E-mail: egodfrey@ymcabra.org. World Wide Web: http://www.blueridgeassembly.org. Contact by e-mail or through World Wide Web site. Application deadline: continuous.

NORTH DAKOTA

A CHRISTIAN MINISTRY IN THE NATIONAL PARKS– NORTH DAKOTA

See A Christian Ministry in the National Parks–Maine on page 107 for complete description.

INTERNATIONAL MUSIC CAMP
INTERNATIONAL PEACE GARDEN
DUNSEITH, NORTH DAKOTA 58329

General Information Residential camp serving 500 students per week in 24 different arts programs. Established in 1956. 120-acre facility located 117 miles from Minot. Features: wooded setting in a state park; 2,000-seat concert hall.

Profile of Summer Employees Total number: 225; typical ages: 18–65. 50% men; 50% women; 5% minorities; 35% college students; 5% retirees; 10% non-U.S. citizens; 20% local applicants. Nonsmokers preferred.

Employment Information Openings are from June 1 to July 30. Jobs available: ▶ 11 *concessioners/housekeepers/maintenance persons* (minimum age 18) at $200–$250 per week ▶ 6 *cooks* (minimum age 18) with cooking experience at $200–$250 per week ▶ 20 *deans/ counselors* (minimum age 21) must be college seniors or graduates at $200–$250 per week ▶ 4 *dishwashers* (minimum age 18) at $200 per week ▶ 1 *first aid technician* (minimum age 21) with CPR, first aid certification, and RN or LPN license at $250 per week ▶ 4 *music librarians* (minimum age 18) with instrumental knowledge at $200 per week ▶ 6 *secretaries* (minimum age 18) with ability to type 50 wpm and knowledge of computers at $200 per week. Applicants must submit a formal organization application, letter of interest, resume, three letters of recommendation. An in-person interview is recommended, but a telephone interview is acceptable. International applicants accepted; must obtain own visa, obtain own working papers.

Benefits and Preemployment Training Free housing, free meals, willing to provide letters of recommendation, names of contacts, on-the-job training, willing to act as a professional reference, opportunity to attend seminars/workshops, and private music lessons at no cost. Preemployment training is required and includes accident prevention and safety, interpersonal skills, leadership skills.

Contact Joseph T. Alme, Camp Director, International Music Camp, 1930 23rd Avenue, SE, Minot, North Dakota 58701. Telephone: 701-838-8472. Fax: 701-838-8472. E-mail: info@ internationalmusiccamp.com. World Wide Web: http://www.internationalmusiccamp.com. Contact by e-mail, fax, or mail. Application deadline: continuous.

THE SOUTHWESTERN COMPANY, NORTH DAKOTA
See The Southwestern Company on page 297 for complete description.

STUDENT CONSERVATION ASSOCIATION (SCA), NORTH DAKOTA
See Student Conservation Association (SCA), New Hampshire on page 200 for complete description.

OHIO

CAMP ECHOING HILLS
36272 COUNTY ROAD 79
WARSAW, OHIO 43844

General Information Camp experience for 650 mentally and physically disabled campers of all ages. Full camping program with highest standards of care for special population campers. Established in 1966. 72-acre facility located 60 miles from Columbus. Features: wooded setting; lake; go-carts; wilderness camping.

Profile of Summer Employees Total number: 40; typical ages: 19–23. 35% men; 65% women; 20% minorities; 20% high school students; 70% college students; 10% non-U.S. citizens. Nonsmokers required.

Employment Information Openings are from June 1 to August 9. Jobs available: ▶ *assistant nurses* (minimum age 21) at $200–$300 per week ▶ 40 *counselors* (minimum age 18) at $175–$250 per week ▶ 20–25 *support staff members* (minimum age 16) at $175–$250 per week. Applicants must submit formal organization application, three personal references, three letters of recommendation. An in-person interview is recommended, but a telephone interview is acceptable. International applicants accepted; must obtain own visa, obtain own working papers, apply through a recognized agency.

Benefits and Preemployment Training Free housing, free meals, possible full-time employment, willing to provide letters of recommendation, on-the-job training, willing to complete paperwork for educational credit, and willing to act as a professional reference. Preemployment training is required and includes accident prevention and safety, first aid, interpersonal skills, leadership skills, caregiving for disabled population.

Contact Shaker Samuel, Camp Administrator, Camp Echoing Hills, 36272 County Road 79, Warsaw, Ohio 43844. Telephone: 740-327-2311. Fax: 740-327-6371. E-mail: campechohl@aol.com. World Wide Web: http://www.campechoinghills.org. Contact by e-mail, fax, mail, or phone. Application deadline: continuous.

CAMP O'BANNON
9688 BUTLER ROAD, NE
NEWARK, OHIO 43055

General Information Residential camp serving children ages 9–14 with the goal of increasing self-esteem. Established in 1922. 169-acre facility located 40 miles from Columbus. Features: main camp; outpost camp; 2 high ropes courses.

Profile of Summer Employees Total number: 22; typical ages: 19–22. 40% men; 60% women; 20% high school students; 80% college students. Nonsmokers preferred.

Employment Information Openings are from June 8 to August 14. Jobs available: ▶ 1 *arts and crafts counselor* with one year of college at $1600–$1800 per season ▶ 8 *cabin counselors* with one year of college at $1600–$1800 per season ▶ *camp director* with college degree (preferred) at $2000 per season ▶ 1 *cook* with ability to cook for 65 or more people at $1500–$1800 per season ▶ 1 *lifeguard* with WSI certification (preferred) at $1600–$1800 per season ▶ 1 *nature counselor* with one year of college at $1600–$1800 per season ▶ 1 *nurse* with RN license at $1800 per season ▶ 3 *outpost counselors* with one year of college at $1600–$1800 per season ▶ 1 *outpost director* with 2 years of college at $2000 per season ▶ 1 *program director* with 2 years of college at $1800 per season. Applicants must submit a formal organization application, three personal references, three letters of recommendation. An in-person interview is recommended, but a telephone interview is acceptable. International applicants accepted; must obtain own visa, obtain own working papers.

Benefits and Preemployment Training Free housing, free meals, health insurance, willing to provide letters of recommendation, names of contacts, on-the-job training, willing to complete paperwork for educational credit, and willing to act as a professional reference. Preemployment training is required.

Contact Ted Cobb, Camp Director, Camp O'Bannon. Telephone: 740-345-8295. Fax: 740-349-5093. E-mail: campobannon@alltel.net. Contact by e-mail, mail, or phone. Application deadline: continuous.

CEDAR POINT
1 CEDAR POINT DRIVE
SANDUSKY, OHIO 44870-5259

General Information Amusement/theme park with 68 rides, 4 resort hotels, a campground, go-karts, ripcord, mini golf, and a water park. Established in 1870. 364-acre facility located 60 miles from Cleveland. Features: 16 roller coasters; 364-acre park; 4 hotels; mile-long sandy beach; adjacent waterpark; campground.

Profile of Summer Employees Total number: 4,000; typical ages: 18–85. 40% men; 60% women; 20% high school students; 60% college students; 20% retirees; 30% non-U.S. citizens.

Employment Information Openings are from May 1 to October 26. Jobs available: ▶ 450–500 *games/arcades staff* (minimum age 18 if housing is required) at $6.25 per hour plus bonus ▶ 450–500 *hotel housekeeping staff* (minimum age 18 if housing is required) at $6.25 per hour plus bonus ▶ 1500 *quick service workers, restaurant staff* (minimum age 18 if housing is required) at $6.25 per hour plus bonus ▶ 850–900 *ride operators* (minimum age 18) at $6.25 per hour plus bonus ▶ 450–500 *sales associates* (minimum age 18 if housing is required) at $6.25 per hour plus bonus. Applicants must submit a formal organization application, online application. An in-person interview is recommended, but a telephone interview is acceptable. International applicants accepted.

Benefits and Preemployment Training Housing at a cost, meals at a cost, on-the-job training, willing to complete paperwork for educational credit, and employee activities program. Preemployment training is required and includes accident prevention and safety, first aid, CPR, interpersonal skills, leadership skills, diversity and sexual harassment awareness training.

Contact Amanda Royer, Assistant Director of Human Resources, Cedar Point, PO Box 5006, Sandusky, Ohio 44870. Fax: 419-627-2163. E-mail: work@cedarpoint.com. World Wide Web: http://www.cedarpoint.com. Contact by mail or through World Wide Web site. No phone calls. Application deadline: August 1.

COLLEGE GIFTED PROGRAMS
OBERLIN COLLEGE
OBERLIN, OHIO 44074

General Information Residential educational academic summer camp for gifted and talented students in grades 4-11. Program blends in-depth academics with recreational and cultural activities. Established in 1984. 440-acre facility located 30 miles from Cleveland. Features: dormitories; campus classroom facilities; campus recreational facilities include pool, tennis courts, and gym; campus library; beautiful college setting.

Profile of Summer Employees Total number: 64; typical ages: 19–70. 50% men; 50% women; 30% minorities; 50% college students; 10% retirees; 10% non-U.S. citizens; 25% local applicants. Nonsmokers required.

Employment Information Openings are from July 18 to August 7. Jobs available: ▶ 1 *administrative assistant (residential)* with good organizational skills and computer knowledge at $2000 per 3-week session (room and board included) ▶ 16–20 *counselors* (minimum age 18) with one year of college completed and experience working with children at $1000 per 3-week session ▶ 3 *directors* with at least 5 years teaching/supervisory experience; master's degree required at $4500 to $7000 per 3-week session ▶ 6 *housemasters/instructors (residential)* with master's degree, teaching, and supervisory experience at $2500 to $3500 per 3-week session ▶ 20 *instructors (non-residential)* with master's degree and teaching experience at $725 to $2900 per 3-week session ▶ 2 *nurses (residential)* with RN license, school experience preferred at $260 per 24 hour period ▶ 1 *secretary (commuting)* with good organizational skills, computer knowledge, and keyboarding skills at $1520 per 3-week session. Applicants must submit formal organization application, resume, academic transcripts, two personal references, two letters of recommendation. An in-person interview is recommended, but a telephone interview is acceptable. International applicants accepted; must apply through a recognized agency.

Benefits and Preemployment Training Free housing, free meals, willing to provide letters of recommendation, willing to complete paperwork for educational credit, and willing to act as a professional reference. Preemployment training is required and includes accident prevention and safety, interpersonal skills, leadership skills, instructional strategies for gifted students.

Contact Charles Zeichner, Executive Director, College Gifted Programs, 120 Littleton Road, Suite 201, Parsippany, New Jersey 07054-1803. Telephone: 973-334-6991. Fax: 973-334-9756. E-mail: info@cgp-sig.com. World Wide Web: http://www.cgp-sig.com. Contact by e-mail, fax, mail, phone, or through World Wide Web site. Application deadline: continuous.

FRIENDS MUSIC CAMP
61830 SANDY RIDGE ROAD
BARNESVILLE, OHIO 43713

General Information Residential camp offering musical instruction to 75 10- to 18-year-olds featuring private music lessons, orchestra, band, jazz, chorus, and musical theater. Established in 1980. 30-acre facility located 30 miles from Wheeling, West Virginia. Features: boarding school dormitories; soccer fields; boarding school main building; woods, rolling hills.

Profile of Summer Employees Total number: 20; typical ages: 18–67. 50% men; 50% women; 5% minorities; 50% college students; 10% retirees; 5% non-U.S. citizens. Nonsmokers required.

Employment Information Openings are from July 9 to August 8. Jobs available: ▶ 1–2 *counselors* (minimum age 19) with leadership skills and experience at $1000 per season ▶ 4–10 *musical instructors* (minimum age 18) with experience in the field at $1000 per season. Applicants must submit a letter of interest, resume, three personal references. An in-person interview is recommended, but a telephone interview is acceptable. International applicants accepted.

Benefits and Preemployment Training Free housing, free meals, willing to provide letters of recommendation, on-the-job training, and travel reimbursement. Preemployment training is required and includes leadership skills.

Contact Peg Champney, Director, Friends Music Camp, PO Box 427, Yellow Springs, Ohio 45387. Telephone: 937-767-1311. Fax: 937-767-2254. E-mail: musicfmc@yahoo.com. World Wide Web: http://www.quaker.org/friends-music-camp/. Contact by e-mail, mail, or phone. Application deadline: continuous.

GIRL SCOUT CAMP MOLLY LOUMAN
LUCASVILLE, OHIO 45648

General Information Girl Scout residential camp that serves campers ages 7-16. General activities include swimming, cookouts, horseback riding, and archery. Specialized activities include adventure travel: backpacking, river canoeing, river rafting, and rappelling. Established in 1929. 160-acre facility located 20 miles from Portsmouth. Features: wooded setting; lake access; use of surrounding public lands; modern, air-conditioned dining hall; staff lodge (air-conditioned); stables.

Profile of Summer Employees Total number: 50; typical ages: 18–25. 4% men; 96% women; 5% minorities; 1% high school students; 80% college students; 1% retirees; 8% non-U.S. citizens; 15% local applicants. Nonsmokers preferred.

Employment Information Openings are from June 15 to August 18. Jobs available: ▶ 2–5 *cooks and kitchen support staff* (minimum age 18) with experience cooking for large groups at $1800–$3200 per season ▶ 20 *general counselors* (minimum age 18) with human relations skills and camping skills at $1800–$2025 per season ▶ 6 *horseback riding instructors* (minimum age 18) with western riding skills and camping skills at $1800–$2025 per season ▶ 4 *lifeguards* (minimum age 18) with good swimming skills, certification/training may be provided at $1800–$2025 per season. Applicants must submit formal organization application, three personal references, BCI fingerprint check. An in-person interview is recommended, but a telephone interview is acceptable. International applicants accepted; must apply through a recognized agency.

Benefits and Preemployment Training Free housing, free meals, formal training, willing to provide letters of recommendation, on-the-job training, willing to complete paperwork for educational credit, willing to act as a professional reference, and opportunity to attend seminars/ workshops. Preemployment training is required and includes accident prevention and safety, first aid, CPR, interpersonal skills, leadership skills.

Contact Becky Foreman, Camp Director, Girl Scout Camp Molly Louman, 1700 Water Mark Drive, Columbus, Ohio 43215. Telephone: 614-487-8101 Ext. 857. Fax: 614-487-8199. E-mail: becky@sealofohio.org. Contact by e-mail, fax, or phone. Application deadline: continuous.

HIDDEN HOLLOW CAMP
5127 OPOSSUM RUN ROAD
BELLVILLE, OHIO 44813-9134

General Information Traditional residential camp serving boys and girls ages 8-15 with activities such as swimming, nature hikes, trail rides, arts and crafts, archery, tennis, woodworking, dramatics, and pond canoeing. Established in 1940. 620-acre facility located 12 miles from Mansfield. Features: pond; wooded setting; Sky High Lodge with beautiful view; 2 tennis courts; 3 heated dorms and 11 cabins; observatory.

Profile of Summer Employees Total number: 30; typical ages: 16–24. 50% men; 50% women; 20% minorities; 49% high school students; 51% college students; 85% local applicants. Nonsmokers preferred.

Employment Information Openings are from June 25 to August 8. Jobs available: ▶ 15–25 *camp counselors* (minimum age 16) with lifeguarding and CPR certification preferred at $165–$220 per week. Applicants must submit a formal organization application, three personal references. An in-person interview is required.

Benefits and Preemployment Training Free housing and free meals. Preemployment training is required and includes accident prevention and safety, leadership skills.

Contact Thelda J. Dillon, Director, Hidden Hollow Camp, 380 North Mulberry Street, Mansfield, Ohio 44902. Fax: 419-522-2166. Contact by mail. No phone calls. Application deadline: April 1.

THE SOUTHWESTERN COMPANY, OHIO
See The Southwestern Company on page 297 for complete description.

STUDENT CONSERVATION ASSOCIATION (SCA), OHIO
See Student Conservation Association (SCA), New Hampshire on page 200 for complete description.

WRIGHT STATE UNIVERSITY PRE-COLLEGE PROGRAMS
3640 COLONEL GLENN HIGHWAY
DAYTON, OHIO 45435-0001

General Information Residential academic enrichment program for motivated students in grades 7-12. Established in 1990. Features: university setting; running/walking trails; campus recreation; university dormitories.

Profile of Summer Employees Total number: 20; typical ages: 19–22. 50% men; 50% women; 100% college students.

Employment Information Openings are from June to August. Jobs available: ▶ 5–10 *residential assistants* (minimum age 19) with experience working in camp setting at $250–$400 per week. Applicants must submit a letter of interest, resume.

Benefits and Preemployment Training Free housing, free meals, willing to provide letters of recommendation, willing to act as a professional reference, opportunity to attend seminars/ workshops, and college credit. Preemployment training is required and includes accident prevention and safety, first aid, CPR, interpersonal skills, leadership skills.

Contact Chris S. Hoffman, Program Coordinator, Wright State University Pre-College Programs, E041 Student Union, 3640 Colonel Glenn Highway, Dayton, Ohio 45435-0001. Telephone: 937-775-3135. Fax: 937-775-4883. E-mail: chris.hoffman@wright.edu. World Wide Web: http:// www.wright.edu/academics/precollege. Contact by e-mail, mail, phone, or through World Wide Web site. Application deadline: continuous.

OKLAHOMA

CAMP RED ROCK
ROUTE 1, BOX 110B
BINGER, OKLAHOMA 73009

General Information Residential camp serving weekly 150 Girl Scouts ages 6–17. Offers general camping, Western horse riding, swimming, archery, rappelling, crafts, low ropes course, and outdoor skills. Established in 1959. 285-acre facility located 60 miles from Oklahoma City. Features: canyon dividing the camp; wooded setting; swimming pool with diving board; sandstone rock outcroppings; dining hall seating 170 family style; cabins and platform tents sleeping 4 each.

Profile of Summer Employees Total number: 22; typical ages: 18–25. 3% men; 97% women; 14% minorities; 27% high school students; 18% college students; 18% non-U.S. citizens; 23% local applicants.

Employment Information Openings are from June 2 to July 24. Jobs available: ▶ 1 *assistant camp director* (minimum age 21) with management and supervisory experience with outdoor and camp programs at $200–$250 per week ▶ 1 *assistant cook* (minimum age 17) with familiarity with kitchen operation at $150–$200 per week ▶ 1 *business manager* (minimum age 21) with current driver's license required and knowledge of bookkeeping and office procedures at $180–$230 per week ▶ 1 *head cook* (minimum age 21) with food service skills for large groups and ability to purchase and plan within a budget at $200–$250 per week ▶ 1 *health supervisor* (minimum age 21) with RN, LPN, or EMT license, ability to adapt to camp life, and knowledge of emotional and physical needs of campers at $200–$250 per week ▶ 1 *pool assistant/lifeguard* (minimum age 17) with current ARC lifeguard certification at $150–$200 per week ▶ 1 *pool director* (minimum age 21) with WSI or equivalent certification, lifeguard certification, ability to teach, and knowledge of pool maintenance at $200–$250 per week ▶ 1–3 *program instructors* (minimum age 17) with ability to plan and implement all camp activities, craft experience, and archery/ropes course certification or experience at $150–$200 per week ▶ 1 *riding director* (minimum age 21) with extensive riding experience, supervisory skills, ability to teach Western riding, and vaulting knowledge a plus at $200–$250 per week ▶ 2 *riding instructors* (minimum age 17) with teaching skills, experience with horses and Western riding, and vaulting knowledge (a plus) at $150–$200 per week ▶ 7 *unit assistants* (minimum age 17) with experience working with youth, leadership ability, and able to teach activities to campers at $135–$150 per week ▶ 6 *unit leaders* (minimum age 21) with supervisory and leadership skills, experience working with youth, and outdoor program at $150–$200 per week. Applicants must submit formal organization application, three personal references. An in-person interview is recommended, but a telephone interview is acceptable. International applicants accepted; must obtain own visa, obtain own working papers, apply through a recognized agency.

Benefits and Preemployment Training Free housing, free meals, formal training, willing to provide letters of recommendation, on-the-job training, willing to complete paperwork for

educational credit, and willing to act as a professional reference. Preemployment training is required and includes accident prevention and safety, first aid, CPR, interpersonal skills, leadership skills, archery NAA certification.

Contact Deborah LaPrairie, Camp Director, Camp Red Rock, 121 Northeast 50th Street, Oklahoma City, Oklahoma 73105, United States. Telephone: 405-528-3535 Ext. 129. Fax: 405-528-4475. E-mail: dlaprairie@redlandscouncil.org. World Wide Web: http://www.redlandscouncil. org. Contact by e-mail, fax, mail, or phone. Application deadline: continuous.

THE SOUTHWESTERN COMPANY, OKLAHOMA
See The Southwestern Company on page 297 for complete description.

STUDENT CONSERVATION ASSOCIATION (SCA), OKLAHOMA
See Student Conservation Association (SCA), New Hampshire on page 200 for complete description.

OREGON

A CHRISTIAN MINISTRY IN THE NATIONAL PARKS– OREGON
See A Christian Ministry in the National Parks–Maine on page 107 for complete description.

B'NAI B'RITH CAMP
PO BOX 110
NEOTSU, OREGON 97364

General Information A complete Jewish camping experience for youth grades 2-11, on the scenic Oregon coast; activities include: athletics, arts and crafts, ropes challenge course, nature, aquatics, Shabbat celebration, trips, and much more. Established in 1921. 14-acre facility located 80 miles from Portland. Features: lakefront; heated pool; ropes challenge course; conference center; heated cabins; tennis courts.

Profile of Summer Employees Total number: 85; typical ages: 17–60. 50% men; 50% women; 90% minorities; 20% high school students; 30% college students; 25% non-U.S. citizens; 76% local applicants. Nonsmokers required.

Employment Information Openings are from June 14 to August 14. Spring break and winter break positions also offered. Jobs available: ▶ 1 *Jewish enrichment director* (minimum age 21) with experience with Jewish studies, first aid/CPR certification, teaching skills, and desire to work with children at a salary dependent on experience ▶ 1 *LIT director* (minimum age 21) with leadership and teaching skills and experience working with children at $1200–$2000 per season ▶ 1 *aquatics director* (minimum age 21) with water craft instructor certification, lifeguard certification, CPR and first aid certification, and management skills at $1200–$1600 per season ▶ 1 *arts and crafts director* (minimum age 20) with two years training and experience in arts and crafts curriculum, teamwork skills, and organizational skills at $1000–$1500 per season ▶ 1 *assistant aquatics director* (minimum age 18) with documented experience, lifeguard certification, and WSI at $1000–$1500 per season ▶ 1 *assistant arts and crafts director* (minimum age

17) at $600–$900 ▶ 1 *assistant athletics director* (minimum age 17) at $600–$900 ▶ 1 *athletic director* (minimum age 20) with teaching skills, training and experience in athletics activities and management, and outdoor skills at $1000–$1500 per season ▶ 2 *bus drivers* with experience driving vehicles from van to 81 passenger, experience with children, DMV record printout, ODOT Medical card, first aid and CPR cards, drug test, and background check at a salary dependent on experience ▶ 1 *camp bookkeeper* (minimum age 20) with degree in accounting, computer skills, problem solving skills, teamwork skills, valid driver's license, first aid, and CPR certification at a salary dependent on experience ▶ 1 *camp store/cafe manager* (minimum age 18) with current food handler's card at $800–$1500 per season ▶ 3 *cooks* (minimum age 18) with experience as cook or assistant cook, food handler's card, first aid/CPR certification, kosher cooking and food service, and experience cooking for large groups at $1800–$2500 per season ▶ 1 *creative arts director* (minimum age 20) with two years training and experience in teaching and delivering creative arts programs and curriculum at $1000–$1500 per season ▶ 1 *dining hall manager* (minimum age 20) with food handler's card, first aid/CPR certification, and experience in camp setting at $1000–$1500 per season ▶ 4 *dishwashers/kitchen helpers* (minimum age 17) with food handler's card, first aid/CPR certification, and desire to work in camp kitchen at $600–$900 per season ▶ *food service manager/head chef* (minimum age 25) with 3 years previous supervisory and cooking experience, first aid/CPR certification, food handler's card, and kosher cooking experience at a salary dependent on experience ▶ 1 *health care assistant* (minimum age 18) with first aid/CPR certification and experience working with children at $1000–$1300 per season ▶ 1 *health care manager* (minimum age 21) with current RN or EMT certification at a salary dependent on experience ▶ 16 *junior counselors* (minimum age 17) with experience working with youth and first aid/CPR certification at $600–$900 per season ▶ 1 *leadership unit head/LIA director* (minimum age 21) with experience at $1400–$2500 per season ▶ 6 *lifeguards* (minimum age 17) with documented experience and lifeguard certification at $700–$1400 per season ▶ 1 *music director* (minimum age 20) with two years training and experience teaching music programs and curriculum and experience working with children at $1000–$1500 per season ▶ 1 *nature director* (minimum age 20) with two years training and experience teaching outdoor skills and environmental studies and first aid/CPR certification at $1000–$1500 per season ▶ 1 *office assistant* (minimum age 18) with office experience, teamwork skills, valid driver's license and good driving record, and first aid/CPR certification at $600–$900 per season ▶ 1 *office manager* (minimum age 21) with a valid driver's license and clean driving record at $1200–$2000 per season ▶ 1 *program director* (minimum age 21) with leadership experience, love of outdoors, supervisory skills, first aid/CPR certification, valid drivers license, and clean driving record at a salary dependent on experience ▶ 1 *programming coordinator* (minimum age 18) with first aid/CPR certification, creativity, and teaching skills at $1000–$1400 per season ▶ 1 *ropes course director* (minimum age 21) with training and documented experience with adventure ropes course programs, CPR/first aid certification, experience working with children, and outdoor skills at $1000–$1600 per season ▶ 2 *roving counselors* (minimum age 20) with previous experience working with children in an overnight camp or educational setting and CPR/first aid certification at $1000–$1200 per season ▶ 16 *senior counselors* (minimum age 19) with first aid/CPR certification and prior experience working with youth in overnight camp or educational setting at $900–$1400 per season ▶ 2 *song leaders* (minimum age 18) with musical versatility at $200–$300 per season ▶ 3 *unit heads* (minimum age 21) with prior camp staff experience, supervisory skills, CPR and first aid certification, and experience working with children and adults at $1200–$2000 per season ▶ 1 *water craft instructor* (minimum age 21) with documented experience and lifeguard certification at $1000–$1400 per season. Applicants must submit formal organization application, three personal references, three letters of recommendation. An in-person interview is recommended, but a telephone interview is acceptable. International applicants accepted; must apply through a recognized agency.

Benefits and Preemployment Training Free housing, free meals, formal training, possible full-time employment, willing to provide letters of recommendation, names of contacts, on-the-job training, willing to complete paperwork for educational credit, and willing to act as a professional reference. Preemployment training is required and includes accident prevention and safety, interpersonal skills, leadership skills.

Contact Michelle Koplan, Camp Director, B'nai B'rith Camp, 6651 SW Capitol Highway, Portland, Oregon 97219. Telephone: 503-244-0111. Fax: 503-245-4233. E-mail: bbcamp@ oregonjcc.org. World Wide Web: http://www.bbcamp.org. Contact by e-mail, phone, or through World Wide Web site. Application deadline: continuous.

CYBERCAMPS–LEWIS AND CLARK COLLEGE
PORTLAND, OREGON
See Cybercamps–University of Washington on page 326 for complete description.

THE INN OF THE SEVENTH MOUNTAIN
18575 SW CENTURY DRIVE
BEND, OREGON 97702
General Information Full-service destination resort. Established in 1970. 40-acre facility located 7 miles from Bend. Features: 2 pools; white-water rafting; canoeing; tennis courts; ice skating, roller skating, roller blading; wooded setting.

Profile of Summer Employees Total number: 201; typical ages: 16–35. 50% men; 50% women; 5% minorities; 10% high school students; 30% college students; 5% retirees; 90% local applicants.

Employment Information Openings are from May 15 to September 6. Spring break, winter break, and year-round positions also offered. Jobs available: ▶ 3 *front desk staff* (minimum age 18) with computer literacy at $8 per hour ▶ *housekeeper* (minimum age 16) at $8 per hour ▶ 2 *lifeguards* (minimum age 18) at $7.50 per hour ▶ *waitstaff* (minimum age 18) with restaurant experience and food handlers permit at $6.90 per hour. Applicants must submit formal organization application, resume, personal reference, letter of recommendation, video if necessary. An in-person interview is recommended, but a telephone interview is acceptable. International applicants accepted; must obtain own visa, obtain own working papers, apply through a recognized agency.

Benefits and Preemployment Training Meals at a cost, possible full-time employment, willing to provide letters of recommendation, on-the-job training, willing to complete paperwork for educational credit, and free recreation. Preemployment training is required and includes customer service training.

Contact Craig Fraser, Human Resources Director, The Inn of the Seventh Mountain, 18575 SW Century Drive, Bend, Oregon 97702. Telephone: 541-382-8711. Fax: 541-382-3517. E-mail: craigf@seventhmountain.com. World Wide Web: http://www.seventhmountain.com. Contact by e-mail, fax, mail, phone, or through World Wide Web site. Application deadline: continuous.

LONGACRE EXPEDITIONS, OREGON
OREGON
General Information Adventure travel program in Oregon emphasizing group living skills, fun, and physical challenges. Programs place equal emphasis on physical accomplishment and emotional growth. Established in 1981. near Portland.

Profile of Summer Employees Total number: 30; typical ages: 21–35. 50% men; 50% women; 10% minorities; 40% college students. Nonsmokers required.

Employment Information Openings are from June 15 to August 1. Jobs available: ▶ 8 *assistant trip leaders* (minimum age 21) with good driving record, WFR, and CPR at $252–$300 per week ▶ 3 *support and logistics staff members* (minimum age 21) with good driving record, WFR, and CPR at $180–$300 per week. Applicants must submit a formal organization application, letter of interest, resume, three personal references, letter(s) of recommendation. An in-person interview is recommended, but a telephone interview is acceptable. International applicants accepted; must obtain own visa, obtain own working papers.

Benefits and Preemployment Training Free housing, free meals, willing to provide letters of recommendation, on-the-job training, willing to complete paperwork for educational credit, willing to act as a professional reference, and pro-deal purchase program. Preemployment training is required and includes accident prevention and safety, interpersonal skills, leadership skills.

Contact Meredith Schuler, Director, Longacre Expeditions, Oregon, 4030 Middle Ridge Road, Newport, Pennsylvania 17074-8110. Telephone: 717-567-6790. Fax: 717-567-3955. E-mail: merry@longacreexpeditions.com. World Wide Web: http://www.longacreexpeditions.com. Contact by e-mail, fax, mail, phone, or through World Wide Web site. Application deadline: continuous.

MEADOWOOD SPRINGS SPEECH AND HEARING CAMP
330 SE EMIGRANT AVENUE
PENDLETON, OREGON 97801-0030

General Information A 39-year-old nonprofit organization that provides a summer camp for children 6 to 16 years of age with speech and hearing disorders. Established in 1964. 143-acre facility located 240 miles from Portland. Features: mountains; wildlife; outdoor camp setting; nature hiking; swimming pool; unique facility.

Profile of Summer Employees Total number: 50–70; typical ages: 18–50. 30% men; 70% women; 1% minorities; 1% high school students; 70% college students; 1% non-U.S. citizens; 27% local applicants.

Employment Information Openings are from July 1 to August 1. Jobs available: ▶ 8 *activities staff* (minimum age 18) with skills in art, crafts, sports, nature, or aquatics at $1000 per month ▶ 17–21 *cabin counselors* (minimum age 18) with ability to provide instruction in daily living skills and reside in unit with campers at $1000 per month ▶ 11 *clinical staff* with experience in speech-language education/interpreting at $1800–$2200 per month ▶ 25 *student clinicians* (minimum age 18) must be college seniors or graduate students in speech pathology program; paid with a stipend. Applicants must submit a formal organization application, letter of interest, resume, personal reference, two letters of recommendation, academic transcripts (for student clinicians only). A telephone interview is required. International applicants accepted; must obtain own visa, obtain own working papers.

Benefits and Preemployment Training Free housing, free meals, willing to provide letters of recommendation, and willing to complete paperwork for educational credit.

Contact Rhonda Hack, Executive Administrator, Meadowood Springs Speech and Hearing Camp, PO Box 1025, Pendleton, Oregon 97801-0030, United States. Telephone: 541-276-2752. Fax: 541-276-7227. E-mail: meadowood@oregontrail.net. World Wide Web: http://www.meadowoodsprings.com. Contact by e-mail, fax, mail, phone, or through World Wide Web site. Application deadline: official deadline is April 15, however applications will be accepted until positions filled.

NORTHWEST YOUTH CORPS
2621 AUGUSTA STREET
EUGENE, OREGON 97403

General Information Mobile, non-residential conservation corps program. Staff are responsible for daily activities (work project, camp operations, and environmental relations) for a crew of 10 high school age youth. Established in 1983.

Profile of Summer Employees Total number: 45; typical ages: 20–30. 65% men; 35% women; 10% minorities; 70% college students; 40% local applicants.

Employment Information Openings are from April 15 to October 15. Jobs available: ▶ 30–45 *field staff* (minimum age 20) with wilderness first aid and CPR and previous leadership/wilderness experience at $80 per day. Applicants must submit a formal organization application, letter of interest, resume, four personal references. An in-person interview is recommended, but a telephone interview is acceptable. International applicants accepted; must obtain own visa, obtain own working papers.

Benefits and Preemployment Training Free housing, free meals, formal training, possible full-time employment, willing to provide letters of recommendation, on-the-job training, willing to complete paperwork for educational credit, and willing to act as a professional reference. Preemployment training is required and includes accident prevention and safety, interpersonal skills, leadership skills, program operation, technical project skills.

Contact Patricia Prisbrey, Youth Services Coordinator, Northwest Youth Corps. Telephone: 541-349-5055 Ext. 236. Fax: 541-349-5060. E-mail: nyc@nwyouthcorps.org. World Wide Web: http://www.nwyouthcorps.org. Contact by e-mail, fax, mail, phone, or through World Wide Web site. Application deadline: continuous.

ROCK SPRINGS GUEST RANCH
64201 TYLER ROAD
BEND, OREGON 97701

General Information Dude ranch with riding, youth program. Established in 1969. 580-acre facility located 180 miles from Portland. Features: riding stables; pool; trout pond; 2 tennis courts; youth center; rural setting.

Profile of Summer Employees Total number: 45; typical ages: 18–22. 34% men; 66% women; 25% high school students; 70% college students; 5% local applicants.

Employment Information Openings are from June 10 to August 30. Year-round positions also offered. Jobs available: ▶ 9 *wranglers* (minimum age 18) with strong horsemanship and interpersonal skills at $1200 per month plus bonus ▶ 5 *youth counselors* (minimum age 18) with genuine interest in and experience with children at $1200 per month plus bonus. Applicants must submit a formal organization application, three personal references. An in-person interview is recommended, but a telephone interview is acceptable. International applicants accepted; must obtain own visa, obtain own working papers.

Benefits and Preemployment Training Housing at a cost, free meals, possible full-time employment, willing to provide letters of recommendation, on-the-job training, willing to complete paperwork for educational credit, and willing to act as a professional reference. Preemployment training is required and includes accident prevention and safety, interpersonal skills, training specific to operation.

Contact Eva Gill, Controller, Rock Springs Guest Ranch, 64201 Tyler Road, Bend, Oregon 97701. Telephone: 541-382-1957. Fax: 541-382-7774. E-mail: eva@rocksprings.com. World Wide Web: http://www.rocksprings.com. Contact by e-mail, fax, mail, phone, or through World Wide Web site. Application deadline: continuous.

THE SOUTHWESTERN COMPANY, OREGON
See The Southwestern Company on page 297 for complete description.

STUDENT CONSERVATION ASSOCIATION (SCA), OREGON
See Student Conservation Association (SCA), New Hampshire on page 200 for complete description.

PENNSYLVANIA

ALLEGHENY CAMP
TYRONE, PENNSYLVANIA 16686

General Information Residential summer camp for girls located on historic boarding school campus. Established in 1975. 350-acre facility located 15 miles from Altoona. Features: dormitory housing; dance studio; 4 riding paddocks; stables for 50 horses; Allegheny Mountains; wooded surroundings.

Profile of Summer Employees Total number: 40; typical ages: 17–25. 100% women; 3% minorities; 5% high school students; 90% college students; 10% non-U.S. citizens; 10% local applicants. Nonsmokers required.

Employment Information Openings are from June 6 to August 15. Jobs available: ▶ 1 *art director* (minimum age 19) with high school diploma, relevant training, and experience at $1850 per season ▶ 2 *assistant counselors* (minimum age 17) with childcare experience at $1200 per season ▶ 2 *barn assistants* (minimum age 17) with experience with horses and familiarity with English Hunt Seat and Dressage at $1200 per season ▶ 1–2 *business assistants* (minimum age 17) with good organization skills and typing ability at $1200 per season ▶ 12 *counselors* (minimum age 18) with high school diploma at $1350 per season ▶ 1 *dance director* (minimum age 19) with high school diploma and experience in ballet, jazz, tap, and hip-hop at $1850 per season ▶ 3 *head counselors* (minimum age 20) with high school diploma at $2080 per season ▶ 1 *program director* (minimum age 21) with leadership experience in camp setting at $3100 per season ▶ 8 *riding instructors* (minimum age 18) with experience teaching English hunt and dressage, CPR training, high school diploma, and riding instructor certification at $2080 per season ▶ 1 *swimming director* (minimum age 20) with lifeguarding certification, WSI certification, and high school diploma at $1850 per season ▶ 1 *theatre director* (minimum age 19) with high school diploma, relevant training, and experience at $1850 per season. Applicants must submit formal organization application, three letters of recommendation, criminal background check upon hiring. An in-person interview is recommended, but a telephone interview is acceptable. International applicants accepted; must apply through a recognized agency.

Benefits and Preemployment Training Free housing, free meals, formal training, willing to provide letters of recommendation, on-the-job training, willing to complete paperwork for educational credit, and willing to act as a professional reference. Preemployment training is required and includes accident prevention and safety, first aid, CPR, interpersonal skills, leadership skills, lifeguard training.

Contact Katherine Adame, Camp Director, Allegheny Camp, Box 308, Tyrone, Pennsylvania 16686. Telephone: 814-684-3000 Ext. 113. Fax: 814-684-2177. E-mail: bestcamp@grier.org. World Wide Web: http://www.bestcamp.org/. Contact by e-mail, mail, or phone. Application deadline: continuous.

BLUE BELL DAY CAMP
PO BOX 184
BLUE BELL, PENNSYLVANIA 19422

General Information Sports and adventure day camp for boys with emphasis on instruction and lesson plans. Established in 1946. 41-acre facility located 15 miles from Philadephia. Features: 10 acres of playing fields; 30 acres of woods; boating pond; river for water skiing; tennis courts; wood shop.

Profile of Summer Employees Total number: 50; typical ages: 23–63. 90% men; 10% women; 4% retirees; 100% local applicants. Nonsmokers preferred.

Employment Information Openings are from June 23 to August 15. Jobs available: ▶ 15–20 *day camp specialists* (minimum age 21) with proficiency in specialty at $375–$450 per week. Applicants must submit resume. An in-person interview is required. International applicants accepted; must obtain own working papers.

Benefits and Preemployment Training Willing to provide letters of recommendation and willing to act as a professional reference. Preemployment training is required and includes general staff orientation.

Contact John Harris, Director, Blue Bell Day Camp. Telephone: 215-646-1897. Fax: 610-584-3577. E-mail: john@bluebellcamp.com. World Wide Web: http://www.bluebellcamp.com. Contact by e-mail, fax, mail, phone, or through World Wide Web site. Application deadline: continuous.

BRYN MAWR CAMP
RR 5, BOX 410
HONESDALE, PENNSYLVANIA 18431

General Information Camp serving 340 girls ages 5–15 for eight weeks. Year-round conference center and mountain retreat. Established in 1921. 135-acre facility located 103 miles from New York, New York. Features: 18 tennis courts; indoor and outdoor climbing; 2 heated pools; 12,000 square-foot gymnastics center; outdoor education center; adventure museum.

Profile of Summer Employees Total number: 140; typical ages: 19–55. 15% men; 85% women; 5% minorities; 2% high school students; 60% college students; 3% retirees; 15% non-U.S. citizens; 5% local applicants. Nonsmokers required.

Employment Information Openings are from June 15 to September 15. Year-round positions also offered. Jobs available: ▶ 5 *English riding instructors* (minimum age 19) at $900–$1900 per season ▶ 4 *arts and crafts instructors* with experience in the field at $1000–$2300 per season ▶ 7 *athletics instructors* (minimum age 19) at $900–$1900 per season ▶ 3 *dance instructors* at $900–$1900 per season ▶ 4 *drama instructors* (minimum age 19) at $900–$1900 per season ▶ 12 *general counselors* (minimum age 19) at $900–$1700 per season ▶ 8 *gymnastics instructors* (minimum age 18) at $1000–$2100 per season ▶ 12 *kitchen assistants* (minimum age 19) at $1100–$1900 per season ▶ 5 *laundry/light housekeeping personnel* (minimum age 18) at $1000–$1500 per season ▶ 2 *nine-month recreation/marketing/sales interns* (minimum age 23) with college degree at $775–$1300 per month ▶ 2 *office staff members* (minimum age 19) with word processing and phone skills at $1100–$2100 per season ▶ 3 *piano/technical theater personnel* (minimum age 21) at $1000–$2100 per season ▶ 4 *registered nurses* (minimum age 21) at $1600–$2900 per season ▶ 5 *ropes challenge/outdoors counselors* with facilitator training at $1100–$2100 per season ▶ 2 *small craft instructors* (minimum age 20) with American Red Cross small craft license/certification at $1100–$1700 per season ▶ 16 *swimming instructors* (minimum age 19) with SLS and WSI certification at $1100–$2100 per season ▶ 20 *tennis instructors* (minimum age 19) with USPTA/USPTR certification and experience teaching tennis to beginners and advanced players at $950–$2400 per season ▶ 4 *waterskiing instructors* (boat drivers must be at least 23 years old) with experience in the field at $1100–$2400 per season. Applicants must submit formal organization application, resume, two personal references, two letters of recommendation. An in-person interview is recommended, but a telephone interview is acceptable. International applicants accepted; must apply through a recognized agency.

Benefits and Preemployment Training Free housing, free meals, formal training, possible full-time employment, on-the-job training, willing to complete paperwork for educational credit, willing to act as a professional reference, opportunity to attend seminars/workshops, travel reimbursement, and uniforms, stipend for accomplishments.

Contact Jane Kagan, Director of Personnel, Bryn Mawr Camp, PO Box 612, Short Hills, New Jersey 07078. Telephone: 973-467-3518. Fax: 973-467-3750. E-mail: jane@campbrynmawr.com. Contact by e-mail, fax, mail, or phone. Application deadline: continuous.

CAMP BALLIBAY FOR THE FINE AND PERFORMING ARTS
1 BALLIBAY ROAD
CAMPTOWN, PENNSYLVANIA 18815
General Information Coeducational residential camp serving up to 155 children ages 6–16 in two- to nine-week sessions. Established in 1964. 500-acre facility located 45 miles from Scranton.
Profile of Summer Employees Total number: 50; typical ages: 22–23. 40% men; 60% women; 60% college students; 5% retirees; 15% non-U.S. citizens; 5% local applicants.
Employment Information Openings are from June 29 to August 30. Jobs available: ▶ *WSI instructors* ▶ *art instructors (all areas)* ▶ *costume instructors* ▶ *dance instructors (all phases)* ▶ *golf instructors* ▶ *music instructors (vocal and instrumental)* ▶ *office staff members* ▶ *riding instructors* ▶ *supervisory staff members* ▶ *technical instructors (lighting and sound)* ▶ *technical theater instructors* ▶ *tennis instructors* ▶ *theater directors* at $750–$2000 per season ▶ *video instructors*. Applicants must submit formal organization application, resume, three personal references, felony check. An in-person interview is recommended, but a telephone interview is acceptable. International applicants accepted; must obtain own visa, apply through a recognized agency.
Benefits and Preemployment Training Free housing, free meals, willing to provide letters of recommendation, willing to complete paperwork for educational credit, and willing to act as a professional reference. Preemployment training is required and includes accident prevention and safety, first aid, interpersonal skills, leadership skills.
Contact Gerard J. Jannone, Owner/Director, Camp Ballibay for the Fine and Performing Arts, Box 1, Camptown, Pennsylvania 18815. Telephone: 570-746-3223. Fax: 570-746-3691. E-mail: jannone@ballibay.com. World Wide Web: http://www.ballibay.com. Contact by e-mail, fax, mail, phone, or through World Wide Web site. Application deadline: continuous.

CAMP CAYUGA
HONESDALE, PENNSYLVANIA 18431
General Information Private coed, nonsectarian camp for children ages 5–15. Family operated since 1957. ACA accredited. Comprehensive facilities. Separate teen campus for ages 13–15. Established in 1957. 350-acre facility located 110 miles from New York, New York. Features: modern cabins with bathrooms; 2 swimming pools; equestrian center with 25 horses; 10 tennis courts; 2 large gymnasiums with stages; separate teen campus for ages 13–15.
Profile of Summer Employees Total number: 135; typical ages: 19–55. 50% men; 50% women; 9% minorities; 98% college students; 2% retirees; 10% non-U.S. citizens; 2% local applicants. Nonsmokers preferred.
Employment Information Openings are from June 19 to August 19. Jobs available: ▶ *4–6 Honda ATV quad-riding instructors* (minimum age 19) with experience riding ATV's and teaching children; at least one year of college completed at $2000 per season ▶ *2–3 academic tutors and ESL instructors* (minimum age 19) with experience tutoring children; at least one year of college completed at $1800 per season ▶ *20–25 activity specialists* (minimum age 19) with at least one year of college completed and experience playing and coaching children in one of the following activities: video camera, model rocketry, radio broadcasting, or roller skating/rollerblading at $2000 per season ▶ *4–6 aerobics instructors* (minimum age 19) with experience in teaching aerobics to children, knowledge of step-blocks, and at least one year of college completed at $2000 per season ▶ *6–8 archery instructors* (minimum age 19) with National Archery Association certification preferred; experience teaching archery to children; at least one year of college completed at $2000 per season ▶ *2–3 art directors* (minimum age 25) with state teacher's license preferred; experience teaching art to children; supervisory, organizational, and managerial skills necessary; kiln and pottery wheel operation knowledge at $2500 per season ▶ *10–12 arts and crafts instructors* (minimum age 19) with experience teaching art to children;

at least one year of college completed at $2000 per season ▶ 2–3 *athletics directors* (minimum age 25) with experience working with children in a sports environment; teachers and coaches preferred at $2500 per season ▶ 4–6 *basketball instructors* (minimum age 19) with experience playing basketball and coaching children; at least one year of college completed at $2000 per season ▶ 6–8 *canoeing and boating instructors* (minimum age 19) with American Red Cross lifeguard and American Canoeing Association certification preferred; experience canoeing and ability to instruct; at least one year of college completed at $2000 per season ▶ 10–12 *ceramics instructors/pottery instructors* (minimum age 19) with experience in kiln and pottery wheel operating and teaching ceramics to children; at least one year of college completed at $2000 per season ▶ 4–6 *chorus/singing instructors* (minimum age 19) with experience in chorus and ability to instruct; at least one year of college completed at $1800 per season ▶ 4–6 *dance instructors* (minimum age 19) with experience in ballet, jazz, and modern dance with teaching experience; at least one year of college completed at $2000 per season ▶ 6–8 *drama instructors* (minimum age 19) with theater experience including directing plays and improvisation; at least one year of college completed at $1800 per season ▶ 2–3 *evening activity directors* (minimum age 25) with experience in organizing and implementing activities; outgoing, good sense of humor, creative personality required at $2500 per season ▶ 4–6 *fishing instructors* (minimum age 19) with experience fishing and ability to instruct; at least one year of college completed at $1800 per season ▶ 10–12 *flying trapeze and circus instructors* (minimum age 19) with experience teaching or coaching children; at least one year of college completed; experience on the flying trapeze and circus skills; strong gymnastic skills helpful at $2000 per season ▶ 24–26 *food service staff (cooks, dining hall service, food prep)* (minimum age 20) with experience in quantity food production required; at least one year of college completed at $2500 per season ▶ 6–7 *golf instructors* (minimum age 19) with experience playing golf and coaching children; at least one year of college completed at $2000 per season ▶ 10–12 *gymnastics instructors* (minimum age 19) with experience on all gymnastics apparatus; experience teaching gymnastics preferred; at least one year of college completed at $2000 per season ▶ 4–6 *head counselors* (minimum age 30) with supervisory skills and experience working with children and young adults at $2500 per season ▶ 10–12 *horseback riding instructors* (minimum age 19) with CHA certification preferred; experience riding and caring for horses and stables; experience teaching children; at least one year of college completed at $2000 per season ▶ 2 *horsemanship directors* (minimum age 25) with CHA certification preferred; experience teaching equestrian skills to children; supervisory, organizational, and managerial skills necessary at $2000–$3000 per season ▶ 2–3 *intercamp tournament directors* (minimum age 25) with teacher's license preferred; experience working with children and young adults; strong organizational and scheduling skills necessary at $2500 per season ▶ 6–7 *lacrosse instructors* (minimum age 19) with experience playing lacrosse and coaching children; at least one year of college completed at $2000 per season ▶ 1–2 *lakefront directors* (minimum age 25) with American Red Cross lifeguard certification or equivalent required; experience instructing canoeing, sailing, and boating; supervisory and managerial skills necessary at $2000–$3000 per season ▶ 6–8 *martial arts instructors* (minimum age 19) with black belt in karate preferred; experience competing and teaching martial arts to children; at least one year of college completed at $2000 per season ▶ 4–6 *mountain biking instructors* (minimum age 19) with experience in biking and ability to instruct; at least one year of college completed at $2000 per season ▶ 2–4 *musical instruments instructors (keyboard, guitar, violin, trumpet, flute, etc)* (minimum age 19) with experience playing an instrument and ability to instruct; at least one year of college completed at $1800 per season ▶ 6 *nurses* (minimum age 25) with RN, LPN or EMT and experience working with children at $2000 per season ▶ 4–6 *office personnel* (minimum age 19) with experience working in a business office, good organizational skills, excellent telephone manner, and administration skills needed at $2000 per season ▶ 4–6 *petting zoo instructors* (minimum age 19) with experience caring for animals (feeding, watering, grooming) at $2000 per season ▶ 2–4 *photography instructors* (minimum age 19) with experience taking photos, developing negatives, printing photos, and darkroom procedures at $2000 per season ► 2–3 *program directors* (minimum age 30) with teaching/coaching license preferred; organizational and supervisory skills needed; experience in scheduling activities and staff at $2500 per season ► 1–2 *receptionists* (minimum age 21) with a good telephone manner, organizational skills, flexibility, and pleasant personality at $2000 per season ► 4–6 *riflery instructors* (minimum age 20) with NRA instructor certification or equivalent preferred; experience with 22-caliber rifles; at least one year of college completed at $2000 per season ► 4–6 *roller hockey instructors* (minimum age 19) with experience as a player and hockey instructor/coach for children; at least one year of college completed at $2000 per season ► 8–10 *ropes course/rock climbing instructors* (minimum age 19) with experience teaching rock climbing and zip line to children; professionally trained individuals; at least one year of college completed at $2000 per season ► 6–8 *sailing instructors* (minimum age 19) with American Red Cross sailing and lifeguard certification preferred; experience teaching sailing to children; at least one year of college completed at $2000 per season ► 2–4 *skateboarding instructors* (minimum age 19) with experience teaching skateboarding to children on half-pipe and street ramps at $2000 per season ► 4–6 *soccer instructors* (minimum age 19) with experience as a player and as an instructor/coach for children; at least one year of college completed at $2000 per season ► 4–6 *softball/baseball instructors* (minimum age 19) with experience as a player and softball/baseball instructor/coach for children; at least one year of college completed at $2000 per season ► 12–14 *swimming instructors* (minimum age 19) with American Red Cross WSI and lifeguard certification or equivalent preferred; experience teaching swimming to children; at least one year of college completed at $2000 per season ► 35–40 *team sports instructors (soccer, frisbee, field hockey, softball, baseball)* (minimum age 19) with experience playing the sport and coaching children; at least one year of college completed at $2000 per season ► 12–14 *tennis instructors and certified tennis professionals* (minimum age 19) with USTA license required for director position; experience playing and coaching tennis; at least one year of college completed at $2000 per season ► 1–2 *transportation directors* (minimum age 25) with driver's license and mechanical skills required; experience driving 15-passenger vans at $2500 per season ► 6–8 *volleyball instructors* (minimum age 19) with experience playing and coaching volleyball and at least one year of college completed at $1800 per season ► 1–2 *waterfront directors* (minimum age 25) with WSI and American Red Cross lifeguard certification or equivalent; pool management and maintenance skills; experience instructing children and supervisory skills at $2800 per season ► 4–6 *weight-lifting instructors* (minimum age 19) with experience in weight training and ability to instruct; at least one year of college completed at $2000 per season ► 4–6 *windsurfing instructors* (minimum age 19) with American Red Cross lifeguard certification or equivalent preferred; experience teaching windsurfing to children; at least one year of college completed at $2000 per season ► 4–6 *wrestling instructors* (minimum age 19) with experience teaching wrestling to children; at least one year of college completed at $2000 per season. Applicants must submit formal organization application, three personal references, two letters of recommendation, copies of certifications (if applicable). A telephone interview is required. International applicants accepted; must apply through a recognized agency.

Benefits and Preemployment Training Free housing, free meals, formal training, willing to provide letters of recommendation, on-the-job training, willing to complete paperwork for educational credit, willing to act as a professional reference, opportunity to attend seminars/workshops, travel reimbursement, and 3-day all expenses-paid winter camp ski reunion, free camp tuition children of senior staff members, free weekly laundry service. Preemployment training is required and includes accident prevention and safety, first aid, CPR, interpersonal skills, leadership skills.

Contact Brian B. Buynak, Camp Director, Camp Cayuga, PO Box 151, Suite PSJ, Peapack, New Jersey 07977. Telephone: 800-422-9842. Fax: 908-470-1228. E-mail: info@campcayuga. com. World Wide Web: http://www.campcayuga.com. Contact by e-mail, fax, mail, phone, or through World Wide Web site. Application deadline: continuous.

CAMP CHEN-A-WANDA
THOMPSON, PENNSYLVANIA 18465

General Information Coeducational residential camp serving 400 campers for a 50 day session. Established in 1939. 183-acre facility located 25 miles from Scranton. Features: heated Olympic-size pool; freshwater lake; indoor fitness center; indoor basketball court; 7 tennis courts; 3 soccer fields.

Profile of Summer Employees Total number: 150; typical ages: 19–24. 52% men; 48% women; 80% college students; 20% non-U.S. citizens. Nonsmokers preferred.

Employment Information Openings are from June 19 to August 17. Jobs available: ▶ 3 *arts and crafts specialists* (minimum age 19) at $600–$1800 per season ▶ 4 *baseball specialists* (minimum age 19) at $600–$1800 per season ▶ 4 *basketball specialists* (minimum age 19) at $600–$1800 per season ▶ 2 *go-cart/all terrain vehicle specialists* (minimum age 19) at $600–$1800 per season ▶ 1 *golf specialist* (minimum age 19) at $600–$1800 per season ▶ 2 *gymnastics specialists* (minimum age 19) at $600–$1800 per season ▶ 2 *lacrosse specialists* (minimum age 19) at $600–$1800 per season ▶ 2 *roller hockey specialists* (minimum age 19) at $600–$1800 per season ▶ 2–4 *ropes/rock climbing/rappelling specialists* (minimum age 19) at $700–$1800 per season ▶ 4 *soccer specialists* (minimum age 19) at $600–$1800 per season ▶ 2 *stage management/scenery staff members* (minimum age 19) at $600–$1800 per season ▶ 3 *tennis specialists* (minimum age 19) at $600–$1800 per season ▶ 2 *volleyball specialists* (minimum age 19) at $600–$1800 per season ▶ 10 *waterfront specialists (swimming, sailing, or waterskiing)* with WSI certification for swimming at $600–$1800 per season. Applicants must submit formal organization application, two personal references, two letters of recommendation. A telephone interview is required. International applicants accepted; must apply through a recognized agency.

Benefits and Preemployment Training Free housing, free meals, willing to provide letters of recommendation, willing to complete paperwork for educational credit, and travel reimbursement. Preemployment training is required and includes accident prevention and safety, interpersonal skills, leadership skills.

Contact Morey Baldwin, Director, Camp Chen-A-Wanda, 8 Claverton Court, Dix Hills, New York 11747. Telephone: 888-268-6535. Fax: 631-643-0920. E-mail: cneier@aol.com. World Wide Web: http://www.campchen-a-wanda.com. Contact by e-mail, fax, mail, phone, or through World Wide Web site. Application deadline: continuous.

CAMP HIDDEN FALLS
RR 2, BOX 720
DINGMAN'S FERRY, PENNSYLVANIA 18328

General Information Seven-week nonprofit residential camp for girls ages 9-17. Established in 1912. 1,000-acre facility located 15 miles from Stroudsburg. Features: horseback riding; in-ground pool; lake for canoes and sail boats; forests; Delaware River nearby; waterfalls.

Profile of Summer Employees Total number: 45; typical ages: 18–25. 5% men; 95% women; 20% minorities; 10% high school students; 70% college students; 5% retirees; 10% non-U.S. citizens; 20% local applicants. Nonsmokers preferred.

Employment Information Openings are from June 9 to August 17. Jobs available: ▶ 14–16 *counselors* (minimum age 18) at $200–$240 per week ▶ 4–5 *lifeguards* (minimum age 18) with WSI, lifeguard training, first aid/CPR, or ability to get training at $210–$250 per week ▶ 4–5 *nature counselors* (minimum age 18) with experience in the field at $220–$240 per week ▶ *program specialists* (minimum age 21) with experience in the field at $220–$240 per week ▶ 4–5 *riding instructors* (minimum age 18) with experience in the field at $210–$250 per week ▶ 1 *waterfront director* (minimum age 21) with supervisory experience and WSI or lifeguarding certification at $280–$320 per week. Applicants must submit formal organization application, three personal references. An in-person interview is recommended, but a telephone interview is acceptable. International applicants accepted; must apply through a recognized agency.

Benefits and Preemployment Training Free housing, free meals, formal training, possible full-time employment, health insurance, willing to provide letters of recommendation, on-the-job training, willing to complete paperwork for educational credit, willing to act as a professional reference, and opportunity to attend seminars/workshops. Preemployment training is required and includes accident prevention and safety, first aid, CPR, interpersonal skills, leadership skills, lifeguarding, archery, boating instruction.

Contact Ann Gillard, Camp Director, Camp Hidden Falls, PO Box 27540, Philadelphia, Pennsylvania 19118. Telephone: 866-564-2030 Ext. 263. Fax: 215-564-6953. E-mail: agillard@gssp.org. World Wide Web: http://www.gssp.org. Contact by e-mail, fax, mail, or phone. Application deadline: continuous.

CAMP LINDENMERE
RR1, BOX 160A
HENRYVILLE, PENNSYLVANIA 18332

General Information Private residential summer camp for children ages 7-17. Established in 1997. 159-acre facility located 90 miles from New York. Features: ropes course; trapeze; riding stages; swimming pool; lake; skateboard park.

Profile of Summer Employees Total number: 130; typical age: 22. 40% men; 60% women; 10% minorities; 30% college students; 50% non-U.S. citizens. Nonsmokers required.

Employment Information Openings are from May 30 to September 1. Jobs available: ▶ 40 *counselors/specialists in all areas* (minimum age 18) with some experience in area at $1400–$2000 per season. Applicants must submit formal organization application, resume, two personal references, background check. An in-person interview is recommended, but a telephone interview is acceptable. International applicants accepted; must apply through a recognized agency.

Benefits and Preemployment Training Free housing, free meals, willing to provide letters of recommendation, names of contacts, willing to act as a professional reference, and travel reimbursement. Preemployment training is required and includes accident prevention and safety, first aid, CPR, interpersonal skills, leadership skills.

Contact Jerry Marcus, Director, Camp Lindenmere, 12773 West Forest Hill Boulevard, Suite 1216, Wellington, Florida 33414. Telephone: 561-791-8988. Fax: 208-723-3288. E-mail: admin@camplindenmere.com. World Wide Web: http://www.camplindenmere.com. Contact by e-mail, fax, mail, phone, or through World Wide Web site. Application deadline: continuous.

CAMP LOHIKAN IN THE POCONO MOUNTAINS
WALLERVILLE ROAD
LAKE COMO, PENNSYLVANIA 18437

General Information Traditional coed summer camp for campers 6 to 15 years old that features 65 daily activities, evening activities, special events, intercamp games, trips, and more. Established in 1957. 1,200-acre facility located 30 miles from Scranton. Features: private lake; swimming pool; 11 tennis courts; 30 horses; 7 sports fields; 14 arts workshops.

Profile of Summer Employees Total number: 200; typical ages: 19–60. 50% men; 50% women; 5% minorities; 83% college students; 2% retirees; 5% non-U.S. citizens; 5% local applicants. Nonsmokers required.

Employment Information Openings are from June 1 to September 30. Jobs available: ▶ 6 *canoeing instructors* (minimum age 19) at $1400–$2500 per season ▶ 12 *creative arts instructors* (minimum age 19) at $1400–$2500 per season ▶ 7 *gymnastics instructors* (minimum age 19) at $1400–$2500 per season ▶ 10 *horseback riding instructors* at $1400–$2500 per season ▶ 10 *lifeguards* (minimum age 19) at $1400–$2500 per season ▶ 3 *mountain boarding instructors* (minimum age 19) at $1400–$2500 per season ▶ 3 *paintball instructors* (minimum age 19) at $1400–$2500 per season ▶ 5 *performing arts instructors* (minimum age 19) at $1400–$2500

Pennsylvania

per season ▶ 4 *pottery instructors* (minimum age 19) at $1400–$2500 per season ▶ 5 *rock climbing instructors* (minimum age 19) at $1400–$2500 per season ▶ 4 *ropes course instructors* (minimum age 19) at $1400–$2500 per season ▶ 6 *sailing instructors* (minimum age 19) at $1400–$2500 per season ▶ 3 *skateboarding instructors* (minimum age 19) at $1400–$2500 per season ▶ 10 *sports instructors* (minimum age 19) at $1400–$2500 per season ▶ 12 *tennis instructors* (minimum age 19) at $1400–$2500 per season ▶ 3 *woodworking instructors* (minimum age 19) at $1400–$2500 per season. Applicants must submit formal organization application, three personal references, three letters of recommendation. An in-person interview is recommended, but a telephone interview is acceptable. International applicants accepted; must apply through a recognized agency.

Benefits and Preemployment Training Free housing, free meals, formal training, possible full-time employment, willing to provide letters of recommendation, on-the-job training, willing to complete paperwork for educational credit, willing to act as a professional reference, and travel reimbursement. Preemployment training is required and includes accident prevention and safety, first aid, CPR, interpersonal skills, leadership skills.

Contact Ian Brassett, Staffing Director, Camp Lohikan in the Pocono Mountains, PO Box 189, Gladstone, New Jersey 07934. Telephone: 908-470-9317. Fax: 908-470-9319. E-mail: mail@lohikan.com. World Wide Web: http://www.lohikan.com. Contact by e-mail, fax, mail, phone, or through World Wide Web site. Application deadline: continuous.

CAMP SPEERS-ELJABAR YMCA
RR 1, BOX 85
DINGMANS FERRY, PENNSYLVANIA 18328

General Information Camp that places emphasis on values of honesty, caring, respect, and responsibility through traditional camp activities. 1,100-acre facility located 70 miles from New York. Features: 42 acre lake; high ropes course; 2 climbing towers; 2 camps; 2 riding rings; wooded and hilly setting.

Profile of Summer Employees Total number: 100; typical ages: 17–25. 45% men; 55% women; 5% high school students; 70% college students; 20% non-U.S. citizens; 5% local applicants. Nonsmokers required.

Employment Information Openings are from June 15 to August 30. Jobs available: ▶ 1–4 *adventure activities specialists* (minimum age 19) with high ropes, climbing tower, and belaying skills at $1900–$2100 per season ▶ *arts and crafts specialists* (minimum age 19) with arts and crafts skills at $1900–$2100 per season ▶ 55–85 *counselors* (minimum age 17) at $1700–$2100 per season ▶ 2 *land activities directors* (minimum age 21) with supervisory and leadership skills at $2200–$2500 per season ▶ 1–4 *ranch specialists* (minimum age 19) with horse back riding skills at $1900–$2100 per season ▶ 1–9 *special needs counselors* (minimum age 18) ▶ 1–2 *transportation coordinators* (minimum age 21) with a clean driving record at $1900–$2100 per season ▶ 2 *trip directors* (minimum age 21) with tripping and leadership skills at $2200–$2500 per season ▶ 5 *unit directors* (minimum age 21) with supervisory and leadership skills at $2200–$2500 per season ▶ 2 *waterfront directors* (minimum age 21) with supervisory and leadership skills at $2200–$2500 per season. Applicants must submit formal organization application, three personal references. A telephone interview is required. International applicants accepted; must apply through a recognized agency.

Contact A. Todd Lennig, Summer Camp Director, Camp Speers-Eljabar YMCA. Telephone: 570-828-2329. Fax: 570-828-2984. E-mail: ycamp@campspeersymca.org. Contact by e-mail, mail, or phone. Application deadline: continuous.

CAMP SUSQUEHANNOCK FOR GIRLS
LAKE CHOCONUT, CARMALT ROAD
FRIENDSVILLE, PENNSYLVANIA 18818

General Information Residential camp for 85 girls ages 7–17. Offers three-, four-, or seven-week sessions. Established in 1986. 750-acre facility located 17 miles from Binghamton, New York. Features: private fresh water lake (natural); wooded setting; 4 tennis courts; 14 saddle horses; large fieldstone lodge; excellent playing fields.

Profile of Summer Employees Total number: 40; typical ages: 18–28. 13% men; 87% women; 60% college students; 6% retirees; 60% non-U.S. citizens; 5% local applicants. Nonsmokers required.

Employment Information Openings are from June to August. Jobs available: ▶ 1 *archery instructor* (minimum age 18) with NAA instructor's certificate at $1000–$2000 per season ▶ 2 *arts and crafts instructors* (minimum age 18) at $1000–$1500 per season ▶ 2 *camp craft (outdoor camping skills)/nature/ecology instructors* (minimum age 18) at $1000–$2000 per season ▶ 2 *field sports/arts staff members (hockey, lacrosse, soccer, volleyball, basketball, dance, drama, and singing)* (minimum age 18) with high school diploma required, team play experience (high school and above), and experience instructing the sport preferred at $1000–$2000 per season ▶ 2 *horseback riders* (minimum age 18) with Horsemanship Association, Pony Club or similar certification preferred; should have experience riding, competing, and handling horses; horsemanship teaching experience preferred at $1000–$2500 per season ▶ 1 *nurse* with RN license at a negotiable salary ▶ 2 *softball instructors* (minimum age 18) with high school diploma required, team play experience (high school and above), and instructing experience preferred at $1000–$2000 per season ▶ 2 *swimming instructors* (minimum age 18) with lifeguard certification at $900–$1500 per season ▶ 2 *tennis instructors* (minimum age 18) at $1200–$2000 per season. Applicants must submit formal organization application, letter of interest, resume, three personal references. An in-person interview is recommended, but a telephone interview is acceptable. International applicants accepted; must apply through a recognized agency.

Benefits and Preemployment Training Free housing, free meals, formal training, willing to provide letters of recommendation, on-the-job training, willing to complete paperwork for educational credit, willing to act as a professional reference, opportunity to attend seminars/workshops, and travel reimbursement. Preemployment training is required and includes accident prevention and safety, first aid, CPR, interpersonal skills, leadership skills, teaching, coaching, officiating, campcraft.

Contact Tarryn Rozen, Camp Susquehannock for Girls. E-mail: tarryn@susquehannock.com. World Wide Web: http://www.susquehannock.com. Contact by e-mail. No phone calls. Application deadline: March 1.

CAMP WATONKA
HAWLEY, PENNSYLVANIA 18428

General Information Residential science camp for 120 boys offering hands-on experience in all areas of science combined with traditional camp activities. Established in 1963. 250-acre facility located 30 miles from Scranton. Features: lake; fishing stream; sports facilities; biking trails; hiking trails; modern buildings.

Profile of Summer Employees Total number: 60; typical ages: 20–40. 95% men; 5% women; 10% minorities; 5% high school students; 55% college students; 20% non-U.S. citizens; 10% local applicants. Nonsmokers required.

Employment Information Openings are from June 15 to August 20. Jobs available: ▶ *archery instructor* should be college student or graduate at $1800–$2500 per season ▶ 3 *arts and crafts staff members* at $1500–$2500 per season ▶ 15 *cabin counselors* should be college juniors or seniors at $1500–$2500 per season ▶ *editors* ▶ *magic instructor* should be college student or graduate at $2000–$3000 per season ▶ 3 *minibike riding instructors* with experience in the field at $1500–$3000 per season ▶ *photography instructor* should be college student or graduate at $1800–$2500 per season ▶ 8 *science instructors* should be college student or graduate at $2000–$3000 per season ▶ 8 *science supervisors* with teaching certification at $2500–$3500 per season ▶ 1 *waterfront director* with ARC certification at $2500–$3500 per season ▶ 5 *waterfront/water sports instructors* with ARC certification at $1500–$3000 per season ▶ 2 *woodworking instructors* with teaching certification at $2500–$3500 per season. Applicants must submit formal organization application, letter of interest, resume. An in-person interview is recommended, but a telephone interview is acceptable. International applicants accepted; must apply through a recognized agency.

Benefits and Preemployment Training Free housing, free meals, formal training, willing to provide letters of recommendation, on-the-job training, and willing to act as a professional reference. Preemployment training is required and includes accident prevention and safety, first aid, CPR, leadership skills.

Contact Donald P. Wacker, Director, Camp Watonka, PO Box 127, Hawley, Pennsylvania 18428. Telephone: 570-857-1401. World Wide Web: http://www.watonka.com. Contact by mail or phone. Application deadline: continuous.

CAMP WAYNE FOR BOYS
PRESTON PARK, PENNSYLVANIA 18455

General Information Private resident camp with sports instruction-focused program offering all land, water sports, and arts and crafts. Established in 1921. 400-acre facility located 40 miles from Binghamton. Features: freshwater lake; 12 tennis courts; 3 indoor gyms; swimming pool; 4 baseball fields; climbing tower/high ropes course.

Profile of Summer Employees Total number: 150; typical ages: 19–65. 75% men; 25% women; 5% minorities; 75% college students; 5% retirees; 15% non-U.S. citizens; 5% local applicants. Nonsmokers preferred.

Employment Information Openings are from June 19 to August 16. Jobs available: ▶ 60–80 *counselors* (minimum age 18) with a minimum of 1 year of college completed at $1500–$2000 per season. Applicants must submit formal organization application, two letters of recommendation. An in-person interview is recommended, but a telephone interview is acceptable. International applicants accepted; must obtain own visa, apply through a recognized agency.

Benefits and Preemployment Training Free housing, free meals, formal training, willing to provide letters of recommendation, on-the-job training, willing to complete paperwork for educational credit, willing to act as a professional reference, and travel reimbursement. Preemployment training is required and includes accident prevention and safety, interpersonal skills, leadership skills.

Contact Peter Corpuel, Director, Camp Wayne for Boys, 55 Channel Drive, Port Washington, New York 11050. Telephone: 516-883-3067. Fax: 516-883-2985. E-mail: info@campwayne. com. World Wide Web: http://www.campwayne.com. Contact by e-mail, phone, or through World Wide Web site. Application deadline: continuous.

CAMP WESTMONT
ROUTE 370
POYNTELLE, PENNSYLVANIA 18454

General Information Residential camp offering all land and water sports, individual and team athletics, arts and crafts, drama and dance, woodworking and ceramics, and circus and gymnastics to 380 campers ages 6–16 for eight weeks. Established in 1980. 225-acre facility located 100 miles from New York, New York. Features: freshwater lake and olympic size pool; wooded setting; 8 tennis courts; 3 soccer fields and 4 baseball fields; flying and stationary trapeze; 2 hockey rinks.

Profile of Summer Employees Total number: 150; typical ages: 18–45. 50% men; 50% women; 5% minorities; 5% high school students; 85% college students; 2% retirees; 10% non-U.S. citizens; 5% local applicants. Nonsmokers required.

Employment Information Openings are from June 15 to August 21. Jobs available: ▶ 80–100 *general counselors* (minimum age 18) with camp experience and experience working with children (coaching, Scouts, or similar) at $1500–$2500 per season ▶ 6–12 *group leaders* (minimum age 25) with camp or teaching experience with children at $2500–$3000 per season ▶ 6–8 *tennis specialists* (minimum age 18) with experience playing and/or teaching tennis at $1500–$2500 per season ▶ 6–10 *waterfront specialists* (minimum age 18) with WSI/lifeguard certification and experience as a swimming instructor or lifeguard at $1500–$2500 per season. Applicants must submit formal organization application, letter of interest, resume, two personal references, two letters of recommendation, photo and copy of proof of age. An in-person interview is recommended, but a telephone interview is acceptable. International applicants accepted; must obtain own visa, apply through a recognized agency.

Benefits and Preemployment Training Free housing, free meals, willing to provide letters of recommendation, on-the-job training, willing to act as a professional reference, and travel reimbursement. Preemployment training is required and includes accident prevention and safety, interpersonal skills, leadership skills.

Contact Jack Pinsky, Owner/Director, Camp Westmont, 14 Squirrel Drive, East Rockaway, New York 11518. Telephone: 516-599-2963. Fax: 516-599-1979. E-mail: campwestmt@aol.com. World Wide Web: http://www.campwestmont.com. Contact by e-mail, fax, mail, phone, or through World Wide Web site. Application deadline: continuous.

CENTER FOR STUDENT MISSIONS–PHILADELPHIA
PHILADELPHIA, PENNSYLVANIA
See Center for Student Missions on page 37 for complete description.

CENTER FOR TALENTED YOUTH/JOHNS HOPKINS UNIVERSITY–DICKINSON COLLEGE
CARLISLE, PENNSYLVANIA
See Center for Talented Youth/Johns Hopkins University on page 131 for complete description.

CENTER FOR TALENTED YOUTH/JOHNS HOPKINS UNIVERSITY–FRANKLIN AND MARSHALL COLLEGE
LANCASTER, PENNSYLVANIA
See Center for Talented Youth/Johns Hopkins University on page 131 for complete description.

CENTER FOR TALENTED YOUTH/JOHNS HOPKINS UNIVERSITY–LAFAYETTE COLLEGE
EASTON, PENNSYLVANIA
See Center for Talented Youth/Johns Hopkins University on page 131 for complete description.

CENTER FOR TALENTED YOUTH/JOHNS HOPKINS UNIVERSITY–MORAVIAN COLLEGE
BETHLEHEM, PENNSYLVANIA
See Center for Talented Youth/Johns Hopkins University on page 131 for complete description.

COLLEGE GIFTED PROGRAMS
BRYN MAWR COLLEGE
BRYN MAWR, PENNSYLVANIA 19010

General Information Residential educational academic summer camp for gifted and talented students in grades 4-11. Program blends in-depth academics with recreational and cultural activities. Established in 1984. 135-acre facility located 11 miles from Philadelphia. Features: dormitories; campus classroom facilities; campus recreational facilities include pool, tennis courts, and gym; campus library; beautiful college setting.

Profile of Summer Employees Total number: 70; typical ages: 19–70. 50% men; 50% women; 30% minorities; 50% college students; 10% retirees; 10% non-U.S. citizens; 25% local applicants. Nonsmokers required.

Employment Information Openings are from June 26 to August 7. Jobs available: ▶ 35 *counselors* with two years of college completed and experience working with children at $1000 to $1300 per 3-week session ▶ 4 *directors* with at least 5 years teaching/supervisory experience; master's degree required, doctorate preferred at $4500–$7000 per year ▶ 7 *housemasters/instructors (residential)* with master's degree, teaching and supervisory experience at $2500 to $3500 per 3-week session ▶ 20 *instructors (non-residential)* with master's degree and teaching experience at $725 to $2900 per 3-week session ▶ 2 *nurses* with RN license, school experience preferred at $260–$300 per day. Applicants must submit formal organization application, resume, academic transcripts, two personal references, two letters of recommendation. An in-person interview is recommended, but a telephone interview is acceptable. International applicants accepted; must apply through a recognized agency.

Benefits and Preemployment Training Free housing, free meals, willing to provide letters of recommendation, willing to complete paperwork for educational credit, and willing to act as a professional reference. Preemployment training is required and includes accident prevention and safety, interpersonal skills, leadership skills, instructional strategies for gifted students.

Contact Charles Zeichner, Director, College Gifted Programs, 120 Littleton Road, Suite 201, Parsippany, New Jersey 07054-1803. Telephone: 973-334-6991. Fax: 973-334-9756. E-mail: info@cgp-sig.com. World Wide Web: http://www.cgp-sig.com. Contact by e-mail, fax, mail, phone, or through World Wide Web site. Application deadline: continuous.

COLLEGE SETTLEMENT OF PHILADELPHIA
600 WITMER ROAD
HORSHAM, PENNSYLVANIA 19044

General Information Residential and day camp serving mostly economically disadvantaged youths ages 7–14 from the Philadelphia metropolitan area. Established in 1922. 235-acre facility located 15 miles from Philadelphia. Features: small lake/pond; low ropes/high ropes course; 2 pools; lighted hard-top for tennis and sports; 6 cabins and large house/dormitory; full-service dining hall.

Profile of Summer Employees Total number: 65; typical ages: 16–30. 50% men; 50% women; 20% minorities; 10% high school students; 80% college students; 40% non-U.S. citizens; 10% local applicants. Nonsmokers preferred.

Employment Information Openings are from June 1 to August 25. Spring break, winter break, and year-round positions also offered. Jobs available: ▶ 2 *adventure staff* (minimum age 21) with experience in outdoor recreation (preferred) and a valid driver's license at $3000–$3500 per season ▶ 26 *cabin counselors* (minimum age 19) with desire to have fun at camp with great kids at $1800–$2500 per season ▶ 2–4 *environmentalists* (minimum age 21) with driver's license (preferred) and background in teaching/sciences/animal care at $2000 per season ▶ 3–4 *pool directors* (minimum age 21) with WSI and LGT certification (training available) at $2000–$3000 per season ▶ 2 *provisions coordinators* (minimum age 21) with driver's license at $2000–$3000 per season ▶ 5 *teachers/naturalists* (minimum age 21) with background in life science, ecology, or environmental education preferred at $225–$275 per week ▶ 3 *trip leaders* (minimum age 21) with driver's license and experience (preferred), training provided at $3000–$3500 per season ▶ 3 *unit leaders* (minimum age 21) with supervisory experience (preferred) at $3000–$3500 per season. Applicants must submit formal organization application, letter of interest, resume, three personal references. An in-person interview is recommended, but a telephone interview is acceptable. International applicants accepted; must apply through a recognized agency.

Benefits and Preemployment Training Free housing, free meals, formal training, possible full-time employment, willing to provide letters of recommendation, on-the-job training, willing to complete paperwork for educational credit, willing to act as a professional reference, opportunity to attend seminars/workshops, and possible certification training for archery, boating, lifeguard, and conflict resolution/counseling. Preemployment training is required and includes accident prevention and safety, first aid, CPR, interpersonal skills, leadership skills, boating, belaying, caving, wilderness first aid, lifeguarding, conflict resolution.

Contact Karyn McGee, Director of Resident Programs, College Settlement of Philadelphia, 600 Witmer Road, Horsham, Pennsylvania 19044. Telephone: 215-542-7974. Fax: 215-542-7457. E-mail: camps@i-bob.com. World Wide Web: http://www.collegesettlement.org. Contact by e-mail, fax, mail, phone, or through World Wide Web site. Application deadline: application by April 15th is preferred.

CYBERCAMPS–BRYN MAWR COLLEGE
PHILADELPHIA, PENNSYLVANIA
See Cybercamps–University of Washington on page 326 for complete description.

DORNEY PARK AND WILDWATER KINGDOM
3830 DORNEY PARK ROAD
ALLENTOWN, PENNSYLVANIA 18104
General Information Amusement park featuring more than 100 rides and attractions, including 4 roller coasters and a waterpark. Established in 1860. 200-acre facility located 50 miles from Philadelphia. Features: 5 designated children's areas; 11 water slides; wave pool; 1921 antique wooden Dentzel carousel; daily live entertainment.

Profile of Summer Employees Total number: 2,500.

Employment Information Openings are from May 1 to October 15. Jobs available: ▶ 350 *food hosts and hostesses* ▶ 100 *game attendants* ▶ 200 *lifeguards* ▶ 180 *merchandise clerks* ▶ 350 *ride operators* ▶ *security staff.* Applicants must submit formal organization application. An in-person interview is required. International applicants accepted; must apply through a recognized agency.

Benefits and Preemployment Training On-the-job training, willing to complete paperwork for educational credit, and scholarships available. Preemployment training is required and includes CPR.

Contact Eileen Minninger, Personnel Manager, Dorney Park and Wildwater Kingdom, 3830 Dorney Park Road, Allentown, Pennsylvania 18104. Telephone: 610-391-7752. Contact by mail or phone. Application deadline: continuous.

FORESITE SPORTS, INC.
632 GERMANTOWN PIKE
LAFAYETTE HILL, PENNSYLVANIA 19444
General Information Organization dedicated to fostering a love of golf by providing beginner and intermediate golfers with the opportunity to learn the fundamental skills of the game. Established in 1998. Located 10 miles from Philadelphia. Features: golf course or range.

Profile of Summer Employees Total number: 10; typical ages: 16–35. 70% men; 30% women; 20% high school students; 50% college students; 90% local applicants. Nonsmokers preferred.

Employment Information Openings are from June to August. Jobs available: ▶ 1–2 *camp counselors* (minimum age 16) at $8–$10 per hour ▶ 10–15 *golf instructors* (minimum age 18) at $10–$15 per hour. Applicants must submit a formal organization application, resume. An in-person interview is recommended, but a telephone interview is acceptable. International applicants accepted; must obtain own visa, obtain own working papers.

Benefits and Preemployment Training Possible full-time employment, willing to provide letters of recommendation, on-the-job training, willing to complete paperwork for educational credit, willing to act as a professional reference, and travel reimbursement. Preemployment training is required and includes interpersonal skills, leadership skills, golf skills.

Contact James Nam, Foresite Sports, Inc. Telephone: 610-825-2441. Fax: 610-825-2681. E-mail: info@forsitesports.com. World Wide Web: http://foresitesports.com. Contact by phone. Application deadline: continuous.

FORT NECESSITY NATIONAL BATTLEFIELD
1 WASHINGTON PARKWAY
FARMINGTON, PENNSYLVANIA 15437

General Information George Washington's first command and battlefield commemorating the opening battle of the French and Indian War and westward expansion along the National Road. Established in 1931. 903-acre facility located 70 miles from Pittsburgh. Features: reconstructed fort and battlefield; visitor center; 19th Century tavern; picnic area; grave site of General Braddock; skirmish site, Jumonville Glen.

Profile of Summer Employees Total number: 2; typical ages: 22–65. 75% men; 25% women; 25% minorities; 50% college students; 25% retirees.

Employment Information Openings are from June 1 to August 25. Jobs available: ▶ 1–2 *interpretive park rangers* (minimum age 18) with public speaking experience and interest in history at $10–$11 per hour. Applicants must submit a formal organization application.

Benefits and Preemployment Training Housing at a cost, formal training, willing to provide letters of recommendation, on-the-job training, willing to complete paperwork for educational credit, and willing to act as a professional reference.

Contact Mary Ellen Snyder, Supervisory Park Ranger, Fort Necessity National Battlefield, 1 Washington Parkway, Farmington, Pennsylvania 15437. Telephone: 724-329-5512. Fax: 724-329-8682. E-mail: mary_ellen_snyder@nps.gov. World Wide Web: http://www.nps.gov/fone. Contact by e-mail, fax, mail, phone, or through World Wide Web site. Application deadline: January 15.

HERSHEYPARK
100 WEST HERSHEYPARK DRIVE
HERSHEY, PENNSYLVANIA 17033

General Information Facility producing four residential shows, song and dance revues, and other types of family entertainment. Established in 1907. 110-acre facility located 100 miles from Philadelphia. Features: 8 roller coasters; clean and green; subsidized housing; physical trainer.

Profile of Summer Employees Total number: 5,000. 50% men; 50% women.

Employment Information Openings are from May 10 to September 3. Jobs available: ▶ 10 *seamstresses/dressers* with experience in the field at $350–$450 per week ▶ 50 *singing/dancing performers* with experience in the field at $420–$480 per week ▶ 4 *sound technicians* with experience in the field at $350–$450 per week ▶ 5 *stage managers* with experience in the field at $400–$500 per week. Applicants must submit a formal organization application, letter of interest, resume, audition. International applicants accepted.

Benefits and Preemployment Training Housing at a cost, willing to provide letters of recommendation, willing to complete paperwork for educational credit, and willing to act as a professional reference. Preemployment training is required.

Contact Cherie Lingle, Entertainment Manager, Hersheypark, 100 West Hersheypark Drive, Hershey, Pennsylvania 17033. Telephone: 717-534-3349. Fax: 717-534-3336. World Wide Web: http://www.hersheypa.com. Contact by fax, mail, or phone. Application deadline: continuous.

JUMONVILLE
887 JUMONVILLE ROAD
HOPWOOD, PENNSYLVANIA 15445

General Information Residential Christian camp serving 250–300 persons of all age levels per week. Established in 1941. 281-acre facility located 50 miles from Pittsburgh. Features: 60-foot tall steel cross; high- and low-elements ropes course; adventure center; campus like setting; mountain location; excellent sports facilities.

Profile of Summer Employees Total number: 45; typical ages: 16–25. 50% men; 50% women; 5% minorities; 10% high school students; 90% college students; 10% local applicants. Nonsmokers preferred.

Employment Information Openings are from May 15 to August 25. Jobs available: ▶ 1 *adventure program coordinator* (minimum age 19) at $192 per week ▶ 2 *adventure staff members* (minimum age 18) at $192 per week ▶ 1 *business manager/truck driver* (minimum age 18, prefer 21 or older) at $210 per week ▶ 2 *cookout staff members* at $192 per week ▶ 5–8 *counselors* (minimum age 18) at $192 per week ▶ 2 *dining room staff members* at $192 per week ▶ 3–4 *dishroom staff members* at $210 per week ▶ 1 *health-care staff member* with paramedic, LPN, or RN license at $192 per week ▶ 1 *information technology coordinator* at $192 per week ▶ 1 *kitchen helper* at $192 per week ▶ 2 *lifeguards* with certification at $192 per week ▶ 3–4 *multimedia specialists and Internet staff* at $192 per week ▶ 2 *multipurpose floaters* at $192 per week ▶ 1 *office assistant/business manager* at $192 per week ▶ 2 *snack shop workers* at $192 per week ▶ 1–2 *songleaders* with musical abilities (guitar playing a plus) at $192 per week. Applicants must submit a formal organization application, three personal references. An in-person interview is required.

Benefits and Preemployment Training Free housing, free meals, willing to provide letters of recommendation, on-the-job training, willing to complete paperwork for educational credit, and willing to act as a professional reference. Preemployment training is required and includes accident prevention and safety, first aid, CPR, interpersonal skills, leadership skills.

Contact Larry Beatty, President, Jumonville, 887 Jumonville Road, Hopwood, Pennsylvania 15445. Telephone: 724-439-4912. Fax: 724-439-1415. E-mail: info@jumonville.org. World Wide Web: http://www.jumonville.org. Contact by e-mail, fax, mail, phone, or through World Wide Web site. Application deadline: March 15.

KENNYWOOD PARK
4800 KENNYWOOD BOULEVARD
WEST MIFFLIN, PENNSYLVANIA 15122

General Information Amusement park servicing more than 1 million guests per season. Established in 1898. 40-acre facility located 7 miles from Pittsburgh. Features: roller coasters; cafe; lagoon; dark rides; pavilions; food concessions.

Profile of Summer Employees Total number: 1,500–1,600; typical ages: 16–26. 47% men; 53% women; 18% minorities; 20% high school students; 70% college students; 10% retirees; 100% local applicants.

Employment Information Openings are from April 15 to September 6. Jobs available: ▶ 1500 *team members (rides, games, and refreshments)* (minimum age 15) at $5.80 per hour. Applicants must submit a formal organization application, personal reference. An in-person interview is required.

Benefits and Preemployment Training Formal training and on-the-job training. Preemployment training is required and includes accident prevention and safety, interpersonal skills.

Contact Joe Barron, Human Resources Director, Kennywood Park, 4800 Kennywood Boulevard, West Mifflin, Pennsylvania 15122. Telephone: 412-461-0500 Ext. 1106. Fax: 412-464-0719. Contact by fax, mail, or phone. Application deadline: continuous.

KEYSTONE TALL TREE SUMMER RESIDENT CAMP PROGRAM
164 SKYMEADOW LANE
AVONMORE, PENNSYLVANIA 15618

General Information A residential camp program with six-day sessions for girls ages 5–17. Serves approximately 400 campers per summer. Established in 1956. 440-acre facility located 30 miles from Pittsburgh. Features: wooded setting; fishing pond; sports field; lodges and tents; horses; canoe pond.

Profile of Summer Employees Total number: 15–20; typical ages: 18–40. 5% men; 95% women; 80% college students; 25% non-U.S. citizens; 75% local applicants. Nonsmokers preferred.

Employment Information Openings are from June 15 to August 15. Jobs available: ▶ 1–4 *archery instructors* must be local personnel with flexible hours ▶ 1–2 *assistant camp directors* (minimum age 21) with parks/recreation/out-of-doors experience at $190–$275 per week ▶ 1 *assistant counselor* (minimum age 18) ▶ 1 *assistant riding instructor* (minimum age 18) ▶ 1 *camp director* (minimum age 25) with BS in education and parks/recreation/out-of-doors experience at $235–$375 per week ▶ 1 *canoeing instructor* must be local personnel with flexible hours ▶ 1 *head counselor* (minimum age 21) with educational background in child development, social work, or early childhood education ▶ 1 *head riding instructor* (minimum age 18) ▶ 1–4 *health supervisors* (minimum age 25) with RN, EMT, paramedic, or physician's assistant license and CPR/first aid certification at $155–$245 per week ▶ 1–4 *kitchen supervisors* (minimum age 25) at $280–$350 per week ▶ 1–4 *lifeguards* (minimum age 18) with CPR/first aid/lifeguard certification (must be local personnel with flexible hours) ▶ 1 *ropes course instructor (usually volunteer)* must be local personnel with flexible hours ▶ 1 *sailing instructor* must be local personnel with flexible hours ▶ 1 *waterfront director* (minimum age 18) with CPR/first aid/ lifeguard certification. Applicants must submit letter of interest, resume, three personal references, three letters of recommendation. An in-person interview is required. International applicants accepted; must apply through a recognized agency.

Benefits and Preemployment Training Free housing, free meals, willing to provide letters of recommendation, on-the-job training, willing to complete paperwork for educational credit, and willing to act as a professional reference. Preemployment training is required and includes accident prevention and safety, first aid, CPR, interpersonal skills, leadership skills.

Contact Ms. Debra Gras, Program Director, Keystone Tall Tree Summer Resident Camp Program, RD 7, Box 368, Kittanning, Pennsylvania 16201. Telephone: 724-543-2681 Ext. 214. Fax: 724-543-6313. World Wide Web: http://www.girlscouts-wpa.org. Contact by fax, mail, or phone. Application deadline: March 31.

LONGACRE EXPEDITIONS
4030 MIDDLE RIDGE ROAD
NEWPORT, PENNSYLVANIA 17074-8110

General Information Adventure travel program in Pennsylvania for teenagers, emphasizing group living skills, physical challenges, and fun. Longacre's challenging programs place equal emphasis on physical accomplishment and emotional growth. Established in 1981. 35-acre facility located 35 miles from Harrisburg. Features: ropes course; climbing wall; wooded setting.

Profile of Summer Employees Total number: 30; typical ages: 21–32. 50% men; 50% women; 10% minorities; 40% college students; 10% local applicants. Nonsmokers required.

Employment Information Openings are from June 15 to August 15. Jobs available: ▶ 24 *assistant trip leaders* (minimum age 21) with good driving record, wilderness first aid, and CPR at

$252–$300 per week ► 1 *equipment manager* (minimum age 21) with good driving record, wilderness first aid, and CPR at $180–$240 per week ► 2 *rock climbing instructors* (minimum age 21) with wilderness first aid and CPR at $300–$450 per week ► 8 *support and logistics staff members* (minimum age 21) with good driving record, wilderness first aid, and CPR at $180–$240 per week. Applicants must submit a formal organization application, letter of interest, resume, three personal references. An in-person interview is recommended, but a telephone interview is acceptable. International applicants accepted; must obtain own visa, obtain own working papers.

Benefits and Preemployment Training Free housing, free meals, willing to provide letters of recommendation, on-the-job training, willing to complete paperwork for educational credit, willing to act as a professional reference, and pro-deal purchase program. Preemployment training is required and includes accident prevention and safety, interpersonal skills, leadership skills.

Contact Meredith Schuler, Director, Longacre Expeditions, 4030 Middle Ridge Road, Newport, Pennsylvania 17074-8110. Telephone: 717-567-6790. Fax: 717-567-3955. E-mail: longacre@ longacreexpeditions.com. World Wide Web: http://www.longacreexpeditions.com. Contact by e-mail, fax, mail, phone, or through World Wide Web site. Application deadline: continuous.

MERCERSBURG ACADEMY SUMMER AND EXTENDED PROGRAMS
300 EAST SEMINARY STREET
MERCERSBURG, PENNSYLVANIA 17236

General Information Summer camps and workshops featuring quality staff with excellent reputations and credentials. 330-acre facility located near Washington, D.C. Features: rural location; wooded setting; dormitories; mountainous region.

Profile of Summer Employees Typical ages: 17–93. 50% men; 50% women. Nonsmokers required.

Employment Information Openings are from June 20 to August 5. Jobs available: ► 1–10 *adventure camps counselors* (minimum age 18). Applicants must submit a formal organization application, resume. A telephone interview is required. International applicants accepted.

Benefits and Preemployment Training Free housing and free meals.

Contact Melody McBeth, Site Coordinator, Mercersburg Academy Summer and Extended Programs. Telephone: 717-328-6225. Fax: 717-328-9072. E-mail: summerprograms@mercersburg. edu. World Wide Web: http://www.mercersburg.edu. Contact by e-mail, fax, mail, or phone.

ONEKA
TAFTON, PENNSYLVANIA 18464

General Information Residential girls camp serving 120 campers in 3½- and 7-week sessions. Established in 1908. 7-acre facility located 30 miles from Scranton. Features: freshwater lake; wooded setting; 3 tennis courts.

Profile of Summer Employees Total number: 35; typical ages: 18–55. 5% men; 95% women; 5% high school students; 95% college students; 30% non-U.S. citizens; 15% local applicants. Nonsmokers preferred.

Employment Information Openings are from June 20 to August 25. Jobs available: ► 1 *aquatic director* (minimum age 21) with WSI, LGT, CPR, first aid, and experience (preferred) at $1800– $2200 per season ► 1 *archery instructor* (minimum age 19) with good personal shooting skills (employee may be sent for further training) at $1000–$1400 per season ► 2 *arts and crafts instructors* (minimum age 19) with experience at $1000–$1400 per season ► 1 *assistant program director* (minimum age 21) with two years of camp experience at $1800–$2200 per season ► 1 *campcraft instructor* (minimum age 19) with experience in the field at $1000–$1400 per season ► 3 *canoeing/kayaking/boating/sailing instructors* (minimum age 19) with LT, CPR, first aid, and WSI certification (preferred) and experience in the field at $1000–$1500 per season ▶ 1 *drama instructor* (minimum age 21) with experience in directing and set design at $1000–$1400 per season ▶ 3 *field sports/hockey/soccer/softball instructors* (minimum age 19) with experience in the field at $1000–$1400 per season ▶ 2 *maintenance helpers* (minimum age 16) at $800–$1000 per season ▶ 1 *music instructor* (minimum age 19) with piano-playing ability and knowledge of show tunes at $1000–$1400 per season ▶ 2 *nurses* with RN license at $2500–$3500 per season ▶ 1 *program director* (minimum age 25) with three years of camp experience and good management and people skills preferred at $2000–$2500 per season ▶ 5 *swimming instructors/lifeguards* (minimum age 19) with LT, CPR, first aid, WSI certification, and experience at $1000–$1500 per season ▶ 2 *tennis instructors* (minimum age 19) with experience at $1000–$1400 per season ▶ 1 *volleyball instructor* (minimum age 19) with experience at $1000–$1400 per season. Applicants must submit formal organization application, resume, three personal references. An in-person interview is recommended, but a telephone interview is acceptable. International applicants accepted; must apply through a recognized agency.

Benefits and Preemployment Training Free housing, free meals, willing to provide letters of recommendation, on-the-job training, willing to complete paperwork for educational credit, and opportunity to attend seminars/workshops. Preemployment training is required and includes accident prevention and safety, first aid, CPR, interpersonal skills, leadership skills, lifeguard training.

Contact Dale H. Dohner, Camp Director, ONEKA, 10 Oakford Road, Wayne, Pennsylvania 19087. Telephone: 610-687-6260. Fax: 610-687-6260. World Wide Web: http://www.oneka.com. Contact by fax, mail, phone, or through World Wide Web site. Application deadline: continuous.

PENNSYLVANIA DEPARTMENT OF TRANSPORTATION
400 NORTH STREET, 5TH FLOOR
HARRISBURG, PENNSYLVANIA 17105

General Information State government agency responsible for the planning, design, construction, and maintenance of Pennsylvania's transportation systems. Established in 1903. Features: walking distance to Capitol; 3 miles to Governor's Mansion; 12 miles to Hershey Park; walking distance to state library; walking distance to Citi Island where basketball games are played and other attractions like baseball are held; centrally located: Philadelphia, Pittsburgh, Washington D.C., New York City, Baltimore.

Profile of Summer Employees Total number: 2,000; typical ages: 18–25. 70% men; 30% women; 10% minorities; 4% high school students; 85% college students; 1% non-U.S. citizens.

Employment Information Openings are from May 1 to October 30. Spring break, winter break, and year-round positions also offered. Jobs available: ▶ *business intern* at $10.31 per hour ▶ *engineering intern* should have completed sophomore year of college at $11.62 per hour ▶ *engineering/scientific/technical interns* should be currently enrolled as a college student and majoring in engineering, math, science, or architecture at $10.31 per hour ▶ *government service interns* should be currently enrolled as a college student in any major at $10.31 per hour ▶ *transportation/construction inspectors* with 2 years of construction inspection experience at $10.31 per hour. Applicants must submit personal data sheet with resume attached. An in-person interview is recommended, but a telephone interview is acceptable.

Benefits and Preemployment Training Formal training, possible full-time employment, willing to provide letters of recommendation, on-the-job training, willing to complete paperwork for educational credit, willing to act as a professional reference, and travel reimbursement.

Contact Recruiting Office, Pennsylvania Department of Transportation, 400 North Street, 5th Floor, Harrisburg, Pennsylvania 17105. Telephone: 717-787-5711. World Wide Web: http://www.dot.state.pa.us. Contact by mail, phone, or through World Wide Web site. Application deadline: April 15.

SALVATION ARMY OF LOWER BUCKS
215 APPLETREE DRIVE
LEVITTOWN, PENNSYLVANIA 19055

General Information Community-based center that offers a full range of service and multi-generational programs. Established in 1865. 8-acre facility located 7 miles from Philadelphia. Features: air-conditioned facility; full-size gym; computer room; craft room; ballfield; church connected to building.

Profile of Summer Employees Total number: 7; typical ages: 18–25. 20% men; 80% women; 10% minorities; 10% high school students; 80% college students; 10% retirees; 90% local applicants. Nonsmokers preferred.

Employment Information Openings are from June 12 to August 30. Jobs available: ▶ 4 *day care counselors* (minimum age 17) with experience caring for children (babysitting, day care, or similar) at $6–$7 per hour ▶ 6–10 *summer camp counselors* (minimum age 18) with any type of childcare background and first aid/CPR (training provided) at $6–$7 per hour. Applicants must submit formal organization application, letter of interest, resume, academic transcripts, two personal references, two letters of recommendation. An in-person interview is required. International applicants accepted; must apply through a recognized agency.

Benefits and Preemployment Training Free meals, willing to provide letters of recommendation, willing to complete paperwork for educational credit, and willing to act as a professional reference. Preemployment training is required and includes accident prevention and safety, first aid, CPR, interpersonal skills, leadership skills.

Contact Maureen C. Carson, Community Programs Coordinator, Salvation Army of Lower Bucks, Appletree Drive and Autumn Lane, Levittown, Pennsylvania 19055. Telephone: 215-945-0718. Fax: 215-945-0607. Contact by fax. Application deadline: January 20.

SHAVER'S CREEK ENVIRONMENTAL CENTER, PENNSYLVANIA STATE UNIVERSITY
RR 1, BOX 325, DISCOVERY ROAD
PETERSBURG, PENNSYLVANIA 16669

General Information Center providing day and residential environmental education and outdoor adventure programming. Established in 1976. 7,000-acre facility located 13 miles from State College. Features: 20 birds of prey; team building low element course; 25 miles of hiking trails; herb and flower gardens; 72-acre lake; hands-on exhibits.

Profile of Summer Employees Total number: 15; typical ages: 20–30. 30% men; 70% women; 10% minorities; 90% college students; 25% non-U.S. citizens; 5% local applicants. Nonsmokers preferred.

Employment Information Openings are from June 3 to August 23. Year-round positions also offered. Jobs available: ▶ 4–6 *environmental education interns* at $150 per week. Applicants must submit formal organization application, resume, three letters of recommendation (international applicants only). A telephone interview is required. International applicants accepted; must apply through a recognized agency.

Benefits and Preemployment Training Free housing, formal training, willing to provide letters of recommendation, on-the-job training, willing to complete paperwork for educational credit, willing to act as a professional reference, and opportunity to attend seminars/workshops. Preemployment training is required and includes accident prevention and safety, first aid, CPR, interpersonal skills, leadership skills, animal handling.

Contact Doug Wentzel, Intern Coordinator, Shaver's Creek Environmental Center, Pennsylvania State University. Telephone: 814-863-2000. Fax: 814-865-2706. E-mail: shaverscreek@outreach.psu.edu. World Wide Web: http://www.shaverscreek.org. Contact by e-mail, fax, mail, phone, or through World Wide Web site. Application deadline: March 1.

SOUTH MOUNTAIN YMCA
PO BOX 147, 201 CUSHION PEAK ROAD
WERNERSVILLE, PENNSYLVANIA 19565
General Information A traditional coed summer camp with both day and resident programs operated by South Mountain YMCA. Established in 1948. 500-acre facility located 12 miles from Reading. Features: wooded setting; pool; tennis/basketball courts; staff lounge with email; laundry facilities; central to Philadelphia, New York City and Washington, D.C.
Profile of Summer Employees Total number: 100; typical ages: 17–28. 45% men; 55% women; 15% high school students; 85% college students; 25% non-U.S. citizens; 25% local applicants. Nonsmokers required.
Employment Information Openings are from June 9 to August 23. Jobs available: ▶ 1–100 *camp counselors* (minimum age 17) at $1200–$3000 per season ▶ 1–2 *rifle instructors* (minimum age 18) at $1400–$1800 per season ▶ 1 *sailing instructor* (minimum age 18) with previous experience with lazers and sunfishes at $1800–$2200 per season. Applicants must submit formal organization application, three personal references, criminal background check (at organization's expense). An in-person interview is recommended, but a telephone interview is acceptable. International applicants accepted; must apply through a recognized agency.
Benefits and Preemployment Training Free housing, free meals, formal training, willing to provide letters of recommendation, names of contacts, willing to complete paperwork for educational credit, willing to act as a professional reference, and certification for certain activities (certified instructor in archery, riflery, horseback riding, lifeguarding). Preemployment training is required and includes accident prevention and safety, first aid, CPR, leadership skills.
Contact Gideon Fetterolf, Director of Resident Camping, South Mountain YMCA. Telephone: 610-670-2267. Fax: 610-670-5010. E-mail: gfetterolf@smymca.org. World Wide Web: http://www.smymca.org. Contact by e-mail, fax, phone, or through World Wide Web site. Application deadline: continuous.

THE SOUTHWESTERN COMPANY, PENNSYLVANIA
See The Southwestern Company on page 297 for complete description.

SPORTS INTERNATIONAL–DHANI JONES FOOTBALL CAMP
EAST STROUDSBURG, PENNSYLVANIA
See Sports International, Inc. on page 134 for complete description.

SPORTS INTERNATIONAL–JAMES THRASH AND CECIL MARTIN FOOTBALL CAMP
READING, PENNSYLVANIA
See Sports International, Inc. on page 134 for complete description.

SPORTS INTERNATIONAL–JOE KRIVAK QUARTERBACK CAMP
SLIPPERY ROCK, PENNSYLVANIA
See Sports International, Inc. on page 134 for complete description.

SPORTS INTERNATIONAL–MARK BRUENER FOOTBALL CAMP
SLIPPERY ROCK, PENNSYLVANIA
See Sports International, Inc. on page 134 for complete description.

STIVERS STAFFING SERVICES–PENNSYLVANIA
See Stivers Staffing Services–Illinois on page 96 for complete description.

STREAMSIDE CAMP AND CONFERENCE CENTER
RURAL ROUTE 3, BOX 3307
STROUDSBURG, PENNSYLVANIA 18360

General Information Residential Christian camp with a focus on providing a quality camping experience for inner-city children, youth, and families. Established in 1942. 140-acre facility located 90 miles from Philadelphia. Features: boating and fishing ponds; outdoor swimming pool; wooded setting with hiking and horse trails; comfortable rustic cabins; 300-foot waterslide; basketball and sand volleyball courts.

Profile of Summer Employees Total number: 60; typical ages: 15–25. 50% men; 50% women; 15% minorities; 25% high school students; 60% college students; 5% retirees; 10% non-U.S. citizens; 60% local applicants. Nonsmokers required.

Employment Information Openings are from June 7 to August 28. Year-round positions also offered. Jobs available: ▶ 20–26 *cabin counselors* (minimum age 18) at $150–$300 per week ▶ 1 *camp nurse* (minimum age 18) with minimum First Aid certifications at $150–$300 per week ▶ 2–4 *dining room workers* (minimum age 15) at $60–$120 per week ▶ 1–2 *horsemanship instructor/wranglers* (minimum age 18) with experience in working with horses at $150–$300 per week ▶ 4–6 *kitchen aides* (minimum age 15) with desire to learn at $60–$150 per week ▶ 1–2 *lifeguards* (minimum age 16) with lifeguard certification at $150–$300 per week ▶ 2–4 *maintenance team workers* (minimum age 15) at $60–$150 per week ▶ 1–2 *program specialists* (minimum age 18) with ability to teach and relate a specific area of expertise to the Christian daily life at $150–$300 per week ▶ 1–2 *water safety instructors* (minimum age 18) with WSI certification at $150–$300 per week. Applicants must submit formal organization application, three personal references. A telephone interview is required. International applicants accepted; must apply through a recognized agency.

Benefits and Preemployment Training Free housing, free meals, formal training, possible full-time employment, health insurance, willing to provide letters of recommendation, on-the-job training, willing to act as a professional reference, opportunity to attend seminars/workshops, travel reimbursement, and tuition assistance. Preemployment training is required and includes accident prevention and safety, first aid, CPR, interpersonal skills, leadership skills, lifeguard training.

Contact Mr. Dale Schoenwald, Director, Streamside Camp and Conference Center, RR #3, Box 3307, Stroudsburg, Pennsylvania 18360. Telephone: 570-629-1902. Fax: 570-629-9650. E-mail: summerstaff@streamside.org. World Wide Web: http://www.streamside.org. Contact by e-mail, fax, mail, phone, or through World Wide Web site. Application deadline: continuous.

STUDENT CONSERVATION ASSOCIATION (SCA), PENNSYLVANIA
See Student Conservation Association (SCA), New Hampshire on page 200 for complete description.

SWARTHMORE TENNIS CAMP
500 COLLEGE AVENUE
SWARTHMORE, PENNSYLVANIA 19081

General Information Operates both a junior and adult camp for resident and day campers. 5 hours daily. Adults 3-day, 5-day, and weekend programs. Juniors 9–18, coed weekly and multi-week sessions. Established in 1981. 325-acre facility located 12 miles from Philadelphia. Features: wooded campus; tennis courts; swimming pool.

Profile of Summer Employees Total number: 12–14; typical ages: 19–40. 80% men; 20% women; 70% college students; 10% non-U.S. citizens. Nonsmokers required.

Employment Information Openings are from June 17 to August 9. Jobs available: ► 10 *tennis instructors* (minimum age 19) with collegiate tennis experience at $265–$285 per week. Applicants must submit a formal organization application, resume, three personal references. International applicants accepted.

Benefits and Preemployment Training Free housing and free meals. Preemployment training is required and includes interpersonal skills, leadership skills.

Contact Lois Broderick, President, Swarthmore Tennis Camp, 444 East 82nd Street, Suite 31D, New York, New York 10028. Telephone: 212-879-0225. Fax: 212-452-0816. E-mail: greatennis@ aol.com. Contact by e-mail, fax, mail, or phone. Application deadline: continuous.

WALDAMEER PARK, INC.
220 PENINSULA DRIVE
ERIE, PENNSYLVANIA 16505

General Information Amusement park and water park with rides, water slides, midway games, arcade, gift shops, refreshment stands, picnic/catering facilities, and entertainment. Established in 1896. 42-acre facility located 90 miles from Cleveland, Ohio. Features: 16 major rides; 11 major water slides; kiddie rides and slides; midway games; food and gift shops; picnic shelters.

Profile of Summer Employees Total number: 400; typical ages: 14–22. 50% men; 50% women; 7% minorities; 70% high school students; 30% college students; 1% retirees; 1% non-U.S. citizens; 95% local applicants. Nonsmokers preferred.

Employment Information Openings are from May 1 to September 7. Jobs available: ► 10 *cashiers* (minimum age 18) ► 30 *food service personnel* (minimum age 16) ► 30 *games attendants* (minimum age 16) ► 30–40 *lifeguards* (minimum age 16) with first aid, CPR, and lifeguard certification ► 20 *picnic staff* (minimum age 18) ► 30–40 *ride operators* (minimum age 18). Applicants must submit a formal organization application, two personal references. An in-person interview is required. International applicants accepted; must obtain own visa, obtain own working papers.

Benefits and Preemployment Training Meals at a cost, willing to provide letters of recommendation, on-the-job training, willing to act as a professional reference, and use of amusement park facility. Preemployment training is required and includes accident prevention and safety, customer service skills.

Contact Steve Gorman, General Manager, Waldameer Park, Inc., PO Box 8308, Erie, Pennsylvania 16505. Fax: 814-835-7435. E-mail: info@waldameer.com. World Wide Web: http://www. waldameer.com. Contact by e-mail or mail. No phone calls. Application deadline: continuous.

YMCA CAMP FITCH
12600 ABLES ROAD
NORTH SPRINGFIELD, PENNSYLVANIA 16430

General Information Traditional residential camp serving 250 campers; special population camp serving 30–70 campers with special needs; specialty camps such as computer, running, and swimming camps serving 30 campers. Established in 1914. 450-acre facility located 20 miles from Erie. Features: location on Lake Erie; 4-acre inland lake; swimming pool; 450 wooded acres and horse trails; soccer and ball fields; many activity areas.

Profile of Summer Employees Total number: 120; typical ages: 17–60. 50% men; 50% women; 15% minorities; 35% high school students; 65% college students; 10% non-U.S. citizens; 60% local applicants. Nonsmokers preferred.

Employment Information Openings are from June 13 to August 31. Year-round positions also offered. Jobs available: ► 1–2 *kitchen stewards* (minimum age 19) with food service/cleaning experience at $150–$200 per week ► 4–6 *special population counselors* (minimum age 18) with camp counselor experience or experience with special populations at $140–$180 per week ▶ *summer camp counselors* (minimum age 18) at $140–$180 per week. Applicants must submit formal organization application, letter of interest, three personal references. An in-person interview is recommended, but a telephone interview is acceptable. International applicants accepted; must obtain own visa, obtain own working papers, apply through a recognized agency.

Benefits and Preemployment Training Free housing, free meals, formal training, willing to provide letters of recommendation, on-the-job training, willing to complete paperwork for educational credit, and opportunity to attend seminars/workshops. Preemployment training is required and includes accident prevention and safety, first aid, CPR, interpersonal skills, leadership skills.

Contact Bill Lyder, Executive Camp Director, YMCA Camp Fitch, 17 North Champion Street, Youngstown, Ohio 44501-1287. Telephone: 330-744-8411. Fax: 330-744-8416. E-mail: campfitch@hotmail.com. World Wide Web: http://www.campfitch.com. Contact by e-mail, fax, mail, or phone. Application deadline: continuous.

RHODE ISLAND

CENTER FOR TALENTED YOUTH/JOHNS HOPKINS UNIVERSITY–ROGER WILLIAMS UNIVERSITY
BRISTOL, RHODE ISLAND
See Center for Talented Youth/Johns Hopkins University on page 131 for complete description.

THE SOUTHWESTERN COMPANY, RHODE ISLAND
See The Southwestern Company on page 297 for complete description.

SPORTS INTERNATIONAL–DAMON HUARD AND MATT LIGHT FOOTBALL CAMP
SMITHFIELD, RHODE ISLAND
See Sports International, Inc. on page 134 for complete description.

SPORTS INTERNATIONAL–JOE KRIVAK QUARTERBACK CAMP
SMITHFIELD, RHODE ISLAND
See Sports International, Inc. on page 134 for complete description.

STUDENT CONSERVATION ASSOCIATION (SCA), RHODE ISLAND
See Student Conservation Association (SCA), New Hampshire on page 200 for complete description.

UNIVERSITY OF RHODE ISLAND SUMMER PROGRAMS
W. ALTON JONES CAMPUS, 401 VICTORY HIGHWAY
WEST GREENWICH, RHODE ISLAND 02817-2158
General Information Residential Earth Camp facility serving 100 campers in seven 1-week sessions focusing on nature awareness and conservation; expedition program for 40 teens in

seven 1-week sessions includes backpacking, kayaking, canoeing, and rock-climbing. Farm and ecology day camp for ages 5–11 utilizes historic working farm and nature preserve. Established in 1962. 2,300-acre facility located 30 miles from Providence. Features: 75-acre lake; 2300-acre property; 40,000 acres of state forests; 10 miles of hiking trails; low ropes challenge course; historic working farm.

Profile of Summer Employees Total number: 50; typical ages: 14–29. 50% men; 50% women; 5% minorities; 10% high school students; 90% college students; 15% non-U.S. citizens; 50% local applicants. Nonsmokers preferred.

Employment Information Openings are from June 16 to August 15. Year-round positions also offered. Jobs available: ▶ 20 *Earth Camp/counselors* (minimum age 18) with CPR/first aid certification and experience working with children at $190–$240 per week ▶ 1 *animal and garden manager* with experience caring for farm animals and gardens at $250–$350 per week ▶ 1 *camp EMT or nurse assistant* (minimum age 20) student nurse with CPR/first aid certification, EMT preferred at $350–$375 per week ▶ 12 *day camp counselors* (minimum age 18) with CPR/first aid certification and experience working with children at $300 per week ▶ 10–12 *field teachers/naturalists* (minimum age 21) with CPR/first aid certification, must have experience teaching children at $250 per week ▶ 2 *lifeguards* (minimum age 18) with driver's license, first aid, CPR, and lifeguard certification at $8–$12 per hour ▶ 10 *teen expedition leaders* (minimum age 21) with driver's license, CPR, first aid, and lifeguard certification; should have experience working with teens and/or outdoor skills at $200–$305 per week. Applicants must submit a formal organization application, letter of interest, resume, three personal references. A telephone interview is required. International applicants accepted.

Benefits and Preemployment Training Free housing, free meals, formal training, willing to provide letters of recommendation, on-the-job training, willing to complete paperwork for educational credit, and willing to act as a professional reference. Preemployment training is required and includes accident prevention and safety, first aid, CPR, interpersonal skills, leadership skills, lesson planning and teaching.

Contact John Jacques, Manager, Environmental Education Center, University of Rhode Island Summer Programs, 401 Victory Highway, West Greenwich, Rhode Island 02817-2158. Telephone: 401-397-3304 Ext. 6043. Fax: 401-397-3293. E-mail: urieec@etal.uri.edu. World Wide Web: http://www.uri.edu/ajc/eec. Contact by e-mail, fax, mail, phone, or through World Wide Web site. Application deadline: continuous.

YMCA CAMP FULLER
619 CAMP FULLER ROAD
WAKEFIELD, RHODE ISLAND 02879

General Information Residential camp serving 250 campers each session with a focus on saltwater sailing and other aquatic activities. General programs offered to campers ages 7–16. Established in 1887. 60-acre facility located 30 miles from Providence. Features: ocean setting; high ropes course.

Profile of Summer Employees Total number: 90; typical ages: 17–25. 50% men; 50% women; 5% minorities; 20% high school students; 75% college students; 15% non-U.S. citizens; 50% local applicants. Nonsmokers preferred.

Employment Information Openings are from June 15 to August 23. Jobs available: ▶ 2 *advanced sailing instructors* (minimum age 21) at $250–$500 per week ▶ 1 *camp nurse* with RN license, first aid, and CPR certification at $500–$550 per week ▶ 2 *division leaders* (minimum age 21) with experience in the field at $275–$325 per week ▶ 20 *senior counselors* (minimum age 18) at $185–$240 per week. Applicants must submit formal organization application, total of four personal references/letters of recommendation. An in-person interview is recommended, but a telephone interview is acceptable. International applicants accepted; must apply through a recognized agency.

Benefits and Preemployment Training Free housing, free meals, willing to provide letters of recommendation, on-the-job training, willing to complete paperwork for educational credit, willing to act as a professional reference, opportunity to attend seminars/workshops, and travel reimbursement. Preemployment training is required and includes accident prevention and safety, first aid, CPR, leadership skills.

Contact Tricia Driscoll, Associate Director, YMCA Camp Fuller, 619 Camp Fuller Road, Wakefield, Rhode Island 02879. Telephone: 800-521-1470. Fax: 401-782-6083. E-mail: fullerkb@ aol.com. World Wide Web: http://www.campfuller.com. Contact by e-mail, fax, mail, phone, or through World Wide Web site. Application deadline: April 1.

SOUTH CAROLINA

CAMP CHATUGA
291 CAMP CHATUGA ROAD
MOUNTAIN REST, SOUTH CAROLINA 29664

General Information Residential coeducational camp serving 165 campers per session in the heart of Sumter National Forest in the Blue Ridge Mountain foothills. Established in 1956. 60-acre facility located 125 miles from Atlanta, Georgia. Features: private lake; surrounded by national forest; football field; screened wood cabins; recreation hall; lodge.

Profile of Summer Employees Total number: 40–50; typical ages: 19–35. 50% men; 50% women; 10% minorities; 75% college students; 5% retirees; 20% non-U.S. citizens; 40% local applicants. Nonsmokers required.

Employment Information Openings are from May 31 to August 10. Jobs available: ▶ 1 *Western horseback riding director* (minimum age 21) with horse experience at $1500–$2500 per season ▶ 1–4 *camp "moms"* at $150 to $225 per week and tuition discounts for children ▶ 25 *counselors* (minimum age 19) at $1400–$2000 per season ▶ 1 *dining hall supervisor* (minimum age 21) with supervisory skills and interest in food service at $1500–$2500 per season ▶ 1–4 *health supervisors* (minimum age 21) with CPR/first aid certification, RN, BSN, or MD, pediatric experience preferred at $200 per week and tuition discounts for children ▶ 1 *nanny* (minimum age 19) at $1500–$2000 per season ▶ 1 *waterfront director* (minimum age 21) with lifeguard certification required, WSI preferred at $1400–$2000 per season. Applicants must submit formal organization application, three personal references. A telephone interview is required. International applicants accepted; must obtain own visa, apply through a recognized agency.

Benefits and Preemployment Training Free housing, free meals, formal training, willing to provide letters of recommendation, names of contacts, on-the-job training, willing to complete paperwork for educational credit, willing to act as a professional reference, opportunity to attend seminars/workshops, and transportation to camp from airport, staff training certifications. Preemployment training is required and includes accident prevention and safety, first aid, CPR, interpersonal skills, leadership skills, archery, riflery.

Contact Kelly Moxley, Director of Personnel, Camp Chatuga, 291 Camp Chatuga Road, Mountain Rest, South Carolina 29664. Telephone: 864-638-3728. Fax: 864-638-0898. E-mail: mail@ campchatuga.com. World Wide Web: http://www.campchatuga.com. Contact by e-mail, fax, mail, phone, or through World Wide Web site. Application deadline: continuous.

THE CITADEL SUMMER CAMP
171 MOULTRIE STREET
CHARLESTON, SOUTH CAROLINA 29409

General Information Structured sports-oriented residential camp for boys and girls ages 10 to 15. Located on the campus of The Citadel, Military College, Charleston, S.C. Approximately 250 campers/3-week section. Established in 1957. 200-acre facility. Features: college campus; boarding center; beach house; full athletic facilities; barracks dormitories.

Profile of Summer Employees Total number: 70; typical ages: 17–23. 85% men; 15% women; 30% high school students; 70% college students; 60% local applicants. Nonsmokers required.

Employment Information Openings are from June 1 to August 15. Jobs available: ▶ 6 *counselor in charge of quarters* (minimum age 19) at $500–$600 per season ▶ 40 *counselors* (minimum age 17) at $850–$2500 per season. Applicants must submit a formal organization application, three personal references, $100 application fee (application available at Web site). An in-person interview is recommended, but a telephone interview is acceptable. International applicants accepted; must obtain own visa.

Benefits and Preemployment Training Free housing, free meals, willing to provide letters of recommendation, and willing to act as a professional reference. Preemployment training is required and includes accident prevention and safety, first aid, CPR, interpersonal skills, leadership skills.

Contact Jenni Garrott, Director, The Citadel Summer Camp, MSC 53, The Citadel, Charleston, South Carolina 29409. Telephone: 843-953-7120. Fax: 843-953-6803. E-mail: summercamp@ citadel.edu. World Wide Web: http://www.citadel.edu/summercamp/. Contact by e-mail, fax, mail, phone, or through World Wide Web site. Application deadline: continuous.

THE SOUTHWESTERN COMPANY, SOUTH CAROLINA
See The Southwestern Company on page 297 for complete description.

STUDENT CONSERVATION ASSOCIATION (SCA), SOUTH CAROLINA
See Student Conservation Association (SCA), New Hampshire on page 200 for complete description.

WILD DUNES RESORT
5757 PALM BOULEVARD
ISLE OF PALMS, SOUTH CAROLINA 29451

General Information Resort offering summer recreational programs for all age groups who are guests at the resort. Established in 1976. 1,700-acre facility located 15 miles from Charleston. Features: 2 18-hole golf courses; 17 Har-Tru tennis courts; 20 swimming pools; 3 miles of beach; marina; conference centers.

Profile of Summer Employees Total number: 850; typical ages: 19–24. 30% men; 70% women; 100% college students.

Employment Information Openings are from May 12 to September 10. Spring break and year-round positions also offered. Jobs available: ▶ 18 *recreation interns* with CPR certification, driver's license, and at least a junior in college at $250 per month ▶ 2 *tennis interns* at $250 per month. Applicants must submit a formal organization application, letter of interest, resume, three personal references, three letters of recommendation. An in-person interview is recommended, but a telephone interview is acceptable. International applicants accepted; must obtain own visa, obtain own working papers.

Benefits and Preemployment Training Meals at a cost, free housing, formal training, possible full-time employment, willing to provide letters of recommendation, names of contacts, on-the-job training, willing to complete paperwork for educational credit, willing to act as a professional reference, opportunity to attend seminars/workshops, and nationally accredited internship program. Preemployment training is required and includes accident prevention and safety, interpersonal skills, leadership skills.

Contact Kyle Markgraf, Recreation Manager, Wild Dunes Resort, 5757 Palmetto Boulevard, Isle of Palms, South Carolina 29451. Telephone: 843-886-2171. Fax: 843-886-2195. E-mail: kmarkgraf@wilddunes.com. World Wide Web: http://www.wilddunes.com. Contact by e-mail, fax, mail, phone, or through World Wide Web site. Application deadline: continuous.

SOUTH DAKOTA

A CHRISTIAN MINISTRY IN THE NATIONAL PARKS– SOUTH DAKOTA
See A Christian Ministry in the National Parks–Maine on page 107 for complete description.

AMERICAN PRESIDENTS RESORT
HIGHWAY 16A
CUSTER, SOUTH DAKOTA 57730
General Information Resort consisting of cabins, campground, and motel units rented nightly from mid-May to mid-September. Established in 1950. 50-acre facility located 40 miles from Rapid City. Features: creek; pool/hot tub; volleyball; cabins; RV/tent sites; wooded setting.

Profile of Summer Employees Total number: 31. 20% men; 80% women; 35% high school students; 35% college students; 10% retirees; 50% local applicants. Nonsmokers preferred.

Employment Information Openings are from May 15 to September 15. Jobs available: ▶ 10 *desk clerks* at $5–$6 per hour ▶ 5 *laundry workers* at $6–$7 per hour ▶ 20 *maids* at $5–$6 per hour. International applicants accepted; must obtain own visa, obtain own working papers, apply through a recognized agency.

Benefits and Preemployment Training On-the-job training.

Contact Jack Strand, Manager, American Presidents Resort, PO Box 446, Custer, South Dakota 57730. Telephone: 605-673-3373. Fax: 605-673-3449. Contact by fax, mail, or phone. Application deadline: May 1.

CUSTER STATE PARK RESORT COMPANY
HC 83, BOX 74
CUSTER, SOUTH DAKOTA 57730
General Information Operator of 4 resorts offering services such as lodging, dining, groceries, gas, and souvenirs and gifts as well as activities that include trail rides, jeep tours, and cookouts. Established in 1989. 73,000-acre facility located 25 miles from Rapid City. Features: wooded setting; freshwater lakes; hiking trails; buffalo safari jeep tours; guided horseback rides; hayride/ chuckwagon cookouts.

Profile of Summer Employees Total number: 300; typical ages: 18–65. 35% men; 65% women; 15% minorities; 10% high school students; 50% college students; 20% retirees; 1% non-U.S. citizens; 20% local applicants. Nonsmokers preferred.

Employment Information Openings are from May 1 to October 15. Jobs available: ▶ 5 *bartenders* (minimum age 21) at $700–$900 per month ▶ 4–6 *bookkeepers* (minimum age 21) at $900–$1200 per month ▶ 15–25 *cook's assistants* (minimum age 18) at $700–$900 per month

▶ 10 *cooks/chefs* (minimum age 18) with ServSafe certification and experience required at $1000–$2000 per month ▶ 18 *dishwashers/buspersons* (minimum age 16) at $700–$800 per month ▶ 17–20 *front desk/reservations personnel* (minimum age 18) at $750–$950 per month ▶ 5–8 *hosts/hostesses* (minimum age 18) at $800–$900 per month ▶ 50–60 *housekeeping personnel* (minimum age 16) at $700–$850 per month ▶ 5–12 *jeep drivers* (minimum age 21) with clean driving record and CPR certification at $750–$900 per month ▶ 8–25 *kitchen/food preparation personnel* (minimum age 18) at $700–$800 per month ▶ 6–8 *maintenance personnel* (minimum age 21) at $900–$1200 per month ▶ 12 *manager trainees* (minimum age 21) with desire to learn the resort business at $1200–$1400 per month ▶ 35–50 *sales clerks* (minimum age 18) at $700–$900 per month ▶ 45–50 *waitpersons* (minimum age 18) at $600 to $750 per month plus tips ▶ 8–14 *wranglers* (minimum age 18) at $800–$1000 per month. Applicants must submit formal organization application, resume, three personal references, photo. An in-person interview is recommended, but a telephone interview is acceptable. International applicants accepted; must obtain own visa, obtain own working papers, apply through a recognized agency.

Benefits and Preemployment Training Formal training, possible full-time employment, willing to provide letters of recommendation, on-the-job training, willing to complete paperwork for educational credit, willing to act as a professional reference, opportunity to attend seminars/workshops, tuition assistance, and room and board are available as part of total compensation package. Preemployment training is required and includes accident prevention and safety, first aid, CPR, specific job training.

Contact Phil Lampert, President, Custer State Park Resort Company, HC 83, Box 74, Custer, South Dakota 57730. Telephone: 605-255-4772. Fax: 605-255-4706. E-mail: e-mail@custerresorts.com. Contact by e-mail, fax, mail, or phone. Application deadline: continuous.

MT. RUSHMORE CONCESSIONS
PO BOX 178
KEYSTONE, SOUTH DAKOTA 57751

General Information Authorized National Park concessionaire. Established in 1951. 25-acre facility located 25 miles from Rapid City. Features: beautiful Black Hills; camping; fishing; hiking; Custer State Park; Badlands National Park.

Profile of Summer Employees Total number: 160; typical ages: 18–70. 50% men; 50% women; 15% minorities; 10% high school students; 35% college students; 20% retirees; 25% non-U.S. citizens; 10% local applicants. Nonsmokers preferred.

Employment Information Openings are from April 15 to October 15. Jobs available: ▶ 82 *food attendants* (minimum age 18) at $6.25 per hour ▶ 60 *gift shop attendants* (minimum age 18) at $6.25 per hour. Applicants must submit formal organization application. International applicants accepted; must obtain own visa, obtain own working papers, apply through a recognized agency.

Benefits and Preemployment Training Housing at a cost, meals at a cost, possible full-time employment, on-the-job training, and willing to act as a professional reference. Preemployment training is required and includes accident prevention and safety, interpersonal skills.

Contact Christina McClanahan, Human Resource Manager, Mt. Rushmore Concessions, PO Box 178, Keystone, South Dakota 57751. Telephone: 605-574-2515. Fax: 605-574-2495. E-mail: cmcclanahan@xanterra.com. World Wide Web: http://www.coolworks.com/showme/rushmore. Contact by e-mail, fax, mail, phone, or through World Wide Web site. Application deadline: continuous.

PALMER GULCH RESORT/MT. RUSHMORE KOA
PO BOX 295, 12620 HIGHWAY 244
HILL CITY, SOUTH DAKOTA 57745

General Information Full-service resort located 5 miles west of Mount Rushmore. Established in 1972. 150-acre facility located 30 miles from Rapid City. Features: proximity to Custer State Park; 2 pools and waterslide; campsites and cabins; lodge motel; wooded setting.

Profile of Summer Employees Total number: 85; typical ages: 18–25. 50% men; 50% women; 5% minorities; 20% high school students; 50% college students; 30% retirees; 15% non-U.S. citizens; 40% local applicants. Nonsmokers preferred.

Employment Information Openings are from May 1 to September 15. Jobs available: ▶ 10–15 *campground registration office/store personnel* (minimum age 16) at $6.50–$6.75 per hour ▶ 10–15 *housekeeping staff members* (minimum age 14) at $6.50 per hour ▶ 4–6 *lodge front desk and registration staff members* (minimum age 16) at $6.50–$7 per hour ▶ 10 *maintenance personnel* (minimum age 16) at $6.50–$6.75 per hour ▶ 3 *reservations staff members* (minimum age 16) at $6.50–$7 per hour ▶ 4 *waterslide staff members* (minimum age 16) with lifesaving, CPR, or first aid certification at $6.50 per hour. Applicants must submit formal organization application, three personal references. A telephone interview is required. International applicants accepted; must apply through a recognized agency.

Benefits and Preemployment Training Housing at a cost, formal training, willing to provide letters of recommendation, on-the-job training, willing to complete paperwork for educational credit, and willing to act as a professional reference. Preemployment training is optional and includes first aid, CPR, hospitality training.

Contact Josh Daiss, General Manager, Palmer Gulch Resort/Mt. Rushmore KOA, Box 295, Hill City, South Dakota 57745. Telephone: 605-574-2525. Fax: 605-574-2574. E-mail: jcdaiss@aol. com. World Wide Web: http://www.palmergulch.com. Contact by e-mail, fax, mail, or phone. Application deadline: continuous.

THE SOUTHWESTERN COMPANY, SOUTH DAKOTA
See The Southwestern Company on page 297 for complete description.

STUDENT CONSERVATION ASSOCIATION (SCA), SOUTH DAKOTA
See Student Conservation Association (SCA), New Hampshire on page 200 for complete description.

TENNESSEE

A CHRISTIAN MINISTRY IN THE NATIONAL PARKS– TENNESSEE
See A Christian Ministry in the National Parks–Maine on page 107 for complete description.

CAMP NAKANAWA
1084 CAMP NAKANAWA ROAD
CROSSVILLE, TENNESSEE 38571-2146

General Information For profit, private organization offering a variety of sports and activities to help young ladies gain confidence and reach their potential in a positive and fun-filled natural environment. Established in 1920. 1,200-acre facility located 100 miles from Nashville. Features: freshwater lake, 150 acres; 11 tennis courts; wooded setting; 24 horses owned by camp; climbing tower with zipline; 6-10 person war canoes.

Profile of Summer Employees Total number: 120; typical age: 19. 3% men; 97% women; 80% college students; 14% retirees; 6% non-U.S. citizens. Nonsmokers preferred.

Employment Information Openings are from June 9 to July 28. Jobs available: ▶ 100 *general counselors and activity instructors* (minimum age 18) with love of children and experience in one or more activities offered at $200–$250 per week ▶ 1–2 *head instructor of riding program* (minimum age 21) with CHA certification (preferred) at $300–$350 per week. Applicants must submit formal organization application, three personal references. An in-person interview is recommended, but a telephone interview is acceptable. International applicants accepted; must apply through a recognized agency.

Benefits and Preemployment Training Free housing, free meals, willing to provide letters of recommendation, on-the-job training, willing to complete paperwork for educational credit, willing to act as a professional reference, and opportunity to attend seminars/workshops. Preemployment training is required and includes accident prevention and safety, interpersonal skills, leadership skills, climbing wall certification class.

Contact Ann Perron, Owner/Director, Camp Nakanawa. Telephone: 931-277-3711. E-mail: campnak@tnaccess.com. Contact by e-mail, mail, or phone. Application deadline: continuous.

CENTER FOR STUDENT MISSIONS–NASHVILLE
NASHVILLE, TENNESSEE
See Center for Student Missions on page 37 for complete description.

CHEROKEE ADVENTURES WHITEWATER RAFTING
2000 JONESBOROUGH ROAD
ERWIN, TENNESSEE 37650-9524

General Information Guided rafting and mountain-biking trips; also ropes course emphasizing team building and camping. Established in 1979. 50-acre facility located 17 miles from Johnson City. Features: located on a river; wooded setting; volleyball courts.

Profile of Summer Employees Total number: 35–40; typical ages: 21–25. 60% men; 40% women; 40% college students; 2% non-U.S. citizens; 58% local applicants. Nonsmokers preferred.

Employment Information Openings are from May to October. Year-round positions also offered. Jobs available: ▶ 1–2 *cook* (minimum age 18) with prior experience as a line or grill cook for 6 months minimum at $6–$8.50 per hour ▶ 1–2 *dishwasher* (minimum age 18) at $5.25–$6.50 per hour ▶ 1–4 *food prep, cooks/cleaning staff members* (minimum age 19) with ability to prepare lunches and perform general cleaning at $5.25–$6.50 per hour ▶ 1–3 *raft guides* (minimum age 18) with responsible, outgoing personalities and Red Cross first aid/CPR certification (salary begins after training completed) at $400–$600 per month ▶ 3 *reservationists/general office personnel* (minimum age 19) with good phone manner and the ability to type 40 wpm at $5.25–$6.50 per hour ▶ 1–3 *servers/waitstaff* (minimum age 18) at $2.35 per hour plus tips with a minimum of $5.15. Applicants must submit a formal organization application, three personal references. International applicants accepted; must obtain own visa, obtain own working papers.

Benefits and Preemployment Training Housing at a cost, meals at a cost, willing to provide letters of recommendation, on-the-job training, and willing to act as a professional reference. Preemployment training is optional and includes first aid, CPR, leadership skills.

Contact Dennis I. Nedelman, President, Cherokee Adventures Whitewater Rafting, 2000 Jonesborough Road, Erwin, Tennessee 37650-9524. Telephone: 423-743-7733. Fax: 423-743-5400. E-mail: ca2raft@usit.net. Contact by e-mail, fax, mail, or phone. Application deadline: continuous.

THE SOUTHWESTERN COMPANY
2451 ATRIUM WAY
NASHVILLE, TENNESSEE 37214

General Information Summer work program for college students selling educational books and software. Positions as independent contractors are available in all 50 states. Established in 1855.

Profile of Summer Employees Total number: 750; typical ages: 18–24. 55% men; 45% women; 100% college students.

Employment Information Openings are from April 25 to October 1. Jobs available: ▶ 4000 *sales-dealers in Southwestern products* (minimum age 18) with ability to relocate and work for summer at a commissioned salary. Applicants must submit signed dealer agreement, letter of credit. An in-person interview is required. International applicants accepted; must obtain own visa, apply through a recognized agency.

Benefits and Preemployment Training Formal training, possible full-time employment, willing to provide letters of recommendation, on-the-job training, willing to complete paperwork for educational credit, willing to act as a professional reference, and opportunity to attend seminars/workshops. Preemployment training is required and includes accident prevention and safety, interpersonal skills, leadership skills.

Contact Trey Campbell, Communications Manager, The Southwestern Company. Telephone: 615-391-2801. Fax: 615-391-2703. E-mail: trey.campbell@southwestern.com. World Wide Web: http://www.southwestern.com. Contact by e-mail or phone. Application deadline: June 15.

STUDENT CONSERVATION ASSOCIATION (SCA), TENNESSEE

See Student Conservation Association (SCA), New Hampshire on page 200 for complete description.

TEXAS

A CHRISTIAN MINISTRY IN THE NATIONAL PARKS–TEXAS

See A Christian Ministry in the National Parks–Maine on page 107 for complete description.

AUSTIN NATURE AND SCIENCE CENTER
301 NATURE CENTER DRIVE
AUSTIN, TEXAS 78746

General Information Living museum with 150 orphaned/injured animals and a focus on outdoor/environmental education including recycling, plants, animals, astronomy, caving, climbing, canoeing, archery, aquatic studies and swimming. Established in 1962. 80-acre facility. Features: pond; animals; 70 acres hiking preserve; on major Austin lake; swimming in local springs; central to many state parks.

Profile of Summer Employees Total number: 41; typical ages: 18–30. 13% men; 87% women; 10% minorities; 5% high school students; 85% college students; 10% local applicants.

Employment Information Openings are from May 15 to August 15. Jobs available: ▶ 24 *summer counselors* (minimum age 18) with desire to work with children in an informal setting at

$6.56–$8.11 per hour. Applicants must submit a formal organization application, three personal references. An in-person interview is recommended, but a telephone interview is acceptable.

Benefits and Preemployment Training Possible full-time employment, willing to provide letters of recommendation, on-the-job training, willing to complete paperwork for educational credit, and willing to act as a professional reference. Preemployment training is required and includes accident prevention and safety, first aid, CPR, interpersonal skills, leadership skills, animal handling, driving safety.

Contact Shannon Kennedy, Public Education Coordinator, Austin Nature and Science Center. Telephone: 512-327-8181. Fax: 512-327-8745. E-mail: shannon.kennedy@ci.austin.tx.us. World Wide Web: http://www.cityofaustin.org/nature-science. Contact by e-mail, mail, or phone. Application deadline: continuous.

CAMP FERN
1046 CAMP ROAD
MARSHALL, TEXAS 75672-1411

General Information Residential camp providing fun, adventure, learning, self-esteem development, and lasting friendships. Established in 1934. 100-acre facility. Located 9 miles from . Features: lake; wooded setting; log cabins; English horseback riding; Red Cross swimming; water skiing; tennis; golf; archery; riflery; trampoline; nature; campcrafts; team sports.

Profile of Summer Employees Total number: 75; typical age: 19. 50% men; 50% women; 100% college students. Nonsmokers required.

Employment Information Openings are from May 26 to August 10. Jobs available: ▶ *waterfront staff members* with WSI, lifeguard, and CPR certification at $125–$150 per week. Applicants must submit a formal organization application, resume. An in-person interview is recommended, but a telephone interview is acceptable. International applicants accepted; must obtain own visa, obtain own working papers.

Benefits and Preemployment Training Free housing, free meals, on-the-job training, and laundry facilities. Preemployment training is required and includes accident prevention and safety, interpersonal skills, leadership skills.

Contact Margaret R. Thompson, Director, Camp Fern, 1040 Camp Road, Marshall, Texas 75672-1411. Telephone: 903-935-5420. Fax: 903-935-6372. E-mail: info@campfern.com. World Wide Web: http://www.campfern.com. Contact by e-mail, fax, mail, phone, or through World Wide Web site. Application deadline: April 1.

CAMP LA JUNTA
HIGHWAY 39 WEST
HUNT, TEXAS 78024

General Information Private residential camp with a focus on individual lifetime activities serving 200 boys in 2- or 4-week terms. Established in 1928. 200-acre facility located 75 miles from San Antonio. Features: spring-fed river; modern stone cabins; hill country setting.

Profile of Summer Employees Total number: 75; typical ages: 17–25. 90% men; 10% women; 5% minorities; 100% college students; 5% non-U.S. citizens; 25% local applicants. Nonsmokers required.

Employment Information Openings are from June 1 to August 5. Jobs available: ▶ *junior counselors* (minimum age 18) at $500–$650 per month ▶ *senior counselors* (minimum age 20) at $650–$750 per month. Applicants must submit formal organization application, three personal references. An in-person interview is recommended, but a telephone interview is acceptable. International applicants accepted; must apply through a recognized agency.

Benefits and Preemployment Training Free housing, free meals, formal training, health insurance, willing to provide letters of recommendation, on-the-job training, willing to complete paperwork for educational credit, willing to act as a professional reference, and travel reimbursement.

Contact Blake W. Smith, Director, Camp La Junta, PO Box 136, Hunt, Texas 78024. Telephone: 830-238-4621. Fax: 830-238-4888. E-mail: lajunta@ktc.com. World Wide Web: http://www. lajunta.com. Contact by e-mail, fax, mail, phone, or through World Wide Web site. Application deadline: continuous.

CAMP LOMA LINDA FOR GIRLS
MO RANCH, HC 1, BOX 158
HUNT, TEXAS 78024

General Information Residential camp serving girls ages 10-15 in two 3-week sessions. Established in 1977. 434-acre facility located 80 miles from San Antonio. Features: freshwater river; dormitory housing; Christian camp; water slide; horseback riding; nature studies.

Profile of Summer Employees Total number: 120; typical ages: 18–28. 50% men; 50% women; 10% high school students; 85% college students; 5% local applicants. Nonsmokers preferred.

Employment Information Openings are from May 31 to September 6. Year-round positions also offered. Jobs available: ▶ 6–12 *counselors/instructors* (minimum age 21) with Christian faith at $1000–$1500 per month. Applicants must submit a formal organization application, resume, two personal references. An in-person interview is recommended, but a telephone interview is acceptable.

Benefits and Preemployment Training Free housing, free meals, possible full-time employment, willing to provide letters of recommendation, on-the-job training, willing to complete paperwork for educational credit, and willing to act as a professional reference. Preemployment training is required and includes accident prevention and safety, first aid, CPR, interpersonal skills, leadership skills.

Contact Human Resources, Camp Loma Linda for Girls, Route 1, Box 158, Hunt, Texas 78024. Telephone: 800-460-4401. Fax: 830-238-4832. E-mail: hr@moranch.com. World Wide Web: http://www.moranch.com. Contact by e-mail, fax, mail, phone, or through World Wide Web site. Application deadline: continuous.

CAMP RIO VISTA FOR BOYS
HIGHWAY 39 WEST
INGRAM, TEXAS 78025

General Information Private residential camp providing 100–150 boys, ages 6–16, with a fun-filled learning experience in a safe, wholesome environment. Established in 1921. 120-acre facility located 75 miles from San Antonio. Features: river; tennis courts; full-size gym; 3 softball fields; lighted football field; golf course.

Profile of Summer Employees Total number: 45; typical ages: 19–23. 100% men; 5% minorities; 10% high school students; 85% college students; 5% non-U.S. citizens; 2% local applicants. Nonsmokers preferred.

Employment Information Openings are from June 1 to August 2. Jobs available: ▶ 45 *cabin/ activity counselors* (minimum age 18) with ability to be good role models and enjoy working with children at $155–$185 per week ▶ 10 *counselors/lifeguards* (minimum age 18) with lifeguard certification at $155–$185 per week ▶ 2 *nurses* with RN/LVN/EMT, experience with children, and field experience at $200–$250 per week. Applicants must submit formal organization application, three personal references, three letters of recommendation. An in-person interview is recommended, but a telephone interview is acceptable. International applicants accepted; must obtain own visa, obtain own working papers, apply through a recognized agency.

Benefits and Preemployment Training Free housing, free meals, formal training, willing to provide letters of recommendation, on-the-job training, willing to complete paperwork for educational credit, and willing to act as a professional reference. Preemployment training is required and includes accident prevention and safety, first aid, CPR, interpersonal skills, leadership skills, child management, liability management.

Contact Mr. James Rice, Camp Director, Camp Rio Vista for Boys, HCR 78, Box 215, Ingram, Texas 78025. Telephone: 830-367-5353. Fax: 830-367-4044. E-mail: riovista@ktc.com. World Wide Web: http://www.vistacamps.com. Contact by e-mail, fax, mail, phone, or through World Wide Web site. Application deadline: May 10.

CAMP SIERRA VISTA FOR GIRLS
HIGHWAY 39 WEST
INGRAM, TEXAS 78025

General Information Private residential camp for girls ages 6–16. Provides a safe, wholesome, fun-filled, learning experience to 96 girls per term. Established in 1982. 120-acre facility located 75 miles from San Antonio. Features: 3/4 miles of riverfront; game fields; golf course; tennis courts; rock gymnasium; 30 activities.

Profile of Summer Employees Total number: 25; typical ages: 19–23. 100% women; 5% minorities; 10% high school students; 85% college students; 10% non-U.S. citizens; 5% local applicants. Nonsmokers preferred.

Employment Information Openings are from June 1 to August 2. Jobs available: ▶ 25 *cabin/ activity counselors* (minimum age 18) with the ability to be good role models and who enjoy working with children at $155–$185 per week ▶ 2 *nurses* with LVN, RN, or EMT certification, experience with children, and field experience at $200–$250 per week ▶ 3 *office staff members* (minimum age 18) with good organizational skills and good telephone skills at $155–$185 per week ▶ 2 *swimming instructors* (minimum age 18) with lifeguard certification at $155–$185 per week. Applicants must submit formal organization application, three personal references, three letters of recommendation. An in-person interview is recommended, but a telephone interview is acceptable. International applicants accepted; must obtain own visa, obtain own working papers, apply through a recognized agency.

Benefits and Preemployment Training Free housing, free meals, formal training, willing to provide letters of recommendation, on-the-job training, willing to complete paperwork for educational credit, and willing to act as a professional reference. Preemployment training is required and includes accident prevention and safety, first aid, CPR, interpersonal skills, leadership skills, child management, liability management.

Contact Debbie Griffen, Camp Director, Camp Sierra Vista for Girls, HCR 78, Box 215, Ingram, Texas 78025. Telephone: 830-367-5353. Fax: 830-367-4044. E-mail: riovista@ktc.com. World Wide Web: http://www.vistacamps.com. Contact by e-mail, fax, mail, phone, or through World Wide Web site. Application deadline: May 10.

CAMP VAL VERDE
1007 CAMP ROAD
MCGREGOR, TEXAS 76657

General Information Residential camp serving 75–100 campers, some economically disadvantaged and others from foster homes, for 1-week sessions. Established in 1948. 397-acre facility located 7 miles from Waco. Features: wooded setting; freshwater pond; swimming pool; dammed river; 2 tennis courts; trails.

Profile of Summer Employees Total number: 25; typical ages: 18–23. 34% men; 66% women; 2% minorities; 1% high school students; 97% college students; 20% local applicants. Nonsmokers required.

Employment Information Openings are from May 23 to July 15. Jobs available: ▶ 25 *counselors* at $650–$800 per season ▶ 2 *horseback instructors* at $650–$800 per season ▶ 4 *lifeguards* with certification at $650–$800 per season ▶ 1 *nurse* with nursing degree at $800–$1000 per season. Applicants must submit a formal organization application, personal reference. An in-person interview is recommended, but a telephone interview is acceptable.

Benefits and Preemployment Training Free housing and free meals. Preemployment training is required and includes accident prevention and safety, first aid, CPR, interpersonal skills, leadership skills.

Contact Keri Knight, Camp Director, Camp Val Verde, 1826 Morrow, Waco, Texas 76707. Telephone: 254-752-5515. Fax: 254-752-5515. E-mail: knight38@hotmail.com. Contact by fax, mail, or phone. Application deadline: continuous.

CAMP WALDEMAR FOR GIRLS
HC 1, BOX 120
HUNT, TEXAS 78024

General Information Private residential skill-building girls camp offering sports, arts, and drama activities for girls ages 9 to 16. Established in 1926. 560-acre facility located 60 miles from San Antonio. Features: beautiful river; trees and hills; 8 tennis courts; 85 horses; buildings/cabins made of rock, tile, and cedar; 45 cabins.

Profile of Summer Employees Total number: 500; typical ages: 17–99. 100% women; 10% minorities; 2% high school students; 80% college students; 2% retirees; 2% non-U.S. citizens; 2% local applicants. Nonsmokers preferred.

Employment Information Openings are from May 27 to August 11. Jobs available: ▶ 5 *arts and crafts (ceramics, jewelry, and weaving) staff members* (minimum age 18) with ability to teach at $450–$700 per month ▶ 2 *fencing staff members* (minimum age 18) with college team playing experience and ability to teach at $450–$700 per month ▶ 5 *gymnastics staff members* (minimum age 18) with team experience at $450–$700 per month ▶ *nurse* ▶ 10 *riding teachers or wranglers* (minimum age 15) with English or Western equitation horsemanship and ability to teach or wrangle at $450–$700 per month ▶ 4–6 *rifle staff members* (minimum age 18) with ability to teach at $450–$700 per month ▶ 21 *swimming staff members* (minimum age 18) at $450–$700 per month ▶ 6 *tennis staff members* (minimum age 18) with varsity high school or college experience and ability to teach at $450–$700 per month. Applicants must submit formal organization application, three personal references. An in-person interview is recommended, but a telephone interview is acceptable. International applicants accepted; must apply through a recognized agency.

Benefits and Preemployment Training Free housing, free meals, formal training, willing to provide letters of recommendation, names of contacts, on-the-job training, willing to complete paperwork for educational credit, willing to act as a professional reference, and travel reimbursement. Preemployment training is required and includes accident prevention and safety, first aid, CPR, interpersonal skills, leadership skills, lifeguarding, rifle instruction, and archery instruction.

Contact Meg Clark, Owner/Director, Camp Waldemar for Girls, 1005 FM 1340, Hunt, Texas 78024. Telephone: 830-238-4821. Fax: 830-238-4051. E-mail: info@waldemar.com. World Wide Web: http://www.waldemar.com. Contact by e-mail, fax, mail, or phone. Application deadline: continuous.

CENTER FOR STUDENT MISSIONS–HOUSTON
HOUSTON, TEXAS
See Center for Student Missions on page 37 for complete description.

CYBERCAMPS–SOUTHERN METHODIST UNIVERSITY
DALLAS, TEXAS
See Cybercamps–University of Washington on page 326 for complete description.

CYBERCAMPS–UT AUSTIN
AUSTIN, TEXAS
See Cybercamps–University of Washington on page 326 for complete description.

KICKAPOO KAMP
216 HUMMINGBIRD LANE
KERRVILLE, TEXAS 78028

General Information Kickapoo Kamp is a private residential girls summer camp providing the following activities: horseback riding, water skiing, gymnastics, arts and crafts, cheerleading, riflery, archery, tennis, ping pong, tae-bo, fishing, drama, canoeing, flags, and aerobic dance. Established in 1925. 300-acre facility located 60 miles from San Antonio. Features: Texas hill country; spring-fed creek with lake; rustic cabins with individual bathrooms; horseback riding program (30 horses); lodge for dining; 2 open buildings for activities.

Profile of Summer Employees Total number: 26; typical ages: 18–23. 100% women; 100% college students. Nonsmokers preferred.

Employment Information Openings are from June 5 to August 3. Jobs available: ▶ 23 *staff counselors* (minimum age 18) with ability to teach an activity at $150 per week. Applicants must submit a formal organization application, three personal references, background check. An in-person interview is recommended, but a telephone interview is acceptable.

Benefits and Preemployment Training Free housing, free meals, willing to provide letters of recommendation, and willing to act as a professional reference. Preemployment training is required and includes accident prevention and safety, first aid, CPR, interpersonal skills, leadership skills.

Contact Laura Hodges, Director, Kickapoo Kamp, 10310 Quail Meadow, San Antonio, Texas 78230. Telephone: 210-690-8361. Fax: 210-690-5731. E-mail: hodges@kickapookamp.com. World Wide Web: http://www.kickapookamp.com. Contact by mail, phone, or through World Wide Web site. Application deadline: continuous.

LAZY HILLS GUEST RANCH
HENDERSON BRANCH ROAD
INGRAM, TEXAS 78025

General Information Resort ranch catering to families and groups. Established in 1959. 750-acre facility located 80 miles from San Antonio. Features: swimming pool; volleyball; basketball; 2 tennis courts; game room; horseback riding.

Profile of Summer Employees Total number: 12; typical ages: 16–23. 20% men; 80% women; 10% minorities; 25% high school students; 75% college students; 30% local applicants. Nonsmokers preferred.

Employment Information Openings are from May 15 to September 5. Spring break positions also offered. Jobs available: ▶ 1 *activities director* (minimum age 16) with enthusiasm and ability to work well with children and adults at $500 to $600 per month plus tips ▶ 1 *office worker* (minimum age 18) with computer experience at $400 per month plus tips ▶ 5 *waiters/waitresses* (minimum age 16) at $400 per month plus tips ▶ 2 *wranglers* (minimum age 18) with Red Cross certification and experience with horses at $400 to $600 per month plus tips. Applicants must submit a formal organization application, three personal references. An in-person interview is recommended, but a telephone interview is acceptable. International applicants accepted; must obtain own visa, obtain own working papers.

Benefits and Preemployment Training Free housing, free meals, possible full-time employment, willing to provide letters of recommendation, on-the-job training, and willing to complete paperwork for educational credit.

Contact Beth Steinruck, Office Manager, Lazy Hills Guest Ranch, Box G, Ingram, Texas 78025. Telephone: 830-367-5600. Fax: 830-367-5667. E-mail: lhills@ktc.com. World Wide Web: http://www.lazyhills.com. Contact by e-mail, fax, mail, or phone. Application deadline: continuous.

MO RANCH
HC1, PO BOX 158
HUNT, TEXAS 78024

General Information Conference center with variety of accommodations for families, individuals, and groups. Established in 1949. 434-acre facility located 80 miles from San Antonio. Features: swimming pool; ropes course; auditorium; fully equipped meeting facilities; crystal clear river front; canoeing; fishing.

Profile of Summer Employees Total number: 120; typical ages: 16–30. 50% men; 50% women; 40% high school students; 10% college students; 1% retirees; 1% non-U.S. citizens; 90% local applicants. Nonsmokers preferred.

Employment Information Openings are from May 1 to September 1. Year-round positions also offered. Jobs available: ▶ *cooks* with quantity cooking experience at $7.50–$8.50 per hour ▶ *housekeeping staff* at $7 per hour ▶ *kitchen staff* at $6.50–$7 per hour ▶ *registration staff* with computer skills preferred at $7 per hour ▶ 2–4 *ropes course/field instructors* with preference for certification or experience in facilitating ropes challenge course groups at $6.75–$7.50 per hour. Applicants must submit a formal organization application, letter of interest, resume, two personal references. An in-person interview is required.

Benefits and Preemployment Training Meals at a cost, possible full-time employment, willing to provide letters of recommendation, on-the-job training, willing to complete paperwork for educational credit, and willing to act as a professional reference. Preemployment training is required and includes management training.

Contact Human Resources, Mo Ranch, Route 1, Box 158, Hunt, Texas 78024. Telephone: 800-460-4401. Fax: 830-238-4202. E-mail: hr@moranch.com. World Wide Web: http://www. moranch.com. Contact by e-mail, fax, mail, phone, or through World Wide Web site. Application deadline: continuous.

MO-RANCH SUMMER CAMPS
2229 FM 1340
HUNT, TEXAS 78024

General Information Residential camp serving boys and girls ages 8–16 in 1, 2, and 3-week sessions. Established in 1979. 434-acre facility located 80 miles from San Antonio. Features: freshwater river; water slide; dormitory; Christian camp; nature studies; horseback riding.

Profile of Summer Employees Total number: 20; typical ages: 18–24. 25% men; 75% women; 20% minorities; 100% college students. Nonsmokers required.

Employment Information Openings are from May 26 to August 6. Jobs available: ▶ 6–12 *counselors/instructors* (minimum age 18) with Christian faith at $150–$175 per week. Applicants must submit formal organization application, resume, three personal references. An in-person interview is recommended, but a telephone interview is acceptable. International applicants accepted; must obtain own visa, obtain own working papers, apply through a recognized agency.

Benefits and Preemployment Training Free housing, free meals, possible full-time employment, willing to provide letters of recommendation, on-the-job training, willing to complete paperwork for educational credit, willing to act as a professional reference, and travel reimbursement. Preemployment training is required and includes accident prevention and safety, first aid, CPR, interpersonal skills, leadership skills.

Contact Human Resources, Mo-Ranch Summer Camps, 2229 FM 1340, Hunt, Texas 78024. Telephone: 800-460-4401. Fax: 830-238-4202. E-mail: hr@moranch.com. World Wide Web: http://www.moranch.com. Contact by e-mail, fax, mail, phone, or through World Wide Web site. Application deadline: continuous.

THE SOUTHWESTERN COMPANY, TEXAS
See The Southwestern Company on page 297 for complete description.

SPORTS INTERNATIONAL–JAY NOVACEK FOOTBALL CAMP
COMMERCE, TEXAS
See Sports International, Inc. on page 134 for complete description.

STUDENT CONSERVATION ASSOCIATION (SCA), TEXAS
See Student Conservation Association (SCA), New Hampshire on page 200 for complete description.

TAG/SOUTHERN METHODIST UNIVERSITY
PO BOX 750383
DALLAS, TEXAS 75275
General Information TAG is an academic, residential program for academically-able middle school students. Established in 1978. Features: beautiful campus; located in Dallas; air conditioned facilities; large library system.
Profile of Summer Employees Total number: 15; typical ages: 19–23. 50% men; 50% women; 100% college students. Nonsmokers preferred.
Employment Information Openings are from July 1 to August 1. Jobs available: ▶ 10–20 *residential assistants* (minimum age 19) at $700 per month. Applicants must submit a formal organization application, two personal references, two letters of recommendation. A telephone interview is required. International applicants accepted; must obtain own visa, obtain own working papers.
Benefits and Preemployment Training Free housing and free meals. Preemployment training is required and includes accident prevention and safety, first aid, interpersonal skills, leadership skills.
Contact Marilyn Swanson, Assistant Director, TAG/Southern Methodist University. Telephone: 214-768-0123. Fax: 214-768-3147. E-mail: gifted@smu.edu. World Wide Web: http://www.smu.edu/tag. Contact by e-mail, fax, mail, or phone. Application deadline: April 1.

UTAH

A CHRISTIAN MINISTRY IN THE NATIONAL PARKS– UTAH
See A Christian Ministry in the National Parks–Maine on page 107 for complete description.

FOUR CORNERS SCHOOL OF OUTDOOR EDUCATION
PO BOX 1029
MONTICELLO, UTAH 84535
General Information Program offering educational adventures using the spectacular Colorado Plateau as an outdoor classroom. 3-day to 2-week programs are available on natural and human history via raft, backpack, van, or skis. Established in 1984. 7-acre facility located 300 miles from Salt Lake City. Features: easy access to 3 national parks; rustic historic homestead.
Profile of Summer Employees Total number: 70; typical ages: 16–55. 70% men; 30% women; 5% minorities; 35% college students; 5% local applicants. Nonsmokers preferred.

Employment Information Openings are from March 1 to October 30. Jobs available: ▶ 4–6 *canyon country youth corps crew leaders* (minimum age 21) with outdoor leadership skills, CPR, and first aid/WFR at $400–$550 per week ▶ 1 *canyon country youth corps educator* with teacher's certificate and outdoor leadership skills at $400–$550 per week ▶ *outdoor education interns* (minimum age 21) with interest in a career in outdoor education and knowledge of the Southwest; First Responder and CPR certification preferred at $75 per week. Applicants must submit a formal organization application, letter of interest, resume, personal reference. A telephone interview is required. International applicants accepted; must obtain own visa, obtain own working papers.

Benefits and Preemployment Training Free housing, free meals, willing to provide letters of recommendation, on-the-job training, willing to complete paperwork for educational credit, and willing to act as a professional reference. Preemployment training is required.

Contact Janet Ross, Director, Four Corners School of Outdoor Education, PO Box 1029, Monticello, Utah 84535. Telephone: 435-587-2156. Fax: 435-587-2193. E-mail: fcs@ fourcornersschool.org. World Wide Web: http://www.sw-adventures.org. Contact by e-mail, fax, mail, or phone. Application deadline: continuous.

THE SOUTHWESTERN COMPANY, UTAH
See The Southwestern Company on page 297 for complete description.

STUDENT CONSERVATION ASSOCIATION (SCA), UTAH
See Student Conservation Association (SCA), New Hampshire on page 200 for complete description.

VERMONT

ALOHA FOUNDATION, INC.
2968 LAKE MOREY ROAD
FAIRLEE, VERMONT 05045-9400

General Information Nonprofit organization offering children's residential camps, day camp, youth wilderness trips, and traditional camp activities. Established in 1905. 1,000-acre facility located 20 miles from White River Junction. Features: wooded setting; freshwater lake waterfront; tennis courts; platform tents; washhouse with electricity and hot water; proximity to White and Green Mountains.

Profile of Summer Employees Total number: 325; typical ages: 21–50. 40% men; 60% women; 20% minorities; 5% high school students; 35% college students; 5% retirees; 25% non-U.S. citizens; 10% local applicants. Nonsmokers preferred.

Employment Information Openings are from June 15 to August 15. Jobs available: ▶ *summer camp counselors* (minimum age 18) at $750–$3000 per season. Applicants must submit formal organization application, three letters of recommendation. An in-person interview is recommended, but a telephone interview is acceptable. International applicants accepted; must apply through a recognized agency.

Benefits and Preemployment Training Free housing, free meals, formal training, possible full-time employment, willing to provide letters of recommendation, on-the-job training, and willing to act as a professional reference. Preemployment training is required and includes accident prevention and safety, first aid, CPR, interpersonal skills, leadership skills, lifeguard training.

Contact Ellen Bagley, Administrative Assistant, Aloha Foundation, Inc. Telephone: 802-333-3400. Fax: 802-333-3404. E-mail: ellen_bagley@alohafoundation.org. World Wide Web: http://www.alohafoundation.org. Contact by e-mail, fax, mail, phone, or through World Wide Web site. Application deadline: June 1.

BURKLYN BALLET THEATRE
337 COLLEGE HILL, JOHNSON STATE COLLEGE
JOHNSON, VERMONT 05656

General Information Classical ballet workshop offers weekly performance opportunity to 136 boys and girls ages 12–20 in one 6-week program. Established in 1976. 100-acre facility located 35 miles from Burlington. Features: mountains; rural village; college campus; university dormitories; library; pool.

Profile of Summer Employees Total number: 20; typical ages: 20–75. 50% men; 50% women; 10% minorities; 25% college students; 1% retirees; 5% non-U.S. citizens. Nonsmokers preferred.

Employment Information Openings are from June 19 to August 3. Jobs available: ▶ 14 *counselors* (minimum age 20) with current professional dance contract or college dance major; salary may be program tuition, room, and board ▶ 1 *registered nurse* should be experienced licensed RN; salary may be child's tuition waiver ▶ 1 *technical director* (minimum age 25) with professional experience or college technical theater major at $100–$200 per week. Applicants must submit resume, in-person/video audition. International applicants accepted; must obtain own visa, obtain own working papers.

Benefits and Preemployment Training Free housing, free meals, formal training, willing to provide letters of recommendation, names of contacts, on-the-job training, willing to act as a professional reference, opportunity to attend seminars/workshops, and tuition assistance. Preemployment training is required and includes interpersonal skills, leadership skills.

Contact Angela Whitehill, Artistic Director, Burklyn Ballet Theatre, PO Box 907, Island Heights, New Jersey 08732. Fax: 732-288-2663. World Wide Web: http://www.burklynballet.com. Contact by fax or mail. No phone calls. Application deadline: April 15.

BURKLYN BALLET THEATRE II, THE INTERMEDIATE PROGRAM
JOHNSON STATE COLLEGE
JOHNSON, VERMONT 05656

General Information Classical ballet workshop for 18 girls ages 8–11 in one 3-week session. Established in 1995. Located 35 miles from Burlington. Features: college campus; rural village; streams and mountains; library; 4 studios; pool.

Profile of Summer Employees Total number: 6; typical age: 35. 10% men; 90% women. Nonsmokers required.

Employment Information Jobs available: ▶ *registered nurse* with experience as a licensed RN at a negotiable salary which may be child's tuition waiver. Applicants must submit a formal organization application, letter of interest, resume, personal reference. An in-person interview is required. International applicants accepted; must obtain own visa, obtain own working papers.

Benefits and Preemployment Training Free housing, free meals, willing to provide letters of recommendation, on-the-job training, willing to act as a professional reference, opportunity to attend seminars/workshops, travel reimbursement, and tuition assistance. Preemployment training is required and includes interpersonal skills.

Contact Angela Whitehill, Artistic Director, Burklyn Ballet Theatre II, The Intermediate Program, PO Box 907, Island Heights, New Jersey 08732. Telephone: 732-288-2660. Fax: 732-288-2663. Application deadline: March 15.

CAMP FARNSWORTH
ROUTE 113
THETFORD, VERMONT 05074

General Information Residential Girl Scout camp for girls ages 6–16 offering four 2-week sessions. Established in 1959. 300-acre facility located 150 miles from Boston, Massachusetts. Features: private lake; variety of terrain: woods, meadows, hills; 50-foot waterslide into lake; high ropes course.

Profile of Summer Employees Total number: 110; typical ages: 18–40. 1% men; 99% women; 5% minorities; 50% college students; 30% non-U.S. citizens; 20% local applicants. Nonsmokers preferred.

Employment Information Openings are from June 16 to August 22. Jobs available: ▶ 1 *adventure director* with experience instructing ropes course at $1800–$3200 per season ▶ 3 *arts assistants* (minimum age 18) with experience teaching in the field at $1500–$1800 per season ▶ 1 *arts director* with supervisory experience at $2400–$3200 per season ▶ 2 *cooks* with quantity cooking experience at $3000–$3800 per season ▶ 1 *counselor-in-training director* (minimum age 21) with camp supervisory experience at $1800–$2400 per season ▶ *driver/shopper* (minimum age 21) with driver's license at $1800–$2400 per season ▶ 2 *health directors* (minimum age 21) with RN, LPN, or EMT license at $2500–$4800 per season ▶ 4 *riding assistants* (minimum age 18) with instructor experience at $1400–$2400 per season ▶ 15–20 *unit assistants* (minimum age 18) with child supervisory experience and high school diploma at $1500–$1800 per season ▶ 12 *unit leaders* with high school diploma, experience supervising adults, and working with groups of children at $1800–$2400 per season ▶ 8 *waterfront assistants* (minimum age 18) with Red Cross or YMCA lifeguard certification (WSI preferred) and experience teaching swimming at $1500–$2400 per season. Applicants must submit formal organization application, three personal references. A telephone interview is required. International applicants accepted; must apply through a recognized agency.

Benefits and Preemployment Training Free housing, free meals, formal training, health insurance, willing to provide letters of recommendation, on-the-job training, willing to complete paperwork for educational credit, and willing to act as a professional reference. Preemployment training is required and includes accident prevention and safety, first aid, CPR, interpersonal skills, leadership skills, child development, camp program.

Contact Beth LaVallee, Camp Director, Camp Farnsworth, One Commerce Drive, Bedford, New Hampshire 03110. Telephone: 603-627-4158. Fax: 603-627-4169. E-mail: blavallee@ swgirlscouts.org. World Wide Web: http://www.swgirlscouts.org. Contact by e-mail, fax, mail, phone, or through World Wide Web site. Application deadline: continuous.

CAMP THOREAU-IN-VERMONT
ONE THOREAU WAY
THETFORD CENTER, VERMONT 05075-9601

General Information Interracial, coeducational, democratic community living for 140 campers and 64 staff members. Established in 1972. 380-acre facility located 25 miles from White River Junction. Features: rural environment; on-site riding facility; 4 clay tennis courts; campsite on 64-acre lake; hiking in nearby White and Green Mountains; fully equipped darkroom and video studio.

Profile of Summer Employees Total number: 65; typical ages: 17–35. 50% men; 50% women; 15% minorities; 8% high school students; 60% college students; 20% non-U.S. citizens; 10% local applicants. Nonsmokers preferred.

Employment Information Openings are from June 13 to August 20. Jobs available: ▶ 3 *counselors/arts and crafts instructors* with CPR/first aid certification and experience at $1500–$2400 per season ▶ 2 *counselors/evening programs instructors* with experience and creativity to design activities for the entire camp at $1500–$2400 per season ▶ 2 *counselors/high-ropes instructors* with experience at $1500–$2400 per season ▶ 2 *counselors/hiking and outdoor living instructors* with experience, familiarity with area, CPR/first aid certification, and Wilderness First Responder or Wilderness EMT (preferred) at $1500–$2400 per season ▶ 12 *counselors/lifeguards* with LGT, CPR/FPR, and first aid certification at $1500–$2400 per season ▶ 2 *counselors/low-ropes instructors* with CPR/first aid certification and experience at $1500–$2400 per season ▶ 2 *counselors/nature (small animals) instructors* with CPR/first aid certification and experience at $1500–$2400 per season ▶ 2 *counselors/photography instructors* with CPR/first aid certification and experience at $1500–$2400 per season ▶ 6 *counselors/small craft instructors* with LGT and canoeing/sailing/kayaking instructor certification at $1500–$2400 per season ▶ 4 *counselors/sports instructors* with CPR/first aid certification and experience at $1500–$2400 per season ▶ 8 *counselors/swimming instructors* with WSI, LGT, first aid, and CPR/FPR certification at $1600–$2500 per season ▶ 2 *counselors/top-rope rock climbing instructors* with experience at $1500–$2400 per season ▶ 2 *counselors/woodshop instructors* with CPR/first aid certification and experience at $1500–$2400 per season ▶ *maintenance staff* with experience at $1400–$2800 per season ▶ *nurses* with RN license, ability to obtain Vermont RN license, and CPR certification at $4500–$5500 per season. Applicants must submit formal organization application, letter of interest, personal reference, letter of recommendation. An in-person interview is recommended, but a telephone interview is acceptable. International applicants accepted; must apply through a recognized agency.

Benefits and Preemployment Training Free housing, free meals, health insurance, on-the-job training, willing to complete paperwork for educational credit, travel reimbursement, and laundry facilities; opportunity to work with diverse, multicultural staff in several different program areas. Preemployment training is required and includes program-specific skill development.

Contact Gregory H. Finger, Director, Camp Thoreau-In-Vermont, 157 Tillson Lake Road, Wallkill, New York 12589-3265. Telephone: 845-895-2974. Fax: 845-895-1281. E-mail: gfinger@frontiernet.net. World Wide Web: http://www.campthoreau-in-vermont.org. Contact by e-mail, phone, or through World Wide Web site. Application deadline: continuous.

CAMP THORPE, INC.
680 CAPEN HILL ROAD
GOSHEN, VERMONT 05733

General Information Summer residential camp that serves children and adults with special needs. Established in 1927. 171-acre facility located 70 miles from Burlington. Features: large pool; tennis court; pond; small stage; cabins; small farm.

Profile of Summer Employees Total number: 25; typical ages: 18–22. 40% men; 60% women; 10% high school students; 90% college students; 25% non-U.S. citizens; 75% local applicants.

Employment Information Openings are from June 18 to August 10. Jobs available: ▶ 1 *camp nurse* with RN, LPN, or EMT license at $3000–$4000 per season ▶ 1 *cook* with previous experience at $3000–$4000 per season ▶ 12 *general counselors* (minimum age 17) with a desire to work with children and adults with special needs at $1600–$1700 per season ▶ 2 *head counselors* (minimum age 18) with two years of college completed at $1800–$2000 per season ▶ 2 *kitchen assistants* (minimum age 16) with previous experience at $200 per week ▶ 5 *specialists (art, nature, music, pool, and sports)* (minimum age 18) with one year of college completed at $1700–$1800 per season. Applicants must submit formal organization application, three personal references. An in-person interview is recommended, but a telephone interview is acceptable. International applicants accepted; must apply through a recognized agency.

Benefits and Preemployment Training Free housing, free meals, willing to provide letters of recommendation, on-the-job training, willing to complete paperwork for educational credit, and willing to act as a professional reference. Preemployment training is required and includes accident prevention and safety, first aid, CPR, interpersonal skills, leadership skills.

Contact Lyle P. Jepson, Director, Camp Thorpe, Inc., 680 Capen Hill Road, Goshen, Vermont 05733. Telephone: 802-247-6611. E-mail: cthorpe@sover.net. Contact by e-mail, mail, or phone. Application deadline: continuous.

CHALLENGE WILDERNESS CAMP FOR BOYS
480 ROARING BROOK ROAD
BRADFORD, VERMONT 05033

General Information Residential camp serving 45 boys ages 9–16 with outdoor skills and wilderness trips. Established in 1965. 650-acre facility located 26 miles from Hanover, New Hampshire. Features: 650-acre forest preserve; 15-acre trout-stocked private lake; Adirondack shelters; blacksmith shop; playing fields.

Profile of Summer Employees Total number: 10–12; typical ages: 21–30. 100% men; 60% college students; 40% non-U.S. citizens. Nonsmokers required.

Employment Information Openings are from June 18 to August 25. Jobs available: ▶ 1 *blacksmithing instructor* (minimum age 21) with ability to be trained at $2000–$2500 per season ▶ 1 *fishing/fly-tying instructor* (minimum age 21) with trout specialty at $2000–$2500 per season ▶ 1 *food services director* (minimum age 21) with outdoorsman and cooking skills at $2000–$3000 per season ▶ 1 *kayak instructor* (minimum age 21) with ACA or BCU certification, LGT preferred at $2000–$2500 per season ▶ 1 *kitchen assistant* (minimum age 21) with outdoorsman skills at $2000–$2500 per season ▶ 1 *marksmanship instructor* (minimum age 21) with .22-caliber and military experience at $2000–$2500 per season ▶ 3 *rock climbing instructors* (minimum age 21) with one 5.10 lead plus two 5.9 seconds at $2000–$2500 per season ▶ 1 *waterfront director* with lifeguard training required, WSI preferred at $2000–$2500 per season ▶ 1 *woodworking instructor* (minimum age 21) with background in carpentry, woodwork, and cabinet-making at $2000–$2500 per season. Applicants must submit formal organization application, letter of interest, resume, three personal references. A telephone interview is required. International applicants accepted; must apply through a recognized agency.

Benefits and Preemployment Training Free housing, free meals, willing to provide letters of recommendation, on-the-job training, willing to complete paperwork for educational credit, willing to act as a professional reference, and outdoor leadership training. Preemployment training is required and includes accident prevention and safety, first aid, CPR, interpersonal skills, leadership skills, water safety rescue.

Contact Dr. J. Thayer, Director, Challenge Wilderness Camp for Boys, 300 Grove Street, #4, Rutland, Vermont 05701. Telephone: 800-832-HAWK. Fax: 802-786-0653. E-mail: rainest@sover. net. World Wide Web: http://www.challengewilderness.com. Contact by e-mail or phone. Application deadline: continuous.

FARM AND WILDERNESS CAMPS
263 FARM AND WILDERNESS ROAD
PLYMOUTH, VERMONT 05056

General Information 5 separate individual residential programs for boys/girls ages 9–17 offering diverse outdoor wilderness activities within Quaker-based communities. Also day camp for boys and girls ages 3–10. Established in 1939. 3,000-acre facility located 23 miles from Rutland. Features: freshwater lake; certified organic farm; Green Mountain National Forest; surrounded by 3000 acres of forest; farm animals; 3-sided cabins.

Profile of Summer Employees Total number: 200; typical ages: 19–24. 55% men; 45% women; 10% minorities; 5% high school students; 75% college students; 2% retirees; 2% non-U.S. citizens; 15% local applicants. Nonsmokers required.

Employment Information Openings are from June 13 to August 18. Year-round positions also offered. Jobs available: ▶ 18 *cooks* (minimum age 18) at $1800–$4000 per season ▶ 120–150 *counselors* (minimum age 18) at $1500–$2250 per season ▶ 6 *nurses* (minimum age 21) with RN license or graduate nursing student status at $3000–$3500 per season. Applicants must submit formal organization application, three personal references. A telephone interview is required. International applicants accepted; must apply through a recognized agency.

Benefits and Preemployment Training Free housing, free meals, formal training, health insurance, on-the-job training, willing to complete paperwork for educational credit, and opportunity to attend seminars/workshops. Preemployment training is required and includes accident prevention and safety, first aid, CPR, interpersonal skills, leadership skills, outdoor skills.

Contact Melissa Zoerheide, Staff Counseling, Farm and Wilderness Camps. Telephone: 802-422-3761. Fax: 802-422-8660. E-mail: melissa@fandw.org. World Wide Web: http://www.fandw.org. Contact by e-mail, mail, phone, or through World Wide Web site. Application deadline: continuous.

GREEN MOUNTAIN CLUB
4711 WATERBURY-STOWE ROAD
WATERBURY CENTER, VERMONT 05677

General Information Club which preserves and protects the Long Trail System and other hiking trails in Vermont. Established in 1910. Located 40 miles from Burlington. Features: wooded setting; mountains; lakes and ponds; hiking trails.

Profile of Summer Employees Total number: 36; typical ages: 18–26. 50% men; 50% women; 20% minorities; 75% college students; 10% non-U.S. citizens; 50% local applicants. Nonsmokers preferred.

Employment Information Openings are from May 15 to October 31. Jobs available: ▶ 15–20 *backcountry caretakers* (minimum age 18) with camping, hiking, and education background at $231–$320 per week ▶ 15–20 *backcountry trail crew* (minimum age 18) with camping, hiking, and trail building background at $231–$320 per week. Applicants must submit a formal organization application, two personal references. A telephone interview is required. International applicants accepted; must obtain own visa.

Benefits and Preemployment Training Free housing, free meals, formal training, possible full-time employment, health insurance, willing to provide letters of recommendation, names of contacts, on-the-job training, willing to complete paperwork for educational credit, willing to act as a professional reference, opportunity to attend seminars/workshops, and tuition assistance. Preemployment training is required and includes accident prevention and safety, first aid, interpersonal skills, leadership skills.

Contact Mr. Dave Hardy, Director of Field Programs, Green Mountain Club. Telephone: 802-244-7037. Fax: 802-244-5867. E-mail: gmc@greenmountainclub.org. World Wide Web: http://www.greenmountainclub.org. Contact by e-mail, fax, mail, phone, or through World Wide Web site. Application deadline: continuous.

KILLOOLEET
ROUTE 100
HANCOCK, VERMONT 05748-0070

General Information Full-season, noncompetitive, coeducational camp serving 100 campers ages 9–14 for 7 or more weeks. Emphasis is on developing techniques in group leadership and individual areas of expertise. Children specialize in a variety of sports and arts activities. Established in 1927. 300-acre facility located 35 miles from Rutland. Features: beautiful valley, streams and woods; flat campus and bicycles; freshwater lake; horses and riding program; all counselors go on hikes and overnight trips.

Profile of Summer Employees Total number: 45; typical ages: 18–30. 50% men; 50% women; 9% minorities; 12% high school students; 65% college students; 4% retirees; 20% non-U.S. citizens; 15% local applicants. Nonsmokers preferred.

Employment Information Openings are from June 19 to August 23. Jobs available: ▶ 1 *boating (canoeing, windsurfing) instructor* (minimum age 19) at $1500–$2300 per season ▶ 1 *drama counselor* (minimum age 19) with ability to direct a musical as well as teach improvisation/ creative dramatics at $1500–$2300 per season ▶ 1 *electronics instructor* (minimum age 19) at $1500–$2200 per season ▶ 1 *fabric arts instructor* (minimum age 19) with sewing skills needed; other fabric arts, such as weaving, knitting or crocheting are useful at $1500–$2200 per season ▶ 2 *horseback riding (English) instructors* (minimum age 19) with Pony Club or equivalent group teaching experience at $1500–$2500 per season ▶ *mountain biking/rock climbing/ camping skills instructor* with teaching experience and other interests at $1500–$2500 per season ▶ 1–3 *music (folk, rhythm and blues/funk) instructors* with interest in working with camper bands, teaching individual lessons, and running group sings at $1500–$2500 per season ▶ 1 *music counselor—piano focus* (minimum age 19) with ability to play piano for the camp musical and help campers with learning their songs (other activity skills desirable, too) at $1500–$2300 per season ▶ 1 *nature instructor* (minimum age 19) with teaching ideas using pond, fields, stream, and woods at $1500–$2200 per season ▶ 1 *secretary* (minimum age 18) with basic skills and enjoyment of working with children at $1500–$2500 per season ▶ 1 *shop counselor (woodworking or crafts)* (minimum age 19) at $1400–$2000 per season ▶ 2 *sports (individual and team) instructors* at $1500–$2400 per season ▶ 1 *stained glass instructor* (minimum age 19) with ability to teach copper foil construction at $1500–$2500 per season ▶ 1–3 *swimming instructors* (minimum age 19) with current WSI and lifeguard certifications at $1500–$2200 per season ▶ 1 *video, filming, and editing instructor* (minimum age 19) with experience with digital camera and editing systems at $1500–$2500 per season. Applicants must submit formal organization application, letter of interest, three personal references, brief biographical statement. An in-person interview is recommended, but a telephone interview is acceptable. International applicants accepted; must apply through a recognized agency.

Benefits and Preemployment Training Free housing, free meals, formal training, health insurance, willing to provide letters of recommendation, on-the-job training, willing to complete paperwork for educational credit, willing to act as a professional reference, opportunity to attend seminars/workshops, and partial travel reimbursement. Preemployment training is required and includes accident prevention and safety, first aid, CPR, interpersonal skills, leadership skills, wilderness first aid.

Contact Kate Spencer-Seeger, Director, Killooleet, 70 Trull Street, Somerville, Massachusetts 02145. Telephone: 617-666-1484. Fax: 617-666-0378. E-mail: camp05748@aol.com. World Wide Web: http://www.killooleet.com. Contact by e-mail, fax, mail, phone, or through World Wide Web site. Application deadline: continuous.

LOCHEARN CAMP FOR GIRLS
LAKE FAIRLEE
POST MILLS, VERMONT 05058

General Information Private residential camp for girls ages 7–16 offering a comprehensive activity program with special emphasis on positive character development of children. Established in 1916. 51-acre facility located 150 miles from Boston, Massachusetts. Features: freshwater lake; wooded setting; lakeside cabins; gymnastics center; 5 tennis courts; 16- horse stable and riding facilities.

Profile of Summer Employees Total number: 75; typical ages: 18–26. 10% men; 90% women; 10% high school students; 80% college students; 10% retirees; 15% non-U.S. citizens. Nonsmokers required.

Employment Information Openings are from June 12 to August 22. Jobs available: ▶ 2 *English-style riding instructors* (minimum age 18) with experience in the field at $2000–$2300 per season ▶ 2 *canoeing instructors* (minimum age 18) with LGT certification or small crafts safety certification at $1850–$2100 per season ▶ 1 *diving instructor* (minimum age 18) with LGT certification at $1850–$2100 per season ▶ 5 *field sports instructors* (minimum age 18) at $1850–$2100 per season ▶ 3 *gymnastics instructors* (minimum age 18) with floor and full apparatus experience, coaching experience preferred at $1850–$2100 per season ▶ *head chef* (minimum age 26) with culinary training, prior experience in cooking, purchasing, and kitchen management at $7000–$9000 per season ▶ 3 *kitchen assistants* (minimum age 18) at $1850–$2200 per season ▶ 2 *leadership trainers* (minimum age 21) with experience in the field at $2000–$2300 per season ▶ 2 *outdoor adventure staff* (minimum age 21) with WFA/First Responder at $2100–$2300 per season ▶ 2 *performing arts instructors* (minimum age 18) with experience in the field at $1850–$2100 per season ▶ 2 *registered nurses* (minimum age 22) with RN (Vermont temporary license), CPR/first aid certification, and pediatric experience at $4000–$4500 per season ▶ 2 *sailing instructors* (minimum age 18) with LGT or small crafts safety certification at $1850–$2100 per season ▶ *secretary* (minimum age 21) with computer/office skills and experience at $2000–$2300 per season ▶ 10 *studio arts instructors* (minimum age 18) at $1850–$2100 per season ▶ 2 *swimming instructors* (minimum age 18) with LGT/WSI certification at $1850–$2100 per season ▶ 4 *tennis instructors* (minimum age 18) with coaching experience preferred at $1850–$2100 per season ▶ 2 *waterskiing instructors/boat drivers* (minimum age 18) with LGT certification and waterski instructors certification at $1850–$2100 per season. Applicants must submit formal organization application, three personal references. A telephone interview is required. International applicants accepted; must apply through a recognized agency.

Benefits and Preemployment Training Free housing, free meals, formal training, willing to provide letters of recommendation, on-the-job training, willing to complete paperwork for educational credit, willing to act as a professional reference, and travel reimbursement. Preemployment training is required and includes accident prevention and safety, first aid, CPR, interpersonal skills, leadership skills, character education, curriculum training, teacher/coach training/LGT.

Contact Rich Maxson, Owner/Director, Lochearn Camp for Girls, Camp Lochearn on Lake Fairlee, Post Mills, Vermont 05058. Telephone: 877-649-4151. Fax: 802-333-4856. E-mail: lochearn@earthlink.net. Contact by e-mail, fax, mail, or phone. Application deadline: continuous.

MOUNT SNOW
ROUTE 100
WEST DOVER, VERMONT 05356

General Information Major ski area. Summer operations include mountain biking, lift service for downhill bikers, kids camp, hotels, golf, golf school, hiking, bus tours, lift rides, schools for biking, and lakes. Established in 1954. 1,000-acre facility located 50 miles from Albany, New York. Features: 2 swimming pools; 2 hotels; wooded setting; 3 lifts operational (summer); golf course (18 holes); climbing wall and in-line skate park.

Profile of Summer Employees Total number: 350; typical ages: 18–60. 70% men; 30% women; 10% high school students; 20% college students; 70% local applicants. Nonsmokers preferred.

Employment Information Openings are from May 31 to October 12. Spring break, winter break, and year-round positions also offered. Jobs available: ▶ *food and beverage staff* (minimum age 18) at $6.50 per hour ▶ *lift operators* (minimum age 18). Applicants must submit a formal organization application. An in-person interview is required. International applicants accepted; must obtain own visa.

Benefits and Preemployment Training Possible full-time employment, willing to provide letters of recommendation, on-the-job training, willing to complete paperwork for educational credit, and free golf/skiing depending on season, discounted bike rentals, use of bike trail network. Preemployment training is required and includes accident prevention and safety, interpersonal skills, leadership skills, guest service cross training.

Contact Charlie Romano, Recruiter/Trainer, Mount Snow, Human Resources, Route 100, West Dover, Vermont 05356. Telephone: 802-464-4221. Fax: 802-464-4135. E-mail: cromano@ mountsnow.com. World Wide Web: http://www.mountsnow.com. Contact by e-mail, fax, phone, or through World Wide Web site. Application deadline: continuous.

POINT COUNTERPOINT CHAMBER MUSIC CAMP
LAKE DUNEMORE, VERMONT 05733

General Information Residential camp serving 50 string players and pianists for three-, four-, or seven-week sessions. Established in 1963. 2-acre facility located 50 miles from Burlington. Features: freshwater; mountains; small student body.

Profile of Summer Employees Total number: 22; typical ages: 19–40. 34% men; 66% women; 16% minorities; 33% college students; 16% non-U.S. citizens; 27% local applicants. Nonsmokers preferred.

Employment Information Openings are from June 15 to August 11. Jobs available: ▶ 1 *activities director* (minimum age 21) with interpersonal skills at $2400–$3000 per season ▶ 6 *activity counselors* (minimum age 19) with WSI, first aid, and CPR certification (preferred) at $1550–$1750 per season ▶ *cooks* with experience in the field at $2200–$6000 per season ▶ 8 *music staff members (4 violinists, 1 violist, 2 cellists, and 1 pianist)* with performing and teaching experience at $2800–$3200 per season. Applicants must submit a formal organization application, resume, three personal references, audition tape for music faculty. A telephone interview is required. International applicants accepted; must obtain own visa, obtain own working papers.

Benefits and Preemployment Training Free housing, free meals, willing to provide letters of recommendation, and willing to act as a professional reference. Preemployment training is required and includes interpersonal skills, leadership skills.

Contact Paul Roby, Director, Point CounterPoint Chamber Music Camp, PO Box 3181, Terre Haute, Indiana 47803. Telephone: 812-877-3745. Fax: 812-877-2174. E-mail: pointcp@aol.com. World Wide Web: http://www.pointcp.com. Contact by e-mail, fax, mail, phone, or through World Wide Web site. Application deadline: continuous.

THE PUTNEY SCHOOL SUMMER PROGRAMS
ELM LEA FARM, 418 HOUGHTON BROOK ROAD
PUTNEY, VERMONT 05346

General Information Boarding and day program for 120 teenage students in visual and performing arts, music, writing, and English as a Second Language. Established in 1987. 500-acre facility located 10 miles from Brattleboro. Features: superb arts facilities; working farm; houses and dormitories; computer lab; miles of biking/running trails; hilltop setting.

Profile of Summer Employees Total number: 45; typical ages: 21–26. 40% men; 60% women; 10% minorities; 30% college students; 10% non-U.S. citizens; 25% local applicants. Nonsmokers required.

Employment Information Openings are from June 21 to August 12. Jobs available: ▶ 15–18 *residential staff/teaching apprentices* (minimum age 21) with experience in arts, music, writing, or English as a Second Language preferred; also residential and outdoor experience and first aid training at $1800 per season. Applicants must submit a formal organization application, letter of interest, resume, three personal references. An in-person interview is recommended, but a telephone interview is acceptable. International applicants accepted; must obtain own visa, obtain own working papers.

Benefits and Preemployment Training Free housing, free meals, formal training, on-the-job training, and willing to act as a professional reference. Preemployment training is required and includes accident prevention and safety, first aid, interpersonal skills, leadership skills.

Contact Tom Howe, Director, Summer Programs, The Putney School Summer Programs, The Putney School, Putney, Vermont 05346. Fax: 802-387-6216. E-mail: summer@putney.com. World

Wide Web: http://www.putneyschool.org/summer. Contact by e-mail or mail. No phone calls. Application deadline: applications accepted from January 1 through March 15.

THE SOUTHWESTERN COMPANY, VERMONT
See The Southwestern Company on page 297 for complete description.

STUDENT CONSERVATION ASSOCIATION (SCA), VERMONT
See Student Conservation Association (SCA), New Hampshire on page 200 for complete description.

SUMMER DISCOVERY AT VERMONT
UNIVERSITY OF VERMONT
BURLINGTON, VERMONT 05401
General Information Precollege enrichment program for high school students at University of Vermont. Established in 1990. Features: sport facilities; beaches; mountains; lakes; major cities nearby; college towns.

Profile of Summer Employees Total number: 20; typical ages: 21–35. 10% minorities; 60% college students; 2% non-U.S. citizens. Nonsmokers required.

Employment Information Openings are from June to August. Jobs available: ▶ 20 *resident counselors* (minimum age 21) with experience working with high school students/children at $200 per week. Applicants must submit a formal organization application, resume, three personal references. An in-person interview is required. International applicants accepted; must obtain own visa, obtain own working papers.

Benefits and Preemployment Training Free housing, free meals, possible full-time employment, on-the-job training, willing to complete paperwork for educational credit, and willing to act as a professional reference. Preemployment training is required and includes accident prevention and safety, CPR, leadership skills.

Contact Rouel Belleza, Operations, Summer Discovery at Vermont, 1326 Old Northern Boulevard, Roslyn, New York 11576, United States. Telephone: 516-621-3939. Fax: 516-625-3438. E-mail: staff@summerfun.com. World Wide Web: http://www.summerfun.com. Contact by e-mail, fax, phone, or through World Wide Web site. Application deadline: continuous.

THE TYLER PLACE FAMILY RESORT
BOX 1, OLD DOCK ROAD
HIGHGATE SPRINGS, VERMONT 05460
General Information Summer family resort with separate activity programs for children, teens and adults. Established in 1933. 160-acre facility located 45 miles from Burlington. Features: freshwater lake; rural setting; indoor/outdoor pools; tennis courts; canoeing, kayaking, sailing, waterskiing, wake boarding; activity programs for children and adults.

Profile of Summer Employees Total number: 220; typical ages: 20–24. 50% men; 50% women; 10% high school students; 75% college students; 1% retirees; 20% non-U.S. citizens; 40% local applicants. Nonsmokers preferred.

Employment Information Openings are from May 25 to September 11. Jobs available: ▶ 1–2 *adult sports and entertainment instructors* (minimum age 20) with adult CPR and first aid, supervisory skills, communication skills, leadership skills, and current college student status (or graduate) at $6.25–$7 per hour ▶ 20–40 *children's, teen's, and head counselors* (minimum age 19) with CPR and first aid training, previous experience, leadership and communication skills at $6.25–$7 per hour ▶ 3–6 *cooks and prep cooks* (minimum age 19) previous experience, hardworking, knife skills at $6.25–$8.50 per hour ▶ 5 *desk clerks* ▶ 10–15 *dining room servers* (minimum age 19) friendly, hardworking, communication skills at $6.25–$7 per hour ▶ 2–4 *lifeguards* (minimum age 19) with WSI with current advanced lifeguarding, CPR, and first aid at $6.25–$7 per hour ▶ 5–9 *watersports instructors* (minimum age 20) with WSI with current advanced lifeguarding, CPR, and first aid; experience in sailing, windsurfing, kayaking, and canoeing at $6.25–$7 per hour. Applicants must submit formal organization application, resume, academic transcripts, three personal references, letter of recommendation. A telephone interview is required. International applicants accepted; must obtain own visa, apply through a recognized agency.

Benefits and Preemployment Training Free housing, free meals, willing to provide letters of recommendation, on-the-job training, willing to complete paperwork for educational credit, willing to act as a professional reference, travel reimbursement, and use of facilities. Preemployment training is required and includes first aid, CPR.

Contact Tasney Tyler Otis, Programs Director, The Tyler Place Family Resort, Box 1, Old Dock Road, Highgate Springs, Vermont 05460. Telephone: 802-868-4000. Fax: 802-868-5621. E-mail: tyler2@together.net. Contact by e-mail, fax, mail, or phone. Application deadline: April 15.

VERMONT STATE PARKS DIVISION
103 SOUTH MAIN STREET
WATERBURY, VERMONT 05671

General Information Division that plans, maintains, operates, designs, and constructs a system of state parks. Established in 1924. Features: freshwater lakes; wooded settings; streams; mountains; waterfalls; beautiful scenery.

Profile of Summer Employees Total number: 200; typical ages: 16–75. 50% men; 50% women; 1% minorities; 15% high school students; 25% college students; 15% retirees; 44% local applicants. Nonsmokers preferred.

Employment Information Openings are from May 1 to October 15. Jobs available: ▶ 10–50 *park attendants* (minimum age 16) with outstanding customer service skills and enjoyment working with others; must work weekends at $7.32–$7.91 per hour ▶ 2–10 *park naturalists* (minimum age 20) with outstanding customer service skills and extensive knowledge of Vermont's natural resources at $8.96–$9.62 per hour. Applicants must submit a formal organization application, letter of interest, resume, two letters of recommendation, 2-6 personal references. An in-person interview is recommended, but a telephone interview is acceptable.

Benefits and Preemployment Training Housing at a cost, willing to provide letters of recommendation, on-the-job training, willing to complete paperwork for educational credit, and willing to act as a professional reference.

Contact Mr. Larry T. Simino, Director of State Parks, Vermont State Parks Division. Fax: 802-244-1481. E-mail: parks@fpr.anr.state.vt.us. World Wide Web: http://www.vtstateparks. com. Contact by e-mail, fax, or mail. No phone calls. Application deadline: April 1.

VIRGINIA

A CHRISTIAN MINISTRY IN THE NATIONAL PARKS–VIRGINIA

See A Christian Ministry in the National Parks–Maine on page 107 for complete description.

CAMP FRIENDSHIP
PO BOX 145
PALMYRA, VIRGINIA 22963

General Information Residential camp with a traditional program, specialized equestrian program, golf, gymnastics, and tennis camps, and adventure trips for teens in one- and two-week sessions. Established in 1966. 730-acre facility located 25 miles from Charlottesville. Features: lake; junior Olympic-size pool; 2 gymnasiums; 80-stall stable; 60-event ropes course; 4 tennis courts.

Profile of Summer Employees Total number: 140; typical ages: 16–40. 50% men; 50% women; 5% minorities; 5% high school students; 50% college students; 15% non-U.S. citizens; 10% local applicants. Nonsmokers preferred.

Employment Information Openings are from June 1 to August 25. Year-round positions also offered. Jobs available: ▶ 1 *arts and crafts director* (minimum age 21) with skills and experience with variety of arts materials at $2000–$3000 per season ▶ 10 *challenge counselors* (minimum age 21) with outdoor skills, driver's license, and adventure skills (preferred) at $2000–$3000 per season ▶ 3 *drivers/maintenance personnel* (minimum age 21) with driver's license at $1200–$1400 per season ▶ 1 *general program staff* (minimum age 21) with camp experience (preferred) and ability to lead camp activities at $2000–$3000 per season ▶ 25 *junior cabin counselors/instructors* (minimum age 16) with teaching skills at $75–$105 per week ▶ 11 *kitchen staff members* at $1000–$2000 per season ▶ 2 *nurses* with RN license at $2000–$4000 per season ▶ 4 *other support positions* (minimum age 16) ▶ 1 *performing arts director* (minimum age 21) with experience/background in performing arts at $2000–$3000 per season ▶ 1 *pool director* (minimum age 21) with WSI, lifeguard instructor certification, and experience supervising pool and lifeguards at $2000–$3000 per season ▶ 8 *riding counselors/instructors* with experience in the field at $1100–$2000 per season ▶ 35 *senior cabin counselors/instructors* (minimum age 19) with teaching skills in a program area at $1500–$2000 per season ▶ 1 *sports director* (minimum age 21) with experience in variety of sports required and teaching or coaching experience preferred at $2000–$3000 per season ▶ 1 *target sports director* (minimum age 21) with archery and riflery instructor's certification at $2000–$3000 per season ▶ 8 *village directors* with college degree and supervisory experience at $2000–$3000 per season ▶ 1 *waterfront director* (minimum age 21) with WSI and lifeguard instructor certification, small craft safety or other related certifications at $2000–$3000 per season. Applicants must submit three personal references, formal organization application (contact for application forms or download from Web site). An in-person interview is recommended, but a telephone interview is acceptable. International applicants accepted; must apply through a recognized agency.

Benefits and Preemployment Training Free housing, free meals, formal training, possible full-time employment, willing to provide letters of recommendation, on-the-job training, willing to complete paperwork for educational credit, willing to act as a professional reference, and opportunity to attend seminars/workshops. Preemployment training is required and includes accident prevention and safety, first aid, CPR, interpersonal skills, leadership skills, specific activity instructor training.

Contact Ray Ackenbom, Director, Camp Friendship. Telephone: 434-589-8950. Fax: 434-589-5880. E-mail: campstaff@campfriendship.com. World Wide Web: http://www.campfriendship.com. Contact by e-mail, fax, mail, phone, or through World Wide Web site. Application deadline: continuous.

CAMP HORIZONS
3586 HORIZONS WAY
HARRISONBURG, VIRGINIA 22802

General Information Summer residential camp for children ages 7-17. Teen adventure and traditional camp programs. Corporate training center and retreat center for schools, churches, and universities in the spring and fall. Established in 1983. 300-acre facility. Features: mountain setting; lake; pool; tennis courts; ropes course; modern cabins.

Profile of Summer Employees Total number: 100; typical ages: 19–45. 40% men; 60% women; 10% minorities; 90% college students; 40% non-U.S. citizens; 20% local applicants. Nonsmokers required.

Employment Information Openings are from June 1 to August 31. Year-round positions also offered. Jobs available: ▶ 20 *adventure counselors/adventure specialists* (minimum age 19) with skills in caving, rock climbing, canoeing, ropes course, and backpacking; CPR/first aid, valid driver's license, and good driving record at $1500–$1800 per season ▶ 2 *custodial/maintenance staff* (minimum age 19) with CPR/first aid certification at $1500–$1800 per season ▶ 6 *department heads* (minimum age 21) with bachelor's degree, experience and skills in education, administration, international education, and counseling; CPR/first aid, valid driver's license, and good driving record at $2200 per season ▶ 20 *general activities counselors* (minimum age 19) with first aid, CPR certification, and experience in any combination of the following: swimming, drama, model rocketry, caving, rock climbing, or sign language at $1500 per season ▶ 60 *general counselors* (minimum age 19) with CPR/first aid, valid driver's license, and good driving record at $1500 per season ▶ 4 *horseback riding counselors* (minimum age 19) with first aid, CPR certification, and knowledge of Western-style horseback riding at $1500 per season ▶ 5 *kitchen staff/cooks* (minimum age 19) with CPR/first aid certification at $1500–$1800 per season ▶ *registered nurse* (must reside at camp) at $500 per week ▶ 4 *village coordinators (unit leaders)* (minimum age 21) with a college degree at $2200 per season ▶ 12 *waterfront counselors* (minimum age 19) with lifeguard, first aid, and CPR certification at $1500 per season. Applicants must submit formal organization application, two personal references, two letters of recommendation, medical form. An in-person interview is recommended, but a telephone interview is acceptable. International applicants accepted; must apply through a recognized agency.

Benefits and Preemployment Training Free housing, free meals, willing to provide letters of recommendation, on-the-job training, willing to complete paperwork for educational credit, and willing to act as a professional reference. Preemployment training is required and includes accident prevention and safety, first aid, CPR, interpersonal skills, leadership skills, ropes course training, lifeguarding.

Contact Ben Swartz, Camp Director, Camp Horizons, 3586 Horizons Way, Harrisonburg, Virginia 22802. Telephone: 540-896-7600. Fax: 540-896-5455. E-mail: camp@horizonsva.com. World Wide Web: http://www.camphorizonsva.com. Contact by e-mail, fax, phone, or through World Wide Web site. Application deadline: continuous.

CAT'S CAP–ST. CATHERINE'S CREATIVE ARTS PROGRAM
6001 GROVE AVENUE
RICHMOND, VIRGINIA 23226

General Information Day camp concentrating on exploration of the visual and performing arts, as well as offering sports, horseback riding, computer, creative writing, river exploration, and elemental/cultural foreign languages. Established in 1978. 16-acre facility located 110 miles from Washington, DC. Features: small college campus-type setting; 2 libraries; sports/athletic complex with pool, regulation gymnasium, track, and weight/fitness room; 3 athletic fields; large dining hall; air-conditioned classrooms.

Profile of Summer Employees Total number: 130–140; typical ages: 14–50. 50% men; 50% women; 9% minorities; 15% high school students; 25% college students; 1% non-U.S. citizens; 98% local applicants. Nonsmokers preferred.

Employment Information Openings are from June 16 to July 25. Jobs available: ▶ 12–15 *instructors* with certification in dance, music, art, theater, physical education, visual or performing arts, art education, or elementary education at $12–$15 per hour ▶ 10–20 *senior counselors* (minimum age 18) with early childhood or education major and experience working with children at $6–$7.50 per hour ▶ *teaching assistants* with training or degree in education and experience working with children at $7–$10 per hour. Applicants must submit a formal organization application, letter of interest, resume, two personal references, two letters of recommendation. An in-person interview is required. International applicants accepted; must obtain own visa, obtain own working papers.

Benefits and Preemployment Training Possible full-time employment, willing to provide letters of recommendation, on-the-job training, willing to act as a professional reference, tuition assistance, and free lunch. Preemployment training is required and includes child development.

Contact Jann Holland, Director, Cat's CAP–St. Catherine's Creative Arts Program, 6001 Grove Avenue, Richmond, Virginia 23226. Fax: 804-285-8169. E-mail: jholland@st.catherines.org. Contact by e-mail or mail. No phone calls. Application deadline: preferred deadline is February; later applications kept on file and used as needed.

CENTER FOR TALENTED YOUTH/JOHNS HOPKINS UNIVERSITY–ST. STEPHEN'S AND ST. AGNES SCHOOL
ALEXANDRIA, VIRGINIA
See Center for Talented Youth/Johns Hopkins University on page 131 for complete description.

CHEERIO ADVENTURES
754 FOX KNOB ROAD
MOUTH OF WILSON, VIRGINIA 24363
General Information Program in adventure tripping and wilderness travel serving campers ages 10-17. Established in 1982. 60-acre facility located 85 miles from Greensboro, North Carolina. Features: on New River; mixture of woodlands and fields; mountain setting; close proximity to many natural forests.

Profile of Summer Employees Total number: 20; typical ages: 19–25. 50% men; 50% women; 20% minorities; 90% college students. Nonsmokers required.

Employment Information Openings are from May 20 to August 3. Jobs available: ▶ 1 *food coordinator* (minimum age 21) with driver's license and experience in the field at $195–$250 per week ▶ 3 *skills coordinators* (minimum age 21) at $225–$260 per week ▶ 1 *transportation coordinator* (minimum age 21) with driver's license at $195–$225 per week ▶ 3 *trip guides* (minimum age 21) at $195–$250 per week ▶ 10 *trip leaders* (minimum age 19) must enjoy working with teens at $195–$225 per week. Applicants must submit a formal organization application, four personal references. An in-person interview is recommended, but a telephone interview is acceptable. International applicants accepted; must obtain own visa.

Benefits and Preemployment Training Free housing, free meals, formal training, health insurance, willing to provide letters of recommendation, on-the-job training, willing to complete paperwork for educational credit, and willing to act as a professional reference. Preemployment training is required and includes accident prevention and safety, first aid, CPR, interpersonal skills, leadership skills, activity skills.

Contact Andrea Galioto, Program Director, Cheerio Adventures, 1430 Camp Cheerio Road, Glade Valley, North Carolina 28627. Telephone: 336-363-2604. Fax: 336-363-3671. E-mail: cheerio-adventures@campcheerio.org. World Wide Web: http://www.cheerioadventures.com. Contact by e-mail, fax, mail, phone, or through World Wide Web site. Application deadline: continuous.

CHINCOTEAGUE NATIONAL WILDLIFE REFUGE
PO BOX 62, 8231 BEACH ROAD
CHINCOTEAGUE, VIRGINIA 23336

General Information National Wildlife Refuge providing habitat for migratory birds and various animals and educating refuge visitors. Established in 1943. 14,000-acre facility located 60 miles from Salisbury, Maryland. Features: beach; maritime forest; lighthouse; saltmarsh; freshwater marsh; migratory birds.

Profile of Summer Employees Total number: 40; typical ages: 18–24. 30% men; 70% women; 90% college students; 2% non-U.S. citizens; 8% local applicants.

Employment Information Year-round positions also offered. Jobs available: ▶ *environmental education interns* with good oral and written communication skills at $125 per week ▶ *field research assistant/wildlife management interns* with background in biology and skills in wildlife management; bird and plant identification helpful at $125 per week ▶ *interpretive interns* with high comfort level in front of big groups at $125 per week. Applicants must submit a letter of interest, resume, telephone interview for finalists. International applicants accepted; must obtain own visa, obtain own working papers.

Benefits and Preemployment Training Free housing, willing to provide letters of recommendation, on-the-job training, willing to complete paperwork for educational credit, and willing to act as a professional reference.

Contact Geralyn Mireles, Refuge Operation Specialist/Volunteer Coordinator, Chincoteague National Wildlife Refuge. Telephone: 757-336-6122. Fax: 757-336-5273. E-mail: geralyn_mireles@ fws.gov. World Wide Web: http://chinco.fws.gov. Contact by e-mail or mail. Application deadline: varies by internship.

CYBERCAMPS–GEORGE MASON UNIVERSITY
FAIRFAX, VIRGINIA
See Cybercamps–University of Washington on page 326 for complete description.

4 STAR SUMMER CAMPS AT THE UNIVERSITY OF VIRGINIA
CHARLOTTESVILLE, VIRGINIA 22905

General Information Residential camp that offers golf, tennis, and academic enrichment courses daily and other sporting events in the evenings. Programs are available for campers ages 9–18. Established in 1975. Located 100 miles from Washington, DC. Features: university facilities; 13 tennis courts; full athletic facilities.

Profile of Summer Employees Total number: 35; typical ages: 19–25. 60% men; 40% women; 10% minorities; 70% college students; 10% local applicants. Nonsmokers required.

Employment Information Openings are from June 24 to August 10. Jobs available: ▶ 1 *evening activities director/recreation director* (minimum age 19) with good organization and planning skills at $1800–$2250 per season ▶ 10 *general counselors* (minimum age 19) with ability to work with young people at $900–$1400 per season ▶ 15 *golf counselors* (minimum age 19) with ability to work with children; should be advanced-level player at $900–$1875 per season ▶ 10 *resident advisors* (minimum age 20) with experience as a resident advisor at a college or university at $1500–$2600 per season ▶ 25 *tennis instructors* (minimum age 19) with some competitive experience; should be advanced-level player at $900–$1400 per season. Applicants must submit formal organization application, letter of interest, resume, three personal references, three letters of recommendation. An in-person interview is recommended, but a telephone interview is acceptable. International applicants accepted; must obtain own visa, obtain own working papers, apply through a recognized agency.

Benefits and Preemployment Training Free housing, free meals, willing to provide letters of recommendation, on-the-job training, willing to complete paperwork for educational credit, and willing to act as a professional reference. Preemployment training is required and includes first aid, interpersonal skills, leadership skills, teaching tennis, golf training.

Contact Ann Grubbs, Assistant Director, 4 Star Summer Camps at the University of Virginia, PO Box 3387, Falls Church, Virginia 22043. Fax: 703-866-7775. E-mail: a.grubbs@4starcamps. com. World Wide Web: http://www.4starcamps.com. Contact by e-mail, fax, mail, or through World Wide Web site. No phone calls. Application deadline: continuous.

FREDERICKSBURG AND SPOTSYLVANIA NATIONAL MILITARY PARK
120 CHATHAM LANE
FREDERICKSBURG, VIRGINIA 22405

General Information Historic park preserving and interpreting four Civil War battlefields in the Fredericksburg area. Established in 1927. 7,340-acre facility located 50 miles from Washington, DC. Features: 4 Civil War battlefields; 2 visitor centers; historic structures; park housing; historical trails; book store.

Profile of Summer Employees Total number: 50; typical ages: 21–40. 50% men; 50% women; 20% minorities; 5% high school students; 40% college students; 5% retirees; 30% local applicants.

Employment Information Openings are from May 19 to September 1. Year-round positions also offered. Jobs available: ▶ 1–5 *park guides* (minimum age 18) with knowledge of the Civil War at $10.85–$12.14 per hour ▶ 1 *seasonal natural resource assistant* (minimum age 18) with knowledge of GIS preferable at $10.85–$12.14 per hour ▶ 1–5 *visitor use assistants* (minimum age 18) with knowledge of the Civil War at $10.85–$12.14 per hour. Applicants must submit a formal organization application.

Benefits and Preemployment Training Housing at a cost, formal training, willing to provide letters of recommendation, on-the-job training, willing to complete paperwork for educational credit, and willing to act as a professional reference. Preemployment training is required and includes interpersonal skills, interpretive skills.

Contact Gregory A. Mertz, Supervisory Historian, Fredericksburg and Spotsylvania National Military Park, 120 Chatham Lane, Fredericksburg, Virginia 22405. Telephone: 540-373-6124. Fax: 540-654-5521. E-mail: greg_mertz@nps.gov. World Wide Web: http://www.nps.gov/frsp. Contact by e-mail or through World Wide Web site. Application deadline: applications are accepted as needed; generally every three months a position is announced and applications will be accepted for a one-week period.

LEGACY INTERNATIONAL'S GLOBAL YOUTH VILLAGE
1020 LEGACY DRIVE
BEDFORD, VIRGINIA 24523

General Information International youth training program in a camp setting that focuses on cross-cultural understanding and leadership training and offers workshops in conflict resolution, the arts, ESOL, international relations, and other programs. Established in 1979. 45-acre facility located 40 miles from Roanoke. Features: wooded setting; pool; short drive to large lake; short drive to mountains.

Profile of Summer Employees Total number: 30; typical ages: 22–45. 40% men; 60% women; 15% minorities; 10% college students; 30% non-U.S. citizens; 1% local applicants. Nonsmokers required.

Employment Information Openings are from June 15 to August 15. Jobs available: ▶ 1 *adventure/outdoor skills instructor* (minimum age 21) with first aid and CPR certification and rock-climbing teaching experience (preferred) at $900 per season ▶ 3 *art instructors* (minimum age 21) with experience in the field; one position requires ability to teach pottery using the wheel and kiln at $900–$1200 per season ▶ 2 *cooks/shift managers* (minimum age 21) with previous experience cooking for large groups, managing others, and some knowledge of vegetarian cooking at $1200 per season ▶ 5 *counselors (female)* (minimum age 21) with demonstrated professional youth work experience at $900–$1200 per season ▶ 4 *counselors (male)* (minimum age 21) with demonstrated professional youth work experience at $900–$1200 per season ▶ 1 *global issues instructor* (minimum age 21) with background and knowledge in international relations and teaching experience at $1200 per season ▶ 7 *kitchen staff members* (minimum age 19) at $1,200 per season or on a volunteer basis ▶ 1 *leadership instructor* (minimum age 21) with experience in the field and ability to teach skills such as event planning, setting priorities, and running meetings at $1200 per season ▶ 2–3 *lifeguards* (minimum age 21) with first aid, CPR, and lifeguarding certification at $900 per season ▶ 5 *prep cooks* (minimum age 19) must enjoy cooking (training provided) at $900 per season ▶ 1 *program coordinator* (minimum age 21) with performing arts background (preferred) and very good organizational and motivational skills at $1200 per season ▶ 1 *sports and games coordinator* (minimum age 21) with ability to lead and guide large groups in various games and sports and familiarity with new games and noncompetitive sports at $900 per season ▶ 1 *theater arts instructor* (minimum age 21) with improvisational theater experience and experience teaching youths at $900–$1200 per season. Applicants must submit formal organization application, resume, 2-3 professional references with phone/fax numbers. A telephone interview is required. International applicants accepted; must obtain own visa, obtain own working papers, apply through a recognized agency.

Benefits and Preemployment Training Free housing, free meals, formal training, health insurance, willing to provide letters of recommendation, names of contacts, on-the-job training, willing to complete paperwork for educational credit, willing to act as a professional reference, and laundry service. Preemployment training is required and includes accident prevention and safety, interpersonal skills, leadership skills, cross-cultural communication, counselor training.

Contact Leila Baz, Co-Director,, Legacy International's Global Youth Village, 1020 Legacy Drive, Bedford, Virginia 24523. Fax: 540-297-1860. E-mail: staff@legacyintl.org. World Wide Web: http://www.globalyouthvillage.org. Contact by e-mail, fax, mail, or through World Wide Web site. No phone calls. Application deadline: most positions filled January through late April.

OAKLAND SCHOOL AND CAMP
BOYD TAVERN
KESWICK, VIRGINIA 22947

General Information Coed residential and day camp for 130 students ages 8-14 with learning disabilities or other academic difficulties. Established in 1950. 450-acre facility located 65 miles from Richmond. Features: riding ring and trails; swimming pool; 2 tennis courts; unique classrooms; gym and recreation center; hiking trails; streams.

Profile of Summer Employees Total number: 70; typical ages: 19–25. 50% men; 50% women; 10% minorities; 75% college students; 25% local applicants. Nonsmokers preferred.

Employment Information Openings are from June 9 to August 8. Year-round positions also offered. Jobs available: ▶ 3–5 *camp counselors* (minimum age 19) with experience working with children, residential camp experience preferred at $3000–$3500 per season ▶ 1 *swimming instructor* (minimum age 20) with lifesaving and WSI certification at $3000–$3500 per season ▶ 1–5 *teachers* with teacher certification, special education preferred at $3600 to $4000 per 7 weeks. Applicants must submit a formal organization application, letter of interest, resume, two personal references, two letters of recommendation. An in-person interview is required.

Benefits and Preemployment Training Free housing, free meals, formal training, possible full-time employment, willing to provide letters of recommendation, and on-the-job training. Preemployment training is required and includes accident prevention and safety, first aid, CPR, interpersonal skills, leadership skills, recreational activity planning, behavior management.

Contact Ms. Carol Smieciuch, Director, Oakland School, Oakland School and Camp, Boyd Tavern, Keswick, Virginia 22947. Telephone: 434-293-9059. Fax: 434-296-8930. E-mail: csoakland@earthlink.net. World Wide Web: http://www.oaklandschool.net. Contact by e-mail, fax, mail, phone, or through World Wide Web site. Application deadline: continuous.

THE SOUTHWESTERN COMPANY, VIRGINIA
See The Southwestern Company on page 297 for complete description.

SPORTS INTERNATIONAL–ART MONK FOOTBALL CAMP
FAIRFAX, VIRGINIA
See Sports International, Inc. on page 134 for complete description.

STUDENT CONSERVATION ASSOCIATION (SCA), VIRGINIA
See Student Conservation Association (SCA), New Hampshire on page 200 for complete description.

WOODBERRY FOREST SUMMER ADVENTURE
WOODBERRY STATION
WOODBERRY FOREST, VIRGINIA 22989

General Information Coeducational boarding school for approximately 100 students grades 7–12. Established in 1889. 1,000-acre facility located 30 miles from Charlottesville. Features: woodlands and river; 6 tennis courts; 4 athletic fields; computer labs/network; 2 pools; golf course.

Profile of Summer Employees Total number: 21; typical age: 21. 60% men; 40% women; 40% college students. Nonsmokers preferred.

Employment Information Openings are from June 17 to August 3. Jobs available: ▶ 21 *interns (math, science, English)* (minimum age 21) with three or four years of college (or recent graduate) at $1500 per season ▶ 30 *teachers (all subjects)* at $2500 per season. Applicants must submit letter of interest, resume, academic transcripts, two letters of recommendation. International applicants accepted; must obtain own visa.

Benefits and Preemployment Training Free housing, free meals, willing to provide letters of recommendation, on-the-job training, willing to complete paperwork for educational credit, and willing to act as a professional reference. Preemployment training is required and includes accident prevention and safety, interpersonal skills, leadership skills.

Contact David McRae, Director of Summer Programs, Woodberry Forest Summer Adventure, Woodberry Forest School, Woodberry Forest, Virginia 22989. Telephone: 540-672-3900. Fax: 540-672-9076. E-mail: david_mcrae@woodberry.org. World Wide Web: http://www.woodberry. org. Contact by e-mail, fax, mail, or phone. Application deadline: February 1.

WASHINGTON

A CHRISTIAN MINISTRY IN THE NATIONAL PARKS– WASHINGTON
See A Christian Ministry in the National Parks–Maine on page 107 for complete description.

CAMP BERACHAH
19830 SOUTHEAST 328TH PLACE
AUBURN, WASHINGTON 98092

General Information Offers eleven day camps (150 campers each), 22 horse camps (24 campers each), junior and teen camp (300 campers each), resident camps, and soccer camp (200 campers). Established in 1973. 160-acre facility located 30 miles from Seattle. Features: wooded setting; indoor pool; large gym; mountain bikes; horses; climbing wall/high ropes course.

Profile of Summer Employees Total number: 120; typical ages: 17–28. 40% men; 60% women; 5% minorities; 30% high school students; 70% college students; 8% non-U.S. citizens; 30% local applicants. Nonsmokers required.

Employment Information Openings are from June 10 to August 31. Spring break, winter break, and year-round positions also offered. Jobs available: ▶ 1 *archery instructor* at $125–$150 per week ▶ 1–2 *bus drivers* (minimum age 21) at $9 per hour ▶ *camp leaders* at a salary dependent upon experience ▶ 1 *canoeing instructor* at $125–$150 per week ▶ 1 *climbing wall facilitator* (minimum age 18) at $125–$150 per week ▶ *counselors* (minimum age 18, but 16 year-olds with CIT experience are also eligible) at $120–$150 per week ▶ 1 *crafts director* (minimum age 21) at $125–$150 per week ▶ 2 *go-cart leaders* at $125–$150 per week ▶ 5 *high ropes course facilitators* (minimum age 18) at $125–$150 per week ▶ 1 *horsemanship instructor/wrangler* at $125–$150 per week ▶ 1 *lifeguard* (minimum age 16) at $125–$150 per week ▶ 1 *mountain bike leader* (minimum age 18) at $125–$150 per week ▶ 1 *nurse* (minimum age 21) at $200 per week ▶ 1 *recreation director* (minimum age 21) at $125–$150 per week ▶ *support staff workers* at $125–$170 per week. Applicants must submit formal organization application, two personal references, two letters of recommendation. An in-person interview is recommended, but a telephone interview is acceptable. International applicants accepted; must obtain own visa, obtain own working papers, apply through a recognized agency.

Benefits and Preemployment Training Free housing, free meals, possible full-time employment, willing to provide letters of recommendation, on-the-job training, willing to complete paperwork for educational credit, willing to act as a professional reference, and college savings plan, college scholarships, contract completion bonus. Preemployment training is required and includes accident prevention and safety, first aid, CPR, interpersonal skills, leadership skills.

Contact James Richey, Program Director, Camp Berachah, 19830 Southeast 328th Place, Auburn, Washington 98092. Telephone: 253-939-0488. Fax: 253-833-7027. E-mail: staff@berachahcamp. org. World Wide Web: http://www.berachahcamp.org. Contact by e-mail, fax, mail, phone, or through World Wide Web site. Application deadline: continuous.

CAMP KIRBY
4734 SAMISH POINT ROAD
BOW, WASHINGTON 98232

General Information Nonprofit youth-serving agency summer camp and environmental education center. Established in 1923. 47-acre facility located 25 miles from Bellingham. Features: 1.5 miles beachfront; Climbing tower; 40 acres of trails; beautiful rustic setting; tree houses and tipis; basketball courts.

Profile of Summer Employees Total number: 35; typical ages: 17–25. 30% men; 70% women; 25% minorities; 10% high school students; 90% college students; 5% retirees; 70% local applicants. Nonsmokers preferred.

Employment Information Openings are from June 20 to August 26. Jobs available: ▶ 1–2 *assistant directors* (minimum age 21) with experience with youth and experience supervising others at $1500–$2000 per season ▶ 10–15 *cabin counselors* (minimum age 17) with experience working with children at $1200–$1400 per season ▶ 1 *climbing instructor* (minimum age 17) with excellent climbing safety skills and experience working with youth at $1250 per season ▶ 4–5 *kitchen staff* (minimum age 16) with Washington food handlers permit at $1200–$2000 per season ▶ *lifeguards* with lifeguarding certification; must be high school graduate (minimum) at \$1200–\$1300 per season ▶ 25–30 *summer camp staff* (minimum age 17) with experience working with youth; must be high school graduate (minimum) at \$1000–\$2000 per season. Applicants must submit a formal organization application, personal references and letters of recommendation in any combination equal to 3. An in-person interview is recommended, but a telephone interview is acceptable. International applicants accepted; must obtain own visa, obtain own working papers.

Benefits and Preemployment Training Free housing, free meals, formal training, willing to provide letters of recommendation, on-the-job training, willing to complete paperwork for educational credit, and willing to act as a professional reference. Preemployment training is required and includes accident prevention and safety, first aid, CPR, interpersonal skills, leadership skills.

Contact Jennifer Brown, Camp Director, Camp Kirby. Telephone: 360-766-6060. Fax: 360-733-5711. E-mail: kirby@campfiresamishcouncil.org. World Wide Web: http://www.campkirby.org. Contact by e-mail, mail, phone, or through World Wide Web site. Application deadline: continuous.

CAMP ORKILA
484 CAMP ORKILA ROAD
EASTSOUND, WASHINGTON 98245

General Information Traditional YMCA resident camp program located on Orcas Island in Washington's San Juans. Established in 1906. 370-acre facility located 48 miles from Bellingham. Features: large Puget Sound waterfront; 100 acre off-shore private island; new marine salmon center/aquarium; fleet of power and sail boats and sea kayaks; farm, garden, and equestrian facilities; fabulous sunsets.

Profile of Summer Employees Total number: 185; typical ages: 19–25. 48% men; 52% women; 10% minorities; 2% high school students; 70% college students; 2% retirees; 10% non-U.S. citizens; 20% local applicants. Nonsmokers required.

Employment Information Openings are from June 14 to August 20. Year-round positions also offered. Jobs available: ▶ 65 *cabin counselors* (minimum age 18) with CPR and first aid certifications at \$1500–\$1900 per season ▶ 20–26 *expedition staff* (minimum age 21) with lifeguarding, wilderness, first responder, and 15 days personal field experiences at \$1800–\$2800 per season ▶ 4 *horse riding instructors* (minimum age 18) with knowledge of horses, riding methods/techniques, basic animal husbandry, and horse training at \$1600–\$2000 per season ▶ 6 *leadership development directors* (minimum age 21) with first aid and CPR certification at \$1800–\$2000 per season ▶ 7 *lifeguards* (minimum age 18) with WSI and/or lifeguard certification at \$1600–\$1800 per season ▶ 3 *ropes course facilitators* (minimum age 20) with CPR and first aid documented experience at \$1800–\$2000 per season. Applicants must submit formal organization application, three personal references, background/driving history check. An in-person interview is recommended, but a telephone interview is acceptable. International applicants accepted; must apply through a recognized agency.

Benefits and Preemployment Training Free housing, free meals, possible full-time employment, willing to provide letters of recommendation, willing to complete paperwork for educational credit, willing to act as a professional reference, and free laundry, Internet access. Preemployment training is required and includes accident prevention and safety, first aid, CPR, interpersonal skills, leadership skills, boating and wilderness medical training.

Contact Griffin Ludwig, Summer Camp Director, Camp Orkila, 909 4th Avenue, Seattle, Washington 98199. Telephone: 206-382-5009. Fax: 206-382-4920. E-mail: gludwig@cs.seattleymca.org. World Wide Web: http://www.seattleymca.org. Contact by e-mail, mail, or phone. Application deadline: continuous.

CAMP RIVER RANCH
33300 NORTHEAST 32ND STREET
CARNATION, WASHINGTON 98014

General Information Resident camp serving approximately 190 girls per session, ages 6–17, and offering a variety of programs including swimming, boating, crafts, environmental education, outdoor skills and outdoor cooking, as well as specialty programs in English and Western riding, biking, backpacking, leadership, and drama. Established in 1951. 430-acre facility located 30 miles from Seattle. Features: freshwater lake; wooded setting; river; climbing wall.

Profile of Summer Employees Total number: 70; typical ages: 17–35. 100% women; 5% minorities; 5% high school students; 80% college students; 10% non-U.S. citizens; 5% local applicants. Nonsmokers preferred.

Employment Information Openings are from June 12 to August 20. Jobs available: ▶ 20 *camp counselors* (minimum age 18) at $1600–$2200 per season ▶ 4 *program coordinators* (minimum age 21) with interest in or ability with horses, arts and nature, water and trips, leadership at $2400–$3000 per season ▶ 6 *program specialists* (minimum age 20) with interest in or ability with horses, arts, nature, waterfront, trips, leadership at $1700–$2200 per season. Applicants must submit formal organization application, three personal references. An in-person interview is recommended, but a telephone interview is acceptable. International applicants accepted; must apply through a recognized agency.

Benefits and Preemployment Training Free housing, free meals, health insurance, willing to provide letters of recommendation, on-the-job training, willing to complete paperwork for educational credit, and willing to act as a professional reference. Preemployment training is optional and includes first aid, CPR, leadership skills, small craft safety (boating), lifeguarding, wilderness first aid.

Contact Margie Culbertson, Camp Administrator, Camp River Ranch. Telephone: 800-878-4685. Fax: 425-333-6236. E-mail: margiemc@girlscoutstotem.org. World Wide Web: http://www.girlscoutstotem.org. Contact by e-mail, fax, mail, phone, or through World Wide Web site. Application deadline: continuous.

CAMP ZANIKA LACHE/CAMP FIRE USA NCW COUNCIL
PO BOX 1734
WENATCHEE, WASHINGTON 98807

General Information ACA-accredited camp located on the shores of Lake Wenatchee in the Wenatchee National Forest: a wonderful setting for campers to enjoy water sports, mountain trails, rivers, forests and streams, great natural beauty and outdoor adventure. Established in 1932. 13-acre facility. Features: freshwater lake; mountain area; ropes/challenge course; forested area; rustic cabins.

Profile of Summer Employees Total number: 35; typical ages: 18–25. 35% men; 65% women; 1% minorities; 1% high school students; 95% college students; 1% non-U.S. citizens; 1% local applicants. Nonsmokers preferred.

Employment Information Openings are from June 10 to August 10. Jobs available: ▶ 1 *archery director* (minimum age 18) with knowledge of archery, instructor certification and/or college course, and experience with children at $1200 per season ▶ 1 *arts and crafts director* (minimum age 18) with training and experience in arts and crafts and experience teaching children at $1200 per season ▶ 2 *assistant camp directors* (minimum age 21) with experience with children and/or bookkeeping, camp staff experience, supervisory experience, experience with camp programming, and organizational skills at $1800 per season ▶ 1 *assistant cook* (minimum age 18) with experience cooking for large groups and Washington State food handlers permit at $1500 per season ▶ 15 *cabin counselors* (minimum age 18) with CPR/first aid training and experience working with children at $1150 per season ▶ 3 *dishwashers* (minimum age 16) with teamwork skills and Washington State food handler's permit at $900–$950 per season ▶ 1 *head cook* (minimum age 21) with CPR and first aid training, Washington State food handler's permit, and experience cooking and ordering for large groups at $2600 per season ▶ 1 *leader and counselor training program director* (minimum age 21) with previous camp counseling and experience with teens required at $1400 per season ▶ 2 *lifeguards* with Red Cross, WSI, or LT, CPR training, and lifeguard experience at $1175 per season ▶ 1 *maintenance person* (minimum age 21) with valid driver's license and ability to operate power and maintenance equipment safely at $3100 for season lasting June 1 to August 31 ▶ *nature director* (minimum age 18) with knowledge of natural science and outdoor environment and ability to teach children at $1200 per season ▶ 1 *ropes course director* (minimum age 18) with documentation or certification of skills, experience in ropes course operation, and experience working with children at $1500 per season ▶ 1 *tripping director* (minimum age 21) with valid driver's license and good driving record, wilderness first aid or woofer certification, basic first aid and CPR training, and backcountry experience at $1500 per season ▶ 2–3 *unit directors* (minimum age 18) with camp counseling experience, youth program experience, supervisory experience, one to two years college experience, valid driver's license, and good driving record at $1300 per season ▶ 1 *waterfront director* (minimum age 21) with WSI or LT certification, supervisory experience, current driver's license and good driving record, and CPR lake guard experience a plus at $1500 per season. Applicants must submit formal organization application, three personal references, $10 fee for limited Camp Fire USA membership. An in-person interview is recommended, but a telephone interview is acceptable. International applicants accepted; must obtain own visa, obtain own working papers, apply through a recognized agency.

Benefits and Preemployment Training Free housing, free meals, health insurance, willing to provide letters of recommendation, on-the-job training, willing to complete paperwork for educational credit, and laundry facilities. Preemployment training is required and includes accident prevention and safety, interpersonal skills, leadership skills, training for position.

Contact Wendy Borden, Outdoor Programs Director, Camp Zanika Lache/Camp Fire USA NCW Council, PO Box 1734, Wenatchee, Washington 98807. Telephone: 509-663-1609. Fax: 509-664-3038. E-mail: camp4@crcwnet.com. World Wide Web: http://www.ncwcampfire.org. Contact by e-mail, fax, mail, phone, or through World Wide Web site. Application deadline: continuous.

CENTER FOR STUDENT MISSIONS–SEATTLE
SEATTLE, WASHINGTON
See Center for Student Missions on page 37 for complete description.

CYBERCAMPS–UNIVERSITY OF PUGET SOUND
TACOMA, WASHINGTON
See Cybercamps–University of Washington below for complete description.

CYBERCAMPS–UNIVERSITY OF WASHINGTON
UNIVERSITY OF WASHINGTON
SEATTLE, WASHINGTON

General Information Technology education for kids ages 7-16 in a well-rounded camp environment. Cybercamps is located nationwide on college campuses. Established in 1997. Features: held on college campuses nationwide; overnight campers stay in the dorms; 1 computer for every camper; small class sizes; fun outdoor activities; project-oriented curriculum.

Profile of Summer Employees Total number: 150; typical ages: 18–35. 50% men; 50% women; 4% high school students; 96% college students; 90% local applicants. Nonsmokers preferred.

Employment Information Openings are from June 1 to August 30. Jobs available: ▶ 30–45 *camp directors* (minimum age 25) with camp experience and/or Bachelor's degree at $700 per week ▶ 100–150 *counselors* (minimum age 18) with experience with children and computers at

$300 per week. Applicants must submit resume, three personal references, online application from Web site. An in-person interview is recommended, but a telephone interview is acceptable.
Benefits and Preemployment Training Free meals, formal training, willing to provide letters of recommendation, on-the-job training, willing to act as a professional reference, and possibility of free housing or housing at cost. Preemployment training is required and includes accident prevention and safety, interpersonal skills, leadership skills, training in curriculum using state-of-the-art software.
Contact Giant Campus/Cybercamps, Cybercamps–University of Washington, 720 Olive Way, Suite 1800, Seattle, Washington 98101, United States. E-mail: summerjobs@cybercamps.net. World Wide Web: http://www.cybercamps.com. Contact by e-mail or through World Wide Web site. No phone calls. Application deadline: continuous.

CYBERCAMPS–UNIVERSITY OF WASHINGTON, BOTHELL
BOTHELL, WASHINGTON
See Cybercamps–University of Washington above for complete description.

ENCHANTED PARKS, INC.
36201 ENCHANTED PARKWAY SOUTH
FEDERAL WAY, WASHINGTON 98003
General Information Amusement/theme park with rides, food stands, and a water park. Established in 1977. 60-acre facility located 16 miles from Seattle. Features: roller coaster; 9 water slides; wavepool; 22 amusement rides; daily shows; retail stores.
Profile of Summer Employees Total number: 800–1,000; typical ages: 16–24. 47% men; 53% women; 30% minorities; 60% high school students; 20% college students; 10% retirees; 5% non-U.S. citizens; 85% local applicants.
Employment Information Openings are from April 11 to October 31. Winter break positions also offered. Jobs available: ▶ 200–250 *lifeguards* (minimum age 16) with water park training course at $7.05–$9 per hour ▶ 300–500 *park employees* (minimum age 16) at $7.01–$10 per hour. Applicants must submit formal organization application, two personal references. An in-person interview is required. International applicants accepted; must obtain own visa, obtain own working papers, apply through a recognized agency.
Benefits and Preemployment Training Meals at a cost, possible full-time employment, health insurance, willing to provide letters of recommendation, on-the-job training, willing to complete paperwork for educational credit, willing to act as a professional reference, opportunity to attend seminars/workshops, and tuition assistance. Preemployment training is required and includes accident prevention and safety, first aid, CPR, interpersonal skills, leadership skills.
Contact Kimberly Zier, Human Resources Manager, Enchanted Parks, Inc., 36201 Enchanted Parkway South, Federal Way, Washington 98003. Telephone: 253-661-8027. Fax: 253-661-8065. E-mail: kzier@sftp.com. World Wide Web: http://www.sixflags.com. Contact by e-mail, fax, mail, phone, or through World Wide Web site. Application deadline: continuous.

LONGACRE EXPEDITIONS, WASHINGTON
BELLINGHAM, WASHINGTON
General Information Adventure travel program throughout the Pacific Northwest including Washington, Oregon, and British Columbia. Challenging programs place equal emphasis on physical accomplishment and emotional growth. Established in 1981.
Profile of Summer Employees Total number: 30; typical ages: 21–32. 50% men; 50% women; 10% minorities; 40% college students; 30% local applicants. Nonsmokers required.
Employment Information Openings are from June 15 to August 10. Jobs available: ▶ 15 *assistant trip leaders* (minimum age 21) with good driving record, CPR, and WFR certification at $252–

$300 per week ▶ 1 *mountaineering instructor* (minimum age 21) with WFR and CPR certification at $300–$400 per week ▶ 1 *rock climbing instructor* (minimum age 21) with good driving record, WFR, and CPR at $300–$400 per week ▶ 2 *sea kayaking instructors* (minimum age 21) with lifeguard training, CPR and WFR certification at $300–$400 per week ▶ 3 *support and logistics staff members* (minimum age 21) with good driving record, WFR, and CPR at $180–$240 per week. Applicants must submit a formal organization application, letter of interest, resume, three personal references. An in-person interview is recommended, but a telephone interview is acceptable. International applicants accepted; must obtain own visa, obtain own working papers.

Benefits and Preemployment Training Free housing, free meals, willing to provide letters of recommendation, on-the-job training, willing to complete paperwork for educational credit, willing to act as a professional reference, and pro-deal purchase program. Preemployment training is required and includes accident prevention and safety, interpersonal skills, leadership skills.

Contact Meredith Schuler, Director, Longacre Expeditions, Washington, 4030 Middle Ridge Road, Newport, Pennsylvania 17074-8110. Telephone: 717-567-6790. Fax: 717-567-3955. E-mail: longacre@longacreexpeditions.com. World Wide Web: http://www.longacreexpeditions.com. Contact by e-mail, fax, mail, phone, or through World Wide Web site. Application deadline: continuous.

MARROWSTONE MUSIC FESTIVAL
11065 5TH AVENUE, NE, SUITE A
SEATTLE, WASHINGTON 98125

General Information A three-week music festival set on the campus of Western Washington University in beautiful Bellingham, WA. Established in 1942. Features: top-notch music facilities; music library; concert hall; Cascade Mountains; university setting; university dormitories.

Profile of Summer Employees Total number: 40; typical ages: 18–25. 50% men; 50% women; 40% minorities; 60% high school students; 40% college students; 7% non-U.S. citizens; 50% local applicants. Nonsmokers preferred.

Employment Information Openings are from July 28 to August 18. Jobs available: ▶ 6–8 *camp counselors* (minimum age 18) with ability to work well with peers and younger students and demonstrate responsibility ▶ 6–12 *interns* (minimum age 18) at $100 per week ▶ 2–4 *librarians* (minimum age 13) ▶ *stage crew* (minimum age 13) ▶ 4–7 *ushers* (minimum age 13). Applicants must submit formal organization application, resume, letter of recommendation, Marrowstone application materials; $35-$50 fee for program costs. International applicants accepted; must obtain own visa, apply through a recognized agency.

Benefits and Preemployment Training Free housing, free meals, willing to provide letters of recommendation, willing to act as a professional reference, opportunity to attend seminars/workshops, and tuition assistance.

Contact Stuart Wolferman, Festival Coordinator, Marrowstone Music Festival. Telephone: 206-362-2300. Fax: 206-361-9254. E-mail: marrowstone@syso.org. World Wide Web: http://www.marrowstone.org. Contact by e-mail. Application deadline: rolling beginning April 1.

MT. RAINIER GUEST SERVICES
PO BOX 108
ASHFORD, WASHINGTON 98304

General Information Operates hotels, food services, and gift shops in Mt. Rainier National Park. Established in 1917. 244,000-acre facility located 100 miles from Tacoma. Features: old growth forests; wildlife; mountain meadows; glaciers; canyons; wilderness.

Profile of Summer Employees Total number: 240; typical ages: 18–75. 50% men; 50% women; 10% minorities; 50% college students; 10% retirees; 30% non-U.S. citizens; 10% local applicants. Nonsmokers preferred.

Employment Information Openings are from May to October. Jobs available: ▶ 20 *cook's helpers/pantry persons* (minimum age 18) with ability to perform prep work plus make salads and sandwiches at $7.25 per hour ▶ 10 *cooks* (minimum age 21) with fine dining cooking experience and ability to work in casual and fine dining restaurants at $8.25–$10.50 per hour ▶ 10 *desk clerks* (minimum age 18) with ability to register guests and handle cash at $7.25 per hour ▶ 30 *fast food attendants* (minimum age 18) with ability to take/fill orders, bus tables, and operate cash register at $7.01 per hour ▶ 20 *housekeeping staff members* (minimum age 18) with ability to clean guest rooms and hotel at $7.01–$7.50 per hour ▶ 5 *janitors (night and day)* (minimum age 18) with ability to clean halls, restrooms, windows, and carpets and empty garbage at $7.25–$9 per hour ▶ 5 *kitchen porters (night and day)* (minimum age 18) with ability to clean hoods, ovens, and floors and assist in dishwashing at $7.25–$8 per hour ▶ 30 *kitchen/utility personnel* (minimum age 18) at $7.25 per hour ▶ 20 *retail clerks* (minimum age 18) with ability to perform retail sales, stocking, and cleaning duties at $7.25 per hour. Applicants must submit formal organization application. International applicants accepted; must obtain own visa, obtain own working papers, apply through a recognized agency.

Benefits and Preemployment Training Housing at a cost, meals at a cost, and on-the-job training. Preemployment training is required and includes accident prevention and safety, CPR, wilderness preparedness.

Contact Personnel Manager, Mt. Rainier Guest Services, PO Box 108, Ashford, Washington 98304. Telephone: 360-569-2400 Ext. 119. Fax: 360-569-2770. E-mail: mtrainierhr@guestservices. com. World Wide Web: http://www.coolworks.com/rainier. Contact by e-mail, fax, mail, phone, or through World Wide Web site. Application deadline: continuous.

THE SOUTHWESTERN COMPANY, WASHINGTON
See The Southwestern Company on page 297 for complete description.

STUDENT CONSERVATION ASSOCIATION (SCA), WASHINGTON
See Student Conservation Association (SCA), New Hampshire on page 200 for complete description.

YMCA CAMP SEYMOUR
9725 CRAMER ROAD KPN
GIG HARBOR, WASHINGTON 98329

General Information Summer camp offering in-camp overnight programs (youth entering 1st-8th grade), out-of-camp wilderness and caravan trip adventures (youth entering 8th-12th grade), and teen leadership experiences (youth entering 8th-12th grade). Established in 1905. 160-acre facility located 20 miles from Tacoma. Features: forested hills; 1/2-mile saltwater shoreline; ropes courses and climbing wall; outdoor pool; waterfront/dock; comfortable cabins.

Profile of Summer Employees Total number: 50; typical ages: 18–30. 45% men; 55% women; 10% minorities; 10% high school students; 45% college students; 5% non-U.S. citizens; 40% local applicants. Nonsmokers preferred.

Employment Information Openings are from June 18 to August 24. Year-round positions also offered. Jobs available: ▶ 1 *adventure areas director* (minimum age 20) with CPR, first aid, ropes course and/or climbing wall experience/certifications; lifeguard preferred at $34–$38 per day ▶ 12–14 *cabin leaders* (minimum age 18) with first aid and CPR certifications, prefer lifeguard certification, and some experience in the field at $22–$28 per day ▶ 1 *camp programs director* (minimum age 20) with first aid and CPR certifications, prefer lifeguard certification, and experience with summer camp programming at $34–$40 per day ▶ 1 *creative arts director* (minimum age 19) with first aid and CPR certification and relevant experience at $34–$38 per day ▶ 1 *health care director* with preference for RN/LPN license in Washington state; minimum requirement is entering final year of degree; EMT desirable at $40–$48 per day ▶ 1 *intern director* (minimum age 20) with staff supervision and camp program experience at $34–$38 per day ▶ 1 *outfitter* (minimum age 20) with CPR, first aid, driver's license, good driving record, and experience with packing and outfitting trips at $32–$36 per day ▶ 1 *pool director* (minimum age 20) with lifeguard certification, first aid, CPR, and experience in the field at $34–$38 per day ▶ 12–14 *senior cabin leaders* (minimum age 19) with first aid and CPR certifications, experience in the field; one year of college and lifeguard certification (preferred) at $26–$32 per day ▶ 1 *skills director* (minimum age 21) with CPR, first aid, experience with many program areas and skills, lifeguard preferred at $34–$38 per day ▶ 4 *teen leaders* (minimum age 20) with CPR, wilderness first aid, safe driving record, and experience in field at $30–$34 per day ▶ 6 *trip leaders* (minimum age 19) with experience in the field; ability to lead bike, backpacking, canoe, or kayak trips; wilderness first aid and CPR certifications at $32–$42 per day ▶ 4 *unit directors* (minimum age 20) with CPR and first aid certification, experience in camping required at $34–$40 per day ▶ 2 *van drivers/assistant outfitters* (minimum age 21) with driver's license, ability to drive trips to remote locations, and assist with trip preparation at $32–$36 per day ▶ 1 *waterfront director* (minimum age 20) with lifeguard certification, first aid, CPR, and experience in the field at $34–$38 per day. Applicants must submit three personal references, three professional references. An in-person interview is recommended, but a telephone interview is acceptable. International applicants accepted; must apply through a recognized agency.

Benefits and Preemployment Training Free housing, free meals, formal training, possible full-time employment, willing to provide letters of recommendation, on-the-job training, willing to complete paperwork for educational credit, willing to act as a professional reference, and travel reimbursement. Preemployment training is required and includes accident prevention and safety, interpersonal skills, leadership skills, working/communicating with children.

Contact Magill Lange, Camping Director, YMCA Camp Seymour, 9725 Cramer Road KPN, Gig Harbor, Washington 98329. Telephone: 253-884-3392. Fax: 253-460-8897. E-mail: campseymour@ymcatacoma.org. World Wide Web: http://www.campseymour.org. Contact by e-mail, mail, or through World Wide Web site. Application deadline: continuous.

WEST VIRGINIA

CAMP TALL TIMBERS
ROUTE 1
HIGH VIEW, WEST VIRGINIA 26808

General Information Summer camp for children. Traditional program including 35 activities. Established in 1970. 112-acre facility located 20 miles from Winchester, Virginia. Features: 112 secluded acres; private lake; swimming pool; 4 tennis courts; basketball and roller hockey courts; athletic fields.

Profile of Summer Employees Total number: 50; typical ages: 19–25. 50% men; 50% women; 90% college students; 1% retirees; 10% non-U.S. citizens. Nonsmokers required.

Employment Information Openings are from June 15 to August 17. Jobs available: ▶ 10–20 *counselors* (minimum age 19) with a desire to work with children and ability to assist with or teach an activity at $1200–$1600 per season. Applicants must submit formal organization application. An in-person interview is recommended, but a telephone interview is acceptable. International applicants accepted; must obtain own visa, obtain own working papers, apply through a recognized agency.

Benefits and Preemployment Training Free housing, free meals, possible full-time employment, willing to provide letters of recommendation, willing to complete paperwork for educational credit, willing to act as a professional reference, and travel reimbursement. Preemployment training is required and includes accident prevention and safety, first aid, CPR, interpersonal skills, leadership skills.

Contact Jerry Smith, Executive Director, Camp Tall Timbers, 11615 Fulham Street, Silver Spring, Maryland 20902-3080. Telephone: 301-649-5577. Fax: 301-681-6662. E-mail: funcamp@ aol.com. World Wide Web: http://www.camptalltimbers.com. Contact through World Wide Web site. Application deadline: continuous.

THE SOUTHWESTERN COMPANY, WEST VIRGINIA
See The Southwestern Company on page 297 for complete description.

STUDENT CONSERVATION ASSOCIATION (SCA), WEST VIRGINIA
See Student Conservation Association (SCA), New Hampshire on page 200 for complete description.

USA RAFT
PO BOX 277
ROWLESBURG, WEST VIRGINIA 26425
General Information Guided whitewater raft trips on the Ocoee, Nantahala, Pigeon, French Broad, Nolichucky, New and Gauley, Cheat, and Potomic Rivers. Established in 1986.
Profile of Summer Employees Total number: 100.
Employment Information Openings are from February to October. Jobs available: ▶ *raft guides* with basic first aid and CPR certification at $1000–$4000 per season ▶ *receptionists/ store clerks* at $5.15 per hour. Applicants must submit a formal organization application. An in-person interview is recommended, but a telephone interview is acceptable.
Benefits and Preemployment Training Housing at a cost and meals at a cost. Preemployment training is required and includes accident prevention and safety, first aid, CPR, interpersonal skills, leadership skills.
Contact Doris Berns, Chief Operating Officer, USA Raft. Telephone: 304-454-2475. Fax: 304-454-2472. E-mail: raft@usaraft.com. World Wide Web: http://www.usaraft.com. Contact by e-mail, fax, mail, or phone. Application deadline: continuous.

WISCONSIN

AURORA UNIVERSITY, LAKE GENEVA CAMPUS
PO BOX 210
WILLIAMS BAY, WISCONSIN 53191
General Information Educational conference center serving families, nonprofit organizations, and groups. Established in 1884. 300-acre facility located 45 miles from Milwaukee. Features: freshwater lake; wooded setting; 2 tennis courts; cabins; 1200 feet of lakefront; 3 piers.
Profile of Summer Employees Total number: 175; typical ages: 14–68. 40% men; 60% women; 50% high school students; 20% college students; 10% non-U.S. citizens. Nonsmokers preferred.

Wisconsin

Employment Information Openings are from May 25 to September 9. Jobs available: ▶ 2 *arts and crafts staff members* (minimum age 16) at $7–$8 per hour ▶ 20–25 *food service workers* (minimum age 14) at $6.15–$6.50 per hour ▶ 3–4 *front desk workers* (minimum age 18) at $7–$8 per hour ▶ 5–6 *golf course staff members* (minimum age 18) at $6–$7 per hour ▶ 4–5 *lifeguards* (minimum age 16) with WSI certification, CPR, and advanced first aid at $7–$8 per hour ▶ 2–3 *preschool/day care staff members* (minimum age 18) at $7–$8 per hour ▶ 3–4 *snack shop clerks* (minimum age 14) at $6.15–$7 per hour. Applicants must submit formal organization application, letter of interest. An in-person interview is recommended, but a telephone interview is acceptable. International applicants accepted; must apply through a recognized agency.

Benefits and Preemployment Training Housing at a cost, meals at a cost, formal training, willing to provide letters of recommendation, on-the-job training, willing to complete paperwork for educational credit, and willing to act as a professional reference. Preemployment training is optional and includes first aid, CPR.

Contact Richard Miller, Director of Personnel, Aurora University, Lake Geneva Campus, PO Box 210, Williams Bay, Wisconsin 53191-0210. Telephone: 262-245-8508. Fax: 262-245-8505. E-mail: rmiller@aurora.edu. World Wide Web: http://www.aurora.edu. Contact by e-mail, fax, mail, or phone. Application deadline: continuous.

BIRCH TRAIL CAMP FOR GIRLS
PO BOX 527
MINONG, WISCONSIN 54859

General Information Residential camp serving 185 girls ages 8–15 in two 4-week sessions including extensive wilderness trips. Established in 1959. 310-acre facility located 55 miles from Duluth, Minnesota. Features: freshwater lake; low and high ropes course; tournament water ski slalom course; wooded setting; 3-sided climbing tower; beautiful rustic area.

Profile of Summer Employees Total number: 90; typical ages: 17–40. 5% men; 95% women; 10% minorities; 10% high school students; 80% college students; 15% non-U.S. citizens; 5% local applicants. Nonsmokers preferred.

Employment Information Openings are from June 8 to August 8. Jobs available: ▶ 25–50 *cabin counselors* (minimum age 18) at $1300–$2400 per season ▶ 1–2 *caretaker's assistants* at $1350–$2200 per season ▶ *housekeepers* at $1350–$2200 per season ▶ *kitchen helpers* at $1350–$2200 per season ▶ 1–3 *nurses* (minimum age 21) with RN, LPN, or graduate nurse at $2150–$3500 per season ▶ 2–4 *rock climbing instructors* (minimum age 20) with prior climbing experience at $1650–$2700 per season ▶ 1–3 *swimming instructors* (minimum age 18) with LGT or WSI certification at $1300–$2000 per season ▶ 3–6 *wilderness trip leaders* (minimum age 21) with LGT certification; canoeing, backpacking, and climbing experience preferred at $1700–$2700 per season. Applicants must submit formal organization application, three personal references. An in-person interview is recommended, but a telephone interview is acceptable. International applicants accepted; must apply through a recognized agency.

Benefits and Preemployment Training Free housing, free meals, formal training, health insurance, willing to provide letters of recommendation, on-the-job training, willing to complete paperwork for educational credit, willing to act as a professional reference, and travel reimbursement. Preemployment training is required and includes accident prevention and safety, first aid, CPR, interpersonal skills, leadership skills, wilderness skills.

Contact Gabe Chernov, Owner/Director, Birch Trail Camp for Girls, PO Box 527, Minong, Wisconsin 54859. Fax: 715-466-2217. E-mail: gabe@birchtrail.com. World Wide Web: http://www.birchtrail.com. Contact through World Wide Web site. No phone calls. Application deadline: May 1.

BOYD'S MASON LAKE RESORT
PO BOX 57
FIFIELD, WISCONSIN 54524

General Information American-plan family resort that rents 18 cabins, serves 3 meals daily, and performs daily maid service for up to 100 guests. Established in 1895. 2,600-acre facility located 250 miles from Madison. Features: 4 freshwater, spring-fed lakes; 2600 private acres; heavily forested, wooded setting; very secluded; miles of hiking/biking trails; very old resort with modern conveniences.

Profile of Summer Employees Total number: 30; typical ages: 17–60. 30% men; 70% women; 7% high school students; 15% college students; 10% retirees; 10% non-U.S. citizens; 75% local applicants. Nonsmokers preferred.

Employment Information Openings are from May 15 to October 15. Jobs available: ▶ 1 *children's recreation supervisor* (minimum age 18) with background in elementary education at $7 per hour ▶ 5 *dining room attendants* (minimum age 18) at $7–$10 per hour ▶ 1 *dishwasher* (minimum age 18) at $7–$10 per hour ▶ 2 *housekeepers* (minimum age 18) at $7 per hour ▶ 1 *pots and pans washer* (minimum age 18) at $7–$10 per hour ▶ 1 *receptionist* (minimum age 18) at $7 per hour ▶ 1 *swing cook* (minimum age 18) at $7–$10 per hour. Applicants must submit formal organization application, resume, two personal references. An in-person interview is recommended, but a telephone interview is acceptable. International applicants accepted; must obtain own visa, obtain own working papers, apply through a recognized agency.

Benefits and Preemployment Training Free housing, free meals, willing to provide letters of recommendation, on-the-job training, and outdoor recreational activities (boating, swimming, hiking).

Contact Richard Simon, Manager/Owner, Boyd's Mason Lake Resort, PO Box 57, Fifield, Wisconsin 54524. Telephone: 715-762-3469. Contact by mail or phone. Application deadline: continuous.

CAMP ALICE CHESTER–EAST TROY
EAST TROY, WISCONSIN

General Information Girl Scouts of Milwaukee area resident camp located on a beautiful lake in the woods of southern Wisconsin serving girls ages 8 to 15.

Employment Information Openings are from June to August. Jobs available: ▶ 3 *adventure trip staff* (minimum age 21) with high school diploma, camping experience, knowledge of Girl Scouts, and desire for adventure at $1900–$2100 per season ▶ 1 *assistant director (camp operations)* (minimum age 21) with two-year degree, knowledge of Girl Scout program, ability to encourage creative thinking, willingness to lead girls in decision-making, team skills, communication skills, and supervisory ability at $2200–$3200 per season ▶ 1 *business manager* (minimum age 21) with two-year degree preferably in business/education, knowledge of Girl Scout program and philosophy, creative thinking skills, ability to manage accounts and maintain inventory, team skills, communication skills, and customer service experience at $2200–$2700 per season ▶ 16 *camp counselors* (minimum age 18) with flexibility, creativity, patience, stamina, communication skills, ability to live outdoors during summer, and leadership initiative at $1800–$1900 per season ▶ 4 *lifeguards/counselors* (minimum age 16) with certificate, lakefront experience, attentive lifeguard certification, safety practices in camp environment, team skills, and ability to work and live in summer camp at $2000–$2200 per season ▶ 1 *lifeguards/trip staff* (minimum age 21) with lifeguarding/smallcraft certification, leadership skills, team skills, and ability to work in summer camp setting at $2200–$2300 per season ▶ 2 *program specialists* (minimum age 18) with ability to work and teach girls ages 8 and up, ability to deliver interesting and active programs, and ability to live and work in outdoor camp setting at $1900–$2100 per season ▶ 1 *small craft instructor* (minimum age 18) with smallcraft instructor certification, ability to teach and encourage 8-14 year old girls, team skills, fun attitude, and willingness to live and work in camp setting at $2000–$2200 per season. Applicants must submit a formal organization application, resume, three personal references. A telephone interview is required.

Benefits and Preemployment Training Free housing, free meals, health insurance, and paid training. Preemployment training is required and includes accident prevention and safety, first aid, CPR, interpersonal skills, leadership skills.

Contact Andrea Yanacheck, Camp Director, Camp Alice Chester–East Troy, 131 South 69th Street, Milwaukee, Wisconsin 53214. Telephone: 414-476-1050 Ext. 159. Fax: 414-476-5958. E-mail: ayanacheck@girlscoutsmilwaukee.org. World Wide Web: http://www.girlscoutsmilwaukee. org. Contact by fax, mail, or phone. Application deadline: continuous.

CAMP INTERLAKEN JCC
7050 OLD HIGHWAY 70
EAGLE RIVER, WISCONSIN 54521

General Information Residential Jewish coeducational camp serving 400 campers ages 8–16. Established in 1966. 110-acre facility located 250 miles from Milwaukee. Features: lakefront; ropes challenge course; lighted tennis courts; north woods setting; Judaic Resource Center; special teen camp program.

Profile of Summer Employees Total number: 95; typical ages: 18–22. 50% men; 50% women; 5% minorities; 90% college students; 5% non-U.S. citizens. Nonsmokers preferred.

Employment Information Openings are from June 18 to August 18. Jobs available: ▶ 1 *crafts instructor* with knowledge of ceramics, tie-dyeing, crafts, and painting preferred at $1200–$2000 per season ▶ 4 *kitchen stewards* (minimum age 21) with experience at $1500 per season ▶ *secretary* (minimum age 19) with experience at $1300–$1600 per season. Applicants must submit formal organization application, resume, three personal references. An in-person interview is recommended, but a telephone interview is acceptable. International applicants accepted; must apply through a recognized agency.

Benefits and Preemployment Training Free housing, free meals, willing to provide letters of recommendation, on-the-job training, willing to complete paperwork for educational credit, willing to act as a professional reference, opportunity to attend seminars/workshops, travel reimbursement, and internship opportunities available. Preemployment training is required and includes accident prevention and safety, first aid, CPR, interpersonal skills, leadership skills.

Contact Howard Wagan, Director, Camp Interlaken JCC, 6255 North Santa Monica, Milwaukee, Wisconsin 53217. Telephone: 414-967-8240. Fax: 414-964-0922. E-mail: ciljcc@execpc.com. World Wide Web: http://www.campinterlaken.org. Contact by e-mail, fax, or phone. Application deadline: continuous.

CAMP MANITO-WISH YMCA
PO BOX 246
BOULDER JUNCTION, WISCONSIN 54512

General Information Facility offering wilderness tripping, canoeing, kayaking, and backpacking for 220 campers ages 11–15 in a 3-week session. Traditional camp programs offer variety when campers are not on the trail. Established in 1919. 300-acre facility located 275 miles from Milwaukee. Features: freshwater lake; north woods setting; wilderness travel; challenge course; Manito-wish Leadership center.

Profile of Summer Employees Total number: 225; typical ages: 17–23. 50% men; 50% women; 15% high school students; 85% college students; 1% non-U.S. citizens; 1% local applicants. Nonsmokers preferred.

Employment Information Openings are from June 5 to August 22. Year-round positions also offered. Jobs available: ▶ 60 *assistant counselors* (minimum age 17) with LGT and first aid/ CPR certification at $144 per week ▶ 60 *cabin counselors/trip leaders* (minimum age 19) with

LGT, first aid, and CPR certification at $170 per week ▶ 20–30 *program area staff* (minimum age 19) with first aid and CPR certification, lifeguard training in some cases at $170 per week ▶ 20 *wilderness trip leaders* (minimum age 21) with Wilderness First Responder certification (training available), CPR, and LGT at $170 per week. Applicants must submit formal organization application, three personal references. An in-person interview is recommended, but a telephone interview is acceptable. International applicants accepted; must apply through a recognized agency.

Benefits and Preemployment Training Free housing, free meals, formal training, health insurance, willing to provide letters of recommendation, names of contacts, on-the-job training, willing to complete paperwork for educational credit, willing to act as a professional reference, opportunity to attend seminars/workshops, and internships. Preemployment training is optional and includes first aid, CPR, leadership skills, lifeguard training, wilderness first aid and first responder, challenge course training, wilderness trips.

Contact Jack Chamberlain, Summer Program Director, Camp Manito-wish YMCA, PO Box 246, Boulder Junction, Wisconsin 54512. Telephone: 715-385-2312. Fax: 715-385-2461. E-mail: jack.chamberlain@manito-wish.org. World Wide Web: http://www.manito-wish.org. Contact by e-mail, fax, mail, phone, or through World Wide Web site. Application deadline: continuous.

CAMP NEBAGAMON FOR BOYS
11451 CAMP NEBAGAMON DRIVE
LAKE NEBAGAMON, WISCONSIN 54849

General Information Residential boys camp for 240 campers from forty different communities and several countries. Established in 1929. 70-acre facility located 30 miles from Duluth, Minnesota. Features: 914-acre freshwater lake; nearby state forests; wooded campsite; proximity to Lake Superior and to Brule River.

Profile of Summer Employees Total number: 115; typical ages: 16–55. 80% men; 20% women; 5% minorities; 27% high school students; 40% college students; 10% non-U.S. citizens; 18% local applicants.

Employment Information Openings are from June 15 to August 15. Jobs available: ▶ 2 *cooks* with experience cooking for large groups at $200–$300 per week ▶ 2 *drivers* (minimum age 21) with clean driving record at $2000–$2400 per season ▶ 25 *junior cabin counselors* (must be juniors or seniors in high school) with skills in water and land sports, tennis, target skills, art, campcraft, and photography at $1000–$1050 per season ▶ 1 *nurse* with RN license at $200–$250 per week ▶ 2 *photography specialists* at $1500–$2200 per season ▶ 25 *senior cabin counselors* (must be college age) with skills in water and land sports, tennis, target skills, art, campcraft, and photography at $1250–$1625 per season ▶ 2 *swimming instructors* with WSI or lifeguard certification at $1250–$2000 per season ▶ 2 *waterfront directors* (minimum age 21) with WSI or Red Cross lifeguard certification at $1800–$2600 per season. Applicants must submit formal organization application, three personal references. An in-person interview is required. International applicants accepted; must obtain own visa, obtain own working papers, apply through a recognized agency.

Benefits and Preemployment Training Free housing, free meals, formal training, willing to provide letters of recommendation, names of contacts, on-the-job training, willing to complete paperwork for educational credit, willing to act as a professional reference, opportunity to attend seminars/workshops, and travel reimbursement. Preemployment training is required and includes accident prevention and safety, first aid, CPR, interpersonal skills, leadership skills.

Contact Judy Wallenstein, Co-Director, Camp Nebagamon for Boys, 5237 North Lakewood, Chicago, Illinois 60640. Telephone: 773-271-9500. Fax: 773-271-9816. E-mail: cnebagamon@aol.com. World Wide Web: http://www.campnebagamon.com. Contact by e-mail, fax, mail, phone, or through World Wide Web site. Application deadline: continuous.

CAMP SILVERBROOK–WEST BEND
WEST BEND, WISCONSIN

Employment Information Jobs available: ▶ 1 *Silverbrook assistant director* with two-year degree, teaching/supervision experience, organization/communication skills, ability to live and work in outdoor setting, and Girl Scout program development at $3700–$4300 per season ▶ 1 *Silverbrook business coordinator* with high school diploma, customer service experience, communication skills, and Microsoft Word and Excel ability at $1700 per season ▶ 13 *Silverbrook counselors* with high school diploma, ability to work with girls 7 and up, enthusiasm, patience, camping skills, and outdoor skills at $1600–$1800 per season ▶ 2–4 *Silverbrook program specialists* with high school diploma, ability to work with children, ability to live and work in outdoor setting, and experience in a program area at $1500–$1700 per season.

Benefits and Preemployment Training Free housing, health insurance, and accident insurance, paid training.

Contact Elise Burns, Camp Director, Camp Silverbrook–West Bend. Telephone: 414-476-1050 Ext. 144. Fax: 414-476-5958. E-mail: eburns@girlscoutsmilwaukee.org. Contact by e-mail, fax, mail, or phone.

CAMPS WOODLAND AND TOWERING PINES
EAGLE RIVER, WISCONSIN 54521

General Information Residential camps on separate sites having four- or six-week seasons. Established in 1946. 400-acre facility located 22 miles from Rhinelander. Features: north woods and lakes; resort area.

Profile of Summer Employees Total number: 60; typical ages: 18–70. 60% men; 40% women; 5% high school students; 80% college students; 5% retirees; 5% non-U.S. citizens; 5% local applicants. Nonsmokers preferred.

Employment Information Openings are from June 17 to August 8. Year-round positions also offered. Jobs available: ▶ *cooks/assistant cooks* with experience at $200–$300 per week ▶ *crafts/Indian lore staff members* at $150–$250 per week ▶ *dishwashers* at $150–$200 per week ▶ *nurses* with RN license at $350–$450 per week ▶ *riflery/archery staff members* with NRA training at $150–$250 per week ▶ *swimming/small craft staff members* with WSI certification at $200–$250 per week ▶ *tennis/gymnastics staff members* at $150–$250 per week. Applicants must submit formal organization application, four personal references. A telephone interview is required. International applicants accepted; must obtain own visa, apply through a recognized agency.

Benefits and Preemployment Training Free housing, on-the-job training, willing to complete paperwork for educational credit, and travel reimbursement. Preemployment training is required and includes accident prevention and safety, first aid, CPR, interpersonal skills, leadership skills.

Contact John Jordan, Owner and Executive Director, Camps Woodland and Towering Pines, 242 Bristol Street, Northfield, Illinois 60093. Telephone: 847-446-7311. Fax: 847-446-7710. E-mail: towpines@aol.com. Contact by e-mail, fax, mail, or phone. Application deadline: continuous.

CENTRAL WISCONSIN ENVIRONMENTAL STATION/ UNIVERSITY OF WISCONSIN–STEVENS POINT
10186 COUNTY ROAD MM
AMHERST JUNCTION, WISCONSIN 54407

General Information Environmental station that provides a foundation for appreciation and understanding of the environment and develops the skills and attitudes needed to deal with present and future environmental problems. Established in 1975. 300-acre facility located 25 miles from Stevens Point. Features: freshwater lake; wooded setting; log cabins; multi-purpose living/teaching building; challenge course.

Profile of Summer Employees Total number: 15; typical ages: 18–30. 50% men; 50% women; 10% minorities; 10% high school students; 90% college students; 10% non-U.S. citizens; 60% local applicants. Nonsmokers preferred.

Employment Information Openings are from June 1 to August 24. Year-round positions also offered. Jobs available: ▶ *assistant summer program director* (minimum age 18) with first aid/CPR, driver's license, experience working with youth, and environmental education or related experience at $180–$220 per week ▶ *counselors/naturalists* (minimum age 18) with first aid/CPR certifications, driver's license, experience working with youth, and environmental education with related experience at $160–$210 per week ▶ *health lodge supervisor* (minimum age 18) with EMT, RN, or advanced first aid training at $150–$190 per week ▶ *summer program director* (minimum age 21) with first aid/CPR, driver's license, experience working with youth and supervising staff, and environmental education or related experience at $300–$350 per week ▶ *waterfront director* (minimum age 18) with WSI, lifeguard certification, and driver's license at $160–$220 per week. Applicants must submit formal organization application, resume, three personal references. An in-person interview is recommended, but a telephone interview is acceptable. International applicants accepted; must obtain own visa, obtain own working papers, apply through a recognized agency.

Benefits and Preemployment Training Free housing, formal training, willing to provide letters of recommendation, on-the-job training, willing to complete paperwork for educational credit, willing to act as a professional reference, and free meals or meals at cost (possible). Preemployment training is required and includes accident prevention and safety, first aid, interpersonal skills, leadership skills, teaching skills, environmental education introduction.

Contact Bobbi Zbleski, Director, Central Wisconsin Environmental Station/University of Wisconsin–Stevens Point, 10186 County Road MM, Amherst Junction, Wisconsin 54407. Telephone: 715-824-2428. Fax: 715-824-3201. E-mail: cwes@uwsp.edu. World Wide Web: http://www.uwsp.edu/cnr/cwes. Contact by e-mail, fax, phone, or through World Wide Web site. Application deadline: continuous.

CLEARWATER CAMP FOR GIRLS
7490 CLEARWATER ROAD
MINOCQUA, WISCONSIN 54548

General Information Traditional residential camp providing caring staff and camping experiences for girls ages 8–16. Established in 1933. 80-acre facility located 25 miles from Rhinelander. Features: 3600-acre headwaters lake; wooded setting; 5-acre island; historical buildings; footbridge from mainland to island.

Profile of Summer Employees Total number: 70; typical ages: 18–75. 2% men; 98% women; 1% minorities; 5% high school students; 85% college students; 1% retirees; 3% non-U.S. citizens; 5% local applicants. Nonsmokers preferred.

Employment Information Openings are from June 7 to August 12. Jobs available: ▶ 2 *English-style riding instructors* with first aid, CPR, CHA, or HSA certification and experience in the field at $2000–$4000 per season ▶ 1–2 *archery instructors* with archery certification preferred and experience in the field at $2000–$2500 per season ▶ 4–6 *canoeing instructors* with lifeguard or emergency water safety, CPR, canoe certification (preferred), and experience in the field at $2000–$2600 per season ▶ 1–3 *cook and assistant cooks* with sanitation certification preferred and experience in the field at $4000–$6000 per season ▶ 2–4 *crafts instructors* with creativity and varied skills in weaving, pottery, and leather at $2000–$2600 per season ▶ 2 *drama instructors* with talent, ability to direct, and creativity at $2000–$2500 per season ▶ 10–25 *general counselors* (minimum age 19) with ability to assist or teach an activity, love for children, willingness and ability to assist youngsters, lifeguard, first aid, CPR certification, and good role modeling at $2000–$3000 per season ▶ 6 *kitchen staff members* (minimum age 16) with cheerful attitude and good work ethic at $1800–$2500 per season ▶ 6 *sailing instructors* with experience handling C scows, CPR/LGT certification, and Red Cross sailing/USRA rating (preferred) at $2200–$2500 per season ▶ 2 *skilled tripping leaders* (minimum age 21) with wilderness water safety, first aid certification, CPR, and LGT at $2500–$3500 per season ▶ 5 *swimming instructors* with CPR, WSI, or lifeguard certification at $2200–$2400 per season ▶ 2 *tennis instructors* with CPR certification and the ability to teach with enthusiasm at $2000–$4000 per season ▶ 2 *trip leaders* (minimum age 21) with campcraft, canoeing, and backpacking experience and first aid, CPR, lifeguard, or wilderness first aid/safety, and wilderness water safety at $2000–$4000 per season ▶ 2 *waterskiing instructors* with boat-driving experience, WSI or lifeguard certification, and waterski instructor course preferred at $2000–$2500 per season ▶ 1 *windsurfing instructor* with lifeguard and windsurfing instructor rating (preferred) at $2000–$2500 per season. Applicants must submit formal organization application, two personal references, three letters of recommendation. An in-person interview is recommended, but a telephone interview is acceptable. International applicants accepted; must obtain own visa, apply through a recognized agency.

Benefits and Preemployment Training Free housing, free meals, health insurance, willing to provide letters of recommendation, names of contacts, on-the-job training, willing to complete paperwork for educational credit, willing to act as a professional reference, opportunity to attend seminars/workshops, and possible travel reimbursements. Preemployment training is required and includes accident prevention and safety, first aid, CPR, interpersonal skills, leadership skills.

Contact Sunny Moore, Director, Clearwater Camp for Girls, 7490 Clearwater Road, Minocqua, Wisconsin 54548. Telephone: 800-399-5030. Fax: 715-356-3124. E-mail: clearwatercamp@ newnorth.net. World Wide Web: http://www.clearwatercamp.com. Contact by e-mail, fax, mail, phone, or through World Wide Web site. Application deadline: continuous.

EASTER SEALS WISCONSIN
101 NOB HILL ROAD, SUITE 301
WISCONSIN DELLS, WISCONSIN 53713

General Information Nonprofit agency providing camping and recreation services to children and adults with disabilities. 400-acre facility located 55 miles from Madison. Features: wooded setting; swimming pool; near resort town; rope course/climbing tower; accessible; air-conditioned.

Profile of Summer Employees Total number: 110; typical ages: 20–25. 20% men; 80% women; 5% minorities; 90% college students; 5% non-U.S. citizens. Nonsmokers preferred.

Employment Information Openings are from June 1 to August 15. Year-round positions also offered. Jobs available: ▶ 4–5 *aquatics specialists* (minimum age 21) with current Red Cross lifeguard certification (required) at $185–$200 per week ▶ 70–80 *counselors* (minimum age 18) with sincere desire to work with people who have a disability at $170–$220 per week ▶ 4–6 *kitchen aides* (minimum age 18) at $160 per week ▶ 3–4 *nurses* (minimum age 21) with first aid training, knowledge of passing medications, seizures, catheterizations, suppositories, colostomy bags, and feeding tubes at $800 per week ▶ 1–2 *ropes specialist* (minimum age 21) with knowledge of facilitating challenge courses for people with disabilities at $200–$250 per week. Applicants must submit formal organization application, resume, three personal references, criminal background check, online application available. A telephone interview is required. International applicants accepted; must apply through a recognized agency.

Benefits and Preemployment Training Free housing, free meals, formal training, willing to provide letters of recommendation, on-the-job training, willing to complete paperwork for educational credit, willing to act as a professional reference, and laundry facilities, workmen's compensation. Preemployment training is required and includes accident prevention and safety, first aid, CPR, interpersonal skills, leadership skills, lifeguarding, ropes course, personal care training.

Contact Chris Hollar, Camp Director, Easter Seals Wisconsin. Telephone: 800-422-2324. Fax: 608-277-8333. E-mail: wawbeek@wi-easterseals.org. World Wide Web: http://www.wi-easterseals. org. Contact by e-mail, fax, mail, phone, or through World Wide Web site. Application deadline: continuous.

MENOMINEE FOR BOYS
4985 COUNTRY ROAD D
EAGLE RIVER, WISCONSIN 54521
General Information Residential boys camp serving 160 boys per program from all over the world. Established in 1928. 80-acre facility located 60 miles from Wausau. Features: lake; golf course; wooded setting; 5 tennis courts; modern cabins with water and electricity; 50 foot climbing wall.
Profile of Summer Employees Total number: 60; typical age: 23. 90% men; 10% women; 5% minorities; 10% high school students; 80% college students; 1% retirees; 10% non-U.S. citizens; 5% local applicants. Nonsmokers required.
Employment Information Openings are from June 8 to August 8. Jobs available: ▶ *golf instructors* ▶ *sailing instructors* ▶ *soccer instructors* ▶ *swimming instructors* ▶ *team sports instructors* at $1200–$1350 per season ▶ *tennis instructors* ▶ *waterskiing instructors/skiboat drivers*. Applicants must submit formal organization application, letter of interest. International applicants accepted; must apply through a recognized agency.
Benefits and Preemployment Training Free housing, free meals, formal training, names of contacts, on-the-job training, willing to complete paperwork for educational credit, willing to act as a professional reference, and travel reimbursement. Preemployment training is required and includes accident prevention and safety, CPR, interpersonal skills, leadership skills.
Contact Steve Kanefsky, Owner/Director, Menominee for Boys, 15253 North 104th Way, Scottsdale, Arizona 85259. Telephone: 800-236-2267. Fax: 480-515-5475. E-mail: fun@ campmenominee.com. World Wide Web: http://www.campmenominee.com. Contact by e-mail, fax, mail, or phone. Application deadline: continuous.

RED PINE CAMP FOR GIRLS
MINOCQUA, WISCONSIN 54548
General Information Private traditional camp providing individual attention for girls ages 6-16, enrolling 130 campers for two-, four-, and eight-week sessions. Established in 1937. 40-acre facility located 30 miles from Rhinelander. Features: only private property on 1200-acre freshwater lake; tennis courts; cabins; surrounded by state land; shower facilities.
Profile of Summer Employees Total number: 50–55; typical ages: 18–45. 10% men; 90% women; 80% college students; 10% non-U.S. citizens; 8% local applicants.
Employment Information Openings are from June 12 to August 16. Jobs available: ▶ 2–7 *English-style riding instructors or stable managers* (minimum age 18) with skill and love of horses and experience in the field at $1300–$2000 per season ▶ 2–10 *arts and crafts, gymnastics, aerobic jazz, cheerleading, and archery staff members* (minimum age 18) with skill and experience in combination of areas at $1200–$1500 per season ▶ 2–6 *canoeing staff members* with emergency and basic water safety (Red Cross) certification preferred, skill and experience in still waters, and knowledge of campcraft at $1200–$1800 per season ▶ *food service staff members* (minimum age 18) with experience in one or more of the following: cook, assistant to cook, general kitchen and dining room help at $1350–$2000 per season ▶ 2–3 *nurses* (minimum age 18) with RN, LPN, EMT or GN license (Wisconsin) at $1500–$2500 per season ▶ 1–2 *sailboarding staff members* (minimum age 18) with experience in the field; Red Cross certification preferred at $1200–$1800 per season ▶ 2–4 *sailing staff members* (minimum age 18) with swimming, LGT, and small craft certification preferred and skill in sailing Sunfish, Puffers, and

Zumas at $1200–$1800 per season ▶ 6–9 *swimming instructors* (minimum age 18) with WSI, LGT, CPR, and first aid certification at $1200–$1800 per season ▶ 2–5 *tennis staff members* with high degree of skill and professional training preferred at $1200–$1800 per season. Applicants must submit formal organization application, resume, three personal references, three letters of recommendation. An in-person interview is recommended, but a telephone interview is acceptable. International applicants accepted; must obtain own visa, obtain own working papers, apply through a recognized agency.

Benefits and Preemployment Training Free housing, free meals, willing to provide letters of recommendation, on-the-job training, willing to complete paperwork for educational credit, willing to act as a professional reference, opportunity to attend seminars/workshops, travel reimbursement, and laundry service. Preemployment training is required and includes accident prevention and safety, first aid, CPR, interpersonal skills, leadership skills, archery and sailing workshops.

Contact Robin Thies, Co-Director, Red Pine Camp for Girls, PO Box 69, Minocqua, Wisconsin 54548. Telephone: 715-356-4571. Fax: 715-356-1077. E-mail: redpinec@newnorth.net. World Wide Web: http://www.redpinecamp.com. Contact by e-mail, fax, mail, phone, or through World Wide Web site. Application deadline: continuous.

SALVATION ARMY WONDERLAND CAMP AND CONFERENCE CENTER
9241 CAMP LAKE ROAD, PO BOX 222
CAMP LAKE, WISCONSIN 53109-0222

General Information Residential Evangelical Christian camping program for Chicago-area Salvation Army, including camps for 120 low-income and at-risk young people for six 8-day sessions. Established in 1924. 145-acre facility located 45 miles from Milwaukee. Features: freshwater lake; upland forest; meadows and prairie; heated outdoor pool and diving tank; gym, tennis and volleyball courts; low ropes course.

Profile of Summer Employees Total number: 90–100; typical ages: 18–26. 50% men; 50% women; 30% minorities; 8% high school students; 90% college students; 2% retirees; 5% non-U.S. citizens; 10% local applicants. Nonsmokers required.

Employment Information Openings are from May 25 to August 14. Winter break and year-round positions also offered. Jobs available: ▶ 1–2 *aquatics assistants* (minimum age 20) with WSI and LTI certification (preferred), leadership ability and supervisory experience at $225–$235 per week ▶ 1 *aquatics director* (minimum age 22) with WSI and LTI certification (preferred), leadership ability, and supervisory experience at $230–$250 per week ▶ *archery director* (minimum age 20) with knowledge/certification in safety and archery at $210–$220 per week ▶ 1 *arts and crafts director* (minimum age 20) with two years of college completed and experience working with children at $210–$220 per week ▶ 12–16 *boys counselors* (minimum age 19) with one year of college completed and experience working with children at $210–$220 per week ▶ 2 *cooks* (minimum age 20) with experience at $240–$280 per week ▶ 12–16 *girls counselors* (minimum age 19) with one year of college completed and experience working with children at $210–$220 per week ▶ 1 *health services assistant* (minimum age 20) with student nurse status or experience in nursing, ARC-PFR and first aid, and experience working with children at $210–$220 per week ▶ 7–9 *lifeguard/support counselors* (minimum age 19) with ARC-LGT (on-site training available) at $210–$220 per week ▶ 1 *nature director* (minimum age 20) with two years of college completed at $210–$220 per week ▶ 1–2 *nurses* (minimum age 22) with BSN or RN license with CPR training (USA certification), PFR, first aid, and experience working with children at $500 per week ▶ 1 *pioneer director* (minimum age 20) with two years of college completed at $210–$220 per week ▶ 6 *program unit directors* (minimum age 20) with two years of college completed, experience working with children, leadership ability, and organizational skills at $210–$220 per week ▶ *ropes director* (minimum age 20) with knowledge/certification in ropes and safety at $210–$220 per week ▶ 6–8 *support counselors* (minimum age 18) with one year of college required at $210–$220 per week. Applicants must submit formal organization application, three personal references, written interview, resume (optional). An in-person interview is recommended, but a telephone interview is acceptable. International applicants accepted; must apply through a recognized agency.

Benefits and Preemployment Training Free housing, free meals, formal training, willing to provide letters of recommendation, on-the-job training, willing to complete paperwork for educational credit, willing to act as a professional reference, and on-site certifications available.

Contact David Ditzler, Director of Camping Services, Salvation Army Wonderland Camp and Conference Center, 9241 Camp Lake Road, PO Box 222, Camp Lake, Wisconsin 53109-0222. Telephone: 262-889-4305 Ext. 304. Fax: 262-889-2043. E-mail: program@wonderlandcamp. com. World Wide Web: http://www.techheadnet.com/wonderland. Contact by e-mail, fax, mail, or phone. Application deadline: June 1.

THE SOUTHWESTERN COMPANY, WISCONSIN
See The Southwestern Company on page 297 for complete description.

SPORTS INTERNATIONAL–WILLIAM HENDERSON AND VONNIE HOLLIDAY FOOTBALL CAMP
DE PERE, WISCONSIN
See Sports International, Inc. on page 134 for complete description.

STIVERS STAFFING SERVICES–WISCONSIN
See Stivers Staffing Services–Illinois on page 96 for complete description.

STUDENT CONSERVATION ASSOCIATION (SCA), WISCONSIN
See Student Conservation Association (SCA), New Hampshire on page 200 for complete description.

SUPERCAMP–UNIVERSITY OF WISCONSIN AT PARKSIDE
UNIVERSITY OF WISCONSIN AT PARKSIDE
KENOSHA, WISCONSIN 53141

General Information Residential program for teens designed to build self-confidence and lifelong learning skills through accelerated learning techniques. Established in 1981. 700-acre facility.

Profile of Summer Employees Total number: 27–30; typical ages: 18–25. 40% men; 60% women; 80% college students; 10% non-U.S. citizens. Nonsmokers preferred.

Employment Information Openings are from June to August. Jobs available: ▶ 1 *counselor* with college degree and PPS credentials, MFCC license, or master's degree in counseling at a salary paid per 10 week session ▶ 3 *facilitators* with presentation skills, college degree, and teaching credentials preferred at a salary paid per 10 week session ▶ *logistics managers* with excellent organizational skills and high school diploma at a salary paid per 10 week session ▶ *office managers* with excellent communication and computer skills, business office experience at a salary paid per 10 week session ▶ 1 *products coordinator* with high school diploma at a salary paid per 10 week session ▶ *site administrators* with experience in camp management at a salary paid per 10 week session ▶ 16–18 *team leaders* with high school diploma and experience with teens at $350 to $600 per 10 week session ▶ 1 *wellness person* with RN license, EMT, or paramedic at a salary paid per 10 day session. Applicants must submit a formal organization application, resume, three letters of recommendation, in-person interview recommended (videotape interview acceptable). International applicants accepted; must obtain own visa, obtain own working papers.

Benefits and Preemployment Training Free housing, free meals, willing to provide letters of recommendation, on-the-job training, willing to complete paperwork for educational credit, and willing to act as a professional reference. Preemployment training is required.

Contact Jen Myers, Staffing, SuperCamp–University of Wisconsin at Parkside, 1725 South Coast Highway, Oceanside, California 92054. Telephone: 800-285-3276 Ext. 109. Fax: 760-722-3507. E-mail: staffing@learningforum.com. World Wide Web: http://www.supercamp.com. Contact by e-mail, fax, mail, phone, or through World Wide Web site. Application deadline: continuous.

YMCA CAMP ICAGHOWAN
899-A 115TH STREET
AMERY, WISCONSIN 54001

General Information Coed residential camp providing opportunities for building self-esteem, confidence, fun, leadership, respect, and appreciation for the environment, self, and others. Serves 120–150 campers weekly. Established in 1909. 120-acre facility located 65 miles from Minneapolis, Minnesota. Features: beautiful wooded island-peninsula; full waterfront setup; cozy, rustic cabins with fireplaces.

Profile of Summer Employees Total number: 50; typical ages: 19–25. 50% men; 50% women; 5% minorities; 20% high school students; 80% college students; 5% non-U.S. citizens; 75% local applicants. Nonsmokers required.

Employment Information Openings are from June 8 to August 30. Year-round positions also offered. Jobs available: ▶ 1 *horseback riding director* with CPR, first aid, and horsemanship safety instructor certification at $130–$160 per week ▶ 1 *nurse* with nursing license at $200–$250 per week ▶ 1 *program coordinator* with CPR, first aid, and lifeguard training at $130–$180 per week ▶ 3 *ropes course directors* with CPR, first aid, and lifeguard training; should have technical skills and experience facilitating ropes course at $120–$150 per week ▶ 1 *sailing/ boating director* (minimum age 19) with CPR/first aid, sailing proficiency, and ability to work with and teach young people at $120–$150 per week ▶ 24 *trail counselors/cabin counselors* with CPR, first aid, and lifeguard training at $115–$145 per week ▶ 1 *waterfront director* with CPR, first aid, and lifeguard training; experience managing pool, lake, and lifeguards at $125–$160 per week. Applicants must submit formal organization application, three personal references, three letters of recommendation. An in-person interview is recommended, but a telephone interview is acceptable. International applicants accepted; must obtain own visa, obtain own working papers, apply through a recognized agency.

Benefits and Preemployment Training Free housing, free meals, formal training, willing to provide letters of recommendation, on-the-job training, willing to complete paperwork for educational credit, willing to act as a professional reference, and internship opportunities available.

Contact Peter Wieczorek, Director, YMCA Camp Icaghowan, 4 West Rustic Lodge Avenue, Minneapolis, Minnesota 55409. Telephone: 612-822-CAMP. Fax: 612-823-2482. E-mail: icghwn@ amerytel.net. World Wide Web: http://www.ymcacamps.org. Contact by e-mail, fax, mail, or phone. Application deadline: continuous.

WYOMING

ABSAROKA MOUNTAIN LODGE
1231 NORTHFORK HIGHWAY
CODY, WYOMING 82414

General Information Mountain lodge located 12 miles from East Gate of Yellowstone National Park. Offering 16 log cabins; main lodge located along Gunbarrel Creek; lodging, dining, and horseback rides in the Absaroka Wilderness Area. Established in 1910. 10-acre facility. Features: mountain setting; creek through property; historic lodge and cabins; horseback riding; close to Yellowstone National Park; blue ribbon trout streams.

Profile of Summer Employees Total number: 12; typical ages: 18–26. 50% men; 50% women; 10% high school students; 80% college students; 10% retirees; 5% non-U.S. citizens; 5% local applicants. Nonsmokers preferred.

Employment Information Openings are from May 1 to September 30. Jobs available: ▶ 1 *cook* (minimum age 18) with cooking experience required at $1000 per month ▶ 4–6 *waiters/waitresses/cabin cleaners* (minimum age 18) with serving and some cleaning experience at $400–$500 per month ▶ 2–4 *wranglers* (minimum age 18) with horse experience (trail guiding, horse care, etc.) required at $600 per month. Applicants must submit a letter of interest, resume, two personal references, two letters of recommendation. A telephone interview is required. International applicants accepted; must obtain own visa.

Benefits and Preemployment Training Free housing, free meals, willing to provide letters of recommendation, on-the-job training, willing to act as a professional reference, and opportunity to partake in ranch activities and horseback riding.

Contact Patti Bates, Owner, Absaroka Mountain Lodge, 1231 Northfork Highway, Cody, Wyoming 82414. Telephone: 307-587-3963. E-mail: batesfam@frontiernet.net. World Wide Web: http://www.absarokamtlodge.com. Contact by e-mail, mail, phone, or through World Wide Web site. Application deadline: continuous.

A CHRISTIAN MINISTRY IN THE NATIONAL PARKS–WYOMING

See A Christian Ministry in the National Parks–Maine on page 107 for complete description.

ALPENHOF LODGE
BOX 288, 3255 WEST VILLAGE AVENUE
TETON VILLAGE, WYOMING 83025

General Information Alpine-style resort lodge with 42 rooms and 2 restaurants providing clientele with personalized service. Established in 1988. 1-acre facility located 260 miles from Salt Lake City, Utah. Features: mountains and rivers.

Profile of Summer Employees Total number: 85; typical ages: 20–25. 60% men; 40% women; 1% high school students; 50% college students; 10% non-U.S. citizens; 39% local applicants. Nonsmokers preferred.

Employment Information Openings are from May 20 to October 12. Year-round positions also offered. Jobs available: ▶ 3 *bellmen* with aptitude for greeting guests in a friendly manner, ability to assist with luggage, run errands, and do light maintenance work at $1040–$1200 per month ▶ 8 *dining room staff members (buspersons and waitstaff)* with tableside experience and wine knowledge at $275–$420 per month ▶ 3–5 *dishwashers* with ability to work quickly at $960–$1040 per month ▶ 8 *food waitstaff members* with interest in working with public and the ability to serve at $370 per month ▶ 2 *front desk clerks* with friendly, outgoing personalities and organizational skills at $9–$10 per hour ▶ 5 *housekeeping staff members* with ability to clean rooms and willingness to do hard work at $1040–$1100 per month ▶ 2–4 *prep or line cooks* with ability to cook in line and work quickly at $1120–$1600 per month. Applicants must submit a formal organization application. An in-person interview is required. International applicants accepted; must obtain own visa, obtain own working papers.

Benefits and Preemployment Training Housing at a cost, free meals, formal training, possible full-time employment, willing to provide letters of recommendation, on-the-job training, willing to complete paperwork for educational credit, and willing to act as a professional reference. Preemployment training is required and includes accident prevention and safety, interpersonal skills.

Contact Mark D. Johnson, Assistant General Manager, Alpenhof Lodge, PO Box 288, Teton Village, Wyoming 83025. Telephone: 307-733-3242. Fax: 307-739-1516. E-mail: mj@alpenhoflodge. com. World Wide Web: http://www.alpenhoflodge.com. Contact by e-mail, fax, or mail. Application deadline: continuous.

BILL CODY RANCH
2604 YELLOWSTONE HIGHWAY
CODY, WYOMING 82414

General Information Guest ranch catering to families with 14 cabins, cookouts, entertainment, daily horseback rides. Established in 1996. 8-acre facility located 135 miles from Billings, Montana. Features: national forest; 30 minutes from Yellowstone; 70 riding horses; white-water rafting; nightly entertainment; 30 minutes from Cody, Wyoming.

Profile of Summer Employees Total number: 20; typical ages: 18–25. 40% men; 60% women; 1% high school students; 90% college students; 2% local applicants. Nonsmokers preferred.

Employment Information Openings are from May 15 to September 30. Jobs available: ▶ 2 *cooks* with some culinary experience at $800–$1500 per month ▶ 5 *horse wranglers* (minimum age 18) with physical ability to perform required duties, valid driver's license, a clean driving record, trailering experience a plus, horseback riding experience required at $500–$700 per month ▶ 6 *housekeepers/waitstaff* at $450–$550 per month ▶ 2 *office assistants* at $600–$800 per month ▶ 1 *prep cook* at $600–$1000 per month. Applicants must submit formal organization application, resume, two personal references. A telephone interview is required. International applicants accepted; must apply through a recognized agency.

Benefits and Preemployment Training Free housing, free meals, willing to provide letters of recommendation, and on-the-job training.

Contact John Parsons, Co-Owner, Bill Cody Ranch, 2604 Yellowstone Highway, Cody, Wyoming 82414. Telephone: 307-587-6271. Fax: 307-587-6272. E-mail: billcody@billcodyranch.com. World Wide Web: http://www.billcodyranch.com. Contact by e-mail, fax, mail, phone, or through World Wide Web site. Application deadline: continuous.

ELEPHANT HEAD LODGE
1170 YELLOWSTONE HIGHWAY
WAPITI, WYOMING 82450

General Information Guest ranch on eastern edge of Yellowstone National Park with lodging, meals, horseback riding, fishing, cookouts, and other activities. Established in 1910. 6-acre facility located 100 miles from Billings, Montana. Features: historic lodge and 12 log cabins; 25 riding horses; Shoshone river fishing; 80 miles from Grand Teton National Parks and 11 miles from Yellowstone National Park; horseback rides in Shoshone National Forest; abundant wildlife.

Profile of Summer Employees Total number: 12; typical ages: 19–22. 40% men; 60% women; 20% minorities; 10% high school students; 80% college students; 2% retirees; 10% non-U.S. citizens; 8% local applicants. Nonsmokers required.

Employment Information Openings are from May to September. Jobs available: ▶ 2 *cooks* (minimum age 18) with experience (preferred), ability to plan and cook meals for crew, and ability to cook on outdoor grill at $650–$850 per month ▶ 2 *experienced wranglers* (minimum age 19) with valid driver's license and ability to drive a horse trailer at $750–$850 per month ▶ 2 *horse wranglers* (minimum age 19) with outgoing personality and physical ability to perform required duties at $650–$750 per month ▶ 5–7 *housekeepers/waitstaff* (minimum age 16) with interest in working with the public and an outgoing personality at $650–$750 per month. Applicants must submit resume, two personal references, letter of recommendation. A telephone interview is required. International applicants accepted; must obtain own visa, obtain own working papers, apply through a recognized agency.

Benefits and Preemployment Training Free housing, free meals, willing to provide letters of recommendation, on-the-job training, willing to complete paperwork for educational credit, willing to act as a professional reference, and laundry facilities, free horseback riding, river rafting, fly-fishing.

Contact Phil Lamb, Owner, Elephant Head Lodge, 1170 Yellowstone Highway, Wapiti, Wyoming 82450. Telephone: 307-587-3980. Fax: 307-527-7922. E-mail: vacation@elephantheadlodge.com. World Wide Web: http://www.elephantheadlodge.com. Contact by e-mail, fax, mail, or phone. Application deadline: continuous.

SIGNAL MOUNTAIN LODGE
GRAND TETON NATIONAL PARK, PO BOX 50
MORAN, WYOMING 83013

General Information Summer resort providing national park visitors with services such as lodging, food, marinas, gifts, guided fishing, groceries, and gasoline. Established in 1984. 30-acre facility located 30 miles from Jackson. Features: employee dormitories; freshwater lake; wooded setting; remote/quiet area; located in Grand Teton National Park; sand volleyball court.

Profile of Summer Employees Total number: 150; typical ages: 19–38. 50% men; 50% women.

Employment Information Openings are from April 25 to October 25. Jobs available: ▶ *accounting personnel (day and night audit)* with experience in the field ▶ *bartenders* (minimum age 21) with serving or bartending experience required ▶ *buspersons* ▶ *convenience store attendants* with cash register experience preferred ▶ *cooks* with experience with fine dining and coffee shop menus ▶ *dishwashers* ▶ *employee dining room staff members* ▶ 3 *float guides/river guides* with experience necessary ▶ *front desk and reservations persons* with typing and interpersonal skills ▶ *gift store sales clerks* with cash register experience preferred ▶ *hosts/hostesses* ▶ *lodging helpers* with ability to make beds, clean, and do laundry ▶ *management and staff positions* with experience in the field ▶ *marina attendants* with ability to handle boat rentals, shuttle guests to and from boats, and pump gas ▶ *pantry personnel* with ability to prepare salads and desserts ▶ *waitstaff* (minimum age 21) with serving experience required. Applicants must submit formal organization application. A telephone interview is required. International applicants accepted; must apply through a recognized agency.

Benefits and Preemployment Training On-the-job training, willing to complete paperwork for educational credit, willing to act as a professional reference, and room and board at $250 per month. Preemployment training is required and includes accident prevention and safety, first aid, CPR, overall orientation.

Contact Megan Dorr, Personnel Manager, Signal Mountain Lodge, PO Box 50, Moran, Wyoming 83013. Telephone: 800-672-6012. Fax: 307-543-2569. E-mail: personnel@signalmtnlodge.com. World Wide Web: http://www.coolworks.com/signalmt/. Contact by e-mail, fax, mail, phone, or through World Wide Web site. Application deadline: continuous.

THE SOUTHWESTERN COMPANY, WYOMING
See The Southwestern Company on page 297 for complete description.

STUDENT CONSERVATION ASSOCIATION (SCA), WYOMING
See Student Conservation Association (SCA), New Hampshire on page 200 for complete description.

TOGWOTEE MOUNTAIN LODGE
PO BOX 91
MORAN, WYOMING 83013

General Information Mountain lodge serving a varied clientele. Established in 1923. 67-acre facility located 48 miles from Jackson Hole. Features: wooded setting; streams; views of Grand Tetons; near Yellowstone.

Profile of Summer Employees Total number: 50–60; typical ages: 18–60. 60% men; 40% women; 5% high school students; 50% college students; 20% retirees; 5% non-U.S. citizens; 20% local applicants.

Employment Information Openings are from June 10 to September 30. Winter break and year-round positions also offered. Jobs available: ▶ 3 *bartenders* (minimum age 21) with an outgoing personality, desire to perform a thorough job, and experience in the field at $5 to $6 per hour plus gratuities ▶ 2 *convenience store clerks* (minimum age 21) with good math skills and an outgoing personality at $6–$7 per hour ▶ 3 *dishwashers* with ability to accomplish tasks neatly and quickly at $6–$7 per hour ▶ 8 *experienced sauté and broiler line cooks* with neat and efficient work habits at $7–$9 per hour ▶ *front desk/reservations persons* with good math aptitude and an outgoing personality at $7–$8 per hour ▶ 2 *general laborers* with efficient work habits at $6–$8 per hour ▶ 9 *housekeepers* with neat appearance and efficient work habits at $6–$7 per hour ▶ 7 *waitstaff* (minimum age 18) with an outgoing personality and desire to perform a thorough job at $4.15 per hour plus gratuities. Applicants must submit a formal organization application, three personal references. A telephone interview is required.

Benefits and Preemployment Training Housing at a cost, meals at a cost, possible full-time employment, willing to provide letters of recommendation, on-the-job training, willing to act as a professional reference, and discounts on horseback riding and other activities.

Contact Ben Wallace, Assistant Residential Manager, Togwotee Mountain Lodge. Telephone: 307-543-2847. Fax: 307-543-2391. E-mail: ben@togwoteelodge.com. World Wide Web: http://www.togwoteelodge.com. Contact by e-mail, fax, mail, phone, or through World Wide Web site. Application deadline: continuous.

WILDERNESS VENTURES
PO BOX 2768
JACKSON HOLE, WYOMING 83001

General Information Organization devoted to leading teenagers on wilderness trips in national parks and forests in the American west and abroad. Established in 1973. Located 280 miles from Salt Lake City, Utah.

Profile of Summer Employees Total number: 110; typical ages: 21–31. 50% men; 50% women; 50% college students; 10% local applicants. Nonsmokers required.

Employment Information Openings are from June 14 to August 20. Jobs available: ▶ 50 *trip leaders* (minimum age 21) with valid driver's license, WFR, and CPR at $1000–$2000 per season. Applicants must submit a formal organization application, letter of interest, resume, two letters of recommendation. A telephone interview is required. International applicants accepted; must obtain own visa, obtain own working papers.

Benefits and Preemployment Training Free housing, free meals, possible full-time employment, willing to provide letters of recommendation, willing to complete paperwork for educational credit, willing to act as a professional reference, and opportunity to attend seminars/workshops. Preemployment training is required and includes accident prevention and safety, interpersonal skills, leadership skills.

Contact Hayes Swinney, Personnel Coordinator, Wilderness Ventures. Telephone: 800-533-2281. Fax: 307-739-1934. E-mail: staff@wildernessventures.com. World Wide Web: http://www. wildernessventures.com. Contact by e-mail, fax, mail, phone, or through World Wide Web site. Application deadline: continuous.

YELLOWSTONE NATIONAL PARK LODGES
PO BOX 165
YELLOWSTONE NATIONAL PARK, WYOMING 82190

General Information Organization offering hospitality services throughout Yellowstone including hotels, restaurants, gift shops, bus/boat/horse tours and campgrounds. Established in 1979. 2,000,000-acre facility located 76 miles from Bozeman, Montana. Features: mountains; geysers/thermal features; waterfalls; lakes; employee residences/pubs/recreation halls; wildlife.

Profile of Summer Employees Total number: 3,500; typical ages: 18–80. 45% men; 55% women; 10% minorities; 1% high school students; 35% college students; 20% retirees; 15% non-U.S. citizens; 10% local applicants.

Employment Information Openings are from May 1 to October 22. Winter break and year-round positions also offered. Jobs available: ▶ 12 *assistant dining room managers* (minimum age 18) with basic supervisory skills and front-of-the-house food and beverage experience at $300 per week ▶ 200 *cooks* (minimum age 18) with cooking experience including hot/cold, broiler, fryer, fast food, or quantity food at $7–$8 per hour ▶ 150 *dining room servers* (minimum age 18) with front-of-the-house serving experience at $3.00 per hour plus gratuities (guarantee of minimum wage) ▶ 50 *employee residence coordinators* (minimum age 18) with experience working with people of a variety of ages, organizational skills, and ability to be self-motivated at $6.50 per hour ▶ 5–10 *food production managers/assistants* (minimum age 18) with knowledge of food preparation and supervisory skills; must supervise BOH operation in a la carte, cafeteria, or employee dining area at $250–$450 per week ▶ 150 *guest services agents* (minimum age 18) with good interpersonal communication and computer/data entry skills at $6.25–$7 per hour ▶ 500 *kitchen help* (minimum age 18) with willingness to learn and work with people at $6.00 per hour ▶ 50 *laundry personnel* (minimum age 18) with willingness to learn to operate high-volume, mechanical laundry sorting and folding machine for all linen for the park at $7 per hour ▶ 7 *painters* (minimum age 19) with a valid driver's license, experience with a brush, roller, airless application, wall preparation, and repair at $7–$10 per hour ▶ 500 *room attendants* (minimum age 18) with willingness to learn and work with people at $6.00 per hour. Applicants must submit formal organization application, two letters of recommendation. International applicants accepted; must apply through a recognized agency.

Benefits and Preemployment Training Housing at a cost, meals at a cost, formal training, possible full-time employment, health insurance, on-the-job training, willing to complete paperwork for educational credit, and opportunity to attend seminars/workshops. Preemployment training is required and includes accident prevention and safety.

Contact Human Resources, Yellowstone National Park Lodges. Telephone: 307-344-5324. Fax: 307-344-5441. E-mail: info@yellowstonejobs.com. World Wide Web: http://www.yellowstonejobs. com. Contact by e-mail, mail, phone, or through World Wide Web site. Application deadline: continuous.

YELLOWSTONE PARK SERVICE STATIONS, INC.
YELLOWSTONE NATIONAL PARK
YELLOWSTONE, WYOMING 82190

General Information Automotive service facilities and information service in Yellowstone National Park. Established in 1947. 2,200,000-acre facility located 90 miles from Bozeman, Montana. Features: geysers; lakes; waterfalls; hiking trails; grizzly bears, elk, wolves; mountaineering.

Profile of Summer Employees Total number: 65; typical ages: 18–24. 60% men; 40% women; 5% minorities; 80% college students; 5% retirees; 10% local applicants. Nonsmokers preferred.

Employment Information Openings are from May 12 to October 16. Jobs available: ▶ 3 *accounting clerks* (minimum age 18) with ability to operate 10-key adding machine by touch, plus computer and communication skills at $270 per week ▶ 18 *automobile mechanics* (minimum age 18) with ASE certification or current enrollment in an ASE program at $320–$400 per week ▶ 50 *service station attendants* (minimum age 18) with good interpersonal skills and desire to work outdoors at $270 per week ▶ 1 *warehouse helper* (minimum age 18) with good driving record and communication skills at $270 per week. Applicants must submit formal organization application, letter of interest. International applicants accepted; must obtain own visa, obtain own working papers, apply through a recognized agency.

Benefits and Preemployment Training Housing at a cost, meals at a cost, formal training, possible full-time employment, health insurance, willing to provide letters of recommendation, names of contacts, on-the-job training, willing to complete paperwork for educational credit, willing to act as a professional reference, and opportunity to attend seminars/workshops. Preemployment training is required and includes accident prevention and safety, leadership skills.

Contact Hal Broadhead, General Manager, Yellowstone Park Service Stations, Inc., PO Box 11, Department WDM, Gardiner, Montana 59030-0011. Telephone: 406-848-7333. Fax: 406-848-7731. E-mail: jobs@ypss.com. World Wide Web: http://www.ypss.com. Contact by e-mail, fax, mail, phone, or through World Wide Web site. Application deadline: June 1.

CANADIAN LISTINGS

BRITISH COLUMBIA

CAMP ARTABAN
1058 RIDGEWOOD DRIVE
NORTH VANCOUVER, BRITISH COLUMBIA V7R 1H8, CANADA
General Information Residential camp with Anglican Church affiliation offering traditional program to 100 boys and girls entering grades 3 through 11 in 7-day sessions. Family and specialty weekend adult camps are also offered. Established in 1923. 63-acre facility located 45 miles from Vancouver. Features: waterfront (salt water) on remote island location; swim tank; canoe and row boats; archery range; crafts log hut; outdoor chapel.
Profile of Summer Employees Total number: 18; typical ages: 17–25. 50% men; 50% women; 30% minorities; 20% high school students; 80% college students. Nonsmokers required.
Employment Information Openings are from June to August. Jobs available: ▶ 1 *chaplain* (minimum age 25) with ability to work with children; should be priest or theology student (Anglican/Episcopalian background preferred) at Can$3000 per season ▶ 1 *first aid attendant* with occupational first aid certification/wilderness first aid or equivalent at Can$3000 to Can$5000 per season ▶ 1 *head cook* (minimum age 25) with supervisory and quantity cooking experience at a negotiable salary ▶ 5–6 *kitchen staff members* (minimum age 17) at Can$2000 to Can$5000 per season ▶ 2 *maintenance staff members* (minimum age 17) at Can$2000 to Can$4000 per season ▶ 1 *registrar/expediter* (minimum age 18) with automobile and insurance, computer skills (Microsoft Office), and data entry skills (will train) at Can$10 per hour ▶ 2 *swimming staff members* (minimum age 18) with WSI and NLS certification at Can$2000 to Can$4000 per season. Applicants must submit a formal organization application, letter of interest, resume, personal reference, letter of recommendation. An in-person interview is recommended, but a telephone interview is acceptable. International applicants accepted; must obtain own working papers.
Benefits and Preemployment Training Free housing, free meals, willing to provide letters of recommendation, on-the-job training, and willing to complete paperwork for educational credit.
Contact Nancy Ferris, On-site Manager, Camp Artaban. Telephone: 604-980-0391. E-mail: office@campartaban.com. World Wide Web: http://www.campartaban.com. Contact by e-mail or mail. Application deadline: February 28.

EVANS LAKE FOREST EDUCATION CENTRE
PO BOX 1893
SQUAMISH, BRITISH COLUMBIA V0N 3G0, CANADA
General Information Residential camp offering environmental education for children 8–11 years old (6-day camp), 10–14 years old (8-day camp) and 13-16 years old (8-day camp) with a capacity of 80 children. Established in 1997. 604-acre facility located 31 miles from Vancouver. Features: freshwater lake; 604-acre demonstration forest; swimming; boating; 15 kilometers of hiking trails; projects and activities to learn about the forest.
Profile of Summer Employees Total number: 25; typical ages: 17–55. 50% men; 50% women; 10% minorities; 60% high school students; 35% college students; 5% local applicants. Nonsmokers preferred.

Employment Information Openings are from July 1 to August 31. Jobs available: ▶ 14 *cabin leaders* (minimum age 17) with counselor training, outdoor experience, and experience with children at Can$65 per day ▶ 1 *instructor* (minimum age 19) with experience working with children, experience in outdoor education, and occupational First Aid or Wilderness First Aid for Leaders certification at Can$95 per day ▶ 3–6 *lifeguards* (minimum age 19) with NLS certification and outdoor education experience at Can$95 per day. Applicants must submit a letter of interest, resume, two letters of recommendation. An in-person interview is required.

Benefits and Preemployment Training Free housing, free meals, willing to provide letters of recommendation, on-the-job training, and willing to act as a professional reference. Preemployment training is required and includes accident prevention and safety, interpersonal skills, leadership skills, child care program.

Contact Matt Thom, Operations Manager, Evans Lake Forest Education Centre, #101 1433 Rupert Street, North Vancouver, British Columbia V7J 1G1, Canada. Fax: 604-904-2260. Contact by fax or mail. No phone calls. Application deadline: April 30.

ONTARIO

BELWOOD LODGE & CAMP
RR#1
BELWOOD, ONTARIO N0B 1J0, CANADA

General Information Residential camp for mentally handicapped individuals ranging from ages 8–85. Established in 1948. 13-acre facility located 15 miles from Guelph. Features: waterfront for pontoons and paddle boats; trampoline; heated swimming pool; animal farm; soccer and baseball fields; archery range, volleyball court, and basketball court.

Profile of Summer Employees Total number: 60; typical age: 20. 45% men; 55% women; 5% minorities; 40% high school students; 40% college students; 50% local applicants.

Employment Information Openings are from June 15 to September 1. Jobs available: ▶ 2 *cooks* at Can$200 to Can$300 per week ▶ 1 *craft director* at Can$225 per week ▶ 10 *junior counselors* at Can$195 per week ▶ *nurse* at Can$350 per week ▶ 1 *program director* at Can$250 per week ▶ 10 *senior counselors* (minimum age 18) at Can$235 per week ▶ 2 *swimming instructors* with lifeguard qualifications at Can$200 per week. Applicants must submit a letter of interest, resume. A telephone interview is required. International applicants accepted; must obtain own visa, obtain own working papers.

Benefits and Preemployment Training Free housing, free meals, on-the-job training, and laundry facilities.

Contact Ms. Chris Murdoch, Director, Belwood Lodge & Camp, RR #1, Belwood, Ontario N0B 1J0. Telephone: 519-843-1211. Fax: 519-843-8398. Contact by fax or mail. Application deadline: continuous.

CAMP FRENDA
SEVENTH-DAY ADVENTIST CHURCH, RR #2
PORT CARLING, ONTARIO P0B 1J0, CANADA

General Information Residential camp serving more than 100 children ages 8–16. 60-acre facility located 100 miles from Toronto. Features: freshwater lake.

Profile of Summer Employees Typical ages: 18–27. 50% men; 50% women; 20% minorities; 20% high school students; 80% college students; 1% retirees. Nonsmokers required.

Employment Information Openings are from June 21 to August 29. Jobs available: ▶ 1 *archery staff member* (minimum age 18) ▶ 1 *canoeing staff member* (minimum age 18) ▶ 1 *glass etching staff member* (minimum age 18) ▶ 3–4 *high ropes course instructors* (minimum age 18) ▶ 4 *horsemanship staff members* (minimum age 18) ▶ 2 *kitchen staff members* ▶ 2 *maintenance staff members* ▶ 2 *outdoor living skills staff members* (minimum age 18) ▶ 1 *photography staff member* (minimum age 18) ▶ 1 *radio broadcasting staff member* (minimum age 18) ▶ 1 *rappelling staff member* (minimum age 18) ▶ 1 *sailing staff member* (minimum age 18) ▶ 1 *silkscreening staff member* (minimum age 18) ▶ 5 *swimming staff members* (minimum age 18) ▶ 1 *tumbling staff member* (minimum age 18) ▶ 4 *waterskiing staff members* (minimum age 18) ▶ *windsurfing staff member*. Applicants must submit a formal organization application, three letters of recommendation, police background check. An in-person interview is recommended, but a telephone interview is acceptable. International applicants accepted.

Benefits and Preemployment Training Free housing, free meals, on-the-job training, willing to complete paperwork for educational credit, and opportunity to attend seminars/workshops. Preemployment training is required and includes accident prevention and safety, first aid, CPR, interpersonal skills, leadership skills.

Contact Cyril Millett, Director, Camp Frenda, 1110 King Street East, Oshawa, Ontario L1H 1H8, Canada. Telephone: 905-571-1022. Fax: 905-571-5995. E-mail: cmillett@ont_sda.org. World Wide Web: http://www.campfrenda.com. Contact by e-mail, fax, mail, phone, or through World Wide Web site. Application deadline: February 30.

CAMP TRILLIUM–CHILDHOOD CANCER SUPPORT CENTRE
200 MAIN STREET WEST
HAMILTON, ONTARIO L8P 4Y4, CANADA

General Information Program offering support and recreational activities to children with cancer and their families. Established in 1984. 120-acre facility located 62 miles from Kingston. Features: private lake; island site; brand new facility; tripping program.

Profile of Summer Employees Total number: 60; typical ages: 18–28. 30% men; 70% women; 10% minorities; 10% high school students; 90% college students; 2% local applicants. Nonsmokers required.

Employment Information Openings are from June 1 to August 30. Jobs available: ▶ 1 *adventure program staff member* (minimum age 18) ▶ 3 *arts and crafts/creative writing staff members* (minimum age 18) ▶ 2 *canoe/kayak specialists* (minimum age 18) ▶ 1 *drama instructor* (minimum age 18) ▶ 3 *outtrippers* (minimum age 18) ▶ 3 *sailing instructors* (minimum age 18) with CYA certification ▶ 4 *waterfront/swimming instructors* (minimum age 18) with NLS and Red Cross certifications. Applicants must submit a formal organization application, letter of interest, resume, two personal references, letter of recommendation. An in-person interview is recommended, but a telephone interview is acceptable. International applicants accepted; must obtain own visa.

Benefits and Preemployment Training Free housing, free meals, willing to provide letters of recommendation, on-the-job training, and willing to act as a professional reference. Preemployment training is required and includes accident prevention and safety, first aid, CPR, interpersonal skills, leadership skills, team building.

Contact Marci Shea-Perry, Director of Programs, Camp Trillium–Childhood Cancer Support Centre, 200 Main Street West, Hamilton, Ontario L8P 4Y4, Canada. Telephone: 905-527-1992. Fax: 905-527-5314. E-mail: marcisp@camptrillium.com. World Wide Web: http://www. camptrillium.com. Contact by e-mail, fax, mail, phone, or through World Wide Web site. Application deadline: January 31.

CENTER FOR STUDENT MISSIONS–TORONTO
TORONTO, ONTARIO
See Center for Student Missions on page 37 for complete description.

GANADAOWEH
RR#3
AYR, ONTARIO NOB 1EO, CANADA
General Information Residential, day, and wilderness camping programs offering Christian education to 100 campers weekly. Established in 1982. 174-acre facility located 15 miles from Kitchener. Features: freshwater lake; wooded setting; 1 sports court; wildlife; high ropes course; pool.
Profile of Summer Employees Total number: 32; typical ages: 17–25. 40% men; 60% women; 10% minorities; 60% high school students; 35% college students; 95% local applicants. Nonsmokers required.
Employment Information Openings are from May 1 to August 31. Jobs available: ▶ 1 *camp nurse* (minimum age 19) should be student nurse at college or university, RN preferred at Can$210 per week ▶ 15 *counselors* (minimum age 16) with counselor training program completed at Can$190 to Can$260 per week ▶ 1 *high ropes instructor* (minimum age 18) with assistant high ropes instructor certification (minimum) at Can$180 to Can$200 per week ▶ 2 *lifeguards* (minimum age 16) with NLS, leaders and instructors preferred at Can$200 per week. Applicants must submit a formal organization application, two personal references, letter of recommendation. An in-person interview is recommended, but a telephone interview is acceptable.
Benefits and Preemployment Training Free housing, free meals, formal training, willing to provide letters of recommendation, names of contacts, on-the-job training, willing to complete paperwork for educational credit, willing to act as a professional reference, and opportunity to attend seminars/workshops. Preemployment training is required and includes accident prevention and safety, first aid, interpersonal skills, leadership skills, Christian program/education development, special needs, child abuse disclosures.
Contact Maja Hipkin, Director, Ganadaoweh, RR 3, Ayr, Ontario N0B 1E0, Canada. Telephone: 519-632-7559. Fax: 519-632-9607. E-mail: camp@ganadaoweh.ca. World Wide Web: http://www.ganadaoweh.ca. Contact by e-mail, fax, mail, or phone. Application deadline: continuous.

NEW STRIDES DAY CAMP
ETOBICOKE CITY HALL, 399 THE WEST MALL
ETOBICOKE, ONTARIO M9C 2Y2, CANADA
General Information The Adapted-Integrated service section provides resources and transition support to individuals with disabilities; also day camp serving 105 individuals with varying special needs. Established in 1977. 525-acre facility located 12 miles from Toronto. Features: sport fields; mini-golf; tennis courts; indoor swimming pool.
Profile of Summer Employees Total number: 5; typical ages: 18–26. 20% men; 80% women; 30% high school students; 70% college students; 90% local applicants. Nonsmokers preferred.
Employment Information Openings are from July to August. Jobs available: ▶ 1 *New Strides director* (minimum age 21) with experience working in camps/recreation and with special needs population; standard first aid/CPR certification; CPI and aquatics helpful at Can$9 to Can$10.50 per hour ▶ *Stepping Up, adult life skills and recreation programmer* (minimum age 20) with standard first aid/CPR certification (aquatic and CPI preferred) and driver's license; should have program planning and recreation experience with a wide range of age and ability within the special population community at Can$9 to Can$10.50 per hour ▶ 1 *community integration coordinator* (minimum age 21) with experience in camps/recreation/playgrounds and one-to-one experience with special needs children; standard first aid and CPR; CPI and aquatics helpful at Can$9 to Can$11.50 per hour ▶ 4–12 *leader positions* (minimum age 18) with standard first aid and CPR certification; background working with special needs individuals; aquatic skills helpful

at Can$7.50 to Can$8.50 per hour. Applicants must submit a formal organization application, letter of interest, resume, two personal references, possible police checks in the future. An in-person interview is required.

Benefits and Preemployment Training Formal training, willing to provide letters of recommendation, names of contacts, on-the-job training, willing to complete paperwork for educational credit, willing to act as a professional reference, and opportunity to attend seminars/workshops. Preemployment training is required and includes accident prevention and safety, first aid, CPR, interpersonal skills, leadership skills.

Contact Miss Sarah Bumstead, Recreationist, Adapted/Integrated Services, New Strides Day Camp, 399 The West Mall, Etobicoke, Ontario M9C 2Y2. Telephone: 416-394-8533. Fax: 416-394-8935. E-mail: sbumste@toronto.ca. World Wide Web: http://www.city.toronto.on.ca. Contact by e-mail, mail, or phone. Application deadline: March 15.

QUEBEC

CAMP NOMININGUE
1889 CHEMIN DES MESANGES
NOMININGUE, QUEBEC J0W 1R0, CANADA

General Information Residential camp for 220 boys ages 7–15 providing a place to cultivate friendships, self-confidence, and a sense of achievement. Established in 1925. 400-acre facility located 120 miles from Montreal. Features: half mile of sandy beach; freshwater lake; 400 acres of woods and fields; 4 tennis courts.

Profile of Summer Employees Total number: 80; typical ages: 18–25. 99% men; 1% women; 15% minorities; 10% high school students; 70% college students; 1% retirees; 50% local applicants. Nonsmokers preferred.

Employment Information Openings are from June 22 to August 25. Year-round positions also offered. Jobs available: ▶ *TOESL instructors* (minimum age 18) must be current student or graduate in university ESL program at Can$235 per week ▶ *archery instructors* (minimum age 18) with CPR, first aid, and instructors certifications at Can$150 to Can$235 per week ▶ *athletics instructors* (minimum age 18) with CPR and first aid certifications at Can$150 to Can$235 per week ▶ *campcraft instructors* (minimum age 18) with CPR and first aid certifications at Can$150 to Can$235 per week ▶ *canoeing instructors* (minimum age 18) with CPR and first aid certifications at Can$150 to Can$235 per week ▶ 1–30 *general counselors* (minimum age 18) with CPR and first aid certifications at Can$150 to Can$235 per week ▶ *golf instructors* (minimum age 18) with CPR and first aid certifications at Can$150 to Can$235 per week ▶ 1–3 *kayaking instructors* (minimum age 18) with CPR and first aid certifications at Can$235 per week ▶ 1 *nature awareness instructor* (minimum age 18) with CPR and first aid certifications at Can$235 per week ▶ *orienteering instructors* (minimum age 18) with CPR and first aid certifications at Can$150 to Can$235 per week ▶ *riflery instructors* (minimum age 18) with CPR and first aid certifications at Can$150 to Can$235 per week ▶ 1–3 *sailing instructors* (minimum age 18) with CPR and first aid certifications and ability to operate motor boat at Can$235 per week ▶ *tennis instructors* (minimum age 18) with CPR and first aid certifications at Can$235 per week ▶ *theater instructors* (minimum age 18) with CPR and first aid certifications at Can$235 per week ▶ 1–3 *windsurfing instructors* (minimum age 18) with CPR and first aid certifications and ability to operate motor boat at Can$235 per week ▶ 1 *woodworking instructor* (minimum age 18) with CPR and first aid certification and ability to operate woodworking machinery at Can$235 per week. Applicants must submit a formal organization application, letter of interest, resume, three personal references. An in-person interview is recommended, but a telephone interview is acceptable. International applicants accepted; must obtain own visa.

Benefits and Preemployment Training Housing at a cost, meals at a cost, formal training, possible full-time employment, willing to provide letters of recommendation, on-the-job training, and willing to act as a professional reference. Preemployment training is required and includes accident prevention and safety, first aid, interpersonal skills, leadership skills.

Contact Grant McKenna, Executive Director, Camp Nominingue, 2700 rue Halpern, St. Laurent, Quebec H45 1R6, Canada. Telephone: 514-856-1333. Fax: 514-856-8001. E-mail: camp@axess. com. World Wide Web: http://www.nominingue.com. Contact by e-mail, fax, mail, phone, or through World Wide Web site. Application deadline: continuous.

STIVERS STAFFING SERVICES–CANADA
See Stivers Staffing Services–Illinois on page 96 for complete description.

LOCATIONS OUTSIDE NORTH AMERICA LISTINGS

BELIZE

LONGACRE EXPEDITIONS, BELIZE
BELIZE

General Information Adventure travel program in Belize for teenagers, emphasizing group living skills and physical challenges. Established in 1981. Near Belize City, Belize.

Profile of Summer Employees Total number: 4; typical ages: 21–30. 50% men; 50% women; 1% minorities; 100% college students. Nonsmokers required.

Employment Information Openings are from June 15 to July 31. Jobs available: ▶ 2 *assistant leaders* (minimum age 21) with scuba certification, WFR, CPR, and lifeguard training at $252–$300 per week. Applicants must submit a formal organization application, letter of interest, resume, three personal references. An in-person interview is recommended, but a telephone interview is acceptable. International applicants accepted; must obtain own visa, obtain own working papers.

Benefits and Preemployment Training Free housing, free meals, willing to provide letters of recommendation, on-the-job training, willing to act as a professional reference, and pro-deal purchase program. Preemployment training is required and includes accident prevention and safety, interpersonal skills, leadership skills.

Contact Meredith Schuler, Director, Longacre Expeditions, Belize, 4030 Middle Ridge Road, Newport, Pennsylvania 17074-8110. Telephone: 717-567-6790. Fax: 717-567-3955. E-mail: merry@longacreexpeditions.com. World Wide Web: http://www.longacreexpeditions.com. Contact by e-mail, fax, mail, phone, or through World Wide Web site. Application deadline: continuous.

U.S. VIRGIN ISLANDS

A CHRISTIAN MINISTRY IN THE NATIONAL PARKS– VIRGIN ISLANDS, WEST INDIES
See A Christian Ministry in the National Parks–Maine on page 107 for complete description.

LONGACRE EXPEDITIONS, VIRGIN ISLANDS
VIRGIN ISLANDS

General Information Adventure travel program in the Virgin Islands for teenagers, emphasizing group living skills and physical challenges. Established in 1981. near St. Thomas.

Profile of Summer Employees Total number: 6; typical ages: 23–30. 50% men; 50% women; 100% college students. Nonsmokers required.

Employment Information Openings are from June 15 to July 30. Jobs available: ▶ 3 *assistant leaders* (minimum age 21) with scuba certification, WFR, CPR, and lifeguard training at $252–$300 per week. Applicants must submit a formal organization application, letter of interest, resume, three personal references. An in-person interview is recommended, but a telephone interview is acceptable. International applicants accepted; must obtain own visa, obtain own working papers.

Benefits and Preemployment Training Free housing, free meals, willing to provide letters of recommendation, on-the-job training, willing to complete paperwork for educational credit, willing to act as a professional reference, and pro-deal purchase program. Preemployment training is required and includes accident prevention and safety, interpersonal skills, leadership skills.

Contact Meredith Schuler, Director, Longacre Expeditions, Virgin Islands, 4030 Middle Ridge Road, Newport, Pennsylvania 17074-8110. Telephone: 717-567-6790. Fax: 717-567-3955. E-mail: longacre@longacreexpeditions.com. World Wide Web: http://www.longacreexpeditions.com. Contact by e-mail, fax, mail, phone, or through World Wide Web site. Application deadline: continuous.

STUDENT CONSERVATION ASSOCIATION (SCA), VIRGIN ISLANDS

See Student Conservation Association (SCA), New Hampshire on page 200 for complete description.

UNITED KINGDOM

GREENFORCE
11-15 BETTERTON STREET, COVENT GARDEN
LONDON WC2H 9BP, UNITED KINGDOM

General Information Nonprofit conservation organization that places individuals on environmental projects throughout the world. Also opportunities for long-term staff positions once volunteer phase is over. Established in 1996. Features: Africa; Amazon; Borneo; Fiji; United Kingdom; Bahamas.

Profile of Summer Employees Total number: 50; typical ages: 18–28. 50% men; 50% women; 25% high school students; 75% college students; 90% non-U.S. citizens.

Employment Information Openings are from January 1 to December 31. Spring break, winter break, and year-round positions also offered. Jobs available: ▶ 180–200 *research assistants* (minimum age 18). Applicants must submit a formal organization application, there is a fee of 2550 British pounds once hired to take part in the program. A telephone interview is required. International applicants accepted.

Benefits and Preemployment Training Free housing, free meals, formal training, possible full-time employment, health insurance, willing to provide letters of recommendation, on-the-job training, willing to complete paperwork for educational credit, willing to act as a professional reference, opportunity to attend seminars/workshops, and tuition assistance. Preemployment training is optional and includes accident prevention and safety, first aid, CPR, interpersonal skills, leadership skills, kit, map, or dive training subject to location.

Contact M. Jones, Director of Operations, Greenforce, 11-15 Betterton Street, London WC2H 9BP, United Kingdom. Telephone: 207-470-8888. Fax: 207-470-8889. E-mail: greenforce@ btinternet.com. World Wide Web: http://www.greenforce.com. Contact by e-mail, fax, mail, phone, or through World Wide Web site. Application deadline: continuous.

SUMMER DISCOVERY AT CAMBRIDGE
NEW HALL COLLEGE, CAMBRIDGE UNIVERSITY
CAMBRIDGE, UNITED KINGDOM

General Information Precollege enrichment program for high school students at Cambridge University in England. Established in 1987. Located 100 miles from London. Features: sport facilities; beaches; mountains; lakes; major cities nearby; college towns.

Profile of Summer Employees Total number: 20; typical ages: 23–35. 10% minorities; 30% college students. Nonsmokers required.

Employment Information Openings are from June to July. Jobs available: ▶ 20 *resident counselors* (minimum age 23) with experience working with high school students/children at $200 per week. Applicants must submit a formal organization application, resume, personal reference. An in-person interview is required. International applicants accepted; must obtain own visa, obtain own working papers.

Benefits and Preemployment Training Free housing, free meals, possible full-time employment, willing to provide letters of recommendation, on-the-job training, willing to complete paperwork for educational credit, and willing to act as a professional reference. Preemployment training is required and includes accident prevention and safety, CPR, interpersonal skills, leadership skills.

Contact Rouel Belleza, Operations, Summer Discovery at Cambridge, 1326 Old Northern Boulevard, Roslyn, New York 11576, United States. Telephone: 516-621-3939. Fax: 516-625-3438. E-mail: staff@summerfun.com. World Wide Web: http://www.summerfun.com. Contact by e-mail, fax, mail, phone, or through World Wide Web site. Application deadline: continuous.

CATEGORY INDEX

Religious Organizations

Retail Trade

Social Assistance

EMPLOYER INDEX

JOB TYPES INDEX